Principles & Practices of Teaching & Training

Sara Miller McCune founded SAGE Publishing in 1965 to support the dissemination of usable knowledge and educate a global community. SAGE publishes more than 1000 journals and over 800 new books each year, spanning a wide range of subject areas. Our growing selection of library products includes archives, data, case studies and video. SAGE remains majority owned by our founder and after her lifetime will become owned by a charitable trust that secures the company's continued independence.

Los Angeles | London | New Delhi | Singapore | Washington DC | Melbourne

Principles & Practices of Teaching & Training

A guide for teachers and trainers in the FE and skills sector

Ann Gravells

Learning Matters
An imprint of SAGE Publications Ltd
1 Oliver's Yard
55 City Road
London EC1Y 1SP

SAGE Publications Inc.
2455 Teller Road
Thousand Oaks, California 91320

SAGE Publications India Pvt Ltd
B 1/I 1 Mohan Cooperative Industrial Area
Mathura Road
New Delhi 110 044

SAGE Publications Asia-Pacific Pte Ltd
3 Church Street
#10-04 Samsung Hub
Singapore 049483

Editor: Amy Thornton
Development Editor: Jennifer Clark
Production Controller: Chris Marke
Project Management: Deer Park Productions
Marketing Manager: Dilhara Attygalle
Cover design: Wendy Scott
Typeset by: C&M Digitals (P) Ltd, Chennai, India
Printed and bound in the UK

First published in 2017 by Learning Matters Ltd

Library of Congress Control Number: 2017945399

British Library Cataloguing in Publication Data

A catalogue record for this book is available from the British Library.

ISBN 978-1-4739-9713-4 (pbk)
ISBN 978-1-4739-9712-7

At SAGE we take sustainability seriously. Most of our products are printed in the UK using FSC papers and boards. When we print overseas we ensure sustainable papers are used as measured by the PREPS grading system. We undertake an annual audit to monitor our sustainability.

CONTENTS

ACKNOWLEDGEMENTS

I would like to give special thanks to the following people who have helped me with the production of this book. They have freely given their time, knowledge and advice, which has resulted in some excellent contributions and additions to the content. Without their amazing proofreading skills and honest feedback, this book would not be what it is, and I am truly grateful.

Audrey Fairgrieve –Teaching, Learning and Assessment Lead at Abingdon & Witney College

Bob Bates – Author and Training Consultant

Dan Williams – Lecturer Post 14 PGCE at the University of Derby @FurtherEdagogy

Daniel Scott – Digital Learning Specialist

Dawn Upton – Director at C&D Training Ltd

Helen Martin – Lecturer at Bishop Burton College

Hilary Read – Author and Director at ReadOn Publications Ltd

Jen McDowell – English Language Arts Teacher at Berlin Intermediate School in Worcester County, Maryland USA

Jonathan White – Author and Librarian at The University of Derby

Lisa Morris – Director at Educating UK & Lead External Quality Assurer at TQUK

Michelle Ellis – Managing Director at ECO Education and Training

Nicola Price – Education Consultant

Paul Warren – Freelance Consultant at @paulw_learn

Peter Adeney – International External Quality Assurer and Examiner

Roisin Kelly – Skills Development Co-ordinator at NICVA

Sharron Carlill – Assistant Principal (Quality and Compliance) at The White Rose Beauty Colleges

Sue Lloyd – Quality Improvement Co-ordinator at North Lindsey College, Scunthorpe.

ACKNOWLEDGEMENTS

I would like to thank my Publisher (Education) Amy Thornton, and my Development Editor, Jennifer Clark for their continued support and guidance.

Every effort has been made to trace the copyright holders and to obtain their permission for the use of copyright material. The publisher and author will gladly receive any information enabling them to rectify any error or omission in subsequent editions.

Ann Gravells
www.anngravells.com

AUTHOR STATEMENT

 Ann has been teaching, assessing and quality assuring in the further education and skills sector since 1983. She is a director of her own company *Ann Gravells Ltd*, an educational consultancy based in East Yorkshire. She specialises in teaching, training, assessment and quality assurance.

Ann holds a Master's in Educational Management, a PGCE, a Degree in Education, and a City & Guilds Medal of Excellence for teaching. She is a Fellow of the Society for Education and Training, and holds QTLS status.

Ann has been writing text books since 2006 which are mainly based on her own experiences as a teacher and the subsequent education of trainee teachers. She aims to write in plain English to help anyone with their role. She creates resources for teachers and learners such as PowerPoints and handouts for the assessment, quality assurance, and teacher training qualifications. These are available via her website: www.anngravells.com

Ann has worked for several awarding organisations producing qualification guidance, policies and procedures, and carrying out the external quality assurance of teaching, assessment and quality assurance qualifications.

She is a consultant to The University of Cambridge's Institute of Continuing Education, Ofqual, and the awarding organisation Training Qualifications UK (TQUK).

Ann welcomes any comments from readers; please contact her via her website www.anngravells.com

Ann Gravells' text books

The teaching, assessment and quality assurance qualification titles change over time. Ann has written books in the past which reflect these titles and has updated them when they have changed. However, the content of the qualifications and the job roles which teachers, assessors and quality assurers carry out remain very much the same.

Ann has now written three generic books aimed at covering all the teaching, assessment and quality assurance qualifications as well as the relevant job roles. It doesn't matter what the qualification title might be called now or in the future or which awarding organisation offers it, these three books should meet the required content of them all.

- *Principles and Practices of Assessment (2015)*
- *Principles and Practices of Quality Assurance (2016)*
- *Principles and Practices of Teaching and Training (2017)*

Ann's first book Delivering Adult Learning was written in 2006 and was aimed at anyone taking the qualification of the same title. This book is no longer in print, but forged the beginning of her writing career and her aim of helping trainee teachers with their role.

Ann is the author of the following text books, many of which are now in new editions (listed here in alphabetical order). Details can be found on her website: www.anngravells.com/books

- *Achieving your Assessment and Quality Assurance Units (TAQA)(2014)*
- *Delivering Employability Skills in the Lifelong Learning Sector (2010)*
- *Passing Assessments for the Award in Education and Training (2013)*
- *Passing PTLLS Assessments (2012)*
- *Preparing to Teach in the Lifelong Learning Sector (2012)*
- *The Award in Education and Training (2014)*
- *What is Teaching in the Lifelong Learning Sector? (2012)*

She is co-author of:

- *Equality and Diversity in the Lifelong Learning Sector (2012)*
- *Passing CTLLS Assessments (2010)*
- *Planning and Enabling Learning in the Lifelong Learning Sector (2010)*
- *The Best Vocational Trainer's Guide (2015)*
- *The Certificate in Education and Training (2014)*
- *Passing Assessments for the Certificate in Education and Training (2014)*

She has edited:

- *Study Skills for PTLLS (2012)*

PREFACE

Congratulations on purchasing this book which should cover everything you need to know to start a career teaching and training those aged 14 and above, in the UK and beyond. The book includes short activities to help you relate theory to practice, gives real examples of teachers' experiences and contains examples of documents a teacher or trainer might use.

I have written the book mainly for new teachers and trainers, whether they are:

- currently teaching

- considering a teaching career

- undertaking a work experience placement

- working towards a teaching qualification

- taking an apprenticeship programme.

However, it will also suit anyone who is more experienced but who would like to refresh their knowledge.

I haven't made reference to too many complex theories within the chapters. Where theories are mentioned, I leave it to you to research them further if you wish. I would recommend anyone taking a high level teaching qualification to read other textbooks besides this one. Different authors write in different ways, theories differ and there will be some topics not covered in this book which can be found in others. I have included reading lists at the end of each chapter with relevant texts and useful websites. I also have a very comprehensive reading list on my website: www.anngravells.com/reading-lists/index

Please read the introduction chapter first as this will help set the scene regarding teaching in the further education and skills sector. The subsequent chapters, although in a logical order, can be read according to what you need to know at any given time. You can refer to the index at the back of the book to locate relevant topics or look in the contents list.

There are some aspects in this book which have previously appeared in my other textbooks, but which have been updated for inclusion in this book.

I hope you gain what you need from the book and I wish you success with your career.

Ann Gravells

www.anngravells.com

Introduction

Introduction

Teaching and training is about helping someone to gain the skills and knowledge they need at a given point in time. The approaches and activities you can use to achieve this will be explained throughout the chapters of this book.

This chapter will explore how to use this book and what the further education and skills sector is. How to work towards a teaching qualification is covered, as is how to obtain a teaching position and evidence your practice.

You can work logically through the book starting with this chapter, or you can just look up appropriate topics in the index (at the back of the book) or the contents, to access aspects relevant to your current area of study or interest.

This chapter will cover the following topics:

- The structure of the book
- The further education and skills sector
- Qualifications and standards for teachers and trainers
- Study skills, academic writing and referencing
- Obtaining a teaching position and progressing further
- Evidence-based practice

The structure of the book

If you are aiming to be, or are a new or inexperienced teacher or trainer, this book is for you. It will guide you through the terminology, principles and practices of teaching and training, to enable you to understand what the role involves, and/or to work towards a relevant teaching qualification if necessary. Although the book has been written with new teachers in mind, it will also prove useful for anyone who teaches in any situation. For example, human resource staff, administrators, technicians, managers, or those in staff development and train the trainer roles. The book will also help experienced teachers and trainers refresh their knowledge of teaching and assessing learning.

Topics covered in the book include:

- the role of a teacher or trainer

- how to plan and prepare sessions for groups or individuals, in the workplace or in a teaching/training environment (on- or off-the-job respectively)

- how to deliver sessions using different teaching and learning approaches and activities

- how to communicate with learners and manage behaviour

- how to assess that learning has taken place

- how to evaluate your own practice to make improvements.

Due to the terminology used throughout the further education (FE) and skills sector, you will find lots of abbreviations and acronyms used within the book. A list of the most commonly used ones can be found in Appendix 1.

Activity |

Take a look at Appendix 1 at the back of this book. This is a list of abbreviations and acronyms, some of which you might not have come across before. Choose five you are not familiar with, find out what they mean, and identify how relevant they are to you at this time.

The term *learner* is used throughout the book to denote anyone taking a qualification, a course or a programme of learning, who might not necessarily call themselves a learner. For example, apprentice, candidate, employee, participant, pupil, student or trainee. The terms course and programme will be used interchangeably throughout the book as they both reflect the way learning can take place. Different organisations use different terms.

This book will try to differentiate between *teaching* and *training*. However, someone who teaches might also train others: for example, teaching theory to a group, followed by training an individual to perform a task based on the theory just learnt. The term *teacher* might therefore be used more than *trainer* in the book. All teaching and training should enable learning to take place. The difference might be that a teacher works in an educational organisation, whereas a trainer works in a workshop or the workplace.

Your role as a teacher gives you the chance to help someone reach their full potential, and it can make a difference to their life and employment prospects. Working through this book will help you understand how to help your learners achieve this. Your job role might be called something other than a teacher or trainer. For example, coach, development officer, facilitator, instructor, lecturer, mentor, professor, supervisor, technician or tutor. Whatever you are called, your purpose will be to educate someone to ensure that learning takes place. Your learners should then be able to put this new learning into practice, demonstrating a change in their behaviour.

There are examples of real teaching situations within each chapter of the book to put the topics into context. There are also activities which you might like to carry out to help put theory into practice. At the end of each section within the chapters is an extension activity. This will stretch and challenge your learning further, for example, if you are working towards a teaching qualification. Completing these activities will help you develop your learning and contribute towards your continuing professional development (CPD). A self-assessment checklist at the end of every chapter will help you appreciate what you have learnt so far.

Depending upon where you are based, some of the legislation, regulations and organisations referred to in this book might only be applicable in England or the UK. If you are teaching internationally, you should check what is current and applicable in the country in which you work.

Example

In the UK, health and safety legislation is covered under the Health and Safety at Work etc. Act (1974). In China, it's known as Workplace Safety Law (2002 amended 2014), and in the USA, it's the Occupational Safety and Health Act (1970).

Throughout the chapters there are examples of completed documents that could be used or adapted for teaching and training purposes. However, do check with the organisation you are working for, in case they have particular documents they require you to use. For the purpose of future-proofing the book, a year has not been added to any dates used within them. When completing any documents yourself, you should always add the year as well as the day and month, to create a full audit trail.

Appendix 2 at the back of the book contains a checklist for teachers and trainers. Although not all the points may apply to you, they might help you ensure that you are covering all aspects of the teaching process. Appendix 3 contains a few tips for new teachers and trainers.

If you are working towards a teaching qualification, you will find it useful to refer to other texts besides this one. A list of relevant books can be found at the end of each chapter.

If your role also involves assessment and/or quality assurance, these topics are covered briefly in this book, although you might like to refer to more comprehensive texts.

Take a look at the list of books and websites at the end of this chapter. Make a list of those which you feel will be helpful to your role. Textbooks are usually available via the online store Amazon (www.amazon.com) which is accessible in most countries. You can often view a sample of a book online prior to making a purchase. If you have an internet connection, access www.anngravells.com/reading-lists/index and look at the reading lists and blogs which are listed. The reading lists contain books in pictures with links to Amazon where you can view a sample. The blogs can help you keep up to date with what's happening in the further education and skills sector.

The further education and skills sector

In the UK, the term *further education (FE) and skills sector* includes the following contexts in which learning can take place (in alphabetical order):

- adult education
- armed, emergency and uniformed services
- charitable organisations
- community education
- further education colleges
- health authorities
- higher education institutions and universities
- immigration and detention centres
- laboratories
- local authorities
- on-site learning centres
- prisoner and offender centres
- private sector learning
- probation services
- public and private training organisations
- schools and academies
- sixth form colleges
- technical colleges
- voluntary sector learning
- work-based learning.

Basically, learning in this sector can occur with anyone from the age of 14 and upwards, whether it be academic or vocational (i.e. theoretical or practical), and it can take place in any environment. In the UK, the term *lifelong learning* is also used. Other terms include adult education, adult and community education, adult and continuing education, and adult learning. The opportunity for people to take further education often gives them chances to do new things. It also gives people the opportunity to improve their skills and knowledge. It could be that they did not do well at school, or are looking for a new interest or a change of job role.

Activity

What is the term used for the further education and skills sector where you work? Why is this term used, and what age range does it encompass? It's useful to know a little about the history of further education and any current national or local initiatives which might affect it. You could search the internet to find this out or talk to your colleagues.

If you are new to teaching, this could be because you have been contemplating a change of profession, or you are required to take a particular teaching qualification because of your job role. Perhaps you have a hobby or a trade you would like to teach to others; you know you are good at it and feel you have the skills and knowledge which you could pass on to others. While this book will guide you through the process of teaching, learning and assessing, it is up to you to ensure you are up to date with your subject knowledge. This is what you will actually teach and is sometimes referred to as a subject discipline or specialist subject. As you will be an experienced practitioner in your *subject*, and also a professional *teacher*, the term *dual professional* is often used to denote your role. This is because you are a professional in two different aspects.

Example

Peter works full time as a plumber. The local college is advertising for plumbing teachers to deliver an evening class. Peter feels he has the necessary skills and knowledge and would like to apply. The advertisement states the successful applicant will be able to take a part-time teaching qualification which will be paid for by the college. If Peter is successful, he can continue with his job, teach an evening class and work towards a teaching qualification. Peter will therefore be a dual professional. A professional teacher and a professional plumber.

Depending upon where and what you will teach, you may not need to be qualified in your particular subject, but be able to demonstrate appropriate occupational skills and knowledge at a certain level. Some subjects require you to have a level above that which you will teach, for example, holding a level 3 qualification to teach it at level 2.

Some subjects might not require you to hold a specific subject qualification at all, but just possess the necessary skills, knowledge and experience. If you are teaching towards an accredited qualification, you will need to find out what the requirements for you to teach it might be. There is often a particular body responsible for your subject. In the UK, it's the Federation for Industry Sector Skills and Standards and you can access their website at: http://fisss.org. They, along with the awarding organisation who accredit and certificate the qualification, will decide what is required by teachers to deliver and assess in each subject area.

Programmes or courses are frequently known as *vocational or technical* (i.e. work or employment related), *non-vocational* (leisure, hobby or interest related) and *academic* (theory related). However, some topics can cover all three aspects.

Example

Kersti works for herself as a horticulturist. She designs gardens for customers and advises which plants are suitable for their environment. The owner of the local garden centre is often asked if there are any short courses regarding garden design. He approached Kersti and she offered to deliver a three-hour session at the garden centre to a group of interested customers. Her session will therefore be vocational (as it could relate to a job), non-vocational (as it could relate to a hobby) and academic (as some theory will be covered). The session will take place in the garden centre and will not be in a classroom. The learners will not receive a certificate but will receive a record of attendance.

Programmes that lead to qualifications are known as *accredited* and an awarding organisation (AO) will issue a certificate to all successful learners. The AO produces a qualification specification and checks that the requirements of it are followed. This is by carrying out ongoing verification or quality measures. All AOs are regulated, in the United Kingdom the regulator is Ofqual in England; it's Qualifications Wales in Wales; the CCEA in Northern Ireland; and the SQA in Scotland (weblinks to these are at the end of this chapter and further details can be found in Chapter 3). Any college or training organisation can apply to an AO to offer accredited qualifications or endorsed programmes of learning, and they are often called a *centre* or a *provider*. An accredited qualification can be offered by several AOs, and is nationally recognised. Endorsed programmes are specifically written by a centre in conjunction with an AO, to meet the needs of particular employers or learners. The AO will still issue a certificate to successful learners; however, it might not be accepted like a nationally recognised qualification would.

Records of achievement or records of attendance could be issued by centres to learners who are on a short programme which is not certificated by an AO. It's good for the learner to have something which shows what they have done, but it only proves achievement or attendance at something specific. For example, an update to the company's policies and procedures, or attendance at a garden design course.

The most important aspect of teaching is to ensure that learning is taking place. If you are currently teaching, your delivery methods might be based on experiences of how you were taught in the past. However, there are many different approaches you could use. This book will hopefully give you new ideas to use in a more engaging and practical way. Chapter 5 includes a table of different teaching and training approaches and activities. Teaching isn't just about being in a classroom; it can take place in many different environments such as the workplace, a voluntary setting, indoors, outdoors or online.

Extension activity

Think back to when you were at school or college. What were your favourite and least favourite subjects and why? How did the teachers impart their skills and knowledge to help you learn? How do you think your experiences as a learner in the past will influence the way you will teach in future?

Qualifications and standards for teachers and trainers

It can be overwhelming making a career move into teaching or training. You might need to achieve certain qualifications or meet particular professional standards prior to commencing your role or while working on-the-job. Having a qualification is a way of demonstrating you have met all the criteria required to be a teacher. Standards are a set of criteria which you can demonstrate on-the-job. They are a way of checking and confirming what you are currently doing.

Most people who choose to teach adults have already had a career for several years in a particular subject area, and wish to impart their skills and knowledge to others. Some training organisations might employ you without a teaching qualification or a specific subject qualification if they feel you have the necessary knowledge and experience. This will depend upon what type of organisation you work for and which country you are in. It might be possible to work towards a teaching qualification once you have started your teaching role, this is known as *in-service*. However, you could work towards a teaching qualification while you are still working in your current job role, known as *pre-service*. You could consider partaking in some voluntary teaching practice to see if it's a career you would want to move into.

Teaching qualifications

In 2013, the Government (in England) removed the requirement for teachers in the FE and skills sector to be qualified. It's now the responsibility of the individual employer, college or university to make the decision as to what qualifications their staff should hold. However, most people in a teaching or training role will want to hold a qualification, and organisations will want to give a quality service to their learners by having qualified staff. There are many countries which do require their staff to hold a teaching qualification and you will need to find out what is applicable to you.

Awarding organisations offer different teaching qualifications ranging from those for new teachers at level 3, to those for more advanced teachers, at level 5 and above. You can find out more about levels in Chapter 4. Some qualifications for teachers are quite short, perhaps a few days for a train the trainer course, or a few weeks for an introductory teaching qualification. Others can take several years and involve *teaching practice*. This is contact with real learners in real situations and is usually a set number of hours throughout the duration of the course (covered in Chapter 14).

The titles of teaching and training qualifications will differ depending upon which country you are in and at which level they are offered. The titles often change depending on government and national initiatives and which AO has produced them. For example, a two-day Level 2 Train the Trainer course aimed at those who need some knowledge of how to train someone in the workplace, or a short teaching course such as the Level 3 Award in Education and Training. This is aimed at new teachers and includes a micro-teach session (covered in Chapter 13). More experienced teachers can take the Level 4 Certificate in Education and Training which involves 30 teaching practice hours. Progression can then be to the Level 5 Diploma in Education and Training or the Level 5 Certificate in Education, also known as the Cert Ed. This can take up to two years on a part-time basis and involves 100 teaching practice hours. There are higher level teaching qualifications such as the Level 6 Professional Graduate Certificate in Education and the Level 7 Post Graduate Certificate in Education (PGCE) for those with a degree.

Working towards a teaching qualification

First, you will need to find a suitable organisation offering the teaching programme or qualification you wish to take. This could be by searching online, talking to colleagues, or approaching a local college, university or training organisation. Once you have applied and been accepted, you will be registered for the qualification with an AO. Your course might involve attending sessions and/or working through online materials. You will learn what it's like to be a teacher and will work through activities to put theory into practice. This might also involve delivering a short session to your peers or to a group of your own learners, known as a micro-teach session (covered in Chapter 13). You might also be observed in your place of work with your own learners (covered in Chapter 14).

Activity

Find out which teaching qualifications are available in your country and the different levels at which they are offered. You could search the internet, talk to colleagues, or contact your local college, university or training organisation. Compare what is offered and make a decision as to what would suit you if you are planning on working towards a qualification. You could also find out if there is any funding available or if your employer would help subsidise you. You might also like to find out if you need to hold any particular subject qualifications at a certain level to be able to teach it. You could then consider applying if you wish.

Once you are signed up to take a teaching qualification you will be allocated a teacher and an assessor. One person might carry out both roles and they will give ongoing feedback regarding your progress and achievement. When producing written work for assessment, you might be able to submit a draft first for informal feedback, before submitting your final work. If you don't pass, you should be referred, usually with the opportunity to resubmit your work within a set timescale.

While working towards a teaching qualification, it would be extremely beneficial for you to have a mentor, someone who can help and support you, not only with advice regarding teaching skills, but also with your specialist subject knowledge. If you are currently teaching or training, your mentor could observe you. They could give you developmental feedback as to how you could improve your interaction with your learners. Conversely, you could observe your mentor to gain useful ideas and tips for delivering your subject.

Some of the assessment methods used for the teaching qualifications include the following (in alphabetical order) which are then explained in more detail later in this section.

- Assessment grids

- Assignments

- Case studies

- Checklists

- Essays

- Evaluation and action plans

- Learner statements

- Observations

- Online assessments

- Portfolio of evidence

- Professional discussion

- Projects

- Questions – written, oral, online

- Reflective learning journal

- Witness testimonies

- Worksheets.

You might be assessed by one or more of these methods through several different activities. Alternatively you might be assessed *holistically*, i.e. having the opportunity to demonstrate several aspects of the qualification at the same time. This saves you having to repeat aspects in different units if they can be assessed at the same time. If you are in any doubt as to how you will be assessed, or the target dates for the submission of your work, you will need to talk to your assessor. Never be afraid of discussing any concerns with them. They are there to help you, and they won't want you to fail.

It's useful to find out how you will be assessed to enable you to understand the process you will go through. When you are answering any questions or writing essays, you might find it useful to set the scene for your assessor. This could be by stating what your subject specialism is, where you are working and the types of learners you have (or will have).

Example

Sara had just signed up to take an introductory teaching qualification. She knew she had to attend 12 evening classes but she did not know how she would be assessed. She approached her teacher who informed her she would have to complete three written assignments and be observed delivering a short session to her peer group. As she did not currently have a teaching role, she was told she could write her assignments using hypothetical responses.

Assessment grids

An assessment grid is a document which lists all the criteria for each of the units of the qualification. Most qualifications are split into smaller units which relate to different topics. You will need to state how you have met the criteria and/or link them to documents and evidence from your teaching practice.

It might be possible to meet the requirements of several criteria from different units at the same time. If this is the case, you will be able to cross-reference your work rather than repeat it.

Assignments

An assignment is a way of ensuring that all the criteria can be met through various tasks or problem-solving activities. The assignment will assess your knowledge and how you can apply it, perhaps through answering questions, holding group discussions, giving presentations to peers, and providing evidence of your teaching practice. You will need time for self-reflection to consolidate your learning as you progress through the assignment. You will be given a target date for completion, and possibly a word count for all written work. You will need to reference any text or quotes you obtain from other sources (covered later in this chapter). This gives credit to the original author and shows you have carried out relevant research. Your assessor should give ongoing feedback, and if you don't fully meet the criteria, you should be given the opportunity to have another attempt.

Case studies

A case study usually consists of a hypothetical or imaginary event for you to consider and analyse. You can then make suggestions regarding how you would deal with the event, which should relate to the qualification criteria.

Alternatively, you could produce your own case study regarding a real situation that you have encountered, again, relating it to the criteria, but keeping it anonymous by not using any names of organisations or learners.

Checklists

A checklist is a list of aspects which need to be achieved which will relate to the qualification criteria. Checklists can be used by you as a form of self-assessment to check your progress so far, or by your assessor to confirm your achievement at a given point. They can be completed and dated when the relevant criteria have been met. Checklists are often used in conjunction with other assessment methods. Don't be tempted to tick something off unless you really understand it and have met the requirements.

Essays

Essays are formal pieces of writing. There will usually be a word count to ensure you remain focused and specific. You might be able to go 10 per cent above or below the figure given. You will have a target date for submission and if you can't meet this for any reason, you will need to ask for an extension.

You will usually have to word process your work in a professional style. If it is acceptable for you to handwrite your responses, make sure your writing is legible and neat. Your assessor should give you guidance as to how to present your work. Always check your spelling, grammar, punctuation and sentence structure. Try not to rely on your computer to check these as it doesn't always realise the context within which you are writing.

Essays often include citing from relevant textbooks, websites and journals (covered later in this chapter).

Evaluation and action plan

An evaluation and action plan is a document which allows you to evaluate your progress and achievement by completing a template at the end of each unit of the qualification. Your writing should clearly evaluate how you have met the criteria. The action plan aspect will help you focus upon the skills, knowledge and understanding required for your development in the future. This could be by considering what other programmes you could take, for example, to improve your research skills, and what other books, journals or websites you might access to help with your continuing professional development (covered in Chapter 12).

Learner statements

Learner statements are a way of writing how you have met the required criteria by giving specific examples of what you have achieved. You might address individual questions which directly relate to each of the criteria, or answer one question which addresses several criteria holistically.

Observations

At some point, you will be observed delivering a session with learners. After the observation you should receive verbal feedback from your assessor. This feedback should also be given to you in written form, either electronically or paper based. You will need to consider the feedback you have received when carrying out any self-evaluation activities.

Teaching practice is a chance to use your new skills and knowledge with your learners (covered in Chapter 14). Never be afraid to try something new or do something differently if it didn't work the first time. No situation is ever the same, as you will be teaching different learners on different occasions, and in different environments. What works for one learner or group, might not work with another.

Online assessments

An online assessment is where you submit your work electronically to an assessor or complete an online test. You will either email or upload it to a learning portal via a dedicated website. There are many online learning tools available, one of the most popular is known as a virtual learning environment (VLE). These sites also enable you to communicate with your assessor and your peers, and to access learning materials.

Online assessment can include *formative* (ongoing) assessment, i.e. receiving feedback from your assessor regarding a draft submission of your work. This feedback will help confirm if you are making good progress or advise you of any areas you need to improve upon. You could then upload your completed work for *summative* (final) assessment when you have completed it.

If you are delivering a session to your learners, your assessor might observe you remotely via the internet. Alternatively, you might be able to make a visual recording for them to view later. You will need to find out if this is allowed and discuss the practicalities of this with your assessor.

Portfolio of evidence

A portfolio of evidence contains proof of your achievement towards meeting the criteria. This could be electronic (for example, digital folders containing various files and documents), or paper based (for example, hard copies of documents placed in a ring binder or folder). It can also include products of your work or references to where they are located. Statements should be made as to how you have met the criteria. Documents such as observation reports, witness testimonies, and materials and resources you have used may be included.

When producing a portfolio, consider quality not quantity. It's not the amount of work (quantity) that matters; a small amount could cover many criteria if it's done well (quality). If you have had to re-do any work, it's best to include your original work as well as your revised work to show progression.

Professional discussion

A professional discussion is a conversation with your assessor rather than questions and answers. It gives you the opportunity to justify how you have achieved the criteria. This could include a discussion on anything you have done previously which might be acceptable: for example, if you have already achieved a unit elsewhere which is included in the qualification you are working towards. This is known as recognition of prior learning (RPL) and you will need to provide evidence of what you have achieved.

Your assessor could verbally explore your knowledge and understanding of the teaching role. This could be instead of having to write about it or answer questions for the sake of it. Having a professional discussion with your assessor is a good way to demonstrate how you have met the criteria, perhaps if you are having difficulty expressing yourself through written work.

A professional discussion can be used as an *holistic* assessment method, meaning several criteria can be assessed at the same time. Your assessor will prompt you to explain how you have met the requirements and ask to see documents which confirm this. They might make written notes during the discussion and/or make a visual or aural recording of your conversation. This can be kept as evidence of your achievement. Prior to the professional discussion taking place, you should agree with your assessor the nature of the content of the conversation to enable you to prepare in advance. You may need to bring along examples of teaching materials you have prepared and used. When you are having the professional discussion, try and remain focused; don't digress but be specific with your responses. At the end of the discussion, your assessor should confirm which criteria you have met and which you still need to work towards.

Projects

A project usually consists of practical activities which can be carried out during your teaching practice, and which are based on the qualification criteria. You should be given a target date for completion, and possibly a word count for any written work. Projects usually take longer in terms of time than an assignment, and might group several criteria together.

Questions – written, oral, online

You may need to produce answers to written or oral questions which will be based around the criteria of the qualification. These could be part of a written test, asked orally, or be completed online. If it's the latter, the online program could give you the results immediately, but might not tell you which questions were answered correctly or not.

If you have answered written questions and met most but not all of the criteria, your assessor might follow this up with some oral questions or a professional discussion to ensure you have the relevant knowledge and understanding.

Reflective learning journal

A reflective learning journal is a way of helping you formally focus upon your learning, pro-gress and achievements. You might be given a template or a document to complete, or you could write in a diary, use a journal, notebook or a word processor. If you are handwriting, make sure your work is legible as your assessor will need to read and understand it. Try and reflect upon your experiences by analysing as well as describing them. Be as specific as possible as to how your experiences have met the criteria. Don't just write a chronological account of events. Consider what worked well, or didn't work well, and how you could do something differently given the opportunity. Try and note which of the qualification criteria you have met as this will help your assessor when they read your journal.

Reflection should become a part of your everyday activities and enable you to look at things in detail as you perhaps would not ordinarily do. There may be events you would not want to change or improve if you felt they went well. If this is the case, reflect as to *why* they went well and use similar situations in future sessions. As you become more experi-enced at reflective writing, you will see how you can make improvements to benefit your learners and yourself (covered in Chapter 12).

Witness testimony

If you are currently teaching, you might have someone who is advising and supporting you at work, such as a mentor. They could observe you with your learners and provide a writ-ten testimony as to what you have achieved. They can confirm which criteria you have met and write a statement to this effect. You will need to check with your assessor if witness testimonies are acceptable or not.

Worksheets

Worksheets include tasks, activities and/or questions for you to carry out. These can be completed during attended sessions, in your own time or as part of an online course.

Worksheets are often used to check progress and might link several criteria together. After completing them, your assessor will check whether your responses can be used to demonstrate achievement of the relevant criteria. They will then give you constructive feedback to help you develop further.

Professional standards

Most countries have professional standards for teachers and trainers to follow. However, these could be called something else, for example, a code of practice, a code of conduct or national occupational standards (NOS). These can take many forms and are either mandatory or voluntary. In England, the Education and Training Foundation (ETF) has a set of Professional Standards for teachers and trainers to follow which were launched in 2014. They are not mandatory, but they give teachers something to aspire to, or to use as a form of self-assessment. If none are available where you work, it might be useful to refer to these as a guide.

The ETF Professional Standards:

- set out clear expectations of effective practice in education and training

- enable teachers, trainers and other practitioners to identify areas for their own professional development

- support initial teacher education and provide a national reference point that organisations can use to support the development of their staff.

There are 20 Professional Standards which relate to three areas:

- *professional values and attributes* – six standards aimed at developing judgement of what works and does not work in teaching and training

- *professional knowledge and understanding* – six standards aimed at developing deep and critically informed knowledge and understanding in theory and practice

- *professional skills* – eight standards aimed at developing expertise and skills to ensure the best outcomes for learners.

www.et-foundation.co.uk/supporting/support-practitioners/professional-standards/ (accessed May 2017)

Professional bodies, associations and networks

It's useful to belong to a professional body, association or network for teachers and trainers, and/or one for your particular subject area if one exists. This will help you to keep your knowledge up to date with what's happening in the sector and with your subject. Belonging to an association should enable you to access relevant resources, training courses and networking opportunities. Some might be free to join, but most rely on payment of a subscription. Some might offer certain benefits like reduced insurance or access to free or subsidised courses and conferences.

The following (in alphabetical order) are a few examples of those available in the UK to teachers, trainers and assessors. You might like to research the following further; most have websites which are listed at the end of this chapter.

Association for Research in Post-Compulsory Education (ARPCE)

The ARPCE aims to sustain and increase individual and collective knowledge (internationally) and use of research in post-compulsory education. This is to enhance its quality and improve public policy-making.

It is subscription free for associates and trustees, who can benefit from discounted attendance at events and conferences, and free online access to the international peer-reviewed journal *Research in Post-Compulsory Education*.

Association of Colleges (AoC)

The AoC exists to represent and promote the interests of colleges and to provide members with professional support services. The AoC was established in 1996 by colleges as a voice for further education and higher education. Its membership includes general and further education colleges, sixth form colleges and specialist colleges in England and Northern Ireland (Wales and Scotland are via partnerships).

Association of Employment and Learning Providers (AELP)

AELP is a trade association for vocational learning and employment providers in England, Scotland and Wales. The majority of its members are independent private, not-for-profit and voluntary sector training and employment service organisations. Membership is open to any provider committed to quality provision and includes FE colleges involved in work-based learning.

Centres for Excellence in Teacher Training (CETT)

These are networks which consist of partnerships of organisations involved in initial teacher training (ITT) and CPD in the further education sector. Their role is to raise the standard of initial teacher education and to improve the quality and consistency of CPD. The centres promote good practice and research, and develop advice and guidance that covers generic teaching issues as well as specific subject resources.

Chartered Institute of Educational Assessors (CIEA)

The CIEA is a professional body dedicated to supporting the needs of everyone involved in educational assessment. This includes senior examiners, moderators and markers, to individuals with an interest in, or responsibility for, assessment in primary schools, secondary schools, colleges, universities, training centres and other educational organisations. Membership is open to everyone with an interest in educational assessment as well as those studying to become teachers.

Chartered Institute of Personnel and Development (CIPD)

The CIPD is the professional body for human resources and people development. It champions better work and working lives. It has a Code of Professional Conduct for its members and has been setting the benchmark for excellence in people and organisation development for more than 100 years. Through its expertise and research, it provides a valuable point of view on the rapidly changing world of work. It sets professional standards and provides the know-how to drive the human resources, and learning and development professions forward.

Chartered Institution for Further Education (CIFE)

The CIFE is a membership body for the higher performing FE colleges and training providers in the UK. It received its Royal Charter in 2015. Its aim is to develop the standing of the FE sector, bringing together training providers to promote and celebrate good practice.

Colleges and training providers with an overall Ofsted grade one or two and in receipt of public funding from the Education and Skills Funding Agency (ESFA) are eligible to apply for membership.

Colleges Northern Ireland (CNI)

Northern Ireland's six regional colleges operate across more than 40 campuses and over 400 outreach community locations. They aim to support, represent and promote the colleges, and positively impact upon their vital contribution to Northern Ireland's economic and social well-being. They provide the voice for the college sector, and advocate on behalf of the sector, including lobbying government departments and other agencies.

Education and Training Foundation (ETF)

The ETF is all about excellence in teaching and learning in England and Wales.

Its mission is to:

- promote the professionalism and status of those working in the post-16 education and training sector, ensuring members gain wider recognition for their expertise and practice

- engage members in the active use, creation and dissemination of existing and new research into effective teaching and learning practice

- bring together members into professional communities of practice through events and community networks, regional, national and online

- provide CPD opportunities which are relevant and impactful, at a reasonable cost.

The ETF operates the membership organisation known as the Society for Education and Training (SET) which is listed towards the end of this section.

General Teaching Council Northern Ireland (GTCNI)

The GTCNI is the independent professional body for teachers in Northern Ireland. It is dedicated to enhancing the status of teaching, and promoting the highest standards of professional conduct and practice. It offers a fresh and authoritative perspective on educational issues by drawing on the experience and knowledge of teachers. It enables teachers to have the opportunity to contribute to, and shape, the future development of the profession.

Institute of Training and Occupational Learning (ITOL)

ITOL is the UK's professional body for trainers and learning and development professionals. In 2000 it was granted 'Institute' status and since that time has become recognised as the premier organisation for everyone involved in the world of training and development.

Learning and Work Institute (LWI)

The LWI is a membership organisation with a diverse set of individual and corporate members including colleges, local authorities, third-sector organisations, universities, businesses and iconic organisations in civil society. It works with a wide range of partners and stakeholders to support the learning and skills sector in providing more and better opportunities for all adults. It also advances the case for adult learning among policy-makers.

National Education Union (NEU)

The NEU was formed in September 2017 from the Association of Teachers and Lecturers (ATL) and the National Union of Teachers (NUT). It represents the majority of teachers and provides a powerful voice for the whole education profession, including support staff, lecturers and leaders working in state-funded and independent schools and colleges. It will be the fourth largest trade union in the UK and the biggest union of teachers and education professionals in Europe.

Society for Education and Training (SET)

The SET is the professional membership organisation run by the Education and Training Foundation (ETF). It is for practitioners working in the post-16 education and training sector. The SET believes that high quality education and training is essential to growth and employment. It supports initial and ongoing professional development, equipping practitioners with the tools and support they need to be excellent in their practice, improving outcomes for learners and employers.

University and College Union (UCU)

The UCU is the largest post-school union in the world, offering support and protection to its members.

Its members include: academics, lecturers, trainers, instructors, researchers, administrators, managers, computer staff, librarians and postgraduates from a university, college, prison, adult education or training organisation.

Ascertain if there is a set of professional standards in the industry or country in which you work. You might need to ask a colleague or carry out an internet search. Locate a copy and find out if they are mandatory or voluntary. Take a look through them, do you feel they adequately reflect what you thought your role would involve? You could also find out what professional organisations are available, or look at the websites of some of those listed here to see if it's worth joining them. Weblinks are at the end of this chapter.

Study skills, academic writing and referencing

If you are working towards a teaching qualification, you will need to be prepared to study in your own time. This will include activities such as research, reading textbooks and reflecting upon your practice. You might also have to use an academic style of writing and reference any quotes you use from sources such as textbooks. You will need to be self-motivated and able to dedicate an appropriate amount of time to this on a regular basis. If you can, set aside time in a place you won't be disturbed so that you can focus on what is required. If you are interrupted, distracted, hungry or thirsty when studying, you probably won't be able to concentrate very well.

It's useful to keep to all target dates for submitting your work and inform your assessor if you can't meet any. Using a diary to forward plan the submission dates could help you manage your time. You could also use your diary to note down details of critical events during your teaching practice to enable you to reflect on them later.

Study skills

If you are unsure of anything while you are studying, or have any concerns, don't be afraid to ask for help. It's best that you get clarification prior to submitting any work for assessment, in case you have misinterpreted or misunderstood something.

Tips for studying:

- Don't miss the first class if it's an attended programme; you will learn so much about the qualification and what is required of you. You will also meet your teachers, assessors and peers to enable you to build working relationships.

- Create a support network with your peers so that you can talk to and motivate each other.

- Check how much time you have for studying each week, and make a commitment to yourself to set a certain amount aside. This could be when you don't have any family or other commitments, or during an evening or weekend. If you commute, you could use this time to read, or use a digital device to listen to, watch or research certain topics online.

- Break your study tasks down into smaller, more manageable parts that will easily fit into your schedule.

- Try not to let your studies overtake your family life. It's important to fit your studies around your other activities yet remember you have made a commitment to achieving a qualification.

- Ask your family and friends to help, for example, talking through the topics you are studying.

- Set yourself realistic goals. Don't try to do too much too soon, just be honest with yourself about what you can achieve in the early stages.

- Don't hesitate to ask for help when you need it, and to network with your peers. You could keep in touch via email, social networking or a specific online learning platform.

- Ask your assessor if there are any past questions and sample answers you can see. This will help you understand what is required and how to structure your own work.

- Don't be tempted to copy anyone else's work or anything from the internet, a book or a journal (without correct referencing) as this is plagiarism. Most organisations use software to check for this. You can't always rely on the online encyclopaedia Wikipedia or some other websites as they might not be factually correct.

If you are attending a taught programme, it would be useful to make notes during the sessions, to which you can refer later. This could be on handouts given by your teacher or printed copies of a visual presentation. If you have a laptop or tablet, you could make notes electronically during the session (providing this is acceptable). When making notes, also try to remain focused on what is happening in the room, otherwise you might miss something. You could write quickly by cutting out vowels, for example, *tchr* for *teacher*. You could also cut out small words such as *an, are, at, is* and *the*. Whichever way you make your notes, make sure you will know what they mean when you look back at them. If you are reading handouts, textbooks and/or journals, you might like to use a highlighter pen or underline certain words to draw attention to them. You could also make notes in the margins, but only do this if they belong to you, not on ones borrowed from others or libraries. If you are using the latter, you could use sticky notes instead.

During attended teaching programmes, you might be required to take part in group work or give short presentations to your peers. Use this as an opportunity to work with others and to gain new skills and knowledge. If you are working towards a qualification via an online or distance learning programme, you might not meet your teacher or your peers in person. However, you might be able to communicate with them either by email or through an online internet-based system, often called a learning platform, or a virtual learning environment (VLE).

You might need support to help you improve aspects such as English, maths and digital skills. This might be available at the organisation where you are studying, or you could attend other relevant programmes. If you don't have access to a computer at home, you could use one at a local library or an internet cafe. Most smartphones enable you to download applications, which might also be appropriate to use.

Make a note of the skills you feel you already have regarding how to study; for example, creating an organised and clear work space and setting a regular time aside each week. How can you improve these skills to make sure you can meet the requirements of working towards a qualification over time? What else do you feel contributes to effective study skills? Research the internet or read a relevant study skills book to find out more. See the books and website lists at the end of this chapter.

Academic writing and referencing

Depending upon the level of qualification you are taking, you may be required to write in an academic way. This will involve citing text from relevant sources such as books, journals and websites. You will need to reference these in a certain way. If you are required to do this, you will need to check with your assessor which academic writing and referencing style to use, and whether it is mandatory or optional. The *Harvard* system is the style that is generally used and standardises the approach. However, other styles could be used; just make sure you are consistent throughout your work. There are many books and websites available which will give you further advice regarding this, some of which are listed at the end of this chapter.

It is important to reference your work to:

- acknowledge the work of other writers, authors and theorists

- assist the reader to locate your sources for their own reference and to confirm they are correct

- avoid plagiarism (i.e. using the work of others without acknowledging it)

- provide evidence of your reading and research

- use existing knowledge and theories to support your writing (whether as a direct quote or paraphrased into your own words).

Referencing from a book

When using text and quotes from different sources, for example, a book, you will need to cite them correctly. This will include using exactly what has been written (including any errors) and stating *the author, date of publication* and *page number* after anything you use. The full details of the book can then be included in a *reference list* at the end of your work.

Example

If you are describing ground rules, you could write the following and cite relevant text from a book to back up what you are saying:

Ground rules should be agreed at the start of a new programme. "Ground rules ... are boundaries and rules to help create suitable conditions within which learners (and yourself) can safely work and learn" (Gravells, 2017, page 185). It is important to establish these early to ensure the programme runs smoothly. If learners do not feel safe, they might not return again, or their learning could be affected.

Any text you insert should be within quotation marks, often known as speech marks (" "). If any words are missed out, using three dots (...) will indicate this. The name of the author, the year of publication of the book and the page number should be in brackets directly afterwards. At the end of your work, you will need a reference list in alphabetical order. This will include the full details of all the books you have quoted from. Some referencing systems use punctuation, others do not; just make sure you are consistent.

Example of the above book in a reference list

Gravells, A. (2017) *Principles and Practices of Teaching and Training.* **London: Learning Matters SAGE.**

When inserting text, make sure you understand what it actually means and how it will fit within your writing. It could be that you agree with what the author has said and it supports what you are saying, or it could be that you totally disagree with it. If so, explain why you agree or disagree, and if it's the latter, state what you might do differently. It's best to write what you think, or what your point of view is, and relate it to your specialist subject when you can.

If the text you use is longer than three lines, indent the paragraph from both margins. Always copy the words and punctuation as it is in the original, even if there are mistakes. You can add [sic] after the error to denote that you are aware of it. Long quotes are always in single line spacing, quotes of three lines or less can be in the line spacing of the main text, for example, if you have used double line spacing.

If a quote is not used within your writing, but the author is still referred to, it will look like this in your text:

Gravells (2017) advocates the agreement of ground rules with learners.

Again, the full book details will go in the reference list.

It's best to use a range of sources to develop your knowledge and understanding. Reading more than one book will help you to gain the perspectives of different authors. You don't have to read the book in full, you can just locate relevant topics by using the index at the back. If you have a look at the index at the back of this book, you will see all the topics are listed alphabetically, making it easy for you to locate the relevant page numbers. The organisation you are taking the qualification with should be able to give you advice regarding academic writing, citing text and referencing your work. They should also provide you with a reading list of relevant textbooks. If not, a reading list is available at www.anngravells.com/reading-lists/teaching.

Referencing a website

The text would be inserted within your writing in a similar way to a book, with the organisation and year it was added in brackets at the end. The month and year is often stated with news updates.

Example

"The Education and Training Foundation today warmly welcomed the Sainsbury review and the Post-16 Skills Plan published today [sic]. ETF Chief Executive David Russell said: 'There is a great deal to like about the review. It is realistic in its assessment of the challenges facing our country. It is serious about setting a reform timescale that can be delivered. And it is unambiguous that our FE and Training system is the solution, not the problem.'" (ETF, 2016)

It would look like this in your reference list, along with the date it was accessed:

Sainsbury Review and Post 16 Skills Plan

www.et-foundation.co.uk/news/sainsbury-review-post-16-skills-plan (accessed April 2017)

The date you accessed it is important as web pages often change or are removed. You might like to take a look at the above web link to read the full article, and to see how the date it was published is available at the beginning of it.

Referencing an online report

The text would be inserted within your writing in the same way as a book.

Example

"Teacher educators have traditionally struggled with convincing learners to work on their portfolios, competing against more traditional assessment demands and the habit of putting the portfolio together at the last minute" (Hopper and Sanford, 2010, page 4).

It would look like this in your reference list, along with the date it was accessed:

Hopper, T. and Sanford, K. (2010) Starting a program-wide ePortfolio practice in teacher education: Resistance, support and renewal. *Teacher Education Quarterly, Special Online Edition.*

www.teqjournal.org/onlineissue/PDFFlash/HopperSanfordManuscript/fscommand/Hopper_Sanford.pdf (accessed May 2017)

There are many other ways of sourcing and referencing information. You might like to obtain further information from your teacher, or from relevant textbooks or websites.

Practise writing some text regarding an educational topic which interests you at the moment. For example, ground rules, or the different ways in which learning takes place. Relate your writing to relevant text from a book (just look up a topic in the index at the back) and use an acceptable form of academic writing and referencing. You could also research how to reference other aspects such as a journal article, a government publication or a video.

Obtaining a teaching position and progressing further

If you haven't obtained a teaching position yet, this section will give you some advice regarding how to do so. It will also help you consider how you can progress further with your teaching career. Learning shouldn't stop just because you have read this book, or you have become qualified, or have gained a teaching or training role. Things change quickly: for example, there might be some new equipment you could use to deliver your subject, or new aspects of technology which you could use with your learners.

Obtaining a teaching position

It can be overwhelming making a career move into teaching, particularly if you have been working in industry for a long while. You might feel you lack confidence at the moment, but self-confidence will come with experience. You can't really think of teaching as a 9–5 job as you will need to spend a lot of your own time preparing your sessions, creating resources and marking learners' work. However, once you have made the decision, you can research jobs which are available for the amount of time you are able to commit. For example, you might like to give up your current career and teach full time, or you might like to teach evening classes while continuing working, or train others in your place of work. You also need to consider what age group you would like to teach, what subject you would like to teach, and where you would like to teach. For example, 16–19 year olds in a college, adult learners attending an evening class in a community centre, offenders in a prison, or new staff at your current place of work (covered in Chapter 2).

If you are not already teaching, consider the subject you would like to teach and why. Is this because you currently work in a similar subject area or because it's a hobby or an interest? Think about the age range of the learners you would like to teach, where you would like to teach and for what time periods.

The time you have available for a teaching role and the type of jobs on offer will determine how you are employed. For example, you could be:

- full time (permanently employed, or on a termly or yearly contract)

- part time (permanently employed or on a temporary contract)

- freelance or peripatetic (working for several organisations and travelling to different locations)

- self-employed (working for yourself and invoicing for work done, without the benefits of being an employee, and possibly requiring business insurance)

- sessional or variable (hourly paid, or on a zero hours contract and just called in when needed)

- supply (providing temporary cover for absent staff via an agency)

- voluntary (unpaid)

- work based (training others in your place of work or their place of work).

The type of contract you are on will determine whether you have time during your working hours for administrative duties, preparation and marking. Not all teachers automatically have this time included. A teaching career requires dedication; you will need to be prepared to work hard and to commit your own time to the role, particularly if you are part time or sessional. Even though you might feel you will get a good hourly rate of pay, you have to take into account that this rate covers you for all the work you do which is outside of these hours. Most organisations now work throughout the year, therefore don't expect to have long breaks like schools do.

When applying for a job, try and resist the temptation of taking whatever might be offered to you. Sadly, there are some organisations that are more focused upon reaching targets and obtaining funding, than the quality of the teaching and learning experience offered. This might not lead to a happy working environment, and you could feel pressured to do things you know are wrong. You could ask what the quality procedures are in the organisation. If there is a good system for supporting staff and ensuring a quality service, it should show the organisation is committed to learning, and not just focused on reaching targets. However, it's always best if you can, to talk to people who currently work in the organisation to find out how it operates.

If you are attending a teacher training course at the moment, you could talk to your teacher and ask them if they know of any teaching opportunities, either now or that might occur in the future. You could even ask if you could sit in on a session which is being delivered in your specialist subject area. This will help you see what is involved, and you could make some useful contacts. You could offer to do some voluntary teaching or to support the current teacher in some way. This would give you some great experience which could help in the future.

Example

Fatima is working towards a teacher training qualification and needs to carry out a certain number of teaching practice hours with learners. She is working full time as an office manager and often carries out training activities with staff on a one-to-one basis. Her teacher has told her that some of this can be classed as teaching practice; however, she also needs to demonstrate she can work with groups. Fatima approached the local college, which said she can sit in on some sessions of the Office Administration course. Fatima hopes that she can then offer to deliver some sessions on a voluntary basis and use this towards her teaching practice. She also hopes to gain some valuable work experience and make some useful contacts at the college. Her aim is to teach evening classes part time in a college environment.

Websites advertising teaching and training jobs

There are many websites available which advertise teaching and training jobs. You might find it useful to look at some of the following and sign up for their job alerts. The following websites were live at the time of publication.

www.cv-library.co.uk/search/teaching-jobs

https://college.jobs.ac.uk

www.eatjobs.co.uk

www.fecareers.co.uk

www.fejobs.com

www.jobbydoo.co.uk/further-education-jobs

www.jobmanji.co.uk/

www.jobs.ac.uk

http://neuvoo.co.uk/en

http://www.nvqjobs.com

www.tes.co.uk/jobs

There might also be relevant forums on professional social networking sites such as LinkedIn (www.linkedin.com) which you might like to join.

Progression

When you are nearing completion of your teaching qualification, you will need to consider how you wish to progress further. You may find it useful to summarise your learning and create an action plan. This could be a list of your strengths and achievements so far, aspects you would like to develop or improve, and how you aim to work towards accomplishing them.

Other things you might like to consider include:

- applying for a professional teaching status if one exists in your country
- applying for a promotion
- attending relevant courses to update your skills and knowledge
- carrying out a work placement
- offering to mentor a colleague
- self-assessing your progress and development towards relevant teaching standards or codes of practice
- working towards a higher level teaching qualification.

If you are not currently teaching, you might like to consider how you can apply for a teaching position.

Professional teaching status

It might be possible for you to gain a professional teaching status which confirms your commitment to your role. This may differ depending upon your qualifications and experience. In England, it's possible to apply for Qualified Teacher Learning and Skills status (QTLS) if you work in the FE and skills sector.

QTLS status is a voluntary process which demonstrates your commitment to being a professional teacher. It is gained by being a paid member of the professional association the Society for Education and Training (SET), which is part of the Education and Training Foundation (ETF). Gaining QTLS status gives parity with the Qualified Teacher Status (QTS) in schools, enabling you to teach in a school or an academy should you wish (this is recognised in English law). However, you do need to have at least a level 5 teaching qualification, be able to demonstrate your English and maths to at least level 2, and pay the required application fee. There is also a *recognition route* for teachers who do not hold a level 5 teaching qualification, but have substantial teaching experience.

Holding QTLS status could help you in your career progression, and you can be added to the SET's online professional status register. Please see this link for details of QTLS status: https://set.et-foundation.co.uk/professionalism/qtls/

Extension activity

If you are currently teaching, find out if there is a professional teaching status you could apply for, such as QTLS in England, once you are qualified and experienced.

If you are not yet teaching, find out where your local colleges or training organisations are. Have a look at their websites or contact them to ask how you could obtain a teaching position. Find out what qualifications and/or experience they expect you to have. If they have any positions available, ask for an application form. If they don't, ask if you can send them your curriculum vitae for them to keep on file, or ask if there are any voluntary teaching opportunities available. Don't be put off by rejection, you need to persevere and stay positive. Alternatively, you could consider delivering some training to colleagues or new staff in your current place of work.

Evidence-based practice

Evidence-based practice is about using what works best when teaching a particular topic or subject. Evidence is confirmation or proof of something, but how do you know what works best if you are a new teacher?

You could try the following:

- talking to other teachers and experts. Discussing what you have done and why it did or did not work. Finding out what they do, why they do it, and why what they do works.

- researching what has been done before. There are many journal papers and books written by educational experts who have tried and tested different ways of doing things. However, there might equally be other experts who contradict them.

- trying something out with your learners, for example, from the research you have read, seeing if it works or not, and considering why. However, what works with one learner or group might not work with another. Don't be put off trying, you can adapt and keep experimenting. You can even be honest with your learners and tell them you are trying something new and would like their feedback.

- carrying out research yourself, for example, you might have to do this as part of a teaching qualification you are taking.

- reviewing what you do and reflecting upon each experience you have, comparing this to research.

If you are a new teacher, you might not really have anything on which to base what you will do when you have your own learners, other than your past experiences as a learner yourself. These experiences might have been positive, for example, a college course with a friendly and helpful teacher. Alternatively, they could have been negative, for example, a school class with a domineering teacher. You will know what worked and did not work for you. However, you can't base how you will teach, on how you were taught, as all situations are different. You also can't teach everyone the same thing at the same time, as learning takes place in different ways and at different times. This is what makes the role of a teacher challenging but interesting. As you progress through this book, you will find out lots of ways of doing things. However, you need to find out what works for you and your learners, in a way that you all feel comfortable with.

Activity

If you have access to the internet, take a look at one or more of the case studies at this shortcut link: http://tinyurl.com/zdat6fw.

Can you use any of the ideas for your own subject? If so, how?

Never be afraid of asking for help, advice and support. There should be colleagues, supervisors and other staff who could help you. Don't think that you have to know everything. It's fine to admit you don't know something and that you would like the benefit of someone else's expertise. It could be that the organisation in which you will teach uses an observation process to support their staff. The person will be able to see you in action with your learners and will give you feedback. Their advice should be based on evidence of what works as they will be experienced specialists. Don't be afraid to ask them some questions and find out what books and research they would recommend you could read.

Example

Alex is a fairly new teacher in a college, having worked there for six months teaching numeracy skills. His organisation uses a system of peer observations to help support each other and share good practice. Jon, another maths teacher, observed one of Alex's sessions. In Jon's feedback, he stated 'You had high expectations of all your learners and took into account their prior knowledge. You were able to set challenging tasks, and all learners were engaged during the session. However, you need to use formative assessment more to ensure learning is taking place by each individual'. This enabled Alex to ask Jon how he used formative assessment with his learners. This led to an interesting and helpful discussion of evidence-based practice.

Whatever you do, sometimes things will go wrong, or something you had planned to do just won't work. Don't panic, just be honest with yourself and your learners, and don't bluff your way out of something. Afterwards, make a note of what went well, and what didn't go well. You can then use this to help evaluate your session and reflect on how you could do things differently next time. You will develop your own strategies as time progresses, and you will also learn from your own experiences.

Extension activity

Research more about what evidence-based practice involves. This could be via the internet by keying in 'evidence-based practice' into an online search engine. Alternatively, it could be by discussing the topic with colleagues, reading current educational research, or visiting a library and reading relevant textbooks or journal articles.

Self-assessment checklist

Do I know about the following?

If not, re-read this chapter, or research the texts and websites listed at the end.

☐ How to use this book

☐ What the FE and skills sector is

☐ The subject I will teach, to whom and in what context

☐ The teaching qualifications I can work towards

☐ The ways I might be assessed for a teaching qualification

☐ The standards which teachers can aspire to

☐ How to study in an effective way

☐ How to write in an academic style

☐ How to cite text and reference work

☐ How to apply for a teaching or a training role

☐ How to progress further once I have achieved my goals

☐ The importance of evidence-based practice upon my role

Summary

This chapter has explored the further education and skills sector and how to become a teacher or a trainer.

You should now be able to explore aspects in more detail, perhaps by working towards a relevant qualification and/or applying for a teaching role. You should also know how to progress further once qualified and experienced.

You might like to carry out further research by accessing the books and websites listed at the end of this chapter, particularly if you are working towards a higher level teaching qualification.

This chapter has covered the following topics:

• The structure of the book

• The further education and skills sector

• Qualifications and standards for teachers and trainers

• Study skills, academic writing and referencing

• Obtaining a teaching position and progressing further

• Evidence-based practice

References and further information

Burton, D. and Bartlett, S. (2009) *Key Issues for Education Researchers*. London: SAGE.

Castle, P. and Buckler, S. (2009) *How to be a Successful Teacher*. London: SAGE.

Clark, R.C. (2015) *Evidence-Based Training Methods: A Guide for Training Professionals* (2nd edition). ATD Press.

Curtis, W. and Ward, S. (2013) *Education Studies: An Issue Based Approach* London: Learning Matters SAGE.

Curzon, L.B. and Tummons, J. (2013) *Teaching in Further Education* (7th edition). London: Bloomsbury.

Denscombe, M. (2014) *The Good Research Guide*. Maidenhead: Open University Press.

Gravells, A. (2015) *Principles and Practices of Assessment*. London: SAGE Learning Matters.

Gravells, A. (2016) *Principles and Practices of Quality Assurance*. London: SAGE Learning Matters.

Gravells, J. and Wallace, S. (2013) *An A-Z Guide to Working in Further Education*. Northwich: Critical Publishing Ltd.

Hargreaves, S. and Crabb, J. (2016) *Study Skills for Students with Dyslexia*. London: SAGE.

Malthouse, R. and Roffey-Barentsen, J. (2013) *Academic Skills: Contemporary Education Studies*. London: Thalassa Publishing.

Pears, R. and Shields, G. (2013) *Cite them right: The Essential Referencing Guide*. Basingstoke: Palgrave Macmillan.

Petty, G. (2009) *Evidence Based Teaching: A Practical Approach* (2nd edition). Cheltenham: Nelson Thornes.

Tummons, J. (2014) *A to Z of Lifelong Learning*. Berkshire: Open University Press.

Tummons, J. (2010) *Becoming a Professional Tutor* (2nd edition). Exeter: Learning Matters.

Websites

Ann Gravells: information and resources – www.anngravells.com

Association for Research in Post-Compulsory Education (ARPCE) – http://arpce.org.uk

Association of Colleges (AOC) – www.aoc.co.uk

Association of Employment and Learning Providers (AELP) – www.aelp.org.uk

Chartered Institute for Educational Assessors (CIEA) – http://ciea.org.uk/

Chartered Institute of Personnel and Development (CIPD) – www.cipd.co.uk

Chartered Institution for Further Education – www.fecharter.org.uk

Colleges Northern Ireland (CNI) – www.anic.ac.uk

Commission on Adult Vocational Teaching and Learning (CAVTL) *It's about work* ... Excellent adult vocational teaching and learning – https://tinyurl.com/l6pbv3e

Council for the Curriculum, Examinations and Assessment (CCEA) – http://ccea.org.uk

Department for Employment and Learning (DEL Northern Ireland) – https://www.delni.gov.uk

Education and Skills Funding Agency (ESFA) – https://tinyurl.com/mdrltn8

Education and Training Foundation (ETF) – www.et-foundation.co.uk

FE Advice – www.feadvice.org.uk

Federation for Industry Sector Skills and Standards (FISSS) – http://fisss.org

General Teaching Council for Northern Ireland (GTCNI) – www.gtcni.org.uk

Institute of Training and Occupational Learning (ITOL) – www.itol.org

Learning and Work Institute (LWE) – www.learningandwork.org.uk

National Education Union (NEU) – www.neu.org.uk

Ofqual – www.ofqual.gov.uk

Ofsted – www.ofsted.gov.uk

Qualifications Wales – www.qualificationswales.org

Reading list for research and study skills – www.anngravells.com/reading-lists/research-and-study-skills

Referencing styles – https://tinyurl.com/lupu2bo

Scottish Qualifications Authority (SQA) – https://tinyurl.com/musjcze

Society for Education and Training (SET) – https://set.et-foundation.co.uk

Study skills – www.back2college.com/top10studytips.htm

       www.barry.edu/pace/current-students/resource-guide/study-skills.html

       www.educationcorner.com/study-skills.html

       www.studygs.net/adulted.htm

University and College Union (UCU) – www.ucu.org.uk

1
The role of a teacher

Introduction

The role of a teacher is about ensuring that meaningful learning is taking place. It also includes many other aspects such as administration tasks, working with others and following relevant guidelines. Being passionate about your subject and enthusiastic in the way you facilitate the learning process will help give your learners an enjoyable and rewarding experience.

This chapter will explore the different aspects of your role, how other people can support you, and how you can deal with any learner behaviour issues. Relevant legislation is covered, as are other aspects which support or impact upon your role.

This chapter will cover the following topics:

- Roles and responsibilities
- Wider professional practice
- Professional boundaries
- Promoting appropriate behaviour and respect
- Creating and maintaining a safe, supportive and effective teaching and learning environment
- Legal, regulatory requirements and codes of practice

Roles and responsibilities

Your main role as a teacher will be to manage and facilitate the learning process. This will be by teaching your subject in a way which actively involves and engages your learners. This might be in the workplace, in a college, or another training or educational environment. However, it's not just about the *teaching*, it's about the *learning* that takes place as a result. You can teach as much as you wish, but if learning is not taking place then your teaching has not been successful.

Most careers are quite challenging and demanding; teaching is no exception to this. You should want your learners to become confident, knowledgeable and independent by the time they leave you. The role can be very rewarding, particularly when you see your learners' achievements and successes, which are as a direct result of your contribution and support. It would be wonderful if your name was remembered by your learners for years to come, as someone who was an inspiration to them.

The subject you teach might be based on a job, a trade or a profession you have, or a hobby or an interest. You will need to make sure you are up to date with your own skills and knowledge in your subject area, as things can change quite quickly. As you progress through this book, you will gain lots of ideas regarding how to teach your subject, i.e. how to pass on your skills and knowledge to others, how to keep up to date, and how to assess that learning has taken place. Assessment can be formal by asking questions to confirm knowledge and/or observing practice to confirm skills. It can also be informal by using discussions, quizzes and other activities. If you don't assess your learners, you won't know what has been learnt.

When you are with your learners, it's best to use clear language at an appropriate level for them, and in terms they will understand. Although you know what you are talking about, this might be the first time your learners have heard it. Therefore, never be afraid of repeating yourself or demonstrating something again. Think back to when you learnt something for the first time, perhaps you didn't take it all in at first. You need to know this will be the same for your own learners. You can always look for aspects such as body language and facial expressions to help you see that they are taking an interest in the subject. Getting to know your learners from when they commence will help you to support them with any particular concerns or needs they might have.

It's best to involve your learners as much as possible to keep them motivated and keen to learn more: for example, by making your sessions interesting and relevant with fun activities. This will help you to engage your learners in the subject and encourage them to leave the session wanting to come back for more. However, you do need to check that they are learning something while they are with you, as well as having fun.

The requirements of your job role will depend upon how many hours you will be working, and where and how your subject will be taught. It will also depend upon the age and experience of your learners, the environment you are in, and any organisational requirements, policies and procedures. This will all become clearer as you progress through the book. If you haven't already read the Introduction chapter, this will help set the scene for your role.

Becoming a good teacher includes being enthusiastic and knowledgeable, being approachable, and taking pride in your work. This should then be conveyed to your learners through your professionalism and passion for your subject.

Example

Jim, a new teacher of English literature, always arrives early to his classes. He ensures he has enough books and handouts, and organises the furniture in a way that encourages communication between everyone. He delivers his subject with passion and enthusiasm using a variety of methods. He includes all his learners by addressing them by name and asking each a question at some point. He remains fair with the support and advice he gives, not favouring one learner over another, and is always polite. He encourages his learners to leave the room tidy, and offers to email additional learning materials if required. His learners see how conscientious and professional he is. They begin to emulate this by being early, being polite and submitting work on time.

A good first impression will help you establish a positive working relationship with your learners. The way you dress, act, respond to questions and offer support, will also influence your learners. They don't need to know anything personal about you, but they will probably make assumptions about you. If asked personal questions, try not to give out any information. By remaining professional, and not becoming too friendly, you will retain their respect. Most teachers of adults are on first name terms with their learners. However, you will need to decide what is appropriate for your situation and the age range of your learners. Establishing routines will help your sessions flow smoothly, for example, always starting on time, setting and keeping to time limits for activities and breaks, and finishing on time.

Often, your personality and mannerisms will be noticed by your learners. You might do things you are not aware of, for example, waving your arms around or fidgeting. It is really useful to make a visual recording of one of your sessions if you can, as you may see things you didn't even realise you did. You might need permission from your organisation and your learners if you wish to do this.

Personal qualities such as arriving early, being organised and smiling when your learners enter the room, will help you all relax at the beginning of the session. Using your learners' names when you get the opportunity will make them feel you are getting to know them as individuals. You could use name cards or badges to help you and the other learners remember people's names in the early stages. Alternatively, you could draw a seating plan and add the names of who sits where. However, this won't help you if people move to different places. Using learners' names as often as you can might help you to remember them.

Observing your learners' body language will help you to see if they are not understanding something or not paying attention. You can then ask a question to refocus them. Don't be afraid of regularly recapping points and repeating topics. Remember, you know your subject, but for your learners it's probably the first time they have seen or heard anything about it.

If you are new to teaching, you may find you are teaching in the same way you were taught at school or college. This could have included lecturing, reading from a book, or copying information from a board which might not have been very effective for you. You won't yet know all the other approaches and activities you could use to make learning interesting and engaging. As you become more experienced, your confidence will grow, and you will be able to experiment with different approaches. Not everything you do will suit all of your learners all of the time. However, if you plan effectively, and choose appropriate teaching and learning methods, you should ensure learning takes place.

If you are ever unsure of anything, make sure you ask someone you work with. You should never feel you are on your own. Teaching can sometimes be an isolated role depending where you work, and you might not always get the opportunity to meet with others regularly. However, there are professional networking sites such as LinkedIn (www.linkedin. com) which have free discussion groups you could join. You could also keep in touch with your colleagues via email or social media.

Activity

How could you create a good first impression with your learners? What would influence this? For example, your own previous experience of attending a session, which was either good or bad.

The teaching, learning and assessment cycle

The teaching, learning and assessment cycle, as in Figure 1.1, is a systematic process which helps ensure your learners have a positive experience and are able to achieve their goals. The process can start at any stage of the cycle and keep on going; however, all stages should be addressed for learning to be effective. Quality assurance should take place continuously to ensure all aspects are being taught and assessed fairly and accurately (covered in Chapter 11). Don't worry if what follows doesn't make sense at the moment as it will be covered in detail throughout the book.

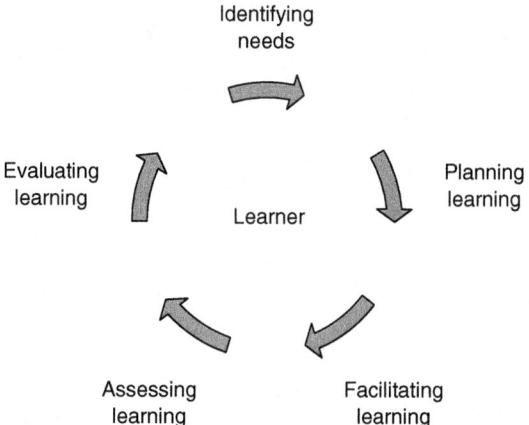

Identifying needs

Evaluating learning

Learner

Planning learning

Assessing learning

Facilitating learning

Figure 1.1 The teaching, learning and assessment cycle

Your role might follow the cycle, with all aspects focusing on the learner, and will briefly involve:

- identifying needs – finding out what your organisation's, your own, and your potential learners' needs are, finding out why learners are taking the programme and what their expectations are, carrying out initial and diagnostic assessments, agreeing individual learning plans, ensuring learners are capable of achieving their goals and progressing to their chosen destination

- planning learning – preparing schemes of work, session plans and materials to ensure you cover the requirements of the programme, liaising with others

- facilitating learning – teaching, training and facilitating learning using a variety of approaches, activities and resources to motivate, engage and inspire learners

- assessing learning – checking your learners have gained the necessary skills, knowledge and understanding at all stages throughout their time with you, using formal and informal types and methods of assessment

- evaluating learning – obtaining feedback from others, reflecting on your role, and all aspects involved with the learning process in order to make improvements.

Obtaining feedback from others, and evaluating your practice can also take place after each stage of the cycle. Running throughout the cycle is quality assurance. This is a system of monitoring all aspects which occur with learners from when they commence the course through to their completion. Good practice for all programmes is to include a system of *internal quality assurance (IQA)*. This might be a formal requirement if you are teaching and assessing an accredited qualification. These are offered by awarding organisations (AO), who will issue a certificate to all successful learners. Depending upon which country you are in, this might be known as an awarding body or an examination board. The IQA process involves a colleague at your organisation monitoring and sampling aspects of everything you do. This will ensure you are being fair to all your learners, making correct decisions and following the relevant policies and procedures. If you are teaching towards an accredited qualification, there might also be an external quality assurance (EQA) system. This involves a person visiting from the organisation that awards the qualification, to ensure all staff are following the requirements correctly.

Most teachers follow the cycle from beginning to end; however, your job role might not require you to be involved with all of them. For example, you might not carry out the *identifying needs* stage as other staff within your organisation will do this. You will, however, need to liaise with them to obtain relevant information to help you plan your sessions. You might be training a member of staff in the workplace and only carry out the *planning learning* and *facilitating learning* stages, as someone else might assess their progress. Again, you would need to liaise with whoever else is involved with your learner to help support them adequately.

To teach effectively involves not only the approaches you use to teach your subject, i.e. discussions, group work and paired activities, but many other factors that go before and after the taught session. This includes:

- planning logically what you will cover during your sessions
- preparing your materials and resources

- assessing that learning has taken place

- giving feedback on progress and achievements

- keeping records and carrying out administrative duties

- evaluating your performance and the experiences your learners have had.

Never underestimate the amount of time you will need to dedicate to the role. You will need good time management skills to ensure you are well prepared and can give a good service to your learners.

Table 1.1 (on pages 38 and 39) lists examples of roles and responsibilities (in alphabetical order) which relate to the teaching, learning and assessment cycle. However, some people might consider a role to be a responsibility and vice versa, depending upon their job requirements. Don't be daunted by the list, you might not need to carry out everything depending upon your job role.

Activity

Look at Table 1.1, make a note of which roles and responsibilities you consider to be the most important for a teacher to carry out. Why do you think this is? Do you think any of the responsibilities should be classed as a role, and vice versa? If you can, discuss this with another teacher and see if you agree or disagree. If you have a job specification, you could compare it to the list. Don't worry if there are any aspects you are unsure of, they will be covered as you progress through the book.

Teaching or training?

Would you consider yourself a teacher or a trainer? You might think that *teaching* occurs in an educational establishment, whereas *training* occurs in the workplace or a workshop. However, that defines the role by the location, rather than the job. You might also think that teaching is a way of someone *imparting* knowledge, and training is a way of enabling someone to *acquire* skills. Whatever you consider the role to be, it's all about the learning that's taking place. This will occur by using different approaches and activities to help your learners gain the relevant skills, knowledge and understanding they need at a given point in time. The process should also help their progression in education, life and work. Throughout this book, the term teacher will be used more than trainer, but it implies both roles.

Activity

What do you consider the difference is between teaching and training? Think about it first, and then research a few definitions. Discuss your response with someone else and see if you agree or disagree. Do you think the two roles are interchangeable?

Table 1.1 Examples of roles and responsibilities

Roles	Responsibilities
Identifying needs	
<ul><li>arranging for suitable initial and diagnostic assessments to take place, for example, to ascertain current skills and knowledge</li><li>attending promotional events to publicise the programme</li><li>carrying out interviews with learners</li><li>identifying any barriers or challenges to learning</li><li>identifying any particular learner, self and organisational needs</li><li>identifying learning preferences</li><li>knowing the boundaries within which to work</li><li>participating in recruitment activities</li></ul>	<ul><li>dressing appropriately</li><li>ensuring learners are on the right programme at the right level</li><li>following organisational policies and procedures</li><li>giving appropriate information, advice and guidance</li><li>helping learners arrange funding/grants</li><li>keeping records</li><li>maintaining confidentiality</li><li>referring learners to other people or agencies when necessary</li><li>undertaking a criminal records check</li></ul>
Planning learning	
<ul><li>agreeing individual learning plans</li><li>contributing to curriculum design</li><li>designing a scheme of work and session plans</li><li>liaising with others</li><li>planning what will be taught and when</li><li>preparing teaching and learning resources and activities</li></ul>	<ul><li>carrying out risk assessments</li><li>collaborating with others</li><li>creating and maintaining a safe, secure, supportive and accessible learning environment</li><li>having a contingency plan</li><li>obtaining a copy of what will be taught and assessed</li><li>setting appropriate targets</li><li>writing realistic aims</li></ul>
Facilitating learning	
<ul><li>carrying out relevant administrative requirements</li><li>carrying out tutorial reviews</li><li>establishing ground rules</li><li>inducting learners to the organisation and programme</li><li>maintaining a duty of care towards your learners</li><li>registering learners for qualifications and exams (or liaising with the person who will)</li><li>using icebreakers and energisers effectively</li><li>teaching in an inclusive and engaging way</li><li>using a variety of teaching and learning approaches and activities to motivate learners</li></ul>	<ul><li>acting and speaking appropriately</li><li>acting professionally and with integrity</li><li>being suitably qualified/experienced to teach your subject</li><li>communicating appropriately and effectively with learners</li><li>completing attendance records</li><li>dealing with behaviour issues as they occur</li><li>differentiating and using appropriate teaching and learning materials and approaches</li><li>engaging and encouraging learning</li><li>following relevant legislation, regulations and codes of practice</li><li>following awarding organisation and external bodies' requirements</li></ul>

Roles	Responsibilities
Facilitating learning (Continued)	
	• following up absences • helping and supporting learners as appropriate • helping learners develop their English, maths and digital skills • incorporating technology during sessions • keeping records of what has been taught and to whom • keeping up to date with developments relating to your subject • maintaining a professional working relationship with learners • monitoring attendance and punctuality • motivating, engaging and inspiring learners • not forcing your own attitudes, values and beliefs upon your learners • promoting appropriate behaviour and respect for others • preparing and tidying the area before and after each session • using appropriate equipment and resources
Assessing learning	
• assessing progress and achievement • ensuring decisions are valid, reliable, fair and ethical • interpreting the assessment requirements correctly • keeping records of individual achievements • preparing realistic formative and summative assessment materials • standardising decisions with others	• assessing work within an agreed time period • checking for plagiarism if applicable • following awarding organisation and external bodies' requirements • giving feedback to learners • informing learners of their right to appeal • maintaining confidentiality • using appropriate equipment and resources • using a variety of assessment types methods
Evaluating learning	
• attending meetings • evaluating how well the programme was planned and delivered • improving the teaching and learning process • liaising with others, e.g. internal/external quality assurers and inspectors • partaking in organisational quality assurance processes • standardising practice with others	• encouraging learner development and progression • evaluating each session you taught, along with the teaching and learning approaches and materials used • helping learners achieve their full potential • maintaining own professional development and subject skills and knowledge • obtaining ongoing feedback from learners and others

Record keeping

Record keeping is a crucial part of the teaching role. This is not only to support the teaching, learning and assessment process, but to provide an audit trail of each learner's progress, and to supply information to others. Records are needed to satisfy auditors, inspectors, regulators, internal and external quality assurers, and to meet your own organisation's requirements. For example, the information and data gathered can inform quality assurance, equality and diversity, and health and safety policies. The information contained in records helps to measure learning, and the effectiveness and appropriateness of the programme overall. Information such as attendance, progress and achievement could be shared with your colleagues if they are also involved with your learners, for example, to look for patterns of non-attendance or behaviour issues.

Records should be kept confidential and secure at your organisation, for example, in a locked filing cabinet or a password protected electronic file. The Data Protection Act (1998) in the UK is mandatory for all organisations that hold or process personal data. In May 2018 this will be replaced with the General Data Protection Regulation (GDPR). The current Act contains eight principles, to ensure that data are:

- processed fairly and lawfully

- obtained and used only for specified and lawful purposes

- adequate, relevant and not excessive

- accurate and, where necessary, kept up to date

- kept for no longer than necessary

- processed in accordance with the individual's rights

- kept secure

- transferred only to countries that offer adequate protection.

Records must be kept for a certain amount of time, depending upon your organisation's requirements, which could be several years. They must be up to date, accurate, factual and legible, whether they are stored electronically or as hard copies. If you happen to be absent for any reason, a colleague will be able to effectively take over if they have access to your records. Data is also useful to your organisation for purposes such as accidents, appeals, equal opportunities, and funding. If accurate records are not maintained, your learners' progress and achievement might not be recognised.

Example

Nigel has set up two lever arch files. One contains all the documentation relevant to deliver and assess the Certificate in Sport and Recreation. This includes a printed copy of the qualification specification, a scheme of work, session plans, and teaching and learning materials. The other contains alphabetical records relating to each of his learners. In these are: application forms, interview notes, initial assessment results, action plans, tutorial review records and assessment results. These files ensure he has everything to hand, not only to carry out his role effectively, but also for auditors and inspectors. His organisation has recently installed computer software to enable all staff to store these records electronically; therefore, Nigel will be able to use the new system when it's introduced. This will save him having to carry heavy files around.

Try and keep on top of your record keeping and administrative work. If you leave it for a while, you may forget to sign or date something. An important record you will need to maintain, and often a legal requirement, is the register or record of attendance. You need to know who is in your session, not only for fire regulations or evacuation procedures, but also to keep track of attendance patterns. If a learner is absent regularly you could find out why, in case they need any individual support due to certain circumstances. Some learners might receive funding based on their attendance and achievement. They will not be happy if they don't receive their full allowance due to incorrect record keeping.

Table 1.2 (on page 42) lists some of the records you might need to keep (in alphabetical order), in relation to the teaching, learning and assessment cycle.

Extension activity

Make a list of the records you will need to maintain for your particular subject, and the reasons why you will need to keep them. If you are currently teaching, find out what the procedures are for keeping records, i.e. where they should be stored and for how long. Can you save them electronically? If so, how will you go about this and will you be required to make backup copies or give copies to anyone else for any reason?

Wider professional practice

Wider professional practice is all about working within the boundaries of your role, following relevant policies and procedures, and contributing to aspects such as quality improvement. It's also about working with colleagues, collaborating with, and being accountable to others, such as stakeholders (covered in Chapter 3).

Teachers are often referred to as *dual professionals*: a professional teacher and a professional subject specialist. Your professional practice will, therefore, involve being a proficient teacher and an expert in the subject you will teach. Keeping up to date with both of these is all part of your professional development (covered in Chapter 12). Having some knowledge of local and/or national government policies, initiatives and reports is also useful in case they will have an impact upon your role.

Table 1.2 Example records

Identifying needs	• application forms • diagnostic test results • enrolment forms • initial assessment results • interview notes • learner contracts • learning preference results • learning support requirements • personal details of learners, e.g. address, contacts, disabilities • registration numbers with awarding organisations • copy of what is to be taught and assessed • targets and funding data
Planning learning	• group profile (details of individual learners) • individual learning plans/action plans • list of books, resources and equipment • risk assessments (plus electrical test results) • scheme of work • session plans • timetables
Facilitating learning	• accident/incident forms • agreed ground rules • attendance records/registers • details of learner progress and behaviour • disciplinary records • evidence of embedding English, maths and digital skills • induction records • learning support records • records of what was taught and when • tutorial review records
Assessing learning	• assessment plans and action plans • achievement data • feedback records and decisions/grades (initial, formative and summative) • tracking sheets
Evaluating learning	• complaints and appeals • continuing professional development (CPD) records • equal opportunities data • inspection reports • internal and external quality assurance reports • minutes of meetings • questionnaire and feedback analysis • retention, achievement and progression data • standardisation records

There will be other people with whom you will need to work or liaise with at some point during your teaching career. These could be people within your organisation (internal) or outside it (external) and could include (in alphabetical order):

- administration staff
- assessors
- budget holders
- career guidance staff
- caretakers
- catering staff
- cleaners
- community leaders
- co-tutors
- council staff
- counsellors
- customers
- e-learning staff
- emergency service personnel
- exam invigilators
- financial support staff
- government officials
- governors
- guest speakers
- health and safety officers
- health care professionals
- human resource staff
- journalists
- inspectors
- internal and external quality assurers
- language translators
- learner/learning support assistants
- maintenance staff
- managers
- mental health staff
- other teachers and trainers
- other training organisation staff
- probation officers
- religious leaders
- reprographics staff
- security staff
- safeguarding officers
- staff development personnel
- social workers
- supervisors
- support workers
- teaching assistants
- technicians
- union staff
- witnesses in the workplace
- work-placement co-ordinators.

When communicating with other people, it's best to be polite, remain professional, and treat everyone with respect, no matter how they treat you. This should be by whatever method you use, i.e. telephone, email, in person or via online face-to-face communications. You will want to build up a good reputation; therefore you should try not to let any personal issues or problems affect your role. You might not yet know about all the different people who can help you; therefore you will need to find out who they are and how you can contact them. There might be an organisation chart you can locate to see who does what and how the lines of communication work.

It would be useful to understand a little bit about the job roles of the people you will work with the most. This would help you to know how they can support you, and how you can support them. However, don't feel you need to support them too much by carrying out aspects of their role for them, otherwise you might be blurring the boundary between your own professional role and theirs.

Activity

How will your role involve you working with other professionals? Make a list of those who you might work with who are internal, and external, to your organisation. It might be useful to ascertain and keep a note of their contact details for when you need to get in touch.

Examples of working with other professionals might include (in alphabetical order):

- attending team meetings and contributing towards issues under discussion

- communicating with administrative staff to ensure that your learners have been registered with the relevant awarding organisation for a particular qualification

- contacting companies to purchase or hire equipment, resources and materials

- getting handouts photocopied by the reprographics department to ensure they are ready in time

- liaising with an internal quality assurer to enable them to sample your work, and/or an external quality assurer from an awarding organisation

- liaising with learning support staff to address individual learner needs

- liaising with the caretaker to ensure the room and/or building is open when you start and secure when you leave

- obtaining technical support when using equipment you are not familiar with

- talking to a learner's supervisor or a witness in their place of work to gain feedback regarding their progress and achievement

- team-teaching or co-tutoring with other members of staff, i.e. planning who will do what and when.

You might experience some issues and need to know who to turn to. You should never feel you have to resolve a situation on your own; there should be others who can help you if necessary. There might be occasions where you are teaching a session in a venue or a building away from the main premises. If this is the case, it would be useful to know who you could contact and how you can contact them in case of an emergency. Having a mobile phone with you, with contact details saved in advance, would be useful.

You might have other roles besides teaching which involve working with others. For example, attending promotional events and conferences, or visiting learners who are taking part in a work placement. If so, always remember you are representing your organisation and should uphold its values and act professionally at all times.

Example

Frieda, an experienced teacher, attended a conference regarding new developments in her subject area of electronics. Although she attended on her day off, she still dressed smartly and wore her name badge. She was polite to everyone she met and ensured she networked with others during the day. She came away with lots of information and the business cards of others she had met. When she returned to her organisation, she produced a report about what she had learnt for her manager and colleagues. She also arranged to demonstrate some practical electronic skills to the staff in her department.

In this example, Frieda maintained her professionalism even though she had attended the conference on her day off.

At some point, you might need to liaise with people who are external to your organisation. For example:

- auditors and inspectors if you are assessing qualifications
- employers and supervisors if you are training and assessing in the workplace
- parents and guardians if you are teaching younger learners
- visiting speakers who are contributing to your sessions.

It might be that you are required to look after relevant people who visit your organisation. If so, you will need to inform reception of their arrival time, perhaps organise parking and refreshments, and be accessible as soon as they arrive. They may need to wear a visitor's badge and sign in and out of the building.

Extension activity

Consider the term professionalism: what do you think it means in relation to your role as a teacher or a trainer? Think about it first, and then research a few definitions. Discuss your response with someone else and see if you agree or disagree. What situations do you think could occur which might lead to a teacher becoming unprofessional? How could you overcome them?

Professional boundaries

There will be professional boundaries within which to work and it's important not to overstep these, for example, by becoming too friendly and personal with your learners. Boundaries are about knowing where your role as a teacher stops. You should be able to work within the limits of that role, but know that it's okay to ask for help when necessary. Don't try to take on too much, or carry out something which is part of someone else's role. If you are ever in any doubt about the boundaries of your role, or how you should act in certain situations, you should ask for advice.

You should be able to maintain appropriate standards of conduct and fulfil your role and responsibilities in a professional way. This will involve not only how you act with your learners, but also with your colleagues, support staff and other staff, for example, external visitors. Having boundaries will help you remain professional in your role.

Example

Navinda had been teaching a group of 16 learners once a week for six weeks. She occasionally emailed them between sessions to inform them of room changes. Two of her learners sent her an email inviting her to join their social networking site. She politely refused to ensure that she remained professional and within the boundaries of her role as their teacher.

You might be informed by your organisation what the boundaries of your role will be, or you might not. Defining the boundaries will help ensure that you can fulfil your duties as a teacher, as well as any other roles you might have. For example, you could be classed as a *personal tutor*, as well as a teacher. The role of a personal tutor is not to become personal with each learner. It is to be their point of contact for help, guidance and support for the duration they are with your organisation. You can be friendly if necessary, but do be careful not to get overfriendly or too personal with a learner. You need to know what is appropriate and what is not, what is part of your role, and what is not.

Example

One of Shammi's learners confided in her that he could not afford to purchase the required resources for the picture framing course, and he may have to leave as a result. Shammi felt she wanted to lend him the money, but knew this was outside of her role. Instead, she advised him how he could apply for a grant and guided him to the right person for this. She did not let his peer group know about his financial situation. As a result, he obtained a grant, purchased the resources and was able to complete the course. He was not made to feel embarrassed in front of his peers, and the relationship between him and Shammi remained professional.

Your role might involve you interviewing learners and deciding whether they can attend the course or not. You might have difficult decisions to make about this; however, you should always be able to get the support of other staff at your organisation. If you make a decision not to accept a learner, you will need to justify your reasons. There might be an *Information, Advice and Guidance* (IAG) department in your organisation who will be able to support you.

If you are a new teacher, you might have been allocated a *mentor*, someone to help and support you as necessary, and you will find it helpful to keep in touch with them and ask for advice when needed.

You might feel that you could do something which another member of staff would normally do, for example, photocopy some handouts instead of disturbing the reprographics staff. However, while you might feel you are doing them a favour, there are probably procedures to follow which will be there to help rather than hinder you in your role.

Example

Celia was due to teach a First Aid session and arrived early to set up the room. She found the computer worked but the interactive whiteboard didn't. She needed to show a video clip which was only available online. Instead of calling the technician, she moved the equipment herself to check the cables. In doing so, she accidentally broke the internet cable. Had she not overstepped the boundary of her role and liaised with the relevant person, she would not have caused any further problems.

There are also professional aspects which you are *bound by* which might hinder or challenge your role. These include policies and procedures, the amount of administrative work you are expected to complete, targets and league tables, or a lack of funding or resources. These aspects can often be interpreted as the *negative* aspects of your role. You might feel they will put pressure on you which could impact upon the teaching and learning process. However, they are something which you will need to be prepared to deal with, and not let it influence the time that you are with your learners. Other staff, and most of all your learners, will not want to know about things like a lack of funding, what you did at the weekend or what you watched on television last night. Save these conversations for more appropriate people and times. Table 1.3 (on page 48) lists some of the boundaries you may encounter (in alphabetical order) in relation to the teaching, learning and assessment cycle.

Activity

Look at Table 1.3 and choose one boundary from each section. How do you feel you could overcome or work within the boundaries you have chosen?

Being professional

When you are with your learners you should always be professional. This can be achieved by the way you act and react, how you remain in control, how fair and ethical you are, and by not demonstrating any favouritism towards particular learners.

Table 1.3 Example boundaries

Identifying needs	• demands from managers • expectations of learners • funding constraints • knowing what advice and/or information can and cannot be given to learners • lack of information regarding learners' requirements • learners not at the required starting level • negative culture within a department or organisation • organisational policies, procedures and administrative requirements • requirements of codes of practice, awarding organisations and external bodies
Planning learning	• access to resources, e.g. photocopying • capability of learners to achieve • financial and funding concerns: organisation and learners • health and safety regulations • lack of access to computers and technology-based learning materials • lack of adequate equipment • not enough knowledge of learners • requirements of, or a lack of, understanding of the course requirements • unsupportive colleagues
Facilitating learning	• ability of learners, e.g. lack of English • barriers to learning such as access, or a lack of specialist equipment, people and resources • behaviour issues • broken or faulty equipment and resources • changes in legislation, codes of practice, policies and procedures • deadlines and targets • disruptive learners • hindering an individual's progress because they are learning more quickly or more slowly than the rest of the group • inability to be flexible when teaching, to take into account the individual needs of learners • inappropriate actions of self or learners • inappropriate seating or working areas • lack of a suitable environment • lack of own subject knowledge • learners' demands or high expectations • learners' lack of motivation • learners' personal and welfare issues • not enough time • own personal problems • requirements of relevant legislation, e.g. risk assessments • safeguarding requirements
Assessing learning	• being biased or unfair with judgements • data protection and confidentiality • demands of administrative duties • giving some learners more support than others • meeting deadlines and targets • not enough evidence from learners to make a decision • not enough time to correctly mark or assess learners' work • passing learners just to achieve targets
Evaluating learning	• awarding organisation's demands, e.g. internal and external quality assurance activities • lack of time to attend training events, standardisation activities or meetings • organisation's targets and demands • own ability to listen to and react to feedback

Example

Elija had a learner, Joel, who was often absent from certain sessions of a full-time course. Each time this happened, Elija would telephone him and leave a message for him to get in touch. If Joel didn't respond, Elija would call again and leave another message. Joel did not respond as he felt he was being harassed. He then gained the confidence to say to Elija that he was having regular hospital appointments which could not be changed, but that he did want to continue with the course. Elija was able to discuss a plan of action regarding what would be missed in order for him to catch up.

In this example it might be sensible to make a telephone call to a learner who has been absent but making repeated calls would be inappropriate.

If you don't know the boundaries or limits of your role, mistakes can happen: some might be minor, but others could be very serious. Sometimes, it could be due to your not knowing what the limits are, other times it could be a lack of training which has led to ignorance of what is right and wrong. If you give your personal telephone number to learners it could be seen as encouraging informal contact, and you may get calls or texts which are not appropriate. You might not want to take your break with your learners or join their social networking sites, as you could become more of a friend than their teacher. It is unprofessional to use unsuitable language, to touch learners in an inappropriate way, or to let your personal problems affect your work.

Examples of being unprofessional can include (in alphabetical order):

- abusing your power over others

- acting as a confidant to a learner who has personal problems

- asking to borrow money from learners

- becoming overfriendly, in person or online

- becoming personally involved with a learner

- giving a learner undue attention

- giving or administering medicine, unless you are a medical professional

- giving gifts or lending money to learners

- hugging learners

- meeting learners outside of the teaching environment

- offering to give learners a lift in your car; you might not be covered by insurance in the event of an accident

- sharing information about learners to third parties who do not have a legitimate interest

- sharing personal problems with learners

- swearing or using inappropriate language in front of learners

- thinking of yourself instead of your learners

- violating your duty of care and position of trust.

There might be situations where you will need to ensure you are not placed in a vulnerable position: for example, by leaving the room door open if you are alone with a young learner. You will also need to inform your learners if they overstep your boundaries, perhaps if an individual asks you to go for a drink with them after class.

Extension activity

Look at the previous bullet list regarding being unprofessional, and see if there is anything else you could add. How do you feel you can protect yourself from becoming vulnerable in your role? How can you ensure that you remain professional at all times?

Promoting appropriate behaviour and respect

Behaviour is all about how you and your learners interact with each other in an acceptable way. Respect is about accepting others for what they are, not being rude to them, or lowering their confidence and self-esteem in any way. Depending upon the age range of your learners, the subject and the environment in which you will teach, you might encounter issues which you will need to deal with immediately. However, it's not just about being *reactive* to a situation. You need to be *proactive* and promote appropriate behaviour and respect whenever possible, to stop issues arising in the first place.

Example

Katherine noticed one of her learners, Alexis, became disruptive when she commenced the debrief after a group activity. She decided to change the format by asking a learner from each group to state how they worked as a team. She asked Alexis to be the first one and he didn't know what to say. Katherine then asked another learner who responded well. As the learners were leaving at the end of the session, Katherine overhead Alexis say to another learner that he had felt embarrassed in front of his friends. He was much quieter in future sessions and paid better attention.

Your organisation should have a behaviour code of practice or a policy, which you might like to take a look at. Having ground rules in place could help avoid any issues. Ground rules, such as not speaking when someone else is speaking, can help to create suitable conditions within which learners (and yourself) can safely work and learn (covered in Chapter 4).

Being a role model for good behaviour might encourage the same from your learners. This can include being polite, showing respect and saying *please* and *thank you*. Welcoming learners to your session when they arrive, with a smile on your face, can give a good impression. Some teachers like to stand at the door as their learners enter. This gives an air of authority, and shows the teacher is in control. Some teachers like to shake hands with each learner as they arrive, to say hello and state the learner's name. This is a little more informal, but still shows the teacher is in control and that they know each learner's name. This might be better than being occupied inside the room and ignoring the learners as they arrive.

It would be wonderful if you could get through a session without any issues arising. Usually, behaviour issues occur because a learner doesn't follow the ground rules, for example, their mobile phone rings, or they do something other than that which you have asked them to do. If this is the case, politely ask them to stop, remind them of the ground rules, and how they are also disrupting their peers' learning. Your learners need to know what is acceptable, what isn't, and why.

Behaviour issues could occur because learners:

- are bored
- are not being stretched or challenged enough
- are seeking attention
- don't understand what you are saying are doing
- have a learning difficulty and/or disability
- have an attention span which is different to other learners.

Behaviour patterns could highlight the need for additional support as disruption could be a way of asking for help. A way of dealing with a situation is to tactfully say to the learner, *'I notice you are not paying attention/are being disruptive, is there any reason for that?'* They might not have anything to say, and will hopefully then focus on the session. However, there might be a valid reason, in which case you can tell your learner you will have a chat with them in confidence later. Alternatively, you could redirect them in some way to focus them on the current task.

Example

Phil has a group of 24 learners and one particular learner, Mike, often disrupts the session. During one session, Mike shouted across the room to another learner 'What did you watch on TV last night?' The other learner did not respond and so Mike shouted again. Phil went over to Mike and asked 'What about this task you are working on, how far have you got? Phil had redirected the situation to be about the work, not the shouting.

In this example, Phil was able to help Mike focus on the task rather than interrupting his peers.

You may find it useful to maintain a record of the individual behaviour of your learners during your sessions. This could help you prepare for future incidents: for example, noting a particular learner who becomes disruptive after a certain time period has elapsed, or another who becomes annoyed when asked to carry out a theory task. This information can be useful when planning future sessions: for example, the timing of breaks, the use of energiser activities, or planning who will work with whom for a paired activity.

Ways to demonstrate and promote positive behaviour and respect include (in alphabetical order):

- admitting to your mistakes rather than bluffing your way out of them
- being consistent, i.e. challenging rule breaking each time it occurs
- being fair to everyone by not having a favourite learner, or by letting some learners get away with things
- being pleasant and polite
- challenging inappropriate behaviour, comments and language
- demonstrating good practice by leading by example
- demonstrating positive body language
- encouraging trust, honesty, politeness and consideration towards others
- ensuring you are non-judgemental
- listening to others' points of view
- praising good practice
- reminding learners of the ground rules
- treating everyone as an individual and with respect
- trying not to talk at your learners, but talk and listen with them
- using learners' names
- using lots of practical activities to stop learners becoming bored
- valuing others' opinions and not imposing your own.

Activity

Take a look at the previous bullet list. What other ways could you demonstrate and promote positive behaviour and respect with your learners?

If you do experience any issues, you will need to handle the situation professionally, i.e. by not becoming emotional and keeping to the facts. If a learner insists on interrupting, you could hold up your hand, palm facing them, in the hope that this stops them. If not, you could ask them to make a note of the questions they were going to ask and state how you will answer them towards the end of the session. This should help to minimise any effect it may have on teaching and learning. If you do need to show disapproval, you could make it clear that it's because of the way they have behaved, not because it's them as a person. Don't just ignore the behaviour thinking it will go away, address it immediately. However, with experience, you will realise that some things can be ignored, providing this does not affect the safety of your learners. For example, if a learner is attention seeking, they might stop when they realise they are not getting the attention they wanted.

Example

Shawn was giving a presentation to a group of 15 learners during a Monday morning session. Three learners in the group began talking among themselves about what they had done at the weekend. Rather than reprimand them, Shawn decided to stop speaking altogether and look at them. They soon realised he was no longer speaking to the group and so stopped talking.

In this example, the learners noticed the silence and then paid attention again.

You can help maintain motivation and promote good behaviour by including all learners during the session. Don't leave anyone out; ensure everyone is asked a question or is involved in some way. Try and keep your sessions active wherever possible, and teach your subject in an interesting and challenging way. Ultimately, you need to find your own way of dealing with situations based upon your experiences. Don't show favouritism, lose your temper, swear, or make any threats. Try to have a positive approach, praise performance and good behaviour, and be consistent and fair to everyone. Most learners respond positively to a well-organised course taught by an enthusiastic teacher who has a genuine interest in them and the subject.

Attitudes affecting behaviour

If you can model good behaviour, and inform your learners that you expect good behaviour from them, this should lead to a positive learning experience. If you have a positive attitude, hopefully your learners will too. They will want to learn, and will not want their peers to affect that learning. Some learners might not have engaged with education in their past, perhaps had a bad learning experience or had a teacher who could not control the group. They will, therefore, have returned to education not wanting these experiences repeated.

It could be that your learners are not attending your course voluntarily, or they may be there for social reasons rather than having an interest in achieving something. They may, therefore, not be as keen as you would like them to be, and you will need to keep them continuously interested and motivated. A way of overcoming this might be to try and relate the subject to their interests and/or their personal or working life.

Example

Sahib was having problems with two learners on his Computing for Beginners course. One would talk over him and the other would use their mobile phone. He decided to spend a few minutes at the beginning of the next session asking each learner in turn (in front of the rest of the group) to state a reason for using a computer which they could relate to their personal or working life. He also asked the group to agree some ground rules which included switching off their mobile phones. This helped the two learners see the relevance of having various computer skills, and helped the other learners feel they were in a positive learning environment.

Betari's cycle of conflict

Betari's cycle of conflict, as in Figure 1.2, also known as Betari's box, is about how attitude affects behaviour. For example, *my attitude affects my behaviour, which affects your attitude which affects your behaviour, which in turn affects my attitude and so on.* It's not clear where the name Betari came from or when it was created; however, attitudes, whether positive or negative, are reflected in behaviour. Positive attitudes should encourage positive behaviour in yourself, as well as in others. This can be through words and actions, verbal and non-verbal messages and body language. If an attitude is positive, it can help others be positive; the same will apply if it's negative.

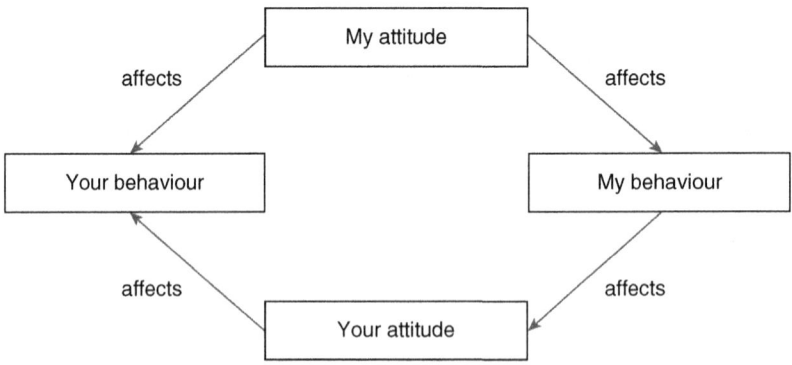

Figure 1.2 Betari's cycle of conflict

Example

Gemma, a learner attending cookery classes, really enjoys the subject. She likes using practical skills and often tries new recipes, makes mistakes and learns from them. Today, she has a different teacher, Abigail, as her usual teacher is absent. Abigail is quick to notice when Gemma is struggling and takes over what she is doing. This continues throughout the session, therefore Gemma now stops when she is unsure of something and calls over Abigail. Because of Abigail's attitude and behaviour towards Gemma's learning, Gemma has adapted her attitude and behaviour to fit in with Abigail.

To change the attitude and behaviour of others you may need to be aware of your own attitude and how it affects your own behaviour. You can then notice how your behaviour affects other people's attitudes and behaviour. You can break the cycle by noticing how the behaviour of others makes you do what you do and by refusing to let it affect you. You will need to recognise negative cycles and turn them into positive ones; this applies to yourself as well as to your learners.

The following are some strategies which you could use with your learners:

- allocate time at the beginning of the course, or each session, to find out what your learners' attitudes are to the subject, i.e. have they had good or bad experiences which might affect their learning?

- ensure all learners can participate in the session and access all equipment and resources

- hold group and individual tutorials with all learners to discuss progress and concerns

- use learners' names, use eye contact and treat each learner as an individual

- make sure everyone is aware of relevant policies and procedures

- negotiate and agree appropriate ground rules

- schedule one-to-one discussions with learners who require additional support

- use a suitable and inclusive icebreaker.

There may be occasions during your sessions where behaviours exist that are offensive, directly discriminate, or are distressing to others. This behaviour may be obvious, but it can also be unintentional and subtle. It might involve a learner using nicknames, teasing, name-calling, or excluding someone. Although it might not have a malicious intent it will still be upsetting. You will need to know what steps your organisation requires you to take, and deal with any inappropriate behaviour as it occurs. There are various ways of managing this depending on the circumstances, such as:

- challenging prejudice, discrimination and stereotyping as it occurs

- creating an acceptable behaviour contract which learners sign up to, and revisit it regularly, perhaps as part of the ground rules

- embracing learner diversity within the group

- encouraging your learners to discuss confidentially any of their own behaviour concerns they have, for example, if they are autistic

- ensuring all resources are inclusive through the use of positive images

- establishing at the start of the programme what the unacceptable behaviours are.

There might also be instances where you do something inadvertently and not really think at the time how it could affect a learner.

Example

Jerome was due to attend a week's summer school programme as part of his Post Graduate Certificate in Education (PGCE). All learners were required to complete a form giving the teacher their name, telephone number and relationship of an emergency contact. The completed forms were left on the teacher's desk where they could be seen by other learners. As a result, it became common knowledge amongst the group that Jerome has a same sex partner. Jerome became distressed as he had not made this public. As a result, he left the course.

In this example, it constitutes a breach of data protection as well as the organisation's confidentially policy. You will be required to treat personal information in the strictest confidence and your learners will trust you with details about their private lives. Information about learners should not become common knowledge via their teacher.

Extension activity

What situations might arise with your learners which could lead to issues with behaviour and/or respect? How could you effectively deal with these situations? Talk to other teachers to find out what experiences they have had, and how they have dealt with them. Research theories of behaviour management, or read relevant texts regarding behaviour. Some are listed at the end of this chapter.

Creating and maintaining a safe, supportive and effective teaching and learning environment

Learners need to know they are safe when they are with you and not in any danger. For example, any equipment and resources should not cause harm, tables and chairs should be in an appropriate layout for the subject, and all areas should be accessible. Safe also relates to learners feeling safe to express their opinions without being ridiculed by others. You have a duty of care to ensure learning takes place in a supportive and effective environment. This duty requires you to take reasonable steps to ensure the safety of your learners. For example, by informing them how to correctly use all relevant equipment and/or to wear protective clothing when necessary.

The teaching and learning environment can be thought of as having three aspects: *physical, social* and *learning* as in Figure 1.3. Each has an impact on the others, and all three aspects should be appropriate and relevant. Some aspects will interact and overlap to ensure teaching, learning and assessment can be effective for everyone. Examples of physical, social and learning aspects are given in Table 1.4 later in this chapter section.

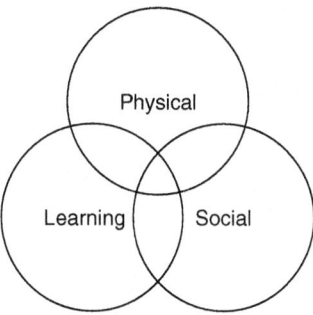

Figure 1.3 Physical, social and learning aspects and how they interact and overlap

Physical

The physical environment is concerned with the surroundings and atmosphere within which learning takes place. This need not be a traditional classroom but could be a training room, workshop, outdoors or another setting such as a community centre. The temperature, lighting and ventilation can all affect the learning that takes place. You may need to close blinds to block out the sun, open a window to let in fresh air or even tidy rubbish away that has been left by the previous occupiers. Different subjects might need different requirements: for example, natural light for drawing and painting, dimmed light to view videos. You will need to find out where light switches are, whether you can adjust heating and ventilation systems, and where fire extinguishers and emergency exits are.

While it is your responsibility to ensure the environment is safe and supportive, you might not be able to control some aspects such as external noise. However, what you can do is ensure that your session is interesting, meaningful and engaging to your learners. You would need to take into account your organisation's health and safety policy and relevant codes of practice. You should not do anything outside of your own responsibility, such as moving heavy equipment. Some resources, particularly electrical ones, require regular maintenance checks and testing. If you see a *portable appliance tested* (PAT) label on a resource which is out of date, you will need to liaise with the relevant personnel in your organisation to ensure that it is safe.

Social

The social environment is concerned with how you help put your learners at ease, establish a rapport with them and help them work and get along together. Using a suitable icebreaker will help learners get to know each other at the beginning of the first meeting. Creating a social and supportive learning environment will include agreeing ground rules. However, the ground rules will depend upon the age and maturity of your learners. Helping learners relax should lead to effective two-way communication and enable learning to take place. You should aim to use eye contact with everyone and use their names whenever possible, so that they feel valued as individuals.

Learners should know that you, their peers, and others if necessary, will make their time meaningful, productive and supportive. Supportive also relates to giving appropriate advice and/or referring your learners to others if you can't help them with a concern they have. You should demonstrate inclusion (i.e. not exclude anyone), and challenge any inappropriate or anti-social behaviour as it occurs.

Learning

The learning environment is concerned with giving your session a purpose by having a clear aim of what you want your learners to achieve, using suitable and varied teaching and learning approaches, resources and activities. How you plan to deliver and assess your subject will be based upon the requirements of what your learner needs to achieve. This might be stated in the programme of learning, qualification specification, work tasks, job specification or set of standards. It might be left to you to decide in what order you do this, and what approaches you take with your learners to achieve it.

Try and plan your session content to flow logically, and make the subject material interesting and stimulating. Encourage your learners to become actively involved, to think for themselves, and to use their existing skills and knowledge to build upon. You can give regular feedback regarding individual progress so that your learners know what they have achieved.

You could encourage peer support by using the *buddy* approach. This enables learners to pair up with someone in the group they feel comfortable with. They can then keep in touch between sessions to discuss the topics and support each other if necessary. This approach is particularly useful if one learner misses a session for any reason and needs to catch up.

Knowing your subject and facilitating it in a meaningful way will help your learners achieve their goals.

Activity

Look at the physical, social and learning aspects in Table 1.4 and add any others which you feel are relevant. Choose at least two from each column. Draw a diagram like that in Figure 1.3 (three overlapping circles) and add your aspects to it. Which do you think will interact and overlap, and why?

You might need to adapt the learning environment to ensure that all learners can access equipment and resources safely. This might involve carrying out a risk assessment to check all equipment is safe to use.

Safeguarding

Safeguarding is the term used to refer to the duties and responsibilities that those providing a health, social or education service have to carry out or perform to protect individuals and vulnerable people from harm. You will have a responsibility to adhere to, and maintain, safeguarding measures as part of your role if you work in the UK.

Table 1.4 Examples of physical, social and learning aspects

Physical	Social	Learning
Ensuring adequate heating, lighting and ventilation	Using a suitable icebreaker to put learners at ease and to create a rapport	Having clear aims of what will be achieved Planning what will take place during each session
Ensuring ease of access to all learning areas, equipment and resources	Agreeing ground rules to help promote appropriate behaviour and respect	Engaging and motivating learners Giving support and encouragement
Ensuring the layout of the room is suitable (e.g. to ensure all learners can see and hear)	Communicating effectively (speaking, listening, body language, eye contact)	Making the session interesting and relevant Summarising, repeating and recapping regularly
Ensuring toilets and refreshment facilities are accessible	Using paired and group activities Drawing on learners' previous skills, knowledge and experiences	Using a variety of suitable teaching, learning and assessment approaches and activities
Ensuring the safe use of equipment, materials and resources	Encouraging learners to listen to you and to each other	Differentiating for individual needs Referring learners elsewhere if necessary
Carrying out risk assessments Minimising hazards Knowing who the first aider is and where they are located	Using learners' names and using eye contact Including all learners during the session Asking questions	Assessing progress and achievement on an ongoing basis
Knowing where fire extinguishers and emergency exits are	Giving adequate breaks at appropriate times	Providing ongoing constructive and developmental feedback
Making sure the room is tidy before and after use	Challenging inappropriate behaviour	Keeping records of what has been taught, and the progress and achievements of all learners

Following the publication of the Safeguarding Vulnerable Groups Act (2006) in the UK, a vetting and barring scheme was established in 2008. This Act created an Independent Barring Board to take all discretionary decisions on whether individuals should be barred from working with children and/or vulnerable adults. Teachers may need to have their criminal background checked via the Disclosure and Barring Service (DBS). The purpose of the DBS is to help employers to prevent unsuitable people from working with children and vulnerable adults.

In 2006, the Department for Education and Skills (DfES), in the UK, produced a document called *Safeguarding Children and Safer Recruitment in Education*. This guidance was aimed at local authorities, schools and further education colleges in England who are responsible for promoting the welfare of children and young people, up to the age of 18 (age 25 for those with learning difficulties and/or disabilities). The DfES has now been replaced with the Department for Children, Schools and Families and the Department for Innovation, Universities and Skills.

Following this, the document *Safer Practice, Safer Learning* (NIACE, 2007) was produced to provide guidance in relation to adults in further education. It recommends that safeguarding duties extend to whole-organisation policies, values and ethos, and include all staff and learners. It is, therefore, everyone's duty to promote the concepts of the safe learner.

The Department of Health (2000) document (in England) *No Secrets* gives a definition of vulnerable adults.

A vulnerable adult is defined as a person 'who is or may be in need of community care services by reason of mental or other disability, age or illness and who is or may be unable to take care of him or herself, or unable to protect him or herself against significant harm or exploitation'. (Department of Health, 2000, page 8)

A vulnerable adult can be put at risk of harm through a variety of actions, inadequate policies and procedures, and failures of people to act. There are six types of abuse defined by the Department of Health:

- physical
- sexual
- psychological/emotional
- financial or material
- neglect and acts of omission
- discriminatory.

A young person or adult could potentially be the victim of any of the above. It is, therefore, your duty to ensure that you take proper steps to safeguard your learners. If a young person or vulnerable adult discloses any abuse to you, take the disclosure seriously and never dismiss any allegation. An allegation of abuse or neglect may lead to a criminal investigation. Asking leading questions, or attempting to investigate the allegations may cause problems for any subsequent court proceedings.

In this respect, don't make any promises regarding confidentiality, particularly if you discover something serious which will have to be reported to an authority as part of the law. Explain to your learner that you will need to report the disclosure and share the information with your organisation's Safeguarding Officer (if there is one) or the person responsible for this (you need to find out who this is at your organisation). They will, where possible, respect the wishes of the individual. However, information will need to be shared with external agencies where it is judged that a person is at risk of suffering significant harm.

Activity

Find out what the policies and procedures are regarding safeguarding at your organisation. What will your responsibilities be and who can you go to should you have any concerns?

Hopefully, the environment you and your learners are in is safe and secure. However, all rooms and equipment should be checked for health and safety hazards. To help ensure that all people in the building are meant to be there, staff, learners and visitors could wear an official name badge. All visitors should be asked to sign in and out of the building, and will possibly need to be accompanied at all times. Anyone not wearing a badge should be challenged if it is safe to do so.

If there is anything you notice, or a learner informs you about which you think could be a potential health, safety or security risk, you must report it. You will also need to be familiar with the organisation's fire and evacuation procedures, and make sure your learners are too.

There could be circumstances where abuse, threatening behaviour, stealing or bullying might occur. You might notice this, or a learner might tell you about it. If so, you will need to treat the matter seriously and follow it up. Your organisation might have a zero tolerance policy of this type of behaviour, and have a particular procedure which will need to be followed.

Learners will need to know who they can talk to, and know where they can feel safe. There are a number of ways in which they could be involved in identifying safe areas.

Example

During a Sport and Leisure session regarding health and safety, the teacher, Warwick, decided to:

- *discuss potential issues and concerns, and what his learners could do if any of these occurred*

- *identify well-being, personal safety and security issues, and how these might be resolved*

- *ask his learners to take digital photographs of safe and unsafe areas inside and outside of the location*

- *encourage his learners to create a display of their pictures and to discuss what they had noticed*

- *share the information with other learners and staff.*

In this example, the learners were able to identity that they were in a safe environment, and to know what to do if they felt unsafe for any reason.

Your learners need to know that their safety and security is of paramount importance to you and your organisation, and that everyone has a responsibility for this. This information can be communicated to your learners in various ways, i.e. through learner handbooks, marketing materials, induction procedures, learner contracts, tutorials, reviews of progress, online information, and learner discussion groups and activities.

Extension activity

What issues might learners encounter regarding their safety and security in the learning environment? How can you maintain a safe and supportive environment for your learners? What can you do if something occurs which is outside of your control?

Legal, regulatory requirements, and codes of practice

Legal aspects relate to laws, regulatory requirements are usually specific to certain industries, and codes of practice vary depending upon the organisation within which you work. It is important for you to keep up to date with all relevant aspects. This will help to ensure that you are remaining current with your skills, knowledge and understanding, and with any changes or updates that have taken place.

Example

Davit wanted to give his learners some handouts rather than ask them to purchase a textbook for the course. He photocopied extracts from a book, but did not add the details of the book to the handouts. Although his organisation paid for a licence to copy extracts, Davit had not realised he had copied more than he was allowed. He had therefore breached the UK Copyright, Designs and Patents Act (1988).

Legislation

This will differ depending upon the context and environment within which you teach. You might also need to be aware of the requirements of external bodies and regulators such as Ofsted (in England) who inspect funded provision, and Ofqual (in England) who regulate awarding organisations.

The following information was current at the time of writing; however, you are advised to check for any changes or updates, and whether they are applicable outside England.

Autism Act (2009) did two key things in England:

- placed a duty on the government to produce a strategy for adults with autism, which was published in March 2010

- produced statutory guidance for local councils and local health bodies on implementing the adult autism strategy. The strategy is to make sure that adults with autism get the help that they need. This guidance was published in December 2010 and updated in 2015.

All people who are autistic share certain difficulties, but will be affected in different ways. Some also have learning disabilities, mental health issues or other conditions, meaning people need different levels of support.

Children Act (2004) provided the legal underpinning for the *Every Child Matters: Change for Children* programme. *Well-being* is the term used in the Act to define the five Every Child Matters outcomes:

- be healthy

- stay safe

- enjoy and achieve

- make a positive contribution

- achieve economic well-being.

Counter-Terrorism and Security Act (2015) will apply if you work with learners who are at risk of becoming radicalised. The Prevent Duty is part of this Act and you should be required to attend a training session at your organisation to ensure you are up to date with the requirements. The Prevent Duty is not about preventing learners from having political and religious views, but about supporting them to use any concerns in non-extremist ways, and to prevent them from becoming radicalised.

Copyright, Designs and Patents Act (1988) relates to the copying, adapting and distributing of materials, which includes computer software and materials found via the internet. Organisations may have a licence to enable the photocopying of small amounts from books or journals. All photocopies should have the original source acknowledged and be within the terms of the licence.

Data Protection Act (1998) made provision for the regulation of the processing of information relating to individuals, including the obtaining, holding, use or disclosure of such information. It will be updated in 2018 to become the General Data Protection Regulation (GDPR).

Equality Act (2010) replaced all previous anti-discrimination legislation and consolidated it into one Act (England, Scotland and Wales). It provides rights for people not to be directly discriminated against or harassed because they have an association with a disabled person or because they are wrongly perceived as disabled (covered in Chapter 9).

Freedom of Information Act (2000) gives learners the opportunity to request to see the information public bodies hold about them.

Health and Safety at Work etc Act (1974) imposes obligations on all staff within an organisation commensurate with their role and responsibility. Risk assessments should be carried out where necessary. In the event of an accident, particularly one resulting in death or serious injury, an investigation by the Health and Safety Executive (HSE) may result in the prosecution of individuals found to be negligent as well as the organisation.

Rehabilitation of Offenders Act (1974) will be applicable if you work with ex-offenders.

Safeguarding Vulnerable Groups Act (2006) introduced a vetting and barring scheme to make decisions about who should be barred from working with children and vulnerable adults. Teachers may need to have their criminal background checked via the Disclosure and Barring Service (DBS). The purpose of the DBS is to help employers to prevent unsuitable people from working with children and vulnerable adults.

Welsh Language Act (1993) places the Welsh language on an equal footing with the English language in Wales, with regard to the public sector.

Regulatory requirements

Public bodies, corporations, agencies and organisations create regulatory requirements, which must be followed if they are applicable to your job role. For example, in education, Ofqual is the regulator of qualifications, examinations and assessments in England.

Regulations are often called *rules* and they specify mandatory requirements that must be met. There will be specific regulations which relate to your specialist subject and you will need to find out what these are. The following information was current at the time of writing; however, you are advised to check for any changes or updates, and whether or not they are applicable outside England.

Control of Substances Hazardous to Health (COSHH) Regulations (2002) applies if you work with hazardous materials.

Food Hygiene Regulations (2006) applies to aspects of farming, manufacturing, distributing and the retailing of food.

Management of Health and Safety at Work Regulations (1999) were introduced to reinforce the Health and Safety at Work etc Act 1974. They require an employer to undertake an assessment of the risks to the health and safety of their employees and others who may be affected by their work activity. For example, use of visual display screens, fire and emergency procedures, and access to first aid. Employees also have a duty to report any concerns.

Manual Handling Operation Regulations (1992) relates to the hazards of manual handling and risks of injury.

Privacy and Electronic Communications (EC Directive) Regulations (2003) applies to all electronic communications such as email and mobile phone messages.

Reporting of Injuries, Diseases and Dangerous Occurrences (RIDDOR) Regulations (1995) requires specified workplace incidents to be reported.

Regulatory Reform (Fire Safety) Order (2005) places the responsibility on individuals within an organisation to carry out risk assessments to identify, manage and reduce the risk of fire.

The Special Educational Needs and Disability Regulations (2014) cover all learners who are aged up to 25 who have special educational needs or disabilities. It stresses the need to inform and involve others, such as parents, guardians and the learners themselves, throughout the learning process.

Activity

Research the regulatory requirements which will apply to the subject you would like to teach in your country. How will they impact upon your role? Take a look at the regulations listed here to check whether they have been updated and if so, what changes have taken place.

Codes of Practice

Codes of practice are usually produced by organisations, associations and professional bodies. They can be mandatory or voluntary and you will need to find out which are applicable to you.

Your organisation should have documented codes of practice such as:

- acceptable use of information technology
- behaviour
- code of conduct
- conflict of interest
- disciplinary
- dress
- duty of care to learners, including personal development, behaviour and welfare
- duty to prevent radicalisation
- environmental awareness
- lone working
- management of information and records
- misconduct
- sustainability
- timekeeping.

There will also be codes of practice which will apply if you belong to a professional association, for example, the Society for Education and Training (SET) in England. Please see the Introduction chapter for further information regarding other professional associations for teachers which might have a code of practice.

Society for Education and Training (SET) Code of Practice

The SET consists of a community of members, which includes: trainers, teachers, assessors, tutors, support staff, mentors, coaches and managers. If you are in England, you might like to join. The membership reaches across the rich diversity of settings in education and training. This includes colleges, independent training providers, adult and community learning, employer providers, the voluntary sector, the justice sector, and the armed services.

The SET Code of Practice sets out the professional behaviour and conduct expected of their members, including mandatory requirements which must be complied with to become and remain a member. It is an important statement of what it means to be part of SET, and the levels of professionalism that are required or encouraged of all of their members. Committing to the Code of Practice is a key part of becoming and remaining a member of the SET.

If you are a teacher who works in the schools sector, and you belong to SET, you are also bound by the Department for Education Teachers' Standards.

Policies and procedures

There will be several policies and procedures in your organisation with which you should become familiar. Some might relate to your role and others will be there to support the learners. Think of a policy as a statement of intent, and a procedure as how the policy will be put into practice. Some of the previously listed codes of practice might be classed as a policy depending upon where you work and how they are interpreted.

Examples of policies include:

- access and fair assessment
- appeals and complaints
- confidentiality of information
- copyright and data protection
- equality and diversity
- health, safety and welfare (including Safeguarding and Prevent Duty)
- internal quality assurance
- plagiarism and cheating
- malpractice.

Policies and procedures should help guide your job role and should reflect the vision and mission of your organisation for the benefit of the learners. They don't need to be long or complicated. They should provide a set of principles to help with decision-making and be reviewed regularly. Procedures should state who will do what and when, and what documentation should be used.

Identify the legislation, regulatory requirements and codes of practice which are relevant to your role, where you work and the subject you will teach. Summarise the key aspects of these and state how they might impact upon your role.

Self-assessment checklist

Do I know about the following?

If not, re-read this chapter, or research the texts and websites listed at the end.

☐ The roles I will carry out as a teacher or a trainer

☐ The responsibilities I have as part of my role

☐ The boundaries of my role and how I can overcome them or work within them

☐ What it means to be a professional

☐ How to work with other professionals

☐ How to remain professional when in contact with learners and others

☐ How to lead by example and model good behaviour

☐ What the physical, social and learning aspects are and how they interact with each other

☐ How to promote appropriate behaviour and respect

☐ How to deal with behaviour issues

☐ How to create a safe, supportive and effective learning environment

☐ The legislation, regulatory requirements, policies, procedures and codes of practice relevant to my role and my subject specialism

Summary

This chapter has explored the various roles and responsibilities you have as a teacher or a trainer. It can be an overwhelming job at times; however, it can be very rewarding. There should always be other people in your organisation who can help and support you.

You should now be able to perform your role in a professional way and promote positive behaviour and respect amongst your learners. You should also know about relevant legislation, regulations and codes of practice which you will need to follow.

You might like to carry out further research by accessing the books and websites listed at the end of this chapter, particularly if you are working towards a higher level teaching qualification.

This chapter has covered the following topics:

- Roles and responsibilities

- Wider professional practice

- Professional boundaries

- Promoting appropriate behaviour and respect

- Creating and maintaining a safe, supportive and effective teaching and learning environment

- Legal, regulatory requirements and codes of practice

References and further information

Beadle, P., (2013) *Why Are You Shouting At Us?: The Dos and Don'ts of Behaviour Management*, London: Bloomsbury Education.

Berry, J. (2010) *Teachers' Legal Rights and Responsibilities: A Guide for Trainee Teachers and Those New to the Profession* (2nd edition). Hertfordshire: University of Hertfordshire Press.

Cowley, S. (2014) *Getting the Buggers to Behave*. London: Bloomsbury.

Dix, P. (2010) *The Essential Guide to Taking Care of Behaviour: Practical Skills for Teachers*. London: Pearson.

Fawvert, F. (2007) *Teaching in Post-compulsory Education*. London: Continuum.

Duckworth, V. (2014) *How to be a Brilliant FE Teacher*. Abingdon: Routledge.

Gravells, J. and Wallace, S. (2013) *The A-Z Guide to Working in Further Education*. Northwich: Critical Publishing Ltd.

HMI (2004) *Every Child Matters: Change for children*. London: DfES.

Lever, C. (2011) *Understanding Challenging Behaviour in Inclusive Classrooms*. Abingdon: Routledge.

Pleasance, S. (2016) *Wider Professional Practice in Education and Training*. London: SAGE.

Plevin, R. (2016) *Take Control of the Noisy Class*. Carmarthen: Crown House Publishing.

Powell, S. and Tummons, J. (2011) *Inclusive Practice in the Lifelong Learning Sector*. Exeter: Learning Matters.

Rogers, B. (2006) *Cracking the Hard Class*. London: Paul Chapman Publishing.

Rogers, B. (2015) *Classroom Behaviour* (4th edition) London: SAGE.

Tummons, J. (2010) *Becoming a Professional Tutor* (2nd edition). Exeter: Learning Matters.

Vizard, D. (2012) *How to Manage Behaviour in Further Education*. London: SAGE.

Wallace, S. (2013) *Managing Behaviour in Further and Adult Education*. London: Learning Matters SAGE.

Wallace, S. (2014) When You're Smiling: Exploring How Teachers Motivate and Engage Learners in the Further Education Sector. *Journal of Further and Higher Education*, 38 (3): 346–60.

Wallace, S. (2017) *Motivating Unwilling Learners in Further Education*. London: Bloomsbury Education.

Websites

Behaviour: Pivotal Education – www.pivotaleducation.com

Behaviour Management Blog by Dan Williams – http://tinyurl.com/hyorsw6

Behaviour Solutions from Dave Vizard – www.behaviourmatters.com

Classroom management free resources – www.pivotaleducation.com/free-resources/

Classroom management free videos – https://tinyurl.com/k5zzvwj

Department for Education (2006) *Safeguarding Children and Safer Recruitment in Education* – https://tinyurl.com/ydx7a9tr

Department for Education Teachers' Standards – https://tinyurl.com/o7hkwwo

Department of Health (2000) *No Secrets* – https://tinyurl.com/pnajc5u

Disclosure and Barring Service – https://tinyurl.com/ceydl2w

FE Advice – www.feadvice.org.uk

Government legislation in the UK – www.legislation.gov.uk

National Autistic Society – www.autism.org.uk

Ofqual – www.ofqual.gov.uk

Ofsted – www.ofsted.gov.uk

Plagiarism – http://plagiarism.org

Prevent Duty online training and resources – http://www.preventforfeandtraining.org.uk

Reading list for behaviour and motivation – www.anngravells.com/reading-lists/behaviour

Resources for teachers and learners – www.anngravells.com/resources/index

Safer Practice, Safer Learning (NIACE, 2007) – http://shop.niace.org.uk/safer-practice.html

Society for Education and Training (SET) Code of Practice – https://tinyurl.com/m23e9p4

2

Factors contributing to learning

Introduction

There are many factors which can contribute to learning taking place. These include the environment, a learner's motivation to learn, the challenges they and you might face, and the different ways in which learning can occur.

This chapter will explore the variety of learners you might teach, their differing age ranges, the locations in which learning takes place and possible challenges. Theories regarding how people learn are covered, as are theoretical principles and models.

This chapter will cover the following topics:

- Teaching and learning environments
- Learner age ranges and modes of attendance
- Motivation
- Challenges
- Learning preferences and styles
- Teaching and learning theories, principles and models

Teaching and learning environments

Teaching and learning can take place in a variety of environments and locations such as: classrooms, the workplace, training rooms, prisons, outdoors and online. Although learning can take place almost anywhere, not all locations and environments will be totally suitable. However, it's *how* you ensure that learning takes place that matters. It helps if you can convey interest, enthusiasm and passion for your subject. It also helps to create a climate which is conducive to learning and mutual respect. Ideally, you should want your learners to leave your session wanting to come back for more.

You might be restricted by the availability of particular rooms or resources; therefore you need to be imaginative with what's available to you. Your learners don't need to know about any organisational problems you might encounter, as your professionalism should enable you to teach your subject effectively. However, you do need to take into account any health, safety and security issues, and let your organisation know if you have any concerns.

You will need to establish a purposeful learning environment where your learners feel safe, secure, confident and valued. The venue, toilets and refreshment areas should all be accessible and appropriate for everyone. However, you might not be able to control these aspects. Having some advance knowledge about your learners will help you check that everything is suitable for them. If it's not, you might want to talk to your learners beforehand to see if any compromises can be reached. You can find out any particular learner needs from the results of initial assessments (covered in Chapter 3) or by talking to your learners. If your session includes a break, make sure you tell your learners what time this will be, and for how long. If you don't, learners might not be concentrating on their learning, but thinking about when they can go to the toilet or where they can get a drink.

What is on the wall, or what is visible from the windows, could have an impact upon learning. If there is a lovely view of trees and birds outside the window, your learners might be more interested in what's happening outside than inside. It might be possible to use blinds or curtains to limit the distraction. If there are posters on the walls with stimulating pictures and words, your learners will probably look at them, and subconsciously take in the information. If learners have carried out activities which involved them creating posters or writing on flip chart paper, these could be added to the walls. Leaving them there as a visual aid could help the learning process. However, you will probably need to check in advance how you can attach things to walls, and whether or not you are allowed to.

Music or sounds can also be useful to aid learning. Tranquil music played as learners enter the room could have a calming effect upon behaviour. Upbeat music while energetic activities are being carried out could stimulate learning. If you do use music, it's useful to bear in mind that certain sounds can bring about memories, some of which might not be good for certain learners. You will also need to be aware of any potential of a breach to copyright legislation which applies to some music. You can get information regarding this from the Performing Rights Society; a weblink is at the end of this chapter. Music is also useful during certain activities for particular subjects such as yoga, tai chi and dancing.

If you are teaching a practical subject, you will need a suitable environment such as a workshop or a laboratory so that you can demonstrate and your learners can practise. If you are teaching a theoretical subject, you may be fine in a room with tables and chairs, but you might need a computer, data projector and/or an interactive whiteboard. Internet and/or wifi access might not always be available, therefore you might like to check in advance. If you are not teaching a practical subject, for example, you are delivering a one day event or a seminar, it could be in a venue you have never been to. If this is the case, it would be useful to telephone, email, or visit in advance to check what facilities are available, and find out how accessible everything is. You could also send out some pre-event materials informing people how to get there, and what facilities are available. Creating a good first impression and being organised should help your learners feel they are receiving a professional service. If they are paying to attend a session with you, they will not expect a second-best service or poor facilities.

Class sizes could affect the learning process, in both positive and negative ways. If you teach on a one-to-one basis or to a small group, you will be able to get to know your learners well and devote more time to them. If you have a large group, this might be more difficult. You might have no control over class sizes; however, you can try using different teaching and learning approaches and activities to get around this (covered in Chapter 5).

Room layouts

An important influence upon the way your session progresses, and how you and your learners can communicate, will be the room layout. You may not be able to control this if the furniture is in fixed positions: for example, a room which has computers on tables, or a laboratory with immobile workstations. Hopefully, the chairs can be moved and this might be a way to ensure all your learners can face you when you need them to hear what you are saying and see what you are doing.

If you can, it is best to create an environment where learners can communicate with each other, and see and hear everything you are doing and saying. Ideally, you should move around the room regularly and interact with your learners, rather than staying at the front of the room or sitting behind a desk.

Some training rooms have a fixed projector with a screen at the front, which all learners will need to be able to see if you are using a visual presentation. However, some modern training rooms now have smaller television screens strategically placed around the room. These enable anyone who is not near the front to see the presentation nearer to where they are seated. If this is the case, you may need to seek technical support if you are not familiar with how to operate the system.

If you can choose the layout of the room, you could decide on the furniture arrangement based on the teaching and learning activities to be carried out. For example, placing tables in groups (also known as cabaret or café style) for group activities, or having tables in rows for a lecture if a lot of learners will be attending.

Tables in groups

This *cabaret* or *café* style is an effective way to enable learners to work together and to interact during group activities. All learners can still see the teacher and any presentation materials being used. The style is informal and the teacher can see everyone. If room permits, tables could be moved so that they are not so close together, or placed at different angles. The teacher could sit beside the desk rather than behind so as not to create a barrier, and move around the room when possible.

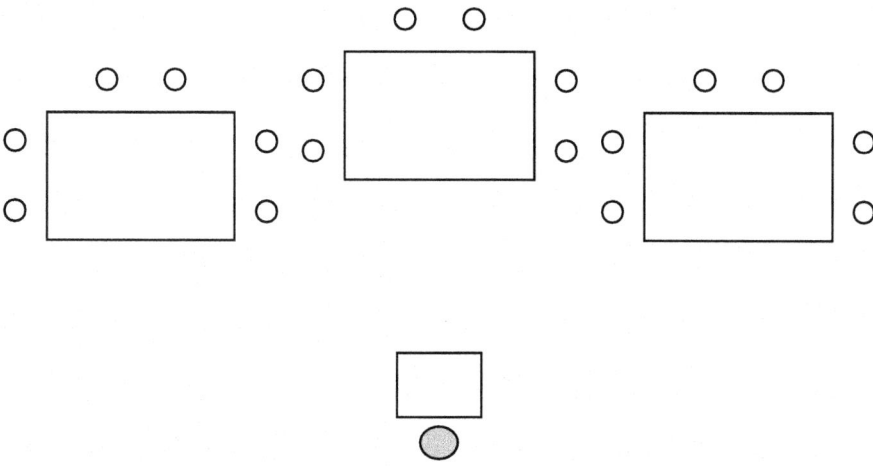

Figure 2.1 Group layout (cabaret or café style)

Tables in rows

This *classroom* style does not lead to effective communication between learners. However, all learners can see what is going on and see the teacher. This layout is useful when presenting information if group work is not required. The teacher would need good voice projection to reach all learners at the back of the room or use a microphone. Without the tables, more chairs could be positioned tightly in rows, allowing many learners to attend

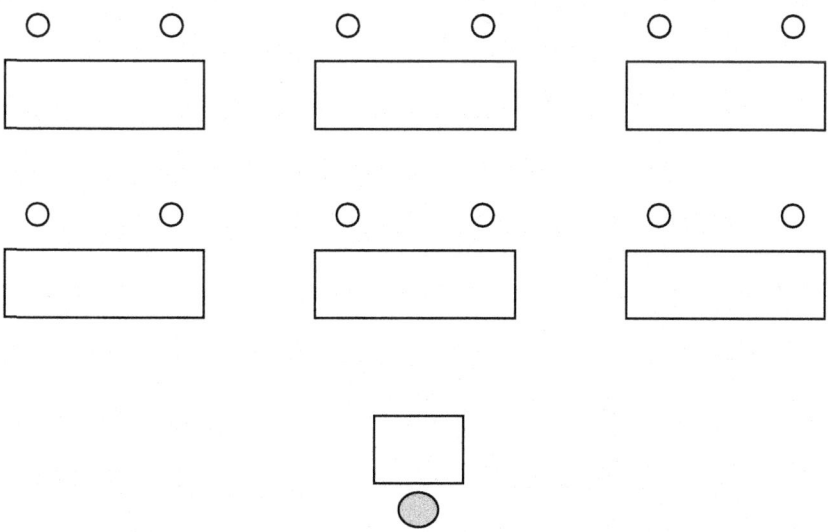

Figure 2.2 Classroom-style layout

a session at the same time. This is known as *lecture* style and could involve the use of benches instead of chairs. If chairs are used, they might have a moveable arm on which to rest notes. If a learner is sitting in the middle of a row and needs to leave the room for any reason, they would disrupt the rest of the row of learners. If there are many rows, learners at the back might not be able to see or hear very well. This style could enable learners to not pay much interest, and the teacher might not notice.

Horseshoe or U-shape

This style allows for large group discussions between the learners and the teacher, but is not good for small group work. Learners can still see the teacher and any presentation materials being used. Learners sitting at the very ends of tables may feel excluded from the group when discussions take place. More tables could be added if necessary to close the gap and create an oblong shape; the teacher then becomes part of the group.

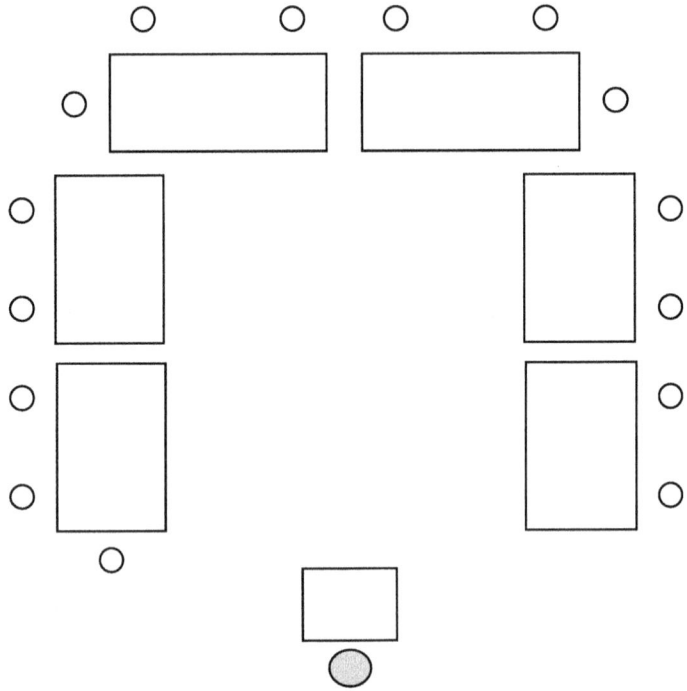

Figure 2.3 Horseshoe or U-shape layout

Boardroom style

This oblong (or it could be a square) style allows for discussions and group work where a large table area is needed. If the teacher sits at the table with the learners, everyone can communicate and see each other. If the teacher sits separately, some learners will have their backs to them, and not be able to see a presentation screen if used.

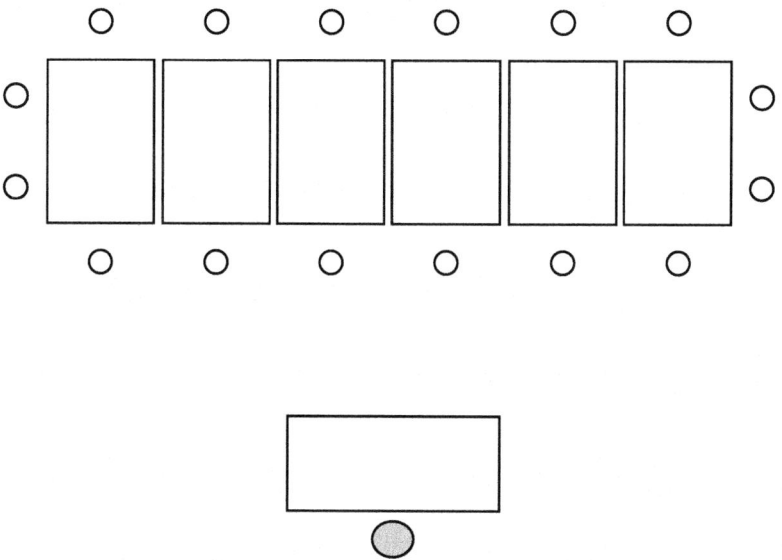

Figure 2.4 Boardroom-style layout

Other layouts

If possible, you could experiment with other layouts (see Figure 2.5 page 76) to see how effective they are for the type of teaching and learning activities which will take place. This can include the teacher as part of the group or not, using tables or not, or a different approach such as chairs in a circle to include all learners as well as the teacher. However, sometimes tables can create barriers.

If you are delivering a session at an external venue, such as a hotel or a conference centre, you might be able to request certain layouts which will be set up beforehand for you. If you need to move the furniture, you should get a member of staff to help you beforehand and again afterwards. You will need to allow space for movement around the room, and for bags and coats to ensure there are no obstructions. If you can, return the room to its original layout at the end of your session.

Activity

Take a look at the figures denoting different styles of room layout. List the advantages and disadvantages of each for your subject. You might like to discuss these with a colleague or friend. How could you overcome any disadvantages? What other room layouts could you use for your subject and why?

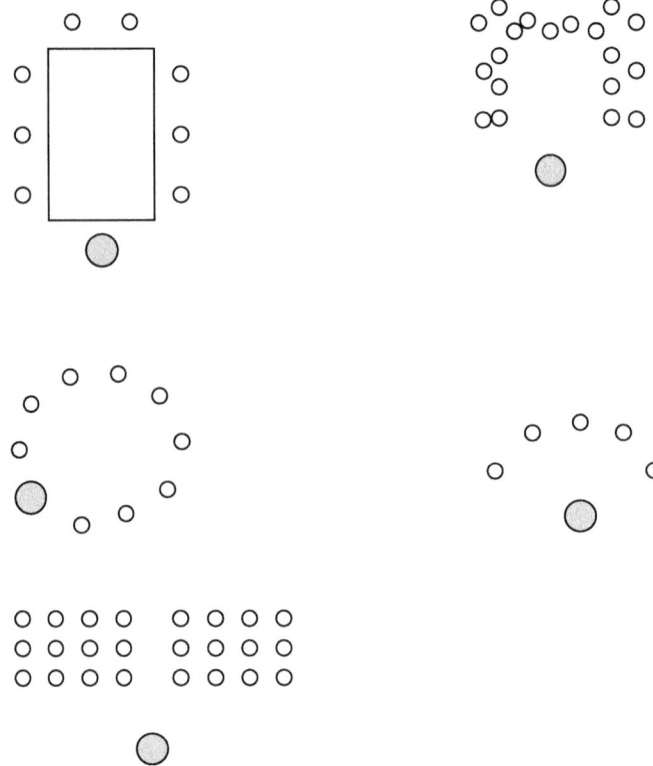

Figure 2.5 Other layouts that could be used

Managing the learning environment

The seating arrangements in a room can have a big impact on learning. People like their comfort zones and you may find that learners will sit in the same place each time they are with you. This is often the place they sat during the first session. This is useful to help you remember their names. You can sketch a seating plan and note who sits where, as well as who has not participated or who has caused disruption. Your sketch and notes will help you plan future sessions, for example, to make sure everyone participates. Remembering and using learners' names will show respect and encourage them to talk to you in confidence if they have any concerns. Some learners like to sit with their friends which might not help them learn from others, or work with others in the group. If you tell your learners from the start that you will move them, for example, when carrying out group activities, they will become used to it. If you suddenly decide half way through a course, they might not take it well. Moving learners around or getting them to work with others can either help or hinder their learning, depending upon the group dynamics and maturity of the learners.

If possible, arrive early to check the layout of the room, and to prepare any materials and equipment. You might find the room hasn't been left in a suitable condition by the previous user and you will need time to prepare it.

Example

Harry arrived at 9.25 a.m. ready for his session which commenced at 9.30 a.m. He found the room was untidy with rubbish on the floor, three chairs were missing, writing was on the board, and the data projector wasn't working. He became very anxious as his learners started arriving. He therefore didn't give a professional impression and was flustered when he commenced the session, missing out some vital information as a result.

In this example, the previous occupant of the room had not left it in a fit state for the next person. If this occurs regularly, it might be an idea to talk to someone who can influence those using the rooms to leave them in a fit state.

There may be instances when you have no option but to arrive at the time the session is due to commence. For example, if another group is timetabled in the room prior to your session. When this is the case, you won't know what state the room will be in. You could ask your learners to wait outside the room for a few minutes until you check it's acceptable. Alternatively, you could let your learners come in, but tell them you need a few minutes to set up. If this is the case, and depending upon the maturity of your learners, you could ask them to chat among themselves about the topic to be covered.

Health and safety considerations

Learners are entitled to learn in a healthy and safe environment. If you see a potential hazard, be proactive and do something about it or report it: don't wait for an accident to happen. In the UK, under the Health and Safety at Work etc. Act (1974), health and safety is not only the responsibility of your employer, but that of you and your learners too. For example, if a learner sees a trailing cable, they should let you know, so that you can report it. Your learners may need to wear protective clothing or use hazardous substances for some activities; you will, therefore, need to find out what your organisation's procedures are for these. You might be using electrical equipment which will need checking regularly by an appointed person in your organisation. You will also need to make sure that any floor surfaces are not slippery, that any trailing wires are out of the way, and any equipment your learners will be working with is safe and reliable. If you are teaching a subject that could be dangerous or hazardous, you may need to carry out risk assessments, which should be documented: for example, if you are teaching hairdressing and using chemicals. If safe to do so, you could include your learners in this process, to help them identify any issues or concerns prior to their use.

You will need to know your organisation's accident, fire, emergency and first aid procedures. You should inform your learners of these during their first meeting with you. If you have any learners who started after the course commenced, you should always give them this information. You could include it in a handout, or it might already be in a learner hand-book or accessible electronically.

You could have learners who have particular individual needs, such as diabetes. They might need to go somewhere private to take medication. You will need to know who they are, what you need to do, and who you need to contact in case of an emergency.

Learner age ranges and modes of attendance

People who participate in further education will be of different ages: for example, learners in a school aged 14–16 or in a college aged 16 and above. The modes of attendance will also vary, for example: part time, full time, learning on-the-job, through distance learning or perhaps in a secure environment such as a prison.

Age ranges

The age range of the learners you will teach may bring interesting challenges, whether you are teaching in a small or a large group, or training individually on a one-to-one basis (covered in Chapter 5). This section will explore some of the age ranges you might come across such as:

- 14–16 year olds
- 16–19 year olds
- adult learners
- mixed age ranges.

14–16 year olds

The 14–16 age group may still be attending compulsory education and certain regulations, safeguarding and disciplinary procedures will apply. For example, you could be teaching in an academy, public, private or free school, college or other organisation. These might have different requirements to a secondary, grammar or comprehensive school.

You might be teaching learners who are in residential care; for example, physically disabled youngsters who are entitled to education, but are not necessarily integrated within mainstream establishments.

Teaching this age group might bring with it issues that you will have to deal with. For example, challenging behaviour, truancy, peer pressure, negative attitudes, disruption, bullying, and the discreet use of mobile phones. Learners might want to be treated as adults but they are still classed as children. It would be beneficial to set clear boundaries and establish routines so that a climate of respect can exist. You will need patience and understanding, and must treat everyone in the group as an individual, remaining firm but fair to all. To help maintain respect, you might not want to be on first name terms, nor reveal anything too personal about yourself.

This age range might be used to a style of teaching different to that you might use with adults. For example, they might have been used to working through worksheets, reading handouts, and preparing for tests and exams. They might not have gained the ability to make notes, to practise skills, or to carry out research and present their findings. You will need to find out what they can and can't do in this respect. Having a structure to your sessions, i.e. starting on time, having frequent changes of activities, recapping points regularly, and finishing on time, might help the attention and participation of your learners.

You might be teaching within a school environment and have to follow their rules and regulations. Alternatively, the learners might come from a school to your organisation. Sometimes, a different environment may alter their behaviour, i.e. they might act more maturely, or act over confidently and become disruptive in front of their peers.

Some learners may have learning difficulties; others may come with a support assistant to help them. However, all learners will have something positive to contribute to the session. You will need to ensure your delivery enables everyone to participate in the learning experience, and does not exclude anyone.

Ensuring your sessions are meaningful, with lots of interesting and practical tasks, will help classroom management. You might be able to relate what you are talking about to your own and your learners' current and past experiences. Bringing your subject to life with anecdotes, and relating it to current topics, trends, and the work place, should help your learners understand what you are talking about.

Younger learners often need lots of praise and encouragement, they appreciate you listening to them and supporting them when necessary. Praise should be about behaviours and attitudes, as well as progress and achievements. Many younger learners like to use technology whenever possible, so incorporating this appropriately could be beneficial. Some learners might not be performing well in other subjects with other teachers. They might, therefore, have a negative attitude towards you and/or the subject. Some might act more maturely, and others quite childishly. You will need to get to know your learners as individuals, and motivate them to learn. This can be quite hard with younger learners if they haven't enjoyed their learning experiences so far. You may need to help build their self-esteem and encourage them more than you would with older learners. Try and be approachable, and listen to what your learners have to say. If you ask a question and they answer wrongly, don't dismiss it, but try and relate their answer to a real situation which is relevant to the subject. Try and include all learners during the session and make them feel their contribution, however small, is valued. If you are enthusiastic about the subject, hopefully they will be.

16–19 year olds

The 16–19 age group includes learners who might still be in compulsory education, apprentices on a training programme, and learners on a part-time, full-time or day release course. Non-attendance might affect their funding allowance if they receive one, and you might be required to sign documents to prove they were present. Some challenges that you may encounter with the 14–16 age range might be the same as those encountered with the 16–19 age range. For example, if learners have to attend as part of a day release programme and are not attending voluntarily, they might not pay as much attention, or even turn up. However, some learners may have been in (or are still in) employment and will have knowledge and experience that can be drawn on during the sessions. You might, therefore, have a mixture of learners in the same group, for example, some who have recently left school, some who have been in employment for a while, and some who are unemployed. As a result, levels of maturity may differ. However, some school leavers might prefer being in an adult environment to a school environment and, as such, pay more attention. Never assume, under- or over-estimate your learners' skills, knowledge and understanding, or make any presumptions about them or their past experiences.

Depending upon your subject, you will find your own ways to reach each individual, giving them confidence to progress with their learning. Always give positive encouragement to retain motivation, and treat all questions from learners as valid, no matter how silly they may seem to you (or them) at the time.

Adult learners

Adult learners, aged 19 and over, are usually motivated to learn, either for their own personal benefit or for professional reasons. They might be retraining to enhance their job role, perhaps as a result of redundancy, or wanting a new challenge or opportunity. Their motivation ensures they are keen and enthusiastic learners, usually attending voluntarily in their own time and probably at unsocial hours. However, some adults might have been told to attend a course either by their employer or as part of a programme to help them gain employment; therefore, their motivation might not be as high as you would like it to be. You might find with some adult learners that they feel they know more than they do. You will need to be tactful at finding out what they do and don't know to help them realise this. You might also feel some learners know more than you. This is nothing to worry about and can be used to your advantage. For example, if you don't know how to use a particular software program very well, you could involve a learner who does. This might make them feel good that they have shown the teacher what to do. However, some older learners might feel they know more than you, and may try to dominate the session. Let them have their say at first and then state that you value their input based on their experience. However, if they do try to dominate, you will have to tactfully ask them not to interrupt you, perhaps because you are short of time to cover everything in the session. Alternatively, when explaining something, you could add the words 'as some of you may know....' or 'some of you might already be familiar with this'. This will show that you are aware of their prior knowledge and experience.

Some adult learners might be apprehensive if they have not attended education for a few years. You will need to reassure them that you are there to help them. Depending upon your subject, there will be ways of integrating your learners' experiences to benefit everyone.

Example

Haani teaches a weekly two-hour information technology course, which will last eight weeks. There are ten learners aged 19 to 65. As part of the first session he asked them to introduce themselves and say a little about their experience of using a computer. He soon realised the older learners had very little experience and three had never even switched on a computer. The younger learners are more confident and have used computers at school and home. He therefore decides to sit a younger learner next to an older learner so they can help and support each other. Each learner will be working individually through a series of tasks at their own pace and can ask each other questions when necessary. They can therefore learn from each other as well as from Haani.

Adults are often used to being active and having self-discipline when it comes to learning. They are frequently confident to ask questions and to challenge theories. They often like to relate new learning to their own experiences. If you are asked a question you cannot answer, say you will find out. Then make sure you tell them the answer next time you see them, or email them in the meantime. While you are expected to have an in-depth knowledge of your subject, you won't know everything and this is fine. It's best to be honest and admit when you don't know something rather than bluff your way out of it.

Quite often, adults are not afraid of making a mistake as they have learnt this through experience, whereas younger learners would not want to embarrass themselves in front of their peers. Adults are often keen to tell you and the group their experiences and how they have learnt from them. Conversely, some adults might lack the confidence to discuss things in front of their peers until they get to know them well.

When teaching adults, try and plan tasks in a logical order, relate theory to practice and involve them with discussions of their own experiences. Always clearly state the aim of your session and what the learners will do. With all learners, you should check their prior knowledge and experience, recap and summarise topics, repeat key points, and ask questions on an ongoing basis to check that learning is taking place.

Adults will usually make the effort to arrive on time, have the necessary materials, e.g. pens, paper and textbooks, and not be disruptive. However, you need to consider their personal circumstances and situations: for example, if you are delivering an evening class and some of your learners have been at work all day, looking after children, travelling far, or haven't yet eaten.

Some adults might have had negative experiences at school or of previous courses they have attended. This might have stayed with them and could affect their current learning. Try and get to know each learner as an individual to enable you to support their learning in an appropriate way. You could be on first name terms with adults and have a more informal delivery style if you feel this is appropriate.

Mixed age ranges

It could be that you will teach a mixture of age ranges within the same group. This could affect the learners' attitudes and the way they act and interact with each other. The demographics of populations are continually changing. What follows is generalised and not meant to be stereotypical, but to give you an idea of the different generations.

The *veteran* generation (aged 65 plus) may have been with the same employer for a long time and be thinking of retiring. They have probably paid off their mortgage, have children who have left home and therefore have different priorities from younger generations.

The *baby boomers* (born 1946–1965) might be working fewer hours and increasing their leisure pursuits, have grown-up children and a low mortgage. This generation will increase over the next few years and may lead to a larger number of older than younger people in the workplace.

Generation X (born 1966–1976) might be mid-career, have had several jobs, and perhaps experienced redundancy and unemployment along the way. They might have a large mortgage and a growing family.

Generation Y (born 1977–1994) might be unemployed, be in training, be first or second jobbers. They could still be living with their parents, have few responsibilities and possibly have debts. They use technology a great deal and the line between work and social use can become blurred.

Generation Z or the millennium generation (born 1995 onwards) have had lifelong access to technology, the internet and social media. Access to multimedia to such an extent can lead to a change in communication methods, which to other generations can look like a lack of social manners. Communication becomes via technology rather than face to face. This can lead to poor spelling and grammar when writing. Personal aspects often take priority over work due to the *immediate* and *switched on* lives they lead. This generation has been subjected to a fame culture through the many reality television shows, and is often influenced by celebrities and fashion.

With these different generations come different aspirations, expectations, attitudes and values towards work. As a result, attitudes might be different towards their peers or indeed towards you as their teacher.

Activity

How do you think the different age ranges of learners could affect the way you teach and the way they learn? What challenges might you encounter with each age group listed and how could you overcome them?

Modes of attendance

The modes of attendance of learners may vary depending upon when and where your courses are offered. Not all learners will attend traditional classes, some might take a distance learning course or learn on-the-job if they are employed. This section will explore some of the modes of attendance you might come across such as:

- apprentice learners

- distance learners

- offender learners

- part-time or full-time

- workplace learners.

Apprentice learners

Apprenticeships are usually for vocational subjects and should lead to a full-time job at the end of the training period. Some apprenticeship programmes also include formal qualifications but all will involve the apprentice working towards a set of standards. Learners who are on an apprenticeship programme will participate in a combination of practical training in the workplace, known as *on-the-job*, and training elsewhere, known as *off-the-job*. Training can also take place *near to the job*, for example, in a separate area such as a mobile unit on a construction site.

If you are involved with an apprentice learner, it might be to carry out training and/or assessment in their place of work. Alternatively, it might be that you are working in a training organisation or a college and the learner comes to you. You might not know much about where the apprentice works, or you might be able to visit them at work to see how they are progressing. You should always liaise with their supervisor regarding what they are doing at work and the progress they are making. It's important to make sure that what you are planning to teach ties in with what the learner is doing in their place of work. Off-the-job training should complement on-the-job training and vice versa.

There will be a set of standards which apprentices will need to have achieved by the end of their programme. You might not be the person who assesses what you have taught, as *end point* assessment (covered in Chapter 10) is usually by someone the learner has not met before. This is a bit like learning to drive, you might teach the person to drive but someone else will assess them during the test. However, you will still need to formatively assess the learner's progress and ensure that they are ready for end point assessment. If the learner is also taking a qualification, the usual assessment requirements will apply. Apprenticeship learners might also be required to take qualifications in English, maths and digital skills. You may need to support them with these skills and liaise with the person responsible for their progress in these subjects.

Distance learners

Distance learners are those that are learning away from the formal teaching environment. They might be isolated from the teacher and their peers. Learners need to be self-motivated, committed and able to devote a suitable amount of time to this type of study. Distance learning could involve the use of technology or the use of learning materials which are sent and returned via the postal service.

Learning is increasingly taking place online, enabling it to occur at any time and in any place where there is an internet-enabled device. Courses can be tailored to meet individual requirements and learners can work at their own pace. If you are teaching online, you might never meet your learners, but communicate via the online program (covered in Chapter 8).

Offender learners

These learners might be in a young offender institution, on remand or detention, or in a prison. It might be compulsory that they attend various training sessions, and while some will be keen to learn, others may not. This will bring its own challenges regarding motivation and there might also be some behavioural issues to contend with. You will need to allow extra time before and after a session to go through the security procedures. If you are teaching in this type of environment you will need to be careful not to allow yourself to become conditioned to situations. You need to remember that your learners are there to gain skills and knowledge to help them upon their release. You will also have strict guidelines and security procedures to follow. It could be that some of your learners are released or moved elsewhere part way through their training. Others might start at different points and will need to catch up on what has been taught so far. Some may drop in and out of your sessions due to the prison regime, perhaps where offenders are attending other activities such as physical education. You might even arrive to teach a session and find that the learners have been locked in their rooms due to operational issues. Some might be in court or with visitors and will miss a session. Keeping an accurate and up-to-date track of individual progress and achievement will be important. Records may need to be passed onto other places if the learners move elsewhere.

Part-time or full-time

Some learners who have employment, family or other commitments might prefer to study on a part-time basis. This could be to spread their learning over a longer time frame, to help with their budgeting and travel constraints. Classes might range from one to three hours a week to one day a week or more.

Full-time learning has different hours and time frames attached depending upon the subject and funding. Some full-time attended classes might only be 16 hours per week, with the rest of the time for self-study. Others could be much more and spread over different days and times. Some courses are classed as *intensive*, meaning the subject is covered quickly in a smaller amount of time. Others might take from a few weeks to several years.

It's useful to keep in touch with your learners between classes as they may need ongoing encouragement to remain motivated, whether part-time or full-time.

The classes might be traditionally attended and take place during the day, the evening or the weekend. Alternatively, they might be by distance learning via a postal or online training programme.

Workplace learners

Workplace learners are those who are learning in their place of work and could be aged 16 and upwards. They might be learning a new task or a procedure, be observed to meet certain standards, or receive training as part of an apprenticeship programme. The way you teach or train in the workplace will usually be on an individual or small group basis. If you are also based in the same working environment as the learners, it will give you the opportunity to spend more time with them. However, it might also mean you are interrupted regularly to give advice and support. You will need to balance your other priorities such as the commitments and deadlines of your own job role.

You might be required to train a learner who is attending your organisation as part of a work experience programme. They could be with you one day a week or for a full week or more. Even though they might not be in paid employment, you should treat them as a member of staff and make them feel welcome. They might have certain tasks they need to learn and carry out as part of their training programme. Therefore, you might need to assess their progress and liaise with staff from the organisation they are from. Work experience isn't about making the tea and carrying out menial jobs; it's about carrying out real job roles, but under supervision.

Extension activity

If you could teach any age range or any type of learner, in any location or environment, what would this be and why? Now consider the reality of who you will teach and where. How different are your responses to the first question and what does this tell you?

Motivation

Motivation is the incentive or reason why someone chooses to do something. It's useful to be aware of what motivates your learners, as their enthusiasm might affect their learning (in a positive or a negative way) and possibly their behaviour. A learner attending a session because they have been told to, may not be as motivated as a learner who is there because they want to be. It's also useful to know what your learners are expecting from the course, as it might differ from what they will receive. Finding out the expectations of your learners and what motivates them, should help you deliver the programme in a way that will lead to successful learner achievement. Expectations could be ascertained during the first session simply by asking. If your learners' expectations don't match with what will take place, tell them why. Learners will want to know what's in it for them and why they should attend. They need to know the value of the course to them either personally or professionally. It could be that they have been recommended to take a course or are on the wrong course and didn't realise it. It's best to find this out at the beginning, rather than part way through.

Motivation is either intrinsic (from within) meaning the learner wants to learn for their own fulfilment, or extrinsic (from without) meaning there may be an external factor motivating them: for example, a promotion at work. Table 2.1 lists some examples of internal and external reasons why people are motivated to learn.

Table 2.1 Examples of intrinsic and extrinsic motivation factors

Intrinsic	Extrinsic
• a passion for the subject • for enjoyment and fulfilment • for personal reasons • for social interaction • the desire to achieve something new • to complete something previously started • to gain confidence • to improve self-esteem and self-worth • to meet people • to overcome personal challenges • to prove to self that something can be achieved	• for a promotion • for professional reasons • the requirement of a job role • to achieve a qualification • to gain a pay rise • to gain acceptance and approval of others • to gain career progression • to please others or make them proud • to prove to others something can be achieved • to receive a bonus or a commission

If learners are keen and proactive towards learning, they should be self-motivated and want to learn. For example, obtaining the relevant resources and textbooks, asking for help when necessary, getting actively involved during sessions, and taking control of their studies. Conversely, if learners are passive, their motivation to learn will be less. For example, expecting the teacher or trainer to supply their resources, not asking for help when necessary, not participating during the session, and not wanting to take control of their studies. Passive learners might blame the teacher or trainer when they don't achieve something, whereas active learners might just blame themselves. If you can be positive and tell all your learners that you believe they can achieve, this will hopefully help to motivate them.

You could motivate your learners by using activities which are interactive rather than just talking to them. People are becoming accustomed to being more interactive due to social media and television. For example, some popular live television programmes encourage their audiences to get involved with online polls, emails and texts. News and weather programmes also encourage interaction by asking viewers to email or upload pictures and videos. This way, people feel engaged, are involved and are active, rather than passive. Keeping your learners active and involved will hopefully keep them motivated to learn.

Activity

If you are currently teaching, do you know what has motivated each of your learners to attend your sessions? If not, try and find out so that you can maintain their motivation.

If you are not currently teaching, think about what motivated you to learn something recently, and how that motivation had a positive or negative impact on what you did. There are useful texts and websites to support motivation and behaviour listed at the end of this chapter, which you might like to read.

Whatever level of motivation your learners have, will be transformed, for better or worse, by what happens during their experience with you. You, therefore, need to promote a professional relationship that leads to individual trust and respect. Some learners may seem naturally enthusiastic about learning, but many need or expect you to inspire and engage them. It's hard to get someone to do something if they can't see a real benefit for themselves. You could try and relate the topic to something they are interested in, such as a hobby or a leisure activity. You could also relate the learning to how it will be applied in practice in the workplace. You might have stories you can tell your learners if you have worked in the subject area previously.

Many factors can affect a learner's motivation to work and to learn, for example: an interest in the subject matter, perception of its usefulness, a general desire to achieve, self-confidence and self-esteem, as well as patience and persistence. Not all learners are motivated by the same values, needs, desires or wants. Some of your learners will be motivated by the approval of others, and some by overcoming personal challenges.

To help motivate your learners you can:

- agree some basic ground rules so that everyone feels safe and secure

- ask open questions to keep them involved (ones that begin with *who, what, when, where, why* and *how* – not closed questions, which just lead to *yes* or *no* responses)

- avoid creating intense competition, although some competition can be engaging and fun

- be aware of attention-span limits (some learners may lose focus quickly)

- give ongoing constructive feedback so that learners know how they are progressing

- give praise and encouragement when it's deserved

- maintain an organised and orderly atmosphere

- make tasks interesting, practical and relevant

- negotiate realistic and achievable targets

- not talking down to your learners or making them feel silly or embarrassed

- offer support when necessary

- stretch and challenge each learner's potential

- treat learners with respect and as individuals

- try not to be too critical, but be positive when you can

- use learners' names to show you know them as individuals

- use icebreakers and energisers to get learners actively working together

- vary your teaching and assessment approaches to reach all learning preferences.

Keeping yourself motivated might also be a challenge. There could be situations that occur which might make you feel like this isn't the job for you. It's hard work being a teacher; however, it's a very rewarding job, and you have the opportunity to help so many people. When times are hard, remember all the good you have done for your learners in the past, and will do in the future. Make sure you have someone you can talk to, such as a mentor. Don't keep things to yourself as any problems or concerns you have might escalate in your own mind. It's probable that your mentor has also experienced what you are feeling, and can give you some useful advice. Things can and will go wrong, just learn from the experiences, be honest with yourself and remember why you wanted to be a teacher.

If you can be enthusiastic and passionate about your subject, this might motivate and enthuse your learners. If not, they might wonder why they should bother attending if you are not showing interest in the subject or are demonstrating that you are not enjoying your job.

Keller's (1987) ARCS model of motivation

Keller (1987) combined existing research on psychological motivation and created the ARCS model: **A**ttention, **R**elevance, **C**onfidence, and **S**atisfaction. Having some knowledge of this model might help you to motivate your learners.

Attention is the first and most important aspect of the ARCS model which is about gaining and maintaining your learners' attention. Keller's strategies for attention include:

- stimulating the five senses – ensuring you reach all learners through sight, hearing, touch, smell and taste, although this might not always be possible

- inquiry arousal – using thought-provoking questions and challenges

- variability – using various delivery approaches, activities and media.

Relevance is the second aspect. To ensure motivation is retained, the learner has to believe the session content is relevant to them. It's about addressing the learner's question of *What's in it for me?* The benefits should clearly be stated to the learner to enable them to see what they will gain.

Confidence is the third aspect. This is to help learners put an effort into their learning and to think they are capable of achieving. Learners should always be given constructive and developmental feedback to help maintain their motivation. Clear targets and deadlines need to be discussed and agreed.

Satisfaction is the final aspect. Learners must obtain some type of satisfaction or reward from their learning experience. This could be in the form of a sense of achievement or of gaining a qualification. Satisfaction could also come from external rewards such as praise from others, a pay rise, more responsibility or a job promotion. Ultimately, the best way for learners to achieve satisfaction is for them to put their new skills and knowledge to immediate use.

Activity

Using the ARCS model of motivation, consider a topic you are going to teach and plan how to gain your learners' attention for each aspect. How will you make this relevant to each learner, ensuring that they feel confident to learn and are satisfied in some way?

Herzberg's (1991) hygiene needs and motivation needs

Herzberg (1991) created a two-level theory with *hygiene* needs and *motivation* needs.

Hygiene needs (also known as maintenance needs) in Herzberg's view, do not provide positive motivation, but their absence causes dissatisfaction. This is in the same way that hygiene prevents disease rather than increasing well-being.

Hygiene needs include factors such as salary, interpersonal relationships, working conditions, style of leadership and types of supervision, security, type of work, working hours and status. They are called hygiene needs as they work like preventative medicine. They can help stop an illness but do not do anything to promote good health. In a teaching context this means that hygiene factors don't motivate learners to do their very best, but they are needed to stop them becoming dissatisfied with their learning experience.

Motivation needs lead to satisfaction. They include factors which allow for: achievement, responsibility, recognition, advancement and challenge. Herzberg suggests that these factors are the ones which encourage people to strive to do well, and motivate them to do their best.

Herzberg believed that hygiene and motivation needs were equally important for satisfaction but that they work in different ways. If the hygiene needs are inadequate, learners will quickly become dissatisfied. However, as these needs are satisfied, trying to motivate them by adding more hygiene needs is an inefficient and short-term solution. A better way would be to appeal to the learners' motivation needs by giving them more responsibility or giving them greater challenges. In this way, they are satisfied and motivated.

Example

Sharron is progressing well towards a beauty therapy course. When she receives compliments from her teacher for keeping her working area clean and tidy, she feels good. However, she doesn't expect compliments every day and isn't demotivated as a result (her hygiene needs are met). The following week Sharron is given the chance to supervise a new learner and enjoys the challenge (meeting her motivation needs).

Maslow's (1987) Hierarchy of Needs

Maslow (1987) introduced a *Hierarchy of Needs* in 1954 which can relate to motivation and the ability to achieve something. He rejected the idea that human behaviour was determined by childhood events. He felt that obstacles should be removed that prevent a person from achieving their goals. He argued that there are five *needs* which represent different levels of motivation which must be met. The highest level was labelled *self-actualisation,* meaning people are fully functional, possess a healthy personality and take responsibility for themselves and their actions. He also believed that people should be able to move through these needs to the highest level, provided they are given an education that promotes growth. Figure 2.6 shows the needs expressed as they might relate to learning, starting at the base of the pyramid.

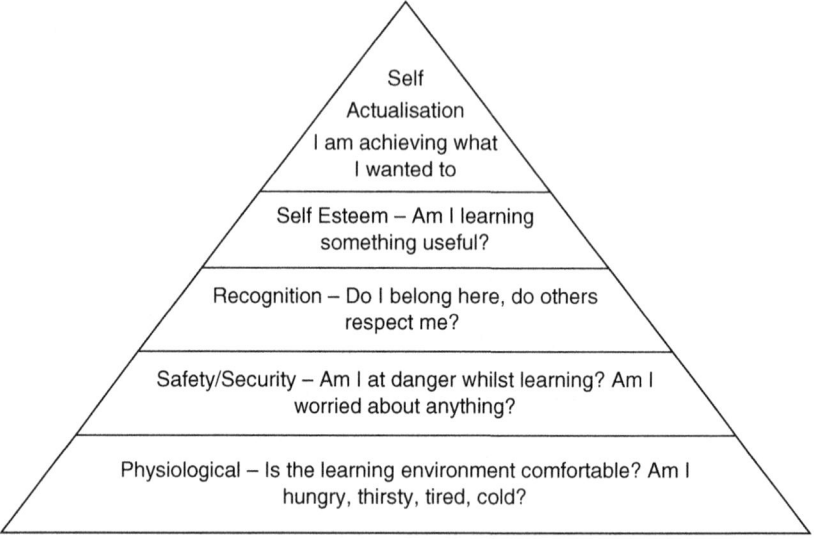

Figure 2.6 Maslow's (1987) Hierarchy of Needs expressed in educational terms

When learners satisfy their needs at one level, they should be able to progress to the next level. Something may set them back a level, but they should want to keep striving upwards. It is these needs that stimulate learning to take place. However, some people may not want to progress through the levels and may be quite content where they are at that moment in their life. There might also be age or cultural factors which could impact upon progression through the levels. You could think of the needs as relevant to your role too. If you are hungry, thirsty, tired or cold as in the first level, you might not perform well.

To help your learners' motivation, try and ensure that the environment you create meets your learners' first level needs. This will enable them to feel comfortable and secure enough to learn and progress to the higher levels. You will need to appreciate that some learners may not have these lower needs met in their home lives, making it difficult for them to move on to the higher levels.

Dawn was due to teach a session from 5 p.m. to 7 p.m. She arrived early and noticed the room was hot and stuffy so she opened the windows. She also realised that most of her learners might not have had a chance to eat something prior to the session. When they arrived she told them they would be able to have an early break to enable them to get refreshments. She kept one window open to let some fresh air into the room and allowed her learners to drink bottled water if they wished.

This example shows how Dawn ensured her learners' first level needs were met, which should then help learning to take place.

While you may be very good at delivering your subject, you might have no control over the environment, and will need to create a suitable learning climate if you can. However, your enthusiasm and passion for your subject should help engage your learners. If you can also make your session interesting, active and varied, your learners will enjoy the experience and remember more about the subject and your delivery, rather than the environment or a lack of facilities.

Extension activity

How can you engage and motivate your learners to progress through each level of Maslow's Hierarchy of Needs? What internal and external factors might affect a learner's motivation? How do you think these factors can be overcome?

Challenges

Throughout your role as a teacher or a trainer you will experience many challenges. These might relate to personal challenges, such as:

- a difference in values and beliefs to that of your employer or your learners

- a disability or a difficulty which might limit access to, or use of, certain areas of a building, resources and/or equipment

- a fear of using new technology

- a lack of money to purchase items which your employer does not supply, e.g. specialist clothing

- family and home commitments

- limited language and numerical skills

- transport issues preventing you from arriving on time.

Others could relate to professional challenges, such as:

- a lack of learner motivation or interest

- a lack of resources and equipment

- a lack of time to adequately plan and prepare sessions

- learner absenteeism

- limited knowledge of the subject you have been asked to teach

- poor learner behaviour

- pressure from managers to achieve targets

- too many meetings to attend

- too much administration work to carry out

- unsupportive colleagues.

You might have colleagues who have experienced the same challenges as yourself and you may find it useful to talk to them. You could find out what support is available within your organisation.

Example

Saira was apprehensive about teaching a group of 25 learners, aged 16–19. She had only taught groups of adults before. Saira approached William, her line manager, for some advice. William had been teaching that age group for many years. He was able to give Saira lots of useful information, particularly relating to behaviour and motivation. Saira was pleased she had approached him. She had thought at first that he would have expected her to have known what to do. However, he proved really helpful and said he would sit in during some of her sessions to give her advice and support if she needed it.

Never think you are on your own; if you are experiencing a challenge, it's highly likely someone else has too.

Activity

Make a list of personal and professional challenges you feel you might encounter throughout your teaching role. How might you be able to overcome them? Will you need to involve anyone else? If so, who could help you and how will you go about contacting them?

Disruptions

To get through a session without any disruptions would be wonderful, but this very rarely happens. You might have a learner who arrives late, an inquisitive learner who always wants to know more, or just someone asking to leave the room to go to the toilet. Whatever the disruption might be, you need to handle this professionally to minimise any effect it might have on teaching and learning.

Usually, disruptions occur because people don't follow the ground rules, for example, their mobile phone rings, they decide to eat or drink, or do something other than that which you have asked them to do. If this is the case, politely ask them to stop, remind them of the ground rules and how they are also disrupting their peers' learning. Other occurrences happen because people are either bored, they don't understand what you are saying or you are not challenging them enough. Could you give them an alternative activity to stretch their learning further? Ideally, it's best not to ignore the disruption but address it immediately.

The late arrival learner

A learner might arrive late for many reasons which might not necessarily be deliberate. Depending upon what is happening at the time, they might take their place quietly or draw attention to themselves by apologising in front of everyone. You could welcome them to the session and give them a quick recap of what is happening. Alternatively, you could tell them you will give them an update regarding what they have missed at an appropriate point during the session.

If a learner is repeatedly late, you will need to find out why to see if it can be prevented. If not, the situation will disrupt the attention of everyone in the group and may make others feel that they shouldn't bother arriving on time either.

The over-enthusiastic learner

Sometimes, a learner can be over-enthusiastic which could have an adverse effect upon the rest of the learners. For example, they interrupt by asking too many questions, they like to tell everyone what they know or they become over-excited or even aggressive. Try not to lose patience with them, you might even find other learners ask them to quieten down before you do. Ways to deal with this situation include:

- moving around the room so that you do not directly face the learner all the time

- holding your hand up in a 'stop' sign when they interrupt you, and then asking them to wait until an appropriate time before speaking

- involving other learners, perhaps by saying *'I appreciate what you are saying; now let's hear from someone else'*

- using group work and activities where they must work with and listen to others.

Make a list of possible disruptions which you might encounter with your learners. Discuss these with a colleague and decide how you could deal with them in an effective way.

Learning preferences and styles

Most people learn in different ways and have a *preference* or a *style* to help them acquire new skills and knowledge and to remember things. Some people prefer the term *preference* to *styles* so as not to categorise a learner. Adults might have developed a preference or style from childhood learning patterns or their experiences of growing up and of working. What suits one learner might not suit another. For example, if a group of people were learning yoga, some might like to watch and listen to the teacher first. Others might want to practise the movements at the same time as the teacher.

All people learn differently, perhaps influenced by experiences in their childhood, school, personal or professional relationships. When you learn something new, you will probably adapt, change or modify your behaviour as a result, and the same will apply with your learners.

Your own experiences of how you learn might influence what you do with your learners. You might deliver your sessions in the style which suits you, but it might not suit your learners. For example, if you like to learn by listening to others, you might want to talk to your learners for most of your session. However, they might not all remain focused or take in what you say. If you can find out what your learners' current preferences are, then you can adapt your teaching approaches to suit.

There are critics of learning styles. In 2004, Professor Frank Coffield and three colleagues carried out a systematic and critical review of learning styles and pedagogy in post-16 learning. The report reviewed the literature on learning styles and examined in detail 13 of the most influential models. The implications for teaching and learning, he states, are serious and should be of concern. Coffield has since written widely on the subject and states ... *it was not sufficient to pay attention to individual differences in learners, we must take account of the whole teaching–learning environment.* (2008, page 31).

It's therefore important to consider other factors which influence learning, such as the environment, not just the preference or style of the individual learner.

Questionnaires and inventories

There are many different versions of questionnaires and inventories which are available. These can determine what preference or style of learning is best for each learner. For example, if they prefer to learn by watching a demonstration, listening to a talk, or to carry out practical activities. Your organisation might have one they would like you to use with your learners, or they might not want them used at all. Some are free and some are paid for; however, not all have been seriously researched in educational fields.

If you do use them, you might prefer to focus on the weaker findings and empower your learners to adapt information in a way that they are comfortable with, for example, by using a digital voice recorder if they are weaker at listening. They can then listen to the recording many times to help improve their listening skills. If a learner needs to improve their visual skills, they can use the image function of internet search engines to look at pictures and graphics.

Your learners might instinctively know what works best for them rather than having it determined for them. For example, they might prefer practical activities rather than reading or writing. This might have developed from previous courses they have attended. Rather than this being their learning preference, you could think of it as their teaching preference. You could ask your learners which teaching preference they have and then adapt your sessions accordingly.

VARK

In 1987, Fleming stated that people can be grouped into four styles of learning: visual, aural, read/write and kinaesthetic, known by the acronym VARK. Table 2.2 gives some examples of characteristics of VARK learners.

Table 2.2 Example characteristics of VARK

Visual (seeing) learners usually:	Aural (listening and talking) learners usually:
are meticulous and neat in appearance	are easily distracted
find verbal instructions difficult	ask questions
create images in their mind	don't like noisy environments
like doodling	enjoy talking and listening to others
like watching videos/DVDs	have difficulty with written instructions
memorise by looking at pictures	hum, sing and whisper
notice details and remember faces	like listening to music
observe rather than act or talk	talk to themselves out loud
Read/write (reading and writing) learners usually:	**Kinaesthetic (doing) learners usually:**
are good spellers	are tactile towards others
enjoy research	do not like reading and are often poor spellers
enjoy studying and writing essays	
have good handwriting skills	enjoy worksheets and discussions
like rewriting what others have written	fidget with pens or other items
	like practical activities
like to read books	like to solve problems by working through them
use a dictionary and thesaurus	
write lists and make notes	use their hands while talking

Table 2.3 Examples of meeting VARK learning preferences

Topic	Visual	Aural	Read/write	Kinaesthetic
Answering the telephone	Watching a demonstration, viewing an electronic presentation and/or online video. Looking at a handout	Listening to instructions and recordings, asking questions	Making notes, reading instructions and handouts	Carrying out the task for real or partaking in a role-play activity
Changing a fuse	Watching a demonstration, viewing an electronic presentation and/or online video	Listening to instructions, asking questions	Making notes, reading instructions	Carrying out the task for real
Decorating a cake	Watching a demonstration, viewing an electronic presentation and/or online video	Listening to instructions, asking questions	Making notes, reading instructions and handouts	Carrying out the task for real
Practising interview skills	Viewing a film or online video, watching others act out an interview	Listening to instructions, asking questions, discussing scenarios with others	Reading handouts, making notes	Partaking in a role play
Remembering historical dates	Viewing a film or online video, looking at a handout or presentation	Listening to instructions, discussing dates with others	Reading textbooks and handouts, researching and writing dates and facts	Researching the internet, partaking in a role play or quiz
Speaking a foreign language	Viewing a video of people talking	Listening to conversations and recordings of people speaking, talking to others	Reading textbooks, writing words and phrases	Having a conversation
Using a digital device, program or app	Watching a demonstration, viewing an electronic presentation or video	Listening to instructions, asking questions	Making notes, reading instructions and handouts	Carrying out a task using a computer or other device
Using fractions	Expressing the fraction as a picture, e.g. ¾ is	Talking through different ways of expressing amounts, e.g. ¾ is 75%	Making notes, reading and researching different uses for fractions	Demonstrating the use of fractions in everyday situations

However, try not to be quick to place learners in one of the four styles, as they may be *multi-modal*, i.e. a mixture of two or more styles, enabling their learning to take place more quickly.

Activity

Think about the subject you will teach. What activities could your learners carry out to cover the visual, aural, read/write and kinaesthetic learning prefer-ences? Do you agree with Frank Coffield that the whole teaching and learning environment has an impact rather than just the learning preferences? If so, how and why?

In 1992, Fleming, along with Mills published their findings in a journal. Other publica-tions have since become available which have different views. Styles and preferences of learning can change over time depending upon many factors, such as lifestyles or par-ticular events. Table 2.3 gives some examples of meeting the VARK learning preferences for various topics. However, it's best to use a mixture of each to ensure variety during your sessions.

Honey and Mumford (1992)

Honey and Mumford suggest learners are a mixture of four styles: activist, pragmatist, the-orist and reflector. This could be interpreted as:

Activist

Activist learners like to deal with new challenges and experiences, often learning by trial and error. They like lots of practical activities to keep them busy and they enjoy a hands-on approach. They love challenges and are enthusiastic.

Pragmatist

Pragmatist learners like to apply what they have learnt to practical situations. They like logi-cal reasons for doing something. They prefer someone to demonstrate a skill first before trying it for themselves.

Theorist

Theorist learners like time to take in information, they prefer to research and read lots of material first. They like things that have been tried and tested and prefer reassurance that something will work.

Reflector

Reflector learners think deeply about what they are learning and the activities they could do to apply this learning. They like to be told about things so that they can think it through. They will also try something, think about it, and then try it again.

Matt has just bought a new mobile phone. He is an activist learner and therefore enjoyed learning to use it by tapping the icons and trying out the functions. If he was a pragmatist, he would have asked someone to show him how to use it. If he was a theorist, he would have read the instructions thoroughly before carrying them out. If he was a reflector, he would have used the functions he was familiar with before thinking about different ways of using them, followed by using the phone's other functions.

It can be useful to ask your learners to complete a learning preference questionnaire. It can be fun and lead to an interesting discussion, as well as helping you plan your approaches to reach all learning preferences. A free online questionnaire is available at www.vark-learn.com.

Retention of learning

Whatever teaching and learning approaches and activities you choose to use with your learners, you will want them to retain what they have learnt. There have been many studies regarding the retention of learning, which are usually expressed in percentages. One is Dale's (1969) Cone of learning and experience, as in Figure 2.7. This shows in percentages how much people remember what they read, hear, see and do. However, Dale said it was not to be used literally, the bands within the cone are not rigid but flexible, and the cone in Figure 2.7 has been adapted, revised and disagreed with over the years.

Using activities from the top of the cone (passive) through to the bottom of the cone (active) might help your learners to realistically experience your subject. They should then remember more because they have *said and done* what they have *read and heard*, i.e. they have put theory into practice.

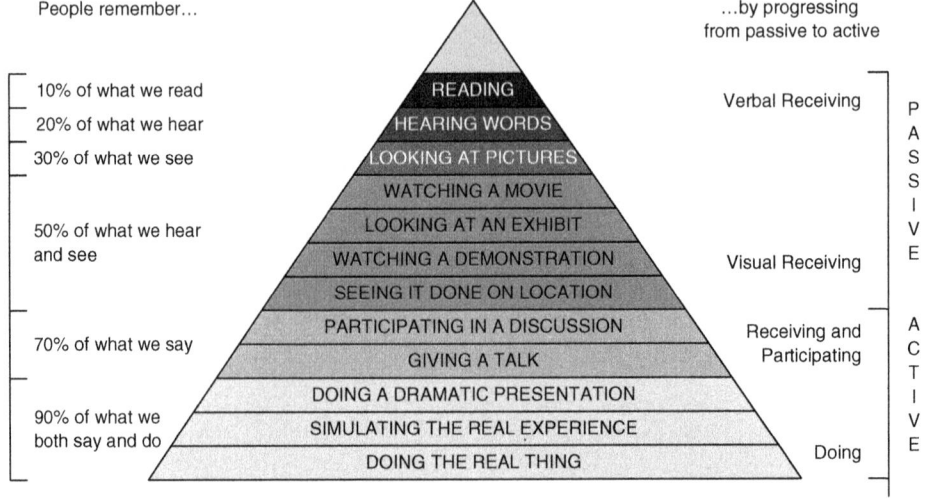

Figure 2.7 Dale's Cone of learning and experience (1969, page 108) adapted

If your learners can incorporate *reading, hearing, seeing, saying* and *doing* during your sessions, their learning retention should increase. Once learners put theory into practice they should begin to understand what they have learnt. Some people learn by imitating or copying others. While they might then be able to perform the task, they might not know *why* they are doing it. Therefore, skills and knowledge are best learnt together to ensure understanding takes place.

Extension activity

If you have access to the internet, go to www.vark-learn.com and carry out the online questionnaire. See what your results are for each of V, A, R and K. Do you think your result adequately reflects the way you learn? If not, why not? Research other theories regarding learning preferences and styles. Find out why some people are critics and others favour them, then make up your own mind if you will use them or not. You might also wish to research critics of Dale's Cone of learning and experience.

Teaching and learning theories, principles and models

There are many teaching and learning theories, principles and models which have been based on ideas, thoughts, experiences and research over many years. Some are quite old, but are trusted; others are fairly recent. This section will briefly explain some of these in (hopefully) an easy to understand way. They are in no particular order, and are often contradictory. For example, whether it's a philosopher's, a psychologist's, a sociologist's or a neuroscientist's perspective. You will need to make your own mind up whether you think they will influence what you do. You might even come up with your own theory or idea to challenge existing ones. All learning should lead to a change in behaviour which demonstrates that learning has taken place. There are many more theories besides those listed here, and there are some textbooks and weblinks at the end of this chapter if you wish to research further.

Sensory theory

Laird (1985) stated that learning occurs when the five senses of sight, hearing, touch, smell and taste are stimulated. Laird's theory suggests that if multi-senses are stimulated, greater learning takes place. You could, therefore, adapt your approaches and resources to enable your learners to use as many of their senses as possible.

The use of sensory stimulation through pictures, videos, sounds, podcasts, objects, smells and other methods can provide learners with a heightened sensory learning experience. This might be more engaging and interactive than a single stimulation.

Max, a curious 18 month old, was playing with a small plastic toy. He looked at it closely, then shook it to see if it made a noise. He followed this by placing it near his nose to see if it smelt. He then put it in in his mouth to see what it tasted like. He didn't like the taste, so he didn't put it in his mouth again. A change in behaviour therefore took place in Max, which demonstrated he had learnt something.

Types and conditions of learning

Gagne (1985) identified five types of *learned capabilities*, which he stated required a different type of instruction. These are:

- intellectual skills

- cognitive strategies

- verbal information

- attitude

- motor skills.

Different internal and external conditions of learning are required for each. For example, for motor skills to be learnt, there must be the opportunity for the learner to practise new skills rather than just observe them. For attitudes, the learner must be able to explore them, perhaps by discussing them.

Gagne believed all teaching and learning sessions should include a sequence of nine events. These should activate the processes needed for effective learning to take place. Each event has a corresponding cognitive process (in brackets) which Gagne stated all teachers should be aware of.

- Gaining attention (reception)

- Informing learners of the objective (expectancy)

- Stimulating recall of prior learning (retrieval)

- Presenting the stimulus (selective perception)

- Providing learning guidance (semantic encoding)

- Eliciting performance (responding)

- Providing feedback (reinforcement)

- Assessing performance (retrieval)

- Enhancing retention and transfer (generalisation)

Example

Ellie, a baking and pastry teacher, ensures all nine events take place in her sessions by:

Gaining attention – showing an example of what the learners will achieve by the end of the session, e.g. an iced wedding cake.

Identifying the objective – stating that the learners will be able to ice a wedding cake by the end of the session.

Recalling prior learning – asking the learners if they have ever iced a wedding cake before.

Presenting stimulus – explaining how they will ice the wedding cake and what they will need to use.

Guiding learning – demonstrating how to ice a wedding cake and showing a short video.

Eliciting performance – encouraging the learners to begin icing a wedding cake themselves.

Providing feedback – informing the learners how they are progressing.

Assessing performance – ensuring the learners are correctly icing the wedding cake by observing and asking questions.

Enhancing retention/transfer – summarising the learning, relating it to real-life situations and explaining what will be covered in the next session.

Behaviourism theory

Behaviourism is about people being conditioned to behave in a particular way, rather than using their own thoughts or feelings. Learning is, therefore, measured by a change in behaviour, which is modified by external influences or *conditioning*. There are many behaviourist theorists, the most well known being Pavlov, Watson and Skinner.

During the 1890s, Russian physiologist Ivan Pavlov was researching the digestive secretions of dogs in response to being fed. He noticed that his dogs would begin to salivate whenever he entered the room, whether he was bringing them food or not. He then rang a bell each time the dogs were fed. After a while, ringing the bell led the dogs to salivate, even though they were not given any food. This became known as *classical conditioning*, as the dogs had been conditioned to associate food with the sound of the bell.

John Watson (1928) believed that everything from speech to emotions are patterns of a stimulus and a response. He believed behaviour could be modified through natural stimuli. He is considered the founder of behaviourism which assumed all behaviour is observable, and can be correlated with other observable events. His research showed that people can be conditioned, and learning is a direct result of this conditioning.

Burrhus Skinner (1974) believed that behaviour is a function of its consequences, i.e. learners will repeat the desired behaviour if positive reinforcement is given. The behaviour should not be repeated if negative feedback is given.

Example

Jamie was sawing a piece of wood as part of a carpentry course and hadn't paid attention to the health and safety regulations. The saw kept slipping and he cut his hand. His teacher administered first aid and then gave him negative feedback. This, along with his experience, ensured he was more careful in future.

Giving immediate feedback, whether positive or negative, should enable your learners to behave in a certain way. Skinner believed the best way to understand behaviour is to look at the causes of an action and its consequences. He called this approach *operant conditioning*, as opposed to Pavlov's *classical conditioning*.

Positive reinforcement or rewards can include verbal feedback such as *That's great, you've produced that document without any errors* or *You're certainly getting on well with that task* through to more tangible rewards such as a certificate at the end of the programme, or a promotion or a pay rise.

Cognitivism theory

Cognitivism is about people constructing their own understanding and knowledge by experiencing something and reflecting on it. Learning is, therefore, an active process of personal interpretation. There are many cognitive theorists, the most well known being Piaget, Vygotsky and Bruner.

Jean Piaget (1959) believed that people construct knowledge rather than receive it. He believed that children are born with a very basic mental structure (genetically inherited and evolved) on which all subsequent learning and knowledge is based. This experience and knowledge is then influenced by their emotional, biological and mental stages of development. Before Piaget's work, there was a common assumption that children are less competent thinkers than adults. Although Piaget's studies were concerned with children, they showed that young children and adults also think differently.

According to Piaget, there are four stages of development in children:

- Sensorimotor (birth to 2 years) learning takes place by touching and feeling, and knowing an object exists even if it can't be seen

- Preoperational (2–7 years) learning continues by thinking about things symbolically, with the ability to arrange objects logically

- Concrete operational (7–11 years) learning takes place by thinking about things rather than trying them out, i.e. the ability to think logically

- Formal operational (11 years and above) learning continues into adulthood by thinking in an abstract way, and by logically testing things out.

The Russian psychologist Lev Vygotsky (1962) believed that the development of language and thought go together. He argued that knowledge and thought are constructed through social interaction which is guided by adults. The origin of reasoning is, therefore, more to do with the ability to communicate with others, than with an interaction with the material world. Unlike Piaget's belief that children's development must precede their learning, Vygotsky argued that culture and social learning tends to precede development. He believed that the environment within which children grew up influenced how they thought, and that learning takes place in the *Zone of Proximal Development* (ZPD), as in Figure 2.8. This is the area between independent problem solving (actual development) and guidance from others (potential development). Effective teaching should take place within this zone, where cognitive growth occurs.

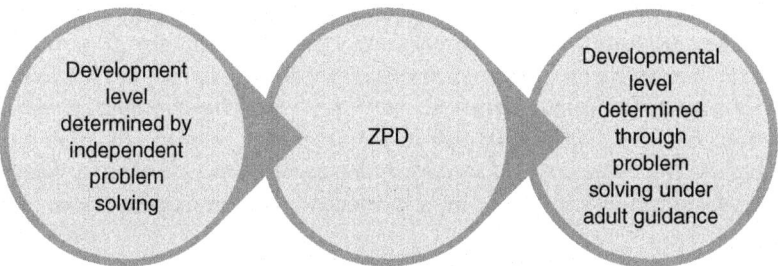

Figure 2.8 Zone of Proximal Development

Jerome Bruner (1960) argued that the purpose of education is not to impart knowledge, but to *facilitate* thinking and problem-solving skills. These skills should be transferable to a range of situations. He believed that behaviour modification was a result of *discovery learning*, rather than being told something. For example, giving the learner the information they need to solve a problem, but not organising it for them. Learners should be active and construct their own knowledge. They should also build on this over time, known as *scaffolding*.

Example

Bob had a new group of learners taking a psychology course. He wanted to introduce them to various theories but did not want to confuse them. He asked them to research four theories and to write a paragraph about each in a simplified way. Once done, the learners discussed their findings among each other. During the next session, the learners researched two more and compared and contrasted them against the original four. This way, the learners were discovering things for themselves and building upon their knowledge. Bob is, therefore, facilitating what they are doing, rather than teaching them.

Humanism theory

The humanism theory emphasises the value of human beings and places the onus of learning away from the teacher onto the learner. Learning is, therefore, based on a natural curiosity and the desire for personal growth and development. Carl Rogers (1959) and others developed the theory of *facilitative learning* based on a belief that people have a natural human eagerness to learn and that learning involves changing your own concept of yourself. This theory suggests that learning will take place if the person delivering it acts as a facilitator. The facilitator should establish an atmosphere in which their learners feel comfortable, are able to discuss new ideas and learn by their mistakes, as long as they are not threatened by external factors.

Example

Vicky is due to teach an evening class in digital photography for beginners. The course does not lead to a qualification; therefore, she has planned to deliver what she thinks is relevant, based on the last time she taught it. However, she remembered being told by an observer of her session last term that she should consider the needs of her learners more. Therefore, at the first session, she decided to encourage her learners to tell her what their expectations of the course would be. This will enable her to facilitate her sessions to meet these. It will also ensure her learners feel included, are comfortable to discuss topics and, as a result, learning will take place as it is relevant to their expectations.

Pragmatism theory

Pragmatists consider thought a tool for prediction, problem solving and actions. It's about dealing with a problem in a sensible way, rather than following fixed ideas.

John Dewey (1938) believed that behaviour modification takes place when the person relates their behaviour to their experiences. He focused on the pragmatic method of inquiry as an ongoing, self-correcting, and social process. He believed problems could be solved through the application of inquiry and experience, rather than being taught.

Activity

Research other pragmatist theorists and compare and contrast them to those of behaviourism, cognitivism and humanism. Do you agree or disagree with any of the theorists? If so, why? You might like to discuss your responses with a colleague or friend.

Pedagogy and andragogy

Malcom Knowles (1975) brought the concept of *pedagogy* and *andragogy* to the fore in education. The *pedagogical approach* places the responsibility for making decisions about the learning process upon the teacher. They may decide to teach the same material in the same order at the same time to all learners. This doesn't allow any flexibility for a learner who may miss a session or is learning more slowly or quickly than others. Pedagogy often relates to formal teaching methods. However, it is possible to teach in a formal manner, yet still involve the learners throughout a session to help make the learning process more engaging.

If your sessions are mainly pedagogical, try to include your learners by asking individual questions to check their understanding. You could also ask pairs of learners to talk about a topic and then discuss it as a whole group. Your subject should never bore your learners; you will need to inspire them to maintain their motivation and interest. Learners will only be bored if the session is delivered in a boring way.

The *andragogical approach* places the emphasis on the learner to take responsibility for the learning process. They can then ensure that they are learning in a way that suits them. This approach allows you to adapt your teaching approaches, activities and materials to suit each learner's progress and development.

The Peter Principle

Peter and Hull (1969) devised the principle that people are promoted to their highest level of competence, after which, further promotion raises them to a level just beyond this and they become incompetent. This theory has been interpreted by different people over time, such as Noel Burch in the 1970s. The Peter Principle levels are as follows.

- Unconscious incompetence – you don't know how to do something, but don't know that you don't know this. To reach the next level, you need to know what it is that you don't know.

- Conscious incompetence – you know what you want to do, and start to appreciate the gap in your competence. To reach the next level, you need to know how to become competent.

- Conscious competence – you can do what you set out to do, but have to give it a lot of attention. Through repeated practice, you can reach the next level.

- Unconscious competence – you can perform a skill easily without giving it a great deal of thought. Once you achieve unconscious competence, you are at a level which suits your ability at the time.

If you are promoted or try something different, you might return to the first level and become unconsciously incompetent again. This is useful to know, as your learners may reach and stay at one of these levels, or reach the highest level and then return to a lower level due to further progression.

Example

Zoe has just started attending a course to learn how to use spreadsheets. She has previously only used a computer for emails and the internet. She doesn't yet know how to use a spreadsheet or the functions it can perform – she is at the unconscious incompetence *level. After learning how to set up a spreadsheet, she now wants to perform some calculations; she knows she wants to do this but doesn't know how. This is the* conscious incompetence *level. Zoe soon learns how to perform calculations and does this at the* conscious competence *level. She isn't quite at the* unconscious competence *level yet, where she can do it without thinking.*

Domains of learning

Bloom (1956) stated that learning often goes through five stages, which should lead to a change in behaviour. These stages are:

- attention

- perception

- understanding

- short-/long-term memory

- change in behaviour.

Starting with gaining your learners' attention, and progressing through the stages should ensure learning takes place, therefore leading to a change in behaviour. The stages relate to your learners' *thinking, emotions* and *actions* which Bloom called *domains* of learning. These domains are known as *cognitive, affective* and *psycho-motor*. Think of cognitive as thinking, affective as emotions, and psycho-motor as actions.

When planning to deliver your subject, you will need to consider which domain you want to reach and how you can progress your learners through the five stages. It's useful to know this when planning your session's aim and objectives (covered in Chapter 4).

Extension activity

How will these theories affect the way you teach and assess your subject? Do you agree with them, or do you have your own theory of how learning takes place? Choose two of the theories which you feel are relevant and research them further, and/or use the weblinks at the end of this chapter to find out about others.

Self-assessment checklist

Do I know about the following?

If not, re-read this chapter, or research the texts and websites listed at the end.

- ☐ The different environments in which learning can take place

- ☐ Different room layouts and the impact they can have upon learning

- ☐ How to manage the learning environment

- ☐ Health and safety considerations in the learning environment

- ☐ The age ranges and varieties of learners

- ☐ What motivates learners

□ Different intrinsic and extrinsic motivation factors

□ Theories of motivation

□ The challenges a teacher faces

□ How to deal with disruptions

□ Learning preferences and styles

□ Different teaching and learning theories, principles and models

Summary

This chapter has explored the different factors which contribute to learning.

You should now be able to manage your sessions in a meaningful way, taking into account the different age ranges of learners, and the different locations where learning takes place. You should also know the theories of how learning takes place.

You might like to carry out further research by accessing the books and websites listed at the end of this chapter, particularly if you are working towards a higher level teaching qualification.

This chapter has covered the following topics:

• Teaching and learning environments

• Learner age ranges and modes of attendance

• Motivation

• Challenges

• Learning preferences and styles

• Teaching and learning theories, principles and models

References and further information

Aubrey, K. and Riley, A. (2016) *Understanding and Using Educational Theories*. London: SAGE.

Bates, B. (2016) *Learning Theories Simplified*. London: SAGE.

Bloom, B.S. (1956) *Taxonomy of Educational Objectives: The Classification of Educational Goals*. New York: McKay.

Bruner, J.S. (1960). *The Process of Education*. Cambridge, MA: Harvard University Press.

Caviglioli, O. (2004) *Thinking Visually: Step-by-step Exercises That Promote Visual, Auditory and Kinaesthetic Learning*. Baldock: Pembroke Publishing Ltd.

Coffield, F. et al. (2004) *Learning Preferences and Pedagogy in Post-16 Learning: A Systematic and Critical Review*. London: Learning and Skills Research Centre.

Coffield, F. (2008) *Just Suppose Teaching and Learning Became the First Priority*. London: Learning and Skills Network.

Dale, E. (1969) *Audio Visual Methods in Teaching* (3rd edition). New York: Holt, Rinehart and Winston.

Dewey, J. (1938) *Logic: The Theory of Inquiry*. New York: Holt, Rinehart and Winston.

Dewey, J. (1963) *Experience and Education*. New York: Collier Books.

Fleming, N. (2005) *Teaching and Learning Preferences: VARK Strategies*. Honolulu: Honolulu Community College.

Fleming, N. and Mills, C. (1992) Not Another Inventory, Rather a Catalyst for Reflection. *To Improve the Academy*, 11: 137.

Gagne, R. (1985) *The Conditions of Learning* (4th edition). New York: Holt, Rinehart and Winston.

Gould, J. (2012) *Learning Theory and Classroom Practice in the Lifelong Learning Sector* (2nd edition). London: Learning Matters SAGE.

Herzberg, F. (1991) *Herzberg on Motivation*. New York: Penton Media Inc.

Honey, P. and Mumford, A. (1992) *The Manual of Learning Preferences* (3rd edition). Maidenhead: Peter Honey Associates.

Illeris, K. (2010) *The Fundamentals of Workplace Learning: Understanding How People Learn in Working Life*. Abingdon: Routledge.

Keller, J.M. (1987) Strategies for Stimulating the Motivation to Learn. *Performance & Instruction*, 26(8): 1–7.

Kidd, W. and Czerniawski, G. (2010) *Successful Teaching 14–19*. London: SAGE.

Knowles, M. (1975) *Self-Directed Learning: A Guide for Learners and Teachers*. New Jersey: Prentice Hall.

Knowles, M., Elwood, F.H. and Swanson, A. (2011) *The Adult Learner* (7th edition). Oxford: Butterworth-Heinemann.

Laird, D. (1985) *Approaches to Training and Development*. Harlow: Addison Wesley.

Maslow, A.H. (1987) (edited by Frager, R.) *Motivation and Personality* (3rd revised edition). New York: Pearson Education Ltd.

Pavlov, I.P. (1927) *Conditioned Reflexes: An Investigation of the Physiological Activity of the Vertebral Cortex*. London: OU Press.

Peart, S. and Atkins, L. (2011) *Teaching 14–19 Students in the Lifelong Learning Sector*. Exeter: Learning Matters.

Peter, L.J. and Hull, R. (1969) *The Peter Principle: Why Things Always go Wrong*. New York: William Morrow and Company.

Piaget, J. (1959) *The Language and Thought of the Child (Vol. 5)*. Psychology Press.

Rogers, C. (1959) A Theory of Therapy, Personality and Interpersonal Relationships as Developed in the Client-centered Framework. In S. Koch (ed.), *Psychology: A Study of a Science. Vol. 3: Formulations of the Person and the Social Context*. New York: McGraw Hill.

Rogers, C. (1994) *Freedom to Learn*. New York: Prentice Hall.

Rogers, A. and Horrocks, N. (2010) *Teaching Adults* (4th edition). Maidenhead: Open University Press.

Senior, L. (2016) *A Teacher's Guide to 14–19 Policy and Practice*. Abingdon: Routledge.

Skinner, B.F. (1953) *Science and Human Behavior*. New York: Free Press.

Skinner, B.F. (1974) *About Behaviorism*. San Francisco, CA: Knopf.

Vygotsky, L.S. (1962) *Thought and Language*. Cambridge, MA: MIT Press.

Vygotsky, L.S. (1978) *Mind and Society: The Development of Higher Mental Processes*. Cambridge, MA: Harvard University Press.

Wallace, S. (2017) *Motivating Unwilling Learners in Further Education*. London: Bloomsbury Education.

Watson, J.B. (1928) *The Ways of Behaviourism*. New York: Harper & Brothers.

Websites

Dan Williams's learning theories blog – https://tinyurl.com/n2v89kz

Health and Safety Executive – www.hse.gov.uk

Institute for Apprenticeships – www.gov.uk/government/organisations/institute-for-apprenticeships

Learning preferences questionnaire – www.vark-learn.com

Learning theories – www.learning-theories.com

www.instructionaldesign.org/theories/ and

http://tinyurl.com/mchvmwe

Learning theory graphic – https://tinyurl.com/ofkjp2d

Noel Burch: Stages of competence – http://tinyurl.com/hgf7394

Performing Rights Society – www.prsformusic.com

Peter Honey – www.peterhoney.com

Reading list for behaviour and motivation – www.anngravells.com/reading-lists/behaviour

3

Supporting learning

Introduction

Supporting learning is about making sure your learners have the necessary opportunities they need to succeed. There are many organisations, agencies and people who can support learners in different ways. These include employers who wish to support their staff to undertake training, stakeholders who supply funding for learning to take place and support agencies to help learners overcome barriers to learning.

This chapter will explore how you can obtain relevant information regarding your learners via initial assessment. How you can work with others to support the learning process is covered, as is the support you might need to carry out your own role effectively.

This chapter will cover the following topics:

- Employers and stakeholders
- Teachers and trainers
- Learners' needs and points of referral
- Barriers to learning
- Learning support assistants
- Initial and diagnostic assessment

Employers and stakeholders

Employers and stakeholders could have an influence on the types of courses offered within an organisation. An employer might wish to support the learning and development of their staff by arranging on- or off-the-job training and/or assessment. If it's part of your role to liaise with learners like these, you would need to communicate with their employer to ensure you are all working towards the same aim. There might also be stakeholders who support the learning process, perhaps financially, or have an influence upon the design of a course. A stakeholder is a person or an organisation who has an interest or a concern in the operation of the organisation and/or the learners.

Employers

Local employers might have an impact upon the curriculum which is offered by your organisation. For example, if you work in a college which is close to several businesses and/or factories, your organisation might be approached to offer training for them. Alternatively, your organisation could approach them to find out if they have any training needs or to inform them of ways in which your organisation could help their staff. If local employers are struggling to hire skilled staff, this could be an area where your organisation could collaborate with them.

When working with an employer, it's important to find out exactly what they need as well as agreeing costs and expenses. This way, there are no hidden surprises or expectations which might not be met. This might include their need for you to provide training, assessment and/or coaching and mentoring support to their staff. If this is the case, you will need to ascertain what is required and agree realistic targets and timescales. It might be that staff can come to your organisation for off-the-job training, or you might go to the company to deliver on-the-job training. Contracts will need to be negotiated and suitable action plans agreed with the individual learners. There might also be some legal and insurance considerations to take into account as well as following certain policies and procedures. Communication with the employer should be ongoing, open and honest. Feedback regarding the employee's progress at work as a result of the training, should be obtained on a regular basis. This will help to ensure the employer is receiving value for money for the investment in their staff.

Different employers will have different needs; these might depend upon the industry, businesses or manufacturing taking place in the local area. If you are delivering or assessing staff in a company which has asked your organisation for this service, they should not be able to dictate changes to your organisation's policies and procedures. However, you will need to respect their own policies and procedures if they are applicable to working on their premises. For example, you might need to obtain security clearance and follow particular procedures in factories, petrochemical works or military installations.

Activity

If you are currently teaching, find out if your organisation is already providing any training or services to local employers and, if so, what these are. If not, what training needs do you think local employers might have? How do you think your organisation could approach them with a view to supporting them, if this is feasible?

Your organisation might partner with or sub-contract some aspects of training and assessment to other companies. If this is the case and you are involved, you will need to make sure they follow the policies and procedures of your organisation, to ensure a consistent approach to the learning process. A partnership agreement should be put into place so that everyone knows the boundaries of their role, what is expected and by when.

You might find it useful to familiarise yourself with the types of businesses in your local area or those intending to locate there: for example, retail, factories, industrial and farming. This could help you to understand the needs of the local businesses and community, perhaps to offer training courses to help the unemployed upskill in anticipation of gaining local employment. You might be able to build up contacts with local employers to enable your learners to partake in work experience with them. This might help the future employability of the learners.

Stakeholders

A stakeholder is a person or an organisation who has an interest in something, for example, the progress of learners. Stakeholders can affect, or be affected by the actions of those involved with the learners. Examples are local authorities, councils, employers or companies that your organisation associates with. Stakeholders in the further education and skills sector can include government departments such as Ofqual and Ofsted, who regulate and inspect accredited qualifications in England, and funding agencies who provide money for training and assessment. In an international context, various national or multinational agencies might be involved with monitoring the quality of training. There might also be government departments similar to those in the UK which will have an impact upon the qualifications offered.

Stakeholders can also include anyone who has an interest in the learner, for example, employers, parents, guardians, carers and/or social workers. These people might need to be kept up to date with the learner's progress and achievement, as well as any personal issues or anxieties they may experience. It would be useful to have a list of names, along with contact details, in case you need to get in touch with them at some time.

If stakeholders are involved with your organisation, it means you, or others will be held accountable in some way. Perhaps by supplying information and data to funding agencies. Statistics might be required such as the number of applications, enrolments, achievements and leavers, as well as progression information. You might be responsible for keeping track of this data or it might be someone in a specific department within your organisation.

Demands might be made upon you and others, such as to achieve organisational key performance indicators (KPIs) or to meet certain targets within a timescale. However, the learner is the most important person so try not to get too obsessed with targets. If you feel a learner, or indeed you, cannot meet a certain target, make sure you talk to the stakeholder to keep them informed. The needs of the different stakeholders as well as their learners should be ascertained. This is so that everyone is clear about what they need to do and when, and are operating transparently.

There are organisations which exist to support teaching and learning, for example, professional associations and networking groups. You can find details of these in the Introduction chapter. Although they are not considered stakeholders, they will have an interest in what you do and how you maintain your professional development. For example, if you belong to a professional association, you may need to keep records of how you are keeping current with your subject skills and knowledge.

The main stakeholders are briefly explained here; however, titles and responsibilities do tend to change, so please check their websites for any updates (listed at the end of this chapter). Different bodies will exist in England, Wales, Scotland, Northern Ireland and internationally.

Awarding organisations

Awarding organisations, also known as awarding bodies, provide accreditation for qualifications nationally and internationally. They will supply a qualification specification, sometimes referred to as a syllabus, qualification handbook or a set of standards. This contains guidance and information regarding the particular qualification offered. Inspections will be conducted by an external quality assurer (EQA), verifier, moderator or quality consultant, to ensure all the requirements are being met. If everything is satisfactory and the learner successfully achieves the qualification, a certificate will be issued. If you are involved with the delivery, assessment and/or quality assurance of an accredited qualification, you will be visited at some point by a representative from the awarding organisation (covered in Chapter 11).

Council for the Curriculum, Examinations and Assessment (CCEA)

The CCEA is a non-departmental public body reporting to the Department of Education in Northern Ireland. It advises the government regarding what should be taught in Northern Ireland's schools and colleges. It monitors standards to ensure that the qualifications and examinations offered by awarding bodies in Northern Ireland are of an appropriate quality and standard.

Department for Education (DfE)

The DfE is a government department responsible for children's services and education, including higher and further education policy, apprenticeships and wider skills in England. It is committed to cutting unnecessary burdens and to giving teachers the freedom and autonomy they need to get on with their jobs. Part of this is about making it easier for teachers to understand how to fulfil their legal obligations and exercise their statutory powers, by making guidance and advisory content clearer and more succinct.

Department for Employment and Learning (DELNI)

DELNI states the qualifications a teacher in further education in Northern Ireland must hold, along with the professional standards teachers should demonstrate.

Education and Skills Funding Agency (ESFA)

The ESFA is sponsored by the Department for Education (DfE) in England. It is responsible for the funding of education for pupils aged 5 to 16, education and training for those aged 16 to 19, apprenticeships and adult education, and for managing school building programmes.

Education and Training Inspectorate (ETI)

The ETI inspects FE colleges in Northern Ireland. Inspection reports and other useful information such as good practice examples can be found on its website; a link is available at the end of this chapter.

Estyn

Estyn is led by Her Majesty's Chief Inspector of Education and Training in Wales. It inspects quality and standards in many areas including schools and further education. The word Estyn is a Welsh word meaning to reach out and to stretch.

Estyn is independent of the National Assembly for Wales and receives its funding from the Welsh Government. It advises them on quality and standards in education and training in Wales.

Institute for Apprenticeships (IfA)

The IfA is responsible for ensuring high quality apprenticeship standards as well as advising government in England on funding for each standard. This is to ensure that the apprenticeship programmes respond to the needs of business and give learners the skills and experience they require to succeed.

The Institute also has an external quality assurance role, as do other appropriate organisations. This is to check the consistency of assessments against the same set of standards from different assessment organisations.

Office for Standards in Education, Children's Services and Skills (Ofsted)

Ofsted inspects and regulates services in England which care for children and young people, and those providing education and skills for learners of all ages. It was originally established to inspect schools; however, it now inspects provision in the further education and skills sector including teacher training, according to a common inspection framework (CIF). Ofsted reports directly to Parliament, and it is independent and impartial. The aim of inspections is to promote improvement and value for money in the services inspected and regulated, so that children and young people, parents and carers, adult learners and employers all benefit. You will need to find out if your organisation is inspected by Ofsted;

it's probable that they will be if they receive any form of government funding. Inspection reports for all organisations can be seen on the Ofqual website, a link is available at the end of this chapter.

Office of Qualifications and Examinations Regulation (Ofqual)

Ofqual is the regulator of qualifications, examinations and assessments in England. It is responsible for maintaining standards, improving confidence in the system, and distributing information about qualifications. Ofqual gives formal recognition to awarding organisations and bodies that deliver and award qualifications. It also monitors their qualifications and activities, including the fees that are charged.

Qualifications Wales

Qualifications Wales is the regulator of non-degree qualifications and the qualifications system in Wales. It is a Welsh government-sponsored body, independent of government, and accountable to the National Assembly for Wales. It ensures that qualifications, and the Welsh qualification system, are effective for meeting the reasonable needs of learners in Wales.

Sector Skills Councils (SSC)

These are employer-led organisations that gather information and labour market intelligence to influence the development of qualifications and apprenticeship programmes in the UK. Each SSC represents an area of business or industry, of which there will probably be one for the subject you will teach, for example, construction, finance or hospitality. For some subjects they are known as Standard Setting Bodies (SSB). All SSCs are members of the Federation for Industry Sector Skills and Standards (FISSS), and are recognised by the government throughout the UK as the independent, employer-led organisations which ensure that the skills system is driven by employers' needs. As a result, they have a major impact on the delivery of publicly and privately funded training throughout the UK. SSCs often produce a set of national occupational standards (NOS) for working in a particular sector.

Scottish Qualifications Authority (SQA)

The SQA approves and quality assures qualifications (other than degrees) which awarding organisations offer in Scotland. It also works with schools, colleges, universities and training organisations to develop and deliver qualifications and assessments.

Partnership working

Partnerships often occur when one organisation isn't able to fulfil a certain activity or programme; therefore, they decide to work with another organisation to achieve it. Partnerships can be very productive to everyone involved; however, they can also be challenging, as the needs of all partners have to be met.

Beta Training Company has been approached by a local car manufacturing firm to deliver and assess a specific off-the-job training programme for their staff. While Beta Training has the staff who are capable of doing most of this, they don't have enough staff with the technical expertise required. They have, therefore, approached a local business that has people capable of this, to partner with them. Beta Training will agree how the two companies will work together for the benefit of the car manufacturer and their staff.

When working in a partnership, it's very important to know who is doing what, by when, and how much money will change hands. Contracts will need to be in place to keep everything legal and professional, and records must be maintained for audit purposes.

Extension activity

If you are currently teaching, find out which stakeholders and/or partners are involved with the operation of the organisation you work for. For example, Ofsted inspectors (in England) or government auditors, partner companies and/or funding providers. How will the needs of these organisations impact upon your role?

Teachers and trainers

Teachers and trainers are the people who will be involved the most with supporting learners. Your needs will vary depending upon your job role, the type of employment contract you have, where you work and the subject you will teach. If you are a new teacher in a training organisation or a new trainer in the workplace, there will be certain things you will need to know before you even meet your learners.

Example

Eliza had been employed at a large call centre for about three years, training new staff on-the-job. While Eliza had enjoyed this role, she has decided she would like to go into teaching and has just been employed in a local college. Her role is to teach communication skills and customer service skills to unemployed adults. She doesn't yet know the finer details of her role and wants to find out. She has decided to make a list of questions before she commences.

If you are already teaching, you will probably know all you need to know at this point in time. However, things do change, therefore it's useful to keep up to date with any developments.

If you are about to start a new role, there will be lots of things you will need to know and questions you would like answered. These could include:

- What type of employment contract do I have and how and when do I get paid?

- Do I have a job specification which outlines my roles and responsibilities? If not, how do I ensure that I perform my role to the best of my ability? Is there a set of professional standards I can work towards?

- How can I get to work on time, i.e. what public transport is available, can I walk or cycle? If I drive, how long will it take, is there a car park close by and will I have to pay for this?

- If I have to travel between different sites or visit learners in their workplace, can I reclaim my costs, and if so, how?

- Do I have administrative time allocated to me for preparation and marking?

- What is the topic or subject I will be teaching? Is there a qualification specification I must follow, or do I need to create the content for a learning programme?

- Where will I be teaching, i.e. in a classroom or other environment? Am I in the same place each time?

- Do I need to carry out any risk assessments or equipment checks?

- When will I be teaching, i.e. do I have a timetable and know the dates and time length of the programmes I will teach?

- Who will I be teaching? If it's a group, how many are there in the group, and what information can I find out about the learners beforehand? For example, if they have any particular learning needs.

- What support is available to me, i.e. administrative support perhaps to create and copy handouts and learning materials?

- What resources and textbooks are already available and accessible? Shall I create a reading list of suitable textbooks?

- If I have to order anything to help teach my subject, how do I go about this?

- Where are the photocopier, computer and printer facilities? Do I have free access?

- How do I access the documents and records I need to use? Are they available electronically or are they paper based? What type of filing system should I use?

- Where can I find out about the organisation's policies and procedures?

- What facilities are available to me and to learners, i.e. refreshments, toilets, lockers?

- Can I have a mentor? If so, who will this be and how will I contact them?

- Will any other staff be available to help my learners, such as learning support assistants or language interpreters?

- If I have any training needs, how can I go about fulfilling these?

- Who do I directly report to, and are there any meetings or events I must attend?

- Am I responsible for any other staff, if so, who are they and what is their role in relation to mine?

Activity

If you are not already sure, try and find out the answers to the questions in the previous bullet list. If you can't answer any or you have any other questions, find out who you can go to at your organisation to get the responses you need.

Ideally, when you start your job role, you will be given an *induction*. This is a process which might include a tour of the organisation, the opportunity to meet the people you will work with and the information you will need. However, if this doesn't happen, you will need to be proactive and ask questions as the need arises.

Personal needs

You might have some personal needs or particular needs of a physical or mental nature which you may need support with. For example, if a teacher has a disability which limits their walking, there might be the opportunity to park closer to the entrance in a designated space, and to teach in a room which is more easily accessible. Some of the learners' needs explained in the next section of this chapter might also apply to teachers. If so, you will need to be prepared to reveal the nature of any needs you have, as you can't expect your employer to help if they are not aware of them.

Other needs might occur throughout your time teaching or training. For example, the need to visit the doctor or dentist. Therefore, you should find out what the policy is at your organisation, as cover might need to be obtained for your classes.

Keeping up to date

Once you are familiar with your job role, you might find that things change, such as developments regarding technology. You will need to keep up to date so that you are giving the best service to your learners. All teachers and trainers should not only be knowledgeable and current in their specialist subject, but they should also know how to use innovative ways to deliver and assess their subject to enable learning to take place. It could be that a topic you are due to teach is one you are not familiar with. You don't need to feel embarrassed if you don't know about something, you just need to be able to research it beforehand.

You might decide to work towards a relevant teaching qualification or attend an event to update your knowledge and/or skills. This might be funded by your employer, or you might have to fund it yourself. Please see Chapter 12 for information regarding continuing professional development (CPD).

| **Extension activity** |

What else do you consider to be a teacher's or a trainer's needs? For example, the need to have patience with learners, the need to manage time, and the need to have a life outside of the job role. Discuss with a colleague any needs you feel you have, how they could be met and how they might impact upon your role.

Learners' needs and points of referral

Some learners will have particular needs which may affect their attendance, behaviour, learning, progress and/or achievement. If you can ascertain these prior to them commencing you will have the knowledge to be able to support them when needed. This is providing it's within the remit of your role. If not, you could refer them to an appropriate person or agency, or ask them to find out for themselves.

Potential learners' needs

The potential needs of learners which you might encounter could be quite diverse, such as a learner requiring privacy to take insulin for diabetes, the need to improve English, or just the need to talk to someone about a concern. Try not to assume that because a disability or a need is not visible, that it doesn't exist. For example, if a learner is in a wheelchair, you can see they have a disability. However, if a learner has diabetes, you cannot see this. This is known as a *hidden disability*.

The phrase *special educational needs and/or disabilities* (SEND) is defined in the English SEND Code of Practice (2014, pages 15, 16) as:

A child or young person has SEN if they have a learning difficulty or disability which calls for special educational provision to be made for him or her. A child of compulsory school age or a young person has a learning difficulty or disability if he or she:

- *has a significantly greater difficulty in learning, than the majority of others of the same age*

- *has a disability which prevents or hinders them from making use of educational facilities of a kind generally provided for others of the same age in mainstream schools or mainstream post-16 institutions.*

At some point, you might encounter learners who have a special educational need and/or have a disability. For example, those who have:

- Asperger syndrome – a lifelong developmental disability that affects how people perceive the world and interact with others

- attention deficit hyperactivity disorder (ADHD) – a behavioural disorder where learners have difficulty controlling their behaviour without medication or behavioural therapy. Although not diagnosed as a learning difficulty, its interference with concentration and attention can make it difficult for a learner to perform well

- dyscalculia – difficulty with calculations or maths

- dysgraphia – difficulty with handwriting

- dyslexia – difficulty with processing written language

- dyspraxia – poor motor co-ordination or clumsiness.

Example

Stuart has been diagnosed with Asperger syndrome and is attending a plumbing apprenticeship course at a local training organisation. He has difficulty in understanding the social and cultural rules that most people take for granted. He therefore misinterprets intentions, behaviour and the conversation of others. On the surface, Stuart appears to be rude and disruptive and constantly interrupts when others are speaking. His teacher is aware of this and has asked Stuart if he can inform the other learners of his situation. Stuart is happy about disclosing this and the group then agree ways of dealing with situations as they arise.

You might find it useful to research different educational needs and disabilities so that you can be proactive at providing relevant help and support. If you notice any potential learners' needs before they become a problem for the learner, you might be able to help. Otherwise, you will need to be reactive to the situation and deal with it professionally and sensitively at the time. Some learning difficulties and/or disabilities could lead teachers and other learners to make wrong assumptions about the learner affected. Hopefully, any needs will have been identified beforehand and communicated to you prior to your learners commencing. However, this might not always be the case; therefore, informal chats or formal tutorials could be an opportunity to discuss any particular needs or concerns, for example, what a learner finds difficult or what has or has not worked for them in the past.

Sometimes, learners might have a Statement of Special Educational Needs (SEN), or an Education, Health and Care Plan (EHC Plan or EHCP). These are the official documents in England which record special needs and supporting notes. These will include the reasonable adjustments schools or colleges need to make, along with what extra support or therapy the learner is entitled to. They will also state targets which the organisation will be expected to follow, and which might be audited as part of an official inspection. You will need to be aware if a learner has one, to enable you to support them, and to differentiate for their needs during sessions. Perhaps you could check with staff in your organisation's administration office.

Activity

Imagine you are due to start teaching a new class of 28 learners aged 16–19 from next week. You have been advised that a learner who is deaf has enrolled on your course and will be supported by a sign language interpreter. What will you need to consider and why? How will you overcome any barriers to their learning and how will this impact upon the learning of the others in the group?

You would need to think about how you might adjust your own teaching style to suit that of the learner. Also, how you might design and organise individual and group activities to ensure everyone can take part. You will also need to consider if you need any specialist equipment. Where an interpreter is present, ensure that there is room for them to sit by the learner. Don't ignore the learner by talking to their interpreter, but ask them how they would like you to communicate with them. If the learner lip reads, make sure they can see you and everyone in the group. More information regarding supporting learners through communication, the use of resources, and equality and diversity can be found in Chapters 6, 7 and 9 respectively.

Group profile

A group profile is a record of all your learners, along with information about each, as in Table 3.1 (on page 122). It is a visual reminder of the names of the individuals in your group. It can be used to support their learning, note any concerns and aid differentiation. The record can be used as an *at a glance* way of seeing the individual needs of your learners and how you can support them. It is also useful to note any attendance, behaviour and motivation concerns. If a regular pattern emerges you can find out why it's happening and address it. For example, a learner might have a health condition which requires regular time out for hospital visits. Work could, therefore, be emailed to them along with information regarding what has been missed.

The group profile can be used for setting additional targets to stretch and challenge individual learners. It can also be used for statistical purposes such as gathering data regarding age, gender and ethnicity. It might be difficult to remember details about each of your learners and the specific needs they may have; therefore, maintaining a group profile could help make this easier for you.

You might want to add a lot of information and there might not be enough room if you are using a paper-based copy. If you can access and use the document electronically, you can expand the space to add more detail.

Activity

Look at the group profile in Table 3.1. What other information would you want to note about your learners and why? For example, what their likes and dislikes are which are relevant to the course and the subject. What would you remove and why? If you are currently teaching, find out if there is a document already available to help you create a group profile. If not, have a go at creating your own using a similar one to that in Table 3.1.

Identifying learners' needs

Identifying your learners' needs can take place as part of the application process, during an interview prior to the course commencing, when they start, or as part of the initial or diagnostic assessment processes (covered towards the end of this chapter). Information, advice and guidance (IAG) should be given to learners regarding their programme choice, which should be clear, unambiguous and impartial to ensure it meets

Table 3.1 Example group profile template

Teacher/ trainer:		Programme/ qualification:	
Number in group:		Start date: End date:	

Name	Age	Gender/ ethnicity	Learning preferences	Prior skills/knowledge/ experience/relevant qualifications and how they relate to learning and progression	Initial and diagnostic assessment results and how they impact on learning and progression	Learning/ learner needs and how they will be supported	Barriers, challenges, health or personal issues and how they will be supported	Attendance, behaviour, and motivation concerns and how they will be addressed	Additional individual targets to stretch and challenge learning and progression

their needs and capability. The application process should ensure learners are on the right programme at the right level. If not, some learners may take a programme which is unsuitable for them or their needs might not be met. You could also inform learners at the earliest opportunity as to how they will be assessed, e.g. assignments, observations or tests. This will ensure that there are no surprises once they have started.

There might be instances where a learner's first language is not that which is used during the training programme. There might be an expectation that they can understand and speak the second language. If this is the case, support could be given if available, or the learner might not be able to participate in the programme.

It might be that you don't have an opportunity to identify your learners' needs, perhaps if they are just attending a short session like a one-day event. In this case, you could find out at the beginning of the event if anyone has any particular needs, perhaps to sit closer to the speaker as they are hard of hearing. Alternatively, you could contact your learners in advance to ask them if they have any requirements.

It's difficult to help your learners if they don't tell you about any specific issues, needs or concerns they might have. You could ask if there is anything you could do to help make their learning experience a more positive one. However, anything you do would have to be reasonable and not seen as favouritism by other learners. Encouraging learners to tell you at an appropriate time would save your learner any embarrassment they might feel when in front of their peers.

Some learners may be uncomfortable or not wish to divulge personal information on application forms or at an interview. You could, therefore, have an informal chat with them to find out if they have any needs or specific requirements.

Example

Bridget's application form and personal statement contained several errors, which led her teacher, Isla, to think she might have dyslexia. Isla arranged to have a chat with her prior to the course starting. Bridget said she had often thought she was dyslexic and wondered if she could find out. Isla was able to arrange for her to have a test via www.dyslexia.uk.net. This confirmed she was and appropriate help and support was then arranged.

If you are ever unsure about how to help your learners, just talk to them. They are best placed to tell you how you can support them.

Learning support and learner support

If you have a learner requiring support for any reason, there is a difference between *learning support* and *learner support*. *Learning* support relates to the *subject*, i.e. help with English, maths and/or study skills. *Learner* support relates to the *person*, i.e. help they might need with any personal issues, and/or general advice and guidance such as financial support, transport, childcare, safety and welfare.

Ideally, prior to or when the learner commences, you could discuss any support requirements they may have. You may need to find out who within your organisation can help, as well as those external to the organisation you could refer them to.

You will need to consider any particular needs or requirements of your learners to ensure they can all participate during sessions. You (or the organisation) may need to make reasonable adjustments to adapt resources, equipment or the environment as stated in the Equality Act (2010) for England, Scotland and Wales. If anything is adapted, make sure that both you and your learners are familiar with the changes prior to use. Some adaptations might need to be discussed with the awarding organisation if the learner is working towards an accredited qualification. This helps ensure fairness and validity.

Challenges to learning and assessment

Some learners may experience certain challenges to learning and assessment which you could support in the following ways, for example:

- Dyspraxia – allow additional time and space if necessary for learners who have poor motor co-ordination.

- Dysgraphia – allow the use of a computer or other suitable media for learners who have difficulty with handwriting.

- Dyscalculia – allow additional time if necessary and use calculators or other equipment for learners who have difficulty with calculations or maths.

- Dyslexia – allow additional time or resources if necessary for learners who have difficulty processing language. Give written questions in a simplified format, for example, bullet points. Ask questions verbally and make an audio or visual recording of your learner's responses; allow the use of a computer for keying in responses rather than expecting handwritten responses.

- A mental or physical disability – use a more comfortable environment where appropriate and available. Allow extra time to complete tasks. Explain where the learner can take medication privately. Dates for assessments could be rearranged to fit around doctor or hospital appointments.

- A hearing impairment – use an induction loop or a sign language interpreter if available. Instructions and questions could be conveyed using sign language. Specialist computer software could be used.

- A visual impairment – use large print or Braille and/or use specialist computer software if available. Ask questions verbally and make an audio recording of your learner's responses rather than expecting them to write.

- Varying work patterns – try to schedule learning and assessment around this if you are teaching one-to-one. If the learner is in a group, make a visual recording of your session, if possible, which they could view later if they can't attend in person. Upload resources and learning materials to an accessible online site or email them to the learner to read in their own time.

- English as a second or other language (ESOL) – if allowed, try to arrange assessments in your learner's first language. Many awarding organisations can translate assessment materials if requested. There are also translation programs, apps and software which could be used. Bilingual assessments could be offered if required.

Points of referral

Your organisation might have support systems in place to meet the individual needs of learners. If this is not the case, you will need to find out who can provide advice and guidance when needed. You should always refer your learners to an appropriate specialist or agency if you can't deal with their needs. Please see Table 3.2 for examples of potential needs and possible points of referral.

Table 3.2 Examples of potential needs and possible points of referral

Potential need of learner	Possible point of referral
access to or fear of technology	specialist colleagues within your organisation and/or internal or external training courses local library or internet café
alcohol or substance misuse	telephone helplines relevant support agencies and websites
childcare concerns	childcare agencies
death in the family	bereavement support agencies
emotional or psychological concerns	health centres, doctors Samaritans or other professionals
English as a second or other language (ESOL)	interpreters, bilingual staff or other specialist colleagues such as learning support assistants
financial issues	banks, building societies Citizens Advice specialist staff with knowledge of funding, grants and loans
hearing impairment	use of a loop system, sign language interpreter or specialist app
health concerns	health centres, doctors, hospitals
limited basic skills such as English and maths	Learning support assistants, specialist colleagues online courses and training centres
sight impairment	enlarged print, magnifiers, Braille
stress or personal/work pressures	counselling services, doctors
transport concerns	public transport websites and timetables

Never feel you have to solve any learner's needs, problems or concerns yourself, and don't get personally involved. Always try and remain professional and impartial. Although you might feel you can help, it's best to seek advice, or refer them to someone who is more suited to help.

Activity

What needs do you think your learners might have and how can you identify them? Make a list of the people or agencies you could refer them to if you are not able to help the learners yourself. Compare these to Table 3.2 and add any other examples.

Reviewing learner progress

It's useful to review the progress of your learners not only to know how they are progressing and what they have achieved, but what they may need to do to improve. It also gives you the opportunity to discuss any concerns or particular needs they may have. Reviews of progress, often called *tutorial reviews* or just *tutorials*, could provide the opportunity to carry out formative assessments in an informal way. They also give your learner the opportunity to ask questions or discuss issues they might have been self-conscious about asking in a group situation. Feedback gained via the review process can help inform the evaluation process for the course and the teacher.

Reviews can be part of timetabled tutorial sessions or take place on a one-to-one basis as the need arises. Informal reviews and discussions can take place at any opportune time; however, formal reviews should always be documented and records maintained. Reviews could take place online rather than in person if appropriate systems are in place for this. This might involve written or spoken chats and/or the use of a webcam.

Reviewing progress enables you to obtain information to help you differentiate effectively. This helps ensure that the needs of your learners are met and that they are being challenged to develop to their full potential. If learners are working towards a higher level qualification, you could give them more autonomy during the review process. For example, ask them to review their progress before meeting you to discuss it. The review process also helps ascertain if learners are experiencing any difficulties, enabling you to arrange for any necessary support or further training. Table 3.3 is an example of a template which could be used for a tutorial review. You will need to find out if your organisation has a particular type of form they wish you to use. If one is not available you could design your own. If the form is a hard copy, it can be signed to denote agreement. However, if it's completed electronically, you will need to check what the requirements are for authenticating it. Any action points should always be followed up.

Activity

What do you consider are the advantages of reviewing a learner's progress? Make a list and then compare it to the bullet points on pages 127 and 128.

Table 3.3 Example tutorial review template

Tutorial review			
Name of learner:		**Teacher/trainer:**	
Location:		**Date:**	
Issues discussed:			
Progress and achievements so far:			
Concerns and/or support required:			
Action points:		Target dates:	
Signed teacher/trainer:		Signed learner:	

Reviewing progress with learners enables you to (in alphabetical order):

- ascertain any issues, concerns or challenges

- confirm progress and achievements

- discuss any confidential or sensitive issues

- give constructive and developmental feedback

- involve your learners, formally or informally

- involve your learners' employers and workplace witnesses (if applicable) to gain more information about their progress and achievements elsewhere

- keep a record of what was discussed and agreed

- motivate your learners

- plan areas for further training and development

- plan for differentiation

- plan future learning and assessments

- plan more challenging or creative assessment opportunities

- review your own contribution to the learning and assessment process

- revise your delivery and assessment materials and resources if necessary

- revise your teaching and learning approaches to meet any particular needs or requirements

- update your learner's action plan or assessment plan.

If possible, at least one formal one-to-one review should take place at some point during every programme. It can be a key aspect of communicating with your learners and making them feel valued as individuals.

Example

Shaheen has a group of 12 adult learners who are attending a weekly evening class in pottery skills from 7 p.m. to 9 p.m. for three terms. He has decided to dedicate one session every term for individual tutorials and reviews of progress. While he is carrying these out the rest of the group will work on projects or use the organisation's library and computer facilities. This enables Shaheen to discuss individual progress, concerns and action points with each learner. It also helps him obtain feedback to evaluate how the programme as a whole is developing.

If there is no set review or tutorial procedure, or you are not required to review your learners' progress, it would still be a useful activity if you have the time. The review process should be ongoing until your learner has completed the programme, even if it is carried out on an informal basis. Regular reviews can help to keep your learners motivated, make them feel less isolated and appreciate how they are progressing.

One-to-one tutorial reviews

The review process should involve arranging a suitable date, time and location and confirming these with your learner. You could also talk to anyone else involved, such as a learning support assistant or a workplace supervisor to obtain their perspective regarding your learner.

When preparing for a tutorial review, try to ensure that the environment meets your learners' basic needs such as feeling safe and comfortable. This will enable them to feel secure enough to discuss things with you and to be motivated to continue. You might want to consider a few things beforehand. For example, finding a suitable area to hold the meeting where you won't be interrupted. However, if you are with a vulnerable learner, a member of the opposite sex or a learner you would rather not be alone with, you might wish to leave the room door open. This will help to ensure the protection of both of you. If you have any concerns about being alone with a learner, you could carry out the tutorial in a location where others are present, such as a library or refreshment area.

You will need to have all your records relating to the learner with you or accessible via an electronic device. Always listen to what your learner has to say without interrupting them; they may not have the opportunity elsewhere to talk to someone about any sensitive issues. If they don't respond immediately when you ask a question, pause and let them think in silence for a moment, rather than pressuring them with further questions. Make sure the level of language you are using is suitable for your learner, and that the pace at which you are speaking is not too fast. Allow time for your learner to hear what you are asking and to have time to respond. You might want to make notes during the conversation or, with the learner's permission, you could make an audio or visual recording. Information regarding communicating with learners can be found in Chapter 6.

The confidentiality of any information your learners disclose to you should be assured, otherwise you could lose their trust and respect. However, you need to know where your boundaries lie, and not get involved personally. There are exceptions to this, i.e. if you have any cause for concern as to your learner's safety. For example, if you suspect bullying or radicalisation, then you must pass this information on to whoever is responsible for safeguarding in your organisation.

A copy of the review record should be signed once completed (if required) and a copy given or emailed to your learner.

Group reviews

If you teach groups of learners, you could carry out a group review at an appropriate time during the programme. This would be to gain feedback to help improve their learning experience. It would not relate to anything personal regarding each individual. A group review can be useful when you need feedback about the types of activities you use during your sessions. It could be that the majority of the group feel some types of activity are not beneficial to them. Asking the learners why could help you plan different types of activities to use.

Prior to the group review, you might want to note down a few questions to ask such as:

- How are you finding the course so far?

- Which activities are best at helping you to understand the topics?

- If you could, what would you change about the course to improve your learning?

Using questions which illicit a full response, such as those above are known as *open* questions. They are better than ones which only give a *yes* or a *no* answer, known as *closed* questions. The latter won't give you anything to work with, and learners might just say *yes* because they think that's what you want to hear. You will need to be careful not to ask any questions in a group situation which could be taken personally. For example, '*What problems are you experiencing?*' A learner might think you are referring to personal problems rather than problems with the course. You will also need to be mindful of learners taking the opportunity to complain about various aspects which are not relevant, or being influenced by what their peers say. In a group situation, if one learner complains, others might back them up and the discussion could get out of control.

Do make a note of what your learners have said so that you can do something with it. If you make any changes as a result, tell your learners, as they will be pleased you have acted on what they have said. Feedback from group reviews can also inform the planning process and be a valuable tool to evaluate the programme as a whole. For example, you might receive feedback regarding other aspects such as the facilities available in the organisation or the changing of break times. If you can't deal with any issues and you feel they are relevant, you will need to talk to someone else in your organisation.

Extension activity

If you are currently teaching, find out if you are expected to carry out one-to-one and/or group tutorial reviews and, if so, how often. If not, perhaps you would like to introduce them, in which case, you will need to allocate suitable time for them during the programme. Are there any formal documents and/or questions you will be required to use? If not, can you create your own, and if so, what would you ask and why?

Barriers to learning

A barrier to learning is something which might prevent or have an impact upon a learner's progress and achievement.

Example

Katie, a learner working towards a dressmaking course, lacked confidence in her ability to do anything on her own. Her teacher, Amy, had a quiet chat with her and found out that she was bullied at school for many years. As a result, she had become very withdrawn and relied upon her sister to help her with most things. As her sister was not attending the dressmaking course, Katie felt she wasn't capable of achieving anything herself. Amy arranged for her to talk to a specialist and, over time, her confidence improved.

Learners' barriers

Some learners face particular barriers which might not be their fault; for example, a lack of public transport to get them to the venue. Others might have a barrier where you are able to help or, if not, you could signpost them to a suitable person or agency. Some of the challenges mentioned previously in this chapter could also be considered a barrier to learning.

Activity

What barriers to learning do you consider might have an impact for your learners? Make a list and then compare it to the following.

The following list includes some of the barriers your learners may experience (in alphabetical order):

- age: much younger or older than others in the group
- bullied in the past
- caring for others which might impinge upon the time available for study
- cultural differences
- costs of education too high
- disability: physical or mental
- family problems or commitments
- fear of embarrassment
- fear of joining an existing group
- fear of returning to an educational environment after a long break
- financial issues
- having to attend on their own and/or not knowing anyone else on the course
- inappropriate learning environment
- inequality, e.g. stereotyped gender roles
- joining a course after it has started
- knowledge of or lack of use of technology
- lack of support at work to be allowed time off
- lack of time to attend regularly
- lack of understanding of people's ethnicity/race/religion/belief
- language concerns
- learning difficulty
- limited access to the learning environment
- limited or no access to childcare
- limited mobility
- medical reasons, an illness or condition which might prevent full attendance
- physical/emotional difficulties
- poor past experiences of teaching and learning
- pre-conceived negative feelings/ideas
- resistance to learn or to being told what to do

- shift work inhibiting regular attendance

- shyness, or a lack of confidence or self-esteem

- specific needs or requirements not catered for

- transient populations (for example, gypsies or asylum seekers) not staying in one place long enough to complete a course

- transport difficulties

- type of teaching, for example, e-learning might not be appropriate for some learners.

These barriers could have a real impact upon whether a particular learner can attend a course, stay for the duration or even achieve their aim. Having some knowledge of these could help you to plan ways of helping and supporting your learners when the need arises.

Teachers' barriers

There might be barriers for you as a teacher which could relate to you personally or professionally. For example, if there is no paper in the photocopier when you need to get copies made, you won't be able to issue any handouts during your next session.

Activity

What barriers do you consider you might have either personally or professionally? Make a list and then compare it to the following.

The following list (in alphabetical order) includes some of the barriers that teachers may experience:

- external factors such as noise and visual distractions during sessions

- interruptions during a session either from visitors or disruptive learners

- lack of ability to control a group of learners

- lack of confidence to carry out certain aspects of the job role

- lack of enthusiasm for the subject or topic

- lack of or availability of suitable equipment and resources

- uncertainty how to make sessions interesting and engaging.

Please see Table 1.3 in Chapter 1 for the boundaries of the teaching role, some of which could also be classed as barriers to teaching.

Look at the two previous bulleted lists and add any more barriers you can think of. Choose three from each list and consider how you could effectively deal with them. If you are currently teaching, find out what the support services and procedures are at your organisation for your learners and for yourself.

Learning support assistants

A learning support assistant (LSA) is a person who provides support to a learner for a particular reason. Their role will vary depending upon the needs of the learners and the context of the learning. LSAs often work on a one-to-one basis or with a small group of learners during a session which has a teacher. An LSA will need to be careful of a learner becoming too dependent or reliant upon them. They are there to support a specific learning difficulty, disability and/or need, not to do the learner's work for them. They should aim for the learner to become independent and autonomous where possible. However, learner safety should always be taken into consideration, for example, if a learner relies on an LSA to prevent any injuries or hazards occurring.

Activities carried out by LSAs could include helping with:

- behaviour for a learner who has Attention Deficit Hyperactivity Disorder (ADHD)
- language support for a learner whose first language is not English
- literacy support for a learner who has dyslexia
- numeracy support for a learner who has dyscalculia
- physical support for a learner who has dyspraxia or who finds it difficult to move about unaided
- sign language interpretation for a learner who is deaf/partially deaf
- visual interpretation for a learner who is blind/partially blind
- study skills support, and/or academic assignment writing and referencing
- writing support for a learner who has dysgraphia.

Example

Omar has ADHD and is not always aware of the impact of some of his actions. Michelle, Omar's LSA, is working with him and his teacher to devise a set of relevant targets to help him. Michelle will help Omar during each session to work towards these targets, which will be reviewed every six weeks. Any progress which still needs to be made will be documented. This is so that Omar can take his targets with him when he progresses to further study or employment.

Other support

Other support could be for the teacher as opposed to the learner: for example, if a teacher has a large class and needs an assistant to support them facilitating the session. These staff are often called *teaching assistants (TAs), classroom assistants (CAs), learning mentors* or *support workers*. The type of contract they are employed on might be on a voluntary basis, by the hour, part time or full time. This might affect the amount of work they can help the teacher with, such as planning sessions and creating and copying resources. Assistants could prove useful at managing group activities, supporting differentiation and providing help when necessary.

Some organisations offer support to learners from a specialist subject tutor, e.g. to improve maths or digital skills. This might be during an additional session which learners can attend on a voluntary basis.

Obtaining support

It's useful to know if there is a dedicated department within your organisation which is responsible for supporting learners and/or teachers. It could be that there are finances or funding available for a specialist team of support staff. If not, it might be worth finding out if other teachers can provide the required support if they have the necessary skills.

Activity

If you are currently teaching, find out if there is a dedicated learning support department within your organisation, and if so, how they ascertain which learners will need support. If there is not a dedicated department, ask a colleague what you will need to do if you have a learner who requires support. If possible, you might like to research online for other training organisations or colleges in your local area which excel with learning support. You could then get in contact with them to find out how they operate to support their learners with a view to sharing good practice.

Working with an LSA

Some LSAs might be undertaking the role prior to becoming a teacher, or they may have been a teacher but changed their mind to be an LSA. Some might have experienced setbacks during their own education, which has given them the confidence and experience to help others. If you work with an LSA who is working towards a qualification, they might ask you to act as a witness and provide feedback of how they have supported your learners. Never assume the circumstances or background of an LSA. Talking will help you both to help your learners in the best way possible.

If the LSA or support worker is going to be present during most or all of your sessions, it's essential to build up a good working relationship with them and to set the boundaries of who will do what. You will need to find out who the LSA is (or if there is more than one) and talk to them prior to their commencing. This will help you to find out how they intend to support the particular learner or group of learners. It will give you the opportunity to state what your expectations are for the learners and what you would like them to achieve regarding your subject. If you have time to meet the LSA prior to their arriving in your session, it will give you the opportunity to have a detailed conversation, rather than a rushed chat at the commencement of the session.

When you create your scheme of work and session plans (covered in Chapter 4), make sure you give the LSA a copy. You may need to explain aspects of these documents. You should have noted on the session plan how you intend to differentiate for the learner whom the LSA is supporting, but you may need to explain any jargon you have used. The LSA might not be a specialist in your subject; therefore, you may need to clarify points as you progress. You might also need to give them some advice regarding a particular task you expect your learners to complete, as they might not be familiar with it.

LSAs may have targets for their learners which are different from your targets. These targets will usually be linked to a specific learning need and designed to enable the learner to eventually work independently and autonomously. These could relate to behaviour, punctuality, focus, concentration and/or social interaction, and may also be linked directly to the funding that your organisation receives for providing learning support. You will need to make sure the LSA knows what is expected of the learner during the session, so that they can assist them to achieve it. The LSA is there to support the learner, if you see them doing any work for the learner, you will need to discreetly discuss this with them. It could be that the LSA accompanies a particular learner to other sessions with other teachers. It might, therefore, be useful to know how the learner is also progressing elsewhere.

It would be useful to make regular eye contact with the LSA during your session, as well as with your learner. There may be difficulties with the learner, or with other learners, that they want to discreetly bring to your attention (e.g. inappropriate use of social media, disengaged learners or a problem with the task you have set). The LSA can often prove to be an extremely valuable second pair of eyes, seeing things you might not. Try and learn to read their signals, and go over to them if it looks like they may need to talk to you.

Try to talk to the LSA at the end of the session. Be honest with them about things you don't understand regarding the learner's needs. Don't be afraid to ask for their feedback about how the session went, and what could be improved for future sessions. Give them the opportunity to inform you about anything which you may have missed. Conversely, let them know about anything that you might have liked them to have done differently.

It could be that if you are inspected or observed at some point; the way in which you work with an LSA will be taken into account. If you have the ability to show that you have a good working relationship with the LSA, it may help to demonstrate your effectiveness and commitment to inclusive teaching and learning.

A good LSA is a highly valuable resource to have in your session. Not only can they support your learners, they can help you see how to help your learner become more independent and autonomous. If they're doing a good job, you might like to tell them so, and give their line manager some feedback too. This might help boost their motivation and commitment, and could be used to positively enhance their performance review or appraisal.

Consider how you could work with an LSA or a support worker before, during and after a session. How would you measure the effectiveness of this and how could you evaluate the resulting success to the learner?

Initial and diagnostic assessment

Initial and diagnostic assessment activities are the formal processes whereby you can ascertain your learners' prior skills, knowledge and understanding. It's also an opportunity to identify any aspects which might otherwise go unnoticed, for example, poor numerical or writing skills. Initial assessment is carried out at the beginning of something, for example, a course or a session. Diagnostic assessment can be carried out at any time, to diagnose any gaps in learning, or any particular learning or learner needs.

Imagine you are visiting the doctor for an ailment. They will ask you how you are feeling and what the signs and symptoms are. This is an initial assessment and diagnosis of your condition, with a view to helping you improve. It's a similar process with a learner, although they are not ill, you will be acquiring information to help them progress further.

Initial and diagnostic assessments can be carried out in person, for example, during an interview, or via an online form, preferably prior to commencement. If they are carried out after the learner has started, time will have been wasted if the programme is unsuitable for them, as they could have been guided to something more appropriate. In the workplace, a *training needs analysis* (TNA) could be carried out with staff to identify areas which require training, perhaps to meet a particular job role.

It might not be your responsibility to interview prospective learners or to carry out initial assessments or TNAs. However, you will need to know the results to enable you to support your learners. If this is the case, you will be basing your judgements on the results rather than the person. Try not to make any assumptions about the learner, you will need to meet them in person to really get to know them.

Initial and diagnostic assessments can help you find a starting point for your learner. They might be carried out separately or they might be combined. Please see Table 3.4 for an example of a combined initial and diagnostic assessment template. You might feel you could use this with your learners, you might want to adapt it in some way first, or there may be forms in your organisation for you to use. The results of initial and diagnostic assessments should help you negotiate appropriate targets with your learners, ensuring that they are on the right programme at the right level with the support they need to succeed.

Examples of initial and diagnostic assessment activities include:

- application/enrolment forms: completed online or as a hard copy, prior to a learner commencing

- interview/discussion: asking your learner why they are applying and ascertaining if they meet any particular entry requirements

- observations: it may be necessary to observe your learner performing a skill, perhaps if they are based in the workplace, before agreeing an appropriate programme and level. Observation during initial assessment activities will give you a sense of how your learner performs, and what they know and can do already

- self-assessment: asking your learner to assess their own skills and knowledge towards the programme requirements. This is often known as a *skills scan* and relies on the learner being honest about their achievements

- structured activities, for example, role plays or simulations to see how a learner performs, or how they can work with others

- tests, for example, in English or maths.

Any initial and diagnostic assessments you use, should have a purpose, and not just be completed for the sake of it. The results should always be used for the benefit of the learners and the learning process.

Activity

Look at Table 3.4 (on page 138) and imagine you will be using the form with your learners. What questions would you change, or what questions would you add or remove, and why?

Once you have the information you require, along with the results of any necessary tests, you can make the decision as to whether the programme or qualification your prospective learner is wanting to take, is in fact the right one for them. If they haven't met any particular entry requirements, you will tactfully need to discuss this with them and guide them elsewhere if necessary. If the learner has been accepted onto the programme, the next step will be to create an individual learning plan (ILP). This will outline what they will be working towards, along with target dates and any support they might require (covered in Chapter 4).

It's all about being *proactive* before learning starts, and *active* when learning is taking place, rather than being *reactive* to a situation when it might be too late to do anything about it.

You will need to keep appropriate records of the results and you might need to discuss these with others who have an involvement with your learners. For example, other teachers or support staff. However, some aspects might need to remain confidential. You will need to find out your organisation's requirements for record keeping and confidentiality of information.

Initial assessment

Initial assessment should be carried out *with* your learner, rather than *to* them. It should be a two-way process to find out about your learner as an individual. It should help you identify why they want to take the programme, and to make sure they are on the right

Table 3.4 Example initial and diagnostic assessment template

Initial and diagnostic assessment		
Separate tests in English, maths and ICT could also be taken		
Name:	Date:	
(Continue overleaf if necessary when answering questions)		
Why have you decided to take this programme/qualification?		
What experience do you have in this subject area?		
What relevant qualifications do you have (if applicable)?		
Have you completed a learning preference questionnaire? If YES, what is your preferred style of learning? If NO, complete the questionnaire at www. vark-learn.com and note your results here:	YES/NO Learning preference results: V: A: R: K:	
Do you have any particular learning needs or requirements we should be aware of? If YES, please state here, or talk to your teacher in confidence.	YES/NO	
What help would you like with written/ spoken English?		Test results English:
What help would you like with maths?		Test results Maths:
What help would you like with digital skills?		Test results ICT:
What help would you like with study skills and academic writing (if applicable)?		

programme at the right level. The process should also help to identify any particular needs they may have, to enable the correct support mechanisms to be available.

Initial assessment is often referred to as assessment *for* learning (AfL), as the results help inform the learning process. Assessment *of* learning (AoL) is about making decisions regarding progress and achievement. Assessment is an integral part of the teaching and learning process, and should not be in isolation from it (covered in Chapter 10). You might need to liaise with others who also have in interest in your learners, for example, workplace supervisors if the learner is combining on-the-job training with off-the-job training.

There could be certain restrictions or entry requirements which a learner must meet prior to starting. However, if the learner has already commenced, it could be that they are on the wrong course if these requirements have not been met. You should not accept learners onto a programme just because you need the numbers to make a group viable, as this might set the learners up to fail.

Initial assessment can:

- allow for differentiation

- ascertain why your learner wants to take the programme, along with their capability to achieve

- ensure your learner is applying for the right type of programme

- find out the expectations and motivations of your learner

- identify any information which needs to be shared with colleagues

- identify any specific additional support needs or any reasonable adjustments which may be required.

Initial assessment can also take place during a session, for example, the first time you take your learners for your subject, or when you change topics. You could ask what they already know or can do, and then build on this. Although you might have obtained some information prior to your learners starting, you might need more as you progress. However, you will need to make sure anything you ask your learners to carry out during the early stages is appropriate.

Example

Tameka was teaching a session to her group of 14 Access to Nursing learners. They consisted of mature learners who had had a career break, many of whom don't have any formal qualifications. In the first week, Tameka asked them to research recent government legislation on health hygiene in hospitals. She also asked them to prepare a written paper with citations and references. Tameka asked the learners to present their paper at the next session. The following week five learners did not return.

This example demonstrates how important it is to recognise that assessment is a continuous process. If the learners' first experience of assessment scares them, they may not return. If any of your learners do not return to your sessions, this may be as a result of an ineffective initial assessment process. You would not want them to become a *withdrawal statistic,* i.e. a learner who has left the programme without achieving anything. This could lead to a bad experience for your learner and have an impact upon your organisation's targets. You could always try and find out why any learners don't return. Perhaps you can telephone them, or liaise with someone in your organisation who is responsible for the recruitment and retention of learners. If you find out that it's because of something you have done, or not done, you can use this to develop and improve in the future.

Diagnostic assessment

Diagnostic assessments can be used to evaluate a learner's skills, knowledge, strengths and areas for development in a particular subject area and identify any gaps. It could be that your learner feels they are capable of achieving at a higher level than the diagnostic assessments determine. The results will give a thorough indication of not only the level at which your learner needs to be placed for the subject, but also which specific aspects they need to improve on. Skills tests can be used for learners to demonstrate what they can do, knowledge tests can be used for learners to demonstrate what they know and understand. Your organisation might have specific tests they require you to use or you might wish to design your own.

It could be that your learner has achieved some units of a qualification elsewhere and might just need to provide proof of this. This is known as recognition of prior learning (RPL). If acceptable, this could mean they would not need any reassessment in the areas in which they have already achieved.

Example

Jasmine had recently moved to another city and signed up to a Level 2 Diploma in a Travel and Tourism course at the local college. She completed a diagnostic assessment process, which was designed to assess her skills and knowledge towards the units of the qualification. Jasmine had started the qualification at another college prior to moving. She was able to provide a certificate as proof of three units which she had recently achieved. Jasmine, therefore, did not need to be reassessed, but still attended the full course to ensure her knowledge was up to date.

Diagnostic assessment can:

- ascertain learning preferences, e.g. visual, aural, read/write and kinaesthetic (VARK)

- enable learners to demonstrate their current level of skills, knowledge and understanding regarding the subject

- ensure learners can access appropriate support for the subject
- give your learner the confidence to negotiate and agree individual learning goals and targets
- identify an appropriate starting point and level
- identify gaps in skills, knowledge and understanding to highlight areas to work on
- identify previous experience, knowledge, achievements and transferable skills
- identify specific requirements: for example, to help improve English, maths, and information and communication technology (ICT) skills.

Types of initial and diagnostic assessments

There are many different types of initial and diagnostic assessments available. Some organisations design and use their own, others purchase and use widely available tests, for example, the system called *Basic Key Skills Builder* (BKSB) to diagnose English, maths and ICT skills. You will need to find out what your organisation uses, how the assessments are implemented and how you can effectively use the results. There's no point using an assessment tool or a test if you are not going to analyse and use the results to good effect. This should be to make sure your learners are on the right programme at the right level and with the right support they need to succeed.

Extension activity

Find out what initial and diagnostic assessments are available at your organisation. Will it be your responsibility to administer these or is there a specialist person to do this? How will you use the results? If you are not yet teaching, investigate suitable initial and diagnostic assessment activities that you could use with your learners in future, perhaps by searching the internet.

Self-assessment checklist

Do I know about the following?

If not, re-read this chapter, or research the texts and websites listed at the end.

- ☐ How employers can support learners and the learning process
- ☐ The role of various stakeholders
- ☐ The needs of a teacher or trainer
- ☐ The needs of learners
- ☐ Points of referral to meet learners' needs

- [ ] What a group profile is and how it can be used

- [ ] The difference between learning support and learner support

- [ ] How to review learners' progress

- [ ] Barriers to learning

- [ ] How to support learners

- [ ] How to work with learning support assistants

- [ ] How to use initial and diagnostic assessments

Summary

This chapter has explored the role of employers, stakeholders and others who are involved with supporting learners and the learning process.

You should now be able to identify and support your learners' needs as well as your own. You should also know how to use the results of initial and diagnostic assessments to help your learners to progress towards achieving an appropriate learning programme.

You might like to carry out further research by accessing the books and websites listed at the end of this chapter, particularly if you are working towards a higher level teaching qualification.

This chapter has covered the following topics:

- Employers and stakeholders

- Teachers and trainers

- Learners' needs and points of referral

- Barriers to learning

- Learning support assistants

- Initial and diagnostic assessment

References and further information

Ayers, H. and Gray, F. (2006) *An A to Z Practical Guide to Learning Difficulties*. London: David Fulton Publishers.

Bates, B. (2016) *A Quick Guide to Special Needs and Disabilities*. London: SAGE.

Delaney, J. and Cope, A. (2016) *Supporting Maths and English in Post-14 Education and Training*. London: OU Press.

Farrell, M. (2011) *The Effective Teachers' Guide to Dyslexia and other Learning Difficulties*. London: Routledge.

Gravells, A. and Simpson, S. (2012) *Equality and Diversity in the Lifelong Learning Sector* (2nd edition). London: Learning Matters SAGE.

Hargreaves, S. and Crabb, J. (2016) *Study Skills for Students with Dyslexia.* London: SAGE.

Powell, S. and Tummons, J. (2011) *Inclusive Practice in the Lifelong Learning Sector.* Exeter: Learning Matters.

Read, H. (2013) *The Best Initial Assessment Guide.* Bideford: Read On Publications Ltd.

Reece, I. and Walker, S. (2007) *Teaching, Training and Learning* (6th edition revised). Tyne & Wear: Business Education Publishers.

Tutt, R. and Williams, P. (2015) *The SEND Code of Practice (0–25 years).* London: SAGE.

Websites

ADHD – https://aadduk.org/symptoms-diagnosis-treatment/

Asperger syndrome – www.autism.org.uk/about/what-is/asperger.aspx

Assistive technology – www.washington.edu/doit/assistive-technology

Basic Key Skills Builder – www.bksb.co.uk

Citizens Advice – www.citizensadvice.org.uk

Council for the Curriculum, Examinations and Assessment (CCEA) – http://ccea.org.uk

Database of self-help groups – www.self-help.org.uk

Department for Education (DfE) – https://tinyurl.com/mk3l5xp

Department for Employment and Learning (DELNI) – www.delni.gov.uk

Disability Equality in Education – https://tinyurl.com/klnsvtn

Disability Rights UK – www.disabilityrightsuk.org

Dyslexia Association – www.dyslexia.uk.net

Education and Skills Funding Agency (ESFA) – www.gov.uk/government/organisations/education-and-skills-funding-agency

Education, Health and Care Plans (EHCP) – https://tinyurl.com/m87vxay

Education and Training Foundation (ETF) – www.et-foundation.co.uk

Education and Training Inspectorate (ETI) – www.etini.gov.uk

EHCP video – http://tinyurl.com/z4cd5q9

Estyn – www.estyn.gov.uk

Free online English audit – http://sagepub.net/LM/audit/audeng.asp

Free online maths audit – http://sagepub.net/LM/audit/audmat.asp

Initial assessment for using technology – http://wip.exeter.ac.uk/collaborate/itest/

Initial and diagnostic assessment materials – https://tinyurl.com/zovyvex

Mental health – www.mind.org.uk

National Autistic Society – www.autism.org.uk

Ofqual – www.gov.uk/government/organisations/ofqual

Ofsted – www.gov.uk/government/organisations/ofsted

Qualifications Wales – www.qualificationswales.org

Reading list for supporting learning – www.anngravells.com/reading-lists/learning-support

Scottish Qualifications Authority (SQA) – wwww.sqa.org.uk

Sector Skills Councils – https://tinyurl.com/kovubha

SEND Code of Practice 0–25 years (2014) – https://tinyurl.com/nr5zqtm

SEND Resources from Pearltrees – https://tinyurl.com/mcuoh5y

SEND Resources from the ETF – http://send.excellencegateway.org.uk

Special Educational Needs lingo by Joe Baldwin – https://tinyurl.com/jzq5ve6

4

Planning and designing teaching and learning programmes

Introduction

Planning and designing teaching and learning programmes is about knowing what you will do and when, to ensure learning takes place. This could be with groups and/or individuals who you may or may not have met before. The starting point will come from the curriculum, which determines the courses, programmes and/or qualifications offered.

This chapter will explore what is involved when planning and designing teaching and learning programmes. The documents you might use such as schemes of work, session plans and individual learning plans will be covered, as will the process learners go through when they commence. This will include an induction, icebreaker and ground rules which all help set the scene for teaching and learning to take place.

This chapter will cover the following topics:

- The curriculum
- Aims and objectives
- Schemes of work
- Session plans
- Individual learning plans
- Induction, icebreakers and ground rules

The curriculum

The term *curriculum* relates to everything which is educational and offered to learners. It is not just a set of standards, a qualification, or a scheme of work. Think of it as everything which an organisation offers. This could include many subject areas as well as additional topics which will benefit the learners.

Example

Alpha College has many departments which offer several subjects, Services to Business being one of them. The curriculum offered within this department includes qualifications such as Health and Social Care, Hospitality and Catering, and Retail Skills. The courses for each cover the subject content of the qualification, plus maths, English, digital literacy skills, employability skills and include a period of work experience.

This example shows the curriculum can be very broad and that other topics will be covered as part of the courses offered.

The curriculum is often based upon the needs of local employers. For example, if there are a few hotels in the area, then hospitality and catering would be a viable option to offer. The curriculum can also be based on a local need, for example, creating youth employment training schemes. Some curriculums are known as *national* as everything offered is the same no matter where the learners are, for example, in a state school. Others are decided by a local authority or a council, perhaps to meet the needs of those living in that area.

The curriculum should always be fit for purpose; there's no point offering a particular course if there is no demand, or if it does not meet the needs of local employers and learners. An organisation will usually have internal systems in place to ensure that what is offered is validated or approved beforehand.

Influences upon the curriculum

Whichever type of organisation you work for, they will need to plan a curriculum based on offering courses and/or qualifications which fulfil the needs of their potential market. This could be to offer training in particular subject areas due to the type of industry in the local area, for example, farming, shipbuilding or car manufacturing. Alternatively, it could be to offer employability skills' training if there is a high level of unemployment locally. It could also be within a company, to offer on-the-job staff training. There are other people and organisations who might be involved in the design or the influence of the curriculum. These include stakeholders, who are covered in Chapter 3.

Often, there are political, social or economic factors which have an influence upon the way a curriculum is put together. This might be the case in the country you are working in. In 2015, David Sainsbury was asked by the government in England to chair a panel of experts to provide clear recommendations for measures that would improve and transform education. *The Report of the Independent Panel on Technical Education* was published along-side the government's *Post-16 Skills Plan* in July 2016. The latter sets out the government's plan to support young people and adults to secure skilled employment, and to meet the needs of the economy. As a result, young people should be given a choice at the age of 16 between two equally high quality options: academic and technical. The academic option is based around theoretical subjects and qualifications. The technical option is built around routes to skilled employment. Each route should be available through college-based courses or apprenticeships, so that young people can choose the mode of learning which suits them best. Some routes might also contain vocational qualifications which can be achieved in addition to the demonstration of skills and knowledge.

Activity

Research the current political, economic, social and technological (PEST) factors which might affect the curriculum offered within your organisation. How will these impact upon your role, if at all?

Types of programmes and qualifications

Once the content of the curriculum has been established, particular courses, programmes and/or qualifications can be offered to prospective learners. These should have appropriate aims and objectives, and are usually supported with a scheme of work and session plans (covered later in this chapter). Please see Figure 4.1 to put these into perspective.

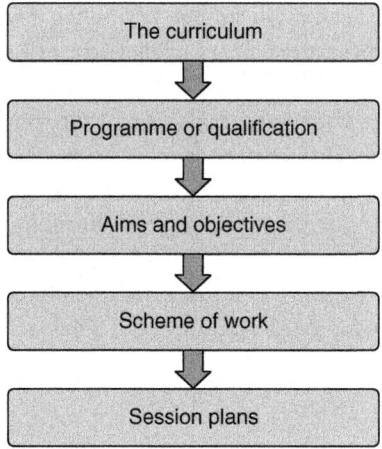

Figure 4.1 The planning process in perspective

Programme models

Programme models are based on how the various aspects of the curriculum will be delivered and assessed: for example, a bespoke training course for a local employer, or to meet the requirements of a qualification. They can range from a few hours for a short course, to those taking weeks, months or years. They could be offered at various times of the day or evening, and at various locations: for example, *on-the-job*, i.e. in the workplace; *off-the-job*, i.e. in a college; *online*, i.e. via an internet-connected device; or *near the job*. An example of the latter could be where trainee construction workers are undertaking some health and safety training in an onsite building near to where they are working.

Examples of different programme models include:

- bespoke training courses for particular employees, either on, off or near to the job

- blended learning which combines technology with traditional learning in any suitable environment

- classroom or workshop learning in a training organisation or the workplace

- conferences, events and seminars in locations such as hotels or specialist centres

- distance and flexible learning via an online or correspondence course

- evening classes in a community centre

- full-time or part-time attendance in a college, training centre, school, academy or university.

The timetabling of a number of sessions for a programme is usually decided by a head of department or a manager within the organisation. If it's for a qualification, a certain number of hours will need to be devoted to it. You might not have any influence upon this, nor the dates, times and rooms you will use.

If there is a demand, *bespoke* programmes could be created to meet a particular company's need. These are often known as *non-accredited* programmes as an awarding organisation has not accredited them as a qualification, nor will they issue a certificate. However, your organisation might issue a *record of attendance*. This will prove a person was there, but not that they necessarily learnt anything. Assessment would need to take place to determine what that person actually learnt, enabling a *certificate of achievement* to be issued. Bespoke programmes are often paid for by the employer or the learner, as funding might not be available. Some bespoke programmes could lead to an accredited qualification if the learners are also able to achieve aspects from qualifications which match the programme content. This would only be providing this route was offered. Alternatively, your organisation could approach an awarding organisation to create a qualification to meet a particular need. This would then be known as an *endorsed* programme.

If the programme you teach is advertised on your organisation's website, in a prospectus, in leaflets or in the local press, make sure you read it to check it is correct. If what you plan to offer is different from that advertised, there may be confusion when your learners commence. Your future learners should be able to have access to appropriate information, advice and guidance (IAG) prior to commencing. This will help them make a choice about what they wish to take, which will help them progress towards reaching their goals.

There might be certain entry requirements before a learner can even apply to take a programme of learning. It might be your responsibility, perhaps as part of the interview process, to ascertain these. Alternatively, it might be that someone else interviews the prospective learners and communicates to you who has been accepted. If your potential learner does not meet any entry requirements, they might not be able to take part.

Example

Phenil is interviewing a prospective learner, Jemma, who wishes to take an advanced computer programming qualification. The entry requirements state that successful applicants must already hold the intermediate level, along with at least level 3 maths and English. Jemma only has the beginner level, along with level 2 maths and English. Phenil explains that she has not met the entry requirements and asks her to apply for the intermediate qualification instead. Jemma is happy to do this, and will also take evening classes to work towards level 3 in maths and English.

In this example, Phenil might have wanted to accept Jemma as he needed a certain number of learners for the course to run. However, Jemma would have struggled to meet the course requirements and would probably have left the course early feeling as though she had failed. Never feel you must accept learners onto a course, just to make it viable, as you are probably setting your learners up to fail.

Product and process models

The product and process models of the curriculum relate to how much can be taught effectively within the timeframe and the way the course content is delivered. Teachers and trainers can often adapt their programmes to include more than is required. For example, a cookery teacher might show learners how to present food in an imaginative way on a plate. This would be in addition to teaching them to cook the particular recipes. Covering purely what is required to achieve a pass is referred to as the *product* model, whereas including more and/or varying the learning experiences relates to the *process* model. Please see Table 4.1 (on page 150) for some examples of the differences.

Product model

The *product* model focuses upon the content of a programme to reach a desired outcome: for example, what learners *must* know to pass an exam, a test and/or obtain a certificate (known as the *product*). The teacher will just teach what *must* be taught to get the learner through, i.e. what is stated in the qualification specification. What *should* be taught, i.e. what is not stated in the qualification specification but would be really helpful to the learner, and what *could* be taught, i.e. what would also be useful to the learner, are not taken into consideration. The product model doesn't add any extra value for the learner. It could be considered a summative model, as it is linked only to the required objectives, outcomes or tasks which the learner must achieve.

Example

Margaret is attending a class in word processing and will be taking an exam on a set date in the near future. Her teacher only has time to focus on what must be taught for Margaret to achieve the requirements of the qualification. There will not be time for Margaret to learn other valuable skills such as keyboarding and file-management.

Process model

The *process* model of delivery focuses on the content of the programme *and* other relevant aspects which *should* and *could* be learnt and applied (known as the *process*). This model adds value for the learner and is related not only to the end product, but to the learning process. A more holistic approach can be taken to the subject, which is centred on the learner. The process model could be considered a formative model, as it is linked to facilitating further learning along the way to achieving the required objectives, outcomes or tasks.

Example

Harold is working towards a Spanish qualification at evening classes. His teacher covers not only what is in the programme requirements (what must be taught) but also what should and could be taught. This will help Harold if he visits Spain in the future, for example, how to use the vocabulary and grammar in different contexts to order a meal, and how to book travel and accommodation.

Table 4.1 Examples of differences between the product and process models
Adapted from Reece and Walker (2007, page 221)

Product model	Process model
Focuses on the objectives, outcomes or tasks, i.e. the end product such as an exam or a test	Focuses on the content, i.e. the learning experiences and activities taking place
Learning is similar no matter where the learner takes the programme	Learning is different as it is tailored towards individual requirements
Learning is just a means to an end, i.e. to obtain a pass	Learning is more valuable and meaningful
Teaching and learning activities are limited to meeting the objectives, outcomes or tasks	Teaching and learning activities can be more imaginative and cover additional topics
Learning can be measured	Not all learning is measurable
Content is fixed	Content can change
Other skills and topics are not included	Other skills can be included, e.g. problem solving, communication, employability and numeracy
Little opportunity is available to extend learning	Provides the opportunity for extended learning, i.e. to stretch and challenge the more capable learners

While adding additional aspects to a programme can benefit the learner, they will be based upon how much time you have, the needs of your organisation and those of your learners. Your organisation might need you to just focus upon the programme requirements, as they may be judged by the achievements of the learners. This might prevent you from using a learner-centred approach, for example, if you are under pressure to cover the content in a certain amount of time.

Spiral model

The spiral model, a theory put forward by Jerome Bruner in 1966, spreads the learning out over time, rather than concentrating it into shorter periods. It introduces topics in a simple way and then repeats them with increasing levels of complexity. This helps to reinforce learning as any issues or concerns can be highlighted early on, with support measures put in place as the learner progresses. Imagine a spiral progressing upwards, which repeats itself as it aims to reach the final outcome, as in Figure 4.2.

Bruner felt that the most complex material, if properly structured and presented, can be understood by any learner.

Key features of the spiral model are:

- the topic is introduced

- the topic is revisited several times throughout the learning process, allowing a logical progression from simple to complex ideas

- the complexity of the topic increases each time it is revisited

- new learning is linked to old learning (and vice versa) and put into context.

This repetitive process continues while all the topics are taught and assessed.

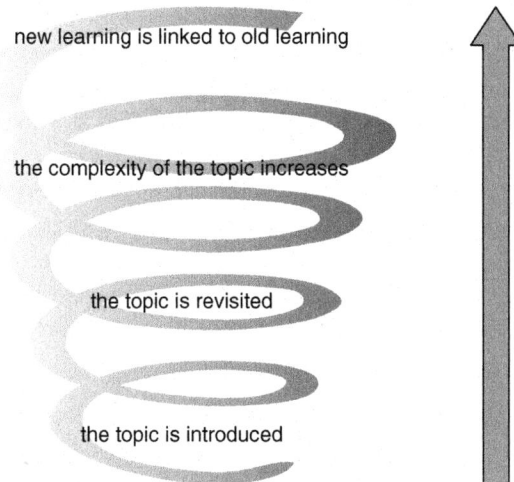

Figure 4.2 Example spiral curriculum model

Linear model

The linear model, a theory put forward by Ralph W. Tyler in 1949, assumes there is an agreed amount of knowledge that needs to be learnt. This knowledge is not repeated, like the spiral model. The teacher must decide how it will be taught and learnt. Tyler's model proposed that teachers should spend equal amounts of time evaluating their session plans, as well as evaluating the learning which is taking place. Imagine a line progressing forwards as it aims to reach the final outcome, as in Figure 4.3.

The linear process goes through four stages:

1. establish the objectives or tasks

2. design teaching and learning activities to achieve the objectives or tasks

3. carry out the activities in an effective way to ensure learning takes place

4. assess learners and evaluate the process.

This process starts and finishes without repeating any aspects.

Figure 4.3 Example linear curriculum model

The hidden curriculum

The hidden curriculum is a term used to denote aspects of learning which are not explicitly taught, i.e. they are *hidden*. They are aspects which are not made obvious, but are demonstrated by teachers and are visible in the learning environment. For example, if a teacher is well dressed in clothing which is suitable for the subject, this could give the message that they take pride in themselves. If rooms and corridors are untidy, with out-of-date posters on the wall, this could give the message the organisation isn't providing a positive learning environment. If an organisation uses sustainable products and has recycling areas for used paper, plastic and cardboard, this gives the message they care for the environment. Other hidden aspects can include the policies and procedures of the organisation, i.e. how up to date and proactive they are in supporting teaching, learning and assessment. The rules and routines which a teacher initiates can also have an impact, i.e. timekeeping, marking and returning work on time. If the culture of the organisation and its staff are not of a positive nature, this could impact negatively upon the learners and the learning taking place.

However, some aspects can be contradictory; for example, if an organisation offers healthy foods and drinks in their refreshment areas, but has vending machines with chocolates and sweets in other areas. This is giving a mixed message to learners.

Think of the hidden curriculum as the values, attitudes and behaviours of others which could influence those of the learners.

Aims and objectives

These are educational terms used to express what you want your learners to achieve and how they will go about it. Using aims and objectives helps you structure your sessions to enable learning to take place. Some programmes or qualifications might already contain the required aims and objectives, which could be called something different, for example:

- assessment criteria
- competency statements
- enabling objectives
- enabling outcomes
- evidence requirements
- indicative content

- knowledge statements
- learning objectives
- learning outcomes
- lesson objectives
- performance criteria
- tasks.

If aims and objectives, or their alternatives, are not provided for you, you will need to write your own. For example, if you are training a staff member to use a new piece of equipment on-the-job, you will need to know what you are going to do, and what you want your staff member to do, to use the equipment safely and effectively.

Aims

When writing an aim, you will need to consider what it is you want your learners to be able to achieve. Your aim is a general statement, and will usually begin with words like: *to appreciate, to be able to, to raise an awareness of.*

Example

Aim: Learners will be able to use a word processor.

You will see that this aim is very broad, and does not state to what extent the learners will use a word processor, just that they will use it.

Other terms that are sometimes used for aims, but are not really good practice to use, include *to know*, and *to understand*. Although these terms do state what you want your learners to achieve, they do not tell you how to check that learning has taken place. This is where objectives will help you.

Objectives

Once you have your aim, you can plan what it is that you want your learners to do to meet it, i.e. the objectives. They will help plan what should be covered and will help you to check that learning has taken place. Objectives are often referred to as *tasks*, i.e. the activities which learners will carry out.

When writing objectives or generating tasks, try not to use words similar to those in your aim, i.e. *Learners will know how to use a computer* because how do you know they know? The only way you will know, is if your learners can complete specific tasks to prove it.

Example

Objective: Learners will switch on a computer, use the keyboard and mouse to open the word processor and create a document.

The key tasks in this objective are *switch on, use, open* and *create*. These are active verbs, i.e. things that the learner has *to do* to prove their knowledge and understanding. They will enable you to assess that your learner is competent.

Objectives should always be SMART to enable you to teach and assess learning effectively. This is an acronym for:

Specific – the objectives or tasks are clearly defined to meet the required aim

Measurable – they can be achieved at the right level for the learner

Achievable – they can be met by all learners

Relevant – they relate to the programme of learning or the qualification requirements

Time bound – the agreed target dates and times can be met.

Being SMART is all about being clear and precise with what you expect your learners to achieve. SMART objectives should always be at the right level for your learners; for example, to *list* is easier than to *evaluate*. Knowing your learners, and the level of the programme or qualification they are working towards, will help you plan which active verbs to use. They should be challenging enough to ensure learning is progressive, yet be inclusive to all learners to ensure they can achieve.

Example

Learners will list the names of the kings and queens of England from 1066 to the present day.

This example shows the objective is SMART by being specific to the subject and at a level to suit all learners in the group. It is measurable, as the teacher will be able to assess each learner's list, and achievable as all learners will be able to do it. It is relevant to what has just been taught; however, it is not time bound. Therefore, the teacher would need to allocate a time for the activity to be achieved, i.e. within 30 minutes.

If the objective was not SMART, it might look like: *Learners will know the kings and queens of England from 1066 to the present day.* This is vague and will not show that learning has taken place. Objectives have to be *specific* to enable learners to demonstrate what they know, understand and/or can do.

If the teacher wants to stretch and challenge their learners further, they could ask them to place the list in chronological order, stating the dates.

Activity

Obtain a copy of the programme of learning, qualification specification, work tasks, job specification or set of standards for your subject. Have a look to see what terminology is used to denote that which you will teach and assess; for example, learning outcomes *and* assessment criteria. *Have a go at writing an aim with associated objectives for a topic you will teach. Check that they are SMART.*

Types of objectives

There are two types of objectives: *behavioural* which enable a learner to demonstrate skills, and *non-behavioural* which enable a learner to demonstrate knowledge and understanding.

Behavioural is when your learners can demonstrate a skill: for example, *learners will switch on a computer.* If you are teaching *skills,* your objectives might include: *demonstrate, perform* and *use.* Behavioural objectives can also relate to attitudes as a learner may need to demonstrate they have the right attitude to carry out a task: for example, *learners will greet customers in a friendly and helpful way.*

Being able to perform a skill and/or demonstrate the right attitude and behaviour should not be in isolation from having the understanding to know *why* it is being performed that way. For example, if you are teaching a practical subject, you will need to observe what your learners can do and know that they understand why they are doing it. Your objectives might, therefore, also include: *describe* and *explain.*

Non-behavioural is when your learners can demonstrate they have gained the required knowledge and understanding. Non-behavioural objectives are more difficult to assess and often contain the words *know, learn* or *understand;* for example, *learners will know the law of gravity.* These words are not good practice and should either be substituted or added to, to make them SMART. For example, *learners will know the law of gravity by explaining how it works.* The addition of the word *explaining* enables you to assess that learning has taken place. You would need to make sure the objectives you are using are at the right level for the subject and your learners. If you asked a level 1 learner to *evaluate* something, they might not be able to. However, they should be able to *list* or *state.*

Once you know the subject you are going to deliver and assess, you should be able to see whether it relates to:

- skills and/or
- knowledge and understanding and/or
- attitudes and behaviours.

This will help you to use appropriate objectives or tasks for your learners to achieve at the right level. Table 4.2 gives some examples of these at different levels of learning; however, they are just a guide and are not all SMART.

Activity

Look at Table 4.2 to see which objectives relate to the subject you will be teaching and/or assessing. Do you feel any are in the wrong column or are at the wrong level for your subject? It's fine if you think this, as many objectives in programmes and qualifications do differ depending upon the context they relate to. You could devise your own list of objectives if they are not supplied for you.

Having clear aims and objectives will help you plan what will be covered during your sessions. They will also enable you to plan how much time is needed to carry out various tasks. You should inform your learners at the beginning of each session what the aims and objectives are, and how they relate to the overall programme or qualification. This will help them appreciate what they are learning and why. You could keep them on display and refer to them regularly to make sure your learners realise how they are achieving them. You could also ask your learners to self-assess themselves by asking them to write down or state how they have achieved the objectives when the session concludes.

Domains of learning

Benjamin Bloom, an American educational psychologist, referred to three domains of learning in 1956: *psycho-motor*, *cognitive* and *affective* as in Figure 4.4. Think of psycho-motor as the hands (skills), cognitive as the head (knowledge and understanding) and affective as the heart (attitudes).

Psycho-motor
The hands
Skills

Cognitive
The head
Knowledge and
understanding

Affective
The heart
Attitudes

Figure 4.4 Bloom's (1956) three domains of learning

Table 4.2 Objectives at different levels

Level	Skills			Knowledge and understanding			Attitudes and behaviours		
Foundation or entry level	Attempt Carry out	Experience Gather	Listen Read	Answer Guess Label	Learn Match	Repeat Show	Adopt Assume	Attend Contribute	Follow Share
1	Activate Arrange Collect Communicate Help	Obtain Record See Separate Sketch	Switch Use View Watch	Access Duplicate Know List Locate	Memorise Name Order Recall	Recap Recognise State Write	Act Adapt Familiarise	Co-operate Comply Imitate	Respond Think
2	Assist Change Choose Connect	Discover Draw Perform Practise	Prepare Present Rearrange Simulate	Associate Compare Decide Describe	Identify Include Incorporate Reorder	Rewrite Select Understand	Accept Consider	Develop Express	Improve Question
3	Apply Assemble Assess Build Calibrate Coach	Check Combine Construct Create Demonstrate Estimate	Facilitate Illustrate Make Measure Supervise Train	Assimilate Contrast Devise Edit Embed	Explain Generalise Grade Guide Infer	Merge Paraphrase Promote Propose Recommend	Appreciate Challenge Determine Discriminate Empathise	Enable Internalise Participate Praise Predict	Relate Review Study Sympathise Visualise
4	Calculate Collaborate Complete Convert Diagnose Explore Inspect	Integrate Maintain Mentor Modify Plan Produce	Quality assure Test Transform Research Search Solve	Analyse Attribute Evaluate Categorise Contextualise	Define Invent Outline Rank	Rate Revise Substitute Summarise Verify	Appraise Command Criticise Critique Debate	Discuss Influence Judge Justify Manipulate	Persuade Rationalise Reflect Support Value

5	Accept
	  responsibility
	Design
	Encapsulate
	Establish
		Examine
		Generate
		Interview
		Investigate
			Manage
			Organise
			Survey
			Teach
				Classify
				Compile
				Compose
					Critically
					  analyse
						Distinguish
						Interpret
						Synthesise
							Argue
							Critically
							  appraise
								Defend
								Differentiate
								Dispute
									Formulate
									Refine
									Suggest

6	Initiate	Operate	Utilise	Critically
				  evaluate
					Extrapolate
					Theorise
						Translate	Conclude
							Critically
							  formulate
								Hypothesise	Justifiably
									  argue

Psycho-motor domain (subject – bricklaying) learners will build a two-foot high wall.

Cognitive domain (subject – geography) learners will state the reasons for coastal erosion.

Affective domain (subject – the environment) learners will discuss their ideas for reducing waste.

Bloom's taxonomy

Bloom chaired a committee of educators in the early 1950s. As a result, in 1956, a framework was published which became known as Bloom's taxonomy (a classification). It includes a hierarchy of six progressive levels ranging from simple to complex as shown in Figure 4.5. Knowledge is first, with those following relating to skills and abilities. This is on the understanding that knowledge is necessary for the skills and abilities to be put into practice.

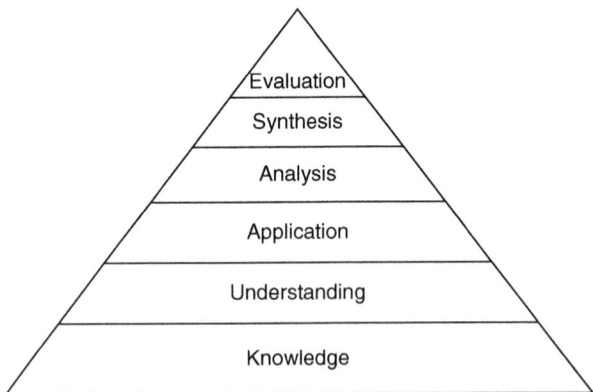

Figure 4.5 Bloom's (1956) six levels of learning

The six progressive levels have associated objectives (active verbs) to denote what learners will be able to know and/or do. They range from *actual* to *abstract* thinking and are:

1. knowledge: to remember and recall facts, e.g. list, recall

2. understanding: to demonstrate knowledge, e.g. describe, identify

3. application: to apply knowledge and understanding to real situations, e.g. demonstrate, explain

4. analysis: to consider, explore and work things out, e.g. appraise, calculate

5. synthesis: to compile ideas and generate new ones, e.g. compose, design

6. evaluation: to make and defend judgements, e.g. critically evaluate, hypothesise.

Using Bloom's taxonomy might help you differentiate the objectives and tasks you want your learners to achieve. Your learners might achieve at different levels throughout their time with you, perhaps if they are taking a long-term programme. This might be by starting with an expression of their knowledge, i.e. by recalling relevant facts, working up to critically evaluating something. You may even have individual learners who are at different levels within the same group. To help you differentiate for this during a session, you could ask them to complete the same task, but in a different way. For example, make a *list* (to demonstrate knowledge), *explain* (to demonstrate understanding) and *appraise* (to demonstrate analysis). All these tasks will enable you to check that learning is taking place.

Table 4.3 lists some objectives which relate to the different levels in Bloom's taxonomy. Please note that they do not always relate to the levels as in Table 4.2.

Table 4.3 Examples of objectives to meet Bloom's taxonomy

Objectives					
Knowledge	**Understanding**	**Application**	**Analysis**	**Synthesis**	**Evaluation**
define	describe	apply	analyse	arrange	argue
list	discuss	demonstrate	appraise	assemble	assess
match	estimate	devise	calculate	compose	choose
name	explain	illustrate	categorise	construct	critically
recall	identify	interpret	compare	create	appraise
recognise	locate	modify	criticise	design	differentiate
repeat	order	operate	debate	invent	estimate
state	select	use	test	summarise	evaluate
					judge

Revised taxonomy

In 2001, Anderson and Krathwohl published a revised version of Bloom's taxonomy. The revision takes attention away from the notion of educational objectives and focuses on a more dynamic concept of classification. The six progressive levels are, therefore, slightly different to those of the original version, as in Figure 4.6.

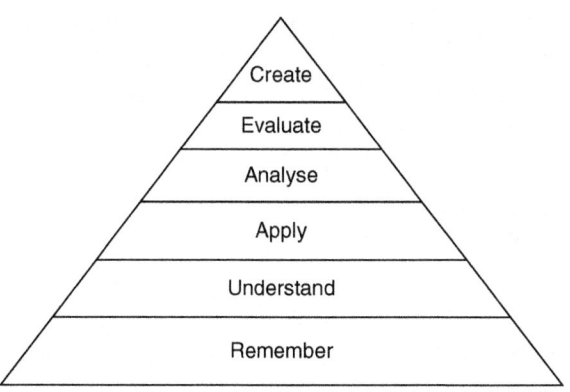

Figure 4.6 Anderson and Krathwohl's (2001) six levels of learning

The revised levels also have associated objectives (active verbs) to denote what learners will be able to know and/or do. These are to:

1. recall facts and basic concepts, e.g. memorise, state

2. explain ideas or concepts, e.g. compare, write

3. use information in new situations, e.g. enable, interpret

4. draw a connection amongst ideas, e.g. evaluate, reflect

5. justify a stand or a decision, e.g. defend, dispute

6. produce new or original work, e.g. critically formulate, initiate.

The objectives in the levels of the revised version do not all match with the original version. However, they will give you an indication of what you want your learners to be able to know and/or do at different points in their learning, if you wish to use them.

Activity

Choose an objective from each of Bloom's levels in Table 4.3 and create a task for your learners to carry out. For example: learners will list ... (knowledge), learners will explain ... (understanding) and so on. This will help you to practise how you can differentiate your subject for different levels of learning, or how you can stretch and challenge your learners if they are capable of achieving more.

Levels of learning

Levels of learning are usually determined by a country's qualification framework. In England, it is known as the Regulated Qualifications Framework (RQF). The levels in the RQF indicate the difficulty and complexity of the knowledge and skills associated with a qualification which is regulated by Ofqual. There are eight levels supported by three *entry* levels, sometimes referred to as *foundation* levels. Entry levels are designed to equip learners with basic skills to progress further. While most qualifications will be assigned a single level, some, such as GCSEs, can span more than one level. A rough comparison of levels 1 to 8 in the RQF to existing qualifications in England is:

1 – GCSEs (grades 3–1: previously D–G)

2 – GCSEs (grades 9–4: previously A*–C)

3 – Advanced level (A level)

4 – Vocational Qualification level 4

5 – Vocational Qualification level 5, Foundation Degree

6 – Bachelor's Degree

7 – Master's Degree, Postgraduate Certificate or Diploma

8 – Doctor of Philosophy (DPhil or PhD).

Qualifications on the RQF have a *size* as well as a level. This refers to the estimated total amount of time it could typically take to study and be assessed for a qualification. This can be anything from a few hours to several years. Size is expressed in terms of total qualification time (TQT). TQT can be thought of as *credits,* i.e. one credit equals 10 hours of learning. This learning time can be contact time with a teacher or assessor, and non-contact time for assignments and self-study. For example, if a qualification has a TQT of 12, it would take approximately 120 hours to achieve (12 × 10).

Qualifications can be at different levels, but require similar amounts of study and assessment time. Likewise, qualifications at the same level can take different amounts of study and assessment time. The RQF replaced the Qualifications and Credit Framework (QCF) and its previous namesake the National Qualifications Framework (NQF) in October 2015. All qualifications on the RQF must be underpinned by a validity strategy that will show how they provide value for learners and employers.

Higher education qualifications, which are not regulated by Ofqual, are offered at universities, or colleges which partner with them. These qualifications are on the Framework for Higher Education Qualifications (FHEQ) and are conferred by bodies with degree-awarding powers.

Extension activity

Find out if there is a qualification framework in the country you are working in. If possible, have a look at it to see how the levels are determined, i.e. what a learner is required to do to achieve at a particular level. These are often referred to as level descriptors. *Have a look at Ofqual's Qualification and Component Levels (2015) at https://tinyurl.com/j6sw9pc to familiarise yourself with what they look like in England.*

Schemes of work

A scheme of work is a document you can use to plan and structure a sequence of teaching and learning sessions. It is also known as a:

- course outline
- learning programme
- schedule of work
- scheme of learning
- structured plan
- study programme.

Having a scheme of work helps you plan what you will do and when. This is useful in case there are any bank or public holidays, which might reduce the number of sessions available.

It's also useful in case you want to book a visiting speaker in advance, take your learners on an external visit, or need to use certain resources which must be prepared in advance. The content should be flexible to allow for any changes, i.e. a cancelled session, and detailed enough in case a colleague needs to cover for you. It should reflect the use of different teaching and learning approaches, resources and assessment methods throughout the duration of the programme. It is a working document which shows what you will do and what you want your learners to do. It should reflect learning in a progressive and logical way through the programme requirements. You wouldn't want to start with something complicated if you haven't covered the basics first.

If you teach the same subject as your colleagues, you could all work together to produce a standardised scheme of work. This will enable all learners to have the same experience no matter which teacher they have. However, individual learners' needs and differentiation will still need to be taken into account. The amount of detail you are expected to include will vary depending upon the context within which you teach. The requirements of your organisation and external inspectors might also have an impact on the detail you need to include. Usually, an organisation will supply their teachers with a standard pro-forma to use. However, if none is available, you could create your own. Please see Table 4.4 for a basic example of a scheme of work. For the purpose of future-proofing the book, a year has not been added to any dates within the documents. When completing any documents yourself, you should always add the year, as well as the day and month, to create a full audit trail.

Starting point for a scheme of work

As soon as you find out what you will be teaching and when, you can create your scheme of work. The starting point for this will usually come from the content of a qualification which will be stated in the awarding organisation's handbook, specification or syllabus. Alternatively, it could be from a programme of learning, work tasks, a job specification or a set of standards. These might be produced in sections, i.e. units or modules which relate to different subjects or topics. While these might be written in a certain order, you can usually decide the order in which you teach them. You could also group some aspects together which are from different units. This would save repetition as there is often an aspect which is repeated in more than one unit. This might relate to a generic topic such as health and safety. Don't worry if there are some aspects you are not familiar with. This is quite normal, as not everyone knows everything. Treat it as an opportunity for you to update your skills and knowledge. Just make sure you feel comfortable and confident prior to teaching the topic. If not, don't bluff your way through something, but be honest with your learners and say that it is new to you. You could always ask your learners what they know and incorporate this into a discussion based on their experiences.

Activity

Have a look at the content of what you will be teaching, i.e. the qualification specification or set of standards. Is it structured in units, modules or some other format? How much time will you have to teach the content, and how will you decide the order in which to do it?

Teacher/trainer A G Smith			Venue: Room 3	

Programme/qualification
Introduction to Information and Communication Technology Level 1

Group composition
10 adults with little or no previous computer experience

Dates
From: 8 Sept
To: 13 Oct

Number of sessions
Six

Number of hours
18 (3 hours per week 6–9 p.m.) plus 2 hours self-study/homework

Aim of programme
To enable learners to use a computer (for basic word processing, spreadsheets, database, internet and email)

Dates	Learning outcomes/objectives *Learners will:*	Teacher activities	Learner activities	Assessment activities	Resources
Week 1 8 Sept	• obtain and discuss information regarding the organisation, programme content and assessment • switch on a computer and use a keyboard and a mouse • complete an online initial assessment and learning preferences questionnaire • discuss previous knowledge/experience of using ICT • use the ICT applications	Facilitate induction, icebreaker, ground rules Explanation of programme and organisation Show video Practical and theoretical demonstration and discussion Recap of session Explanation of next session	Discussion Initial assessment Differentiated activities based upon results of learning preferences and to meet individual needs Practical activities Listening and questioning	Oral questions Observation Online initial assessment Discussion Quiz	Computers Interactive whiteboard Workpacks Internet access Flipchart Handouts Exercises Quiz
Week 2 15 Sept	• create, save and print documents using a word-processing program	Recap previous session Demonstration of word processing Discussion of uses of a word processor, link to learners' experiences Recap of session Explanation of next session	Discussion Differentiated activities based on learners' experience Practical activities Listening and questioning	Observation Oral and written questions Gapped handout Practical activities Quiz	Computers Interactive whiteboard Workpacks Handouts Exercises Quiz
Week 6 13 Oct	• use all ICT programs • carry out a formal assessment activity • complete an evaluation form • discuss opportunities for progression	Recap all sessions Explain and discuss formal assessment process, those not taking it will continue with individual exercises Explain case study activity Facilitate programme evaluation Explain progression opportunities	Discussion Differentiated activities to meet assessment requirements Practical activities Formal assessment activities Listening and questioning	Formal assignment Observation Questions	Computers Interactive whiteboard Exercises Case study activity Assignments Evaluation form

If you are delivering a non-accredited programme, there might not be a qualification speci-fication for you to refer to. You might, therefore, need to devise your own content. This is where the use of aims and objectives will really help you to plan what you will do, as in the previous section of this chapter. Some programmes are nationalised, i.e. they are the same no matter where a learner takes it. Schemes of work for these might be provided, and often, changes can't be made without approval.

Example

Janine is a freelance first aid trainer. She has been asked by a company to teach a First Aid at Work programme to 12 members of their staff. The programme is a national one, i.e. it is the same no matter where in the country learners take it. The scheme of work for the programme is provided by the organisation which accredits it. Janine, therefore, does not have to create her own, but has been told she can make minor amendments to meet any particular learner needs.

Planning your scheme of work

When planning your scheme of work, it is useful to know something about your learn-ers; for example, their previous knowledge and/or experience, their learning preferences, and/or any individual requirements or needs they may have (covered in Chapter 3). You might have found this out prior to your learners commencing, if not, you will need to find this out during the first session. You could add this information to a group profile as in Chapter 3 Table 3.1. This is a visual reminder of the individuals in your group to support their learning, to note any concerns and aid differentiation. This will enable you to plan your teaching and learning activities in a progressive way for each learner to achieve their maximum potential.

You might like to put yourself in the place of your learners when planning what to do and when. This way, you can see things from a beginner's perspective to ensure you keep things simple during the earlier sessions. Start with the *known* and move onto the *unknown* or *unfamiliar*, checking the progress of your learners as you go. You might want to achieve too much in the early stages, which could confuse your learners. Try to break your subject down into manageable chunks, topics or tasks which a learner who knows nothing about it can easily follow.

You may need to check if you will have the same venue or room for all the sessions, and what facilities, equipment and resources are available. It might be that you have to book some equipment in advance. Knowing which date you will use it will help with your plan-ning, particularly if it's not available when you would like it to be.

Your scheme of work should show a variety of teaching, learning and assessment activi-ties to meet all learners' needs, and keep the subject interesting for them. The activities you choose to use will differ depending upon the *subject* you are teaching, the *context* and *environment* you are teaching in, as well as the *length* of each session. You might need to show how you will embed additional skills such as English, maths, and information and computing technology (ICT) (covered in Chapter 5). It would be useful if you could plan time for tutorial reviews, to enable you to talk to each of your learners on a one-to-one basis at some point during the programme.

The very first session should include an induction, icebreaker and ground rules (covered later in this chapter). All subsequent sessions should begin with a recap of the previous session, time for questions, and an introduction to the current session, i.e. the objectives. They should end with a recap of the objectives and an explanation of the following session.

Depending on how long the programme will last, it would be useful to include an evaluation activity to obtain feedback part way through, as well as during the final session. At the end of the programme you could give details of how your learners can progress further, i.e. what steps they can take to continue their learning and development.

Rationale

A rationale such as using the *five Ws and one H* format of **who, what, when, where, why** and **how**, will help you plan your scheme of work, for example:

- who: the learners

- what: the aims and objectives you want your learners to achieve

- when: the number of sessions and hours, dates and times

- where: venue or environment

- why: the programme or qualification learners will be working towards

- how: the teaching and learning approaches, resources and assessment methods.

Activity

Create a rationale for your course using the five Ws and one H. What else will you need to consider prior to producing your scheme of work? How will you find out this information?

There are a number of aspects to consider when creating your scheme of work. You could use the following points to help you.

☐ obtain the qualification specification (if it's an accredited programme) or other relevant documentation

☐ devise your own programme content (if it's non-accredited)

☐ break the content down into a logical order, with manageable chunks of learning in an appropriate amount of time

☐ find out what rooms, facilities, equipment and resources are available, or which need to be obtained

☐ know the dates and times when learners will be attending, and any bank, public and religious holiday dates which might reduce the number of sessions

☐ find out aspects about your learners, e.g. age range, ability, prior knowledge, learning preferences

☐ obtain any information about the subject or partake in any training yourself

☐ allow time for an induction, initial assessment, icebreaker and ground rules in the first session

☐ embed additional skills such as English, maths and ICT

☐ plan activities and materials which can be differentiated and are inclusive to all

☐ liaise with others

☐ plan self-study or homework activities

☐ devise teaching, learning and assessment materials

☐ upload materials to an online or virtual learning environment (VLE)

☐ allow time for tutorial reviews

☐ evaluate the programme and your own performance

☐ keep up to date with changes to the subject, and to legislation, policies and procedures.

Once you have created your scheme of work, you may need to show it to your line manager for their approval. Once approved, you could give a copy to your learners, or make it available electronically. However, as it is a working document, you might make changes to it which could confuse your learners. Giving a copy to them might also have the disadvantage that if they think a forthcoming topic is not interesting to them, they won't attend. Alternatively, you could give your learners a list of the topics rather than the full scheme of work.

Sometimes, teachers might have *administrative time* allocated each week as part of their timetable. This can be used for planning sessions, creating resources and marking work. However, many teachers don't get this time allocated; therefore, creating a scheme of work, which can be very time consuming, might need to be carried out during your own time. However, the more time you take to plan what will go into your scheme of work, the easier it will be to design your individual session plans.

Extension activity

Create a scheme of work for at least six sessions based on your specialist subject. Use your organisation's template or design one with similar headings to that in Table 4.4. Think carefully about what you want to achieve during each session, and don't try to do too much in the early stages.

Session plans

A session plan is a document which should be produced prior to each session you will teach. It is also known as a:

- learning plan

- lesson plan

- teaching and learning plan

- training plan.

It is an expanded version of each individual session from your scheme of work. Although the content on a session plan is very similar to that stated on a scheme of work, it is much more detailed. Think of the scheme of work as an overview of the full programme which is supported by session plans for each date. It will help you to effectively manage the time that you are with your learners, what you will do and what your learners will do. If you are only delivering one session rather than a series of sessions, a session plan can be used instead of a scheme of work. It might be that you are teaching a programme which already has the session plans prepared for you. If this is the case you will need to familiarise yourself with them, and find out whether you can make any changes or not.

Try not to prepare too many session plans in advance, as circumstances or dates may change. If you create a full set of session plans from your scheme of work, perhaps spanning several months, the information for each will not be fresh in your mind. You might also change the content of a subsequent plan based upon what happened in a current session. It's good to be flexible and adaptable with the content of your session plans. You will be responding to what happens on the day and what you plan to do might not always take place. When deciding on the content to include, it's useful to ask yourself *'If a colleague had to take over my session, would they be able to do so by using my session plan?'*

If your organisation is inspected by Ofsted (in England), they require to see evidence of planned learning. This can be in any format, which your organisation, or you, can choose to use. Table 4.5 is a sample session plan for the first session from the previous example of a scheme of work. There are many different designs of session plans; some are meant to only take five minutes to create, are more visual and are called a *five-minute session plan*. An example is given in Table 4.6. This type of plan saves repetition, but does not always include the timings of the activities. An alternative plan relates to the three stages of a session, i.e. the introduction, development and conclusion (beginning, middle and ending). An example is given in Table 4.7.

Once you have a set of session plans, providing the programme doesn't change, you can adapt them in the future for different groups of learners rather than starting again. However, don't think that because everything worked well the last time that it will be the same again this time, as you will have different learners with different abilities and needs.

Table 4.5 Example session plan

Teacher/trainer	A G Smith		Date	8 September	Venue	Room 3
Programme/ Qualification	Introduction to Information and Communication Technology Level 1 (Ref 1.1)		Time Duration	6-9 p.m. 3 hours	Number of learners	10
Aim of session	To induct learners to the programme, organisation and assessment requirements To enable learners to use a computer					
Group composition	10 adults with little or no previous computer experience of computers (4 female, 6 male, age range 19–55). Initial assessment during this session will identify any prior skills, knowledge and understanding along with learning preferences. One learner has dyslexia and requires handouts on pastel coloured paper, therefore all handouts issued will be the same colour. All learners will complete all the planned activities, most will complete a gapped handout, and some will complete an additional activity if there is time.					

Timing	Learning outcomes/objectives/tasks Learners will:	Teacher activities	Learner activities	Assessment activities	Resources
6.00	Obtain and discuss information regarding the organisation, programme content and assessment	Explanation and discussion	Listen and ask questions	Oral questions	Handouts Flipchart, paper, pens Interactive whiteboard
6.20	Complete an icebreaker	Facilitate icebreaker	Partake in icebreaker	Observation	Handouts
6.40	Agree ground rules	Facilitate ground rules	Discuss and agree ground rules	Discussion	Flipchart
6.50	Switch on a computer and use a keyboard and mouse	Show video via internet Practical demonstration	View video Observe demonstration Switch on computer Use keyboard and mouse to work through differentiated workpacks	Oral questions	Video via internet Computers Workpacks – differentiated based on experience Exercises Interactive whiteboard
7.30 Break					
7.45	Complete an online initial assessment and learning preference questionnaire	Facilitate initial assessment	Complete online assessments	Observation Online initial assessments	Computers connected to the internet
8.15	Discuss previous knowledge/ experience of using ICT	Discussion	Discussion	Oral questions	
8.25	Use a word processor	Facilitate practical activities	Use computer and workpacks Complete gapped handout	Oral questions Observation Written questions Gapped handout	Interactive whiteboard Workpacks Exercises
8.50	Switch off the computer	Summarise session Explain next session	Log off Hear a summary of this session and next session Ask questions	Oral questions Quiz	Flipchart Quiz

Table 4.6 Example five-minute session plan

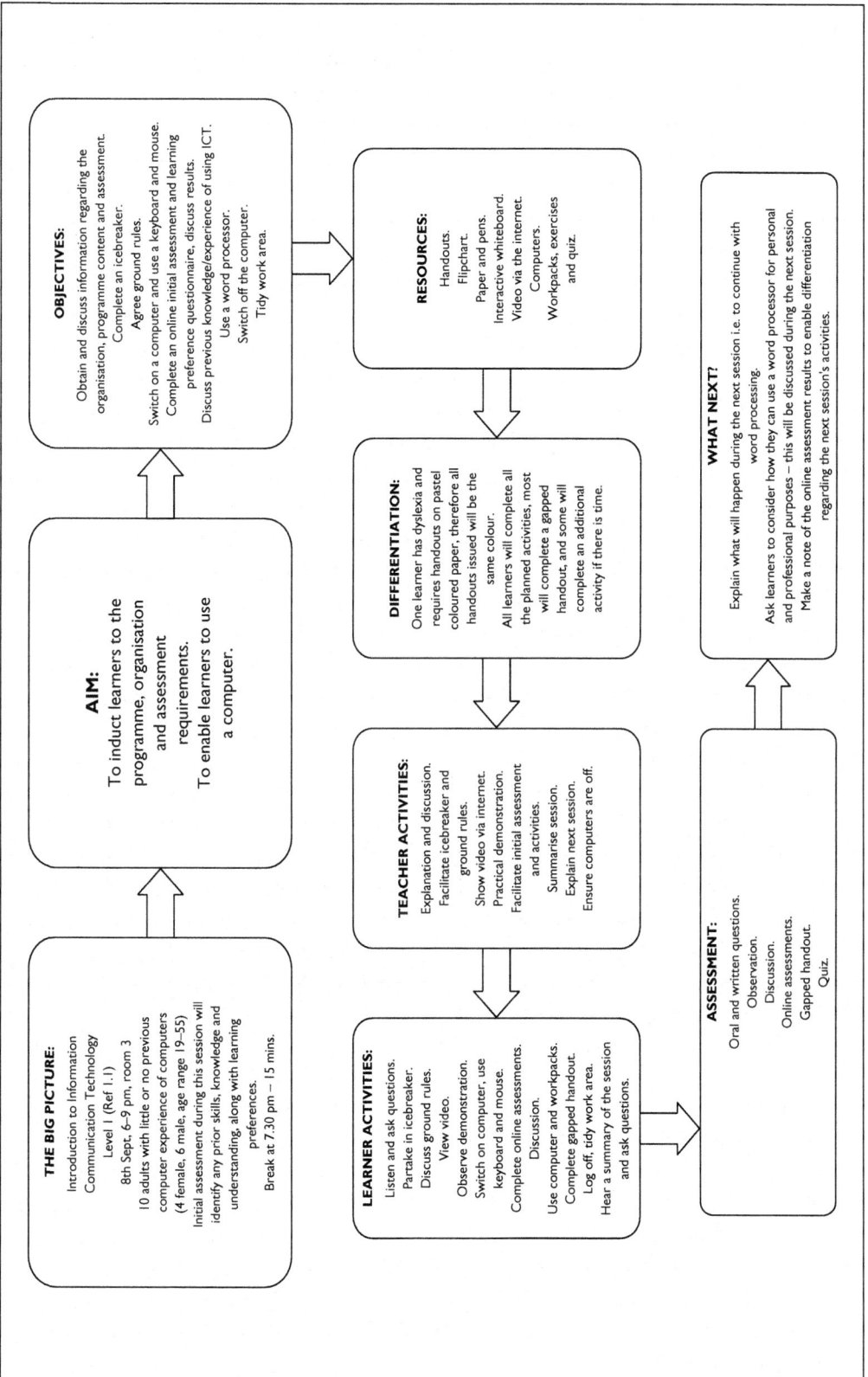

THE BIG PICTURE:

Introduction to Information Communication Technology Level I (Ref 1.1)
8th Sept, 6–9 pm, room 3
10 adults with little or no previous computer experience of computers (4 female, 6 male, age range 19–55)
Initial assessment during this session will identify any prior skills, knowledge and understanding, along with learning preferences.

Break at 7.30 pm – 15 mins.

AIM:

To induct learners to the programme, organisation and assessment requirements.
To enable learners to use a computer.

OBJECTIVES:

Obtain and discuss information regarding the organisation, programme content and assessment.
Complete an icebreaker.
Agree ground rules.
Switch on a computer and use a keyboard and mouse.
Complete an online initial assessment and learning preference questionnaire, discuss results.
Discuss previous knowledge/experience of using ICT.
Use a word processor.
Switch off the computer.
Tidy work area.

RESOURCES:

Handouts.
Flipchart.
Paper and pens.
Interactive whiteboard.
Video via the internet.
Computers.
Workpacks, exercises and quiz.

DIFFERENTIATION:

One learner has dyslexia and requires handouts on pastel coloured paper, therefore all handouts issued will be the same colour.
All learners will complete all the planned activities, most will complete a gapped handout, and some will complete an additional activity if there is time.

TEACHER ACTIVITIES:

Explanation and discussion.
Facilitate icebreaker and ground rules.
Show video via internet.
Practical demonstration.
Facilitate initial assessment and activities.
Summarise session.
Explain next session.
Ensure computers are off.

LEARNER ACTIVITIES:

Listen and ask questions.
Partake in icebreaker.
Discuss ground rules.
View video.
Observe demonstration.
Switch on computer, use keyboard and mouse.
Complete online assessments.
Discussion.
Use computer and workpacks.
Complete gapped handout.
Log off, tidy work area.
Hear a summary of the session and ask questions.

ASSESSMENT:

Oral and written questions.
Observation.
Discussion.
Online assessments.
Gapped handout.
Quiz.

WHAT NEXT?

Explain what will happen during the next session i.e. to continue with word processing.
Ask learners to consider how they can use a word processor for personal and professional purposes – this will be discussed during the next session.
Make a note of the online assessment results to enable differentiation regarding the next session's activities.

Table 4.7 Example three-stage session plan

Teacher/trainer	A G Smith	Date	8 September	Venue	Room 3
Programme/ Qualification	Introduction to Information Communication Technology Level 1 (Ref 1.1)	**Time Duration**	6-9 p.m. 3 hours	**Number of learners**	10
Aim of session	To induct learners to the programme, organisation and assessment requirements To enable learners to use a computer				
Group composition	10 adults with little or no previous computer experience of computers (4 female, 6 male, age range 19-55) Initial assessment during this session will identify any prior skills, knowledge and understanding, along with learning preferences. One learner has dyslexia and requires handouts on pastel coloured paper, therefore all handouts issued will be the same colour. All learners will complete all the planned activities, most will complete a gapped handout, and some will complete an additional activity if there is time.				
Learners will:					
Introduction 6–6.50 p.m.	• Partake in an induction: the organisation, programme content and assessment • Complete an icebreaker • Agree ground rules				
Development 7.45–8.50 p.m.	• Watch a video • **Break 7.30 p.m.** • Switch on a computer and use a keyboard and mouse • Complete an online initial assessment and learning preference questionnaire, discuss the results • Discuss previous knowledge/experience of using ICT • Use a word processor				
Conclusion 8.50–9 p.m.	• Switch off the computer • Find out about the content of the next session • Tidy work area				

The three stages of a session

When planning what to cover during each session, think of it as being in three stages: the introduction, development and conclusion, as in Figure 4.7. In other words, having a beginning, middle and ending.

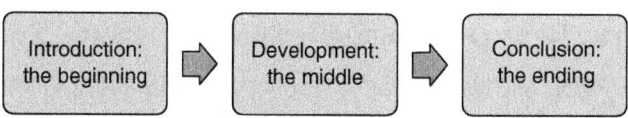

Figure 4.7 The three stages of a session

Each stage should contain the activities a learner will carry out. It's good to establish a routine of how you will progress though the three stages, particularly the way you start and end each session. This lets your learners know how you work, and helps them know what they will do and when.

When you are planning what to do in each stage, ask yourself *'if I was a learner, would I learn something new, and would I enjoy how I was learning it?'* If you don't think you would, it's probable your learners wouldn't either.

If your organisation doesn't require you to use a formal session plan, you could make notes of what you aim to achieve during each of the three stages, as in Table 4.7. This type of plan is useful if you are delivering a one-off session, rather than a series of sessions.

An alternative use for the three-stage plan is to list what *you* will do during each stage, rather than what your *learners* will do. This might be useful if you are facilitating a short event, a seminar or a meeting. Noting what you will do can act like a checklist to make sure you cover everything in the right order.

The introduction stage

If this is your first meeting with your learners, make sure you introduce yourself, explain the facilities of the organisation, the requirements of the programme, carry out an icebreaker and agree a few ground rules. This is a lot to cover; however, don't let all this take over the session. Your learners might wonder when they are going to start learning something to do with the subject.

If it's not the first session, your introduction should include the aim of the session and a recap of the previous session (if applicable). This should hopefully arouse interest and link to previous learning. You could carry out a *starter activity* to gain attention and focus learning, for example, a short quiz to check previous knowledge (covered in Chapter 5). Alternatively, you could carry out a quick initial assessment question regarding what your learners already know about the topics you are going to cover. This will help you draw on their knowledge throughout the session, and relate new learning to previous and current knowledge. You can also carry out any practical matters such as taking a record of attendance, reminding learners of any important issues, and perhaps recapping the ground rules.

The development stage

The development stage is where teaching and learning will take place, it should be in a logical sequence for learning to progress. Try not to move on to a new topic until you know all your learners have understood the current topic. You could include a variety of theory and practical approaches, individual, paired and group activities to help maintain motivation and interest (covered in Chapter 5). The session isn't about you and how much talking you are doing, it's about your learners and how much learning is taking place.

You will need to engage and include your learners, perhaps by asking questions and holding discussions with them. If you don't vary your activities, your learners may become bored, lose concentration or become disruptive. Don't be afraid to try something different, for example, a paired activity instead of a group discussion. Don't assume your learners will know something, and don't expect too much from them at first. They don't know what you know and they will need time to assimilate new skills and knowledge before they fully understand it. You could plan to differentiate the activities during your session. For example, by what *all, most* and *some* learners will achieve, i.e., a wordsearch (all), a multiple-choice test (most), a crossword (some).

The conclusion stage

Your conclusion should include a summary of what has been covered and relate to the objectives. If you have time, you could ask your learners which objectives they feel they have met as this will help check their understanding.

If you have a large group, you could finish with a *closing activity*. This enables learners to attach relevance to what they have learnt (covered in Chapter 5). Always allow time for any individual questions from your learners, and to discuss any homework, self-study or other issues. You can then state what the aim of your next session will be (if applicable).

If you are unsure what to say to formally end your session, simply say, *Thank you, I've enjoyed my session with you today.* If you are due to see your learners again for another session, you could say, *Thank you, I look forward to seeing you all again on* ... Plan time at the end for clearing up; you don't want to be rushed, particularly if you have another session. You could ask your learners to help tidy up if applicable.

You might find that some learners stay behind at the end of the session to talk to you about something in confidence. If you don't have to rush to another session, your learners will probably appreciate you taking this extra time.

Activity

Watch one of the main news programmes on television. Notice how the presenters introduce the stories, then explain them in more detail and recap them at the end. Often there are two presenters, one male and one female, the camera shots change and there are videos and pictures to support the stories. They will have planned and prepared well and have a contingency plan in case anything goes wrong. This is how you could think about planning your sessions, i.e. what will go in the three stages and how you can add variety. When you watched the pro-gramme, did you take into account what the presenters looked like, how they spoke and what they were wearing? Did this distract you in any way? Do you think you might distract your learners in a subconscious way?

Newsreaders have an autocue to read from; they also have the news written on paper as a contingency plan. They will have a script which shows the timings for the news stories and who will read them. As the news is always a live programme, timings are crucial. This is just like your session, it has to follow the introduction, development and conclusion stages and complete within the allocated time.

Timings

You will need to know how long each session is to consider how much time to allocate to the various teaching, learning and assessment activities. When planning, try to use 30 per cent of the time for your teaching activities and 70 per cent of the time for learner involvement and assessment activities as in Figure 4.8. This will help keep your learners active and add variety and interest. However, this is more difficult if you are giving a lecture where you are required to speak for a certain amount of time. You could, therefore, con-sider asking questions and using quick polls or surveys to add a bit of variety.

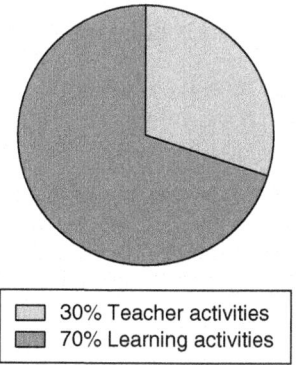

30% Teacher activities
70% Learning activities

Figure 4.8 Teaching and learning activity time

If your session includes a break, don't forget to allow time for this, and know that it takes a few minutes for learners to settle again once they return. Time will go quickly so be prepared to remove something from your plan, or reduce your timings of other activities if necessary.

When creating your plan, your timings can be expressed as actual times, e.g. 6 p.m., 6.05 p.m., and so on, or how long each activity will take, e.g. 5 minutes, 10 minutes and so on, or both. This will help as a visual reminder to where you should be at any point. Don't feel you have to adhere strictly to these. If something isn't working well, you can cut it down and increase the timing for something else. Be prepared to make changes as you progress through your session as you never know what will happen.

Example

Maya was 15 minutes into her health and social care class when the fire alarm sounded. She followed the fire drill and escorted her learners to the meeting place. Fortunately, it was a false alarm, but it had taken 30 minutes out of the session. When they all returned, Maya quickly checked her session plan to see what she could adapt without it adversely affecting the session.

Be prepared; it's better to have too much than not enough. Unused material can be carried forward to another session or given as work to be carried out during self-study time. Consider any learners who may finish tasks early: can you give them something else to do, perhaps to challenge their learning further? It's useful to have a few spare activities or worksheets just in case.

Activity

What do you need to consider when creating a session plan and why? Compare your notes to the following list.

Aspects to consider when session planning

There are a number of aspects to consider when creating your session plan. You could use the following points to help you.

- ☐ The overall aim of your session, i.e. what you expect your learners to achieve.

- ☐ Objectives, learning outcomes or tasks, i.e. how your learners will achieve your aim. Are they SMART, how do they link to the programme or qualification, in what order will you cover them and why?

- ☐ Breaks, remember to allocate time for these. If learners are late back, this will impede upon the rest of your session.

- ☐ Group composition, i.e. the details of individual learners and any specific needs to enable differentiation to take place.

- ☐ How will you introduce the session?

- ☐ Teacher activities, i.e. what you will be doing and for how long. Try and keep these to 30 per cent of the time.

- ☐ Learner activities, i.e. what your learners will be doing and for how long. How will you keep your learners motivated and interested? How will you ensure inclusion and differentiation? Do you have any spare activities in case some learners finish early, or which are at a higher level to stretch and challenge others? What could you remove or cut down on if you run out of time?

☐ Assessment activities: how will you assess that learning has taken place?

☐ Resources, i.e. what you will need to create and/or use. Do you need to check if something is available and working, arrange for any photocopies to be made, or reserve anything in advance? Do you have a contingency plan in case something doesn't work?

☐ How will you summarise the session?

You may find it useful to have your session plan visible or accessible for you to refer to and to check your timings, perhaps paper based or on an electronic device. You could highlight key words to glance quickly at as an aid to keep you focused. Alternatively, you could prepare *cue cards*, small pieces of card with key words or statements on, which you hold in your hand, or have visible close by. These can act as prompts, particularly if you have a lot of complex information to remember. If it's on a small device, you could keep hold of it as you progress through the session, perhaps if you are moving around the room. You could also revise it if you have to adjust any timings, or add notes regarding what did and didn't work. If it's stored online, be aware that if you lose the internet connection you will not be able to access your session plan.

Workshop plan

If you have a group of learners all working towards something different during the same session, a session plan could be adapted for this purpose. This will then be known as a *workshop plan*. Please see the example template in Table 4.8. The document enables you to plan what each individual learner will be working towards and how they will be assessed. This is useful if you have roll-on-roll-off learners, i.e. those who start and end on different dates. Often, a workshop might run all year round, with learners starting on a date to suit them rather than the organisation. For example, a computer workshop where learners can progress at their own pace, using different programs. They can be assessed, or entered for a test or external exam when they are ready. This poses challenges for the teacher, as they need to keep track of what each individual is doing. They also need to be adaptable, as they will not be teaching the same topic, at the same time, to all the learners. However, small group teaching could take place when required, perhaps if a few learners need to know something before they can progress further.

Workshops can include realistic working environments (RWEs) such as those for motor vehicle maintenance, hair and beauty, and catering, where learners carry out real activities for real people. They can also include simulated working environments (SWEs) where learners use workpacks and complete pre-prepared tasks to learn skills, such as computing and office practice.

Extension activity

Plan a session for at least one date from your scheme of work using a similar format to that in Tables 4.5, 4.6 or 4.7. Make sure you have an appropriate aim and suitable objectives for the level of your learners. Think about the three stages, the resources you will need, how you can differentiate, and how you will check that learning is taking place.

Table 4.8 Example workshop plan

Teacher/trainer		Date		Venue	
Programme/ Qualification		Time Duration		Number of learners	
Aim of session					
Group composition					

Name	Objectives/ learning outcomes/tasks	Learner activities	Assessment activities	Resources
Learner 1				
Learner 2				
Learner 3				
Learner 4				
Learner 5				

Individual learning plans

An individual learning plan (ILP) is similar to a scheme of work, but it's for one learner rather than a group of learners, see the example template in Table 4.9. The ILP can be updated at any time and can be used to review ongoing progress towards meeting the planned targets.

Other terms for an ILP include:

- an action plan (AP)

- an individual development plan (IDP)

- a personal learning plan (PLP)

- a personal development plan (PDP).

As soon as you know who your individual learner is and what they are aiming to achieve, you can create an ILP. When you commence your first session with an individual learner, you will go through a similar process to that which you would go through with a group.

Table 4.9 Example individual learning plan

Learner:	Teacher:
Start date:	Expected achievement date:
Programme/qualification title & level:	

Programme/qualification aims:

Results of initial and diagnostic assessments:
Learning preferences:
Individual needs and support requirements:
Resources required:

Targets:

Including any additional skills

Units/objectives/learning outcomes/tasks:	Target date	Achievement date

General comments:

Signed teacher:	Signed learner:
Date:	Date:

Reviews/updates to plan:		
Date	Teacher comments	Learner comments

Example

Imran has a new learner, Charlie, starting next week. Charlie is working towards an apprenticeship programme and will be attending off-the-job training with Imran one day a week. Imran has a copy of the apprenticeship standards so that he can discuss them with Charlie. He has planned to carry out an induction to explain about the course and will include a short icebreaker so they can get to know each other. He will also agree a few ground rules and then ask Charlie to complete an initial and diagnostic assessment. The results of the assessments will be used to agree appropriate targets and dates for the off-the-job training. Imran will also liaise with Charlie's workplace supervisor. This is to make sure the on- and off-the-job training aspects are appropriately matched to cover the topics which are relevant at the time.

The ILP should be agreed with your learner, signed and dated. If you are completing documents electronically, you will need to find out what the policy is in your organisation as to whether an email address or electronic signature is required. You could give your learner a copy or make it accessible electronically, so that they know what they will be doing and when.

Activity

If you are going to be working with individual learners, what will you need to consider when completing an ILP with them and why? Compare your notes to the following list.

Aspects to consider when completing an ILP

There are a number of aspects to consider when completing an ILP with a learner. You could use the following points to help you.

- Do your learner's expectations match those of what they will be working towards? If not, you will need to inform them why not.

- Do you need to include additional skills such as English, maths and ICT, or set targets for any other skills?

- Is there a clear link between the targets on the ILP, the teaching, learning and assessment activities, and the aims and objectives?

- Is your learner aware of the targets, what is required and by when?

- Are the targets realistic and achievable?

- Is your learner able to discuss any concerns or support needs?

- How can you use the results of initial and diagnostic assessments to support the learning process?

- Can you use regular tutorial and review sessions to discuss and update the ILP with your learner?

RARPA

If you are facilitating a programme which does not lead to a formal qualification, you will still need to plan and record your learners' targets and progress. This is known as *recognising and recording progress and achievement in non-accredited learning* (RARPA).

There are five processes to RARPA.

1. Aims – these should be appropriate to the individual or group of learners.

2. Initial assessment – this should be used to establish each learner's starting point.

3. Identification of appropriately challenging learning objectives – these should be agreed, renegotiated and revised as necessary after formative assessment, and should be appropriate to each learner.

4. Recognition and recording of progress and achievement during the programme – this should include assessor feedback, learner reflection and reviews of progress.

5. End of programme – this includes summative assessment, learner self-assessment and a review of overall progress and achievement. This should be in relation to the learning objectives, and any other outcomes achieved during the programme.

If you use the RARPA system, you will need to check what records you need to complete and maintain. There may be standard templates for you to use or you may need to design your own.

Extension activity

If you are working with learners on an individual basis, find out what documents you will need to complete. If none are available, create one similar to that in Table 4.9 and, if possible, have a go at using it with a learner. How was the experience? Would you change anything and if so, what and why?

Induction, icebreakers and ground rules

During the first session with your group, or with an individual learner, you will need to allocate time to explain the requirements of the course, and the facilities and services of the organisation. This is known as an *induction,* and is a chance for you to create a good first impression. Learners will notice aspects such as how you present yourself, how helpful and organised you are. They may make a judgement about you based on this. Therefore, try not to get too friendly or too personal, but remain professional. Once you get to know your learners after a few sessions, you could be a little less formal if it's appropriate.

What first impression would you like to portray to your learners? Will you act formally or informally, will you be serious or light-hearted? How do you think this will impact upon the learners and the learning process?

Whichever way you wish to convey yourself, you might want to remain consistent throughout all the time with your learners. Alternatively, you might want to be firmer in the early stages and then relax a little later on. Do be careful not to overstep the boundaries of your role by becoming too friendly with your learners or by joining their social networking sites.

When your learners first start, you won't want to put them off the course by talking for a long time. Therefore, the first session is a good time to introduce learners to each other (if they haven't already met), perhaps with a practical activity known as an *icebreaker*. This will help your learners to feel comfortable and enable them to get to know each other, as well as you. Establishing *ground rules* once your learners have relaxed a little will help underpin appropriate behaviour and respect throughout their time with you.

Induction

The time taken to carry out the induction process might depend upon how much information you need to cover with your learners. It could range from 10–15 minutes at the beginning of the first session, or take the whole of a session, perhaps, if initial assessments or diagnostic tests are also included in the process. You will need to carefully plan what you will cover, as you won't want to overload or confuse your learners during the early stages of their course. Don't forget to introduce yourself at the beginning, otherwise your learners might be wondering who you are and might not focus on what you are saying.

There may be some administrative aspects to be completed during the first meeting with your learners, such as filling in relevant forms. Try not to let this take over, your learners will want to leave their first session having learnt something interesting about the subject. However, if this is the case, you could name the first session an *induction session*, so that learners are aware that they won't be commencing the subject straight away.

If you have any learners who start the course later, make sure you spend some time with them to cover what they have missed and to introduce them to the other learners. Making them feel welcome and included as part of the group could help them settle in. If you can pair them with an existing learner, they will have someone they can talk to from the start.

Your organisation might have a checklist of general points for you to follow and you may need to add specific points regarding your subject. If an induction checklist isn't provided for you, you could create your own based on the example in Table 4.10. However, don't just work through it and tick each aspect off; try and make the topics interesting and relevant by including your learners when you can. Most of the information could also be included in a learner handbook, either electronic or paper based. If you have the opportunity to contribute to the handbook, an electronic version could be made in an interactive way. Maps, photos, 360 degree videos and weblinks could be included. This might be more interesting for the learners to access and use, and may help them to remember key points.

Table 4.10 Example induction checklist

Induction Checklist

Organisation

- ☐ an introduction to the teacher and the organisation
- ☐ other staff who learners might need to contact, i.e. names, roles and contact details
- ☐ tour of the site
- ☐ where to go for help and advice
- ☐ policies and procedures, for example, health, safety and security
- ☐ evacuation procedures/first aid in case of an emergency
- ☐ what learners can expect from the organisation
- ☐ what you expect from your learners (can be linked to ground rules)
- ☐ methods of keeping in touch if necessary, for example, telephone, email, online
- ☐ procedures to follow in case of absence or lateness
- ☐ enrolment/registration/form filling

Programme

- ☐ icebreaker
- ☐ ground rules
- ☐ learners' expectations
- ☐ programme/qualification details
- ☐ items learner may need to purchase such as specialist clothing and textbooks
- ☐ assessment details and target dates
- ☐ attendance dates
- ☐ break times
- ☐ coursework/self-study/homework
- ☐ appeals and complaints procedures
- ☐ provision for learning and learner support
- ☐ tutorial review procedures
- ☐ costs and methods of payment, if applicable, or access to funding
- ☐ commitment both during the programme and in learners' own time
- ☐ available resources and how to access them
- ☐ initial and diagnostic assessments
- ☐ possible guests/visiting speakers/external trips
- ☐ progression opportunities

Facilities

- ☐ toilets, refreshments, parking, smoking
- ☐ disabled access and facilities
- ☐ crèche and childcare facilities
- ☐ classrooms, training rooms and learning environments
- ☐ computer and library facilities, how to access online resources
- ☐ opening and closing times of services and buildings
- ☐ travel and transport arrangements
- ☐ how to access advice, guidance and welfare information

Activity

Devise an induction checklist regarding the information you will need to cover with your learners, i.e. the organisation, the programme and the facilities offered. Now add any specific aspects which relate to your particular subject. How can you make the induction process interesting rather than it becoming a tick list of things to do? If you are currently teaching, obtain a copy of your organisation's checklist, if there is one, and compare it with yours.

Often, the information you will need to cover during the induction might involve you talking for a long time and your learners might be become bored. You could change this by asking your learners to find things out for themselves, perhaps in pairs or small groups, and then reporting back to the full group. Alternatively, you could create a visual presentation which includes text, pictures, sounds and short videos. You could even invite a previous learner to talk to your group; they will be able to answer any questions your new learners might have, from their perspective. If you have carried out an icebreaker prior to the induction process, your learners might feel more relaxed and at ease to talk in front of their peers.

Giving your learners a copy of the induction checklist or making it available electronically, will help act as a reminder of what was covered. Often, so much information is given out during the first session that learners can easily forget some important points. You could keep a copy which has been signed and dated by each learner as a record. This will show any inspectors that the induction process actually took place.

Learners' expectations

Learners often have an expectation of what they want to achieve, or how they expect to learn and be assessed. If you can obtain this information it will help you match what they expect with the programme content. If you ask the learners and they state their expectations out loud, you could make a note perhaps on flip chart paper to refer to later. Alternatively, you could ask for their expectations as part of an icebreaker or by asking learners to write on sticky notes. If there are any expectations that will not be met for some reason, make sure you explain why this is. Sometimes, learners have a pre-conceived idea of things they expect to do during the sessions. Giving them the opportunity to mention this will enable you to say if they can be met or not. Otherwise, learners might complain that the course wasn't what they expected, so it's best to make things clear from the start. Keeping a record would be useful for you to refer to at the end of the programme. This way, you can check that your learners have had their expectations met as they might have forgotten.

Icebreakers

Some learners can be quiet, shy, nervous or apprehensive when they start a new programme or meet strangers. Carrying out an icebreaker is a good way of everyone getting to know each other and encouraging communication to take place. Some learners may already know each other, or have carried out an icebreaker with another teacher or trainer they currently have. Knowing this beforehand will help you decide upon an appropriate and suitable icebreaker to use and saves repetition. You could carry out the icebreaker before covering the induction requirements. This will encourage your learners to relax and give them the confidence to speak or ask questions in front of others. Always introduce yourself first, otherwise learners may be wondering what your name is or whether you are just someone facilitating the first session.

Icebreakers can be quite simple; for example, asking your learners to introduce themselves in front of the group. However, this can be a bit intimidating if none of the learners have met before. A way around this is to form the group into pairs and ask them to talk to each other for five minutes about their interests, reason for attending, how they are feeling and any expectations they have. They may find they have something in common and create a bond. You can then ask each person to introduce the person they have been talking to. People may not feel comfortable talking about themselves to a group of strangers, so another person introducing them might take any anxiety away.

A good idea to help you remember names is to note these down when the learners introduce each other, perhaps on a rough sketch of a seating plan. It's likely they will return to the same position next time. You could also make a note of something about them, perhaps a hobby they have mentioned which you could use in a future conversation. This shows that you are taking an interest in each learner as an individual.

If you don't have time for introductions, you could issue name badges for learners to wear or name cards to place in front of them. This acts as a visual reminder to others and helps you remember and use their name when speaking to them. The next session you have with your learners could be an opportunity to use their names when they enter the room. You could say, *'Hello Ella, hello Bill, hello Ramona ...'* as each one enters. If you get their name wrong, you could say *'I'm just trying to remember your names, hopefully I'll get it right next time'*, with a smile on your face.

More complex icebreakers can involve games or activities, but the outcome should be for your learners to relax, enjoy the activity, communicate and find out each other's names. An example is in Table 4.11 (on page 184) which you might like to adapt and use. Icebreakers can help retain attention, keep motivation high and help the group to bond and work together. All learners should be included and you will want to manage the activity carefully to ensure everyone can take part. Ascertaining in advance if anyone has any difficulties or disabilities could save any embarrassment. You may wish to include yourself in the icebreaker or just observe what is happening. If you include yourself, don't get too personal, resist the temptation to be everyone's friend by revealing personal details and try to remain professional.

Example

*Alana has a new group of 14 learners and she wants them to carry out an icebreaker which gets them moving about and talking. Her aim is to get them to find out each other's names and something about themselves. She has devised a game of **people bingo** as in Table 4.11. As a result, the learners really enjoyed finding out about each other and having some fun at the same time.*

Table 4.11 Example icebreaker

Icebreaker – People bingo All learners are to stand in an area where they can move around and mingle with everyone else. Insert **one name** in each box after talking to a learner. The same name **can** be used more than once – but you must only ask one question at a time and then move onto someone else. Shout **BINGO** when you have filled in a line, diagonal or column. If there is time, you will be told if you can then continue to fill all the boxes.				
speaks a foreign language	owns a cat	has a job	has been to Europe	has a mobile device with them
has blue eyes	doesn't like carrots	rides a motor bike	is a vegetarian or vegan (or knows someone who is)	lives within six miles of here
lives more than six miles from here	likes Chinese or Indian food	owns a dog	enjoys gardening	likes swimming
likes sport	has come here in a car	has brown eyes	is nervous about attending this course	has green eyes
has a bicycle	is going on holiday soon	has been to Africa, Asia or India	likes to get up early	is wearing something black

Energisers

Icebreakers can also be used during an established session, perhaps after a break or after lunch to help learners refocus. These are called *energisers* and can be subject-specific such as a quiz, or a fun activity or game which gets learners moving about and working together.

Ajit's learners were often a little lethargic after returning from lunch. He decided to give them an activity which would focus their concentration and keep them active. As each learner entered the room, he gave them a piece of paper with a word written on which related to the current topic. He asked them to keep walking around the room until they had thought of a sentence which used the word. Once done, they could return to their original seating position and discuss the sentence with whoever was sitting closest. This helped them to focus their knowledge regarding the topic, to move about and to talk to other learners. Ajit then gave some example sentences he had created and checked if his learners had anything similar. This then prompted a discussion about the topic which focused his learners' attention.

Whichever way you use an icebreaker or an energiser, it should be designed to be a fun and light-hearted activity to:

- build confidence

- create a suitable learning environment

- enable learners to talk confidently in front of their peers

- encourage communication, motivation, interaction, teamwork and inclusion

- establish trust and respect

- get the programme off to a good start

- help learners relax

- introduce learners to each other

- reduce apprehension and nervousness

- reduce intimidation.

Activity

Imagine you have a new group of 16 learners starting next week who have never met before. What sort of icebreaker would you use with them and why? There are many examples available online; a few websites are listed at the end of this chapter if you would like to research them.

Ground rules

Ground rules, also known as *group rules, class rules,* a *group contract* or a *learning agreement,* are boundaries and rules to help create suitable conditions within which learners (and yourself) can safely work and learn. They can help underpin appropriate behaviour and respect for everyone in the group. They can also help establish the group norms and ensure that sessions run smoothly. If rules are not set, problems might occur which could disrupt the session and lead to misunderstandings or behaviour problems. You may find that your learners welcome a set of ground rules as it can give them a sense of order and safety.

It is best to agree the ground rules during the first session with learners, perhaps after the icebreaker once everyone is feeling more relaxed. If you are working on a one-to-one basis rather than with a group, it's still useful to agree a few ground rules. This way, you should be able to maintain a professional working relationship.

Ground rules should always be discussed and negotiated with your learners rather than forced upon them. Involving your learners in the decision-making process will help give them ownership of what has been agreed. Some ground rules might be renegotiated or added to throughout the programme, such as changing break times. Others might be non-negotiable such as the health and safety requirements. These might already be stated in a learner handbook, agreement or learner contract, or be accessible via the organisation's intranet. You would need to make sure all learners have a copy, and know that they are in addition to any other rules agreed as a group. The types of ground rules you agree with your learners might depend upon their age and maturity. For example, mature learners might arrive early with the expectation of starting on time; younger learners might expect to use their mobile devices during the session.

When establishing ground rules, you will need to have an idea of what will be non-negotiable, i.e. because of organisational requirements, and what can be negotiable.

Example

Non-negotiable ground rules:

- *Be respectful towards others and the environment*
- *Follow health and safety guidelines*
- *Be ready to work and to contribute*

Negotiable ground rules:

- *Eating or drinking during sessions*
- *Use of mobile phones and electronic devices*
- *Break times*

Having a few ideas in mind before agreeing the ground rules with your learners can help you to lead a discussion. Having clear rules which everyone understands will help your learners feel comfortable and able to participate. You might like to change any negative ground rules into positive ones; for example, *no eating or drinking during sessions* could become *eat and drink outside of the session*. Ideally, you should be a role model and set a good example for your learners by not breaking any of the rules yourself. Also, if you have too many rules, learners might become over-cautious of what they can and can't do and this could affect the learning process.

If your learners attend sessions with other teachers, it is a good idea to discuss with them what was agreed to ensure consistency. You might also take your learners for other subjects and, therefore, have a core list of rules for all sessions, with some specific ones for each particular subject.

Ways to establish ground rules

One way to establish ground rules is by a process of discussion and negotiation. This could take place after a suitable icebreaker, when learners are feeling a little more relaxed. A discussion will enable your learners to recognise what is and is not acceptable, giving them a sense of ownership and responsibility when they have an idea for a rule. It also enables learners to begin working together as a group and encourages aspects such as listening, compromise and respect for others.

Alternatively, your learners could write down the rules individually, then discuss them in pairs and join into fours to create a poster or a list. One person from each group could present their ideas to the full group and agreement can then take place.

Another way would be to ask your group what has made learning difficult on previous courses they have attended. They will usually come up with answers like mobile phones ringing, people interrupting others or arriving back late from breaks. You can then use these to start creating a list to build upon with the group.

If you have learners who don't yet feel comfortable at contributing ideas for the rules, you could ask them to write something on a piece of paper anonymously. You could then collect them in and discuss which are viable or not.

Once agreed, a copy could be given to each learner or be made accessible electronically.

Ways to maintain ground rules

Keeping the ground rules visible throughout the sessions can act as a reminder of what is and is not acceptable. It can also enable them to be amended or added to as necessary. Any learners who have commenced the programme late will be able to see them. It's useful to refer to the rules at the beginning of the session and when a rule is broken. For example, if a learner is late, they must be reminded that it is a requirement that all sessions start promptly, otherwise they might not make the effort to arrive on time for subsequent sessions. If other learners see that you don't say or do anything, they will feel the ground rules have no value. You, therefore, need to be consistent with everyone. However, there might be occasions when a learner cannot help being late due, perhaps, to transport issues.

If a learner breaks a rule, you may find their peers reprimand them before you need to. You might like to ask your group to decide upon fun penalties or consequences for when a rule is broken. This could be a token penalty, perhaps donating a few coins to a group fund. Your learners can then decide what to do with the fund at the end of the programme, such as giving it to a local charity. If it's more serious, the learner's name could be written on a wall chart. A marker could be added to their name each time a rule is broken, in the hope that this visual reminder will stop them reoffending. Three points could lead to disciplinary action or removal from the session. Ultimately, you will need to find your own strategy for dealing with learners who break the rules, depending upon the age and maturity of those in the group.

If no rules have been broken by the end of a session, you could thank your learners for following them. This will act as a reminder of their existence and send a positive message to your learners.

If you can lead by example, you will help create a culture of mutual compliance which should enable effective teaching, learning and assessment to take place.

Extension activity

What methods would you use to establish ground rules with your learners? Write down a few examples of ground rules which would be non-negotiable and ones which you could negotiate. What would you do if a learner broke a ground rule?

Self-assessment checklist

Do I know about the following?

If not, re-read this chapter, or research the texts and websites listed at the end.

☐ How a curriculum is structured and why

☐ The different curriculum models

☐ What the hidden curriculum refers to

☐ How to write aims and objectives

☐ The difference between behavioural and non-behavioural objectives

☐ Qualification frameworks and levels of learning

☐ How to create a scheme of work

☐ How to create a session plan

☐ What an ILP is and how to agree one with an individual learner

☐ What information could be included as part of the induction process

☐ How to facilitate an icebreaker

☐ How to agree and maintain ground rules with learners

Summary

This chapter has explored how a curriculum is formed, and how you can plan and design a programme of learning with groups and/or individuals.

You should now be able to devise relevant aims and objectives (or tasks) to structure appropriate schemes of work, session plans, workshop plans and individual learning plans. You should also know how to devise a suitable induction programme, carry out an ice-breaker and agree ground rules with learners.

You might like to carry out further research by accessing the books and websites listed at the end of this chapter, particularly if you are working towards a higher level teaching qualification.

This chapter has covered the following topics:

- The curriculum

- Aims and objectives

- Schemes of work

- Session plans

- Individual learning plans

- Induction, icebreakers and ground rules

References and further information

Anderson, L. and Krathwohl, D.A. (2001). *Taxonomy for Learning, Teaching and Assessing: A Revision of Bloom's Taxonomy of Educational Objectives*. New York: Longman.

Bloom, B.S. (1956) *Taxonomy of Educational Objectives: The Classification of Educational Goals*. New York: McKay.

Bruner, J.S. (1966) *Towards a Theory of Instruction*. New York: WW Norton.

Dennick, R. and Exley, K. (2004) *Small Group Teaching: Tutorials, Seminars and Beyond*. Routledge: Abingdon.

Reece, I. and Walker, S. (2007) *Teaching, Training and Learning: A Practical Guide* (6th edition). Tyne and Wear: Business Education Publishers.

Tummons, J. (2012) *Curriculum Studies in the Lifelong Learning Sector*. Exeter Learning Matters.

Tyler, R.W. (1949/2013) *Basic Principles of Curriculum and Instruction*. Chicago: University of Chicago Press.

Websites

Curriculum models – https://tinyurl.com/mr5rmhn

Five-minute session plan – www.5minutelessonplan.co.uk

www.teachertoolkit.me/the-5-minute-lesson-plan/

Icebreakers – https://tinyurl.com/pubvpxv

https://tinyurl.com/z458l2y

https://tinyurl.com/msnnzo5

Objective writing (from TeachOnline) – http://tinyurl.com/qe5r3t6

Ofqual's Qualification and Component Levels (2015) – https://tinyurl.com/j6sw9pc

PEST – https://tinyurl.com/c2kz85

Post 16 Skills Plan – https://tinyurl.com/h6ukgbf

Reading list for teaching and learning – www.anngravells.com/reading-lists/teaching

RARPA – https://tinyurl.com/hmb55m5

Regulated Qualifications Framework (RQF) – https://tinyurl.com/lssm74y

The Report of the Independent Panel on Technical Education (Sainsbury Report) – https://tinyurl.com/zzkl9vu

5

Managing and facilitating learning

Introduction

Managing and facilitating learning will be your main role as a teacher or a trainer. If this is done in a passionate and enthusiastic way, it should help motivate and inspire your learners. They will then be able to understand and put into practice their newly acquired knowledge and skills.

This chapter will explore how you can work with learners in groups or on an individual basis. Various activities you could use to help them become independent and autonomous are covered, as are functional and wider skills. These skills include English, maths, and information and communication technology (ICT).

At the end of the chapter you will find a table containing examples of teaching and learning approaches and activities which you could use with learners.

This chapter will cover the following topics:

- Managing learning
- Facilitating group learning
- Facilitating individual learning
- Coaching and mentoring
- Functional skills and wider skills
- Teaching and learning approaches and activities

Managing learning

Managing the learning process will be a big part of your role; using various teaching and learning approaches and activities will help to do this. Think of these as the techniques which can enable learners to be *actively engaged* during the session and not just *passively listening* to you talking. What you use will depend upon the subject you are teaching, the context and environment you are teaching in, the length of each session and any particular learner's needs. They should be fit for purpose, i.e. to enable learning to take place. They should not be used for the sake of it or because you like to do things in a certain way. It's not about you, it's about your learners and the learning which is taking place. You can teach all you like but if your learners don't learn anything, it's meaningless. Please see Appendix 2 for a checklist to help you manage and facilitate your sessions.

When managing the learning process, you will be looking for a change in behaviour in your learners. This change might relate to the performance of a skill, the demonstration of understanding and/or a change in behaviour and attitudes. This way, you are able to see the progress and achievement your learners are making.

Formal teaching approaches include lectures, demonstrations, instruction and presentations which are usually teacher-centred, known as *pedagogy*. Informal approaches include discussions, group work, practical activities and role plays, and are usually learner-centred, known as *andragogy*. Wherever possible it's best to use a mixture of the two and vary the activities used and the time spent on each. Activities are the tasks you can use with your learners and examples are given later in this chapter. This will ensure that all learners are included and can participate, and will enable you to assess that learning is taking place.

Example

Tom teaches history and feels that although he gives a formal presentation and backs this up with handouts, his learners are not actively participating in any way. He decides to make his session more practical by introducing group discussions and role plays regarding historical events. Several learners approach him after the session to say how much they enjoyed it and how it enabled them to understand the subject more. He has also set up an online system to encourage interaction between learners outside of the sessions. He uploads videos and audio clips for learners to access and encourages online discussions regarding historical facts. He has decided to finish each session with a quiz to check the learners' knowledge in a fun way. Tom's sessions are now inclusive and active, his learners are more motivated and he can see that learning is taking place.

There is an old Chinese proverb:

I hear – I forget

I see – I remember

I do – I understand.

When you hear lots of information you may find it difficult to remember it all. If you can see something taking place that represents what you hear, you should remember more. However, if you actually carry out the task which relates to what you have heard and seen, you may well understand the full process and remember how to do it again. Doing it again, perhaps by showing someone else how to do it, will help reinforce the newly learnt skills and knowledge. These are aspects to consider for your subject when you are planning the approaches and activities to use with your learners.

Activity

Does your subject mainly relate to skills (practice), knowledge (theory) or attitudes (behaviours)? If it's practical, how can you demonstrate skills to learners in a way that enables them to practise for themselves? If it's theoretical, how can you impart knowledge in a way that shows your learners have understood? If it's to change behaviour, how can you have an impact upon your learners for this to take place?

To be a good teacher involves not only having the skills and knowledge of your specialist subject, but the ability and enthusiasm to communicate this to others. You also need to check that learning has taken place. Teaching and learning should not be in isolation from the assessment process. You can check that learning is taking place each time you are with your learners. This can simply be by observing practice or asking questions. If your learners are working towards a qualification, there will be formal methods of assessment such as an examination, assignment or an observation in the workplace. However, you can devise informal methods to use with your learners to check ongoing progress (covered in Chapter 10).

While you might be extremely knowledgeable and experienced with your subject, until you try and teach it to someone else, you won't really know if you are good at teaching or even if you will enjoy it. The starting point will be to decide what it is your learners need to know and in what order. You can then decide how you will facilitate the learning process using a variety of approaches and activities. Varying what you do during your sessions will give your learners more chances to engage with the subject. There may be times when you find that your learners know something that you don't. This is fine; don't be embarrassed as you can acknowledge your learners' input and encourage other learners to contribute too. Your learners can also learn from each other. They won't all have had the same experiences as each other; therefore, you can embrace this during your sessions.

Attention spans

An attention span is the amount of time which a learner can concentrate without being distracted. This will probably vary according to the age of your learners. Often, younger learners will concentrate less and older ones more. Being able to focus without being distracted is crucial for learning to take place.

Most healthy teenagers and adults are able to sustain attention on one thing for about 20 minutes (Cornish and Dukette, 2009, page 73). They can then choose to refocus on the same thing for another 20 minutes. This ability to renew concentration enables people to stay on task for as long as necessary. However, there are other factors to take into consideration, such as self-motivation, ability, tiredness, thirst and hunger. If a learner is really hungry, their concentration may lapse as a result. If you find your learners losing focus, ask them if there's anything distracting them, as you might be able to help resolve it, for example, opening a window if the room is too warm.

When planning what to do during your sessions, try and use several short activities to enable your learners to stay focused. If you do need to use longer activities, try and break these down into 20 minutes for each, with a chance for a discussion or something different in between.

You might find that attention spans are decreasing due to the use of modern technology. For example, searching the internet, changing television channels and using electronic devices and mobile phones can reduce concentration time. If you have learners who use electronic devices regularly, they may have reduced attention spans and need to move on to other tasks more frequently. If applicable, you could incorporate the use of their devices, for example, researching current topics online and creating a presentation regarding their findings or completing an interactive quiz (covered in Chapter 8).

Cognitive Load Theory

When planning to teach your subject, you should always consider how to maximise the learning which will take place. Cognitive Load Theory (CLT) devised by Sweller (1988) suggests that a person's working memory can only handle a limited amount of information. When teaching, you should seek to minimise the burden on working memory to maximise learning.

Sweller advocates building upon prior knowledge by activating the long-term memory first through the use of discussions and activities. This will bring information into the working memory so that it can be dealt with more easily. Another method to minimise the burden on working memory is to combine both visual and verbal information when presenting new content to learners. This is a theory which you might like to research further and try out with your learners.

Routines

Whether you are teaching groups or individuals in a classroom, the workplace or another environment, it's useful to follow a routine. This lets your learners know how you operate and helps them know what they will do and when. This could include the aspects which are carried out during the beginning, middle and ending of a session (covered in Chapter 4). For example, you could commence with a starter activity and end with a closing activity.

Starter activities

A starter activity can help to gain attention and focus learning from the start of a session. It should grab your learners' attention and make them inspired to learn and to want to participate. It should set everyone into a learning mode, yet still be meaningful. A starter activity, sometimes referred to as a *welcome activity*, can also have another use if a learner arrives late. If it's a fun activity, any learners who arrive late will realise they have missed something good. It might encourage them to arrive on time in future. However, try not to let the starter activity take up too much time, or let digression and discussions occur. If they do, you might not be able to adjust your timings for the other activities you have planned to use.

Example starter activities

Starter activities can include the following:

- a gapped handout, crossword or a puzzle to test knowledge

- a discussion about a relevant news event

- a paired/small group/full group discussion to open up thinking about the current topic

- a quiz where the group is split into teams and you ask questions, perhaps in the form of a multiple choice to ascertain knowledge about the topic to be taught

- asking learners in pairs or small groups to devise a question based on what they think will be covered during the session. They can then ask the question at the end of the session to another pair or small group (as a closing activity).

You may need to carry out a quick debrief regarding the starter activity if it is not apparent why you used it.

Activity

Design a starter activity to use with your learners. It should aim to grab their attention and make them want to learn more. If possible, use the activity and evaluate how effective it was. What would you change and why?

Progressing through the session

When commencing a session, if you are unsure what to say to gather your learners' attention, start with *Welcome to the session, today we will ...* in a louder than normal but assertive voice. This should gain the learners' attention and enable you to introduce the starter activity.

When progressing from the starter activity to the main body of the session, make sure you have recapped any previous session, and then inform your learners what it is that will be covered during this session. It's useful to have a session plan to guide you and to state the aim and objectives (covered in Chapter 4). Always check if your learners have any prior knowledge and/or experience of the current topic. This can simply be done by asking questions; you can then draw upon this as you progress through the session. Never assume your learners know or don't know something, always check.

If you are nervous, breathe deeply and pause for a second or two; it might seem a long time to you but it won't to your learners. Focus your thoughts, relax and enjoy what you are doing. A tip if nerves do take over is to place your tongue on the roof of the inside of your mouth for a few seconds, no one will notice and you should feel better.

As you continue with your planned approaches and activities, allow time for questioning and for repeating and reinforcing important points. Only move on when you are sure your learners have understood the current topic. Incorporate the knowledge and experience of your learners and, if you can, give relevant anecdotes to bring the subject to life. Try and relate what you are teaching to how the learners will benefit from it.

Try and ensure your session flows progressively, i.e. is delivered in a logical order and assesses progress before moving on. When changing topics, try to link them together somehow or summarise one before moving on to the other. Break aspects down into smaller manageable chunks. For example, if you are teaching a learner how to spell the dog breed of Chihuahua, break it down into three small chunks, i.e. Chi, hua, hua.

Try not to use the word *obvious* as things are only obvious to you. Show interest, passion and enthusiasm for your subject and encourage your learners to take pride in their work. Use tone and inflection to emphasise key points and don't be afraid of silent pauses; they will give you time to refocus and give your learners time to consider what you have said. Use eye contact when you can and use your learners' names as this shows you are interested in them as individuals. You might want to move around the room rather than stay in the same position at the front. This will give you a chance to check that your learners are focused and shows them you are in control.

If you feel you are overrunning on your timings, don't be afraid to carry something over to the next session, cut it out altogether, or give it as homework or self-study material. Alternatively, you can adjust the timings of the other activities to reduce or increase them as necessary. Don't feel you must keep to the number of minutes you have written on your session plan for each activity. It's more important to ensure learning is taking place than to keep to your timings. If your learners tend to ask lots of questions and you are running short of time, ask them to write them on a piece of paper or a sticky note. You can collect them in and address them at the end of the session or at the beginning of the following session. If your learners have access to an online learning environment, you could post your responses on there.

When you summarise at the end of the session, try not to introduce anything new as this might confuse your learners. However, you should explain what will be covered in the next session (if applicable) and make clear what homework or self-study activities the learners need to do. You should allow some time for questions from your learners and then you can finish with a closing activity if you wish.

Try not to end a session with 'Does anyone have any questions?' as often only those who are keen or confident will ask. This doesn't tell you what has been learnt and might exclude some learners who might be shy, or do not want to embarrass themselves in front of the group. If you want to ask questions, try the *pose, pause, pick* method (covered in Chapter 10). This will enable all learners to think of a suitable response.

Closing activities

Closing activities are useful if you find you have some spare time towards the end of your session, or if you want to establish it as part of your normal routine. They are short activities to enable learners to attach relevance to what they have learnt. If a learner has to leave a few minutes early for any reason, they might only miss the closing activity rather than any important points.

You could hold a quiz by placing your learners in small groups and letting them confer on the answers. You could prepare and ask five questions based on the topic just learnt. A point could be allocated to the winning team and points built up throughout the programme. Some sort of reward could be given to the winning team at the end of the programme, or they might just like the fact they have received the most points. This method could be a fun way of closing the session and is also a good way to informally assess learning has taken place.

You could be adventurous and ask your learners to come up with an idea for a closing activity. You will need to give them time to think about this, and could even create a starter activity based on the learners devising a closing activity. If you did this, you would need to guide your learners with their ideas, which could then be used over several sessions.

Example closing activities

Closing activities can be similar to opening activities and include the following:

- a gapped handout, crossword or a puzzle to test knowledge gained during the session

- a question to each learner in turn to ask for one aspect from the session that has had the most impact upon their learning

- a question to each learner in turn to say one word that sums up the session for them. If there is time, you can ask them to explain why, or to use more words

- a question to pairs or small groups to come up with one way of putting the new learning into practice

- a quiz where the group is split into teams and you ask questions, perhaps in the form of multiple choice to ascertain knowledge about the topic covered

- asking learners to create their own summary to the session and to present it in turns throughout the programme – within a strict time limit

- asking learners to state which objectives they have met

- asking pairs or small groups to review what has been covered during the session and to decide on one question to ask another pair or group.

If you are short of time, but still want to carry out a closing activity, you could carry out one of the following:

- ask the learners to write a question or a comment on a piece of paper and hand it to you on the way out. You could then respond to them at the beginning of the next session

- stand at the door and ask the learners to say one word or phrase that sums up the session for them, on their way out

- ask learners to close their eyes and then rate how much they feel they have learnt from the session by holding up their hand – on a scale of 1–5 where one finger denotes not a lot and five fingers denote a lot. Doing it with eyes closed removes any peer pressure.

Extension activity

Design a closing activity to use with your learners. Use the activity and evaluate how effective it was. What would you change and why?

Discuss with a colleague how can you can gain the attention of your learners at the commencement of the session and maintain their motivation to learn through to the end. What do you think will impact upon how you manage the learning process and what can you do about it?

Facilitating group learning

A group is often considered as being three learners or more. One learner is an individual, two learners are a pair. Groups of learners are usually based in an educational environment which is fit for purpose, such as a classroom, conference room or seminar room. Individuals are usually in their own normal working environment or a room suitable for individual teaching or training. However, you might have a group of learners but, at some point during the session, work with an individual learner on a one-to-one basis. This could be if they need some extra support to understand a topic or a task.

When working with a group of learners, you will need to accept that this is a collection of individuals, each with different needs and wants. Individuals often behave differently in a group situation from when they are with others on a one-to-one basis. Group dynamics can change; for example, when new learners start a course later than others, when the venue or seating arrangements alter or if there are personality clashes between learners.

Always make late starters welcome and perhaps buddy them with another learner so that they don't feel alone. Try and make sure you include everyone at some point during each session. This can be by talking to them individually, using eye contact, using their name and asking questions. If learners always sit in the same place each time they are with you, it might not give them the opportunity to get to know the rest of the group. If you explain when the learners start the course that you will move them around regularly, they will come to accept it.

Working with groups can have limitations, for example:

- higher level learners might feel they are not being stretched and challenged enough

- interruptions, distractions and behaviour issues could impede progress

- learners could be excluded by their peers

- learners could digress from the task

- learners could finish an activity before others, resulting in nothing to do

- lower level learners could fall behind

- peer pressure could occur

- personality clashes might happen

- some learners may dominate or others might not take part

- the dynamics might change as the course progresses and some learners gain more confidence.

It takes practice to control a group and to deal with any situations as they happen. You might like to arrange to observe an experienced teacher or trainer to see how they manage their groups.

Individual personalities and the roles learners take on when part of a group may impede the success or the achievement of the task. There are many theories regarding how people act when part of a group; here briefly are two of them.

Belbin's team roles

Belbin (2010, page 23) defined team roles as: ... *a tendency to behave, contribute and interrelate with others in a particular way*. Belbin's research identified nine clusters of behaviour, each of which is termed a *team-role*. Each team-role has a combination of strengths which the individual contributes to the team, as well as allowable weaknesses. It's important to accept that people do have weaknesses; therefore, if you can focus on their strengths you will be able to help manage these. Please see Table 5.1 (on page 200) for the contributions and allowable weaknesses of each team role.

The nine team-roles are grouped into *action, people* and *cerebral* roles:

- action-oriented roles: Shaper, Implementer and Completer Finisher

- people-oriented roles: Co-ordinator, Teamworker and Resource Investigator

- cerebral roles: Plant, Monitor Evaluator and Specialist.

You might notice your learners taking on one or more of these roles while working together on a group activity.

Sometimes groups or teams become problematic, not because their members don't know what they are doing, but because they have problems accepting, adjusting and communicating with each other as they take on different roles. Knowing that individuals within teams take on these different roles will help you to manage group work more effectively. For example, if a group of learners need to work together on a project, you could make sure there is a mixture of the *action, people* and *cerebral* roles within the group.

Table 5.1 Team Role Summary Descriptions, reprinted with kind permission from www.belbin.com

Team Role	Contribution	Allowable Weaknesses
Plant	Creative, imaginative, free-thinking. Generates ideas and solves difficult problems.	Ignores incidentals. Too preoccupied to communicate effectively.
Resource Investigator	Outgoing, enthusiastic, communicative. Explores opportunities and develops contacts.	Over-optimistic. Loses interest once initial enthusiasm has passed.
Co-ordinator	Mature, confident, identifies talent. Clarifies goals. Delegates effectively.	Can be seen as manipulative. Offloads own share of the work.
Shaper	Challenging, dynamic, thrives on pressure. Has the drive and courage to overcome obstacles.	Prone to provocation. Offends people's feelings.
Monitor Evaluator	Sober, strategic and discerning. Sees all options and judges accurately.	Lacks drive and ability to inspire others. Can be overly critical.
Teamworker	Co-operative, perceptive and diplomatic. Listens and averts friction.	Indecisive in crunch situations. Avoids confrontation.
Implementer	Practical, reliable, efficient. Turns ideas into actions and organises work that needs to be done.	Somewhat inflexible. Slow to respond to new possibilities.
Completer Finisher	Painstaking, conscientious, anxious. Searches out errors. Polishes and perfects.	Inclined to worry unduly. Reluctant to delegate.
Specialist	Single-minded, self-starting, dedicated. Provides knowledge and skills in rare supply.	Contributes only on a narrow front. Dwells on technicalities.

© BELBIN® 2012   'BELBIN®' is a registered trademark of BELBIN UK.   www.belbin.com

Tuckman's Group Formation theory

Tuckman (1965) devised a Group Formation theory of *forming, storming, norming* and *performing*. This was amended in the mid-1970s to add *adjourning* (also known as *mourning* or *deforming*). There have been various adaptations of this theory over time, which you might like to research further.

Tuckman advocated that groups go through different stages to reach their conclusion. These are:

Forming – this is the *getting to know you* and *what shall we do* stage. Individuals may be anxious and need to know the boundaries and code of conduct within which the team will work.

Storming – this is the *it can't be done* stage. It's where conflict can arise, rebellion against the leader or another person can happen and disagreements may take place.

Norming – this is the *it can be done* stage. This is where group cohesion takes place and norms are established. Mutual support is offered, views are exchanged and the group co-operates to work towards the task.

Performing – this is the *we are doing it* stage. Individuals feel safe enough to express opinions and there is energy and enthusiasm towards achieving the task.

Adjourning – this is the *we will do it again* stage. The task is complete and the group separates. Members often leave the group with the desire to meet again or to keep in touch.

Being aware of the stages that groups go through, and informing your learners that this might occur, could help you all see why things happen the way they do. Depending upon the activity, the stages might happen over a short- or a long-term time frame. You might even see all the stages occur during one activity where the learners have a tight deadline. Alternatively, you might have a group of learners which gets stuck at one of the stages and you will need to intervene to help them move on.

Activity

Plan an activity that your learners could carry out in small groups. If possible, carry it out and watch how the team develops through Tuckman's stages. How many stages did they go through and was the activity achieved within the time allocated? Did you have any learners who were disruptive or worked well with some learners and not others? If so, what could you do next time to ensure everyone is performing on task? If you have the opportunity, observe another group activity and watch for learners taking on one or more of Belbin's team roles.

Managing and facilitating small group activities

If an activity is to be carried out in small groups, knowledge of your learners will help you decide if they have the maturity to team up themselves or whether you need to group them. If it's the former, you might find the same learners group together each time, i.e. those they get along with. If it's the latter, you might like to decide who will work with whom to help learners get to know others. You could decide by aspects such as: learning preferences; levels of ability; knowledge and experience; or just randomly. If you are carrying out several activities, you could mix your learners in a way that gives them the opportunity to work with everyone over time. Try not to do anything that could be conceived as stereotyping, e.g. grouping males separately from females, or older learners separately from younger ones. Groups of four to six are a good size for learners to have the opportunity to work together and achieve the task. If you ask particular learners to create their own groups by choosing their peers in front of everyone, it could cause problems. For example, those learners left until last to be chosen might feel that they were not wanted. If you have an odd number of learners, resist the temptation to be part of one of the groups yourself, as this could give an unfair advantage to them. It would also mean you might lose the overview of what other learners are doing. It's fine to have some groups with more learners than others, as this can be addressed when another activity takes place. You might find it useful to keep a note of who has worked with who over time.

You will need to be careful of learners with strong personalities as they might dominate and change the group dynamics. Equally, you will need to make sure quiet or shy learners are able to participate and are not excluded in any way. It would be good to agree some ground rules for small group activities. For example, respecting others' opinions and not speaking over someone else.

Whenever you set a group activity or a task, make sure you give very clear instructions regarding what you want your learners to do, how they will achieve it and how you will assess them. You could leave the instructions on display somewhere as a visual reminder or give them as a handout. You will need to set a time limit and you might find it useful to remind learners at regular points how long they have left. If the activity counts towards the achievement of a qualification, you will need to make the decision as to how each individual learner has met the requirements.

If your learners need any particular resources to carry out an activity, you will need to make sure they are prepared in advance, such as handouts or instruction leaflets. If something isn't available or is not working, it will take time to sort out and your learners will be left with nothing to do while waiting. However, if this does happen, ask your learners to discuss the current topic until you are ready.

While your learners are busy working in their groups, you might like to move around them, watching and listening to what is taking place. If you feel a learner is taking over, you will need to prompt them to let someone else have a say. If a learner is not participating, you will need to prompt them to become involved. Alternatively, you could move learners to different groups while the activity is taking place. If you are going to do this, pre-warn your learners it might happen. Otherwise, they might get defensive and not move. Try and observe that the learners are staying on task and are not digressing. If they do, re-focus them back to the activity, point out the instructions and inform them how much time they have left. Some learners might ask you questions regarding the activity or need clarification. Try not to lead them in any way that gives them an unfair advantage over the other groups. Instead, ask them some questions to get them thinking and discussing the task themselves. You can then do this with the other groups so that you are being fair to all.

If a group finishes early, you might find it useful to have something pre-prepared that they can do. Otherwise, they might become talkative, disruptive and noisy. You could ask them to discuss a particular topic among themselves, give them some reading and/or research to carry out, or ask them to help another group which has not finished yet. However, the latter might change the group dynamics.

If a member of each group will need to report back to the full group at the end of the activity, you will need to decide who this will be or leave it to the learners to decide. If it's the latter, a confident learner might volunteer or no one might volunteer. The person reporting back could also be the group leader, whose role is to keep the group on task, or it could be another learner. If you choose a different learner each time, all learners will get the chance to carry out the roles. If the activity involves making notes, you will need to decide if this will be the group leader, the person reporting back or another learner. If these roles are not clear from the start, time could be wasted. You could keep a note of who has carried out each role over time.

Concluding group activities

When the time is drawing to an end, prompt the groups to finish what they are doing. If a group asks for more time when all the others have finished, it would not be fair to give it. However, if all the groups have not finished, you could decide to extend the activity and then adjust the rest of your session timings accordingly.

If the groups have a nominated person who will report back to the full group, check that they are ready to do this. Reporting back might simply be by the group leader staying in their current position (sitting or standing) and speaking out loud, or moving to the front of the room. Alternatively, all members of the group could be involved in delivering a presentation. If technology is available, learners could use it to create a summary of the activity, for example, via an interactive whiteboard. You will need to decide the order in which the group leaders will report back, and allocate a time limit to how long they can take.

It's always useful to carry out a debrief of the activity and provide feedback to each group whether they met the objective or not. Your feedback could be focused on each group's ability to achieve the task, as well as the individual contributions each learner has made.

Facilitating an event

Your role might include facilitating short events, as well as, or instead of, full programmes of learning. You might never have visited the venue where it will take place or even have met your learners. Finding out where the venue is and what facilities are available is useful. You might need to see where power sockets are, test presentation equipment, order refreshments and/or arrange the seating in a certain way.

Sending out some pre-event materials can often be useful. This can include a copy of the programme, details of where the venue is, what refreshments (if any) are provided, availability of wifi, transport links and parking details. The clearer you can be the better, so that you are not inundated with questions. You might even want your learners to prepare something in advance or carry out some work before attending. It would be useful to give your learners a contact name, email address and telephone number just in case of queries.

It's useful to have a sign-in sheet ready, and to be available to meet everyone as they arrive. You might like to give people a name badge to wear and ask them to introduce themselves to the person they sit next to as they take their places. If you only have a list of names of who will attend, you won't know anything about your learners, what their prior knowledge or experience is and what they wish to gain from the event. You could carry out a quick initial assessment at the beginning of the session, perhaps as a starter activity. However, this will take time. Alternatively, you might be able to get in touch with them beforehand to find this out. The more detail you have before the event starts, the better able you will be to facilitate the learning process to meet their requirements.

You could carry out certain *housekeeping* aspects at the commencement of the session. This might include stating the times of breaks, where certain facilities can be accessed such as toilets and refreshments, along with information regarding fire procedures, facilities for smokers and how to access wifi. If you can deliver this information with humour, and not take too long about it, you will help retain your learners' attention. You might wish to agree a few ground rules, such as switching mobile devices to vibrate and taking calls out of the room if they are urgent.

Example

Agatha introduced herself to the group. She then explained the times of the breaks, where the toilets are and where smokers could go. She gave details of what refreshments would be provided and when, and what to do in case of an emergency. She did this by pretending to be a flight attendant and waving her arms to show where the exits are. She then told everyone that they could keep their mobile devices on if they wished, providing they were set to silent. She then jokingly said, 'Now that we've got that out of the way, we can take flight'.

Using humour, as in this example, can help people relax at the commencement of a session.

If your learners have been asked to attend an event, they might not be as self-motivated as if they had chosen to attend for themselves. Some learners might have firm expectations of what they want to gain by attending. If you haven't been able to ascertain these beforehand, you could ask them to write them on a sticky note which you can collect in and stick to a wall or board. When you have an opportune moment, you could look through them to see what you can or can't address. Sticky notes are also useful for learners to write questions on throughout the event, perhaps if there is not enough time for questions, or if some learners are shy about talking in front of others. You can collect them in and respond to the questions towards the end.

You could end the session by revisiting the original expectations. If you haven't been able to meet any, state why. It could be that some requests were unreasonable as they did not relate to the programme. You could then ask everyone to set themselves an action point. For example, 'How will you benefit from what you have learnt today?' or 'How will you put theory into practice back at work?' The learners could state this out loud, write it down or email it to themselves and copy you in. If it's the latter, you could email each person in about a month's time to see how they are getting on. You could also issue an evaluation form or a link to an online survey to gain feedback. You, or your organisation might want to give the learners a record of attendance. This is proof they attended the event but is not proof of what was achieved.

When everyone has left, make sure you leave the room tidy, collect in any feedback forms and keep the attendance list. You will need to analyse the feedback you have received, with a view to making improvements for the next time (covered in Chapter 12).

Team-teaching

Team-teaching (or co-teaching) is useful when a new teacher commences their role, as they can have the support of an experienced teacher until they feel confident. It's also useful when working with large groups of learners. However, it can prove costly to have two or more people take a session together on a long-term basis.

If you are team-teaching a session with a colleague, you will need to plan in advance which aspects will be covered by whom, and who will deal with any questions or issues. Hopefully you will know the person you are working with and you will both be able to utilise each other's strengths. You might decide one of you will introduce the session and the other will close the session, with you both taking in turns for the different topics and activities throughout. You will need to plan the session together and decide who will create and copy any necessary resources and materials.

Team-teaching takes practice as personalities and delivery styles may differ. However, it is useful where a complex subject is being taught as different delivery techniques can be used. The experience and knowledge of the different teachers can be drawn upon. The teachers don't have to agree on everything, they can instigate discussions and debates to challenge the learners. If you don't get along with the person with whom you are team-teaching, you will need to put any differences aside. You don't have to like them; you just have to be professional at what you do for the sake of your learners. There's no point deliberately interrupting them or embarrassing them as this won't look good, and you might lose the respect of your learners. However, you do need to take some risks and be open minded when working with someone else.

Extension activity

Imagine you are due to facilitate a six-hour one-day event with 30 people you have never met before. You will be team-teaching with a colleague you have never worked with. The session plan and all the resources and materials have been designed for you. There are four different small group activities of 30 minutes each to be carried out during the day. How would you prepare for the event and manage the session and group activities? All you know is the learners' names and email addresses. How could you work effectively with your colleague to give a good experience to the group?

Facilitating individual learning

Working with an individual on a one-to-one basis may sound like the ideal teaching approach. If the learner is motivated and you both get on well, a professional working relationship can help learning to take place. However, if your learner is not very motivated and/or you don't both get on well, things could be different. You will need to be professional and ensure that your time with each learner is meaningful. You will be spending quite a lot of time together and although this will enable you both to get to know each other well, you must not blur the boundaries of your role. It could be easy to get too personal or too friendly by discussing things which are not connected to the learning programme.

Individuals often act differently depending upon the situation and the other people they are with at the time. How you and your learner act towards each other might also be different depending upon the context, environment or circumstances you are in. Different issues will arise when teaching or training an individual, as opposed to working with groups. It takes practice to remain focused upon the topic and the learning taking place, without giving the individual an inappropriate amount of attention and support.

When you commence your first session with an individual learner, you will probably go through a similar process to that which you would go through with a group. For example, carry out an induction, icebreaker, agree ground rules, and complete an initial and diagnostic assessment. The results of these can form the foundation of what your learner needs to work towards. When working with an individual, you could use an individual learning plan (ILP) as in Chapter 4 Table 4.9. This will help you to structure the learning process.

Task analysis

To help you plan an individual session with a learner, perhaps if you are covering one topic rather than a series of topics, you could devise a *task analysis*. This is sometimes referred to as a *skill's analysis* or *critical path analysis*. This enables you to break down the topic into smaller stages. It's useful if you are training someone in a practical skill, perhaps on-the-job or in a workshop. It's useful to have an aim and objectives to help you plan the steps involved.

Example

Aim: the learner will print double-sided copies of a document using a photocopier. The objectives would then be all the smaller stages which the learner will carry out to achieve the aim. Assessment would be by observation and questions, and the resources would be the photocopier and the printing paper.

Sometimes, it's hard to break down a topic into smaller relevant stages, and to plan how to check progress along the way. Although you will be experienced with the topic, it might be easy to forget something or to do things in the wrong order. Using a template like the one in Table 5.2 might help you to plan the steps involved. It will enable you to list the objectives, i.e. all the smaller stages, in the order in which you will demonstrate them. You can then include the knowledge which you will need to impart as you demonstrate each practical step. If you wish, you can adapt the template to add how you will assess your learner, along with timings for each step.

Table 5.2 Example task analysis template

Task			
Aim		**Resources**	
Step	**Objectives (practical steps)**	**Knowledge required**	
1			
2			
3			

Activity

Imagine you are training a learner to make a cup of tea (the aim) and they have never done this before. Using the aspects as in Table 5.2, write down all the smaller practical steps (the objectives) that your learner will need to do. If you can, ask a colleague or a friend to do the same. Compare what you have both produced. Did you miss anything out or get something in the wrong order? Many people carrying out this activity start with switch the kettle on. *However, the learner would need to know what a kettle is, where it is, whether water is already in it, how to add more water, where the tap is to get the water, whether they take the kettle to the tap or use a jug of water to fill it and so on. You can see that the list of the smaller stages could be quite long. Other aspects such as health and safety would also need to be included as you wouldn't want the learner to scald themselves.*

Some practical tasks can be quite complex. Breaking them down into smaller stages, with an explanation of each, can make them much easier for a learner to be able to do and understand. You could demonstrate the task first and then ask your learner to carry it out. You will then be able to see if they can do it and ask questions to check their knowledge and understanding.

EDIP

EDIP is an acronym for **E**xplain, **D**emonstrate, **I**mitate and **P**ractice. Allen's (1919) four-step training method was originally devised for training shipyard workers in the USA. It is now widely used by the British and American forces and is a useful method when teaching a practical subject. It can be used when training groups or individuals although it's particularly useful for the latter.

- **E**xplain clearly to your learner in words they can understand, all the main points of the task you are about to demonstrate and why. Keep the points brief and simple.

- **D**emonstrate the task slowly so that your learner can see exactly what you are doing.

- **I**mitate. Demonstrate the task again and this time ask your learner to mirror and copy what you do at the same time. Reiterate the main points as you progress.

- **P**ractise. Ask your learner to carry out the task on their own. Correct any errors and answer any questions they might have.

This method isn't very flexible as it was designed to get people performing a task quickly. It doesn't allow for a two-way conversation. However, if you wish to use this method you could include questioning.

With EDIP, learners might be able to learn and perform a task quickly, but not really understand why they are doing it. If you are delivering a practical training session to an individual, make sure you have a clear aim of what you want them to do and objectives that will enable them to achieve it. You can then go through a logical process to demonstrate the activity, followed by both of you doing it together, and then your learner doing it on their own. Think of this as *I do it, we do it, you do it*. EDIP is quite a formal method of demonstrating a task; however, you could adapt it to suit your circumstances. For example, you could add another stage so that the learner demonstrates the task to someone else as in Figure 5.1. This gives the learner the opportunity to try out the task more than once. If the task will become part of their job role, they may need to try it out several times before they become fully competent.

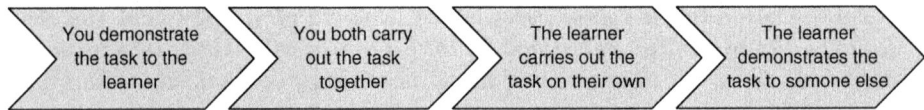

Figure 5.1 Stages of demonstrating a task to an individual

The following checklist might help you when planning to demonstrate a practical task to a learner.

Checklist for demonstrating a task

- ☐ *Make sure you know what you are doing. You might want to use a task analysis which shows how the activity is broken down into logical steps.*

- ☐ *Position yourself so that your learner can see what you are doing, check if they are left- or right-handed.*

- ☐ *State the aim and objectives, set these in context, i.e. why the learner is doing it and how they will benefit from it.*

- ☐ *If your learner is going to make something, show an example of the finished item so that they can see what they are aiming towards.*

☐ Help make your learner feel at ease by talking to them and asking if they have ever done anything like this before. If they have, you can discuss and build on their knowledge – go from the known to the unknown.

☐ Demonstrate the task, explaining as you go along but don't overload your learner with too much information. You will know your topic well, but this might be the first time your learner has seen or heard about it. Don't rush, and look at your learner regularly to check they are watching what you are doing.

☐ Gauge any learner reactions and respond accordingly.

☐ Encourage your learner to ask questions throughout.

☐ When you have finished, ask your learner to explain what you have just done. This will help you know if they have forgotten anything. If they really did not understand the task, you might need to demonstrate it again.

☐ If possible, both of you can then carry out the task together. Give them time to think, don't rush them. You could have a handout or pictures and text for your learner to refer to as they progress.

☐ When they have finished alongside you, ask some questions to check their understanding.

☐ Finally, ask your learner to demonstrate the task on their own. Ask questions as they are doing it and let them learn from their mistakes if it's safe to do so. Don't be tempted to do anything for them. You could ask them to talk through what they are doing as they perform it.

☐ When they have finished, ask your learner how they think they have done. This can promote self-assessment and help them realise what they might have done wrong.

☐ Make a decision as to their competence and provide feedback.

☐ Agree on any development points.

☐ If another person is available, you could ask your learner to demonstrate the task to them. This will give them further experience and help you see how they are performing.

☐ Relate the task to the job role or the next aspect of the learning programme.

Extension activity

Think of a practical task which you could demonstrate to an individual learner for your specialist subject. Ensure you have a clear aim and objectives. You might like to use a task analysis to ensure you don't miss anything out. If possible, carry out the activity with a learner and evaluate how effective the process was. What would you change and why?

Coaching and mentoring

Coaching and mentoring might form part of your job role, but how do these roles differ from being a teacher or a trainer? You could think of coaching as giving practical training in the short term, and mentoring about giving advice and support in the long term. Both of these roles could be considered part of teaching or training depending upon the context in which you work. Opportunities for coaching and mentoring might occur naturally: for example, demonstrating a task to a learner in the workplace (coaching) or guiding a learner how to search for employment opportunities (mentoring). Both roles should be about helping the learner to become as independent and autonomous as possible.

Coaching could occur with more than one learner at the same time and usually relates to skills, knowledge and understanding. Mentoring is usually carried out on a one-to-one basis and relates to knowledge and understanding.

It's useful to treat the coaching and mentoring roles in a similar way to the teaching or training roles. It's a good idea to carry out an induction and initial assessment and to agree a few ground rules. You could adapt an individual learning plan to become a coaching or a mentoring plan. It could include aims, objectives, targets and timescales and be updated as the learner progresses. Coaching and mentoring could occur spontaneously as the need arises, or be planned for certain dates and times. Both roles require patience and good communication skills.

Example

Ainsley, Brian's mentor, is due to meet him for the first time next week. As they both work in the same organisation, they are aware of each other but do not know each other well. They have agreed to meet for an hour to discuss what Brian would like to gain from the mentoring process. This will help Ainsley recognise the areas he can help and guide Brian with. Future meetings will then follow a plan.

Learners should be encouraged to think for themselves, reach their own decisions and set their own action points. Sessions should always end on a positive note, with both parties knowing what will happen next. If at any stage the relationship breaks down to an irrecoverable point, the learner should be referred to someone else.

There will come a point when the learner is totally independent and no longer needs the coach or mentor. This is good and means the learner is now confident and knowledgeable to carry out their role on their own.

There is not enough room in this book to explore coaching and mentoring in detail. There are many good textbooks available and links to these are listed at the end of this chapter.

What do you consider to be the differences between coaching and mentoring? Research definitions online and in textbooks to find out about different models and theories. You could also discuss them with a colleague or friend to see what they think.

Advantages and disadvantages to the roles

Both roles can have similar advantages and disadvantages.

Advantages

- A professional working relationship can be built up over time.

- It can be formal or informal and occur as and when needed.

- The learner has someone to go to if they have any concerns, problems or just need someone to talk to.

- The learner might progress more quickly with the right coaching/mentoring.

- The coach/mentor can act as a source of expertise, be an impartial listener, provide advice and guidance and help the learner to explore issues for themselves.

- The coach/mentor can facilitate access to different experiences, activities and people.

- The pace and approach of learning can be geared to the needs of the learner.

- The process can improve the confidence of the learner.

Disadvantages

- If unsupervised, the learner might make mistakes which could be dangerous.

- It can be time consuming.

- Resources and equipment may need to be prepared in advance.

- The learner may become dependent or reliant on the coach/mentor and not think things through for themselves.

- The learner might need support when the coach/mentor is not available.

- The learner might not feel that they can question or disagree with the coach/mentor.

- The learner might not feel that they want to do what the coach/mentor has advised.

- The coach/mentor might be frustrated if the learner does not take their advice.

- The learner might not find out different ways of performing the task, having only ever been shown one way to do it.

- The coach/mentor and the learner might not get on.

- The coach/mentor might have been assigned to the learner rather than being the right person for the role; therefore, they do not take it seriously.

- The coach/mentor might resent the learner for the amount of their time they take up.

Extension activity

Imagine you are an experienced teacher who has been in the role for five years. A new teacher has just commenced and you have been allocated to them as their mentor (or coach if you wish). What would you do first and why? How could you encourage the new teacher to become confident, knowledgeable and independent over time?

Functional skills and wider skills

Functional skills consist of English, maths, and information and communication technology (ICT). English includes other terms such as language and literacy, and maths includes the term numeracy. Depending upon which country you work in, these skills might be called something else such as Basic Skills, Skills for Life, Key Skills, Core Skills or Essential Skills. They are designed to help learners to function confidently, effectively and independently in life and at work. Qualifications are available in England for the functional skills, which could be taken additionally, or as part of a learning programme such as an apprenticeship.

Wider skills is the term used for the skills which are associated with education, employment and life in general. They include: Working with Others, Improving Own Learning and Performance, and Problem Solving. They are skills which can be transferred to different situations and contexts to help a learner progress further. They are often referred to as *transferable skills*.

Whenever possible, you should try and embed functional and wider skills during your sessions. This will hopefully increase the learners' employability and career aspirations. However, you might feel some of your own skills need improving first; therefore, you could partake in further training yourself. If you are not competent you will not set a good example to your learners. For example, if you spell words wrongly in a handout, have difficulty making calculations or can't use a digital device, your learners may lose confidence in you. Teachers should be able to demonstrate the *minimum core* personal skills of language, literacy, numeracy and ICT (covered in Chapter 14). You should have enough knowledge to make the skills relevant to the subject. For example, maths doesn't have to be about complex equations, it can be about using numerical skills such as planning a household budget, working out the cost of a shopping list, calculating the amount of paint needed to decorate a room, or comparing gas and electricity prices.

Functional skills

Functional skills are designed to help learners to:

- apply their knowledge and understanding to everyday life

- engage competently and confidently with others

- solve problems in both familiar and unfamiliar situations

- develop personally and professionally as positive citizens who can actively contribute to society.

Rather than treating the skills as separate subjects, try and embed them as part of the specialist subject. This will help your learners to engage with real situations in the subject area. Opportunities might arise naturally or you might need to be creative and imaginative.

Example

Sanjay is due to teach a catering course and plans to improve his learners' functional skills as follows:

English (language) – discussing recipes, talking and listening to others, planning and creating a menu.

English (literacy) – reading recipes, researching and reading healthy eating magazines and books, writing a list of ingredients, designing posters to promote and sell the finished products.

Maths (numeracy) – calculating weights and costs of ingredients, measuring amounts, estimating calorific values, cooking times and temperatures, dealing with money to buy ingredients and to sell completed products, working out profit margins.

ICT – using a word processor to produce the menu, researching relevant websites, emailing other learners, creating and giving presentations using an electronic whiteboard, creating a podcast, making videos, taking photos of the finished products and uploading them to a virtual learning environment (VLE), website, app or electronic portfolio, using social media to promote and sell the products.

In this example, the learners will naturally have the opportunity to use English, maths and ICT skills without realising they have been embedded. A discussion could take place afterwards to ascertain if the learners realised how they had used the different skills. If you are struggling to think how you can embed the skills, you could ask your learners how they feel the various skills could be used as part of the subject.

Other ways of helping learners utilise these skills can include making deliberate mistakes and asking your learners to look for them. For example, you could make five spelling mistakes which your learners need to look out for during a presentation. However, you will need to make sure they are not distracted from the topic by just looking for the errors. When assessing a learner's written work, rather than point out an error they have made with a particular word, point out the sentence and ask them to find it for themselves.

You could think of ways of using the following activities when planning to embed English, maths and ICT skills during your sessions:

- English Language: speaking, listening, discussing, role play, interviews, presentations

- English Literacy: reading, writing, spelling, grammar, punctuation and syntax

- maths: calculations, interpretations, evaluations and measurements

- ICT: using online applications, e-learning programs, word processors, spreadsheet packages, a VLE, emails, podcasts, webcasts, videos, searching the internet.

Wider skills

Depending upon where you work, it might be a requirement for you to incorporate aspects of the wider skills during your sessions or as separate topics. Alternatively, there might be specialist staff who will support your learners with them.

The wider skills include:

- *Working with Others* which focuses on teamwork, planning, organising and carrying out work with other people.

- *Improving Own Learning and Performance* which focuses on recognising the skills of being an effective learner and the importance of reflection.

- *Problem Solving* which focuses on the skills of recognising problems and identifying, evaluating and seeing through possible solutions.

These skills might occur naturally during activities with your learners; however, sometimes they need to be taught. For example, if a learner prefers to work on their own, they might not be used to communicating and working with others as part of a team.

Additional wider skills are known as *personal learning and thinking skills* (PLTS). They are skills that, together with the functional skills of English, maths and ICT, are essential to success in learning, life and work.

The six areas of PLTS are:

- *Independent enquirers:* planning and carrying out investigations and taking informed decisions.

- *Creative thinkers:* generating ideas, tackling problems and finding imaginative solutions.

- *Reflective learners:* setting goals for learning and work, monitoring performance and reviewing progress.

- *Team workers:* working collaboratively with other people, taking responsibility and resolving issues.

- *Self-managers:* being organised, showing enterprise and responding to new challenges.

- *Effective participators:* playing a full part in studies and the workplace or the wider community.

Qualifications are available in England for the wider skills, which could be taken additionally, or as part of a learning programme such as an apprenticeship.

Employability and employment skills

Employability skills and employment skills could be considered the same; however, there are differences between them. Employability skills are the skills that make someone employable, for example, reliability, trustworthiness and honesty. Employment skills are the skills required to perform a job effectively, for example, knowledge and experience of the vocational area along with English, maths and ICT skills. Your learners will benefit from having these skills to help them progress further. You might like to incorporate aspects within your sessions, as separate sessions, or as additional work for the learners to carry out in their own time.

Employability programmes aim to:

- build self-esteem and self-awareness

- develop learners' interpersonal skills, written and verbal communication skills, and teamworking skills

- develop learners' personal learning and thinking skills (PLTS)

- develop learners' personal, social, health and economic knowledge (PSHE)

- develop the attitudes and behaviours required in the workplace

- empower learners to adapt to change, retrain and/or progress further

- enable learners to experience the reality of life in the workplace

- encourage learners to take control of their direction to fulfil their potential

- help learners to compete in and succeed in their chosen career

- increase learners' employment prospects by raising their skills such as language, literacy, numeracy and ICT

- meet the needs of learners who wish to obtain, gain and sustain employment

- provide valuable accreditation of current skills and/or knowledge.

You might like to incorporate activities and role plays with your learners to help them improve aspects such as producing a professional looking curriculum vitae (CV), searching for and applying for jobs, and developing interview techniques.

Activity

Create your own list of employability skills and employment skills. Consider which you think are the three most important for each. Discuss with a colleague or friend the advantages and disadvantages of those chosen. Decide on the best ways of achieving them with your learners.

There are other areas in which you could promote skills, knowledge and understanding with your learners. For example:

- *British Values*: researching and discussing what these mean (covered in Chapter 9).

- *Citizenship*: discussions based on nationality, politics and the state.

- *Enterprise:* setting up a small business, creating a website and an online ordering system.

- *Personal development, behaviour and welfare (PDBW):* discussing time keeping, positive behaviour and good conduct, acting professionally, having self-confidence, looking after personal health and well-being, making decisions, maintaining good attendance, punctuality, staying safe, respecting others, taking responsibility.

- *Sustainability*: how to recycle, reuse and reduce usage of products.

Learners who possess skills in these areas should be able to progress in education, training and employment, and make a positive contribution to the communities in which they live and work.

Extension activity

Find out which of the functional skills and wider skills you may need to incorporate into your subject. If you are not required to use any, consider the ones you feel would help your learners the most, such as those to gain employment. How could you provide opportunities for your learners to learn about and use these skills? Design an activity to incorporate these skills and, if possible, try it out with your learners. Evaluate how effective it was and consider what you would change and why.

Teaching and learning approaches and activities

Teaching approaches can be formal and informal and include demonstrations, discussions, group work and presentations. Activities are the tasks which your learners can carry out as part of the approaches you use. However, some approaches could also be classed as activities depending upon what you are doing at the time – it's just terminology. Do consider that what works with some learners might not work with others. Therefore, it might be trial and error at first, but don't be afraid to try something new or to make a mistake and learn from it.

If you just talk to your learners about your subject, how do you even know they are listening? Furthermore, if you just show them how to do something, how do you know they can do it for themselves? Using different activities and involving your learners doing or saying something will help learning to take place. Teaching is all about making sure learning is taking place. Please see Table 5.3 at the end of this section for the strengths and limitations of various approaches and activities you could use for teaching and learning.

Activity

If you are currently teaching, discuss with your colleagues the approaches and activities they use with their learners and why. Are there any you hadn't thought of using but now might like to?

If you are not teaching, take a look at Table 5.3 for some ideas of approaches and activities you could use.

Time fillers

If you find you have spare time during a session, or if some learners finish an activity before others, it's useful to have a few spare activities to use. You could create a gapped handout, crossword, puzzle or wordsearch to use when necessary. They could be paper based or available electronically. Alternatively, you could ask a question to an individual, a pair or a small group, which prompts them to think further about the current topic. It's best to keep your learners active and learning, rather than asking them to talk amongst themselves just to fill in time. Alternatively, you could have a few prepared ideas you could use.

Example

Lizzie had been facilitating an activity in small groups with her hairdressing learners. One of the groups had finished well before the others, so Lizzie quickly thought of an activity for them to carry out. She asked them to write the word HAIRDRESSING down the left hand side of a piece of paper. She then asked them to write a related sentence next to each letter. This enabled the learners to continue working on something which was relevant to their course. To start them off, she gave them an idea for the first one: H = health and safety should always be taken into consideration when working with hair dye.

Extension activities to stretch and challenge learners

You might have some learners who are capable of achieving more than is required. You can help increase their development by using extension activities to stretch and challenge their potential further. Stretching is about improving the capability of learners and challenging helps them to do more.

Not all learners achieve at the same time at the same level; therefore, using extension activities can help meet their needs. This can be carried out on an individual or a group basis depending upon your learners. You can also use these activities as time fillers if appropriate or when the need arises. It's useful to create a bank of activities in advance, perhaps by creating an *extension box* (or a *virtual box* if your learners all have access to digital devices) which contains various activities.

These could include:

* gapped handouts with missing words of increasing difficulty

* multiple choice questions which start off easy and get harder

* open questions requiring an answer of a particular word count, e.g. 150 words

* past test paper questions for learners to attempt in a certain time

* pictures or statements to identify which is the odd one out (at different levels of learning)

* tasks which use objectives of gradually increasing active verbs, e.g. list, describe, explain, analyse

* topics to compare and contrast which increase in difficulty

* worksheets which introduce new topics and include questions to check understanding.

Example activities to use with learners

The activities you use with your learners must relate to the topics being covered, which in turn relate to the programme, qualification, job specification or set of standards which the learner is working towards. It takes time to plan, prepare and use them, but they will enable your learners to explore the topics in a far more interesting and inspirational way. This can be more engaging than just listening to you talking or watching you demonstrate something. Whatever activities you choose to use, it might be an idea to work through them first, looking at them from a learner's perspective. You will need to decide if the activity will be carried out individually, in pairs or small groups. You will also need to give clear instructions and set a time limit for completion. Make sure you de-brief the activity afterwards and state how it relates to the subject.

Examples of various activities you could use with learners are covered throughout most of the chapters in this book. Some are listed overleaf; however, you could design and create your own, for example, a board game, a quiz, a crossword or a puzzle. Chapter 8 contains example websites you could look at with a view to creating these online.

A/B/C/D responses

Learners write the letters A, B, C and D on separate pieces of paper. You can ask a question and give four possible answers, one for each of A, B, C and D. Learners then hold up the letter to denote the response they think is correct. You may need to repeat the question and responses, or reduce them to three instead of four if learners can't remember them all. Alternatively, you could have the questions and responses on display as part of a presentation. If you have the opportunity, you could create and laminate a set of A, B, C and D cards and re-use them as and when required. Discussions could take place regarding the responses if any were wrongly answered.

Card activities

Using strips of card or thick paper (or paper which can be laminated and cut into strips) to match, list, order or group items. For example:

- List about 10 separate questions and answers relating to the current topic. Learners can match the answers to the questions. A discussion can take place if any were matched wrongly.

- List a few topic headings and related points (for example, recipes [headings] and ingredients [points]). Learners can list the points under each heading. A discussion can take place as to what is correct or not.

- List a few actions that need to be carried out in a certain order (for example, the procedures which must be carried out for a certain process to occur). Learners can then place them in the order in which they think is correct. A discussion can take place as to what is correct or not.

- List a few headings with related items which learners need to group together. For example, different aspects of a particular job and the tools required for each. Learners need to group the tools according to the jobs. A discussion can take place as to what is correct or not.

- Write some sentences which are true and some which are false regarding the current topic. Learners need to place them in two columns: true and false. A discussion can take place as to what is correct or not.

Creating leaflets and posters

In small groups, learners could create a leaflet or a poster, in hard copy or online, to summarise the current topic. Alternatively, each member of the small group could research a different topic prior to discussing it within their group, and then creating a poster together. A discussion can take place regarding how all the groups approached the activity and what they learnt from it.

Identifying similarities and differences

Give pairs of learners two or three relevant topics and ask them to identify the similarities and differences between them. Each pair can then join another pair and discuss their responses; this is known as *snowballing* as the pairs can keep increasing. A full group discussion and debate can then take place.

Jigsaw puzzles

This is a small group activity where learners need to assemble a picture like a jigsaw puzzle. Find a few pictures which relate to the subject and cut them into smaller shapes (you could laminate them if you have this facility). For example, if you have 30 learners you could cut five pictures into six smaller shapes (one shape per learner). Mix the shapes and give one to each learner who will have to communicate with the others to find out who has the missing pieces to complete the jigsaw. You could have a copy of the completed pictures on separate tables for the learners to locate first. Alternatively, you could try not showing a complete picture if you would like to challenge your learners further. However, this will take much longer for them to achieve.

Some groups will finish more quickly than others; you can, therefore, set them a task based on the picture. For example, if the group are studying travel and tourism, the jigsaw could be a map of a country. The learners can then state things about that country such as its currency, major tourist attractions, transport links, the language spoken and the colours of the flag.

Open activities

These are activities in which you pose a question, but leave it open to your learners how they answer it. For example, posing a topical and relevant question and letting your learners (as individuals, pairs or small groups) decide how they will answer it. They might choose to discuss it amongst each other; research textbooks or the internet; create a poster or a display; a cartoon strip or a drawing; write an article, poem, song or a blog; act out a short play; or anything else which inspires them. A time limit must be set and you will need to check what has been achieved. You might need to guide your learners with some ideas if they are struggling to decide on their own. Feedback will need to be given as to whether or not the question was successfully answered.

Points of view

If your subject, for example, politics, could have opposing views, you could ask learners to research a particular angle and then justify their reasons for it as part of a discussion. If learners do have a personal view, this might challenge them to understand other views. You would need to make sure an argument did not occur which might get out of control.

Reading, researching and presenting

Learners read and/or research the current topic or an upcoming topic (using textbooks, journals, newspapers and the internet). They can then give a short (timed) presentation to the full group using appropriate resources. A discussion can take place regarding how the groups approached the activity and what they learnt. An alternative to a presentation could be to create a visual display either manually or electronically.

True/false questions

Learners write the words 'true' and 'false' on separate pieces of paper. You can ask a closed question and they hold up their response. You could plan questions which are based around difficult ideas or concepts and which lead to a critical discussion if learners get the answer wrong. If you have the opportunity, you could create and laminate a set of true and false cards and re-use them as and when required.

Using sticky notes and mini whiteboards

Ask a question to the full group then each learner must write their response on a sticky note or a mini whiteboard (or a piece paper). Learners then stick the sticky note on the wall or hold up the mini whiteboard for you to see. Learners (and you) can look at and discuss the different responses. Instead of asking a question, you could ask the learners to summarise the current topic in three bullet points or 10 words, and write these on the sticky note or mini whiteboard.

Alternatively, learners could do this activity in pairs and discuss the responses amongst each other. You will need to discuss their responses with them in case any are wrong.

Sticky notes can also be used throughout a session for learners to write questions on, perhaps if they don't want to interrupt or embarrass themselves in front of their peers. The sticky notes could be stuck on the wall and you could address the questions to the full group either at an appropriate time during the session or towards the end.

Writing a newspaper article or a blog

Learners could read newspaper articles/blogs which relate to the current topic and then write their own. You could ask your learners to write from a particular perspective, e.g. positive or negative, or to be unbiased. A discussion can take place regarding how the groups approached the activity and what they learnt as a result. Alternatively, learners could read something and then re-write it in their own words to demonstrate their understanding.

Extension activity

Devise four different activities for your subject which you could use with your learners, perhaps based on the previous examples. Make sure you have clear instructions and an idea of how long they will take. Consider the strengths and limitations of each. If possible, use at least one of the activities with your learners and evaluate how effective it was. What would you change and why?

Table 5.3 Examples of teaching and learning approaches and activities

Approach/activity	Description	Strengths	Limitations
Assignments	A longer-term activity based around a particular subject area which can provide evidence of learning Can be practical or theoretical	Can challenge a learner's potential or be used to consolidate learning Can be formative or summative Can encourage learners to research aspects further	If set by an awarding organisation, the teacher needs to ensure all aspects of the syllabus have been taught beforehand Must be individually assessed and written feedback given which can develop learning further Can be time consuming to produce and to mark
Blended learning	Using more than one method of teaching which often includes the use of technology	Combines traditional and technological learning Formal teaching can be supported with informal learning	Not all learners may have access to the technology Some learners might prefer traditional-based learning
Brainstorming (sometimes referred to as a thought shower)	A list or a drawing of suggestions or ideas regarding a particular theme, topic or problem	Quickly stimulates thoughts and ideas Can be carried out individually or in a paired or group situation Builds on current knowledge and experience Can be teacher led or group led Can be refined and used as a basis for other activities	Some learners may not contribute or might be judgemental and overpowering Ideas might be given too quickly in a group to note down Time limits must be set

Approach/activity	Description	Strengths	Limitations
Buzz groups	Short topics to be discussed in small groups	Can break up a more formal session Enables learners to work together and focus their ideas Checks knowledge and understanding Doesn't require formal feedback Can be impromptu or a time filler activity Once learners have spoken in a small buzz group they might have the confidence to speak in front of the full group	Learners may digress Specific points could be lost Checking individual learning has taken place may be difficult Time limits must be set Feedback should be taken from each group otherwise they may think the activity was meaningless
Case studies	Can be a hypothetical situation, an actual event, or an incomplete event, which learners can discuss or act on	Can make topics more realistic, enhancing motivation and interest Can be carried out individually or in a paired or group situation Builds on current knowledge and experience Can be differentiated to stretch and challenge particular learners	Time limits must be set If carried out as a group activity, roles should be defined Must have clear outcomes Time should be allocated for a de-brief and/or feedback
Closing activity	A short activity at the end of a session to enable learners to attach relevance to what they have learnt	Helps find out what each learner has gained from the session Different activities can be used If a learner has to leave early, they will only miss this activity and not the summary of the session	Some learners might feel it's trivial or time wasting Sessions might over-run due to the use of the activity

(Continued)

Table 5.3 (Continued)

Approach/activity	Description	Strengths	Limitations
Coaching	A one-to-one or small group activity which can occur spontaneously	Ideal for on-the-job training Ongoing advice and guidance can be given Takes account of individual needs	Not suitable for large groups Can be time consuming
Collaborative working	Involves pairs or groups of learners working together to solve problems, to create a product or to complete a task	Enables learners to work together and learn from each other Can involve the use of technology	Not all learners might want to take part Needs careful planning
Copying	Learners copy written work or what the teacher has demonstrated	A teacher-centred method which might suit some learners	It shows the learner is capable of copying something, but they might not understand what they are doing
Critical incident analysis	Learners explore something critical (which has occurred or which might occur) to understand it and to find alternative ways of reacting and responding to it A critical incident is one which has a positive or negative effect on something or someone	Useful to help learners anticipate a situation and discuss how they would react Can challenge assumptions Gains different points of view which can be explored, e.g. why learners made their decisions or arrived at certain conclusions If the analysis is based on a real incident, learners could benefit from the experience of those involved	Learners might recall aspects in a different manner to which they actually occurred The teacher needs to guide the learners to a successful conclusion
Debates	Learners or guests present a case to learners, with subsequent arguments, questions and discussions	Learner centred Allows freedom of viewpoints and demonstrates understanding	Some learners may not get involved, others may dominate The teacher needs to manage the debate carefully and keep track of time Learners may need to research a topic in advance Can generate inappropriate behaviour

Approach/activity	Description	Strengths	Limitations
Demonstration	A practical way of showing learners how something works	Can set a good example of how to do something Can inspire learners to try it out for themselves Can be supported with handouts and practical activities, i.e. getting the learners to do it for themselves	Equipment might not be available or in working order Learners in larger groups might not be able to see what is going on The teacher might go too fast and/or learners might miss something The demonstration can be overdone or overcomplicated if not broken down into smaller stages There might not be enough resources for all learners to have a go Some learners might be quicker or take longer than others Some learners may not pay attention or get bored watching a long demonstration Can be time consuming to set up Questions must be asked to check knowledge and understanding
Dictation	Reading text out loud for learners to note down	Gives emphasis to key points – should be used in moderation Can be followed up with learners carrying out research regarding what was dictated	Learners might not understand what they are writing Some learners may get behind and miss points Does not allow for clarification or questions

(Continued)

Table 5.3 (Continued)

Approach/activity	Description	Strengths	Limitations
Didactic	A teacher-centred approach where knowledge is imparted to learners	Presents a view of what is right and moral, from the teacher's perspective of knowledge of the subject	A passive approach Very little inclusion of learners (if any)
Discovery learning	Learners try out a skill or carry out a task before being taught about it	Learners can experiment and discover aspects for themselves (providing it's safe to do so) A discussion can take place about what they have experienced, followed by having another go if necessary	Careful planning is required Learners need to be gently directed and encouraged A clear purpose is needed
Discussion	Learners explore a topic or the teacher can introduce a topic for the learners to discuss	All learners can participate and share knowledge and experiences Smaller groups could discuss different topics and then pass on their findings to the other groups for further discussion Learners might feel more comfortable talking rather than writing	Some learners may be shy or not want to be involved Some learners might dominate others Teacher needs to make sure all learners can contribute Easy to digress Teacher needs to keep the group focused A time limit must be set
Distance learning or open learning	Learning which takes place away from the organisation offering the programme/ qualification Work can be issued to learners via post, email or a web-based application	Learning can occur at a time and place to suit the learner Can be combined with other learning methods, e.g. blended learning	Could be a long gap between submitting work for assessment and receiving feedback Self-discipline is needed Targets must be clearly agreed Learner may never meet teacher/ assessor

Approach/activity	Description	Strengths	Limitations
Drawing	Illustrations to show how something works (by the teacher and/or learner)	Several drawings can be used to show how something works in a simple way	Needs explaining carefully Some learners might not be good at drawing
e-learning/online learning	Learning which is supported or enhanced using information and communication technology (ICT) Learning which takes place in a virtual learning environment (VLE) via a device connected to an intranet or the internet	Learning can take place anywhere a digital device is available Learning can be flexible Ongoing support can be given	Learners need access to a digital device and need the skills to use it A reliable internet connection may be required Self-discipline is needed, along with clear targets for achievement Authenticity of learner's work may need validating Technical support may be required
Essays	A formal piece of written or word-processed text, produced by the learner to address a specific subject area	Useful for higher level subjects Can check a learner's English skills Can confirm knowledge and understanding Can encourage further reading, research and study	Not suitable for some learners Requires clear assessment grading criteria Marking can be time consuming Plagiarism can be an issue
Exam/test past papers	Learners can work through past papers to gain an idea of the structure of a future exam or test	Gives learners an idea of how to approach an exam or a test A discussion can take place to ascertain how the learners felt about the process, and how they approached answering the questions	Time limits need to be set Can be daunting to some learners Teacher needs to invigilate the activity as though it was a real exam or test Papers should be marked and individual feedback given, which can be time consuming

(Continued)

Table 5.3 (Continued)

Approach/activity	Description	Strengths	Limitations
Experiential/ experimental	Practical tasks enabling learners to act out, experience or experiment with a particular topic	Learners can put theory into practice Learners can be in control, find out things for themselves and learn from their mistakes (if it's safe to do so) Can be exciting and engaging	Not all learners may want to participate Some learners may lack confidence or not want to embarrass themselves in front of their peers Can be time consuming
Extension activity	An additional task which can be used to stretch and challenge learners' potential further	Can be used when learners finish a task earlier than others Ideal for differentiation Can be used to extend a learner's thinking about a topic	Some learners might feel pressured to complete them when they are not able to, i.e. peer pressure Can be demeaning if some learners see others completing them, they may feel left behind
Flexible learning	Learning that can take place at a time and place to suit the learner and/or using different delivery approaches within a session to meet particular challenges	Suits learners who cannot attend formal sessions Ideal for varying the pace of a session	Ongoing support and monitoring of achievement is required Not all learners are motivated to this style of learning
Flipped learning	The work normally carried out during an attended session is flipped with what would be carried out elsewhere, e.g. swapping classwork and homework	Enables discussions to take place during the session based on what has been learnt outside of the session	Requires learners to carry out what is required before attending the session Some learners might not feel comfortable studying outside of the session Takes time for the teacher to plan what the learners will do as homework, and to manage the activities during the class session

Approach/activity	Description	Strengths	Limitations
Formal instruction (pedagogy)	The teacher imparts knowledge or demonstrates skills to learners	Suits learners who prefer to watch and listen	Not effective with all learners as the process is teacher led Learners must assimilate the knowledge at the pace of the teacher Might not take into account previous learners' experiences and knowledge
Games	A fun way of learning to enable problem solving and decision making to take place	Board or card games can be designed to make learning enjoyable Physical games put theory into practice Online games can develop digital skills Can be used to open or close a session Assesses learning so far Encourages interaction and healthy competition	Needs to be well prepared in advance Learners need to remain focused and all given a chance to take part Objectives need to be clear Careful supervision is needed Game rules should be followed
Gapped handout	Blank spaces within a handout for learners to fill in the missing words from sentences	Different versions for different levels of learners could be devised Useful to fill in time during a session	Some learners might find it too easy Learners who complete them slowly might get left behind
Group work	Enables learners to carry out a specific activity by working with others	Allows interaction between learners Learners learn from each other's experiences and knowledge Encourages participation and variety Rotating group members over time enables all learners to work with each other Can be practical or theoretical	Careful management by the teacher is required regarding who is in the groups All group members need to be clear regarding the requirements Potential for personality clashes One person may dominate

(Continued)

Table 5.3 (Continued)

Approach/activity	Description	Strengths	Limitations
Group work (Continued)			Time limits must be set Learners might get left out or be too shy to contribute Ground rules might be needed to keep the group on track Time is needed for a thorough de-brief and feedback
Guided learning	Creates a bridge between whole group learning and independent learning with guidance from the teacher	Enables learning to take place in a group context, followed by individual independent learning	Not all learners like this method Needs careful planning and timing
Handouts	Written and/or visual information/drawings/text/ pictures to promote and support learning	Useful for learners to refer to after a session Can incorporate questions for learners to answer as a homework or self-study activity Can be differentiated More information could be covered in handouts which is not covered during the session	Should be used in conjunction with other activities Need to be adapted for any special learner requirements, e.g. a visual impairment Should be produced well in advance Spelling, grammar, punctuation and syntax must be accurate
Homework	Activities carried out between sessions, e.g. further reading and research Learning doesn't have to stop just because the session has ended	Learners can complete at a time and place that suits them Maintains interest between sessions Encourages learners to stretch and challenge themselves further	Target dates must be set Learners might not do it Must be discussed, or marked/ assessed and individual feedback given, otherwise learners might feel it's meaningless

Approach/activity	Description	Strengths	Limitations
Icebreakers/ energisers/team-building exercises	A fun and light-hearted way of introducing learners and topics	A good way of learners getting to know each other, and for teachers to observe behaviours and attitudes Can revitalise a flagging session	Not all learners may want to take part Some learners may see them as insignificant Careful explanations are needed to link the exercise to the topic
Individual/ independent learning (andragogy)	Learners carry out tasks on their own and are in control of their own learning	Some learners might prefer working on their own and enjoy this type of activity Learners could set their own targets and methods of meeting the required outcomes Develops independent learners and encourages autonomy	Some learners might prefer to work with others or be led by the teacher Teacher must carefully plan what each learner will do and what will be achieved by when
Informal instruction	Learning which takes place outside of the formal environment or which is delivered in an informal way	Suits learners who prefer a more informal or relaxed way to find out about something Learners can interrupt the teacher and ask questions	Not effective with all learners
Instruction	Formal method of teaching whereby the teacher shows or tells the learner what to do to achieve a particular skill; the learner then performs this or rephrases it	If on a one-to-one basis it can be a good method of pacing learning to suit the individual learner Learners can see/hear what they need to do/know and then try it themselves Learners could show or talk through a task to their peers to demonstrate their understanding	If demonstrated/told to a group, some learners may get left behind or forget what to do Might need to be supported with a handout or further information/ activities Appropriate positioning is required if an aspect is demonstrated, e.g. left-handed learners of right-handed teachers Instructions need to be very clear and unambiguous

(Continued)

Table 5.3 (Continued)

Approach/activity	Description	Strengths	Limitations
Interactive whiteboard	Teachers and/or learners use a board with various technological functions including linking to the internet	Good for group work and presentations	Not all learners can use it at the same time Not all learners might be able to see what is taking place
Journal or diary	Learners keep a record of their progress, their reflections and thoughts	Develops self-assessment skills Relates theory to practice (if learners are undertaking work experience) Helps assess English skills	Should be specific to the learning taking place and be analytical rather than descriptive Learners need to be guided as to how to write in a particular way to meet the programme criteria Content needs to remain confidential between the teacher and learner Can be time consuming to read
Lecture	Traditional *teacher-centred* technique of imparting information	Ideal for imparting knowledge to large groups Useful for teaching theoretical subjects Key points can be prepared in advance, perhaps on small cards as prompts to read Can be supported with videos, images, text and sounds Useful if learners need to know a lot about a topic in a short time	Learners are passive, they might not listen and may lose concentration Learners may not feel they can interrupt or ask questions to clarify points Learners need good listening and note-taking skills Good voice projection and clarity of speech is required by the teacher Learners need to work at the pace of the teacher Difficult to know if learning has taken place

Approach/activity	Description	Strengths	Limitations
Mentoring	One-to-one support by someone other than the teacher who is usually experienced in the subject	Expertise and knowledge can be passed on through ongoing advice, guidance and support Times can be arranged to suit all parties	Can be time consuming Mentor and mentee might not get along
Micro-teaching	A short teaching and learning session Usually a simulated session taught by a trainee teacher in front of their peer group	Enables learners to practice in a safe environment Can be recorded to aid self-evaluation Peer feedback can be given	Not all learners enjoy the experience Recording equipment, if used, can be difficult to manage while observing learners Some peers might not give constructive feedback
Mind maps/spider grams	A visual way of organising Information and making plans. Learners can draw a circle with a key point in the middle of a page. They then branch from this with subheadings to explore and develop aspects further	Learners are active Topics can be explored in a fun and meaningful way Links between ideas are easy to see New information can easily be added Can be created by using technology	Not all learners may want to contribute nor understand what to do One learner may dominate Needs careful supervision Large paper, a board and marker pens or electronic devices are required
Mnemonics	Remembering things by associating the first letters of words with something else For example, Richard of York Gave Battle In Vain (RYGBIV) is Red, Yellow, Green, Blue, Indigo, Violet for the colours of the rainbow	A quick way of remembering facts	Demonstrates knowledge but not understanding Some learners might get the letters mixed up

(Continued)

Table 5.3 (Continued)

Approach/activity	Description	Strengths	Limitations
Models	Useful where the real object cannot be seen Life models can be used, e.g. in art classes, or machinery models in engineering	Learners have a chance to see how something looks and/or works, and to ask questions	Must be clearly explained and demonstrated May require funding to purchase Needs careful planning and preparation Should be supported with a handout of detailed instructions on how to use
Paired work	Enables learners to carry out a specific activity with a peer, e.g. problem solving or checking each other's work Can be practical or theoretical	Allows interaction between learners Learners learn from each other Encourages participation and variety Pairs can link up as fours and so on to share their experiences and knowledge (known as snowballing) Tasks could be differentiated to stretch and challenge particular learners	Careful management by the teacher is required regarding time limits Each pair must be clear about the requirements Learners need to get along with each other The teacher could nominate who will work together, perhaps placing one knowledgeable learner with one less so Difficult to assess individual contributions Time is needed for feedback from each pair and to check what they have achieved
Participative learning	Includes everyone in the learning process	Fosters mutual learning Enables learners to work together and learn from each other Creativity and enthusiasm could evolve	Learners must be prepared to participate in the activities Learners need to get along with each other Individual contributions must be taken into account

Approach/activity	Description	Strengths	Limitations
Peer learning/tasks/ assessment	Learners gaining skills and/or knowledge from their peers Learners setting tasks for their peers to carry out Learners assessing their peers	Helps learners to engage with the subject Enables learners to work together in an informal way to learn from each other's experiences and knowledge Learners can support each other throughout the session or programme Learners can create tasks based upon the topic, and provide feedback to each other	There may be personality clashes between learners which prevent learning taking place Not all information given by learners may be correct If learners are creating tasks, they will need to fully understand the topic/ subject If learners are giving feedback, they must understand how to do it effectively
Plenary	An opportunity to summarise the session, recap what has been learnt, and relate it to the aims and objectives	Could be combined with a closing activity to gain feedback from the learners Formally ends the session and links to the next session (if applicable)	Enough time has to be planned for it
Podcast	A digital, audio or video file which can be uploaded to the internet	Can supplement learning for many topics A video could be taken of the session for learners to access and view later	Some learners might not be able to access them, or have the skills to May encourage non-attendance if learners prefer to watch the session from their device at home
Pose, pause, pick questioning technique	Ask a question, then pause for a few seconds so that all learners are thinking about a response. Then pick a learner to answer the question by stating their name	Enables all learners to consider the answer if they think they might be asked	Chosen learner might not know the answer

(Continued)

Table 5.3 (Continued)

Approach/activity	Description	Strengths	Limitations
Presentations	Similar to a lecture with greater use of audio-visual aids	Interaction can take place between the teacher and learners Effective use of media can make presentations stimulating, motivating and inspiring Learners could carry out research and present their findings to others, rather than the teacher doing it	Some learners may not pay attention or might get distracted Too many slides with too much detail can be daunting, learners often read the slides rather than listening to what is being said by the presenter Needs to be interactive and to the pace of the learners, otherwise they might be left behind
Problem solving	Enabling learners to find things out for themselves	Helps learners to become more autonomous and take responsibility for their own learning Enables learners to communicate with others if working in pairs or groups	Needs careful planning of what is required Timings need to be specified and kept to
Projects/project-based learning	A long-term activity enabling learners to provide evidence of, or consolidate their learning and experiences	Can be interesting and motivating Can be individual or group led Learners could choose a relevant topic to cover the learning outcomes, leading to autonomous learning Can involve real life problem-solving opportunities	Clear outcomes must be set, along with a time limit Must be relevant, realistic and achievable Progress should be checked regularly If a group is carrying out the project, be aware of each individual's input, don't let one person dominate Thorough feedback should be given

Approach/activity	Description	Strengths	Limitations
Questions	A key technique for checking understanding and stimulating thinking	Can be online, written or oral Enables the learner to think about what they are learning Can challenge a learner's potential An effective way of testing knowledge when open questions are used	Closed questions only gain a yes or *no* response which doesn't demonstrate knowledge Questions must be unambiguous More than one question should not be asked in one sentence or confusion could occur Learners might struggle to answer oral questions in front of their peers Written questions might be misinterpreted or misunderstood Questions might be too easy and not stretch or challenge the learners enough Time constraints might be necessary
Quizzes	Fun activities to check learning by the use of panel games, online activities or other practical ways	Learners are actively involved Useful backup activity if spare time is available Can be fun Learners could mark their own or their peers' responses	Can seem trivial to some learners Dominant learners might take over Shy learners might not get involved De-brief is required
Reading	Learners work from relevant texts/books/journals and other suitable documents including online reading	Learners could choose what they wish to read providing it is relevant Learners can read to themselves or out loud to the group; however, the latter might demoralise some learners who lack confidence at speaking in front of others Learners can explain to the teacher and/or each other how they have understood a topic	Reading and note taking skills are required Learners can get bored or easily distracted May need to have differentiated texts to account for a range of levels within the group

(Continued)

Table 5.3 (Continued)

Approach/activity	Description	Strengths	Limitations
Reading (Continued)		Learners could write a summary of the main points and identify any mistakes or misconceptions Encourages further learning	
Recognition of prior learning (RPL)	Assessing what has previously been learnt, experienced and achieved to find a suitable starting point for further learning and assessment	Helps to build new knowledge and skills logically Ideal for learners who have achieved certain aspects prior to commencement Should be no need for learners to duplicate work, or be reassessed Values previous learning, experiences and achievements	Takes time to find out what each learner knows and/or can do already, and can be hard to evidence Checking the authenticity and currency of the evidence provided is crucial Awarding organisation approval might be required if it's towards an accredited qualification Previous learning, experiences and achievements might not be relevant in relation to current requirements Can be time consuming for both learner to prove, and the assessor to assess
Repetition, reciting or rote learning	Learners repeat, aspects such as important figures, dates or poems For example, the times tables: 1×6 is 6, 2×6 is 12 and so on	A good way of remembering useful figures, facts or poems	Does not test knowledge and understanding, only the ability to repeat, recite or recall something
Reports	Learners produce a document to inform, recommend and/or make suggestions based on a given topic	Useful for higher level learners Encourages the use of research techniques	Good writing skills and the use of referencing might be required Learners need to interpret and evaluate key points to demonstrate

Approach/activity	Description	Strengths	Limitations
Research	An in-depth way of finding out answers or more information regarding a topic	Learners can use the internet, read textbooks, access journals and other documents during class time or in their own time Learners could choose what they want to research providing it is relevant	Learners need to know how to research and what to do with their findings Learners might not know how to apply their research to real situations Time is needed to check what has been researched and to ensure it is relevant
Rhyme and Rap	Reciting and recalling phrases or songs to aid memory For example, 30 days has September, April June and November	Learners can create their own phrases or songs to help them remember points Can be fun	Can seem trivial to some learners Does not test knowledge and understanding, only the ability to recite or recall something
Role play	A practical activity to demonstrate learning Can be used to act out a hypothetical situation or scenario to see how learners would respond	Can see how a learner reacts to certain situations Can help improve self-confidence Encourages participation in a safe environment Can be a fun method of learning Can lead to debates Links theory to practice Gives learners the opportunity to demonstrate communication skills Learners can observe and give peer feedback	Can be time consuming Clear roles must be defined Not all learners may want, or be able to participate Time limit should be set Some learners may get too dramatic Time is needed for a thorough de-brief

(Continued)

Table 5.3 (Continued)

Approach/activity	Description	Strengths	Limitations
Self-assessment	Learners decide how they have met the assessment criteria, or how they are progressing at a given point in time	Promotes ownership, learner involvement and personal autonomy Encourages learners to check their own work before handing in for assessment Encourages reflection Promotes individual thinking regarding progress and achievements	Some learners may feel they are doing better or worse than they actually are Assessor needs to discuss progress and achievements with each learner to confirm their decisions Learners need to be honest and specific about what they have achieved Some learners might not be able to identify what they still need to do to complete any gaps
Seminars	A presentation of ideas, followed by questions and a discussion	An informal teaching approach If a learner leads the seminar, it can help them to gain confidence at speaking to their peers Can lead to worthwhile discussions	Learners need specific topics or a paper/thesis to present Teacher needs to agree topics well in advance along with a running order of who will lead first A time limit needs to be set and kept to Some learners might not pay attention or want to participate
Senses learning	Learners use some or all of their senses, e.g. hear, see, smell, taste and/or touch	Can be fun Useful for certain subjects, e.g. cookery	Unless followed with an assessment activity, it might be difficult to determine what learning has taken place

Approach/activity	Description	Strengths	Limitations
Simulation	An imitation activity carried out when the real activity would be too dangerous. For example, the evacuation of a building when the fire alarm goes off, there's no need to set fire to the building for a simulated evacuation	Enables learners to demonstrate what they might do in the real situation Learners may realise things about themselves they were not aware of	Careful planning is needed Can be time consuming Specialist equipment may be needed Not all learners may be able to participate fully May not be taken seriously by some learners Thorough de-brief needed
Starter activity	A short activity at the beginning of a session to settle learners and focus their attention towards learning It could be a quiz to test knowledge gained so far, a discussion to open up thinking about the current subject, or an energiser activity focusing upon the session topic	If a learner arrives late, they only miss the starter activity not the introduction to the session	Some learners might feel it's trivial or wasting their time unless they can see how it relates to the subject
Surveys	Gaining information from others	The survey can be created by the teacher to gain feedback from learners either online, written or verbally Surveys can be short or long term Learners can design and use a survey to find things out from others	Permission may be required depending on the type of survey used Ethics and confidentiality required Quality of question content is important Could be time consuming to analyse

(Continued)

Table 5.3 (Continued)

Approach/activity	Description	Strengths	Limitations
Talking	The teacher or a learner talks about a topic	Preparation is needed regarding what to say and how to relate it to what needs to be learnt	Some learners might not listen attentively Is usually one-way communication, i.e. not enabling learners to ask questions
Tasks	Practical or theoretical activities carried out by an individual, in pairs or a group which are relevant to the topic being taught	Learners are active Useful backup activity if spare time is available Can be individual, paired or group based Can develop group interaction, communication and learner confidence Learners can relate the activities to real life situations Help and advice can be given as needed	Can be time consuming to plan and prepare Not all learners may want to participate Clear objectives should be set The task must be clearly explained Time limit required Time needed for feedback or a de-brief
Task analysis/skills analysis	The breakdown of a task or a job into its smaller component parts	Demonstrates or lists a logical progression or an order of something Enables learners to follow a precise order	Time consuming to think about and break down Some aspects could be missed
Teaching/training/tutoring	Educating learners in a subject, furthering their skills, attitudes, behaviours, knowledge, and/or understanding	A variety of approaches (as listed in this table) can be used depending upon the subject, learners, context and environment If planned well, can motivate and inspire learners Encourages progress, achievement, development and progression	Some learners might not respond well to formal teaching methods Takes time to plan and prepare teaching and learning activities and materials

Approach/activity	Description	Strengths	Limitations
Team-teaching (co-teaching)	Facilitating a session with a colleague	Enables learners to see different teaching and learning approaches Teachers can bring their experiences to the learning process, as well as personal anecdotes Shares the responsibility of a session between teachers	Some learners might get confused with more than one teacher in the room Teachers need to carefully plan who will do what and when One teacher might dominate Teachers might not get on
Technology-based learning *(also see blended learning, and e-learning/online learning)*	Using relevant equipment, media and materials, e.g. those which incorporate visual, audio and digital uses	Can show real events to learners Enables learners to be active Can generate discussions and improve communication Gives learners responsibility for their own learning	Can be time consuming to plan and prepare Learners need to remain focused Learners may need to be supervised There could be a lack of equipment A reliable internet connection might be needed
Tests	Written questions (e.g. open, closed, multiple choice) to test knowledge and understanding Practical activities to assess skills	Formally checks learning at a specific point in time Short tests can be used to fill in time towards the end of a session or to extend learning Useful for individual learners who like to be challenged further	May need to be carried out in supervised conditions Time limits required Can be stressful to learners Feedback may not be immediate If set by an awarding organisation, the teacher needs to ensure all aspects of the syllabus have been taught beforehand

(Continued)

Table 5.3 (Continued)

Approach/activity	Description	Strengths	Limitations
Tutorial reviews	A one-to-one or group discussion between the teacher and the learner/s with an agreed purpose, e.g. discussing progress and achievements so far	A good way of informally assessing a learner's progress and/or giving feedback An opportunity for learners to discuss issues or for informal tuition to take place	Needs to be in a comfortable, safe and quiet environment as confidential issues may be discussed on a one-to-one basis Tutorial may overrun Records should be maintained and action points followed up
Undoing	Learners can *undo* or *take apart* an object to learn how it was put together An example is taking a plug apart to see how it was originally wired	Goof for developing practical skills Needs to be demonstrated by the teacher first Useful in practical sessions	Objects/resources need to be available for all learners Needs to be supported with further information and careful guidance
Viewing, e.g. a video/TV/DVD/ webinar and online recordings	Watching a recording or a live programme via various media including the internet	Can be used to show good and bad practice to generate discussions Can show alternative ways of doing something if the teacher does not have the resources to do this Learners could make and then watch a recording of themselves performing a task and identify what needs improving	Not interactive All learners need to be in a position to see the screen and hear the sound Doesn't demonstrate understanding, only the ability to watch Some learners might not pay attention Extra tasks should be set or questions asked to check knowledge and understanding after viewing
Virtual learning environment (VLE)	An online platform for teachers to upload learning materials and to interact with learners	Enables learners to access materials outside the sessions Can be used for online learning instead of attending sessions	Not all learners might be computer literate or have the skills to use it Not all learners have internet access

Approach/activity	Description	Strengths	Limitations
Virtual learning environment (VLE) (Continued)		Allows online interaction between other learners and the teacher Assignments can be accessed by learners and uploaded once complete The teacher can provide feedback via the VLE and records are automatically maintained	
Visiting speakers	An expert in the subject area speaks to the learners	Can add variety and expertise to a topic from someone with a different perspective to the teacher A discussion can take place beforehand regarding what questions the learners want to ask the speaker	Must be arranged well in advance Some speakers may charge a fee or cancel beforehand Time should be allowed for questions and discussions Some learners might ask inappropriate questions
Visits/field trips	Learners visit a venue relevant to the subject such as a museum	Learners can be involved with fact finding and planning Can be active, interesting and stimulating Makes the subject real Can put theory into practice Can be discussed in subsequent sessions Can link with projects and assignments Can be a welcome change to routine	Needs careful planning Organisational and health and safety procedures must be followed Needs finance, e.g. for transport or entrance fees Learners need to be well briefed and prepared Ground rules must be agreed for how learners will behave Supervision usually required De-brief needed

(Continued)

Table 5.3 (Continued)

Approach/activity	Description	Strengths	Limitations
Watching	Learners watch something taking place, e.g. a live demonstration, a film clip or a video	Questions can be asked to check knowledge Can enable learners to see things they might not otherwise be able to Learners could discuss what was good or not, or how they would do what they have just seen, but in a different way	Not interactive Learners might be distracted Doesn't demonstrate understanding
Webcast	Videos and information uploaded to the internet Similar to podcasts	A useful way of distributing additional information to support current teaching	No interaction between learners Not all learners might have internet access
Worksheets	Interactive documents which learners read, followed by responding to questions or carrying out practical activities	Informal activity which can be completed individually, in pairs or groups Helps put theory into practice Useful for lower level learners or to set as homework or self-study material Can be created at different degrees of difficulty to address differentiation	Some learners may consider them inappropriate Too many worksheets can be boring to some learners Learners might not be stretched and challenged enough
Workshops	An opportunity to share practice, use activities and develop knowledge and understanding in a real or simulated working environment	Enables learners to work at their own pace in a safe environment Learners can support each other and learn from each other's experiences	Individual support and supervision might be required Suitable worksheets might need to be produced to enable learners to progress at their own pace

Self-assessment checklist

Do I know about the following?

If not, re-read this chapter, or research the texts and websites listed at the end.

☐ How to impart skills and knowledge in a way that enables learning to take place

☐ How to create and use starter and closing activities

☐ How to facilitate group learning

☐ How learners might act according to Belbin's team roles

☐ What Tuckman's Group Formation theory involves

☐ How to facilitate individual learning

☐ How to facilitate an event

☐ How to create a task analysis

☐ What EDIP is and how to use it

☐ What coaching and mentoring involve

☐ What functional skills and wider skills are

☐ Different approaches and activities to use with learners

Summary

This chapter has explored how you can manage and facilitate learning in groups or on an individual basis.

You should now be able to use various activities to help learners become independent and autonomous in the subject or vocational area they are working towards. You should also know how to embed functional skills and wider skills into your sessions as necessary.

You might like to carry out further research by accessing the books and websites listed at the end of this chapter, particularly if you are working towards a higher level teaching qualification.

This chapter has covered the following topics:

• Managing learning

• Facilitating group learning

• Facilitating individual learning

• Coaching and mentoring

• Functional skills and wider skills

• Teaching and learning approaches and activities

References and further information

Allen, C.R. (1919) *The Instructor: The Man and the Job: A Handbook for Instructors of Industrial and Vocational Subjects.* USA: J B Lippincott Company.

Allen, D. (2017) *Teaching English and Maths in FE: What Works for Vocational Learners?* London: Learning Matters SAGE.

Armitage, A., Bryant, R., Dunnill, R., Flanagan, K., Hayes, D., Hudson, A., Kent, J., Lawes, S. and Renwick, M. (2012) *Teaching and Training in Lifelong Learning.* Maidenhead: Open University Press.

Avis, J. and Fisher, R. (2014) *Teaching in Lifelong Learning.* Maidenhead: Open University Press.

Beevers, K. (2016) *Learning and Development Practice in the Workplace.* London: Kogan Page.

Belbin, M. (2010) *Team Roles at Work.* Oxford: Elsevier Science & Technology.

Cornish, D. and Dukette, D. (2009) *The Essential 20: Twenty Components of an Excellent Health Care Team.* Pittsburgh: RoseDog Books.

Cowley, S. (2013) *The Seven R's of Great Group Work (The Alphabet Sevens.)* CreateSpace Independent Publishing Platform.

Delaney, J. and Cope, A. (2016) *Supporting Maths and English in Post-14 Education and Training.* London: OU Press.

Dennick, R. and Exley, K. (2004) *Small Group Teaching: Tutorials, Seminars and Beyond.* Routledge: Abingdon.

Duckworth, V. (2014) *How to be a Brilliant FE Teacher.* Abingdon: Routledge.

Duckworth, V. and Maxwell, B. (2015) Extending the Mentor Role in Initial Teacher Education: Embracing Social Justice. *International Journal of Mentoring and Coaching in Education,* 4 (1), 4–20.

Egolf, D. (2001) *Forming Storming Norming Performing: Successful Communication in Groups and Teams.* Lincoln, USA: Writers Club Press.

Garvey, et al (2014) *Coaching and Mentoring.* London: SAGE.

Gravells, A. (2010) *Delivering Employability Skills.* Exeter: Learning Matters.

Harvey, B. and Harvey, J. (2012) *Creative Teaching Approaches in the Lifelong Learning Sector.* Maidenhead: Open University Press.

Howell Major, C. (2015) *Teaching for Learning.* New York: Routledge.

Ingle, S. and Duckworth, V. (2013) *Teaching and Training Vocational Learners.* London: SAGE.

Lancer, N., Clutterbuck, D. and Megginson, D. (2016) *Techniques for Coaching and Mentoring.* New York: Routledge.

Petty, G. (2014) *Teaching Today: A Practical Guide* (5th edition). Cheltenham: Nelson Thornes

Read, H. and Gravells, A. (2015) *The Best Vocational Trainer's Guide.* Bideford: Read On Publications Ltd.

Rogers, A. and Horrocks, N. (2010) *Teaching Adults* (4th edition). Maidenhead: Open University Press.

Sweller, J. (1988). Cognitive Load during Problem Solving: Effects on Learning. *Cognitive Science,* 12: 257–85.

Websites

Belbin's team roles – www.belbin.com

Challenging learning toolkit from TES – https://tinyurl.com/n95yf3n

Citizen Maths – www.citizenmaths.com

Free online English and maths support – www.bbc.co.uk/skillswise/0/

Free online initial assessment for using technology – http://wip.exeter.ac.uk/collaborate/itest/

Free online English audit – http://sagepub.net/LM/audit/audeng.asp

Free online maths audit – http://sagepub.net/LM/audit/audmat.asp

Functional skills resources – https://tinyurl.com/qxsc9ov

National Association for Numeracy and Mathematics in Colleges – www.nanamic.org.uk

PLTS – https://tinyurl.com/zcxkudz

PSHE – https://tinyurl.com/lz4wf97

Reading list for coaching and mentoring – www.anngravells.com/reading-lists/coaching-and-mentoring

Reading list for teachers and trainers – www.anngravells.com/reading-lists/teaching

Resources for teachers – www.anngravells.com/resources/index

Small group teaching – https://tinyurl.com/mgdpr53

Tuckman's Group Formation theory – https://www.mindtools.com/pages/article/newLDR_86.htm

6

Communication

Introduction

Communication is about passing on information from one person to another. It is also a manner of expression through the use of body language, tone of voice, and gestures. The first time you meet your learners they will probably make a subconscious judgement about you, and you will probably make one about them. These judgements often turn out to be wrong; therefore, it is important not to make any assumptions about your learners based on how they look or communicate. Understanding how to communicate effectively will help you to support your learners in a meaningful way and ensure that learning takes place.

This chapter will explore different ways of communicating with learners and others. Barriers to communication are covered, as are various communication theories.

This chapter will cover the following topics:

- The importance of communication
- Reading, writing, speaking and listening
- Verbal and non-verbal communication
- Barriers to communication
- Interpersonal and intrapersonal skills
- Theories of communication

The importance of communication

Communication is the key to encouraging learner motivation and respect, managing behaviour and disruption, and becoming a successful teacher or trainer. It should always be to the level of your learners, appropriate and effective. For example, if you need to write on a board while speaking to your learners, don't do both at the same time. If you face the board, they may not hear you speak and you might miss something happening in the room. If you don't communicate effectively, i.e. convey what you want your learners to hear in a way that they can interpret it, things may be misunderstood and learning might not take place.

When communicating, it needs to be in a way that the recipient can interpret and understand the message you are wanting to convey. If you speak, you expect the recipient to listen. However, they might be thinking about something else and not really focus on what you are saying.

Activity

Think of the last time you spoke to someone and you felt that they didn't really listen to you or understand what you said. Why do you think this was, and what could you do differently next time?

Communication is much more than what is spoken or written. It includes how you portray yourself and the messages you give out perhaps without realising. For example, your facial expressions, body language and the way you act and speak. The person watching you might interpret things differently to the way you feel you are portraying them. For example, if your arms are folded it could be perceived as a barrier. Communication is also about how you write, as the text could be interpreted differently when read. It's useful to read anything you have written, such as a handout, to try and understand it from the point of view of the reader.

Communication is also about considering and using an appropriate method, depending upon the recipient and the situation.

Example

Stephanie urgently needed to contact her colleague Neil to let him know of a room change for his next class. She knew he would be in the staff room at break time; therefore, she went to see him face to face. That way, she knew he would get the message and she could gauge his reaction to her request. If she had sent an email or a text message, she wouldn't know if Neil had received it.

In this example, Stephanie had used an appropriate method of communication for Neil and the situation.

There are many methods of communication you could use depending upon the situation. These include:

- verbal: speaking, i.e. face to face, telephone conversations, making digital recordings, video conferencing

- non-verbal: i.e. body language, appearance, dress, facial expressions, eye contact, gestures, posture, and the way you portray yourself

- written: i.e. letters, memos, reports, texts, progress reviews, worksheets, handouts

- visual: i.e. notice boards, adverts, posters, videos

- digital: i.e. emails, completing forms, online chats, social networking.

Activity

Consider the advantages and disadvantages of each of the different communication methods in the previous bullet list. Give an example of when you would use each. In some cases, more than one method of communication may be needed. For example, you might have an informal chat with a learner and follow it up with an email to confirm what was discussed. If you have time, you could carry out a search via the internet to see what you find regarding different communication methods and skills.

You will need to develop the skills which enable you to use all the methods of communication which are appropriate, and to decide which is the most suitable for a particular situation and person.

One of the skills of communicating effectively is projecting *confidence* when you are speaking. You may not feel confident when meeting a new group of learners for the first time; you might even feel quite nervous. You could imagine that you are an actor playing a character role to help you remain composed and focused. Your knowledge of, and passion for, your subject should help your confidence.

You will need to plan what you want to communicate along with how and when you are going to do this. Your learners don't know what you know, that's why they want to learn. When communicating, try and keep things simple, there's no need to talk quickly and/or use a lot of jargon, as it takes time for your learners to assimilate new knowledge.

Communicating with learners

Your main communication will be with your learners, although you will at times communicate with colleagues and others who can support your role. Always make sure that what you are communicating is accurate, unambiguous and not biased in any way. You won't want to confuse your learners as they might misinterpret something. Try and show your professionalism, not only in what you say, but in the way you say it. Professionalism can also be demonstrated with your behaviour, attitude, body language and the way you dress and act. A confident and genuine smile, a positive attitude, self-assurance and the use of eye contact and learners' names should help put everyone at ease, including yourself. The language you use when speaking and writing should reflect equality and inclusiveness, be relevant to the subject and level, and not offend anyone in any way. You should never use racist, discriminative or inappropriate words.

You might have a learner whose first language is not that which is to be used during the course. If so, you will need to find out how proficient they are with the language to be used. It might be that they would need to improve their second language skills prior to commencing. Alternatively, support could be given or translation software could be used.

Successful communication also includes listening, i.e. using eye contact and nodding, not interrupting, and not being judgemental when responding to what you've heard. It also includes other qualities that you can convey such as empathy and sympathy. *Empathy* and *sympathy* can be classed as skills of communication. You can express empathy when you have personally experienced something your learner has gone through. You can only sympathise when you haven't. However, don't be too keen to reveal to your learners any personal information about yourself that might affect the teacher/learner relationship. You may feel you are gaining a learner's confidence but you might also lose their respect. However, if there is anything that might affect the way you communicate, for example, a stutter or a disability, it's best to explain how this might have an impact. This way, your learners should be supportive and compassionate. Learners might tell you things that need to remain confidential, or they may discuss things with you that you cannot deal with; therefore, you may need to liaise with others when necessary.

Example

Marilyn had just finished her session with a group of 16–19 year olds working towards a Level 3 Diploma in Retail Skills. One of her learners, Jenna, asked to talk to her in confidence. She confided that she was pregnant and didn't know how to tell her parents. Marilyn listened to what she said and could empathise as she had been in the same situation at that age. However, she did not reveal this to Jenna as it was personal. With Jenna's agreement, Marilyn arranged a meeting with the training organisation's counsellor who was more qualified to help.

This example shows how important it is to support learners, but to keep anything personal to yourself. If one learner gets to know something about you, they could tell others and you might not want them knowing certain things.

When speaking to a group, you may have to practise with your voice projection, but don't shout, just speak a little louder and slower than normal, and always check that your learners can hear you. Sometimes nerves might make you speak faster or make nervous sounds like coughing or laughing. You could always record yourself for part of a session to listen to afterwards. You might be surprised at how you sound; you can then consider if you need to change anything.

Don't expect your learners to remember everything the first time you say it. It's fine to repeat or rephrase key points regularly. You might get frustrated if you are asked questions regarding points you have already explained. Try not to say things like 'I just told you that' or 'Can't you remember what I just said?' If a learner asks you to repeat something, don't embarrass them in front of their peer group; they may feel they can't ask you anything again. If one learner has asked you, others are perhaps thinking the same. If you are ever asked something you are unsure of, don't bluff your way through it. Tell your learners you will find out and then make sure you get back to them.

Learning occurs best in an active, not a passive environment, where communication is a two-way process. Try and watch for signals from your learners to check they are understanding what you are saying.

Example

Diane was explaining a complex topic and noticed one of her learners, Josh, was making a strange expression, furrowing his brow as if he didn't understand. As Diane regularly uses eye contact with her learners, she soon observed this. So as not to embarrass him, she rephrased to the group what she had just said. She was able to see from Josh's smiling and nodding face that he now understood. She also noticed a few other learners nodding too. To double-check Josh's understanding, she asked an open question to the group but nominated him to answer, which he successfully did.

Communication is an essential skill of a teacher, whether it's used verbally, non-verbally or in written or electronic form. Used effectively, it will enable you to share your knowledge and skills with your learners, enabling learning to take place.

Communicating with others

At some point, you will need to communicate with others: for example, colleagues, managers, visitors, and inspectors. You may also have to attend meetings or take part in video conferences. Wherever you are with other people, they might make assumptions about you based upon what they see and hear. You may have to write reports and respond to emails. The way you express yourself when writing is as important as when you are speaking. Always remain professional and leave any personal issues behind, otherwise these might impact upon your role. It is important that you have an organised and appropriate approach to communications with others. For example, not making a phone call to a colleague when you should be supervising a group activity.

The way you communicate might be influenced by your personality. For example, you might prefer to use an informal method such as emails, rather than formally meet in person. There are so many different ways to communicate now rather than in person. For example, telephone, online chats, social media, video conferencing and so on. Whichever method you use, you will need to make sure that what you convey is understood by the recipient and is in accordance with your organisation's guidelines.

You might not be liked by everyone; however, you are performing a professional role and you are not there to be everyone's friend. Don't take it personally if you feel someone doesn't like you; it's probably the situation they don't like rather than you as a person.

Records of communication

Records should always be maintained of all formal communications. This will enable them to be referred to at a later date, for example, if there is any doubt about what was actually said in a meeting, or if actions which should have been completed have not been. If you are in regular contact with learners, you will probably review their progress formally. This would involve a discussion about how they are progressing, and you will probably agree new achievement targets. If you didn't keep a record of this, you or the learner might forget what was discussed. Although you might feel it's time consuming, if clear, factual and specific records are kept, things should not be misinterpreted or forgotten.

Records can be kept electronically or as hard copies, and should always conform to any confidentiality, organisational and data protection requirements (covered in Chapter 1).

Extension activity

Think back to the last time you communicated with other professionals, for example, during a meeting. How did you act and react to them? What would you do differently next time? Consider how you normally communicate with people. Do you prefer a formal or an informal approach and why?

Reading, writing, speaking and listening

The four skills of language are *reading, writing, speaking and listening*. Using these in positive ways should help you to communicate effectively with your learners and others.

Reading and writing

As part of your job role, you may need to read lots of documents. For example, the qualification specification (or whatever is to be taught and assessed), minutes of meetings, and inspector's or quality assurer's reports. You will not only need to read them, but interpret them, understand them and act on any action points if necessary.

You may also need to create lots of documents, for example, schemes of work and session plans. You might need to produce handouts and learning materials, respond to emails and create visual presentations (covered in Chapter 7). The way you write these will be interpreted by your learners in a certain way which might not be the way you intended.

Some tips for reading include:

- being active, i.e. getting involved with what is written to really understand it. You may need to carry out further reading to gain more information or facts. You could re-write what you have read into your own words to demonstrate your understanding.

- being critical – evaluating what you have read and taking your own point of view. This could be when marking a learner's work. However, you must remain objective and keep to the marking criteria, rather than being subjective with your own opinions.

- making notes – writing down anything you don't understand to follow it up, i.e. looking up words in a dictionary that you are not familiar with.

- scanning – looking for key words, i.e. if you don't have a lot of time to read a full document. If you are researching information regarding a topic you are going to teach, you could look up key words in the contents or index of a text book to quickly locate what you are looking for.

- skimming – moving your eyes quickly over headings and text to look for the main points. In this way, you can see if it's relevant to you, or if you need to read it further.

Some tips for writing include:

- asking a colleague to proofread your work

- avoiding too many slang words, abbreviations, acronyms or jargon

- checking to see if anything could be misinterpreted – remember that the tone of how you write it might not be the same as how someone else reads it

- considering who will read your text, for example, if they have any visual disabilities

- ensuring your text covers equality, differentiation and inclusiveness

- expressing numbers in a certain way when including them in sentences. For example, *five days later*, rather than *5 days later*. This applies when the number is less than 10 or it begins a sentence. The number 10, or anything greater than 10, should be written as a number not a word, for example, *there were 15 in the group*.

- issuing a reading list, website list and/or a way to guide learners where they can obtain further information

- keeping sentences short and to the point, in a suitable font and size

- keeping your text logical and progressive

- not cutting out vowels in words

- not including too many facts or dates

- not mixing terms, for example, learner, student and candidate; just choose one and keep to it

- not putting too much on one page, i.e. spread things out and use spacing accordingly

- not raising any questions which are left unanswered

- not using a lot of exclamation marks (!) or needless emoticons (☺)

- not using too many CAPITAL LETTERS as it might appear you are shouting

- proofreading your work for spelling, grammar, punctuation and sentence construction errors

- reading what you have written as though a learner is reading it, to check it won't be misinterpreted or that the tone is not coming across as negative

- standardising documents and email signatures in accordance with the organisation's identity and branding

- using correct referencing if you are citing from books

- using visuals to back up your text, i.e. illustrations, pictures, graphs and diagrams when possible

- using language that suits the reader and is appropriate to the level of learning (please see Chapter 7 regarding checking the readability of text)

- using subject headings, underlining, bullets, italics or emboldening to emphasise points and break up large sections of text.

Speaking and listening

Speaking and listening involves *oral* and *aural* skills. You might be able to convey orally, i.e. verbally, what you want your learners to hear, but unless they have aural skills, i.e. listening skills, they won't really hear what you are saying. There is a difference between hearing and listening. If you go to the supermarket to get some shopping, there will probably be music playing in the background. You will hear this music as you progress with your shopping, but you don't deliberately set out to listen to it. It's the same with your learners, they might hear what you are saying, but whether they are listening or not might be another matter. To ensure that they are listening, you could regularly ask questions to check they have heard what you have said (covered in Chapter 10). If your session involves you speaking quite a lot, you could try and break this up by asking questions, showing a short video or asking your learners to carry out an activity based on what you have said. If you are talking a lot, they might stop listening and start thinking about other things, and you might not notice.

Example

Gracie planned to teach a one-hour session regarding employment law to a mature group of learners. She had made lots of notes and the more she researched the subject, the more she found to say. When she taught her session, she actually spoke for 40 minutes out of 60. When she asked some questions towards the end, she found her learners struggled to answer them. On reflection, she realised she should have involved her learners more and made the session about them, not her. She decided next time she would involve her learners from the start by asking what their experiences of the topic are. She would then be able to link these to what she had to say and ask questions throughout the session. She also decided to show a short video which her learners could discuss and to use a fun quiz towards the end of the session.

This example shows how Gracie made her session interactive and used various ways of communicating. This would help to ensure her learners are paying attention and to check that learning was taking place.

You should never assume that all your learners will understand or hear what you are saying. In fact, you should never assume anything. When commencing a session, it's a good idea to ask if everyone can hear you. Those at the back of the room might not be able to, and they might be too polite to tell you. Conversely, a learner might shout at you to speak up and interrupt the flow of what you are saying. You might have some learners who are hard of hearing; they might like to sit closer to you to hear you or to lip read. You could practise your voice projection or see if there is a microphone you can use if you are speaking to a large group.

You might also need to develop your own listening skills, to make sure you can hear what your learners are saying, no matter where they are positioned. Don't be afraid of asking them to speak up, or to repeat what they have said so that other learners can hear them too. It can be very frustrating for a learner to ask a question, which you then answer, but some of the other learners in the room didn't hear the question or the response. Listening skills also include non-verbal language such as nodding and smiling to show that you have heard what has been said.

Some tips for speaking include:

- allowing time for questions (by you and from your learners) but not getting too side-tracked by these

- asking if everyone can hear you (and see you if they are hard of hearing or will be lip reading)

- asking questions regularly to check that learners are listening and understanding

- avoiding ambiguity and misunderstandings by explaining things well

- backing up explanations with handouts and/or visual images

- being aware of your body language so that you are not appearing negative when speaking, i.e. by folding your arms

- being aware of your posture and gestures

- emphasising key words, repeating things, and summarising key points regularly

- ensuring you have the required subject knowledge, introducing and conveying this confidently, convincingly, passionately and enthusiastically

- explaining new or unusual words, jargon and acronyms

- giving constructive and positive feedback when applicable

- introducing points in a logical and progressive order

- not complicating your speech by including too much too soon

- not speaking too quickly

- not losing the point of what you are trying to convey

- recognising group dynamics, encouraging shy learners to get involved and managing over-confident ones

- remaining focused

- speaking a little more slowly and loudly than normal

- trying not to say *erm, yeah, okay, you know,* or saying *does that make sense?* (the latter may only gain a *yes* response as learners feel that is what you want to hear, ask open questions instead)

- trying not to say *obviously,* as things are only obvious to you

- using active listening skills

- using learners' names

- watching and listening to your learners for their reactions to what you are saying.

Some tips for listening include:

- avoiding interrupting

- avoiding reaching conclusions or hasty judgements

- leaving your emotions, arguments and thoughts behind

- limiting distractions if possible

- listening for a key word which will help you clarify what is being said

- stopping talking

- using body language such as nodding and smiling to convey you are listening

- using eye contact, but not in a threatening way

- watching your learners' body language for signs they don't understand something.

Effective listening only takes place when the person who receives the information interprets and understands it the way the deliverer intended. It can be easy to say something, and think you said it in a way that your learner will understand, only to find them asking you to say it again or to re-phrase it.

Activity

Think about the last time you heard something important. This might have been some information from a colleague or a family member, or perhaps you just listened to the news on the television or radio. Did you really listen to what was being said, or did you just tune into the parts that interested you? Was your mind wandering elsewhere or were you distracted by something? How could you improve your listening skills?

Active listening

Active listening is about focusing on what is being said. What someone says and what you hear can be very different. Often, personal assumptions and beliefs can distort what is heard. Try to use *active* listening skills. This includes repeating back or summarising what was said, to ensure that you have understood it. It also includes using positive body language and facial expressions to show you are listening. You might consider that you are a good listener; however, if you interrupt, look away, or get distracted, you may miss something which is said. If you are unsure what someone has said, ask them to repeat it or say, *'Did you mean ...?'* Questioning this way demonstrates that you are actively listening and confirms the communication between you and your learner.

Communication should always be a two-way process. If you can't listen to what your learners say or answer their questions satisfactorily, communication will break down. You might be distracted by external noises or interruptions and may not be able to concentrate on what is being said at the time. Listening to what is said is different from hearing what is going on in the background. You may need to pay more attention and to keep focused on what your learners are saying. When your learners speak to you, they might say things which you will need to react to in a certain way. Listening for a key word will help you respond appropriately.

Activity

Read the following sentences from learners. Decide what the key word is in each. How could you respond effectively?

1. *I'm sorry I'm late; I've got problems at home.*

2. *I don't think I can do this assignment; it's too hard.*

3. *You explain the topics well but go too fast for me to take it all in.*

1. The first key word is *problems,* you might like to ask the learner if there is anyone that can help out to ensure they arrive on time in future. You don't need to know what the problems are, unless the learner wishes to talk to you about them.

2. The second is *hard.* You could ask the learner why they are finding that the assignment is hard. Perhaps you could break the assignment down into smaller parts to help them.

3. The third is *fast.* If this learner feels this way maybe others do too. You could speak a little more slowly next time and vary your delivery techniques. For example, by involving your learners with questions or using activities to change the pace.

Active listening involves listening with a purpose; that is, to hear what you want to hear and yet remain able to listen to all that is being said. Try not to let other things distract you. If you find it hard to remember what is being said, repeat key words in your head or make notes to help you. This is a skill you can encourage your learners to develop too.

Understanding a little about your own personal communication style will help you create a lasting impression upon your learners and enable you to become a better listener. If you are aware of how others see and hear you, you should be able to adapt accordingly.

Verbal and non-verbal communication

It's good to be aware of your verbal (speech) and non-verbal (body language and visual aspects) communication so that you can adapt them if necessary. Non-verbal communication includes facial expressions, eye contact, gestures, posture, dress and appearance. There are some aspects of your non-verbal communication that you might not be able to control, such as facial flushing, blinking rapidly, or clearing your throat. However, there are some you might be able to control, such as winking, giving a thumbs-up sign or laughing. You may also need to take into account the way you speak, i.e. your pitch and tone of voice, or your accent or dialect.

When you are with your learners face to face you will demonstrate a mixture of verbal and non-verbal communication methods, as in Table 6.1 (on page 262). You can plan what you are going to say and control the way you do it, but you might not be able to plan your non-verbal signals. For example, you might plan to introduce a complex topic to your learners which could be misinterpreted if not conveyed in a logical order. Speaking too quickly or giving too much factual information will not allow learners time to assimilate their new knowledge. Poor body language or poor voice projection, too many gestures or facial expressions might prevent your learners from listening to what you are saying. Handouts with too much text or jargon, or which contain spelling errors, may lead to confusion.

Facial communication

The way you communicate by using your face can have a big impact upon the way your learners react to you. If you smile your eyes will appear to smile with you. This can be used to reassure a learner and to convey your personality. However, be cautious of having a fixed smile which might not look genuine. If you smile when speaking on the telephone, your voice will come across better than if you don't. Your face can express many emotions, i.e. sadness, happiness, anger, frustration, excitement and so on. You should try and match your facial expressions to what you are talking about at the time.

You might be good at using eye contact with learners, but looking away from a learner while you are talking or listening can appear ignorant. Too much eye contact could appear as staring and come across as threatening. Are you aware of how long you blink for? A long blink might be interpreted as shutting yourself out or becoming bored. Eye contact can convey involvement, intimacy and intimidation. Knowing how long to look at someone and the facial expressions you use at the same time, will come with experience.

Table 6.1 Examples of verbal and non-verbal communication

Verbal communication	Non-verbal communication
• being relaxed and natural when speaking • being conscious of your accent, dialect, pitch and tone when speaking • having a clear voice • not using too much jargon or acronyms • projecting your voice to suit the environment • smiling when speaking, when the other person cannot see you (e.g. on the telephone as it makes your voice sound better) • using humour appropriately • using an appropriate level of language to suit the learners and the subject • using pauses and pacing effectively when speaking • using visual aids to support what you are talking about	• acting genuinely • acting professionally • being aware of gestures and facial expressions • conveying a genuine interest in others by smiling and nodding • demonstrating good posture and movement • having a warm confident manner • limiting internal and external distractions • looking sincerely at people • moving naturally and easily • positioning yourself so that others can see and hear you • projecting positive body language • taking care of your appearance • using active listening skills • using good eye contact (not too short or too long) • wearing appropriate dress

Activity

Watch a television chat show or an interview with the sound turned down for a few minutes. Look at the body language and facial expressions as the host is asking questions and how they react to their guest. Can you gauge if the host is conveying involvement, intimacy and/or intimidation just by their facial expressions and use of eye contact? Turn the sound up and notice what they say and do to involve their guests. Would you do this differently and if so, in what way? Can you transfer any of these techniques to your own communication skills?

Body language

Your body language can communicate your interest in something or someone. Some people are quite open and extrovert, whereas others are closed and introvert. You might have some bad habits you are not aware of but which could inhibit effective communication. When speaking, are you aware of the gestures you are making and, if so, are they really necessary? They could be distracting: for example, rocking backwards and forwards while standing, waving your arms about or fiddling with something. If you don't know what to do with your arms, just clasp your hands gently in front of you; don't fold them as that can appear negative.

Do you slouch, hunch your shoulders, fiddle with a pen, or place your hands in your pockets? Do you walk about a lot, or lean in too close when talking to someone? When listening to someone, are you aware of what you are doing, not only with your body language, but your facial expressions and eye contact? You might not be aware of what you are doing but it might be having a negative impact upon your communication skills. Ideally, you need to be as relaxed as possible to come across as natural and convincing.

Appearance and dress

How you appear and dress might be influenced by the subject you teach, your culture and/or the organisation you work for. For example, you might have to wear a particular item of clothing for health and safety reasons or wear a uniform. It's best to dress in a way that portrays you as a professional and which is appropriate for the subject you are teaching. How you style your hair (and wear make-up or jewellery if relevant) will also say something about you. Unbrushed hair and too much make-up could lead to your learners looking at that, rather than focusing upon what is being said. A lack of personal grooming and cleanliness could affect the way others perceive you.

Example

Rahul taught at a school where dress was an important factor, both for teachers and learners. One morning, he was late out of bed and didn't have time to dress appropriately. His shirt was not pressed and he had forgotten his tie. There was a mark on his jacket and his shoes were unpolished. When he walked into the classroom his learners made disapproving noises and looked at each other in disbelief. Rahul tried to turn this to his advantage by talking about the importance of time management and organisation. However, his learners were not impressed. His manager also reprimanded him in the staff room later, which embarrassed him in front of his colleagues.

You might work in an organisation where informal dress is quite acceptable. However, your learners might still make a subconscious judgement about you which will be based on how you dress, act and speak. This judgement could be totally wrong, but is part of human nature. If you are communicating visually online, you should still make an effort regarding your appearance and dress to give a good impression.

Have you ever found yourself watching the news or weather on television, only to be thinking about what the presenter is wearing or how they styled their hair, and not taking in what they are saying? This might occur with your learners as they might be pre-occupied looking at your appearance and dress. They might not hear what you are saying or take you seriously. You never get a second chance to make a first impression.

Speech

The way you speak can help or hinder communication. For example, if you have a strong accent or dialect and your learners are not familiar with it, they might not understand what you are saying. It's best to ask them as you might be able to consciously speak a little more slowly and clearly once you know. The way you project your voice can also have an impact. If you don't speak loudly enough, learners at the back of the room might not hear you. There are other aspects to be aware of, such as becoming monotone when speaking, the tone of voice being used, or saying 'erm' a lot.

Example

Jerry, a rugby trainer, had dressed appropriately in the required kit for the first session with a new group. He was keen to set a good example of what a rugby player should wear and how they should act. However, when Jerry started speaking, his learners started laughing as he had a high-pitched voice. This appeared inconsistent with Jerry's image and became a barrier to communication. However, Jerry was unaware of this and just thought he had unruly learners. A colleague later told him, and he was able to work on the tone of his voice to lower the pitch.

To help the way you speak, try and become aware of your breathing and how relaxed you are. If you are nervous, you might speak quickly and more quietly than normal. When you speak or read text in front of learners, try not to be monotonous. You will know what you are talking about, and will probably have explained it many times. However, this will be the first time your learners hear it and they will want you to express yourself with enthusiasm and to make the topic interesting. Emphasising key words in sentences will show their significance. You won't want to come across as boring; therefore, be passionate about what you are talking about, and enjoy what you are doing. Your learners' futures are at stake and teaching is a big responsibility to have. Some people are naturally approachable, personable and likeable. However, you don't need to be liked by your learners to be a good teacher; you just need to communicate in a way that will help learning to take place. If you have a sense of humour, it could endear you to your learners, and make the sessions fun. However, you don't need to be telling jokes all the time, getting too friendly or using terms of endearment like 'mate' or 'pal'. You are a professional person and you won't want to give the wrong impression to your learners and others.

Your verbal and non-verbal communications should not be a barrier to teaching and learning, nor should any distractions. If you are in any doubt as to how well you are communicating, just ask your learners to tell you. If you can lead by example and project passion and enthusiasm for your subject, hopefully your learners will enjoy their time with you, and learning will take place.

Extension activity

If you are currently teaching, ask a colleague or your mentor to observe one of your sessions with a particular focus on how you communicate. Alternatively, make a visual recording of your session (with any necessary permissions) and watch this afterwards. You may be surprised at what you see. Perhaps you have mannerisms you weren't aware of when communicating, such as waving your arms about or repeatedly saying 'erm'.

Barriers to communication

A barrier to communication is anything that inhibits or prevents one person from receiving and understanding the message the other is trying to convey. It's not a physical barrier, but something that impedes the message getting through. When communicating, you should want to get your message across so that it is understood in the same way that you convey it. This will involve effort on behalf of the person sending the message, and the person receiving it. This is known as encoding and decoding. The sender will encode the message by talking, and the receiver will decode it by listening, as in Figure 6.1. The receiver should then feedback to the sender in some way, perhaps via their body language or by asking a question. This will help the sender know that the receiver has understood (or not) what they were trying to convey.

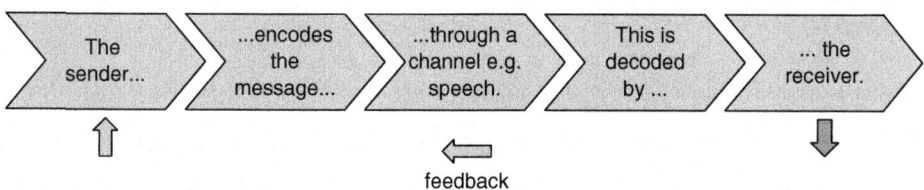

feedback

Figure 6.1 Encoding and decoding

Barriers can get in the way of effective encoding and decoding. If the sender does not transmit the message in a way the receiver can interpret and understand it, a breakdown in communication will take place. This could be a misinterpretation of what was said or a complete misunderstanding of it. If the channel used is not speech, but is written material, the receiver might read it in a totally different way to that which the sender intended. If the recipient is not present at the same time as the sender they cannot provide feedback to show that they have understood (or not).

Example

Aadi was talking enthusiastically to his new ballroom dancing learners at their first meeting. He was explaining the different titles of the dance moves of which he was familiar with, but his learners had never heard before. He could tell via their bemused faces that they were not understanding what he was saying. He soon realised he needed to introduce the names of the dance moves gradually throughout the course, perhaps at the same time as he demonstrated them. He also decided he would create a handout with pictures of the moves and their titles. One learner asked if she could make a visual recording of them practising the moves, so that she could view it later to help her remember. Aadi was fine with this and the rest of the group asked for a copy to help them too.

In this example, Aadi had not taken into account that it was the first time his learners had heard the titles of the dance moves. He was encoding the message, but his learners were not able to decode it. Through feedback, he was able to make a change.

External barriers

External barriers are those which are outside of your control. They can include the layout of the room, for example, fixed seating positions or the suitability of the environment. Always check that your learners are seated in areas of the room where they can see and hear you. If not, they might miss what you are saying or doing. You might also miss something they say or do. You could move tables and chairs if possible and if it's safe to do so. However, you might be in a room which is just not suitable and you will need to make the best of it if you can't move elsewhere.

Example

Andrew was teaching a group of learners working towards a biology qualification. They were based in a large science lab which had immovable work benches. Each bench had a sink, taps and various pieces of equipment fixed to it. This was fine for practical sessions; however, it was unsuitable for theory sessions. Andrew therefore asked his learners to move their chairs towards the front of the lab when they covered theory. There was room for them all to sit closer together; they could see and hear what he was talking about and still work in pairs to discuss various topics. Although this was not perfect, it did enable the learners to cover the theoretical topics in a more meaningful way.

Asking the learners to move, as in this example, helped to remove the barriers that might have hindered learning taking place.

Noise can also be a barrier. For example, if an airplane passes overhead or there is some other external noise, you (or your learners) should stop speaking until it passes. If the noise is going to be prolonged, such as roadworks outside the building, you could see if it's possible to move to another room. Noise can also be a distractor if it's from other learners, for example, if learners are working quietly in pairs on a topic, but a few others in the room start talking rather loudly. You would need to manage this in an appropriate way, perhaps by asking them to speak a little more quietly as they are disturbing the other learners. Setting ground rules and reminding learners to respect others might help with any issues that occur.

There might be times when you are interrupted which could cause a barrier to communication. For example, other people coming into your room when everyone is busy working on a task. This would disrupt the flow of the session and learners could become distracted. If you are expecting a visitor, such as an inspector or quality assurer, you will need to warn your learners that this will occur. It's best to ask them to behave as normal while the visitor is with you. Otherwise, they might want to please you by acting in a way they would not do normally. You might also be interrupted by people coming into your session whom you didn't expect, but who need to ask you something. Your learners will be looking at them and wondering what is going on. You could introduce the person, and then ask your learners to discuss a topic between themselves for a few minutes until you are free again.

A visual distraction could occur, for example, something happening outside the window. If most of your learners begin looking outside, it would be wise to ask them to stop looking. However, this would then generate interest in the other learners to see what is happening. You could instead draw attention to it for a minute and then ask your learners to focus back on what they were doing.

Whether the room is too cold or too hot can also be a barrier to effective communication. Learners might be focusing on trying to keep warm or when they can get some fresh air, rather than focusing on you. You will need to be aware of your learners' body language, for example, if learners start putting on their jackets. This should be a signal that they are cold. Conversely, if they start removing a jumper or cardigan, they will be too hot. You might be able to adjust the heating or open/close a window. Access to refreshments can also inhibit communication. If learners are thinking about when they can get something to eat or drink, they will not be focusing upon the topic. When you first meet your learners, you could explain when the breaks will be, and where they can get refreshments and when. You also might like to agree if they can have bottled water with them or not. You should explain where the toilet facilities are, and whether they need to ask if they can leave the room if they need to.

Equipment and technology can cause a barrier to learning, for example, if a learner is unable to use a piece of equipment due to a learning difficulty and/or disability, or another is not confident at using a computer. If possible, check everything is working before use and that it is appropriate and suitable for all learners to access and use.

Activity

What external barriers might you and your learners experience regarding communication? How could you help to resolve them to ensure communication remains effective?

Internal barriers

Internal barriers are those which relate to yourself or to a learner. They can include a lack of motivation, resistance to instruction, bad previous experiences of teaching and learning, or a learning difficulty or disability. Whenever possible, you need to find out what you can about your learners' internal barriers, to be able to support them. This could take place as part of the initial assessment process, or as a one-to-one discussion at an appropriate time. Your learners will be best placed to know what works for them so never be afraid to ask them. You will also need to realise what your own internal barriers are, for example, a lack of confidence when using new technology.

Example

Freya was due to teach maths to a group of 19–24 year olds. She was not confident at using the interactive whiteboard but wanted to give it a go. During the session, she kept getting things wrong and her learners began losing attention. When she realised this, she stopped using the interactive whiteboard and reverted to using a standard board. Her learners were then able to follow what she was doing. Afterwards, Freya asked her supervisor if she could attend a training session to learn how to use the interactive whiteboard properly.

Once you are aware of any barriers you can do something about it. Never be afraid to ask for help and support, you should not be expected to know everything.

Some learners might not be very good at speaking and listening, for example, if English is not their first language. Furthermore, they might misinterpret something you are saying, or be too polite or shy to ask you to clarify something they are unsure about. If you have a learner who has Asperger's syndrome, they might take what you say quite literally; therefore, you will need to be very clear with what you are saying. Some cultures don't advocate interrupting a speaker, or asking questions, or challenging what was said. If you are aware of this, you can ask lots of open questions to help you check that your learners have understood what you have been saying.

You might have learners who are partially or fully deaf or blind, or who have a learning difficulty or disability which might affect the way you, and other learners, communicate with them. Some might have a learning support assistant (covered in Chapter 3) with them, who will need to be accommodated next to them in the room. You would need to find out how you can make the learner's experience a rewarding one. Talk to both the learner and their assistant to find out how you can help. Never make any assumptions about what they might need or not need.

You might need to talk to someone else in your organisation to arrange for specialist people or equipment to be available, for example, an audio loop, Braille equipment, or a sign language interpreter. Some learners might attend sessions with a guide dog. If there is a dog in the room, don't encourage the other learners to approach it, as the dog is a working dog and should not be distracted.

Extension activity

What internal barriers might you experience as a teacher? How could you help to resolve them to ensure communication remains effective with your learners? What internal barriers do you think your learners might encounter? How could you help to resolve them?

Interpersonal and intrapersonal skills

A way of differentiating between *inter*personal and *intra*personal skills is to regard interpersonal skills as those which occur *between people* and intrapersonal skills as those which occur *within a person*.

Interpersonal skills are about the ability to recognise distinctions between other people, to know their faces and voices, to react appropriately to their needs, to understand their motives, feelings and moods, and to appreciate such perspectives with sensitivity and empathy. Possessing interpersonal skills can help you develop your personal and professional relationships.

Ways to improve interpersonal skills include:

- being a mentor to others
- meeting new people at work, social groups, clubs, meetings and events
- participating in workshops or seminars
- spending time each day practising active listening skills with friends, family, colleagues and others
- starting a support/network group in person or online.

Intrapersonal skills are about having the ability to be reflective and access your inner feelings. Having this ability can enable you to recognise and change your own behaviour, build upon your strengths and reduce your limitations. This should result in quick improvements, developments and achievements as people have a strong ability to learn from past events and from others.

Ways to improve intrapersonal skills include:

- attending courses, e.g. Neuro Linguistic Programming (NLP), Transactional Analysis (TA) and Emotional Intelligence (EI) (covered later in this chapter)
- developing an interest or hobby
- keeping a reflective learning journal or diary
- meditation or quiet time alone to think and reflect
- observing people who are great leaders, motivators, speakers or positive thinkers
- reading self-help books
- setting short- and long-term goals and following these through.

Look at the previous bullet lists of how to improve interpersonal and intrapersonal skills. What do you think you can do to improve your own skills? If you can, put them into practice and then evaluate how you have improved.

Howard Gardner (1993) defines intrapersonal intelligence as: *sensitivity to our own feelings, our own wants and fears, our own personal histories, an awareness of our own strengths and weaknesses, plans and goals.* (Gardner, 1993, page 263). He is best known for his theory of multiple intelligences of which there are eight, interpersonal and intrapersonal being two of them. The other six are:

- linguistic – the ability to use language to codify and remember information; to communicate, explain and convince

- logical – also known as mathematical intelligence; the capacity to perceive sequence, pattern and order, and to use these observations to explain, extrapolate and predict

- musical – the capacity to distinguish the whole realm of sound and, in particular, to discern, appreciate and apply the various aspects of music (pitch, rhythm, timbre and mood), both separately and holistically

- naturalist – the ability to recognise, appreciate, and understand the natural world; it involves such capacities as species discernment and discrimination, the ability to recognise and classify various flora and fauna, and knowledge of and communion with the natural world

- physical – also called kinaesthetic intelligence; the ability to use your body in highly differentiated and skilled ways, for both goal-oriented and expressive purposes; the capacity to exercise fine and gross motor control

- visual-spatial – the ability to accurately perceive the visual world and to re-create, manipulate and modify aspects of your perceptions.

According to Gardner, individuals possess all of these intelligences. However, they are not all present in equal proportions (in extreme circumstances it may appear that an individual is severely lacking in one or more). The particular combination of intelligences and their relative strengths can form a profile that is unique to each individual. Some people are more intelligent than their peers; others appear superior at certain tasks, are more capable of manipulating information or more readily see the solutions to problems. Some are more expressive or more capable of learning new tasks quickly.

Austin is working towards an electrical installation qualification. He can communicate well with his teacher and peers (interpersonal and linguistic skills), he can also calculate, use approximations and measurements to good effect (logical and visual-spatial skills). He is good at thinking and reflecting about what he is doing (intrapersonal skills) and manipulating himself to reach awkward areas when fitting cables (physical). The two intelligences of musical and natural do not apply to him and he does not feel the need to utilise them for the job he is aiming for.

Gardner's eight intelligences have been debated and amended by many other theorists over time. They can be compared to various learning preference theories, for example, Honey and Mumford's (1986) Activist, Pragmatist, Reflector and Theorist (covered in Chapter 2). Being aware of differing intelligences with your learners, and in yourself, might help you consider alternative ways of communicating.

Extension activity

Research interpersonal and intrapersonal skills further. What do you consider their meanings to be? How can you differentiate between the two when teaching and communicating with learners and others?

Theories of communication

People act differently depending upon the situation they are in and the people they are with at the time. You might find that on a one-to-one basis a colleague is quite mature but in a meeting they can be rather disruptive and immature. There are many more theories of communication besides those listed here and you will find some weblinks at the end of this chapter if you wish to research further. Some theories regarding communicating in teams are covered in Chapter 5. You will need to make your own mind up whether or not you think the theories will influence what you do with your learners. You might even come up with your own communication theory to challenge existing ones.

Transactional Analysis

Berne's (1973) Transactional Analysis (TA) theory is a method of analysing communications between people. Berne identified three personality states; the *child*, the *parent* and the *adult*. These states are called *ego states* and people behave and exist in a mixture of these. This is due to their: past experiences, gestures, vocal tones, expressions, attitudes, vocabulary and the situation they are in at the time.

TA assumes all past events, feelings and experiences are stored within and can be re-experienced in current situations. You might see this with learners who take on a different state depending on who they are with. For example, acting like a child and asking for help from a teacher, but acting like an adult with their peers.

Transactions are verbal exchanges between two people: one speaks and the other responds. If the conversation is complementary, i.e. adult to adult, as in Figure 6.2, then the transactions enable the conversation to continue.

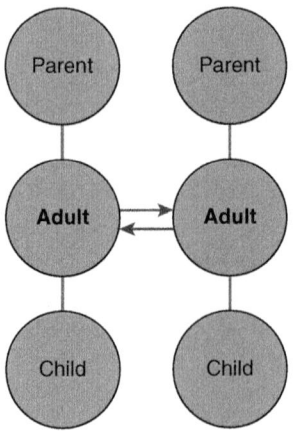

Figure 6.2 Complementary adult-to-adult communication

If the transactions are *crossed*, as in Figure 6.3, i.e. parent to child, the conversation may change its nature or come to an end.

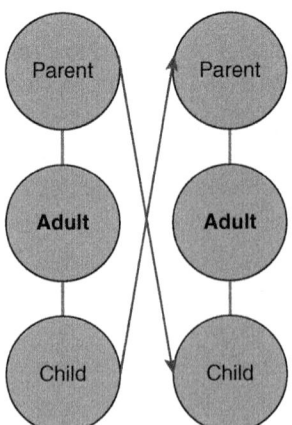

Figure 6.3 Crossed parent-to-child communication

Berne recognised that people need *stroking*. Strokes are acts of recognition which one person gives to another and can be positive or negative. They are not physical but are words of appreciation or otherwise. Giving or receiving *positive* strokes develops emotionally healthy people who are confident in themselves and have a feeling of being *okay*. You could consider giving feedback to a learner to be like stroking. Negative strokes (or feedback) can lead to a person being demoralised if not given in a skilful way.

Example

Ibrahim was working towards an introductory teaching qualification and wanted to prove to his assessor how good he was. He kept saying to himself, I'll be okay if I produce all the required work to please my assessor and I don't make any mistakes. *By doing this, Ibrahim felt he would be looked upon more favourably and receive strokes of appreciation in the form of positive feedback. He felt the feedback would encourage and motivate him.*

Understanding a little about the different ego states of the child, parent and adult will help you see how your learners take on different roles in different situations, particularly during group work where some may become quite childish or dominate and take control.

If you ever feel like a *child* at work, it may be because your supervisor is operating in their *parent* state and you are responding in your *child* state. Your *child* state makes you feel small, afraid, undervalued, demotivated and rebellious. These feelings may make you undermine, withdraw, gossip, procrastinate, plot revenge, or attempt to please in order to be rewarded. In this *child* state, you will find it very hard to become a successful professional. If you realise that you have moved into a particular *state*, it is possible to change if you need to. When you feel your *child* state about to make you withdraw, gossip or undermine, you can choose instead to participate, find out the facts and resolve your differences in the *adult* state.

As a teacher, you may find yourself acting like a *parent*. You may have learnt this from your parents' responses to you years ago. The *parent* state makes you feel superior, detached and impatient. Being in this state can make you harden your tone, not listen to people, shout, bribe others into complying, or criticise them more than encourage them. When you feel your *parent* state about to make you criticise or take over, you can choose instead to speak warmly, be patient, listen and find enjoyment in the challenge by acting in the *adult* state.

The best option is to remain in the *adult* state. As an *adult*, you feel good about yourself, respectful of the talents and lives of others, delighted with challenges, proud of accomplishments and expectant of success. These feelings make you respond to others by appreciating and listening to them, using respectful language, perceiving the facts, considering alternatives, and having a long-term view and enjoyment of work and life. However, it is very difficult to consistently be in the *adult* state. You may find yourself adapting to different situations and responding and reacting to the states other people have taken on. However, trying to remain in the adult state should help you gain confidence and respect from your colleagues and learners, as well as performing your job role satisfactorily.

Activity

Do you find you act in the child, parent or adult state with any particular people? If so, why do you think this is and would you change anything if you could? The next time you talk to a colleague, observe how they act and react to you and vice versa.

Emotional intelligence

Emotional intelligence (EI) is a behavioural model, given prominence in Daniel Goleman's book *Emotional Intelligence* (1995); however, work originally began on the model in the 1970s and 1980s by Howard Gardner.

The EI concept argues that IQ (Intelligence Quotient) or conventional intelligence, is too narrow as there are wider areas of EI that dictate and enable how successful people are. Possessing a high IQ rating does not mean that success automatically follows.

Goleman identified five domains of emotional intelligence:

- knowing your emotions

- managing your emotions

- motivating yourself

- recognising and understanding other people's emotions

- managing relationships, i.e. the emotions of others.

The principles of EI provide a new way to understand and assess people's behaviour, attitudes, interpersonal skills, management styles, and potential. This could be useful if you have groups of learners who aren't always working in a consistent manner. By developing EI, Goleman suggested that people can become more productive and successful at what they do, and help others to be more productive and successful too. He also suggested that the process and outcomes of developing EI contain aspects which are known to reduce stress for individuals and organisations. This can help improve relationships, decrease conflict, and increase stability, continuity and harmony. Becoming aware of your own emotions and how they can affect what you do could help you develop more fulfilling and professional relationships with your colleagues and learners.

Neuro Linguistic Programming

Neuro Linguistic Programming (NLP) is a model of interpersonal communication concerned with relationships and experiences. Interpersonal skills are those which take place *between people,* in contrast to intrapersonal skills which are *within a person.*

The model can be useful when providing feedback to learners to help influence their development. NLP is a way to increase self-awareness and to change patterns of mental and emotional behaviour. Richard Bandler and John Grinder, the co-founders of NLP in the 1970s, claimed it would be instrumental in finding ways to help people have better, fuller and richer lives. They created the title to reflect a connection between neurological processes (neuro), language (linguistic) and behavioural patterns (programming). These have been learned through experience and can be used to achieve specific goals. The model was based on how some very effective communicators were habitually using language to influence other people.

NLP training should help turn negative thoughts into positive thoughts. It provides the skills to define and achieve outcomes, along with a heightened awareness of the five senses (sight, hearing, touch, smell and taste).

NLP techniques can be used to:

- coach learners how to gain greater satisfaction from their contributions

- enhance the various skills of learners

- improve own and others' performance

- improve an individual's effectiveness and productivity

- set clear goals and define realistic strategies

- understand and reduce stress and conflict.

NLP provides questions and patterns to make communication more clearly understood. For example, all thoughts and behaviours have a structure and all structures can be re-programmed. For example, do you regularly use jargon, complex terms or clichés without thinking? Your learners might not understand what you are talking about because you assume they already have the knowledge. If so, you will need to try and re-programme yourself to stop doing this.

Extension activity

Arrange to observe a colleague, preferably in your subject area, to watch how they interact with their learners. Are they using any of the theories of communication which have been mentioned in this chapter?

If you can't carry out an observation, watch or listen to influential people on the television, radio or via the internet. Ask yourself what it is about them that makes them communicate well (or not). Can you emulate the good points yourself? If so, try them out when you can.

Self-assessment checklist

Do I know about the following?

If not, re-read this chapter, or research the texts and websites listed at the end.

- ☐ The importance of communication

- ☐ Different methods of communication

- ☐ Different communication skills, e.g. those associated with reading, writing, speaking and listening

- ☐ How to improve reading, writing, speaking and listening skills

- ☐ How to use active listening skills

- ☐ The difference between verbal and non-verbal communication skills

☐ How to improve facial communication and body language

☐ How appearance and dress can affect communication

☐ Examples of external and internal barriers to communication and how to overcome them

☐ How transactional analysis can affect communication

☐ The difference between interpersonal and intrapersonal skills

☐ How to use NLP techniques

Summary

This chapter has explored how communication can be used to pass on information from one person to another in a positive way.

You should now be able to communicate effectively with learners, as well as other people and professionals you will come into contact with. You should also know about various communication theories to help you support your learners in a meaningful way.

You might like to carry out further research by accessing the books and websites listed at the end of this chapter, particularly if you are working towards a higher level teaching qualification.

This chapter has covered the following topics:

• The importance of communication

• Reading, writing, speaking and listening

• Verbal and non-verbal communication

• Barriers to communication

• Interpersonal and intrapersonal skills

• Theories of communication

References and further information

Appleyard, N. and Appleyard, K. (2010) *Communicating with Learners in the Lifelong Learning Sector.* Exeter: Learning Matters.

Ashmore, A. and Robinson, D. (2015) *Learning, Teaching and Development.* London: SAGE.

Bates, B. (2016) *A Quick Guide to Special Needs and Disabilities.* London: SAGE.

Beattie, G. (2016) *Rethinking Body Language: How Hand Movements Reveal Hidden Thoughts.* Abingdon: Psychology Press.

Berne, E. (1973/2016) *Games People Play: The Psychology of Human Relationships.* London: Penguin Books Ltd.

Gardner, H. (1993/2011) *Frames of Mind: Theory of Multiple Intelligences*. New York: Basic Books.

Goleman, D. (1995) *Emotional Intelligence*. London: Bloomsbury.

Gould, J. (2012) *Learning Theory and Classroom Practice in the Lifelong Learning Sector*. London: Learning Matters SAGE.

Stewart, I. and Joines, V. (2012) *TA Today: A New introduction to Transactional Analysis*. Kegworth: Lifespace Publishing.

Websites

Association for Neuro Linguistic Programming – www.anlp.org

Emotional Intelligence – www.unh.edu/emotional_intelligence/index.html

Reading list for teaching and learning – www.anngravells.com/reading-lists/teaching

Transactional analysis – www.ericberne.com/transactional-analysis/

7

Resources

Introduction

Resources are all the items which you can use to help with your job role and to teach and assess your subject. They include: books, handouts, equipment, objects and people. The main purpose of using resources is to stimulate learning, add impact and promote interest in your subject.

This chapter will explore different types of resources and how you can use them for your role and with your learners. Creating and using various types of presentations, handouts and worksheets is covered, as is how to evaluate their use. Electronic resources are covered in Chapter 8.

This chapter will cover the following topics:

- Physical resources
- People as resources
- Creating and adapting resources
- Meeting the individual needs of learners through resources
- Visual presentations, handouts and worksheets
- Evaluating resources

Physical resources

Physical resources are those which are tangible and real. They can be seen, touched and used by you and your learners. For example, an interactive whiteboard, a textbook, a piece of equipment or a handout. Depending upon your subject and what is or is not already available, you may need to create your own, or adapt someone else's resources. This might be a worksheet or a complex working model used to demonstrate a topic. You might have to acknowledge your organisation's resource constraints and make best use of what is available. Using visual aids such as adding posters to the wall of a room can help to reinforce points. They can often be purchased quite cheaply or found free via the internet. Learners may not always look at them consciously, but subconsciously they will glance at them and hopefully take in the information.

Resources are often referred to as *learning materials* or *supplies*. The main principle of using them should be that they are accessible and inclusive to all learners. They should enable all learners to acquire new skills, knowledge and understanding. They can also be used to reinforce points and consolidate learning. Most learners like variety; they won't want to get bored. Using resources can therefore help capture and stimulate interest. You will need to plan what to use and when, and be prepared to devote time to creating and practising using them. A list of example resources is in Table 7.1 (on page 280), electronic resources are covered in Chapter 8. After using a resource, you could evaluate the effectiveness of it to modify or change it for future use.

There might be some external resources your learners could benefit from accessing, which could give them valuable experience that relates to the subject. For example, museums, exhibitions and conferences. You might have to organise the visit yourself, including taking any safeguarding measures into account and arranging transport and/or funding. Alternatively, there might be someone in your organisation with responsibility for this. If there isn't time for external visits during the course, you could recommend that your learners undertake the visit in their own time. This would be providing they have the maturity and the finance, if applicable. Make sure you discuss the experience with your learners afterwards and/or ask them to write about it. This way, you can check what they have learnt and what impact it has had.

The purpose of resources

The main purpose of using resources is to stimulate learning, add impact and promote interest in your subject. Whichever resources you choose to use, you will need to make sure they are fit for purpose, are at the required level of learning, are relevant and are accessible to everyone. To help you decide what sort of resource to use, it might help to consider why you want to use it to ensure learning can take place. For example, to:

* aid revision
* assess learning
* consolidate learning
* encourage learning
* support teaching.

Table 7.1 Examples of resources

Information and communication technology	Objects	External resources	People	Other
• 3D printers • Audio, visual and digital recorders • Augmented reality • Blogs, vlogs, podcasts, forums, wikis • Calculators • CDROMs/DVDs • Computers/laptops/netbooks/tablets • Digital cameras • Gaming • Handheld devices • Interactive whiteboards • Internet/Intranet • Microscope • Mobile phones and smartphones • Personal digital assistants • Photocopier • Programs, software and applications • Radio • Scanners • Social networking sites • Television • Video conferencing • Virtual learning environment (VLE) • Virtual reality goggles • Visual presentations • Voting technology • Wearable technology • Webcam	• Animals • Apparatus • Artefacts • Games and board games • Laminator • Models • Plants • Puppets • Robotics • Samples of products • Specimens • Sports equipment • Subject-specific resources • The *real thing* • Tools • Toys	• Cinema/theatre/concert • Conferences • Events • Exhibitions • Field trips • Lectures • Libraries • Museums • Specialist shops • Sports/leisure centres **Visual aids** • Chalk board • Charts • Display board • Flannel/sticky/magnetic boards • Flip chart paper and pens • Learning wall • Maps • Mini whiteboards • Overhead projectors (OHPs) • Photographs • Posters • PowerPoints and other presentation software • Projectors and data projectors • Slides • Videos • Whiteboard	• Internal, e.g. colleagues, teachers, trainers, managers, mentors, technicians, administrative staff, support staff • External, e.g. employers, supervisors, work-based witnesses • Friends and relatives • Information, advice & guidance and careers staff • Learners • Manufacturers and suppliers • Other professionals such as agency staff, quality assurers, awarding organisation personnel, subject experts • Visiting, expert and guest speakers • Volunteers • Yourself	• Advertisements • Binoculars • Books • Catalogues • Card sort activities • Comics • Drones • Epidiascope • Food and cooking ingredients • Gapped handouts • Handouts of information • Headsets • Information leaflets • Instruction, guidance and training sheets • Instruction books • Journals • Magazines • Manuals • Newspapers • Original documents • Periodicals • Photocopies of documents • Promotional literature • Publicity materials • Puzzles and quizzes • Reference books • Reports • Stationery • Telescope • Textbooks • Wordsearches/crosswords • Worksheets/workbooks

Don't just use a resource for the sake of it. Whatever you use should have a real purpose and benefit to your learners. For example, you might think that using an electronic presentation will add variety to your session, but some learners might not pay attention to it or they might get distracted. If you have access to the internet during your session, you could try something different, for example, the free Prezi online presentation program (https://prezi.com) or others such as those listed in Chapter 8. These programs utilise more interactive activities than PowerPoint can and they might help gain learners' attention more. However, a new program will take time to learn to use.

When using resources, you will need to plan how much time to devote to their use with learners. It might be that you want to demonstrate how to use a piece of equipment, and then let your learners have a go. If you don't have enough for all learners and they have to share, it might take longer than you had planned. It's also worth noting that some learners might not want to share with some other learners, or that one learner might dominate its use. Careful planning of who will work with who can help with this. It is important that all your learners get the chance to have a go or they might feel left out. You could therefore plan to reduce the time for something else if this happens. You will also need to consider how long the resource is going to take you to prepare and/or set up, and if any finance is required. There might not be a budget available for resources so you might have to make the best of what you have. If you don't have the latest version of something make sure you inform your learners what is currently available and/or show a video or pictures of it.

Always have a clear rationale to justify the resources you have chosen to use. Using the: *who, what, when, where, why* and *how* rationale is a good basis for determining how relevant, purposeful and effective your resource will be.

Activity

Think of a resource you would like to use with your learners for your subject. For example, a handout or a piece of equipment. What is its purpose, i.e. to aid revision, assess learning, consolidate learning, encourage learning and/or support teaching? Write a rationale for: who, what, when, where, why and how it will be used. This should help you focus on its relevance to the topic you will be covering.

Resources can be used to (in alphabetical order):

- act as an aid to memory
- add variety
- add visuals and pictures to show what you are talking about
- aid revision
- allow for differentiation
- assess learning
- consolidate learning

- create interest

- enable learners to try things out for themselves

- encourage learning

- increase understanding

- inspire, excite and motivate learners

- promote equality

- provide relevant information

- reinforce key points

- stretch and challenge the capability of learners

- stimulate the senses, e.g. sight, hearing, touch, smell and taste

- support teaching.

If you will be demonstrating and explaining how to use a piece of equipment, keep what you say as simple as you can. You will be familiar with it but it might be the first time your learner has seen and used it. Often, manufacturers' instructions can be quite complicated. You could therefore write some instructions yourself. If so, work through them yourself to check that they are aimed at a beginner before giving them to your learners. After a learner has used the equipment, you could ask them to demonstrate its use to another learner, if safe to do so. This would show you what they have learnt. You could even ask your learners to write the instructions themselves. This would reinforce their learning in their own words. If a resource you are using is not effective with some learners, try changing the experience rather than the resource. For example, changing a group activity to become an individual one.

When using resources, you may have to deal with unexpected situations which might occur. It is useful to have a contingency plan just in case.

Example

Jack was due to deliver a food hygiene session to a group of 12 learners just after lunch. He had created a digital presentation and saved it to a memory stick. He arrived half an hour early, only to find a notice on the door stating he had been moved to another room. In the other room were two circular tables that would seat six learners comfortably, but only four chairs at each. He switched on the computer and realised the version of his presentation was newer and it wouldn't work. However, because he was early he was able to locate and ask the caretaker to bring four extra chairs. He had printouts of the presentation which he could give to each learner. He also had time to go to the office and resave the document in a previous version. While there, he saved it to the organisation's hard drive, which was accessible from any room, just in case a problem occurred with his memory stick. As Jack had a contingency plan, he was able to deliver the session effectively.

Preparing for unforeseen circumstances comes with experience. Whenever you are due to meet your learners, ask yourself, *What would I do if something isn't available or doesn't work?* For example, you might prepare a digital presentation and make copies as handouts that you can give your learners. However, if you can't get copies made in time, you can still deliver your presentation, and offer to email a copy to your learners, upload it to a virtual learning environment (VLE) or get photocopies made later. Try not to rely totally on presentation software when teaching: use different approaches and activities to add variety and maintain interest.

Obtaining resources

When you first start your role as a teacher or a trainer, you will need to find out what resources are currently available to you. It might be that you are based in the same room for all your sessions, which has suitable equipment and resources within it. If so, you will need to check that anything you will use is in working order and is safe. This might involve asking someone in your organisation to check it, for example, if it's electrical. You wouldn't want you or your learners to have an accident. Some equipment might be out of date, but still useable. If there isn't enough funding to purchase the latest piece of equipment, it might be that there is a video available online which learners could watch. This would give them an idea of how things advance and change. You could even ask your learners to research information about newer models, and then report back to the rest of the group. There might be some equipment in other areas of the building which you could take your learners to see being used. Alternatively, you could contact local organisations to see if your learners could visit to see the equipment in operation, for example, a printing press.

You might be lucky in that there could be some funding available to purchase equipment or resources. If so, you would need to check if you have to use an approved supplier or whether you can choose your own to save money. Often, you will just have to make the best of what is available or what you can legitimately obtain. You could contact local organisations to ask if they have any relevant equipment or resources which they no longer need. Often, they will be happy to donate them to educational organisations, for example, computers and printers. If you need to use devices with internet access, but don't have enough at your organisation, you could let your learners use theirs. If most learners have their own devices, they would probably be happy to use them during sessions when relevant. This is known as bring your own device (BYOD); however, you would need to agree some ground rules, such as not checking personal social networking sites. Sharing could take place if not all learners have their own device.

Resources, such as visual presentations, handouts and worksheets could be created by a team of staff who all teach the same subject or topic. There's no point your creating a handout if there is one available already. These could be held centrally on a computer system for electronic access or saved remotely in the cloud for access on any device with an internet connection. Always make sure you have a backup copy in case of any issues which might occur. If you attend standardisation meetings with colleagues, this would be a good time to find out what is available and what could be created or updated. If there is a bank of materials which you could access, you can then amend and update the materials to suit your session and learners. If they are shared electronically, you will need to decide if they can be amended by anyone or re-saved elsewhere. When creating and saving a bank of resources, make sure they are organised into categories, e.g. topics. This will save time when accessing them in the future. Adding a footer with the document title, file location and date will help you to keep track of them.

Before you create any of your own resources, take a look online. There are lots of resources and learning materials freely available, for example, handouts and worksheets.

Activity

If you have access to the internet, carry out a search for resources for your particular subject area, e.g. science resources. You might find a lot of them are for schools rather than further education; however, you might be able to download, save and adapt them. You will need to check that they are appropriate, whether there are any copyright restrictions and if you can have unlimited use. You might need to acknowledge the source if you print or use anything with learners.

Often, qualifications have reading lists of recommended textbooks for learners to refer to. These are usually listed in the qualification specification (if applicable). If not, you could create your own list for your learners of relevant books. If there is a learning resource centre (LRC) at your organisation, you could check if any relevant books are available there or, if not, if they could be ordered. You could reserve a session with a member of the LRC staff to show your learners around. If they become familiar with the LRC they might feel more confident to use it regularly. However, not all organisations have library facilities available. You may have to find out from a public library what books, computer facilities, and other useful resources they have available for your learners to borrow or use.

To help you decide which books are appropriate, you could carry out a search via an online book store for your particular subject. If learners need to have their own copy, they could also search the internet to find where they are the cheapest, so that all learners can benefit. Alternatively, your organisation might get a discount for a bulk order via the publisher, which they could then pass on to the learners. Publishers are often happy to give away free inspection copies of textbooks to teachers if you provide feedback or recommend the books to your learners.

Activity

If you have access to the internet, carry out a search for your subject via an online book store, e.g. Amazon (www.amazon.com). See what books are available and who publishes them. Then have a look at the publisher's website to see if they offer a free inspection copy. You might need to register first so that the publisher can check you are a legitimate teacher. When you receive and have read the book, remember to provide feedback to the publisher. If a reading list of relevant textbooks does not currently exist for your subject, have a go at creating one to issue to your learners.

Some resources might be available for you to use in your organisation on a booking system. For example, a television or an overhead projector might be kept centrally. When booked for a certain date and time, it will be placed in your room ready to use. If you have to move any equipment yourself, you will need to be careful or ask someone to help. If you are using electrical equipment you will need to ensure cables are out of the way, as they could become a tripping hazard. You will also need to ensure your learners follow all health and safety regulations.

Example

John is teaching a do-it-yourself woodwork programme to a mixed group of adults in a community learning centre. He has been teaching this group for a while and knows most of them really well. In this session, the learners are using battery-powered drills to make holes in pieces of wood. They have used these drills before and John therefore assumed they knew the procedures regarding health and safety. One particularly important point is that only one learner operates a drill at any one time. One drill was not working properly and a learner held the drill bit while another learner tried to switch it on. Fortunately, John saw what was happening and yelled across the room. A serious accident was averted – this time. John realised he needed to recap the health and safety guidelines at the commencement of each session.

Always be careful with any equipment both you and your learners will use. You might find it useful to recap the safety advice each session and to ask some questions to check your learners' understanding.

Extension activity

Look at the list of resources in Table 7.1 and make a list of the ones you could use for your subject, and add any of your own. Choose three and consider how they will stimulate learning, add impact and promote interest in your subject. What are the advantages and disadvantages of each?

People as resources

Teachers are one of the most effective resources available to learners. You will want to provide a stimulating and interesting environment in which learning can take place. Learners who have a good experience usually state that this is because they have had a good teacher. Where there is a poor experience, this might also be due to the teacher. It's a big responsibility on your own, particularly if you are new to the role. You could consider asking other relevant people to help, providing they are willing and able. For example, they could talk to your learners about their experiences of the subject.

Activity

Make a list of all the people you could contact who could be a valuable resource for your subject. Consider what value they could add to your sessions and how your learners will benefit.

People you could contact (who are explained below) include:

- colleagues
- expert speakers
- friends and family
- learners
- mentors
- supervisors and witnesses
- support staff.

Colleagues

Colleagues can be a vital source of expertise and you should not be afraid to ask for help and advice from them. It's useful to build working relationships with them and others in your organisation, as well as from different organisations, so that both you and your learners can benefit from the exchange of expertise. You might like to ask a colleague to co-deliver a session with you, or ask them to deliver a topic they are more experienced in. This would depend upon how much time they will have to spare. Having a different person to that which your learners are used to can add another dimension to the subject.

Expert speakers

You could ask experts from industry, business and commerce who work in the area of your subject to speak to your learners. This would add variety to your sessions and enable your learners to ask questions that they might not ask you. They will be known as *guest speakers*. They can provide additional knowledge as they are an authority on their subject. This could include people working in industry, authors, politicians and journalists who can bring a different and new perspective to your subject. You might even learn something yourself. If you know of, or can get in touch with someone who is an authority in the subject area you are teaching, why not ask them? You might need to seek approval from your organisation for them to visit, and find out if they can be paid (or not) for their time and expenses. You will need to give them some advance information, for example, the number in your group, what topics you are covering at the time, and what they might like to talk about. Do remember that you want it to have an impact upon your learners; it's not just a way of giving you free time while they are speaking. When they arrive, they will need to sign in at reception and follow your organisation's guidelines for visitors. You will need to introduce them to your learners and state why they are there. If you can give some advance notice to your learners, they will have time to think of some questions they would like to ask. You should remain present with the visitor while they are with your learners, as your organisation will have safeguarding procedures to follow.

Friends and family

It might be that you have friends and family members who are knowledgeable regarding your subject. This could be if they operate a business or work in your subject area. You might be able to arrange a visit for your learners to see them working, or ask them to come and speak to your learners. The same arrangements for expert speakers visiting your organisation would apply.

Learners

Learners can be considered a valuable resource. Those who have completed their course and left could be asked to return to give a talk to your current learners. This would be a great opportunity for them to talk to someone who has been in their position. Learners could ask questions about how the course has helped them personally and professionally, and how they applied for various jobs. The same arrangements for expert speakers visiting your organisation would apply.

Mentors

A mentor is someone who is a specialist in the subject you wish to teach. They might be a colleague in the same organisation as you, or from another organisation. They could sit in on a session you are delivering to give you help and advice and/or help out when necessary.

Supervisors and witnesses

You might have learners who are employed or are taking part in a work experience programme. They should have a supervisor and/or witness who provides support and feedback in their workplace. They can be a useful source of help for learners as they will have knowledge of the subject and be able to apply it to a workplace context. It might be your responsibility to check they have the time to commit to the role and that they are appropriately experienced.

Example

Haseem has a group of 12 learners working towards an accountancy qualification. As part of the programme, each learner has the opportunity to spend one day a week (for six weeks) in a local accountancy firm. Haseem made contact with several interested firms and arranged to visit to discuss how the learners could benefit. He ensured each firm had a named mentor who was appropriately

(Continued)

(Continued)

experienced to give support and advice. He talked through the qualification criteria and arranged to keep in touch regularly. Most mentors also offered to be a witness and gave a statement as to what the learners had achieved.

Support staff

Support staff such as administrators, learning support assistants, technicians and volunteers can also give help to you and your learners. You would need to find out who they are and how they can help you. If they are present during your session, it's important that they are included and kept informed regarding the learners and the progress they are making.

Extension activity

If you are currently teaching, contact at least one of the people on the list you created for the previous activity. Ask if they would be willing to come and talk to your learners. If they will, agree it with your organisation, arrange a suitable date and time and discuss the topic you would like them to talk about. When they arrive, follow your organisation's procedures for visitors and remain with them during their stay. Make sure you introduce them to your learners and state why they are there. Encourage your learners to ask appropriate questions. Afterwards, evaluate how it went and ask your learners what impact the talk has had upon them.

Creating and adapting resources

Creating and adapting resources and learning materials requires an in-depth knowledge of the programme and subject you are teaching. If learners are taking a qualification, there will be certain criteria which they will be required to achieve. If you are teaching a programme which doesn't lead to a qualification, there will still be certain criteria to follow. These criteria might be produced by your organisation, or you may have to produce them yourself. You will need to obtain all this information before considering what resources will best support your subject.

At some point, you may need to create your own or adapt someone else's resources or materials. This could be a handout of useful information, a practical activity, a board game, a worksheet, a project or a complex working model used to demonstrate a topic. Once you know what is currently available you will have a starting point. If there is already a bank of resources, take a look at what's there to see if anything is relevant for your subject and learners and if you can amend and use it.

Wherever possible, resources should reflect your learners' interests as well as the subject. For example, enabling learners to choose a project which reflects their own interests will help their motivation, progress and achievement.

Maureen teaches digital skills to a group of young people who are working towards a sport and leisure qualification. During the first few sessions, Maureen issued worksheets to enable the learners to use various computer skills. However, after two sessions, she noticed a lack of motivation and a lot of disruption from her learners. She therefore decided to redesign the worksheets so that they were sports and leisure related. The revised materials provided a combined approach to using computer skills as well as the area of interest of her learners. Maureen found the learners became much more motivated and there was less disruption as a result.

Too often, teaching is worksheet and handout driven. This might be easier for the teacher but could be boring for the learners. Using resources and materials effectively in order to support learning is challenging. However, it can be exciting for you as a teacher, and engaging and motivating for your learners. Try and be creative and innovative when selecting resources for your course. For example, could you make a visual recording of your session and upload it to a VLE for learners to watch again later? This would be useful if a learner wanted to recap something or had missed a session. However, it could lead to absenteeism as learners might feel they don't need to attend if there will always be something they can watch. A VLE can be useful to upload resources to for your course, as learners can access them and communicate with each other in their own time.

Activity

If you are currently teaching, find out if there is a VLE you can use with your learners at your organisation. If so, create an area for your subject and upload some electronic resources for learners to access. You might need some training to help you in the early stages. There are some free VLE programs available online if your organisation doesn't have one; just carry out a search via the internet for free VLEs.

It's possible you may have updated or revised many of your own resources in the past, either based on feedback, the success (or otherwise) of their use or to meet any individual learner's needs. However, you will need to make sure they are still fresh, professional looking and current, i.e. reflecting the latest developments regarding your subject.

Property rights

If you create any resources as part of your job role (even if it's during your own time), you might find your work contract doesn't allow them to remain your property. It might entitle your organisation to have the rights over them or you could have the rights yourself. Intellectual property is something unique that you physically create. An idea is not intellectual property, for example, an idea for a book doesn't count, but the words you've written will. Having intellectual property rights will stop anyone else taking or copying:

- the names of your products or brands

- your inventions

- the design or look of your products

- things you write, make or produce.

Copyright, designs, patents and trademarks are all types of intellectual property protection. Some types of protection can apply automatically, for example, writing the word *copyright* along with your name and the date on any original work you produce, perhaps if you write blogs or magazine articles. Others types you will have to apply for.

You can own intellectual property if you:

- created it (and it meets the requirements for copyright, a patent or a design)

- bought intellectual property rights from the creator or a previous owner

- have a brand that could be a trademark, e.g. a well-known product name.

Intellectual property can:

- have more than one owner

- belong to people or businesses

- be sold or transferred.

If you are using, adapting or copying the work of others, you will need to check that you are not in breach of any copyright legislation. The Copyright Designs and Patent Act (1998) in the UK covers copying, adapting and distributing materials, including applications and materials found via the internet. It may be that you will have to ask the author's permission to use their materials, and they may need to be acknowledged for their work on your resource. You will also need to be careful if you are copying anything from the internet. The source might not be reliable, or you could accidentally plagiarise the work of others.

Resource box

A resource box is literally a box full of items which can be used to support teaching and learning. It could be a shoe box, a small crate or even a carrier bag. It can contain things which you can use for your role such as pens and board markers, and resources which are relevant to your subject such as gemstones for geology. You can place all sorts of items in it and use them whenever you need to. For example, anything which is small and easily carried which is relevant to you and your subject, such as (in alphabetical order):

- board markers

- calculator

- chalk

- cloths

- cough sweets/snacks/water

- drawing pins

- electronic presentation remote control
- eraser/rubber
- fuzzy felt boards plus letters
- hole punch
- paper
- paper clips
- pencil sharpener
- pencils
- pens
- plastic wallets

- reusable adhesive
- ruler
- scissors
- sellotape
- small clock
- spare USB stick/memory card
- stapler and staples
- sticky notes
- string
- treasury tags
- whiteboard cleaner

If you let your learners use anything from your resource box, it might be an idea to keep a check of who has borrowed what. This will help ensure everything is returned again. If you have lots of items which are being shared around, you could count them out at the beginning of a session then count them in at the end. Issuing and collecting them in this way will save time during the session, you could even nominate a learner to do this. However, if something does go missing, it might be difficult to challenge a learner. Items could also be lost or broken and you might just have to accept that this will happen.

You will probably need to purchase some of these items yourself, unless there is some funding available or the items are freely given to staff. You can build up these types of resources over time, and keep them somewhere safe until you need them.

You could also have lots of small items, which, although not directly relevant to your subject, can be made to be if required, for example, small soft/sponge balls. You can use them for an activity if you feel the need arises, you have spare time during a session or you need to energise your learners.

Example

Olivia's group of 14 hospitality learners were not paying much attention after the lunch break. She was covering a theoretical subject but felt her learners needed to do something practical. She asked all her learners to stand up and form a circle at the front of the room. She gave a small soft ball to one of her learners and asked them to ask a question which related to hospitality, followed by gently throwing the ball to another learner. The learner who caught the ball had to answer the question. If they got it correct, they could ask a question and throw the ball to another learner and so on. If they got it wrong, they could throw the ball to another learner to answer.

In this example, Olivia helped energise her learners by using a practical activity based around the theory she was covering. When managing activities like the one in the example, you will need to ensure everyone can participate and will remain focused. If learners are unable to stand up for any reason, they could remain seated. If the question is asked before the ball is thrown, all learners will be thinking about an answer as they won't know if they will be nominated or not. If the name of a learner is given prior to the question being asked, the other learners might not think about an answer. You can devise activities like this using all sorts of items; you just need to be creative.

Sticky notes are a useful resource, not only for making notes yourself, but to give to learners. If some learners are apprehensive about asking questions during a session, if there are some sticky notes on their tables, they could write their question on one. You could periodically collect them in and address all the questions to the full group. This way, the question can remain anonymous and no one would be embarrassed or afraid to ask it in front of their peers. You can also use sticky notes to create a *graffiti wall*. You could ask a question and learners can write their response on one and stick it on the wall. Again, they can be anonymous and it also creates something visual for learners to go and look at. Sticky notes could be used for many reasons, i.e. ideas, concerns, compliments or anything that you would like to obtain learner input or feedback on.

Extension activity

Create a resource box and/or a bank of electronic resources, either on your own or with colleagues. Think of lots of different resources you could add to your box, not only to help you, i.e. pens and board markers, but ones that could be used during activities with learners. If you are setting up a bank of electronic resources, find out what is currently available in your organisation, or what you could share with colleagues. If you don't know how to use a piece of equipment or a particular resource at your organisation, ask a colleague how you can arrange to have some training.

Meeting the individual needs of learners through resources

Learners may have individual needs which you will need to take into account when using resources, for example, by simplifying the wording in a handout you use for different levels of learning. You will also need to consider the fact that some learners might not have access to certain resources away from your sessions, for example, the internet or relevant textbooks. If some learners can't afford to purchase any resources which are a requirement of the course, you could ask at your organisation if there is any funding available to help them.

Differentiation

Depending upon your learners' needs, you might need to differentiate some of the resources you use. For example, a learner who has dyslexia might prefer a handout in a larger sized font which is printed on pastel coloured paper. Rather than do this for that one learner, you could do it for all your learners. That way, no one is singled out. If you can't get coloured copies printed, you could give the learner a coloured plastic wallet within which they can place the handout. This will change its colour and hopefully make it easier to read. Tinted glasses are also available and the learner might already have a pair which they bring with them. You could also check if there is a particular type of font they prefer, and whether left justified text is easier for them to read than fully justified text.

You might have learners of different levels within the same group. You could create an activity for everyone to carry out, but which is slightly different. For example, a gapped handout for lower level learners, a wordsearch for intermediate learners and a crossword for higher level learners. Or you could use the same questions but in a different way.

Example

Colin had a mixed ability group of learners working towards a bricklaying course. He wanted to check their knowledge regarding the building materials which could be used to create a garden wall. He gave all his learners a product catalogue and asked them to list *the materials they would use. He knew all his learners would be able to do this, but he wanted to stretch and challenge some further. He gave his learners the option to* explain *why they had chosen the items as well as* calculate *the amounts they would use for a particular sized wall. In this way, all learners were listing the materials, most learners were also explaining and some were also calculating.*

In this example, all the learners were able to carry out the activity based around using the product catalogue. However, Colin was able to stretch and challenge some of his learners further by using the same resource.

You might need to consider how adaptable your resources can be to stretch and challenge your learners, and how they could be used in other contexts. A handout you use with your current group, might or might not be suitable for use with another group. Therefore, resources may need to be adapted to suit future learners' needs and changes or developments which may occur.

Everyone is different, but all your learners deserve to be treated with an equal level of respect with equal access to all resources. You will need to be proactive in coping with differences, perhaps by talking to your learners and finding out exactly what they require. This will help ensure their learning is effective from the start of their programme. When you are considering any required changes or alterations to resources, you will need to make sure they are reasonable. You should keep in mind that your organisation has a legal responsibility to comply with the Equality Act (2010) and the Welsh Language Act (1993) in the UK. The latter placed the Welsh language on an equal footing with the English language in Wales with regard to the public sector.

Activity

If you are currently teaching, think about your current learners and the individual needs they have. How might these affect the type of resources you would use? How could you address their needs with the use of differentiated resources?

Assistive resources

You might have some learners who would benefit from using assistive resources. These include anything that will help the learner and the learning process. For example, a desk that can be raised higher to accommodate a wheelchair. Whenever possible, you need to find out what you can about your learners' needs, to be able to support them. This could take place as part of the initial assessment process or as a one-to-one discussion at an appropriate time. Your learners will be best placed to know what works for them, so never be afraid to ask them. However, always consider what they can do, not what they can't do. It could be that they have a learning difficulty and/or disability that can be supported by using various assistive resources. These could include (in alphabetical order):

- braille smart watches
- communication boards, e.g. fuzzy felt and letters rather than pen and paper
- computers with special screens, keyboards and pointing devices
- desks on risers to accommodate a wheelchair
- digital voice recorders
- grab tools to pick up or reach for small items
- items for left-handed use
- magnifiers to increase text size or view small items
- mobility devices to help a learner move around
- positioning and attaching devices for keeping things securely in place
- smartphone applications such as those which translate speech to sign language, or English to other languages (and vice versa)
- special or adjustable seating
- talking clocks
- technology and speciality software, e.g. for speech recognition, Braille translation, and other uses
- tinted glasses for learners who have dyslexia.

It might be that you, or someone in your organisation, could make an adaptation or modification to something. If anything is adapted, it will need to be checked prior to use to ensure it is safe and that it meets the needs of the learner and any qualification requirements.

Other apparatus which can help in the learning environment include: ramps, lifts, grab bars, hearing loops, automatic door openers, hoists, remote switches, senses and remote controls. It might be possible to borrow, hire or lease some specialist equipment if this option is available to you.

There may be other resources and help to learners such as: support for the production of digital resources, photocopying facilities, childcare and transport. This is all something you will need to find out when you commence your role.

Meeting learning preferences with resources

If you have not yet identified the way your learners learn, i.e. their learning preferences (covered in Chapter 2), you could ask them to take a short online questionnaire. This will be able to find out if they are predominantly visual, aural, read/write or kinaesthetic. Examples of resources to meet these are in Table 7.2. A free questionnaire is available at www.vark-learn.com if you would like your learners to try it, or you can print it out for them to complete if they don't have internet access. This way, you can plan which resources will be best for your learners. However, not all teachers agree with the use of learning preference questionnaires; you will need to make your own decision and/or check what your organisation's policy is.

Table 7.2 Examples of meeting learning preferences with resources or activities

Visual	Aural	Read/write	Kinaesthetic
Boards: interactive, whiteboard, chalk board, flip chart	Digital and taped recordings	Annotating handouts	Computers and digital technology
Charts, cartoons, maps, posters, drawings	Group and paired discussions	Equipment manuals and instruction books	Equipment and materials
Demonstrations	Guest speakers	Gapped handouts	Games and gaming
Handouts		Journals	Models
Presentation/video or film clip		Magazines	Practical task-based activities
Pictures/photographs		Textbooks	The *real thing*
		Worksheets	Role-play activities

When you can, it's best to use resources which will meet the needs of more than one learning preference to help increase learning. For example, if you are talking about a topic (aural), you could write the key points on a board (visual) and ask learners to take notes (read/write). You could then make this practical by asking learners to research the topic further using their own device (kinaesthetic) followed by a presentation to their peers or a role-play activity.

Extension activity

Take a look at Table 7.2. What other resources or activities could you add to each column? What resources or activities could cover more than one learning preference at the same time? Devise an activity which could reach all learning preferences and then try it out with your learners. Evaluate how effective it was and why.

Visual presentations, handouts and worksheets

Visual presentations, for example, an electronic presentation, handouts and worksheets are useful resources to add variety to your session and to focus attention. However, try not to rely on them too much but try something different when you can. For example, rather than use a visual presentation which you just talk through, put the onus on your learners to research and present a topic. All visual presentations should be used to support what you are doing, but not be a substitute for it.

All documents you use should be appropriate in terms of level, quality, quantity and content and be relevant to the subject and the learning which is expected. Text and pictures should not include stereotypes of people. They should portray all aspects of society, i.e. people from different races and cultures, and who are able bodied or disabled. You should always check the spelling, grammar and punctuation of any learning materials you use, otherwise you could come across as unprofessional. If you are unsure, ask a colleague to read through it for you. If a learner does notice an error, don't make excuses but thank them and say you will amend it for future use. You could add your name, date and organisation name as a footer on all documents to show where they originated. You may also find it useful to add a file name and version number to keep track of any changes, and where you have saved them if they are electronic documents.

Hard copies of your materials will enable your learners to refer to them during and after the session, to annotate on and to recap important points. However, you might not always be able to get copies made in time. You could consider uploading them to a shared drive, a cloud-based folder, an intranet or VLE to aid sustainability, or you could email them to your learners. Learning doesn't have to stop just because the session has. Learners can read things in their own time and make a list of questions to ask you when they next see you.

Readability

There are ways of checking that the text you use is of the right level for your learners; this is known as *readability*. There are many systems available for checking this. One is The Fog Index, which was devised by Robert Gunning in 1952 as part of his PhD dissertation and later referred to in his 1968 publication. He observed that most high school graduates were unable to read complex text, and felt that newspapers and business documents were full of *fog* and unnecessary complexity. The Fog Index estimates the number of formal years of education someone will need to understand the text the first time they read it. For example, a Fog Index of 10 would mean someone needs to be aged around 15 to understand the text, i.e. they have had 10 years of formal education (if they commenced school at age 5). It is based on the amount of words used with three syllables, i.e. the more syllables there are, the increased difficulty there will be of reading and understanding it. If you have a mixed age group of learners, you should aim for a Fog Index of 12 or less. As a rough guide, a Fog Index of 17 is graduate level.

Using the Fog Index can help you work out if the text you are using is of the right level for your learners. Do be careful of the amount of jargon or specialist terminology you are using. Always make sure you explain any to your learners and check that they understand them before moving on. You could ask your learners to write what they mean in their own words to help reinforce their learning.

Activity

If you have access to an internet-enabled device and a document such as a handout, copy and paste a paragraph of the text into the free online Fog Index calculator at: http://gunning-fog-index.com. The program will then calculate the Fog Index of the text. If the result is not of the right level for your learners (i.e. 12 or less of 3+ syllables) you will be able to make changes to ensure it is more suitable.

You can also carry out this activity with text from books, websites or other resources you are considering using with your learners.

Manually calculating the Fog Index

If you don't have access to an internet enabled device, you can calculate the Fog Index manually; however, it is a bit confusing and consists of the following five steps.

- Step 1: Choose a sample paragraph of at least 100 words and count the number of words and sentences.

- Step 2: Divide the total number of words in the sample by the total number of sentences, to arrive at the Average Sentence Length (ASL).

- Step 3: Count the number of words which consist of three or more syllables which are NOT (a) proper nouns, (b) combinations of easy words or hyphenated words, or (c) two-syllable verbs which are made into three, i.e. by adding -es and -ed endings. This will give you the Percent Hard Words (PHW).

- Step 4: Add the ASL from Step 2 and the PHW from Step 3.

- Step 5: Multiply the result by 0.4 to arrive at the Fog Index figure.

The mathematical formula is: Grade Level = 0.4 (ASL + PHW). ASL is the Average Sentence Length (i.e. the number of words divided by the number of sentences) and PHW is the Percentage of Hard Words. You might be lost at this point but don't be too concerned. As long as you are aware of the readability concept, you can manually scan your documents to see if there are too many, or not enough, words of three syllables or more.

SMOG index

Other versions of the Fog Index are available, for example, the SMOG index which stands for the *Simple Measure of Gobbledygook*. This was developed by G H McLaughlin in 1969. The calculation is easier than the Fog Index and consists of three steps which will give a slightly different result to the Fog Index.

- Step 1: Count the words of three or more syllables in three 10-sentence samples.

- Step 2: Estimate the count's square root (from the nearest perfect square).

- Step 3: Add 3 to your figure.

Readability scoring software is available at: https://readability-score.com.

Visual presentations

Visual presentations include electronic presentations, slide projectors, overhead projectors (OHP) and handheld devices. Most presentations can incorporate text, pictures, graphs, charts, video clips, sounds and more. Rather than your using them during a session, you could train your learners to use them instead. They can then research topics and give presentations to their peers. They could also use their own devices to make short video clips regarding a topic to show to their peers. This keeps them active rather than passive and learning is more likely to take place as a result. You will need to agree some ground rules beforehand, perhaps to ensure one person does not dominate the activity and that everyone has a chance to contribute.

You could also use television, film and internet clips as part of a visual presentation. However, if it's quite long, perhaps over 15 minutes, you could pause it and discuss an aspect of what has been seen, then return to it again. This will help retain attention and help you check that learning is taking place. Otherwise, while learners are passively watching something, you won't know if they are learning anything. Alternatively, just show the most important aspects of something. Learners could always watch the full version in their own time. If learners are watching something on their own device or via a personal computer (with headphones), keep walking around the room and check they are watching what they should be. You could issue a handout at the end, which contains questions that learners can answer. You can discuss the responses afterwards as a full group activity or collect them in for checking, depending upon time.

Boards

If you don't have access to electronic or visual presentation equipment, you might have to use traditional boards, e.g. a whiteboard, chalk board or flip chart paper. You might be able to prepare these in advance if you have access and have the time. Otherwise, you will need to write on them while you are with your learners. This will mean you are not facing them and you could miss something happening in the room. Try and write small amounts of text, then discuss what you have written with your learners before adding more. You could give them a short activity to carry out while you are writing. For example, to discuss a topic in pairs and think of a question to ask you.

You could use the board as a jotter throughout a session, to add key points as you are talking, rather than to add lots of text all at once. Alternatively, you could delegate this to a learner to do. Learners could take turns as the course progresses so that everyone gets the chance or you could ask for volunteers. However, you might end up with the same learners each time, which is not fair to the others.

Using coloured marker pens or chalks will help to emphasise key points. You could also draw diagrams or charts to help clarify what you are saying. Always make sure you are writing legibly and that everything can be seen from the back of the room.

When using board markers, there is a difference between *permanent* markers, and *board* markers. The latter will wipe clean, whereas the former will not. It can be very frustrating going into a room with a whiteboard where someone has used a permanent marker by mistake. Although some of it may wipe off, the writing is often still visible and can be very distracting. Sometimes, writing over the permanent marks with a board marker, then wiping it straight off, might bring the permanent marks off. Special cleaning fluid or wipes can be purchased to clean whiteboards. This is something you might like to keep in your resource box, along with some cleaning cloths. You should always clean the board when you are finished, this makes it easier for the next person coming in and shows you are being professional.

Mini whiteboards

Mini whiteboards are a useful resource if they are available (or pieces of A4 paper if not). For example, you could ask a question then each learner can write their response on it. They can then hold it up for you to see. This saves embarrassment if a learner is unsure if they have answered correctly, or if they lack confidence in speaking in front of the group.

Learners can use whiteboards during the session to ask a question; for example, they can write the question on their board and then hold it up. Learners can also use them to provide feedback during the session. If they don't understand something, they can draw an unhappy face symbol ☹ and show it to you. Alternatively, if you have been explaining something complex, your learners could draw one of three faces to show: they understand ☺, are unsure 😐, or don't understand ☹. This way, you get instant feedback.

Flip charts

If you are using flip chart paper, the sheets might be part of a pad which is attached to a stand. The stand might have legs which are easy to trip over, or it might be portable and sit on a table. You might need to move it around the room, so make sure there is plenty of space to manoeuvre. You will need to practise your writing skills, as it's easy to start large but then go smaller, or the text begins to lean down at an angle. You could prepare the flip chart sheets in advance, so that they are all ready to use when needed. However, only have on display the one you are referring to at the time, otherwise they could become a distraction. Alternatively, you could pre-prepare your sheets by writing in pencil, then go over it with a marker pen when you are ready to refer to it.

Completed sheets could be removed from the stand and pinned to the wall if you need them on display all the time. You will need to check if you can pin, or stick them to the wall in some way, as some organisations are not happy about this in case the walls become marked.

Individual sheets of flip chart paper can be a good resource to use with learners. You can set a small group activity and they can make notes or brainstorm a topic by writing on them. They can then talk through what they have created to the rest of the group. You will need a good supply of working marker pens for this and plenty of paper. Alternatively, you could place blank sheets of flip chart paper around the room, on the wall or a table, for learners to write on. Furthermore, you could create a display and add some text or pictures as a starting point. This enables learners to add to them and learn from their peers as a topic or project progresses. You could also create a *learning wall*. This is a blank area of a wall, or sheets of flip chart paper, where each learner can have their own *brick* in the wall. The brick is a pre-drawn box or a coloured piece of paper, which each learner can write or draw on with what they have learnt. Alternatively, they could write on a sticky note and add this to their brick. This can show how much learning has taken place by each individual over time.

If your organisation supplies you with flip chart pads, keep them rolled rather than folded when not in use. This will prevent them from becoming creased. A more modern version of flip chart paper is available which can attach to walls without marking them. This type also acts like a whiteboard and can be cleaned and reused; however, it is usually quite expensive.

Overhead projector (OHP)

An OHP is a projector which is portable and can be moved from room to room if necessary. It uses a mirror to project an image or text from clear plastic, known as a transparency. This can be pre-prepared or written on during the session. However, some OHPs can be heavy and cumbersome to move. They contain a bulb, which, if not working, will not enable you to use the machine. It has to be adjusted to make sure the focus is correct when the image is projected. This is usually done by moving the lens and mirror up and down a pole support or moving the OHP closer or further away from the screen. You should always check that the OHP is working prior to use by plugging it in, and do be careful where the cable goes so that no one can trip over it. Check that the machine itself will not block the view for a learner. It needs to be positioned directly in front of the screen for it to project on to correctly. If not, you might need to move it, the screen or the learner.

You can create the transparencies in advance by using coloured OHP marker pens or photocopying directly onto them. If it's the latter, special transparencies will need to be used. Some marker pens are permanent; therefore, you cannot delete what you have added.

Non-permanent pens will enable you to amend or reuse a transparency if necessary. Remember that whatever you write needs to be legible and visible from a distance.

When using an OHP, you can stand near to it and face your learners. You can refer to the transparency on the OHP rather than the one projected onto the screen. When you place a transparency on the OHP all the material becomes visible. If you don't want your learners to see everything at once, use a piece of paper to cover up some areas. You can then move the paper to reveal what you want to be seen. Do be careful not to block the projection with your hand or body and give your learners time to comprehend what is visible before removing the transparency. It's best not to leave the OHP switched on when not in use as the bulb could overheat and stop working.

Tips for using visual presentations

- Always check the equipment and projector are connected and working. Make sure the image is appearing clearly on a screen or a blank wall. Check that the program and version in which you saved your presentation is compatible with the one to be used, and make a backup copy.

- Don't include too much text or use fancy fonts, too many colours and/or animations, as this could distract from the points you want to make.

- Check if you need to insert a logo on each slide as a footer, or use a particular font and size for consistency throughout the organisation.

- Large, bold plain fonts are easier to read, for example **Arial, _Comic Sans_** or **Verdana.** Serif and script fonts are thought to be more difficult to read, for example Times New Roman and _Brush Script_. The font size should be readable from the back of the room. Using combined upper and lower case is preferable to using all UPPER CASE as the latter can appear as though you are shouting.

- Be consistent with the colours and backgrounds you use, for example use black text on a white background. Blue-eyed people sometimes struggle to see red, orange, green or yellow text, particularly if it's on a coloured background. Red and green could cause confusion for learners who are colour blind. Some learners who have dyslexia might prefer pastel colours. You could check which fonts and colours your learners prefer by asking them. How you see them may be very different to how your learners see them. If you can, check your presentation on the actual equipment you will use as the colours might differ to those on the device you created it on.

- Use bullet points, three or four per slide, and try not to read them verbatim. Expand on each point and discuss them with your learners. Schedule the bullets to come in line by line, otherwise your learners will be reading ahead of you if they are all visible. Involve learners where possible by asking open questions to make the presentation a two-way process and use anecdotes to bring your subject to life.

- Graphs, pie charts and diagrams are often easier for learners to understand than tables; however, don't make them too complex. It's better to use several slides with a few pieces of information on rather than one slide with too much on.

- If you have time, incorporate a short video or sounds to bring your topic to life and add variety. However, do check any copyright restrictions and/or fair use policies. If you are connected to the internet you can insert the website link into your slide for easy access. Don't forget to check in advance that the site is still accessible.

- If you need to refer to the same slide more than once, copy it rather than moving back through your presentation, otherwise you could lose your place.

- Use a remote control for moving through your slides. This enables you to walk around the room rather than standing next to the keyboard. The remote control communicates via a device which usually plugs into a USB slot in the computer. Don't forget to remove it at the end or you may forget it. Alternatively, you could use a tablet or a smartphone which connects remotely to the presentation. If you don't have a remote device, you could ask a learner to be your assistant and give them a nod when you want the slide moving on.

- Press the letter B on the keyboard to black out the screen, or W to white out (for PowerPoints), for example, if you don't want a slide on display for a few minutes while you focus on something else. Pressing B or W again will restore it.

- If your presentation is given via an electronic whiteboard, you could use features such as adding text and drawings with the pen-like device. You can then save and email it to your learners, print it or upload it to a VLE. Don't use normal whiteboard markers as they will not function correctly.

- Involve your learners; ask them to use the presentation equipment and/or electronic whiteboard whenever possible.

- Don't rely on using too many presentations. Vary your delivery by using other types of equipment, different resources, and teaching and learning approaches.

- Have a paper copy of the presentation for yourself in case something goes wrong. You can then refer to it rather than having nothing. You can also hold it during the presentation and remain facing your learners, rather than looking at and talking to the screen.

- If you want your learners to make notes throughout the presentation, you can print a copy using the *handout* function. That way, they can have several slides on one A4 page with room for making notes. Printing one slide per A4 sheet is just a waste of paper. If you are not sure how to do this, ask someone to show you.

- Supporting handouts can be given at the end, which include further information such as websites and reading lists, rather than squashing it into the presentation.

Activity

Look at the previous bullet list regarding visual presentations to see which points are relevant to you and whether you follow them or not. What else could you add to the list and why?

Handouts

Handouts are useful to give to learners as a summary of what they are learning. However, if you give a handout at the beginning of the session, you may find your learners begin reading it and don't focus on what you are saying. If you can, issue handouts at an appropriate time and talk through the content. Ask questions regularly to ensure your learners have understood what is on the handout. Otherwise, issue them at the end of the session and ask learners to read them later to help reinforce what has been covered. Alternatively, to aid sustainability, you could upload handouts to a VLE or email them to your learners.

Using pictures as well as text and not putting too much information on a handout will make it easier to read. If you were given one handout with a lot of written information in small text, and another with text in a larger more pleasing font with a few pictures, which one would you prefer? It would probably be the latter; therefore, the same might apply to your learners. Pictures and visuals can aid retention of what has been read or heard. Unfortunately, there isn't enough room in this book to insert many to help aid your retention.

Handouts should be regularly updated and adapted for your particular group of learners. Don't give a handout to learners that you have been giving out for years as things change. If you photocopy handouts, make sure you keep the original separately, as copying from a copy can leave marks and make it difficult to read.

Tips for using handouts

- Make the text easily readable, in an appropriate font and size. It should be clearly written and unambiguous. Read through it as though you were a new learner reading it for the first time.

- Don't put too much text or too many pictures on one page and don't mix fancy fonts. It might look good to you, but might not be easily readable by your learners.

- Keep plenty of *white space,* the blank area around the text/pictures. This makes the information stand out clearly. If there is too much on a handout your learners may find it difficult to read and not absorb all the information. Use wide margins, or leave gaps if you would like your learners to make notes somewhere.

- A single sheet, one sided or double sided, is best; too many pages will take too long for your learners to assimilate the information. If you do use more pages, always staple in the top left corner and number each page so they don't get mixed up.

- If you have created the handout yourself, type your name, filename, version number and date as a footer. This will enable you to locate it again to make future changes and ensures you are using the most recent version.

- Consider numbering paragraphs or using numbers instead of bullet points. That way you can direct your learners to important points.

- Make sure the information is up to date. You may need to revise something if there have been changes or developments to your subject.

- If you are issuing several handouts during a session, you could print them on different coloured paper for ease of reference when you are talking about them.

- If you use pictures of people, make sure they represent all aspects of society and that you have any relevant permissions.

- If you cite from books, make sure you use correct referencing.

- A list of relevant references or websites is useful to encourage your learners to research further after the session.

- Arrange to have them copied in good time, just in case there is a problem with the photocopier or printer. Have a few spare copies in case you have more learners than you expected and don't forget one for yourself.

- If possible, give handouts towards the end of the activity they refer to. If you give them too early, your learners may fiddle with them and read through them rather than focusing on the activity.

Activity

Look at the previous bullet list regarding handouts to see which points are relevant to you and whether you follow them or not. What else could you add to the list and why?

Worksheets and workbooks

Worksheets are like handouts but they include activities for learners to carry out based on the information within them. They are suitable to use with lower level or new learners, as a fun team activity or to fill in time at the end of a session. They should not be relied upon as the main teaching and learning approach. However, they can add variety to a session, prove useful as a learning aid, and be used as a formative assessment activity to consolidate learning.

Example

Most of Farida's learners in her English for speakers of other languages group cannot tell the time by looking at a clock face. She realised they only had a digital watch or referred to a digital clock image on their phones. She therefore planned a session to teach them to tell the time. She used a large clock to demonstrate on the hour, past the hour, and to the hour. Discussions took place as to how a clock face differs from a digital image. She located and showed a short video in the learner's own language to help reinforce what she had explained in English. She then created various worksheets which had pictures of clocks showing various times. The learners had to look at the pictures and write the time underneath each. Worksheets were good in this situation as the learners could progress at their own pace and Farida could see if they were getting the responses right or wrong. Any wrong answers enabled her to explain to the learner why.

In this example, Farida used the worksheets to help assess learning, which enabled her to see each individual's progress. They were used as an additional activity and did not replace the normal interaction between Farida and her learners. An example of a worksheet for a teacher training course which is based on the use of resources is in Table 7.3. It gives information and then enables the learners to answer questions. Peer discussions could take place to compare responses; however, you should always take the time to check each individual learner's responses and provide your own feedback. When using worksheets and workbooks, it might help your learners if you ask questions based on how they can put theory into practice, i.e. how their knowledge will help them in their current or future employment. This will help them to see some significance to their responses.

Table 7.3 Example worksheet

Resources for teachers and learners	
Read the following text and then answer the questions	
Resources are all the aids, books, handouts, items of equipment, objects and people that you can use to help teach and assess your subject. The main purpose of using resources is to stimulate learning, add impact and promote interest in your subject.	
What resources can you use for your subject and why?	
Whichever resources you use, you will need to make sure they are fit for purpose, are at the required level of learning, are relevant, and are accessible to everyone. You will need to decide if the resource is to aid revision, assess learning, consolidate learning, encourage learning and/or support teaching? Knowing what you are aiming for will help you consider how the resource can be used for the benefit of learning.	
How can you make sure your resources are fit for purpose, at the required level of learning, relevant and accessible?	
Experts from industry who work in your subject area could be invited to speak to your learners. This would add variety to your sessions and enable your learners to ask questions that they might not ask you. They can provide additional knowledge as they are an authority on their subject. For example, authors, politicians and journalists can bring a different and new perspective to your subject. They are known as guest speakers; however, there might also be other people you know who could talk to your learners, for example, colleagues and mentors, other learners and support staff in your organisation.	
Are there any guest speakers you could invite to talk to your learners? If so, who are they and how could you get in touch with them? How could you ensure they add real impact to the learning process?	

Worksheets are usually single or double-sided A4 sheets of paper. If they incorporate assessment activities you will need to check if your learners have carried them out correctly. However, this might not show you whether the learner really understands a topic, or whether they have just copied the answer from somewhere or guessed it. Workbooks include many pages and can progressively build up knowledge over time. The learner reads the text and then completes various tasks. These could include answering questions, or carrying out various activities, for example, on a computer or other device. If you are teaching a continuous programme, where learners can start and finish at any time, a workbook is a useful resource to aid individual learning. Learners will be able to work at their own pace, and take relevant assessment activities when they are ready.

Gapped handout

A *gapped* handout (sometimes called a *cloze sentence* or *cloze test*) contains sentences with missing words that learners need to complete. They can be used to assist note taking and consolidation of a topic. If one is given out when a new subject is introduced, learners can add the key words and then refer to them again later. They can be given out at the end of a session to enable learners to remember what they have heard during the session. However, this might only test memory and recall abilities rather than an understanding of the topic.

Gapped handouts can be useful if your subject involves a lot of jargon or acronyms. You can list the missing words at the top of the handout, add more words or don't give any words as a challenge. The activity can be carried out individually, in pairs, or small groups.

Example

Roger's new group of engineering learners seemed to be struggling with some of the terminology and phrases he used. He decided to create a gapped handout which contained sentences with missing words. His first one was: A _____ _____ is a type of load which varies over time. He included 10 sentences in the handout and listed 15 phrases for learners to choose from. When he gave the activity to his learners, they found it fun to complete, and they realised they had been getting confused with some of the terminology. This enabled a discussion to take place to clarify their answers and discuss the terminology used. If you are wondering, the answer is a dynamic load.

Instruction and training sheets

Instruction and training sheets are a combination of a handout and a worksheet. They can include: guidance on how to do something, drawings to instruct how to use something or maps to locate things. They should all have some form of assessment such as questions to answer, or things to do.

Example

Donna wanted to assess her art and design learners' knowledge regarding different types of brushes and paints. She decided to create a training sheet which had pictures of brushes and tins of paints on. She included them in a treasure hunt-style map, with questions relating to items she had hidden around the room. Learners had to locate where the items were hidden once they had worked out the correct answer. When she evaluated the activity, feedback from her learners said they had enjoyed it.

In this example, Donna was able to check that learning had taken place by observing her learners in action.

You might need to be creative when designing instruction and training sheets and make sure that they are clearly written and fit for purpose. You may find it useful to ask a colleague to work through them beforehand, to ensure that what you expect will actually work. They should be used to reinforce learning in an active way but, like worksheets, they should not be totally relied upon.

Extension activity

Create a visual presentation, handout, worksheet, workbook or instruction sheet for your subject. Take into account the previous bulleted points. You could also check some of the text you use via one of the readability indexes to see if it's at an appropriate level for your learners. If possible, use the resource with your learners and ask for their feedback to evaluate its appropriateness.

Evaluating resources

It's useful to evaluate the resources you have used to improve or amend them. For example, it could be that a handout you used was not read thoroughly by your learners, i.e. there was too much text on it or it was too complex. Alternatively, it could be that you used a working model to demonstrate something but it didn't function on the day. It's best to practise with your resources in advance of using them with your learners, just in case anything could go wrong.

Example

Laura designed a card activity to use with her political history learners. She printed cards with key dates on, and then the activities which occurred on each. She had planned for her learners to match each activity with the relevant date. However, when she gave the cards to her learners to carry out the activity in groups, she realised she had mixed them up. Each group did not have the correct amount of each type of card. This caused confusion and none of the groups were able to complete the activity.

This example shows that had Laura checked all the cards were grouped accurately, this would not have happened.

When using resources, it's useful to remember that what works with one learner or group might not work well with others. This could be due to their learning preferences, group cohesion, current knowledge or other internal or external influences. When evaluating if something worked or not, make sure you take all factors into consideration, not just whether or not it worked. For example, ask your learners how they felt about using it or what they would recommend could be changed. If you do decide to change something, don't do it for the sake of it; if it works, hopefully it will continue to work. You might like to reflect on the effectiveness of all the resources you use and discuss this with a colleague or your mentor. They might be able to give you some valuable feedback and advice.

Activity

Create a resource activity, perhaps similar to the one in the previous card example. If there are lots of acronyms or jargon words for your subject, you could add these to separate pieces of card for your learners to match with their meanings. If you are currently teaching, try the activity with your learners and then evaluate it. Would you make any changes? If so, what and why?

There are many different ways of evaluating something, for example, self-evaluation, peer evaluation and obtaining feedback from others (covered in Chapter 12).

Checklist for evaluating resources

When evaluating your resources, you could ask yourself the following.

☐ *What was the purpose of the resource, i.e. to aid revision, assess learning, consolidate learning, encourage learning and/or support teaching?*

☐ *Did the resource do what I expected? If not, why not?*

☐ *Did it support and reinforce learning effectively?*

☐ *Did it reach all learning preferences, i.e. was there something to look at (visual), did I talk about it and could learners discuss it (aural), was there something written and/or could learners make notes (read/write) and was there something practical for learners to do (kinaesthetic)?*

☐ *Were all learners able to access and use it correctly?*

☐ *Was there enough of everything for everyone?*

☐ *Did it motivate the learners to want to achieve more?*

☐ *Was it up to date and relevant to the subject?*

☐ *Was it active or passive? Do my learners prefer to be actively engaged when using resources, such as a working model, rather than passively reading a handout?*

☐ *Was it easy for me to create? Can I update it easily?*

☐ *If it was a document/visual presentation, did I (or the learners) notice any mistakes? Would I change anything for the next time I use it?*

☐ *Can I share it with others and/or save it to an electronic resource bank or keep it in my resource box?*

☐ *Can I adapt it to use with other learners and/or groups?*

☐ *Did I encounter any problems setting it up and using it? Was it too time consuming or cumbersome?*

☐ *Did I carry out any necessary risk assessments?*

☐ *Was it of a high quality and professional looking?*

☐ *Did it cause any confusion or was anything ambiguous?*

☐ *What were the overall strengths and weaknesses?*

Although the above questions mainly require a yes/no response, you should ask yourself why, or what you could do differently, for each one. After evaluating how effective a resource was, you can then make any necessary changes before using it again.

Extension activity

Use a resource with your learners, perhaps one that you have never used before to challenge yourself. You might like to create something, such as a board game, a working model, a visual presentation or something else. Use it with your learners and then evaluate it by using the previous checklist. What would you change and why?

Self-assessment checklist

Do I know about the following?

If not, re-read this chapter, or research the texts and websites listed at the end.

☐ The different physical resources I can use with my learners

☐ The purpose of resources

☐ How to obtain resources

☐ The people I could use as a resource

☐ How to create resources such as handouts and visual presentations

☐ What to add to a resource box

☐ How to create an electronic resource bank

☐ How to meet the individual needs of learners through resources

☐ The different assistive resources available to support learners

☐ How to create and use a worksheet or workbook

☐ How to calculate a readability score

☐ How to evaluate the resources I have used

Summary

This chapter has explored how using resources will add variety to your sessions and help learning to take place.

You should now be able to create and adapt resources to use for your subject. You should also know that anything you use is for the benefit of your learners, and not just something to make your job easier.

You might like to carry out further research by accessing the books and websites listed at the end of this chapter, particularly if you are working towards a higher level teaching qualification.

This chapter has covered the following topics:

* Physical resources

* People as resources

* Creating and adapting resources

* Meeting the individual needs of learners through resources

* Visual presentations, handouts and worksheets

* Evaluating resources

References and further information

Bates, B. (2016) *A Quick Guide to Special Needs and Disabilities*. London: SAGE.

Best, B. and Thomas, W. (2008) *The Creative Teaching and Learning Resource Book*. London: Continuum.

Gunning, R. (1968) *The Technique of Clear Writing* (Revised edition). Columbus: McGraw Hill.

McLaughlin, G.H. (1969) SMOG Grading – a New Readability Formula. *Journal of Reading*, 12(8): 639–46.

Websites

Assistive technology – www.washington.edu/doit/assistive-technology

Assistive technology Jisc – https://tinyurl.com/md5pbkf

British Assistive Technology Association – www.bataonline.org

Copyright – www.copyrightservice.co.uk

Dropbox file sharing in the cloud – www.dropbox.com

Dyslexia Association – www.dyslexia.uk.net

Gunning Fog Index calculator – http://gunning-fog-index.com

Intellectual Property Office – https://tinyurl.com/l7kohn6

Online games and teaching resources – https://tinyurl.com/mtkwmrn

Online presentations – www.prezi.com

Readability scoring – https://readability-score.com

Reading list for teaching and learning – www.anngravells.com/reading-lists/teaching

Resources Centre – www.heacademy.ac.uk/resources

SMOG calculator shortcut – http://tinyurl.com/jpu5h4v

Using computers and technology: free guides – http://digitalunite.com/

8

Technology enhanced teaching and learning

Introduction

Technology enhanced teaching and learning is about using a range of information and communication technology to enhance and reinforce knowledge and understanding. It's an area that is constantly evolving as new resources, programs and internet-based applications frequently become accessible. Courses can now be taken online and/or supported with learning materials which are accessible outside of traditional taught sessions.

This chapter will explore how you can use technology to enhance your own role and the experience of your learners. The use of social media for educational purposes is covered, as is how to stay safe online.

This chapter will cover the following topics:

- The role of technology in teaching, learning and assessment
- Learning technology
- E-learning
- Social networking and social media
- Using digital technology
- Online safety and security

The role of technology in teaching, learning and assessment

Technology is about the application of knowledge for practical purposes, such as using a new piece of equipment or machinery. Digital technology is about using electronic systems and devices which generate, store and process data. These can include computers, tablets, smartphones, 3D printers, virtual reality goggles and game consoles. Encouraging your learners to use technology and digital technology will help increase their knowledge and skills in areas which relate to their learning.

The internet is a fantastic way of communicating with others and for accessing aspects of digital technology online. This is usually via a wired connection, a non-wired connection known as wifi, a mobile telephone network or a satellite. It can be accessed by subscribing to a paid for or a free connection via a service provider. Many resources can be downloaded while online, i.e. saved to your own device, and then accessed and used when offline. If you are saving any confidential data, records or information regarding your learners, it will need to be in accordance with any relevant legislation and guidelines.

Not all areas of all countries have internet access and you would need to check if it is available and accessible where you are located. Some countries and organisations restrict access to certain websites. This could be because they don't want people to access those which they deem to be inappropriate. A website is a collection of pages of information which is accessible via the internet. The internet was invented by Sir Tim Berners-Lee and it became available to the public in 1991. He had wanted to create a system for sharing and distributing information not just within a company, but globally. He produced three fundamental technologies that are still the foundation of today's World Wide Web (often just referred to as the *web*):

- HTML: hypertext markup language; the formatting language for the web

- URI: uniform resource identifier; a unique address to identify websites, now known as a URL: uniform resource locator

- HTTP: hypertext transfer protocol; enables access to other linked websites and resources across the web.

Websites are located by keying in the website address in an internet browser (if you know the address, e.g. www.anngravells.com) or by using a search engine (e.g. Google, Bing, Yahoo) to find a particular area of interest. A good educational search engine is https://scholar.google.co.uk.

Anyone can create a website providing they have the knowledge to do so and have an internet connection. Most website addresses begin with the three letters *www* which is an acronym for the *world wide web*. For example, www.anngravells.com.

There are many educational websites which offer free or inexpensive online resources, most of which can be downloaded for you to use in your own time. Examples of these are listed throughout this chapter and at the end; however, some websites might not be available when you try to access them, or might have a different address as they often change.

Technology enhanced learning (TEL), *edtech* (short for educational technology) and *information and communication technology* (ICT) are terms that are often used for incorporating technology for the purposes of enhancing teaching and learning. It's not just about using programs such as word processors and databases, it's about using what is currently available and what is emerging: for example, using online presentation tools (Prezi), creating and/or accessing multimedia (YouTube) and collaborative writing (Google Drive). These are accessed via the internet and often stored *in the cloud,* i.e. not on an individual's computer or device. This means they are accessible on any internet-connected device. Please note that the spelling of program for a computer *program* is different to the spelling of *programme,* which refers to a course of learning.

An organisation's own version of the internet is known as an *intranet.* You could think of this as a private internet which is only accessible to those who have been given the right to use it (whereas the internet is available to the public). A range of information and services can be available securely, which would not normally be available to the public. Examples are policies and procedures, resources and company handbooks. Intranets can also have secure areas for teachers and learners to access relevant course materials via a password.

If your learners have their own device, they might expect to use it to connect to the internet as part of the learning process. However, not all learners will own their own device and might not be familiar with using them. Some learners might be *digital natives,* i.e. they were brought up with digital technology or are very familiar with it. You might, therefore have some learners who know more than others, or you. This is nothing to be concerned about and can be used to your advantage. For example, asking an experienced learner to pair with an inexperienced learner. You could also ask an experienced learner to demonstrate an aspect of using technology to the rest of the group. This could generate a discussion and enable you to benefit as well as the learners. Don't be embarrassed to tell your learners that you don't know how to use something. It's best to be honest than to bluff your way through something. Your learners will respect you for being truthful and will often be happy to tell you what they know.

The term for people who were not brought up with technology and who are just getting to know about it is *digital immigrant.* Some teachers who are new to using technology often try to make sense of it by relating it to what they already know.

Example

Daniel, a biology teacher, had never used an interactive whiteboard before but he had used a whiteboard. When one was installed in his classroom, he soon learnt to write on it with the special pens and to annotate on the projected photographs. He was able to make a screencast (video) of what he had done. He could then upload this to YouTube for his learners to view again later. As he gained in confidence, he learnt to use tools such as the pointer, the spotlight, the calculator and the magnifier. He was soon involving his learners by showing an image of a skeleton and asking them to take turns to add the names of the bones. Once the image was correctly completed, a copy could be printed for everyone as well as saved for future access.

It would be worthwhile for your learners to use digital technology when possible, as it is bound to form a part of their professional or personal lives. It could be that your subject is more practical than theoretical and doesn't lend itself to using technology. If this is the case, you could ask your learners to carry out some research via the internet regarding a particular topic. They might find some interesting facts or useful information and videos to help them. For example, a guitar teacher could ask their learners to research the different types of strings used and how to replace them. Learners could also decide which areas of digital technology they could use to support their learning. This could stretch and challenge them to find out about particular software. This could be a good activity for self-study which would enable them to report back during the following session.

The *digital divide* is a term that denotes the gap between those who have access to ICT and the internet and those who do not (or who have restricted access). It can relate to individuals, households, businesses, geographic areas or demographic categories. The divide between regions or countries in the world is referred to as the *global digital divide*.

Digital literacy skills is the term often used for being able to use, to understand, and to benefit from ICT. This includes all the devices which will store, retrieve, display, manipulate, send or receive information electronically in a digital format. For example, personal computers, tablets, smartphones and interactive whiteboards. Technology is advancing very quickly and there are new products and devices becoming available. ICT should be used whenever possible to engage and stimulate your learners. It might also help raise learner confidence if they haven't used ICT much in the past. You might already deliver and assess your subject online, or use a blended approach of traditional teaching supported with access to technology. Learners today live in a world of easy access to the internet and often use tablets and/or smartphones as part of their everyday activities. Therefore, you could consider how you can incorporate this into your sessions to make learning interactive. However, don't be too keen to overload your learners by using too much too soon; make sure you get the balance right by using other resources.

For your own job role, digital technology can make a huge difference to the teaching, learning and assessment process. It can make things easier, for example, by creating and saving documents online to enable them to be accessed at any time in any place. Many aspects of your role could be carried out digitally, such as completing the attendance register, marking work and messaging colleagues.

Technology can be accessed via different devices and used in different environments, for example, through:

Open environments (such as social networks/media, discussion forums/boards and anywhere else freely accessible on the Web) – the content can be seen, shared, commented upon by anyone.

Closed/restricted environments (such as groups, networks and media where membership is by invite only or is shared with only a selected community/audience. Parts of virtual learning environments (VLEs), such as group work activities can be thought of in this way) – the content is only available to invited or registered users.

Private/personal environments (such as email accounts, personal storage in the cloud, personal areas of institutional portals and VLEs) – the environment and its content is only available to you. You may be able to customise the environment and possibly communicate or share some content with others through it (White, 2015, page 31).

Whichever environment you are using with your learners, you will need to check that your learners are able to access a suitable device and are capable of using it. There are advantages and disadvantages to using technology, please see Table 8.1 for some examples.

Activity

Look at Table 8.1 and add any other advantages and disadvantages that are not listed. Are there any personal and/or organisational barriers which might prevent you from using anything with your learners? If so, how can you overcome them?

Table 8.1 Examples of advantages and disadvantages of using technology

Advantages	Disadvantages
<ul><li>accessible and inclusive</li><li>addresses sustainability, i.e. no need for paper copies</li><li>an efficient use of time</li><li>auditable and reliable</li><li>available and flexible, i.e. resources and materials can be accessed at a time and place to suit teachers and learners</li><li>cost-effective, i.e. available to many learners in large online classes, and can save on the purchase of printed copies of textbooks or the printing of handouts and resources</li><li>gives immediate results from online tests and polls</li><li>learners can *bring your own device* (BYOD) to use during sessions</li><li>on demand, i.e. tests can be taken when a learner is ready and results can be immediate</li><li>documents can be saved in the cloud, i.e. they are stored remotely and can be accessed anywhere at anytime via an internet-enabled device</li></ul>	<ul><li>finance is required to purchase or upgrade equipment, some software might be expensive for the initial purchase</li><li>it could lead to copying, cheating and plagiarism by learners</li><li>the identity of the learner and the authenticity of their work must be checked</li><li>it is time consuming to initially set up</li><li>it might create barriers if a learner cannot access it, is not confident to use it or has health concerns which prevent using it</li><li>learners/teachers/assessors accessing the internet via their own devices might run out of credit if paying for wifi or accidentally download a virus</li><li>learners might misuse or abuse certain aspects of technology</li><li>power cuts/low broadband speeds/limited wifi networks can affect connections and access</li><li>an internet connection is often required to access certain websites</li><li>security of data could be compromised</li><li>some people might be afraid of using technology or certain devices</li><li>some organisations block access to certain sites</li><li>there might not be enough resources available for all learners to use at the same time</li></ul>

ICT resources

ICT use can encompass a wide variety of resources, methods and media, for example, using (in alphabetical order):

- applications (apps)
- audio, video, digital and online clips (creating or viewing, recorded or live)
- augmented reality
- blogs
- calculators
- calendars and diaries (online)
- chat rooms
- cloud computing applications
- computer programs
- digital cameras, camcorders and video recorders
- discussion boards
- distance/online/open learning
- e-assessments
- electronic brain games
- email (text and video, with or without attachments)
- e-portfolios and e-assessment
- e-readers
- file sharing websites
- gaming software
- graphic organisers
- interactive and online programs and educational games
- interactive whiteboards linked to the internet
- internet/intranet access
- laptops, netbooks and tablets
- mobile phones and smartphones
- online discussions
- online voting
- podcasts (digital audio files)
- presentation software
- robotics
- scanners
- simulators
- software and programs
- social networking and social media
- smartboards
- three-dimensional printers
- translation software
- video conferencing and video email
- virtual learning environments (VLE)
- virtual reality goggles
- webcasts
- webinars
- websites which are interactive for creating and using surveys, polls and questionnaires
- wikis

Activity

Look at the previous bullet list and note those which are accessible to you that you could use for your subject. Now think how you could use them effectively with your learners. Is there anything else you could add to your list? How confident are you at using those you have mentioned and how could you become confident at using others?

You will need to find out what is available for your own and your learners' use, and what technical support is available. It could be that you are teaching in an environment which has access to all types of technology and technical support, for example, wifi-enabled computers, digital recording equipment, tablets and smartphones. However, do you know if technical support would be available at the times you might need it? If you are planning on using visual or audio devices to record your learners during an activity, you would need to find out if this is acceptable and, if so, under what conditions. This could include obtaining permissions from others who might appear in the recording. You will also need to find out what prior knowledge and experience your learners have. This will enable you to utilise it if they know something you don't, and to build on it if they don't. The term *digital media* refers to any audio, video, games and images which have been digitally compressed (encoded) so that they can easily be transmitted via computer networks.

There might be a learning resource centre (LRC) or a library within your organisation, or a public library which is accessible locally. They are no longer places that just contain books; many have computers and devices which are permanently connected to the internet, photocopying facilities, and other resources such as journals, magazines, newspapers and periodicals (manual and electronic). If there is an LRC or library at your organisation, you could arrange for a member of their staff to give your learners a short tour of the facilities. Often, they will have a licence to enable learners to access and read texts and journals online from their own devices at a time to suit.

Some organisations have a set of devices, such as tablets, which the teacher can reserve for use with their learners. If this is the case where you work, you will need to find out how you go about reserving them, and whether you need to collect and return them or if someone else will. They are often stored in a lockable trolley, which can be wheeled to and from the learning environment. Ideally, you will need to track their issue and return to make sure none go missing. If any devices develop a fault, you will need to report this, otherwise the next group who use them will experience problems. You will also need to check if the batteries are fully charged beforehand or if there is access to power sockets.

Open education resources (OER) are digital resources which are uploaded, exchanged and shared by teachers and assessors online. If you can carry out an internet search for a topic you are planning to teach, you will probably find lots of sites with free resources you can use. You might need to register with the site first, or reciprocate by uploading a resource of your own before downloading another. If you are using any materials you have found online, you will need to acknowledge the creator and/or the source of them.

If you have computer and internet facilities within the learning environment, try and make use of them whenever possible. However, don't try and overuse them, as your learners might feel they would like some traditional interaction with you and their peers. You will also need to make best use of what you have, rather than focusing on what you don't have.

Extension activity

Find out what aspects of ICT are available for you to use or to access in the organisation you are working in. Do you need to request to use anything in advance or is it always accessible? Is there a permanent internet connection or wifi access for staff and learners? Is there a specialist technology department with technical support if you need it? If so, they might be able to give you advice and guidance on what to use for your subject. If you use any of your own electronic devices in your workplace, will you need to have them checked to ensure they are safe to use? Finding out all this information prior to using ICT can save you time when planning what to use and when.

Learning technology

Learning technology is all about utilising the different aspects of TEL and ICT. This includes online sources, resources and media to enhance the teaching, learning and assessment process. However, you do need to know your own strengths and limitations. If you don't feel very confident at using something, you could invite someone who is familiar with it to deliver an awareness session to your learners, perhaps as part of the induction process. This would also help increase your own skills and knowledge. It's useful to know what your strengths and limitations are so that you can do something about it. There are many free tutorial videos regarding using technology, which you might like to access. Some of these are listed at the end of this chapter, and others are available by searching video sites such as YouTube.

When planning to incorporate technology into the teaching and learning process, you could ask yourself the following questions:

- Do I feel confident at using it? If not, who can help me?

- If the learners will use it, do they know how to? If not, how can I show them?

- Will I need any technical support? If so, how can I go about this?

- Are the devices and/or software accessible? If not, what do I need to do? Will the devices need charging up beforehand?

- Do I need an internet or wifi connection? If yes, how can I make sure it is reliable?

- How much time will I need to plan and prepare for its use?

- How can I make sure the resources are presented well and are accessible?

- What will I do if something goes wrong?

- Will it enhance what the learners are doing and increase their understanding of the subject?

As you begin to use various aspects of technology, you will soon find out what works and what doesn't. It's a learning process for you as well as your learners.

The FELTAG report *Paths Forward to a Digital Future for Further Education and Skills* (2014) recommended an increase in the use of technology in the UK (i.e. 10 per cent of learning to be online) and for learners to take responsibility for their own learning. If the programme you deliver and assess does not incorporate the use of technology, you could encourage your learners to access and use it in their own time.

Activity

Find out if there are any government reports or other recommendations for using technology for teaching and learning purposes. Take a look at the FELTAG report Paths Forward to a Digital Future for Further Education and Skills (2014) which can be accessed at: http://feltag.org.uk/ What impact do these type of reports have upon your job role?

Technology is only as good as the person using it; therefore, both you and your learners would need to know how to use it effectively. It should always be used in a way that educates and informs, for example, to illustrate a point, to promote a discussion, and to further skills, knowledge and understanding. It should not be relied on as a means to entertain learners.

Wherever possible, you should try and involve your learners with the use of ICT during and after their sessions with you. For example, giving small groups the responsibility for researching a topic during the session, then collaborating between sessions to produce a presentation of their findings. The presentation could be delivered during the following session. Their peers could provide feedback via an online survey or questionnaire that has been devised by them beforehand. This will help build on and improve the learners' digital literacy skills.

Software is the term used for programs and applications which run on a computer or other device, whereas hardware is the computer and other items such as printers. If you use software for presentations, you could incorporate pictures and graphics as well as text to make your presentation more visual. You are probably familiar with Microsoft PowerPoint; however, there are other innovative presentation programs such as:

- Haiku Deck (www.haikudeck.com)

- Keynote (www.apple.com/uk/keynote/)

- My simpleshow (www.mysimpleshow.com)

- Office Mix (https://mix.office.com)

- Prezi (www.prezi.com)

- Powtoon (www.powtoon.com)

- Slideshare (www.slideshare.net).

They can be fun to use, are a little bit different to PowerPoint, and can increase the engagement of learners. Videos and links to websites and resources can be embedded, as well as sounds, pictures and text. However, as most are saved to the cloud, internet access is required to retrieve them. Free alternative versions of the Microsoft programs (including PowerPoint) are available at: www.openoffice.org/download.

A wireless remote control is useful when using a presentation. It enables you to move around the room and use it to move through the slides, rather than stand next to the keyboard tapping a key. It's useful to have a contingency plan in case anything doesn't work, i.e. an activity which learners can carry out while you resolve the problem. Things will at some point go wrong, or just not work. When this happens, try not to get flustered or angry in front of your learners. Stay calm and move onto something else.

Activity

Take a look at the online interactive map at this link regarding ways of using technology with learners: http://tinyurl.com/gqzpa7h. It was produced by All Aboard (http://allaboardhe.org), a project funded by Ireland's National Forum for the Enhancement of Teaching and Learning. It will give you lots of ideas of things to do with your learners. If you click on various areas, you can see more information about them.

Some learners may be quite concerned about using ICT; for example, a learner with epilepsy may need regular breaks from a computer screen. Ideally, you will have ascertained this as part of the initial assessment process (covered in Chapter 3). However, it's best to check if your learners have any anxieties about using technology, including any health-related concerns or physical conditions which could affect access.

You could let your learners bring their own laptops, tablets, smartphones and e-readers to use during sessions. This could be for reading downloaded texts and/or writing notes rather than using textbooks, pen and paper. Learners could use their devices to access the internet for research or other activities. This is known BYOD, which is an acronym for *bring your own device*. If there are not enough computers or devices at your organisation for learners to use, BYOD is a good way of incorporating the use of technology. However, don't forget to agree some ground rules for their safe use.

Example

Jacqui wanted to use technology with her beauty therapy learners. As all her learners had their own mobile devices she felt she could incorporate their use somehow. She created an online quiz based on the topic of the session, which her learners were able to access via their own devices. They completed the quiz individually and then compared their results in pairs. The activity went well and Jacqui now uses other apps with her learners, such as voting tools and surveys.

Any electronic devices which are not owned by the organisation in which they are being used might need to be tested first. In the United Kingdom, the Republic of Ireland, New Zealand and Australia this is known as PAT testing which stands for portable appliance testing. A PAT test is carried out by a trained person to ensure the device is safe to use. These tests can help detect any potential problems before they occur. Always check the equipment is working and that the programs you use are appropriate and relevant for your learners.

Supporting learners

Never assume your learners are capable or confident at using technology; always carry out an initial assessment to ascertain their prior skills, knowledge and understanding. They, and indeed you, might need some training, for example, how to access, log on and use a particular program. The use of technology can also assist when differentiating activities to meet a particular learner's requirements. For example, using a screen reader or text enlargement software for a learner who is partially sighted. *Assistive resources* or *adaptive technology* are the terms used to denote devices and their use for people with disabilities or difficulties. Their use can lead to greater independence by providing enhancements to or changing the methods of use. This should enable learners to accomplish tasks they might not have been able to do without it.

Technological advances have made an enormous difference to learners who have particular needs, enabling them to access suitable learning opportunities. This is predominantly true for learners who have physical or sensory impairments, or those who have learning difficulties. Technology can provide a means of access to learning for those who:

- are hearing impaired
- are visually impaired
- have a degenerative condition which is physically tiring
- have a first language which is not the one used during the course
- have difficulty in speaking
- have difficulty with manipulation and fine motor control.

Please see Chapter 7 for further information regarding supporting learners using assistive resources.

Extension activity

Research what technologies are available to help learners who have particular needs and how you could use them. Take a look at the assistive technology websites listed at the end of this chapter for some guidance. Find out what specialist equipment or software is available in your organisation to help learners, and whether you need any training to use it.

E-learning

E-learning, short for *electronic learning,* is about using electronic learning technologies, devices, tools and systems with learners: for example, data projectors, interactive whiteboards and virtual learning environments (VLEs). They don't always have to include the use of the internet.

Electronic books (e-books) and journals can also be classed as using e-learning. Some are free or inexpensive and they are easily accessible via a computer or a device with an e-reader program. Many will play audio, read the text out loud, and contain links to relevant websites where the reader can find more information. Some organisations pay for a licence to enable staff and learners to have electronic access rather than having to purchase printed copies. You could encourage your learners to access chapters of relevant e-books before and after taught sessions. This would help to increase their knowledge and understanding and could be used as the basis of a group discussion during the session. Learners with any particular disabilities might find they can view the texts in a range of formats. Amazon offers a free Kindle e-reader app here: https://www.amazon.co.uk/kindle-dbs/fd/kcp

Activity

What opportunities can you identify to use e-learning with your learners? Find out what is available within your organisation or via the internet that you could use. Are there any e-books available for your subject? You could search publishers' websites to find out. You might like to talk to your colleagues to see what they use and how effective it is with learners.

E-learning includes the use of different models of teaching and learning, including:

- online/distance learning
- virtual learning environments (VLEs)
- blended learning
- flipped learning.

An explanation of each of these follows.

Online/distance learning

Qualifications and courses can be delivered online (either at, or at a distance from, the training venue) where learners can access a program via a specialist website or a *platform*. A platform is the device and operating system which runs the software such as a desktop computer, tablet or smartphone. This is ideal for learners who might have difficulty attending a particular venue or wish to learn at times and places convenient to them. It's sometimes referred to as *remote learning* as the learner is remote from the venue, their teacher and peers. However, remote learning doesn't always occur online. Correspondence courses can be entered into where learning materials are paper based and sent and returned via a postal service.

Online learning requires learners to access a computer or a device with a reliable internet connection, which could be in a library or another suitable location rather than at home.

Some learners may prefer or need to learn when and where it is convenient for them. Many organisations now offer online courses, which learners can commence and complete at any time. Some online courses can have hundreds of learners and are known as MOOCs, which is an acronym for massive open online courses. These are often free and open to anyone who is interested in a particular subject being offered, and who has an internet connection. The downside of this for a tutor is the number of learners allocated to them will vary. Many learners tend to drop out and a lot of time might be needed to manage the learning process effectively.

If you want your learners to work together as part of an online community, you could carry out activities as though you are with the group in person. This could include introductions, carrying out an icebreaker, agreeing ground rules and encouraging them to interact with each other and yourself. Good interpersonal skills, approachability, enthusiasm and a strong commitment to supporting learning will help you to establish and maintain motivation and interaction with your learners.

Example

Marlon is the tutor for a group of 100 learners who are about to commence an online course in psychology. He does not know anything about the learners. His first task is to welcome everyone to the course and to ask them to create an online profile. This will enable him and the other learners to see who they are working with. He informs them that he will post topics for discussion in the forum, which everyone should contribute to. He tells them how they can access information regarding the course content, how they will be assessed and the target dates for assignments. His second task is to agree some ground rules, such as how learners should behave online. His third task is to carry out an icebreaker to help the learners communicate and to feel confident at using the program. Marlon appreciated that some learners would drop out of the course but that he would do his best to motivate and support them on an ongoing basis.

The key issues regarding online learning are:

- availability and access to the software being used, familiarity with ICT, internet availability and download speeds

- being isolated, some learners might not like the idea of being on their own for the learning process

- encouraging learners to update their profiles, to agree a social etiquette and communicate with others within the online community

- ensuring learners are fully aware of what they need to do, along with target dates

- ensuring the authenticity, safety and security of the learners, their work and data

- knowing when to intervene or moderate in a situation that might become out of control, for example, discussing sensitive issues which are not related to the subject

- motivating learners to establish a routine, for example, to commit regular times for study, to partake in discussion forums and to meet deadlines for the submission of work

- differing screen sizes, therefore some people might struggle to read on a small screen

- the amount of support each individual will require.

Online roles

If you are working with learners who are undertaking an online course, you might be home based or work from an office in the organisation which employs you. You might never meet your learners face to face. This could have its own challenges such as confirming the identity of the learner and the authenticity of their work.

You might have a job specification which includes one more of the following roles:

- e-tutor/online tutor

- e-assessor/online assessor

- e-moderator/online moderator.

An explanation of each of these follows and some might overlap. The roles will require you to encourage, motivate and challenge your learners, as well as demonstrate certain skills such as communication, empathy and time management.

E-tutor/online tutor

E-tutors are often referred to as online tutors and are available to support learners throughout their time on a particular course. However, this might not always be at the time the learner needs the help. They might expect an instant response if they post a question. You will need to inform learners when you are available online, and when you will respond to questions when offline. However, don't just leave your learners to it; make sure you regularly check how they are progressing and carry out an online tutorial if necessary.

Learning materials will need to be uploaded to the online program in advance. It could be that you are not familiar with the content of them if they have been created by someone else. You might therefore want to work through them first, in case you are asked any questions about them. If you are creating the learning materials, make sure any instructions you include are clear. Don't assume your learners will understand what you are asking them to do. Read everything you create from a learner's perspective and check for spelling and grammar errors.

An e-tutor will facilitate the learning process by encouraging the learners to progress through the learning materials. E-tutors should be careful of using too much jargon, or assuming their learners will understand things. Knowledge of using ICT and the particular program used will be required, as will the ability to solve some technical issues or know who to contact if they can't be dealt with. E-tutors need to be aware that learners have a life outside of the course and that sometimes this might hinder their access and progress. Learners will also need to appreciate that their tutor might not always be accessible when they want them to be.

Action plans and target dates for the submission of work should be agreed. The online tutor will be able to assess and provide feedback electronically. Communication will be via the program, which can be live, or recorded for accessing later (text, audio or visual). This enables all communications to be tracked. The online tutor and the learners can create a profile of themselves and upload a photo if they wish. This helps make the interaction a more personal one as you can see a picture of the person and learn a little about them.

E-assessor/online assessor

E-assessors are often referred to as online assessors and will either combine their role with that of an online tutor or purely be an online assessor. The latter means they are only assessing the work which a learner submits; they are not facilitating learning or checking if learners have worked through the course materials beforehand.

Online assessment can be used in addition to other traditional assessment methods during an attended session. For example, learners could complete a multiple-choice test, which will automatically be marked online and gives instant results. The system could generate different questions for each learner so that no two tests are the same. Tests can be taken on demand when a learner is ready and can be taken anywhere there is a suitable device with access to the software. However, supervision might be necessary for some online tests, and grades might be meaningless without detailed feedback. An online system is able to track all submission dates and grades, and give a detailed visual analysis of each learner's achievements. Quality assurance can also be integrated and tracked.

When assessing work that has been uploaded online, there should be the facility for you to add electronic comments. This can be via the software, or you could download the document to a computer and add comments via a word processor, before uploading it for the learner to see. This will create a record of what was submitted and when, along with a copy of the comments and feedback. Anything you assess must always be valid, authentic, current, sufficient and reliable (covered in Chapter 10).

Be careful how you write your feedback as it could be interpreted differently when read by a learner. You need to remember that whatever you write might be permanent and accessible for a long time; therefore, don't use any inappropriate language or anything you might regret later.

If you are an online assessor, you will still need to get to know your learners as individuals. This will help you when assessing that their work is authentic. For example, if you know how your learner responds in the discussion forums, but their writing is very different when completing assessment activities, then you might be concerned that the work is not their own.

E-moderator

E-moderators are often referred to as online moderators. They are not usually performing the role of a tutor or an assessor at the same time, but are facilitating and supporting the interactions of others. This could be where learners are on a course that does not lead to a qualification. The learners will work through materials and resources and discuss them with their peers. These types of courses are usually for personal and professional development and often delivered through a MOOC approach.

The e-moderator's role is to welcome the participants and encourage them to interact with their peers. This interaction could be via live chat rooms, where conversations can happen quickly if many learners are taking part. Learners will need guidance regarding how to use the system and what the protocols are for posting and responding to comments. This is to ensure learning stays on track and that nothing inappropriate is discussed. An e-moderator might also manage and moderate video conferences, online forums and the exchange of resources.

Synchronous and asynchronous learning

Online learning can by *synchronous*, i.e. the learner and the teacher are online at the same time, or *asynchronous*, i.e. at different times.

Synchronous learning

This is where the tutor and learners can communicate in real time. However, everyone needs to agree to log onto their computer or device at the agreed time. It's like arriving to attend a class, but it's a virtual environment rather than a physical environment. A reliable internet connection is required and, ideally, the tutor and learners should be in a quiet place where they won't be interrupted by others.

The advantages of a synchronous learning environment are:

- attendance is automatically tracked: a record is made of when the learners log on and off

- tutors can choose from a variety of technologies to deliver the subject, i.e. slide presentations, a shared whiteboard, audio and video conferencing

- learners can work together in pairs or groups and the teacher can see how they are communicating to achieve a task

- there is live interaction with the learners during a discussion. A learner can indicate when they want to *speak* (either verbally or by keying in a message) by choosing an option to virtually raise their hand. Most programs enable learners to see and speak to each other and the tutor. Learners will need to have enabled their audio and video facilities in advance, i.e. speakers, a microphone and a webcam. If a learner wishes to communicate something in confidence, they can ask to go to a private chat room.

- tutors can use online questions and quizzes which are automatically assessed

- assessment and feedback records are maintained and are trackable.

Asynchronous learning

This can take place anywhere and at any time. Learners can log on when they have time and can interact with the various tasks and resource materials that have been uploaded.

They can leave messages for their peers and their tutor, which will hopefully have been responded to by the next time they log in. Discussion *threads* (virtual conversations) are a great way to gain and share knowledge. However, the tutor will need to keep an eye on what is being discussed in case anything inappropriate is posted. Learners from across the world and in different time zones can participate in the same course. This can add a welcome diversity where different opinions and ideas can be shared and discussed.

The advantages of an asynchronous learning environment are:

- learning can take place at a time and place to suit each learner

- many learners can participate

- learners from different areas or countries can take part, enabling a wide variety of knowledge to be shared.

Activity

What do you consider the challenges to be of using synchronous and asynchronous learning? Discuss this with a colleague or friend to compare your responses.

Virtual learning environments (VLEs)

These are often referred to by the acronym VLE and are like a virtual classroom where learners can take a course, and/or access materials and resources to support a course they are attending. They include a range of online collaboration, communication and tracking tools. They can be accessed via an organisation's intranet or stored in the cloud and accessed via the internet.

A type of VLE is known as Moodle, which is classed as a free open source software learning management system. This means that organisations can use and adapt it to suit their own requirements. Moodle is an acronym for modular object-oriented dynamic learning environment. Learners can access the VLE by logging on with a user name and password, which the organisation creates in advance. If your organisation doesn't have their own VLE, you can check out what is available online. They might be free to use for a small number of learners. For example:

- Canvas (www.canvasvle.co.uk)

- Course Sites (www.coursesites.com)

- Edmodo (www.edmodo.com)

- Educadium (www.educadium.com)

- Nearpod (www.nearpod.com)

- Simple VLE (www.simplevle.com).

VLEs are useful to support traditional face-to-face courses or for purely online courses. For online learning, they can be used for learners to work through course materials, interact with their tutor and peers, and upload completed work for assessment and feedback.

VLEs are a useful way for learners to access:

- assessment information and assignments

- chat rooms for communicating with peers

- course information

- learning materials, resources and activities

- message facilities to communicate with their tutor

- projects for collaboration

- synchronous or asynchronous discussion forums

- video and audio clips, pictures and sounds.

Blended learning

When technology is combined with traditional face-to-face methods of teaching and assessment, it is known as *blended learning*. It's a great way to encourage learners to use aspects of digital technology to support their learning. For example, learners could use the internet to research further a topic which a teacher has just explained. It's about making best use of what's available at the time to support teaching and learning and to add variety.

In the UK there is a blended learning consortium; you might like to check their website for further information: http://www.blc-fe.org/.

At the time of publication, a free online course regarding blended learning was available at: https://www.futurelearn.com/courses/blended-learning-getting-started.

Flipped learning

The term *flipped* learning relates to flipping the work normally carried out *during* a session, to that which is carried out *away* from the session. Examples include learners using multimedia, i.e. watching videos, listening to podcasts and collaborating with their peers while away from the face-to-face session. They will then discuss this during the next session and contextualise it to the subject. This gives the teacher the opportunity to give a more personalised and interactive approach when with their learners. The teacher becomes more of a facilitator of learning, guiding and supporting learners to find things out for themselves. It puts the emphasis on learners to research theory outside the session so that they can apply their knowledge during the session by interacting and collaborating with others.

Extension activity

If you are not already using online learning, VLEs, blended learning or flipped learning, have a go at planning to use one or more of them in some way. You might need to check what is currently available at your organisation and whether you need further training or technical support. If nothing is available, you could set up your own online VLE and upload resources and learning materials. Just search the internet for 'free simple VLE', many of which are accessible via the cloud.

Social networking and social media

Social *networking* is about connecting and communicating with friends, family and other people who share an interest (i.e. a network of people). It can be used to build up contacts with other professionals and future employers. Social *media* is about using technology to turn communication into an interactive dialogue. However, you might consider some networking sites to be social media sites and vice versa depending upon the situation in which they are used. Both can be used by teachers and learners, providing everyone is aware of how to stay safe online. Please see the section towards the end of this chapter regarding safety and security. Most social networking and social media sites are free to join; however, you might need to pay for extra facilities if you wish to use them.

Learners might already belong to a social networking site and/or access social media on a regular basis. They might therefore expect to have access to these during sessions. If you are using them with your learners, you will need to agree some ground rules. This might include accessing relevant sites for educational purposes only and not accessing personal sites.

Some learners might struggle with speaking in front of their peers but might feel comfortable communicating via social networks or social media sites. This can be useful if particular learners are shy or feel intimidated to ask questions or respond to others orally. When writing, learners might key in words as abbreviations or miss out vowels (e.g. B4 for before). If you can make sure they are not doing this when using them for educational purposes, it can help improve their spelling and grammar. It can also help them focus on a topic and not digress. For example, Twitter only allows the use of 140 characters when posting a message.

Your learners might want to find out more about you and search the internet to see if you have an online presence. Do be careful with any information you post about yourself that can be accessed in the public domain. It's best to politely decline any requests from learners to join their personal social networking sites. You are not their *friend*, you are their teacher.

Social networking

There are many social networking sites available that teachers and learners can join to discuss their interest in a particular area. These include:

Facebook (www.facebook.com)

LinkedIn (www.linkedin.com)

Google+ (https://plus.google.com)

Twitter (www.twitter.com).

To join a social network, you will need to go to the relevant website and create an account. This will involve writing a bit about yourself, known as a *profile* and uploading a photo. Some people join under an assumed name, and/or use a photo which is not of themselves. It's always wise to be careful when communicating with anyone you don't know and to be cautious of what people write. Once joined, you can choose to *follow* people or organisations by updating your settings to be notified when they post anything. Alternatively, you can just view what has been posted in the public areas. You can choose to respond to discussions other people have started, or start a discussion yourself. You might find it useful to set up a social network purely for your learners to access, which is based on your subject.

Example

Sadiq created a page on a popular social networking site purely for his subject and learners. He updated the site settings so that the page was not open to the public. Sadiq added links to relevant videos and encouraged his learners to view them and to respond to the discussions he posted. Using the site enabled his learners to access information in their own time and to keep in touch with their peers. Sadiq could check the site to see what his learners were discussing with a view to incorporating the topics during future sessions. The site therefore became a way of communicating, collaborating, sharing and learning.

With most social networking sites, there is usually an option to communicate privately rather than publicly; again, be careful of what you say to people you don't know. What you post (text and images) can easily be taken out of context and can be accessible for many years. If you are ever unsure, don't post anything in a public forum which you would not willingly say to a total stranger you have just met. This is also useful to tell to your learners. You might like to ask them to carry out an online search for their own name using different search engines. They might be surprised what they find, and this information could also be found by current and future employers as well as family members.

There are some negative sides to social networking sites, besides people who join with an assumed name. Sometimes people post nasty or untrue comments, or *troll* others. Trolling is about annoying, mocking or upsetting others by posting inflammatory and derisory comments. This can be hurtful to the person on the receiving end. Social networking sites can also be a target for others to steal personal information and identities and use them immorally. A positive side is that social networking enables people to keep in touch and to receive information quickly. A *digital citizen* is a person who is acting responsibly when participating in social activities using the internet and digital technology.

Online communities

An online community is a virtual community consisting of a group of people with a common interest, for example, a particular educational subject. Communication is via the internet, often using social networking or social media to post questions and discuss various topics.

There are many educational online communities which you will be able to search for and join. These might relate to your particular subject area, or to teaching, training and assessment in general. You can post a question and receive responses from people who are in a similar situation to yourself. Popular professional discussion forums can be found at LinkedIn (www.linkedin.com). Some forums are open to anyone to join; others you will need to request to join.

Example

Manuel had been teaching his subject of physics for many years. He felt his lessons were becoming a bit repetitive. He decided to find out how other physics teachers incorporated the use of technology with learners. He joined LinkedIn (www. linkedin.com) and searched the 'groups' for 'teaching physics'. He was surprised at how many groups there were and so asked to join a few. He was soon able to post a question to start a discussion and received some very helpful responses.

You might like to carry out a search for your subject in the LinkedIn groups or other relevant social networking sites. This would connect you with people who might be able to help you with ideas for teaching your subject.

Twitter is another way of creating an online community (www.twitter.com). Anyone can set up a Twitter hashtag (#) for a particular topic and then everyone with an interest can log onto their Twitter account at an agreed time. Questions can be asked and anyone who responds can include the particular hashtag in their reply (e.g. #maths). Sometimes, the live conversation moves quite quickly and it's easy to get left behind. If you can't keep up or can't participate live, you can type the hashtag in the Twitter search box later to see what has been discussed. A popular group in the UK is UKFEchat (#ukfechat) who meet online most Thursday evenings at 9 p.m. UK time for one hour. Outside of this time, the particular hashtag can be added to any comment posted on Twitter to enable it to appear in a later search.

You, and your learners, will need to remember that anything posted will be attributed to your/their name and will not be anonymous.

Social media

Media relates to information which is accessible via newspapers, magazines, radio and television. Social media relates to information and materials which are accessible via the internet. Using social media is a way of transmitting information very quickly to a lot of people. This can include text, videos, pictures, documents, blogs and vlogs. A blog (weblog) is a succession of written posts about various topics, a bit like a diary. The term comes from using the last letter of *web* before the word *log*. A vlog (video log) is a video version of a blog. The term *going viral* is often used when people spread the message that they have seen and it gets seen by thousands of people very quickly.

There are lots of social media sites available which can help support your subject. These enable your learners to communicate with each other and for you to upload learning materials, videos and images for them to access. You might consider the use of social media sites for personal use; however, they can be used in imaginative ways for teaching and learning purposes. These include:

- Blogger (www.blogger.com)

- Flickr (www.flickr.com)

- Instagram (www.instagram.com)

- Periscope (www.periscope.tv)

- Pinterest (www.pinterest.com)

- Snapchat (www.snapchat.com)

- Storify (www.storify.com)

- Ted Talks (www.ted.com/talks)

- Tumblr (www.tumblr.com)

- Vimeo (www.vimeo.com)

- Vine (www.vine.co)

- WhatsApp (www.whatsapp.com)

- Wordpress (www.wordpress.com)

- YouTube (www.youtube.com).

Activity

If you have access to the internet, have a look at various social networking and social media sites such as those mentioned in the bullet lists in this chapter. You could join some to use for professional networking regarding your subject.

You could generate your own social media page by going to a relevant site and creating an account. You can see what others are posting in public areas, add materials yourself, or just choose to search for a person or a topic that you would like to follow. When you follow someone, you can amend the site settings to automatically be notified when they post something. This is useful if you want to keep up to date with what influential people in your sector are talking about.

Some educational organisations block access to certain sites. However, some of the sites they block can actually be a really good source for your subject, such as videos regarding various topics. However, if you do have access to, and plan on showing any videos to your learners, you are best watching them yourself first, as you can't always trust the source. Not all the information that is posted online is genuine. If it's being used to support educational purposes, the origins will need to be confirmed.

You could use social media sites to encourage your learners to communicate, engage in discussions and support each other outside of the learning environment. Learning opportunities should reflect the way society is today, which includes working in online social environments. You may need to enlighten your learners in how to get the best out of communicating online, how to be effective collaborators, how to interact with others in a polite way and how to stay safe in the virtual world.

Extension activity

If you currently have a group of learners, discuss the advantages and disadvantages of using social networking and social media for educational purposes. If possible, ask your learners to research different sites with a view to creating a page for their subject. You could then create the page with your learners and set the privacy setting so that it is not accessible by the public. Learners in turn could post a discussion based on a relevant topic and include links to relevant websites and resources they have researched.

Using digital technology

When using various aspects of digital technology with your learners, it's best to try it out yourself first. Some things will work well, others won't. This could be because of an issue with the particular software, the way you demonstrate it or the way learners respond when using it. However, you will need to be aware that some learners might be reluctant to use it or not wish to use it all. It might be useful to inform your learners prior to their starting the course, which aspects of technology will be used and why.

Examples of using digital technology for teaching and learning can include (in alphabetical order):

- accessing blogs, vlogs, chat rooms, social networking sites, social media and discussion forums to help learners communicate and collaborate with each other

- accessing cloud storage facilities which teachers and learners can use to upload, share, collaborate on and access from various online devices

- accessing digital media for visual/audio recording and playback

- annotating images and videos (www.thinglink.com)

- checking learners' assignments for plagiarism with specialist software (www.grammarly.com/plagiarism)

- creating a private YouTube channel and empowering learners to make and add videos for their peers to review and comment on (www.youtube.com)

- creating a Twitter hashtag for a topic (#) and encouraging learners to use it during a session, then checking the comments later by searching for the hashtag (www.twitter.com)

- creating a wiki for learners to collaborate with their peers. They can contribute to a discussion with a trackable history of changes (www.wikispaces.com)

- creating an online glossary either in a VLE or as a document saved to the cloud; learners can add new words, acronyms, jargon and phrases with meanings. A completed list can be downloaded by each learner at the end of the course

- creating and using live webinars for learners to view if they can't attend a session (www.freeconferencecall.com) or filming the session and uploading it to a VLE or video sharing site for later access

- creating and using online and on-demand tests which can give instant results: for example, diagnostic, learning preferences and multiple-choice tests

- creating electronic portfolios for learners to save and access their work

- creating online discussion and chat forums which allow asynchronous (taking place at different times) and synchronous (taking place at the same time) discussions

- enabling BYOD (bring your own device) where learners use their own devices for learning and assessment (ground rules should be agreed)

- enabling internet access on various devices for research to support assignments and presentations

- encouraging learners to keep an online diary, blog, vlog or reflective learning journal

- setting a task for learners to carry out by asking them to come up with technological ideas to complete it

- synchronising online calendars with members of staff for meetings, or with learners for attending online or onsite sessions

- using computer software for learners to complete assignments, save and back up their work (to the computer, a storage device, or the cloud)

- using educational gaming software, augmented reality and virtual reality

- using email for electronic submission of assessments, communication and informal feedback on progress

- using interactive whiteboards for teachers and learners to use

- using mobile phones and tablets for taking pictures, creating video and audio clips and communicating with others

- using networked systems to allow access to software and documents from any computer linked to the system (an *intranet*)

- using online voting, surveys and questionnaire apps to use during or after a session (a list of websites is available later in this chapter)

- using puzzle software for creating fun activities either to be used online or printed and used as paper copies, for example, crosswords, quizzes, flash cards and domino type games (a list of websites is available later in this chapter)

- using scanners for copying and transferring documents to a computer

- using VLEs to access and upload learning materials and assessment activities

- using web cameras or video conferencing if you can't be in the same place as your learners and you need to see and speak with them.

Activity

Design an activity for your learners to carry out using technology. Looking at the previous bullet list might give you some ideas. For example, you could create an activity for learners to collaborate on via cloud computing regarding a relevant topic. If possible, use the activity with your learners and then evaluate how effective it was. What changes would you make and why?

Software

Software is a general term for programs and applications (apps) which can be used on computers and other devices such as tablets and smartphones. You might already be familiar with using some software such as a word processor or a presentation program. However, you might not be familiar with any specialist software for your subject such as a computer aided design (CAD) program. Your organisation might have to purchase or use some programs under a licence agreement.

You will need to find out what is available and what will work effectively on the devices you have, for the benefit of teaching and learning. There are thousands of different programs and apps for personal and professional use and more are becoming available daily. Some will work on all devices (known as multi-platform or cross-platform) and some will only work on a computer. Some are free to use but often include advertisements. If you use any of these with your learners, you will need to know that the adverts are appropriate. Often, if someone searches for something via the internet on their device, and then they use the device for something else, adverts will pop up based on their original search. You might therefore have no control over this.

Online voting, surveys, quiz and questionnaire apps

These can be fun to use during or after a session to obtain responses to questions and/or gain feedback from learners. Time is needed beforehand to create the questions, learners will need to be informed how to respond to them and an internet connection is needed. The app will automatically analyse the data. They are a good way to engage learners during a session, can be quick and easy to use and most have free basic use. These include:

- Google forms (www.google.com/forms)

- Plickers (https://plickers.com/)

- Quizlet (https://quizlet.com)

- Socrative (wwwl.socrative.com)

- Survey Monkey (www.surveymonkey.com)

- Typeform (www.typeform.com)

Puzzle software and learning activities

Puzzle software can be used to create fun learning activities either to be used online or printed and used as paper copies. As a change from you creating them, you could ask your learners to create one to use with each other. This could be a way of consolidating their knowledge so far, perhaps in pairs or small groups. Once completed by another pair or small group, a discussion could take place regarding any aspects which were incorrect, and how this impacted on those completing the activity.

The software can include crosswords, jigsaws, flash cards, word searches and domino-type matching card games. Some will involve downloading software first, whereas others can be used online and most have free basic use. These include:

- Archers: puzzles and crosswords (www.archersoftware.co.uk/crossword)

- Classtools: games, quizzes and activities (www.classtools.net)

- Crossword compiler (www.crossword-compiler.com)

- Discovery Education: puzzles and wordsearches (www.discoveryeducation.com)

- Eclipse Crossword (www.eclipsecrossword.com)

- Hemitech Laboratory: learning activities (www.mmlsoft.com/index.php/products)

- Hot Potatoes: interactive activities (http://hotpot.uvic.ca)

- Kahoot: learning games (www.kahoot.com)

- Mathsnet: mathematical activities (www.mathsnet.net)

Activity

Find out what software is available for you and your learners to use. Have a go at creating an activity to determine how useful it would be to the learning process. Alternatively, access one from the previous bullet lists. Is there is a specialist program which you feel your learners would benefit from using for your subject? If so, research how much it would cost and under what terms it can be used. It might be worth approaching your organisation to ask if they could purchase it or if they can use it under a licence.

Cloud computing

Cloud computing is a way of storing and accessing information, data, pictures, sounds and videos via the internet, rather than saving them to a computer or other device. They are not literally saved in clouds in the sky, but on a remote server used by the company which has designed the program or app. Most have free basic use. These include:

- Box (www.box.com)
- Dropbox (www.dropbox.com)
- Evernote (www.evernote.com)
- Google drive (www.google.com/drive/)
- Google for Education (www.google.co.uk/edu)
- Lino (http://en.linoit.com)
- Microsoft Office 365 (https://products.office.com)
- Padlet (www.padlet.com)
- Pinterest (www.pinterest.com)
- Screencast-o-matic (https://screencast-o-matic.com).

Once you have created an account, you can choose to give access to others to view your stored information, to collaborate and edit, or just keep it there for your own use.

The advantage of saving to the cloud, is that storage space is not required on your own device and you can access your documents via the program or app from anywhere with an internet connection. You also don't risk damaging any storage devices such as memory sticks or cards. The disadvantage is that if you can't gain access, perhaps because the internet connection is not working, you can't access your documents.

If you have a reliable internet connection, using an appropriate program or app via the cloud is a good way to help learners collaborate on documents and presentations. Any documents created should follow copyright guidelines and relevant legislation (covered in Chapter 7).

Online messaging, voice and video calls

There are many online messaging, voice and video programs and apps which are available for communicating in real time. They can be for sending and receiving messages, pictures, videos, voice and video calls and most have free basic use. Some apps let you communicate with more than one person at the same time, and can be used for live transmissions and video conferencing, known as *streaming*. Some apps can be also be used for webinars. This is a web-based seminar where people attend online rather than in person onsite.

These include:

- Google Hangouts (http://hangouts.google.com)
- GoToMeeting (www.gotomeeting.com)
- Imo (www.imo.im)
- MailVu (www.mailvu.com)
- Microsoft Teams (https://products.office.com)
- Oovoo (www.oovoo.com)
- Skype (www.skype.com)
- Snapchat (www.snapchat.com)
- Todaysmeet (www.todaysmeet.com)
- Webex (www.webex.com)
- Whatsapp (www.whatsapp.com).

There are also messaging and chat options within popular social networking sites such as Facebook and Twitter, some email programs and some mobile providers' own networks.

Example

Rashid teaches drama to a group of 16 learners once a week. One of his learners, Rick, has broken his arm and is unable to attend the forthcoming session. He emailed Rashid to ask if he would stream the next session to him live via Skype. Rashid checked with his group to see if they were happy to be included in the live stream and they were. At the beginning of the session, Rashid positioned his mobile phone where the camera could view him and the room and called Rick's Skype number. When Rick accepted the call he was able to see everything that was happening. This ensured he did not miss any of the session. Rashid emailed Rick the handouts from the session and made another Skype call a couple of days later to talk to Rick in real time about any questions or concerns he had.

Keeping up to date

Technology is constantly evolving and advancing. No sooner have you got used to using a particular program or app, it might change. The websites listed in this chapter might be out of date by the time you check them. However, a quick internet search might find a suitable alternative. It can also be confusing as there are so many different websites and apps which are available to access. Having the time to choose and use what's appropriate can often be difficult. However, communicating with others can help share knowledge. This could be with colleagues or those in a similar subject area as yourself, either through an online forum in a social networking group or via online chats and messaging. To help you keep track of relevant websites and resources you have located on the internet, there are online programs which you could use and most have free basic use.

These include:

- Diigo (www.diigo.com)
- Evernote (www.evernote.com)
- Pearltrees (www.pearltrees.com)

Websites for keeping up to date with technology

Searching the internet for your particular subject area will often locate many different websites, some might be appropriate and others might not. If you use any information you find online, it's useful to check that it's genuine, and then reference your source (i.e. the webpage link and date) when including it in a handout for learners.

The following websites are useful to gain up-to-date information regarding developments in technology as well as with teaching and training.

- Association for Learning Technology – www.alt.ac.uk/
- Digital Unite – www.digitalunite.com
- Excellence Gateway (resources) – www.excellencegateway.org.uk
- FE Advice – www.feadvice.org.uk
- Foundation Online – free courses – www.foundationonline.org.uk/course/index.p...
- Future Learn free courses – www.futurelearn.com/
- Open University free courses – www.open.edu/openlearn/free-courses
- Teacher Training Videos – www.teachertrainingvideos.com/

Extension activity

Take a look at some of the websites in the bullet list above and see how useful the information is to help you keep up to date. Research other sites which could be useful for keeping up to date with technology and with your particular subject.

Online safety and security

Teachers and learners need to be aware of how to stay safe and secure when using ICT. How you and your learners use it for teaching and learning purposes might differ from how it's used for personal or social reasons. You will need to remember that you are in a position of authority and trust. As such, you have a responsibility to make sure your learners are safe when using it and that they are not vulnerable in any way to the acts of others. Your organisation might have a *digital strategy*. This might state how ICT, the internet and email should be used to good effect. There should also be policies and procedures in place regarding the safeguarding of learners when using ICT. They will have been produced with your own, and your learners' safety and security in mind. You will need to make sure that your learners are aware of them, and that both they, and you, adhere to them. Copies might be available via your organisation's intranet, on an online or real notice board, or included in staff and learner handbooks.

These might include:

- acceptable use policy
- code of practice.

Acceptable use policy

An acceptable use policy will usually state how often and for how long users within the organisation can access and use ICT and internet devices. When learners leave the course, any accounts with user names and passwords should be deleted. The policy will often state that usage will be monitored to help prevent access to unsuitable or inappropriate websites. The policy should also cover aspects such as cheating and plagiarism by learners. Access to personal social networking sites might not be allowed during teaching and learning sessions. However, educational networking sites might be considered useful and acceptable. User names and passwords should only be used by the people they are intended for.

Code of practice

A code of practice relates to how teachers and learners should behave when using ICT, the internet and email. Everyone should be cautious about revealing personal details such as their home address, telephone numbers and passwords. You might want to warn your learners about fake websites and scam emails, and advise them not to click on any dubious links or files in case they contain a virus.

You will need to look out for, and confront, certain aspects regarding the behaviour of others, which should be included in the Code of Practice, such as not:

- accessing inappropriate sites or extremist material
- creating rumours about others which are untrue
- deliberately damaging equipment or software
- downloading or installing inappropriate software
- grooming people; i.e. building an emotional connection for the purpose of exploitation
- hacking; i.e. gaining unauthorised access to data in a computer system
- making threats or blackmailing others
- partaking in criminal or terrorist activity
- partaking in cyber bullying or trolling
- radicalising others; the process of making someone adopt a radical position regarding social issues or politics

- sharing information and/or images of others without their permission

- using inappropriate language

- using insults or abusing others online.

You could incorporate a discussion around these bullet points when agreeing ground rules with your learners at the beginning of the course. Alternatively, you could ask your learners to use digital technology to collaborate and create a poster or a mind map. Popplet (www.popplet.com) and MindMeister (www.mindmeister.com) might be worth checking out for this. You can always revisit the ground rules at any time to add to or amend them, in the light of situations which have occurred. You could agree a ground rule that if learners are using the internet during a session, they should not be accessing any personal accounts they have. It might be that you and your learners have to sign a document to agree to certain terms and conditions regarding the appropriate use of ICT. If you do see behaviour that breaches the Code of Practice, you will need to follow the relevant procedure within your organisation.

Following policies and agreeing some ground rules will help ensure that the use of technology is reasonable and safe.

Activity

Locate and read the policies and/or relevant codes of practice which relate to using ICT and accessing the internet. You will probably find they are quite detailed and might contain a lot of jargon. If you are unsure of the content, ask someone for clarification. If you don't understand something, your learners probably won't either. You may also need to find out who to report any inappropriate behaviour to, and what your responsibilities are.

Staying safe online

Staying safe online is not something that occurs automatically. Everyone needs to take responsibility for what they do and don't do. *Digital resilience* is the term for understanding the relationship between technology and risk, and being positive about dealing with it.

Example

Helen, a learner, had recently joined a social networking site and posted some photos of herself and places she had visited. She soon gained a few online friends and became excited when they liked something she had posted. People she didn't know began asking to be her friend and she accepted all the requests. She felt she needed to have lots of friends who would like what she posted. However, this soon got out of hand when her so-called friends starting criticising her. Helen was not aware of the privacy settings she could use or who her online friends really were. She decided to cancel her account. She realised that what happens in the real world is much better than in the virtual world. She also found she had more time to do other things as she was not obsessed with looking at her online account.

If your organisation is inspected by Ofsted in England, they will be looking at how learners are able to stay safe online, and that they understand the potential risks and dangers of using and misusing technology.

Teachers and learners can contribute to staying safe online by (in alphabetical order):

- backing-up documents and data to a separate drive

- being aware of scams (a dishonest scheme or fraud)

- being careful when using wifi networks as others might be able to access their device and its contents

- changing passwords regularly, making them complex and not revealing them to anyone

- checking the privacy settings on social networking sites so as not to reveal anything personal to strangers

- covering a webcam when it's not in use

- following relevant policies, procedures, codes of practice and legislation

- keeping personal and professional networking accounts separate

- not accessing insecure or untrusted websites

- not getting friendly with strangers online; they might not be who they seem

- not meeting strangers in real life who you have met online; they might not be who they say they are

- not posting anything in a public forum which you would not willingly say to a total stranger

- not purchasing anything from an insecure site

- not uploading pictures or videos of yourself unless you are happy that other people can access and use them for purposes you might not have intended

- only using the communication channels provided by your organisation, i.e. a secure email account, VLE or intranet

- reporting sites or users which you are seriously concerned about

- thinking before you post; once your text/pictures are online, they might be accessible for many years, even though you think you have deleted them

- using anti-virus and/or anti-spyware software and a firewall to stop unauthorised access to a computer or a device and its contents.

An aspect to consider when using computers, devices, keyboards and mice, which are shared among others, is hygiene. Germs can linger and then be caught and spread by everyone who uses them. Washing hands regularly, and/or using cleansing wipes or antibacterial liquid can help to prevent this. Having good hygiene is something to be aware of, particularly in times of coughs and colds.

Extension activity

Create an activity for your learners to carry out which is based around staying safe and secure online. For example, place your learners in small discussion groups to research and agree a few dos and don'ts. They can then create a short presentation to deliver to the rest of the group.

Self-assessment checklist

Do I know about the following?

If not, re-read this chapter, or research the texts and websites listed at the end.

☐ The advantages and disadvantages of using technology

☐ Identifying different technologies to use for my role and with learners

☐ What cloud computing is and how learners can collaborate using it

☐ What open education resources (OER) are

☐ What a virtual learning environment (VLE) is

☐ How to support learners' needs with the use of ICT

☐ What e-learning is

☐ How to use online, blended and flipped learning

☐ The difference between synchronous and asynchronous learning

☐ How to use social networking and social media for teaching and learning purposes

☐ How to keep up to date with technological developments

☐ How myself and my learners can stay safe and secure online

Summary

This chapter has explored how technology enhanced teaching and learning can help to enhance and reinforce knowledge and understanding.

You should now be able to use aspects of technology for your job role and to add variety to your sessions. You should also know which software can be used to improve the learning experience.

You might like to carry out further research by accessing the books and websites listed at the end of this chapter, particularly if you are working towards a higher level teaching qualification.

This chapter has covered the following topics:

- The role of technology in teaching, learning and assessment

- Learning technology

- E-learning

- Social networking and social media

- Using digital technology

- Online safety and security

References and further information

Allen, M. (2016) *Guide to E-learning: Building Interactive, Fun and Effective Learning Programs for any Company.* New Jersey: John Wiley & Sons.

Berners-Lee, T. (2000) *Weaving the Web: The Past, Present and Future of the World Wide Web by its Inventor.* Knutsford: Texere Publishing.

Elkins, D. and Pinder, D. (2015) *E-Learning Fundamentals: A Practical Guide.* Virginia: ATD Publications.

Haythornthwaite, C. and Andrews, R. (2011) *E-learning Theory and Practice.* London: SAGE.

Ingle, S. and Duckworth, V. (2013) *Enhancing Learning Through Technology In Lifelong Learning: Fresh Ideas: Innovative Strategies.* Maidenhead: McGraw Hill.

Ofqual (2009) *Authenticity – A Guide for Teachers.* Coventry: Ofqual.

Passey, D. (2013) *Inclusive Technology Enhanced Learning.* Abingdon: Routledge.

Poore, M. (2013) *Using Social Media in the Classroom: A Best Practice Guide.* London: SAGE.

Salmon, G. (2011) *E-moderating.* Abingdon: Routledge.

Salmon, G. (2013) *E-tivities* (2nd edition). Abingdon: Routledge.

Starkey, L. (2012) *Teaching and Learning in the Digital Age.* Abingdon: Routledge.

Stein, J. (2014) *Essentials for Blended Learning: A Standards-Based Guide.* Abingdon: Routledge.

Stowell, L. (2016) *Staying Safe Online.* London: Usborne Publishing Ltd.

Taylor, A. (2016) *The Learningwheel: A Model of Digital Pedagogy.* Northwich: Critical Publishing.

White, J. (2015) *Digital Literacy Skills for FE Teachers.* London: SAGE.

Websites

Please also see all the websites listed throughout this chapter

Assistive technology – www.washington.edu/doit/assistive-technology

Assistive technology Jisc – https://tinyurl.com/md5pbkf

British Assistive Technology Association – www.bataonline.org

CPD resources – http://lfutures.co.uk

Developing Digital Literacies – www.jisc.ac.uk/guides/developing-digital-literacies

Digital learning resources – www.gillysalmon.com/digital-learning.html

Digital pedagogy – http://learningwheel.co.uk/2016/06/english-language/

Digital Unite – www.digitalunite.com

Effective Assessment in a Digital Age: A Guide to Technology-enhanced Assessment and Feedback (2010) – www.jisc.ac.uk/digiassess

FELTAG Report (2014) *Paths Forward to a Digital Future for Further Education and Skills* – http://feltag. org.uk/

Flipped classroom – www.knewton.com/infographics/flipped-classroom/

Free technology – www.freetech4teachers.com

Initial assessment for using technology – http://wip.exeter.ac.uk/collaborate/itest/

Innovating Pedagogy – http://proxima.iet.open.ac.uk/public/innovating_pedagogy_2016.pdf

Joint Information Systems Committee (JISC) – www.jisc.ac.uk

Moodle – https://docs.moodle.org/32/en/About_Moodle

Online free courses in various subjects – www.vision2learn.net

www.futurelearn.com

www.opencolleges.edu.au/

www.open.ac.uk

Online safety – http://tinyurl.com/jmunerk and http://tinyurl.com/o6khvla

Online videos for using ICT – www.teachertrainingvideos.com

Plagiarism – www.plagiarism.org and www.plagiarismadvice.org

Reading list for e-learning – www.anngravells.com/reading-lists/e-learning

Teaching with digital technology – https://tinyurl.com/kbtgja6

Using Microsoft programs – https://tinyurl.com/kxxus4t

9

Equality and diversity

Introduction

Equality and diversity is about giving people fair and equal chances, yet valuing and respecting their differences. The further education and skills sector is a diverse one with teachers, support staff and learners from a wide variety of backgrounds, cultures, religions, beliefs and faiths. This can bring challenges, but also rewards for those willing to share their experiences and work together.

This chapter will explore how to promote aspects of equality and diversity within your role. Ways to encourage inclusion during your sessions as well as differentiate for different learners' needs are covered, as is how to demonstrate good practice.

This chapter will cover the following topics:

- Equality and diversity
- Inclusive practice
- Differentiation
- Culture
- Discrimination
- Demonstrating good practice

Equality and diversity

Equality for learners is about their right to have fair access to attend and participate in their chosen learning programme. This should be regardless of age, ability and/or circumstances. However, there could be certain entry requirements, which might need to be met for some qualifications or courses. Equal opportunity is a concept underpinned by legislation in most countries. It should provide relevant and appropriate access for the participation, development and advancement of all individuals and groups within society. In the past, equality has often been described as *everyone being the same* or *having equal opportunities*. Nowadays, it can be described as *everyone being different, but having equal rights*.

Diversity is about valuing and respecting the differences in learners. If you have two or more learners, you will experience diversity.

Combined together, equality and diversity will help embrace learners' experiences, cultures and differences. This should enable each individual's maximum potential to be achieved in a safe and positive learning environment. In a diverse and multicultural society, recognising and accepting individual differences is part of embracing equality and diversity.

Equality and diversity policy

Your organisation should have an equality and diversity policy which both you and your learners should be aware of. However, having a policy is not enough. There should be a *working group* or a *committee* to ensure that it is monitored and regularly reviewed. If the organisation is small, there might be a named person instead of a group. There should be an action plan to ensure equality and diversity are promoted and advanced within the organisation. The content of the policy should be understood and practised by all staff and learners.

Example

Zeta Training aims to ensure that equality and diversity are promoted and advanced amongst all its staff and learners. Any unfair or unlawful discrimination, whether direct or indirect, will be abolished to promote a climate of equality and respect. All staff and learners can expect to work in an environment free from harassment and bullying.

Zeta Training fully supports all principles of equality and diversity and opposes any unfair or unlawful discrimination on the grounds of ability, age, colour, culture, disability, domestic circumstances, employment status, ethnic origin, gender, gender reassignment, learning difficulties, marital status/civil partnership, pregnancy and maternity, nationality, political conviction, race, religion or belief, sexual orientation and/or social background.

The policy could also include assurances to learners, for example, to:

- ensure that individuals are valued in their achievements, and progression opportunities are recognised

- ensure that reasonable adjustments can be made for learners' needs

- have a philosophy of equity as opposed to exclusivity

- place the learner at the centre of the learning process

- provide a curriculum and support which are relevant to each learner

- provide an inclusive learning environment, i.e. not excluding anyone

- take account of the diverse range of support needed to enable individuals to participate and learn, and utilise any learning aids or adaptations to resources (covered in Chapter 7).

Activity

Locate the equality and diversity policy within your organisation. Does it include assurances similar to those in the previous bullet point list? Would you recommend any changes to the policy? If so, what and why? Make sure that your learners know where to access the policy and what to do if they have a problem or a complaint.

If you had difficulty locating the policy, your learners might too. It could be that it's called something else, for example, an *Equal Opportunities Policy*. Having looked at it, would you know what to do if you or a learner had a problem or a complaint? This information should be accessible to all staff and learners. Usually, a policy will be accompanied by a procedure which may be located elsewhere. This will state the process that should be gone through, within specific timeframes, if there was a problem or a complaint, and what will be done about it.

The policy should be regularly monitored, for example, gathering information and data for statistical purposes such as recruitment and enrolment, and providing support with any problems or complaints. Monitoring the implementation of the policy will also help ensure that there is no unintentional discrimination. The policy should be reviewed regularly, for example, if there are any legislative or organisational changes. Having a policy often leads to a *reactive* situation where problems are dealt with afterwards. Policies should really be designed to prevent or respond to events or problems. It's best to be *proactive* and avoid problems occurring in the first place.

Keeping up to date

Ideally, organisations should invest in equality and diversity training and development for all their staff. This will help create a culture of support and commitment by all. Attending staff training sessions and keeping up to date with equality and diversity issues can help raise your awareness. It should also give you the confidence to respond to your learners' particular needs and any discriminatory or challenging behaviour.

Information regarding equality and diversity for staff might be incorporated into and/or be accessible via (in alphabetical order):

- course reviews

- curriculum and team meetings

- external conferences

- external quality assurance visits and reports

- induction programmes

- information leaflets

- internal quality assurance processes

- mentoring

- online information and support programmes

- peer support and/or session observations

- staff handbook

- staff training sessions

- the organisation's intranet.

If you get the opportunity to partake in relevant continuing professional development (CPD) such as attending training events and conferences, it could help you improve your knowledge. You could also carry out relevant research via the internet. This should ultimately have an impact upon your learners' experiences (covered in Chapter 12).

Your organisation should support equality and diversity, for example by:

- following up problems and complaints by the relevant person within the required timescales

- having a current and relevant policy which is promoted, monitored and regularly reviewed

- having a wide range of relevant services to support learning and learners

- informing staff of current legislation and how it impacts on their role

- making sure the teaching environment and resources are appropriate, fair and inclusive

- promoting staff awareness of the diverse nature of those in today's society

- raising awareness through relevant staff training and development

- reflecting equality and diversity in the safer recruitment and selection of staff and learners

- removing barriers which could prevent access and participation

- supporting staff and learners as necessary.

Find out what information there is regarding equality and diversity in your organisation, perhaps in a staff handbook or via their intranet. See if there are any training and development opportunities you could participate in. What external agencies are there in your local area which can give advice regarding equality and diversity? Knowing this might be useful if the need arises.

Attitudes, values and beliefs

Most people have their own attitudes, values and beliefs, often based on past experiences or how their friends and colleagues act. It could be that yours are based on what other people currently do in your organisation, or what your family and friends do, rather than making your own decisions and choices. It's difficult if you don't know any different, i.e. you just do what other people do. However, as part of your teaching or training role you will need to build up a climate of trust, openness and honesty with your colleagues and your learners. This should help you all to respect people who have different attitudes, values and beliefs to your own. However, if someone has extremist or radical views, which are just not right and moral, you should report it to someone in authority. Some countries have different attitudes to certain communities or groups of people which you might feel you have to go along with. However, you will know what is right and wrong and you should act accordingly.

What do you consider the meaning to be of the words attitudes, values and beliefs? Write your own meaning and then research definitions and compare them to yours or discuss them with a colleague or friend. What do you think your attitudes, values and beliefs have been based on? Would you change them, and if so, why? For example, if you have the attitude that other people are here to help you, you could change this to you helping them instead.

You could think of *attitudes* as being a way of thinking, feeling or acting about something. For example, Henry has the attitude that all his learners are capable of achieving the qualification.

Values are the basic principles that help decide what is right and wrong. For example, Mark values the friendship of his other learners in the group, as they all support each other when necessary.

Beliefs are about the feeling that something is true, or that it exists. For example, Jayne's belief in religion gives her hope when times are difficult.

People will have different attitudes, values and beliefs to other learners and to you. This should not prevent you all working together and respecting each other unless someone has ulterior motives to do harm. Learners should always be supported to achieve their maximum potential in a safe environment, without being excluded or discriminated against, for example, because their belief requires them to attend a particular cultural event, but yours doesn't. Having knowledge of the dates of relevant religious festivals and cultural events will help when planning your programme delivery. Some religious festivals may require learners to be absent so they can attend certain events either at a place of worship or with their families. A discussion with learners around these events would prove useful. You might be able to authorise their absence in line with the policies of your organisation. You will also need to be aware of anything which might impact upon learning, for example, if a learner is fasting as part of their faith. This may affect their ability to concentrate; therefore, you would need to be aware of this.

Example

Fatima is due to fast as part of Ramadan and will not be eating or drinking during daylight hours. She explained to her teacher beforehand that she may feel tired and find it difficult to concentrate. Her teacher was understanding and told her she could leave the room if necessary. Her teacher also offered to email Fatima any work that she might miss, and to have a tutorial after Ramadan to go through the materials with her.

Using activities with learners based around equality and diversity, and those which reflect the local community and society, could help your learners be more understanding and tolerant of each other. You could encourage learners to sit next to different people each time they are with you and to work with others during activities. This will help them integrate and communicate during the sessions. You will also need to prepare your learners for the world outside their own living and working environment. Sometimes, communities live and work together in certain areas of the country and don't get the opportunity to meet and mix with people from different races and cultures. It could be that your organisation is inspected at some time, and you may need to demonstrate how you are embedding aspects of equality and diversity. For example, you could use pictures in handouts and visual presentations, which reflect all aspects of society. This could include people of different abilities, ages, cultures, genders and races.

When you are with your learners, try to make sure you:

- are non-judgemental

- challenge any direct or indirect discrimination, stereotyping, prejudice, harassment, bullying and biased attitudes by yourself or others

- do not have favourite learners or give some more attention than others

- do not indulge the minority at the expense of the majority

- ensure particular groups are not offended; for example, faith or religion

- ensure individual learners are not disadvantaged or overly advantaged

- reflect on your own attitudes, values and beliefs so that you are not imposing these upon your learners

- treat all learners with respect and dignity

- use questions which are worded so as not to cause embarrassment to learners.

If you have access to the internet during your session you could search for a short equality and diversity video which you could show to your learners. Alternatively, your organisation might have their own videos you could access. This would help to generate discussions based on relevant topics. Other activities could involve discussions around perceptions and stereotypes, for example, most fire-fighters are male and most nurses are female. If the opportunity arises, impromptu discussions could take place.

Example

Leah was teaching a group of hair and beauty learners who were three weeks into a two-year day release programme. There were 12 females and two males. During a group activity, Leah overheard one of the females make a remark that the males must be gay if they were on this programme. After the activity, Leah took the opportunity to open up a group discussion as to why there is sometimes a perception that males must be gay if they are in this profession. Leah ensured each learner was able to voice their opinion and by the end of the session the learners' perceptions had changed.

Try to encourage learners not to make assumptions: for example, *foreigners always take the jobs of British people,* or *mothers always take time off work to look after their children.* If conversations like these occur, take the opportunity to challenge them. You may have to challenge your own attitudes, values and beliefs at some point. However, as a professional, you are first and foremost a teacher, and your personal opinions must not interfere with the teaching and learning process.

Sometimes, assumptions are made about people because of how they look or act, this might be deliberate on their part to *fit in* with a particular group for fear of discrimination. You will need to get to know your learners as individuals, to encourage them to be themselves, and to promote an inclusive culture within your groups. This can lead to greater confidence and a sense of belonging on the learner's part, better communication within the group and respect for individual differences.

Learners may have attitudes, values and beliefs which they have inherited from others, without having the opportunity to develop their own. These could include set ways of thinking, or pre-conceived ideas of others that are not based on fact. Ignorance should be no excuse for treating someone unfairly. Part of your role should be to encourage a climate of acceptance and support, informed by fact, and not based upon a person's background, upbringing, culture or religion. Your learners need to accept that they may have different attitudes, values and beliefs to other learners, but that these should not interfere with the group cohesion or the learning process. The same might apply to you and you don't have to believe or agree with all your learners, but you must not let your personal opinions influence others. You must also be careful not to be biased in any way towards a particular type of group or learner.

British values

If you work in education in Great Britain, you will need to consider how you can promote fundamental British Values. If your organisation is inspected by Ofsted, they will be looking for evidence of this. However, perhaps it's not just about British Values, it could be considered everyone's values.

According to Ofsted, 'fundamental British Values' are:

- democracy

- the rule of law

- individual liberty

- mutual respect

- tolerance of those with different faiths and beliefs, and for those without faith.

Learners will need to know about these and understand how they affect their role in society. They will need to know what is right and wrong, and how they should respect the law. They should also know how to accept responsibility for their actions, respect others, and understand how they can contribute to society in a positive way. If you get the opportunity, you could hold a discussion with your learners based around the values. Some curriculum areas might include the values as a specific topic.

Ways to promote the values can include:

- discussing and researching how democracy and the law works in Britain, for example, comparing it to governments in other countries

- encouraging learners to make independent choices and express their views, with the knowledge that they are in a safe, secure and supportive environment

- exploring with learners what it means to be British, and what they think the values mean

- holding discussions which give learners the opportunity to learn how to defend their points of view and respect others' views

- inviting guest speakers from different faiths and beliefs to talk to learners and answer any questions they have

- preparing learners for life and employment in a modern civilised society

- promoting democracy in action by encouraging learners to speak up, knowing they will be listened to

- using learning materials which represent all aspects of society

- enabling learners to vote for members to be on educational committees.

The British Values are taken from *The Prevent Strategy* (2011). There is also the *Prevent Duty*, which is part of the Counter-Terrorism and Security Act (2015). The Prevent Duty is not about preventing learners from having political and religious views, but about supporting them to use any concerns in non-extremist ways, and to prevent them from becoming radicalised by others. You might be required to attend a training session at your organisation to ensure you are up to date with the Prevent Duty requirements. There are some free online resources you might like to access, which are listed at the end of this chapter.

Activity

Research information which is available online regarding British Values and discuss these with a colleague. Obtain a copy of, or access online, the Prevent Strategy and the Prevent Duty. You will find weblinks at the end of this chapter. How will they impact upon your role? If you have any concerns, there should be a nominated person in your organisation who you will be able to talk to; you might like to find out who this is.

The Equality Act (2010)

The Equality Act (2010) replaced all previous anti-discrimination legislation and consolidated it into one Act (for England, Scotland and Wales). It provides rights for individuals and those associated with them, not to be directly discriminated against or harassed.

To ensure you comply with the Equality Act (2010) you will need to be proactive in all aspects of equality and diversity. You should make sure your delivery style, teaching, learning and assessment activities and resources promote and include all learners in respect of the Act's nine *protected characteristics*. These are known as the *personal attributes* of individuals and groups who are likely to be discriminated against. They are:

- age

- disability

- gender reassignment

- marriage and civil partnership

- pregnancy and maternity

- race

- religion or belief

- sex

- sexual orientation.

All nine protected characteristics are covered in the employment duties of the Act. However, the protected characteristic of marriage and civil partnerships is not included in the education duties of the Act.

Examples of the protected characteristics are:

Age: older people, younger people.

Disability: physical or sensory impairments, mental health difficulties, long-term medical conditions, learning difficulties, neurodiverse conditions such as dyslexia, autism, tourettes or attention deficit hyperactivity disorder (ADHD). For an impairment to be a disability, its effect on normal day-to-day activities must be substantial. The Equality Act (2010) defines substantial to mean *more than minor or trivial.*

Gender reassignment: transsexual people, transgender people, men and women with a transsexual history or who are in the process of becoming a transsexual person.

Marriage and civil partnership: married people, people in a civil partnership, single people.

Pregnancy and maternity: pregnant women, people on maternity leave, women who have recently given birth.

Race: colour, nationality, ethnic or national origin, heritage.

Religion or belief: people from different faith groups, people with a philosophical belief, people with no religion or belief.

Sex: male, female.

Sexual orientation: gay and lesbian people, bisexual people, heterosexual/straight people.

When preparing your teaching materials and resources, you should try to use representations of people with protected characteristics as well as those without.

When possible, it's best to find ways of talking about and integrating the protected characteristics during your sessions. You could create activities based around them, or the opportunity might occur naturally.

Example

Marta was teaching cookery skills to a mixed group of learners from various backgrounds and faiths. As Chinese New Year was approaching, she decided to use it as a theme and create different menus based on Chinese food. This opened up a discussion about the Chinese culture, which the group found interesting and meaningful. Marta decided she would research aspects of other cultures, faiths, religions and beliefs to incorporate them during her sessions throughout the year.

Other opportunities could include:

- celebrating local and national events

- creating and using crosswords, word searches, puzzles or quizzes based around aspects of equality and diversity

- discussing issues when they arise during your sessions, such as learners' perceptions of: disability; older people; different races and cultures

- discussing events in the news such as racist attacks, or an issue in a particular television programme such as disability or ageism

- drawing upon the experiences of learners within your group

- embracing individual differences and experiences

- mixing different learners during group and paired activities, so that everyone gets the opportunity to work with other learners

- visiting museums, heritage and cultural buildings.

The Equality Act has seven different *types of discrimination* which can be legally protected against:

1. Associative discrimination: direct discrimination against someone because they are associated with another person with a protected characteristic. For example, a learner receives verbal abuse because they are friends with a transsexual learner.

2. Direct discrimination: discrimination because of a protected characteristic. For example, not accepting an older learner onto a course because all the other learners are younger.

3. Indirect discrimination: when a rule or a policy which applies to everyone can disadvantage a person with a protected characteristic. For example, a hotel is unwilling to give a hotel reception learner a work placement as she wears a burqa. They felt their guests would rather see the receptionists' faces.

4. Discrimination by perception: direct discrimination against someone because others think they have a protected characteristic. For example, a learner taunting another learner because they have a stammer, even though it's not a disability.

5. Harassment: behaviour deemed offensive by the recipient. For example, a male learner telling a female learner that she has to go on a date with him, otherwise he will tell everyone she is gay.

6. Harassment by a third party: the harassment of people by those not directly employed by an organisation. For example, an outside building contractor makes racist remarks to an Asian learner.

7. Victimisation: discrimination against someone because they made or supported a complaint under equality legislation. For example, a Muslim learner feels victimised because they made a complaint that there is not a suitable area within which to pray.

In countries outside the UK, there will be different legislation. If this applies to you, you might like to research what the current legislation is and how it impacts upon your role.

Activity

How can you promote equality and value diversity during your sessions? Design an activity you could use with your learners which will enable them to discuss relevant topics relating to equality and diversity. If you have a chance, carry it out and evaluate how effective it was.

The term *advance*

The term *advance* has replaced the word *promote* which was previously used in legislation. The intention being to move forward, to get somewhere and to achieve improved outcomes for your learners.

Advance involves organisations having due regard to:

- encouraging learners with a relevant protected characteristic to fully participate in activities where participation is disproportionately low

- removing/minimising disadvantages experienced by learners who share a protected characteristic which are connected to that characteristic

- taking steps to meet the needs of learners who share a relevant protected characteristic that are different from the needs of learners who don't share it.

Valuing equality and diversity

If you ever feel unsure as to whether you, or other learners and colleagues are valuing equality and diversity, just ask yourself the following:

- Is this fair?

- How would I feel in this situation?

- Would I want to be treated this way?

If your answer is a negative one, then make sure you do something about it. However, you may not always have the answer to these questions, especially where there is a difficulty in meeting the conflicting needs of learners.

The changing and diverse nature of society can pose many challenges for individuals, groups, employers and teachers. To truly value equality and diversity, it would be moral, fair and decent if inclusion and acceptance became the norm. This will demonstrate to everyone that any issues do not just affect minority groups. The rights and needs of each person should be taken into account, and they should not be those of the majority. You should also be careful not to indulge the minority to the detriment of the majority. The learning environment can be enriched through the diversity of your learners and their experiences.

Extension activity

If you are currently teaching, ask your learners to watch the news or a particular television programme (in their own time). Ask them to note any key issues regarding equality and diversity and to bring their notes to the next session. You can then place your learners into pairs and ask them to discuss the key issues and how they felt about them. If you have time, you can then place the pairs into fours for further discussion. From this activity, you will be able to see how your learners view equality and diversity. You will be able to walk around the room and listen to what they are saying, or hold a full group discussion. You could take the opportunity to challenge any negative aspects and link to how the issues might affect people who work in the area or profession they are studying.

Inclusive practice

Inclusive practice is about ensuring all your learners have the opportunity to be involved, to contribute and to be included in the learning process. It's also about recognising and treating all learners equally and fairly, without directly or indirectly excluding anyone.

Inclusive practice is about attitudes as well as behaviour as learners can be affected by the words or actions of others. You are not teaching a group of learners who are all the same, but a group made up of individuals with different experiences, abilities and needs. These can be recognised, embraced and respected during your sessions. When you are with your learners, try to promote a positive culture of equality of opportunity whereby all your learners can attend, participate and feel safe and valued. If you can develop the conditions for learning that are based on respect and trust, and address the needs of individual learners, you will have created an effective teaching, learning and assessment environment.

Activity

What do you feel the term inclusive practice *means? Are there any policies or regulations within your organisation regarding inclusive practice? If so, find out how they will impact upon your role. How can you ensure all your learners feel included during each of your sessions?*

The best way to ensure that you are effectively including all learners, and treating them fairly, is to talk to them. If asked, learners will usually tell you if they have any particular needs, whether that is from a religious or cultural point of view or if they have a learning difficulty and/or disability. However, it's difficult to help your learners if they don't tell you about any specific issues, needs or concerns they might have. You could ask them if there is anything you could do to help make their learning experience a more positive one. Try and ascertain what they *can do* rather than what they *can't do*. However, anything you do to accommodate their needs would have to be reasonable, and not seen as favouritism by other learners. Encouraging learners to tell you in confidence could save your learner any embarrassment they might feel in front of their peers. Sometimes, inclusive practice might naturally occur, particularly if learners are proactive about their needs.

Example

A group of four learners decide to go out for dinner to celebrate their achievements. One is a vegetarian, the second is dairy intolerant, the third doesn't eat fish and the fourth has no preference. They all want to eat at the same restaurant and choose from the same menu. They checked in advance that the restaurant they had chosen caters for all nutritional needs. This ensured they will all be included as part of the group and can order from the same menu, therefore be treated equally.

This example shows the diverse requirements of the group are taken into account to differentiate for their needs, and ensure that no one is excluded.

The initial assessment process might have helped you to ascertain information regarding your learners; however, not all are forthcoming in the early stages to disclose their particular needs to you. Building up a good working relationship over time will hopefully help your learners feel able to talk to you.

Ways to promote inclusion

Ways to promote inclusion with your learners during a session can simply be by using their names when they arrive and when talking to them, using eye contact, speaking personally to them and asking individual questions. Recognising each learner and not ignoring them in any way can help them feel at ease.

Example

Rezaul is a learner who struggles to read small text on handouts and visual presentations. He told this to Jude, his teacher, when he commenced the course. Rather than make any assumptions about how to help him, Jude asked Rezaul what she could do to make his learning experience better. He asked if he could sit near the front of the room when visual presentations were used. He also asked to have the handouts emailed to him in advance, so that he could use his own device during the sessions to open and view them in a way that he could see them better.

In this example, Rezaul was not excluded from any of the activities taking place during the session.

Access to resources can have an impact on whether learners are excluded from some activities. For example, if a learner can't afford the course textbook, they could be at a disadvantage. Ideally, relevant books should be available from a library or learners might be able to access an electronic version. Some courses might require learners to purchase items, for example, cooking ingredients for a catering course. If a learner has financial problems and they are willing to talk to you about it, there might be the opportunity to obtain a grant or a loan. You could find out what is available by talking to someone in your organisation who will know about these things. You could also encourage your learners to find out this information for themselves. This could help promote their confidence and reduce their reliance on others finding out things for them.

Ideally, you should consider how you can promote inclusion throughout all aspects of teaching, learning and assessment. Table 9.1 (on pages 362 and 363) gives examples of how to promote inclusion in an educational organisation.

Extension activity

Look at Table 9.1. Choose one aspect from each section and consider what you could do to promote inclusion within your organisation and/or your sessions for each. Discuss your responses with a colleague and contemplate what other aspects you could add to the table and why.

Table 9.1 Examples of ways to promote inclusion

Identifying needs	• ascertaining learners' specific and additional needs as well as their aspirations for the future • ensuring all learners can complete application and enrolment forms, perhaps by using different languages, font sizes, electronic and paper-based copies • ensuring interview notes are kept regarding any support requirements needed and that these are communicated to relevant people, for example, dyslexia, epilepsy, diabetes • ensuring learners have had access to impartial initial advice and guidance (IAG) to consider all their options • ensuring programmes are offered at times everyone can attend (if appropriate) • exploring flexible programme delivery or blended learning approaches • finding ways to overcome barriers such as finance, childcare, transport • removing physical barriers to enable learners to access information, staff, documents and buildings, for example, by using access ramps • using initial assessment results to plan individual learning
Planning learning	• ensuring a programme is in place that responds to the needs and aspirations of all learners • using appropriate and accessible equipment and resources • agreeing individual learning plans/action plans • creating resources and materials which positively promote all aspects of society, equality and diversity • creating schemes of work and session plans to reflect how you will include all learners during sessions • differentiating your teaching approaches and activities to address individual differences, for example, levels or speed of learning • ensuring off site visits are accessible by all, for example, transport and stairs • ensuring the environment is accessible to all • planning opportunities to develop learner motivation, self-esteem and confidence • planning your delivery to meet the needs of all learning preferences

Facilitating learning	• using a variety of teaching and learning approaches to suit all learners
	• adapting resources as necessary
	• avoiding favouritism and positive discrimination
	• being approachable and accessible, enabling your learners to feel comfortable to talk to you
	• being aware that everyone has different experiences, interests, skills and knowledge which will affect their ability to develop and learn
	• carrying out an icebreaker or energiser which doesn't exclude anyone
	• agreeing suitable ground rules
	• challenging stereotyping, discrimination and prejudice as it happens
	• drawing on personal experiences of learners during each session
	• encouraging group discussions and activities where everyone can participate
	• encouraging group work where learners can mix with all members of the group over a period of time
	• encouraging respect and promoting understanding of learner differences
	• ensuring learners have access to facilities, resources and equipment which is appropriate for the subject and level of learning
	• ensuring newcomers to a group are made to feel welcome and are included
	• ensuring the language and jargon used is at an appropriate level
	• following up absences and ensuring learners have access to any missed material
	• identifying where modifications or changes are needed to ensure everyone is included
	• involving all learners within your session, using their name, using eye contact and asking individual questions
	• not excluding any learner for any legitimate reason
	• providing a safe and supportive environment where everyone's contribution is valued
Assessing learning	• adapting assessment activities where possible to meet any particular requirements or needs (if appropriate)
	• encouraging all learners to progress further and reach their full potential
	• ensuring assessment planning is individual, appropriate and relevant
	• giving ongoing developmental feedback at a level to suit the learner
	• recognising and valuing individual achievements
Evaluating learning	• communicating with colleagues to ensure they are aware of any learner requirements or issues
	• evaluating your delivery to ensure you have included all learners fully during your session
	• liaising with the awarding organisation regarding any modifications required to the assessment activities for a qualification (if applicable)
	• obtaining feedback from your learners and others in different ways, for example, verbally, written or electronically

Differentiation

Differentiation is about using a range of different approaches and resources to meet the needs of individual learners: a small group within the main group or the full group. This should help to reduce barriers to learning, stretch and challenge learners and hopefully keep everyone interested and motivated. It is very rare that a teacher or trainer has a group of learners who are all at the same level of ability, with the same prior knowledge and experience and with the same needs. However, they might all be working towards the same outcomes or the same qualification. This will make your job more challenging but exciting and interesting. You might want to pitch all your sessions at the same level, perhaps because you don't have time to prepare or to think how you can differentiate. Although this might be easy for you, it won't help your learners. If you have a mixed ability group you will have some learners who might be slower or quicker at learning than others. Learners who work quickly might soon get bored, and those who need more time might get left behind. Think of differentiation as a way of adding variety to your sessions, to ensure learning by everyone is taking place. You don't have to differentiate everything you do, but you might like to differentiate what the learners do. This could alleviate boredom and aid motivation and interest.

Differentiation is ideal when carrying out activities with learners and can take place in several ways. For example, you could differentiate by:

- **ability:** learners could be given a word search, a crossword, a multiple-choice quiz or a problem-solving activity which are all based around the same topic but differentiated for their ability at the time. To help stretch and challenge learners, they could all start with a word search and progress through the other activities according to their capability. Graduated questions could also be used. For example, producing questions which get progressively harder and use more complex language. Learners could have a time limit within which to achieve a certain number of questions. They could choose to start at the beginning or choose those questions they feel they can complete.

- **activity/task:** learners could answer questions by choosing a different activity or task, for example: designing a poster, creating a presentation, producing a mind map or writing an essay.

- **learning outcomes:** you, or your learners, could choose a relevant activity at an appropriate level for them to meet the required learning outcomes.

- **learning preferences:** learners could work through tasks which relate to their preferred way of learning. For example, visual learners could create a mind map or a poster, aural learners could hold a discussion, read/write learners could research books and websites and write up their findings, kinaesthetic learners could create a role play. If the activity relates to group work, mixing learners with different preferences can help ensure everyone is involved.

- **level:** learners who are working towards the same subject but are aiming towards a different level could answer relevant questions based on the level. For example, some questions could require open or closed responses (level 1), others might require descriptions (level 2), explanations (level 3) or analysis (level 4).

- **prior knowledge and/or experience:** learners could discuss or research a topic based on what they already know and/or can do. Alternatively, you could mix learners with different levels of experience so that they can work together and learn from each other. This is ideal for encouraging peer support and feedback.

- **support:** learners study the same topic and use the same resources and materials, but have different amounts of support depending upon their needs. This support could be from the teacher and/or learning support assistants or in the form of additional learning materials.

When differentiating the approaches and activities you will use, you could move the learners around the room so that they are working together according to what they are doing at the time. Alternatively, you could mix the learners so that they are in different pairs or groups for different activities. Often, learners sit in the same place each time, next to the same person. Moving your learners regularly could help them integrate, communicate and work with others. If you tell your learners at the start of the course that you will regularly move them, they will come to expect it.

Activity

What will you need to know about your learners to plan for effective differentiation of teaching, learning and assessment? Look at the previous bullet list, what other ways could you use for differentiation and why?

When preparing your session plan, it should show how you will differentiate with the use of various approaches and activities. For example, if you have a mixed ability group, you could note what *all, most* and *some* of your learners will do. Planning different activities which *all* your learners are capable of achieving, as well as what *most* or *some* can achieve is a way to differentiate. However, some learners might feel they are capable of achieving more than you have given them. That's fine, as you could give them something else to challenge them. It's best they start at their current level and work upwards, rather than feel demoralised because they couldn't achieve the higher level first.

Example

Paul has a mixed group of level 1, 2 and 3 learners working towards a Certificate in Customer Service. He knows the full group will be able to answer questions based on the level 1 programme, most will be able to answer from both level 1 and 2, and some will be able to answer questions based on level 3. He will therefore devise a different set of questions for all, most *and* some *of his learners. His session plan therefore has a section that denotes what* all, most *and* some *learners will do.*

Differentiating in this way helps stretch and challenge learners, but does take time to plan and prepare.

You could create a record known as a *group profile* (covered in Chapter 3) to help you remember certain aspects about your learners. This will include details of each learner, i.e. what they are aiming towards, any individual needs, their level of ability and so on, to enable differentiation and support to take place. It's a useful document to refer to as you progress through your session. Initial assessment is a good way to gain the information that you need to plan effectively; however, not all your learners may reveal things during this process. If you can encourage your learners to let you know of anything that you can do to help them, for example, if they prefer to see a particular font on handouts, you should be able to improve their learning experience. Simply asking, *Is there anything I can do to help the way you learn?* could help ascertain this. Alternatively, ask yourself, *What can I do to give everyone a valuable and meaningful learning experience?*

Sometimes things will happen which you couldn't plan for. For example, you might plan to carry out an activity but after a discussion about the current topic, you realise you want to do something different. This is fine, you don't have to keep rigidly to your plan, and it shows you are taking your learners' needs into account. When you reflect on how the session went afterwards, you can consider why you made the change, and whether you need to do anything differently next time.

Acknowledging and embracing the diverse nature of your learners' ages, experiences, culture and backgrounds should help you include all learners and bring your subject to life. Some learners might have experienced things you haven't and they might be happy to share these with the group. Some learners may work more quickly than others. Giving them an extension activity could help develop, stretch and challenge their learning further, without compromising the learning of others. Stretching is about improving the capability of learners, and challenging helps them to do more. If possible, you could keep a set of pre-prepared extension activities handy for when you need them (covered in Chapter 5).

Differentiating your teaching, learning and assessment approaches should lead to more confident learners who feel included, are motivated to learn and are able to achieve and progress further. If your learners have access to digital applications, there are some educational apps which automatically differentiate activities according to the user's strengths and limitations. You might like to research what is available for your subject. While it may take longer to plan and prepare your sessions to differentiate effectively, you will hopefully find your learners are more engaged and motivated rather than being bored and uninterested.

Extension activity

Think how you can use differentiation during a future session with your learners. For example, by creating different activities based on the same topic. If you are currently teaching, create a differentiated activity, try it with your learners, and evaluate how effective it was. What would you do differently and why?

Culture

Culture can be thought of as *the way of life, or the way things are done* within an organisation. It's the ideas, beliefs and behaviours of a particular group of people, for example, those of other teachers in your organisation. If other teachers always dress in smart clothing, you might feel you must do the same. Sometimes, people accept the *way things are* and don't always question them, but subconsciously begin to follow them. For example, if other teachers in your organisation don't clean the boards and tidy the room when they finish, you might feel you shouldn't bother either. However, you can begin to change this culture by cleaning the board and leaving the room tidy each time you finish a session. When other teachers see how much nicer it is to go into a tidy room with a clean board, they too might start to leave the room clean and tidy. Culture can be infectious, both in a good way and in a bad way.

Example

Mary, a childcare teacher, always arrived around five minutes late to her Tuesday morning session. Her learners began arriving late too, as they thought there was no point being on time if Mary wasn't. They therefore developed a culture of being late and began attending other sessions late too. However, one learner felt that valuable learning time was being lost due to this. She asked Mary why they couldn't start on time. It transpired that Mary used public transport, which was often delayed. The group then agreed to start later and finish later for this session and began attending the other sessions on time.

Sometimes, you might not realise that you, or others, are setting a bad example, which could become the norm if not challenged. If you feel your organisation isn't very proactive at promoting a positive culture in any areas, there's no reason to be complacent just because others are. If other people see your positive attitude and the proactive way in which you work, this may help improve the way they work, and ultimately the culture in your organisation. You may need to consider how you can create a positive culture with your learners. Encouraging them rather than discouraging them could help. For example, saying that they can achieve if they work hard, rather than they won't if they don't.

You can help create a positive culture with your learners by (in alphabetical order):

- agreeing ground rules so that learners know the boundaries

- being aware of the impact of certain behaviours upon others

- being genuine in your desire to be fair

- being respectful to the needs of learners from different races and cultures, even when this might cause a negative impact within the group

- being sensitive and respectful to the thoughts, feelings and opinions of others

- challenging negative situations as they occur

- creating a *can do* attitude among your learners

- creating a positive atmosphere of trust, tolerance and respect

- demonstrating your knowledge and commitment to advancing equality and diversity

- integrating learners to enable them to work with others they wouldn't normally work with

- leading by example

- raising awareness of the differences between people

- remaining professional at all times

- showing empathy by putting yourself in the other person's position, and imagining how they might think and feel, and encouraging this in your learners when necessary

- using an appropriate icebreaker to help everyone get to know each other

- valuing the experiences of others, and incorporating this into your sessions.

Activity

What does the term culture *mean to you? Write your own definition and then talk to a colleague or friend about what they think. Research other definitions and compare them to yours. Think about the culture in your organisation, both with staff and learners, do you think it's positive? If not, what do you think could be done to improve it?*

You really need to get to know your learners as individuals, to encourage them to be *themselves* and to promote an inclusive culture within your groups. This can lead to greater confidence and a sense of belonging on the learner's part, better communication within the group, and respect for individual differences. Having a positive attitude in front of your learners and leading by example, should help create a positive culture among everyone.

Extension activity

Do you feel that you demonstrate a positive culture or have you been influenced by the way other people do things? Are there things happening in your organisation or which occur during sessions with your learners, that you would like to change? If so, what can you do about it?

Discrimination

Discrimination is about treating a person or a group differently, often in a negative manner, usually as a result of a prejudice or ignorance. It is about people being thought of as having a different worth or value, and/or being given fewer opportunities as a result. However, not all treatment is discriminatory. Discrimination occurs when differential treatment cannot be objectively and reasonably justified. Sometimes, assumptions are made about people because of how they look or act. This might be deliberate on their part to *fit in* with a particular group for fear of discrimination from others.

The Equality Act (2010) for England, Scotland and Wales prohibits discrimination on a wide range of grounds including the nine protected characteristics previously mentioned in this chapter. There are two types of discrimination.

Direct discrimination: is where a person is less favourably or unfairly treated because they have a protected characteristic. This could arise because of assumptions, stereotyping, fear, ignorance or prejudice. For example, a learner requests an extension for a piece of written work and tells her teacher that the reason is that she is affected by medication she is taking for schizophrenia. The teacher doesn't consider this a valid reason for an extension and declines the request. This is likely to be direct discrimination. The teacher cannot argue that it was not their intention to discriminate; the law only considers the end effect. Direct discrimination also covers *association discrimination* or *perception discrimination*. This is direct discrimination against someone because they associate with a person who has the protected characteristic, or because they are perceived as having a protected characteristic.

Example

Holly sees Ali, a Bangladeshi learner, being subjected to racially abusive language. She complains that this has affected her, even though she is white and not the subject of the abuse.

Indirect discrimination: is when something occurs where a rule, a practice or a policy that appears to be fair (because it applies equally to everyone) can be a disadvantage to some people.

Example

A training organisation has installed a lift to give access to the learning support centre which is on a higher floor. However, there is a set of six steps outside the main entrance, which does not have an access ramp. This means anyone who uses a wheelchair must use the entrance at the back of the building. This is likely to be indirect discrimination. Wheelchair users are therefore not able to use the main entrance like able-bodied people.

In some instances, *positive discrimination* is permitted by equality legislation, i.e. if it's designed to redress a perceived injustice. Positive discrimination includes any activity that helps:

- address a disadvantage experienced by learners who share a protected characteristic

- meet the needs of learners who share a protected characteristic, when these needs are different from those who don't share a protected characteristic

- address disproportionately low participation in learning.

Example

A training organisation has decided to offer a female-only gymnastics class. This is because they undertook research in the local community and received feedback that females were unlikely to take part if males were present.

Learners could be personally affected by discrimination and/or prejudice when attending sessions. This might relate to a disability, age, religion, or sexual orientation, which could result in non-attendance or non-achievement. Ideally, you need to ensure all your learners value each other and that the basic rights they are entitled to, for example, to learn in a comfortable and safe environment, are met.

Activity

Do you feel you have discriminated against anyone you work with, or a learner, whether intentionally or not? If you have, how do you think that person will have felt, and what could you do differently next time?

If at any time, you or your learners feel that discrimination has taken place, then there are some logical steps you could take:

- Clarify and discuss the problem.

- Get help and advice from the named person within your organisation, i.e. the equality and diversity officer, or safeguarding officer.

- Try to resolve the issue informally.

- Complain formally within your organisation.

- Complain to an external person or organisation.

- Report it to the police, depending upon the severity of the incident.

- Take legal advice.

Harassment

Harassment is any behaviour that is deemed offensive by the recipient. Learners can claim they find something offensive even when it's not directed at them. Organisations are also potentially liable for the harassment of their staff and learners by people they don't directly employ, for example, visitors and contractors. However, there might be different cultural and social perceptions as to what is considered to be harassment. You could include a workshop during a session with your learners to try and address these perceptions. For example, if the subject is religious studies, learners who have personal experiences could talk to the full group about them. You could also invite guest speakers from different cultures, religions and beliefs to talk about their experiences and answer learners' questions.

Any form of harassment can be stressful and intimidating for the victim. Bullying is also a form of harassment and may constitute a hate incident or a crime.

Examples include:

- ignoring someone

- intrusive questioning about ethnic origin

- racist and/or sexist comments or jokes

- the display or circulation of offensive materials or books

- unfair allocation of activities and tasks

- unnecessary references to sex and gender

- unwanted physical contact

- verbal or physical abuse, taunting or teasing.

If you experience any of these taking place among your learners you will need to address it immediately. This could be by having a quiet word with the offending learner, or intervening immediately to stop a more serious situation from developing, such as verbal or physical abuse. There might be instances of peer pressure among learners which you notice. For example, if a learner ridicules another because they are not wearing the latest designer clothing. The other learner might feel they must purchase some, even if they can't afford it. If you see any peer pressure like this, you could talk to the full group. You could explain why people don't have to conform to what others do and how negative peer pressure could affect others. It could be that they didn't even realise what they were doing.

Carole's group of sociology learners were carrying out an activity in small groups. She noticed the learners in one group were giggling and looking at another group where Frank, another learner, was talking with a stutter. She went over to the group and asked them why they were giggling. They said it was funny the way that Frank spoke. Carole asked them to put themselves in Frank's position, i.e. how difficult it must be for him to speak in front of others. The learners hadn't appreciated it from Frank's perspective and said they would not do it again.

Stereotyping

Stereotyping is an over-generalised assumption, belief or judgement about a person or a particular group of people which might not be true. It can be based on your own and/or other people's opinions or experiences. For example, *older people are not good at using technology.* Both you and your learners will need to be careful not to make any general assumptions. If a learner does say something which you feel is stereotyping, challenge them to justify why they said it. If they can't justify it, it would be useful to hold a discussion with the full group about how stereotyping can affect others' feelings. If the opportunity arises, you could ask your learners to draw or look at some pictures of people, for example, a footballer, a construction worker and a doctor's receptionist. They could then write a sentence about each. It would be interesting to see what they draw and what they say, to see if they have made any assumptions.

Assumptions can sometimes occur without the person realising what they have done. They might think they are doing it for the right reasons, but the recipient takes it differently.

Example

Anka, a prospective learner whose first language is Polish, but who does speak a little English, went to her local community centre to enquire about English courses. She was asked when she had arrived in this country and how long she had been unemployed. The receptionist assumed Anka was not born in this country and did not have a job. In fact, she was born in this country and was working part time. The question was for the purposes of obtaining funding for her to take the course, but the receptionist did not say this. Anka asked if everyone who made enquiries was asked the same questions or if it was only asked of certain groups of people. She felt the receptionist was treating her unfairly, when she was only trying to help.

In this example, the receptionist thought she was being helpful, but Anka perceived it differently.

Examples of groups of learners who may be subjected to stereotyping include (in alphabetical order):

- asylum seekers

- disaffected young people

- homeless people

- immigrants

- offenders (ex or current)

- older people

- people with learning difficulties and/or disabilities

- people who have mental health problems

- pregnant teenagers

- single parents

- those whose first language is not English

- transient people.

The individuals within those groups should all have a right to learn, no matter what circumstances have led them to being in that group.

When people are stereotyped, they may feel less like an individual and feel hurt by what has been said. For example, a teacher assuming that a learner whose parents are both doctors will also become a doctor. Stereotyping can also include a positive assumption, for example, *men are better car drivers than women*. While this is a positive general statement about men, it implies the opposite of women.

Extension activity

Find out what you can about various beliefs, faiths and religions by choosing three from the following: Agnostic, Atheism, Buddhism, Christianity, Hinduism, Islam, Jehovah's Witness, Judaism, Mormon, Paganism, Rastafarianism, Shinto, Sikhism, Taoism or any others you would like to research. Compare and contrast them and then discuss your findings with a colleague. Do you feel your new knowledge will help you with your understanding of equality and diversity among your learners? If so, how?

Demonstrating good practice

To demonstrate good practice regarding equality and diversity, relevant aspects need to be embedded throughout your role. Table 9.2 at the end of this chapter is a checklist you might like to refer to regarding demonstrating good practice.

If there is a positive culture within an organisation, staff should naturally embrace equality and diversity policies, enabling learners to attend and participate in a safe and secure environment. For example, identifying learners' specific and additional needs; designing a programme that responds to these needs and aspirations; using appropriate approaches, activities and resources to support learning; giving learners access to fair assessment and gaining feedback from learners and others.

Activity

Imagine you have a new group of learners commencing next week. What can you do to demonstrate good practice regarding equality and diversity, both prior to their arrival and when they commence?

Before the start of your course, you could find out if any of your learners has already shared information about themselves to someone else in your organisation. They may have previously completed a course in another subject. If they have completed an enrolment form they might have been asked if they wish to disclose any learning difficulty and/or disability. At this early stage some learners will willingly share this information and some will not. Some learners may not see themselves as having a disability but recognise that they have particular needs or requirements. If a learner has been disadvantaged in the past, they may not tell anyone about any difficulties they currently have. You could try to create an atmosphere whereby your learners feel they can talk to you in confidence. For example, if they want to tell you about any particular needs they feel might not get addressed. Learners might feel much more confident about disclosing something from the beginning of the course, if they feel that the organisation has a positive and supportive attitude.

It is good practice to:

- talk to your learners to find out how you can help them (before, at the beginning and during the course)

- find out how long any necessary changes and/or adjustments to the environment or equipment will take

- keep your learner informed about progress and timescales.

Example

During Steph's interview to attend a drama course, she told her prospective teacher William, that she has the early stages of Parkinson's disease. She finds it difficult to sit still for long periods of time and doesn't want the other learners to know. William was able to reassure her that there would be plenty of opportunities for practical activities involving movement. This alleviated Steph's concerns and she therefore looked forward to commencing the course.

The impact in this particular example is that the learner will come to the first session less worried than she would have otherwise been, and enjoy an effective and relaxed learning experience. This information should be noted in documents such as the group profile and individual learning plan (ILP) as a reminder. It will also provide evidence of the steps taken to support the learner should it be required, perhaps as part of an inspection. More importantly, it will demonstrate how the learner is being supported in a proactive way.

Your learners' experiences of your organisation may have already begun before they arrive for their first session. They may have obtained information perhaps from a brochure or a website.

Example

A course leaflet for English for Speakers of Other Languages (ESOL) has been produced in English for potential learners. It includes details of free child-care provision and free transport to the venue. Many prospective learners in a remote location of the community, whom this course is aimed at, cannot read English very well. Therefore, this information is not accessible to them. Following an analysis of the potential learners in this community, the leaflet has now been produced in two other languages. An audible version is also available via the organisation's website.

This example shows how important it is to find out certain information in advance to be able to support the learners who will be attending the course.

A good time to carry out discussions and activities regarding equality and diversity would be during the early stages of the course, for example, if your learners partake in an induction programme which informs them about the course and the organisation. You could set aside some time to discuss your organisation's policy along with how everyone can be treated with respect. You could create some practical activities to enable learners to recognise different attitudes, values, beliefs and cultures. Alternatively, if you have access to the internet, search for *equality and diversity quiz*. You will find lots of online activities that your learners could have a go at, which might lead to some interesting discussions.

Extension activity

Look at Table 9.2. Choose one aspect from each section and consider what you can do to demonstrate good practice within your organisation and/or sessions. Discuss your responses with a colleague and contemplate what other aspects you could add to the table. If you are currently teaching, after the next session you deliver, evaluate how effective you felt you were at demonstrating good practice with regards to equality and diversity. Think about what further training and/or development you might need, along with ways of addressing this.

Table 9.2 Checklist for demonstrating good practice

Identifying needs	☐ Do your publicity, recruitment and guidance materials contain all the information needed to represent those for whom it is intended?
	☐ Do you provide information, advice and guidance to help learners choose the right programme based on their needs and/or to progress further?
	☐ Is the application and interview process fair to all?
	☐ Can you identify any potential learning difficulties and/or disabilities and take reasonable steps to address these prior to the learner commencing?
	☐ Are your learners given the opportunity to discuss what it is they aspire to, any potential or additional support requirements and needs they may have, and any barriers to learning?
	☐ Do you need to make reasonable adjustments to the environment, equipment and/or resources in any way?
	☐ Can learners take an initial assessment relating to language, literacy, numeracy and digital skills if relevant?
	☐ Is there a specific initial assessment/skill scan/diagnostic test available in your subject area to help identify a learner's current skills and knowledge?
	☐ Is there an opportunity for your learners to take a dyslexia test if necessary?
	☐ Can you agree a differentiated individual learning plan with each of your learners?
Planning learning	☐ Does your scheme of work reflect the subject in a diverse yet inclusive way?
	☐ Does your scheme of work reflect the requirements of the Ofsted common inspection framework (if applicable), embrace equality and diversity, and reflect differentiation?
	☐ Does your scheme of work build upon topics in a logical way, taking into account any identified needs, the results of learning preference tests and initial assessments?
	☐ Does your scheme of work take into account any specific dates that learners may not be able to attend, or dates and events that can be celebrated?
	☐ Can you provide a choice of learning opportunities at a variety of times and places?
	☐ Can you plan time for tutorials – group and individual? Group tutorials can be an opportunity for equality and diversity activities and discussions to raise learner awareness.
	☐ Does the teaching environment you have been allocated fulfil the needs of your subject and learners and is it safe and accessible?
	☐ Do your session plans take into consideration the individual needs of your learners and show how you will differentiate for them?
	☐ Do you use an induction checklist to ensure all aspects of the course, qualification and the organisation are stated?
	☐ Is time allocated during induction for information and discussion regarding equality and diversity including policies, complaints and appeals?
	☐ Can you include a workshop or a session regarding equality and diversity, or invite expert speakers?
	☐ Can you communicate with others who are involved with your learners, for example, carers, teachers and workplace supervisors?

Planning learning (Continued)	☐ Do your resources represent the diverse range of your learners and society? ☐ Do you need to adapt any resources to suit your learners, for example, the use of large print or coloured paper? ☐ Do you check all visual presentations, handouts and documents to ensure they are legible and readable by all learners, without using too much jargon? ☐ Can you create extension activities to stretch and challenge higher level learners or those who finish a task earlier? ☐ Can you make your teaching and learning materials accessible electronically? ☐ Do you need to obtain or arrange for any specialist equipment or support? ☐ Do you maintain a group profile and update it regularly?
Facilitating learning	☐ Can you use an appropriate and inclusive icebreaker? ☐ Can you agree suitable ground rules with your learners which include aspects of equality and diversity? ☐ Do you use a variety of stimulating teaching activities, methods and resources to cover all learning preferences? ☐ Do you treat your learners as individuals, using their names when possible? ☐ Can all learners access the learning environment and use all relevant equipment and materials safely? ☐ Is the environment conducive to learning, for example, layout, accessibility? ☐ Is the language you use appropriate, non-discriminatory and at the right level? ☐ Do you manage discussions to ensure learners' language is appropriate and non-discriminatory? ☐ Do you make good use of occasions when opportunities naturally occur regarding equality and diversity? ☐ Do you ensure individual learner needs are met and differentiated for all abilities? ☐ Do you treat all learners fairly? ☐ Do you ensure all learners treat each other with respect? Do you challenge negativity? ☐ Do you encourage teamwork? ☐ Do you present materials and topics in a way that embraces equality and diversity? ☐ Can you build in sufficient time for group activities to advance equality and diversity, bearing in mind any cultural clashes that may occur? ☐ Is diversity included within your teaching and learning resources, for example, referring to a variety of cultures, faiths, religions and traditions? ☐ Are pictures of people from all aspects of society visible in your resources? ☐ Can you confidently challenge prejudice, discrimination and stereotyping as it occurs? ☐ Can you put your own attitudes, values and beliefs aside if they conflict with your learners', or at the very least do not let them affect teaching and learning? ☐ Do you use appropriate body language and non-verbal communication? ☐ Is equality and diversity an agenda item for team meetings? Are meaningful topics discussed and acted upon? Are there opportunities for staff training?

(Continued)

Table 9.2 (Continued)

Assessing learning	☐ Is assessment planned with all learners?
	☐ Are appropriate assessment types and methods used for all learners?
	☐ Is assessment fair and not discriminative against any learner?
	☐ Can you use alternative forms of assessment, for example, reading questions to a learner who is visually impaired?
	☐ Do you need to contact the awarding organisation to obtain extra time for assessments or exams due to language barriers or physical difficulties (if applicable)?
	☐ Do you provide feedback on an individual basis, giving developmental support where necessary, at a level to suit each learner?
	☐ Can you rephrase questions if they are not understood by the learner?
	☐ Do you differentiate for learners' abilities and needs?
	☐ Are your learners aware of the appeals procedure?
	☐ Are you keeping relevant records of progress and achievement?
Evaluating learning	☐ Do learners have the opportunity to evaluate their programme in an anonymous way?
	☐ Can all learners understand the questions being asked and complete the necessary forms? Can the forms be available electronically?
	☐ Do you collect an adequate range of data including ethnicity, retention, achievement, progression, destinations?
	☐ Do you analyse the data collected and do something positive with it?
	☐ Can you follow up any feedback from learners or others?
	☐ Can you evaluate each session delivered and note any equality and diversity issues that occurred?
	☐ Can you foster links with the local community to improve your own knowledge?
	☐ Can you take any further training to benefit yourself and your learners?

Self-assessment checklist

Do I know about the following?

If not, re-read this chapter, or research the texts and websites listed at the end.

- ☐ What the terms equality and diversity mean
- ☐ How an equality and diversity policy should look
- ☐ How to keep up to date with equality and diversity issues and legislation
- ☐ How attitudes, values and beliefs can impact upon others
- ☐ The Equality Act (2010) for England, Scotland and Wales
- ☐ What inclusive practice is and how to promote inclusion
- ☐ What differentiation is and how to differentiate for different learners' needs
- ☐ What culture is and how to promote a positive culture with learners
- ☐ The differences between direct and indirect discrimination
- ☐ How harassment can affect learning and how to deal with it
- ☐ What stereotyping is and how it can affect learners
- ☐ How to demonstrate good practice regarding equality and diversity

Summary

This chapter has explored various aspects regarding equality and diversity.

You should now be able to give your learners fair and equal chances, and value and respect their differences. You should also know how to encourage inclusion during your sessions, as well as differentiate for different learners' needs.

You might like to carry out further research by accessing the books and websites listed at the end of this chapter, particularly if you are working towards a higher level teaching qualification.

This chapter has covered the following topics:

- Equality and diversity
- Inclusive practice
- Differentiation
- Culture
- Discrimination
- Demonstrating good practice

References and further information

Gravells, A. and Simpson, S. (2012) *Equality and Diversity in the Lifelong Learning Sector* (2nd edition). London: Learning Matters SAGE.

Hiddleston, P. and Unwin, L. (2012) *Teaching and Learning in Further Education: Diversity and Change.* Abingdon: Routledge.

Knowles, G. (2011) *Diversity, Equality and Achievement in Education.* London: SAGE.

Patel, J. and Yafai, G. (2016) *Demystifying Diversity: A Handbook to Navigate Equality, Diversity and Inclusion.* London: Gilgamesh.

Peart, S. (2014) *Equality and Diversity in Further Education.* Northwich: Critical Publications Ltd.

Powell, S. and Tummons, J. (2011) *Inclusive Practice in the Lifelong Learning Sector.* Exeter: Learning Matters.

Race, P. (2014) *Making Learning Happen.* London: SAGE.

Spencerley, L. (2014) *Inclusion in Further Education.* Northwich: Critical Publications Ltd.

Thompson, N. (2011) *Promoting Equality: Working with Diversity and Difference.* Basingstoke: Palgrave Macmillan.

Zaidi, N. (2015) *Embedding Equality and Diversity into the Curriculum – A Literature Review.* London: Education and Training Consultants Ltd.

Websites

Differentiated teaching and learning activities – www.tes.com/teaching-resource/challenge-toolkit-6063318

Disability Equality in Education – www.worldofinclusion.com/inclusion_education.htm

Disability News Service – www.disabilitynewsservice.com

Disability Now – https://disabilitynow.org.uk

Disability Rights UK – www.disabilityrightsuk.org

Equality and Diversity Forum – www.edf.org.uk

Equality and Human Rights Commission – www.equalityhumanrights.com

Legislation in the UK – www.legislation.gov.uk

Mental health – www.mind.org.uk

Ofsted British Values – https://tinyurl.com/kwhrog7

Prevent Duty: free resources from the Education and Training Foundation – www.preventforfeandtraining.org.uk

Prevent Strategy – https://tinyurl.com/z8xwwut

Workplace Bullying – www.workplacebullying.co.uk

10

Assessing learning

Introduction

Assessment is about checking if learning has taken place. It enables you to ascertain if your learners have gained the required skills, behaviours, knowledge, and/or understanding at a given point. It also provides your learners with an opportunity to demonstrate what progress they have made and what they still need to do.

This chapter will explore the purpose of assessment and how it can be used to assess learning both on- and off-the-job. Different types of assessment such as holistic, formative and summative are also covered, as are methods of assessment such as observation and questioning. How to make decisions and provide feedback to learners are covered, along with the risks that might be involved.

This chapter will cover the following topics:

- The purpose of assessment
- Assessment both on- and off-the-job
- Assessment types and methods
- Questioning techniques
- Minimising risks
- Making decisions and providing feedback

The purpose of assessment

Assessment is a process whereby you can check the progress that a learner has made, what they have achieved so far and what still needs to be done. It can take place in any environment, for example, a classroom, a training workshop, the workplace or an outside location. It is a measure of learning at a given point and the results should not be influenced by anything other than the learner's ability. They can be used to determine if a learner can gain a certificate and/or a qualification or to confirm competent performance at work. If you don't plan for and carry out any assessment activities with your learners, you will not know how well, or what, they have learnt.

Assessment should not be confused with evaluation; assessment is of *learning*, whereas evaluation is of the *programme* which the learner is working towards. Assessment specifically relates to an individual learner's progress and achievements, as well as identifying how they can develop and improve. Evaluation is a tool which monitors quality assurance. It includes obtaining feedback from your learners and others, for example, employers, line managers and quality assurers. Evaluation should help you to improve the overall learning experience as well as your own practice (covered in Chapter 12).

Before you can carry out any assessment activities with your learners, you will need to know what you are going to assess, why, and where it will take place. This will help you to plan what to do and when, and to agree it with your learners. You will also need to know when your learners will be ready for assessment, as some aspects might need to be taught first.

Activity

What is the subject that you will assess and why will you assess it, i.e. to check progress at regular intervals? Where will assessment take place, i.e. in the workplace, in a classroom or somewhere else? How will you know when your learners are ready to be assessed?

If you see your learners regularly, perhaps if you are teaching as well as assessing them, you can assess that learning is taking place each time you see them. This is called *informal* assessment and could simply be by watching what your learners are doing and/or asking questions to check their knowledge and understanding. *Formal* assessment will count towards the achievement of something, such as a qualification, whereas informal assessment is to check progress. However, assessment should not be in isolation from the teaching and learning process. For example, if you are assessing in the workplace, you (or someone else) might carry out a short training session if your learner hasn't quite met the requirements. Alternatively, you could be assessing an online programme (covered in Chapter 8) in which you never meet your learner, but they will be working through training materials before you assess their progress.

There are some assessors who do not teach or train, but will just assess, make decisions and provide feedback. This might be where competent staff are demonstrating their skills regarding their job role or are being assessed to ensure they are meeting performance management or service standards. These assessors might be employed in the same organisation as their learners, be freelance, or might work for a college or training organisation and visit learners in the workplace as required.

Assessment for learning and assessment of learning

There is a difference between assessment *for* learning (AfL), and assessment *of* learning (AoL). Assessment *for* learning is usually a *formative* process and is often informal. It will ascertain the progress that a learner has made so far in order to plan further learning and development. It's called formative assessment because it is ongoing throughout the learning process. It's also a chance for a learner to make a mistake or to get something wrong and to learn from this. Assessment *of* learning is usually *summative* and often formal. It confirms whether learning and achievement have taken place (or not). It's called summative assessment because it occurs at the end of an aspect of learning. This could be *modular*, i.e. after a unit or a module is completed, or *linear*, i.e. when the whole course has been completed.

If your learners are working towards a qualification, there will be *formal summative* methods of assessment that you will need to use, such as an assignment or a workplace observation. However, you can devise *informal formative* methods to use with your learners to check their progress at any time, such as discussions, role plays or quizzes. Assessment should always focus on improving and reinforcing learning as well as measuring progress and achievement. It should help your learners understand what they have achieved so far and what they need to do to improve and/or develop further.

Example

Jim has devised an informal formative quiz based on a popular television game show. He uses it to ask questions to his group of learners at the end of each theory session. Using this method also introduces an element of fun to the subject. The quiz is to assess knowledge and understanding towards the Level 1 Motor Vehicle Studies qualification. Jim then uses the formal summative activities provided by the awarding organisation to assess each learner's achievement at the appropriate time.

The assessment cycle

The assessment cycle (Figure 10.1, on page 384) is a systematic process which could be followed to provide your learner with a positive assessment experience. Depending upon the subject you are assessing and whether it is academic (theory or knowledge based) or vocational (practical or performance based), you will usually follow the assessment cycle.

The cycle will continue until all aspects of the programme or qualification have hopefully been achieved by your learner, or perhaps not if they decide to leave.

Throughout the cycle, standardisation of assessment practice between assessors should take place (covered in Chapter 11). This will help to ensure the consistency and fairness of assessment decisions, and that all assessors have interpreted the requirements in the same way.

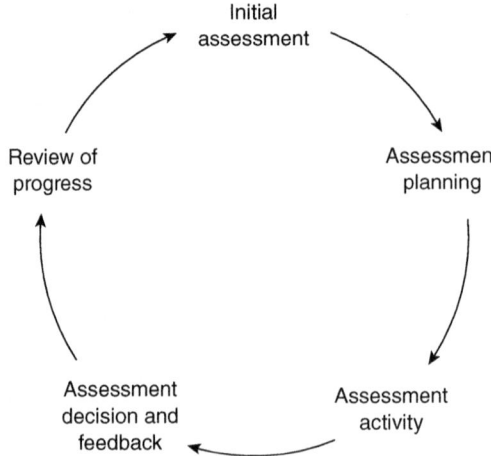

Figure 10.1 The assessment cycle

- **Initial assessment** – ascertaining information regarding your learners: for example, any specific assessment requirements they may have or any further training and support that they may need. This information can be obtained in a range of ways, for example, application forms, interviews, diagnostic tests and discussions. This process might not always be carried out by you but the information obtained must be passed on to you. Initial assessment is known as assessment *for* learning, because it helps prepare learners *for* assessment and identifies their potential.

- **Assessment planning** – agreeing suitable types and methods of assessment with learners, setting appropriate target dates and involving others as necessary, such as colleagues, witnesses or workplace supervisors.

- **Assessment activity** – using relevant approaches and activities, for example, observation, questioning, assignments or gathering appropriate evidence of competence. Assessment can be formative (usually ongoing and informal to check progress, e.g. a discussion) and/or summative (usually at the end and formal, e.g. a test). Summative assessment is often known as assessment *of* learning because it counts towards the achievement *of* something.

- **Assessment decision and feedback** – making a judgement of success or otherwise or allocating a grade and advising how to achieve a higher grade in future. Providing constructive and developmental feedback and agreeing upon any further action that may be necessary.

- **Review of progress** – reviewing progress and achievement and discussing any other issues that may be relevant to the learning and assessment process.

The cycle can then begin again with an initial assessment regarding the next area to be assessed. Records should be maintained throughout all aspects of the assessment cycle and quality assurance activities should take place on an ongoing basis (covered in Chapter 11).

Assessment should be a regular and continual process; it might not always be formalised as you might be informally watching what your learners are doing, asking them questions, and reviewing their progress whenever you are in contact with them. If you also teach or train, your learners will be demonstrating their skills, behaviours, knowledge and/or understanding regularly, for example, through various tasks, discussions and activities. It's good practice to provide your learners with constructive and developmental feedback when assessing them informally. This will help them realise what progress they are making. If they haven't reached a certain standard, you should still provide feedback regarding what they have done well so far, and how they can improve and develop further. If you feel that it is difficult to make a decision with the assessment activities you have used, you could discuss your concerns with other assessors. You may need to redesign some activities to make them more specific and/or unambiguous. If most of your learners are achieving everything with ease, perhaps you need to be more challenging with the tasks you set. If most are not, perhaps you are doing something incorrectly or at the wrong time, i.e. assessing something which your learners are not familiar with or that they don't understand.

Assessment can help your learners by:

- acknowledging what progress has been made

- addressing issues where there are gaps in learning

- ascertaining areas for development

- confirming achievements

- diagnosing any areas of concern to enable support to be arranged

- encouraging discussions and questions

- ensuring that they are on the right programme at the right level

- identifying what is yet to be learnt

- maintaining motivation

- seeing any inaccuracies, e.g. spelling or grammar errors in a written task or mistakes during a practical task.

Liaising with others

There might be other people who are involved with your learners' development. For example, if you assess learners but someone else teaches them, it would be useful to know who this person is to communicate with them. Some learners might have a mentor or a supervisor in the workplace and/or other teachers, trainers and assessors. You will need to communicate with these people to ensure that you are aware of what is taking place and when.

You may need to inform others of any particular learner requirements or safeguarding concerns. However, do be aware of any sensitive or confidential issues relating to your learners which they may not wish you to divulge to others.

If your programme is quality assured, internal and external quality assurers will sample your work to ensure that your judgements and decisions are correct and fair. Inspectors might also need to talk to you or observe you. They will usually inform you in advance regarding what they need to do. It's useful to be prepared for this and to have all your records up to date.

The starting point for assessment

If you are going to assess accredited qualifications, the starting point should be the *programme handbook* or *syllabus*, often known as a *qualification specification*. An accredited qualification is offered via an awarding organisation (AO) who will issue a certificate to a learner upon successful achievement. Depending upon which country you are in, this might be known as an awarding body or an examination board. The qualification specification should state how your subject is to be assessed and quality assured and is usually available from the AO's website. It will give information and guidance in the form of an *assessment strategy*. This should state the experience, professional development and qualifications that assessors and internal quality assurers should have. It will also state how the subject should be assessed, and whether assessment activities are provided for you, or if you need to create your own. Alternatively, you might be assessing non-accredited qualifications. These are programmes of learning that do not lead to a formal qualification or a certificate which is issued by an AO. However, a company certificate, a record of achievement or a record of attendance might be issued instead.

When planning to carry out assessment activities, you will need to know when your learners are ready to be assessed. There's no point in assessing them if they haven't learnt everything as you will be setting them up to fail. If a learner has been absent for any reason, you will need to make sure that they are up to date regarding what they have missed, prior to assessing them. Carrying out a formative assessment well before a summative assessment can help both you and your learner see how ready they are.

The timing of assessments can make a difference to a learner: if you plan to assess on a Friday before a holiday period, your learners might not be as focused; equally so first thing on a Monday morning. However, this is difficult if you only see your learners on these particular days. If you are planning a schedule of assessments throughout the year, you will need to consider any public or cultural holidays. There is no point in planning to assess only on Mondays if the majority of these fall on public holidays.

Some formal assessment dates might not be able to be changed, for example, a national test which must be taken by all relevant learners on the same day and at the same time.

Extension activity

If you are assessing learners who are working towards an accredited qualification, find out which the awarding organisation is for your particular subject and access their website. Locate the qualification specification and look at the assessment strategy to ensure that you can meet the requirements. If you are going to assess non-accredited programmes of learning, obtain and familiarise yourself with the standards or the programme that you will assess.

If you are not currently assessing, have a look at a few different qualification specifications to familiarise yourself with their layout and content. These can usually be located on any awarding organisation's website.

Assessment both on- and off-the-job

Assessment activities should take place in a suitable environment. This might be *on-the-job* if you are assessing vocational learners such as apprentices, employees and trainees in their place of work. Alternatively, it might be *off-the-job* if you are assessing academic learners working towards a qualification. Some programmes might be a mixture of vocational and academic subjects, with assessment taking place in workshops or a realistic working environment (RWE). An example of an RWE is a commercial hairdressing/beauty salon within a college. Members of the public can visit, and to the learners, they are real customers. However, learners are supervised and the public know that they are in a training environment. Other programmes might have a mixture of on-the-job and off-the-job assessment.

Examples of different locations and assessment methods are:

- classroom or training room: practical and theoretical tasks, tests, discussions, role plays, projects and presentations

- lecture theatre or hall: exams, multiple-choice tests and written questions

- library or home: assignments, online activities and case studies

- outside environment: practical activities and projects

- workplace: observations, questions and reviewing evidence produced by learners

- workshop/RWE: simulations, practical activities and tests.

There is a great deal of terminology involved with assessment, such as the term *competence statements*. These are simply statements of what a learner must do, for example, *the learner will greet customers in a polite and helpful manner*. The terminology which is used in the assessment process is to determine what a learner must be able to understand and/or do. Other terms include (in alphabetical order):

- assessment criteria
- assessment instruments
- candidate proficiencies
- common core standards
- content area

- knowledge statements
- learning outcomes
- learning standards
- national occupational standards (NOS)
- objectives

- performance criteria
- performance indicators
- performance outcomes
- performance tasks
- professional dispositions

- proficiency statements
- range statements
- skills statements
- success statements.

Whatever the terminology used, you will need to interpret what the assessment requirements are to make sure that your learners can achieve them.

Assessment planning

Assessment planning is a fundamental part of the assessment process. If it is not carried out correctly and comprehensively, problems may occur which could disadvantage your learners or prevent them from achieving. There is a lot to think about, and you will need to take into account aspects such as: equality of opportunity, health and safety, safeguarding, inclusivity and differentiation. Never assume everything is fine just because your learners don't complain. Always include your learners in the assessment planning process in case there is something you don't know, that you need to act upon.

You could start by devising a rationale using the *five Ws and one H* format of *who, what, when, where, why* and *how*. This information should always be agreed with your learners beforehand so that everyone is aware of what will happen and when. Whether you are assessing on an individual basis (i.e. observation in the workplace) or a group basis (i.e. a test in the classroom), the assessment planning process should be formalised and agreed with your learners.

Assessment planning should provide opportunities for both you and your learners to obtain and use information which is relevant to their progress and achievement. It should also be flexible and responsive, for example, by including the use of technology (covered in Chapter 8).

Your learners should know what they are working towards, the criteria that will be used to assess them, how they will be assessed and the date, time and place for assessment. You should also plan how and when you will provide feedback. This could be orally immediately after the assessment activity, the next time you see your learner, by email or another means. However, the sooner the better so that nothing is forgotten.

Informal assessments will not require an assessment plan, for example, role plays, questions and quizzes if they are only to check ongoing progress. However, anything which counts towards the achievement of something will need to be formally planned for.

To effectively plan how you will assess your learners, you will need to use methods which are ethical, safe and fair.

- Ethical: the methods used are right and proper for what is being assessed and the context of assessment. The learner's welfare, health, safety and security are not compromised.

- Safe: the learner's work can be confirmed as valid and authentic. There should be little chance of plagiarism, confidentiality of information should be taken into account and learning and assessment should not be compromised in any way, nor the learner's experience or potential to achieve. (Safe in this context does not relate to health and safety but to whether the assessment methods are sufficiently robust to make a reliable decision.)

- Fair: the methods used are appropriate to all learners at the required level, taking into account any particular needs. All learners should have an equal chance of an accurate assessment decision.

Example

If you provide your learners with the information to answer questions this is unethical. If you allow your learners to copy text from the internet without quoting their sources, it will be deemed unsafe. If you provide some learners with more help than others this is unfair.

The planning process

Depending upon whether you are assessing on-the-job or off-the-job, the planning process may differ. An *assessment* plan (usually for on-the-job) or an *action* plan (usually for off-the-job) should be agreed with each learner. It's like a contract towards achievement of their qualification, standards, criteria, job role or whatever is to be assessed. It is sometimes referred to as an *assessment scheme* or a *scheme of assessment*. Careful assessment planning and prior knowledge of your learner's previous achievements are the key to ensuring everyone involved understands what will take place and when. The plan can be reviewed and updated at any time. Rather than completing a separate feedback form when a learner has achieved something, the planning document could perform a dual function. Some organisations might use different documents which perform a similar role, such as individual learning plans (ILPs) or personal learning plans (PLPs) (covered in Chapter 4). Later in this chapter section there is an example of an on-the-job assessment plan in Table 10.1 and an off-the-job action plan in Table 10.2. For the purpose of future-proofing the book, a year has not been added to any dates within the documents. When completing any documents yourself, you should always add the year, as well as the day and month, to create a full audit trail.

Always ask your learners if there is anything you can do to help make their assessment experience a positive one. For example, ensure you face your learners when speaking to assist anyone hard of hearing, or use written questions instead of oral questions (or vice versa) if necessary. If you use printed handouts make sure that they are in a font, size and colour which suit any particular learner requirements.

Assessment planning should always be SMART.

- **S**pecific – the activity relates only to what is being assessed and is clearly stated.

- **M**easurable – the activity can be measured against the assessment requirements, allowing any gaps to be identified.

- **A**chievable – the activity can be achieved at the right level.

- **R**elevant– the activity is suitable and realistic, relates to what is being assessed and will give consistent results.

- **T**ime bound – target dates and times are agreed.

Apprenticeship assessment plan

In England, the term *assessment plan* for an apprenticeship programme is not the same as an assessment plan for a learner working towards a qualification. An apprenticeship assessment plan outlines the way in which the full programme will be assessed for a particular occupation. It might or might not also include a relevant qualification. If it does, the normal qualification requirements of formative and summative assessment will apply.

While the nature and methods of assessment will differ between occupations and job roles, all assessment plans will focus on the end-point (synoptic) assessment process and will:

- explain in detail what will be assessed (i.e. skills, behaviours, knowledge)

- explain how the apprentice will be assessed (i.e. which method or methods will be used to judge competency at the end of the apprenticeship programme)

- indicate who will carry out the assessment (i.e. who will be the assessor(s) for each aspect of the end-point assessment) and who will make the final decision regarding the competency and grading descriptors. Grades of distinction, merit, pass and not yet achieved (NYA) will be used

- propose quality assurance arrangements to make sure that the assessment is reliable and consistent across different locations, employers, training and assessment organisations.

If you are an end-point assessor, your role will not include training apprentices towards the aspects which you will assess. You might therefore be working for an *apprenticeship assessment organisation (AAO)* and will have never met the apprentice prior to assessing them.

If you are the apprentice's trainer, you will need to prepare your apprentice for end-point assessment and will need to see the assessment plan to find out what's involved, for example, ensuring the apprentice knows how to take part in a professional discussion or how to give a presentation. If the apprentice is also working towards a qualification, it's probable you will be able to train as well as assess providing you meet the requirements of the qualification's assessment strategy.

Each subject to be assessed will have an *apprenticeship standard* which outlines details of:

- the occupation/job profile

- the knowledge, skills and behaviours required to perform the job role

- entry requirements

- the level of the programme and the typical time allowed to achieve it

- whether any qualifications are also included which must be achieved prior to the apprentice taking the end-point assessment, along with any other subjects such as English and maths

- links to relevant professional association registration and progression (if applicable)

- when the standard will be reviewed.

The standard will be used by the person training the apprentice to ensure all aspects are met. However, the standard should not be treated like a list which is ticked off when the apprentice has achieved something. This is often referred to as the *tick box culture*, i.e. ticking things off and then moving on to something else. While the apprentice might feel they have achieved something, they might not be able to competently do it again in a month's time. The apprentice will need to demonstrate their competence over time, not just on one occasion, hence the use of end-point assessment.

Assessing on-the-job

If you are going to assess learners on-the-job, i.e. in the workplace, this will usually be on a one-to-one basis. You might be employed in the same organisation as the learner and can therefore be flexible with the dates and times for assessing. You might carry out formative as well as summative assessment. Alternatively, you might work for an assessment centre and just carry out summative assessments, with someone else carrying out formative assessment. This might occur with apprentices, therefore you will need to communicate with the learner and their assessor to ensure they are ready for assessment. Looking at the relevant standards or the qualification specification will help you plan effective activities to use according to what is required. You will need to discuss these with your learner (and possibly their supervisor), to ensure that you all interpret the requirements in the same way. Standards and qualifications often change; therefore, you would need to ensure that you are working with the latest version.

Vocational qualifications are an excellent way for competent learners to demonstrate what they have learnt in their own work environment and to gain a certificate. However, if there are aspects of the qualification with which they are not familiar, training will need to take place first. An initial and/or diagnostic assessment would greatly help identify what may need to be learnt before any formal assessment takes place.

If you are assessing on-the-job, the most commonly used methods are:

- observations of skills and behaviours

- examining work products and evidence

- asking questions – written or oral

- holding discussions with your learner, often known as professional discussions

- obtaining witness testimonies, for example, from a learner's supervisor

- reading your learner's written statements and reflective accounts of how they performed certain tasks, and confirming these with their supervisor

- recognising your learner's prior learning (RPL)

- the learner self-assessing themselves against the standards or outcomes.

On-the-job assessment activities will need to confirm the learner has the required skills and behaviour, as well as knowledge and understanding.

Example

John, a trainee in a chemical plant, could hold a discussion with his assessor about what actions would be taken in the event of a chemical leak. This would cover the knowledge aspect; however, the understanding, skills and behaviours would only be demonstrated during a simulation or a real chemical leak.

In this example, John could only demonstrate what should happen in the event of a chemical leak, not what would really happen. A simulation might not reflect reality as people might panic and act differently under the circumstances.

Having knowledge does not imply understanding. For example, you know that the earth is round but do you understand why? When assessing knowledge, it might be sufficient for a learner to know enough to get by, such as knowing certain historical dates but not the reasons why. However, in other areas, understanding must also be demonstrated. If you can, try to use a variety of at least two or three different assessment activities to keep the process interesting, for example, observation, oral questions and looking at work products. This way, you are ensuring that you are assessing not only learner performance and behaviour, but knowledge and understanding.

Assessment should be a two-way process between yourself and your learner; you need to plan what you are going to do, and they need to know what is expected of them and when. It could be that you will assess units or aspects in a different order from those stated in the standards or requirements. For example, instead of assessing Unit 1 before Unit 2, you might decide with your learner that Unit 2 could be assessed first as they are already performing those aspects at work. However, they might also naturally cover aspects of other units which had not been planned for. This should not be discounted, but can be assessed holistically.

If you visit learners in their place of work, it is best to plan ahead to enable assessment of relevant activities at appropriate times. If you have several learners in the same or different locations, planning ahead will enable you to assess learners who are in close proximity. This will help to ease the time and cost spent travelling. Out of courtesy, notify your learner's supervisor or manager in advance in case there is any reason why they cannot accommodate you on a particular day. You will also need to check travel, transport and/or parking arrangements.

If your learner works shifts or during the weekend, you will need to visit when they are working, as it isn't fair to ask them to change their work patterns just to suit you. If for any reason an assessment is cancelled, make sure that a revised date is scheduled as soon as possible and inform all concerned. Always confirm your visit a few days beforehand, just in case there is any reason why the assessment cannot go ahead.

Table 10.1 Example assessment plan (on-the-job)

Assessment plan		
Learner: Irene Jones **Assessor:** Jenny Smith		
Qualification/unit: Level 1 Certificate in Hospitality & Catering (Unit 101)		
Aspects to be assessed	**Assessment details**	**Target date**
Unit 101.3 *Be able to help maintain a hygienic, safe and secure workplace*	An observation will take place on February 6th at the County Leisure Centre to assess competence in the work environment towards unit 101.3. The awarding organisation's observation form will be used for this purpose. A witness testimony will be obtained from Irene's supervisor. If any other aspects are seen during the observation which meet the criteria of other units, these will be taken into account.	6 February
Unit 101.4 *Know how to maintain a hygienic, safe and secure workplace*	Oral questions and a professional discussion will take place to assess unit 101.4.	6 February

Assessing off-the-job

If you are not assessing competence in the work environment or an RWE, you will probably be assessing an academic qualification or a non-vocational programme. You might also be responsible for teaching or training as well as assessing. This would enable you to get to know your learners before you assess them. However, depending upon your job role, someone else might teach the learners and you might only be responsible for assessing them.

If you are assessing off-the-job, i.e. in a classroom or other environment, the most commonly used methods are:

- assignments

- case studies

- essays

- observations

- peer assessments

- professional discussions

- projects

- puzzles and quizzes

- simulations

- tests

- written and oral questions.

You will need to carry out some form of planning with your learners, even if it's only agreeing target dates for the submission of assignments or planning ahead for the dates of tests or exams. Your learners will need to know what they are working towards, when they will be assessed, and how, e.g. by assignments. This information could be in the form of an action plan rather than an assessment plan. The action plan would contain the details of the assignments which can be updated with achievement dates, and be added to or amended as necessary.

Activity

If you will be assessing learners in a classroom or other environment (off-the-job), what will you need to find out? For example, what will be assessed and when, and the dates the learners will be with you. Will anyone else be involved in the assessment process? If so, how will you communicate with them to ensure that assessment takes place at the right time?

If you are teaching as well as assessing, you will need to prepare a scheme of work to show what you will teach and when, and how you will assess that learning has taken place (covered in Chapter 4). When planning this, make sure you have taught all the required material before carrying out any formal assessments. You may need to ensure appropriate time is planned for assessment activities during your sessions, or in between sessions, i.e. an assignment. You will also need to plan adequate time for you to carry out marking and assessment, make a decision and provide feedback to your learners. It's best to stagger the formal assessment activities so that you don't overload or put too much pressure on your learners, or yourself, throughout the programme.

If your learners will be taking an exam, this will need to be planned and invigilated according to the awarding organisation's requirements. Some assignments may also need to be completed under supervised conditions. You would therefore need to ensure you have taught everything in good time. You could use past exam papers as a formative assessment activity. This is good revision and will help to check the progress of your learners beforehand. This will also give them an idea of the structure that will need to be followed regarding their responses to the questions asked.

If your learners are working towards an accredited qualification, you will need to ensure they have been registered with the appropriate awarding organisation. It might not be your responsibility to carry out this task, but you should communicate with the relevant person. If learners have not been registered, the awarding organisation is not responsible for them and the results of their assessments might be deemed invalid.

Table 10.2 Example action plan (off-the-job)

Action plan			
Learner: Marcia Indira		Assessor: Abbi Cross	
Qualification/unit: Level 2 Business, Administration and Finance (Unit 1)			
Criteria	Assignment questions	Target date	Achievement date
Learning outcome 2: Be able to develop a business enterprise idea	Q1 – Generate a range of ideas for a business enterprise	7 October	
	Q2 – Compare the viability of the business enterprise ideas	14 October	
	Q3 – Select and develop a business idea	21 October	
	The total word count for all answers should be within 10% of 2000 words. Pictures, tables and charts are in addition to this.		

Extension activity

Find out what documentation you will be required to use for assessment purposes, for example, assessment plans, action plans or ILPs/PLPs. Can you complete them electronically? Where and how will you file them? Who else will need to see them and why?

Assessment types and methods

Assessment *types* are different from assessment *methods*. The *method* is how the *type* is used. For example, a *type* of assessment is *initial* and the *method* used could be *oral questions*. You will probably use different assessment types and methods depending upon whether you are assessing knowledge and/or performance. Knowledge is usually assessed by assignments, essays, questions and tests. Performance is usually assessed by observations, discussions and simulations.

You might have all the information provided for you regarding which types and methods of assessment to use. If not, you will need to carefully select these to suit your subject, the situation and your learners.

Assessment types

Five frequently used assessment types are:

- initial

- diagnostic

- formative

- summative

- holistic.

Initial and diagnostic assessments are the formal processes whereby you can ascertain your learners' prior skills and knowledge. It's also an opportunity to identify any aspects which might otherwise go unnoticed, for example, poor numerical or writing skills. Initial assessment, as the word implies, is carried out at the beginning of something, for example, a course or a session. Diagnostic assessment can be carried out at any time to diagnose any gaps in learning, or any particular learning or learner needs (covered in Chapter 3).

Formative assessment should take place continually and is usually carried out informally to check progress, identify any support requirements and inform further development. Assessing your learners on a formative basis will enable you to see if they are ready for a summative or final assessment. Formative assessment is usually informal, devised by yourself, and often called assessment *for* learning because it helps prepare learners *for* formal assessment.

Summative assessment usually occurs at the end of a session, programme, topic, unit or full qualification. It is a measure of achievement rather than progress. This type of assessment can often be quite stressful to learners and sometimes leads to a fail result, even though the learner is quite capable under other circumstances. Summative assessment is usually formal, devised by the awarding organisation that accredits the qualification, and is often called assessment *of* learning because it counts towards the achievement *of* something.

Holistic assessment enables learners to demonstrate several criteria from different aspects or units at the same time. You might be able to observe naturally occurring situations in addition to what had originally been planned. For example, if you are watching a learner perform a task and they also do something which had not been planned for but which occurs naturally during the activity. Don't discount this, but inform your learner you were able to assess them for these other aspects as well.

Holistic assessment is beneficial to all concerned when assessing occupational competence, particularly in a work environment. It can save duplication and repetition. It could be that you carry out a holistic assessment and find your learner is competent at most but not all of the criteria you planned to assess. If this is the case, you can still sign off what they have achieved and then update the assessment plan to assess the remaining criteria on another occasion. Alternatively, you might be able to ask questions or hold a professional discussion with your learner to evidence any gaps (if this is acceptable). If so, you would need to keep a record of what was asked along with the responses your learner gave. Without records, there's no proof of what has occurred and therefore what has been achieved.

Assessment methods

There are several different assessment methods you could use, for example, observations, professional discussions, questioning, tests and exams. If assessment activities are not provided for you, you will need to devise your own. However, these should be based on the requirements of what is to be assessed. You will need to use appropriate and valid ways of assessing your learners, at a point when you know your learners are ready to be assessed.

Activities to formally assess learners' achievements are often provided by an awarding organisation (if you are assessing an accredited qualification). You should be able to devise your own informal assessment activities to check ongoing progress with your learners. Depending upon what is being assessed, some informal activities could also be used as formal activities if they are acceptable.

Examples of formal assessment methods are:

- assignments
- case studies
- essays
- examinations
- multiple-choice questions
- observations
- professional discussions
- projects
- recognition of prior learning
- reviewing learner evidence
- tests
- witness testimonies
- written questions.

Examples of informal assessment methods are:

- crosswords
- discussions
- gapped handouts (sentences with missing words)
- journals/diaries
- peer and self-assessment
- puzzles
- practical activities
- questions: oral, written, multiple choice
- quizzes
- role plays
- simulation
- worksheets and workbooks.

If you are assessing a programme whereby the assessment activities are provided for you, for example tests or exams, there is often the tendency to teach purely what is required for the learner to achieve a pass. They may therefore not gain valuable additional skills and knowledge. Teaching to pass tests does not maximise a learner's ability and potential to use their skills and knowledge in different situations.

All assessment methods should be suitable to the level of your learners. A level 1 learner might struggle to maintain a journal of their progress and a level 2 learner may not be mature enough to accept peer feedback. A level 3 learner may feel a puzzle is too easy and so on. Some learners may respond better to informal assessment rather than formal assessment. You will need to consider the assessment requirements for your subject, and how you can best implement these, without changing the assessment criteria.

Example

Wendy sees her group of learners once a week as part of an art and design programme. Each week, she commences the session by asking some questions regarding the topics covered in the previous week. This is informal formative assessment *to check progress. Towards the end of term, she will issue an assignment. This is* formal summative assessment *to confirm their achievement.*

In this example, Wendy used informal and formal assessment on a formative and summative basis.

If you are responsible for devising your own assessment activities, you might decide to choose ones which are easy for you to mark, for example, multiple-choice questions. You might not have a lot of time for marking, therefore the more time you spend preparing something suitable and relevant, the easier the marking will be. There's no point making assessment activities complex unless it's a requirement of the qualification or you need to challenge higher level learners further. Equally, lower level learners can easily become demoralised if the activities are unattainable.

If you assess group work, such as presentations or role plays, you will need to assess each individual's contribution towards the assessment requirements. Otherwise you could be passing the whole group when some learners may not have contributed much at all. If you are related to, or know personally the learners you will assess, you might need to notify your organisation of any conflict of interest. They may also need to notify the relevant awarding organisation if the qualification is accredited.

Learning outcomes and assessment criteria

If there is a qualification specification for your subject, certain terminology will be used, for example, *learning outcomes* and *assessment criteria*. These are often referred to as *the learner will*, and *the learner can*, respectively.

Example

Unit: Behaviour in a business administration environment

Learning outcome The learner will:	Assessment criteria The learner can:
1. Understand how to communicate in a business administration environment	1.1 Communicate appropriately with others in a business administration environment 1.2 Use appropriate language for a business administration environment
2. Know how to behave appropriately in a business administration environment	2.1 State the importance of workplace values 2.2 Give examples of appropriate workplace behaviour

If you look at the learning outcomes in the example, you can see the words *understand* and *know* are used. These would indicate that the learner needs this knowledge and understanding prior to being assessed. The assessment criteria have key words: *communicate, use, state* and *give examples*. These will give you a good idea of which assessment methods to use. For example, to assess that a learner can *communicate*, you would need to observe them in action. To assess that a learner can *give examples*, you would need to ask questions (either oral or written, or as part of an assignment, project or case study).

Usually, the first words are the key words which can be used to determine how the criteria will be assessed. Words such as: *describe, explain, list* and *state* are knowledge based. Words such as: *demonstrate, use,* and *apply* are performance based. Knowing which relate to each should help you to plan how you will assess your learners.

Activity

Find out the key words which relate to the assessment of your subject. If they are not given for you, i.e. in a qualification specification, you may need to write your own. Can you easily recognise which are knowledge based and which are performance based?

Never be afraid to try something different or to be flexible, particularly with formative assessments that you can design yourself to check progress. You could use puzzles, quizzes or crosswords as a fun and active way of informally assessing progress. You could even try letting your learners design their own assessment activities if appropriate. This would help them analyse what is to be assessed and to devise suitable ways of achieving it.

When using any assessment activity, you need to ensure that it is inclusive and differentiates for any individual needs, learning difficulties and/or disabilities (LDD) (covered in Chapter 3). If you are assessing towards a qualification, you may need to check if it's possible to make any changes with the awarding organisation. Always follow health and safety guidelines, and carry out any relevant risk assessments and adhere to safeguarding standards (where applicable).

Peer and self-assessment

Peer assessment involves a learner assessing another learner's progress. Self-assessment involves a learner assessing their own progress. Both methods encourage learners to make decisions about what has been learnt so far, take responsibility for their learning and become involved with the assessment process.

For peer and self-assessment to be effective, your learners will need to fully understand what needs to be assessed, how to be honest with their decisions and how to provide feedback. Throughout the process of peer and self-assessment, learners can develop skills such as listening, observing and questioning. However, the results of peer and self-assessment are not usually counted towards meeting the requirements of a qualification, as you should make the final decision. However, in the workplace, peer assessment might be counted as proof that the learner has met the requirements of a job role, for example, if the peer is a colleague.

Examples of peer-assessment activities include:

- assessing each other's work and giving written or oral feedback
- giving grades and/or written or oral feedback regarding peer presentations
- holding group discussions before collectively agreeing a grade and providing feedback
- suggesting improvements to their peers' work
- producing a written statement of how their peers could improve and/or develop their practice in certain areas.

Examples of self-assessment activities include:

- awarding a grade for a presentation they have delivered
- suggesting improvements regarding their skills and knowledge
- compiling a written statement of what they could do differently or how they could improve their work.

Extension activity

Take a look at the qualification specification or the criteria of the subject that you will assess. Consider which assessment types and methods you could use for both formative and summative assessment. State the advantages and disadvantages of each.

Questioning techniques

Questions are a really useful method of formative assessment to ensure your learners are acquiring the necessary knowledge and understanding before moving on to a new topic. They can also be used as summative assessment at the end of a programme, perhaps as part of a test or an exam.

Questions can be oral or written, and can be *open* requiring a full answer or *closed* requiring a 'yes' or 'no' answer. They can be aimed at one learner, i.e. directly using their name, or to a group, i.e. indirectly to everyone. If you are asking questions orally to a group of learners, ensure that you give each learner the chance to respond. Don't just let the keen learners answer first as this gives the ones who don't know the answers the chance to stay quiet. You could tell your learners that you are going to use a particular questioning method beforehand. For example, pose a question, pause for a second and then pick a learner to answer the question. This way, all learners are thinking about the answer as soon as you have posed the question, and are ready to speak if their name is picked. This is sometimes referred to as *pose, pause, pick* (PPP). *Pick* could also be *Pounce*. If you use this process, make sure you have enough questions for everyone in the group so that no one is left out. If your nominated learner doesn't know the answer, ask them to guess. That way they still have to think and can't opt out. If they still don't know, tell them they made a good attempt and then move on to another learner.

To ensure you include everyone throughout your session, you could have a list of their names handy and tick each one off after you have asked them a question. This is fine if you don't have a large group. If you do, make sure you ask different learners each time you are in contact with them. Another technique is to write each learner's name on small pieces of paper, fold them up and place them in a bowl. You (or a different learner each time) can choose a piece of paper. This way, no one knows whose name will be called. By not placing the names back in the bowl, you can keep track of how many learners still need to be asked a question.

When asking questions, try and only use one question in a sentence, as more than one may confuse your learners. For example, *'What plants will grow in arid conditions, which countries would this include and how much rainfall do they need?'* This is three questions, and your learner might not remember what you have asked, or only address part of the question.

Try not to ask *'Does anyone have any questions?'* as often only those who are keen or confident will ask. This doesn't tell you what your learners have learnt. Try not to use questions such as *'Does that make sense?'* or *'Do you understand?'*, as your learners will often say 'yes' as they feel that's what you expect to hear or they won't want to embarrass themselves. However, if you find yourself doing this, follow it up by asking *why* it makes sense, or *how* they understand it, to gain clarification.

You might also need to realise that your learners might not understand a question, not because of the way you have phrased it, but because they don't comprehend some words.

Example

Nicola was teaching history to a group of learners aged 14–16. She asked them to carry out an activity regarding placing certain historical events in chronological order. Many of her learners got it wrong. What Nicola didn't realise beforehand was that some learners did not know what the word chronological meant.

This example shows it's always useful to make sure your learners have a level of language and comprehension which is relevant to that which is being assessed.

When questioning:

- allow enough time for your questions and your learners' responses
- ask open questions, i.e. those beginning with *who, what, when, where, why* and *how*
- avoid trick or complex questions
- be aware of your posture, gestures and body language
- be conscious of your dialect, accent, pitch and tone of voice
- don't ask more than one question in the same sentence
- if you must use closed questions, generate activity and energy within a group by asking learners to all stand up, then ask them to sit down for a *yes* answer (or vice versa)
- know that some learners might be shy, therefore direct your questions to a table of learners (if you have small groups) to help encourage their input
- make sure you don't use closed questions to elicit a *yes* response too often, learners may feel that is what you want to hear but it doesn't confirm understanding
- make sure your learners understand the language and terminology used
- use active listening skills to show you are concentrating on hearing what they have to say, for example, by using eye contact and nodding
- try not to say *erm, yeah, okay, you know,* or *does that make sense?*
- try not to use a lot of jargon or acronyms or, if you must, make sure your learners understand them
- use eye contact when talking to an individual learner, or use eye contact as you ask a question to a group by alternating looking at each learner for a split second as you speak
- use learners' names when possible
- watch your learners' reactions and body language.

Types of questions

Types of questions can include: open, closed, probing, prompting, clarifying, leading, hypothetical, reflective and rhetorical. Some questioning techniques are better than others and it will take practice to use the ones which are most effective for your particular learners and the subject.

Example

Open: 'How would you ...?'

Closed: 'Would you ...?'

Probing: 'Why exactly was that?'

Prompting: 'What about ...?'

Clarifying: 'Can you go over that again, or expand further?'

Leading: 'So what you are saying is ... '

Hypothetical: 'What would you do if ...?'

Reflective: 'If you could do that again, how would you approach it?'

Rhetorical: 'Isn't that a great display that Peter has put together for his practical assignment?'

Rhetorical questions are good for engaging your learner in conversation, but they usually only require your learner to agree or disagree with you. They should be followed up with another type of question to elicit knowledge.

When asking oral questions, make sure you allow enough time for your learner to answer. If your learner can't answer, and you have time during the session, you could ask them to discuss it in a pair or group, or research it and come back to you. If they are finding things out for themselves, they are more likely to remember than if you tell them the answer.

Activity

Research how to create and use other question types, such as multiple-choice questions. Varying the types of questions that you use can help keep the assessment process interesting to both you and your learners.

If you are using the same questions with different learners at different times, be careful as they may collude and share their answers with each other. You may need to rephrase some questions if your learners are struggling with an answer, as poor answers are often the result of poor questions. For essay and short-answer tests you should create sample answers to have something with which to compare. If there are several assessors involved, you could all answer the questions and then compare all the responses. This will help ensure the questions have been interpreted correctly, aid the standardisation process and give consistent marks to learners. If you issue any assessment activities to be carried out during self-study time, you will need to plan your own time accordingly to ensure you are able to assess all the work that will be submitted by a certain date. It could be that your organisation expects you to assess and provide feedback within a certain time period, for example, seven days. You will need to find out what the requirements are so that you can meet them.

Minimising risks

Assessing a learner and confirming their success can be very rewarding; however, there are risks involved. Being aware of these will hopefully help you to minimise or prevent them from occurring. The risks apply not only with regard to the health, safety and welfare of all concerned, but also what might occur in your own area of responsibility for your particular subject. Just ask yourself what could possibly go wrong and, if you think of something, then there is a risk.

Learner risks

You will need to minimise risks such as putting unnecessary stress upon learners, over-assessing, under-assessing or being unfair and expecting too much too soon. Some learners might not be ready to be observed regarding a practical skill, or feel so pressured by target dates for a theory test that they resort to colluding or plagiarising work. If learners are under pressure, or have any issues or concerns that have not been addressed, they could be disadvantaged and might decide not to continue with the programme.

Plagiarism and authenticity

When assessing written work, you will need to be aware that some learners, intentionally or not, might plagiarise the work of others. Plagiarism is the wrongful use of someone else's work. Authenticity is the rightful and confirmed use of your own work. Learners should take responsibility for referencing any sources used in all work submitted, and may be required to sign a declaration or an authenticity statement. If you suspect plagiarism, you could type a few of the learner's words into an internet search engine or specialist software to see what appears. There are many free plagiarism checkers available via the internet. If you discovered plagiarism, you would need to challenge your learner as to whether it was intentional or not and follow your organisation's plagiarism procedure.

Example

Gary was marking assignments from his English literature learners and noticed that two of them had included an identical paragraph. He typed a few of these words into a search engine. He found that they were from an assignment which a previous learner had uploaded to a study skills' website. He decided to challenge his learners. They both said they had left their work until quite late and hadn't realised they couldn't copy and paste text from the internet. Gary reminded them about the Acceptable Use Policy *and said that anything they had used which belonged to someone else should have been correctly referenced. He then gave them a different assignment and discussed the importance of managing their time to meet deadlines.*

Unfortunately, some learners do cheat, copy or plagiarise the work of others. Sometimes this is deliberate, and at other times it is due to a lack of knowledge of exactly what was required, or a misunderstanding when citing quotes within work. If you feel the work that has been submitted to you might not be the actual work of your learner, ask them some questions about it. This will confirm their knowledge or otherwise. If you still feel it isn't their work, you will need to confront them and let them know you will take the matter further. At this point your learner may confess or they may have what they consider a legitimate excuse. However, you must be certain the work is their own, otherwise it could be classed as fraud.

It is easier to compare the work of your own learners as you are familiar with them; however, other assessors in your organisation might also assess the same programme with different learners. In this case, the internal quality assurer may pick up on issues when they are sampling learners' work. It is difficult to check and compare the work of all learners; therefore, the importance of authenticity must be stressed to everyone at the commencement of their programme and continually throughout. Asking learners to sign and date hard copies of work, or adding a statement to electronic work is a useful way of getting them to accept responsibility.

If you are assessing the work of learners you have not met, for example, by e-assessment, it can be very difficult to ensure the authenticity of their work. Your organisation might require each learner to attend an interview at some point and bring along some form of photo identification such as a driving licence, passport or employee card.

If assessors and learners are completing and/or submitting documents electronically, there might not be an opportunity to print them to add a real signature to confirm authenticity. However, many companies are now accepting a scanned signature or an email address, providing the identity of the person has been confirmed beforehand. If learners are using an online system to upload their work towards a qualification, an awarding organisation might check that staff do not have access to their passwords. This could be seen as maladministration.

Some ways of checking the authenticity of learners' work includes:

- spelling, grammar and punctuation – you know your learner speaks in a certain way at a certain level, yet their written work does not reflect this

- work which includes quotes from sources which have not been referenced – this is direct plagiarism and could be a breach of copyright

- word-processed work which contains different fonts and sizes of text – this shows it could have been copied from the internet or from someone else's electronic file

- handwritten work that looks different from your learner's normal handwriting, or is not the same style or language as normally used, or the submission of word-processed work when the learner would normally write by hand

- work that refers to information you haven't taught or is not relevant to the question.

The Copyright, Designs and Patents Act (1988) is the current UK copyright law. Copying the work of others without their permission would infringe the Act. Copyright is where an individual or organisation creates something as an original and has the right to control the ways in which their work may be used by others. Normally, the person who created the work will own the exclusive rights. However, if the work is produced as part of your employment, perhaps if you created several handouts or a workbook for your learners, then normally the work will belong to your organisation. Learners may be in breach of this Act if they plagiarise or copy the work of others without making reference to the original author.

Assessor risks

There are risks on your part as an assessor; for example, pressure to pass learners quickly due to funding and targets might lead you to allow something that you normally wouldn't. There is also the risk that you might unknowingly offer favouritism or bias towards some learners over others.

A risk to yourself could be if you carry out assessments in the work environment and visit places with which you are not familiar. You might need to travel early or late in the dark, find locations on foot, take public transport or drive to areas with which you are not familiar. If you are visiting places on your own, you will be classed as a lone worker and your organisation should have a policy for your protection. Having a mobile phone is helpful in such situations. If not, note where the nearest public phone or shop is. You may find it useful, if you use satellite navigation when driving, to search the internet beforehand for the postcode you are visiting. The results will show you a street map and pictures of the local area to enable you to visualise where you are going.

The type of employment contract you have might also pose a risk. For example, you might be part time and work for more than one organisation, be working for an agency or for yourself on a freelance basis. If you don't have a permanent contract, it could be difficult to determine who you report to if you have any concerns. Standardisation of practice might also be difficult if assessors are not all in the same location or working for the same organisation. Using communication technology could be a way of staff meeting virtually.

Your role might not give you access to the resources that permanent members of staff have and you may need to provide your own resources such as personal protective equipment (PPE). There's also the risk of pressure upon you if your learners are allocated to you on a case load basis. For example, you might only be paid if your allocated number of learners complete the qualification.

Activity

Have you ever been placed in a difficult situation which could cause a risk to yourself? If so, why do you think it happened and what would you do differently next time?

Other risks

Besides risks to learners and to yourself, there are other risks which you might encounter. If you are assessing in the work environment, you might come across employers who are not very supportive of their staff. For example, someone might make it difficult for you to visit at a certain time in order to carry out a formal assessment. If you can, try to build a good working relationship with your learner's employer or supervisor.

You might not be allowed to assess close friends or relatives, or if you can, your decisions might need to be countersigned by an impartial assessor and be quality assured. If you are assessing an accredited qualification, the awarding organisation will be able to provide you with guidance regarding this.

Extension activity

Make a list of the risks that you might encounter when assessing learners and state how you will overcome them. Try to list ones which have not been mentioned in this chapter. You might like to discuss your responses with a colleague or friend.

Making decisions and providing feedback

Once assessment has taken place, a decision needs to be made and feedback provided to the learner. This will inform them what has or has not been achieved, and what will happen next. It is quite a responsibility to confirm an achievement (or otherwise) as it can affect your learner's personal and professional development. Your learner may need to pass certain criteria to achieve a promotion at work or they may want to achieve a qualification for personal or professional fulfilment. Feedback therefore has to be meaningful to the learner, and not just something that you have to do. Praise should not be used at the cost of being sincere or if you are concerned that you might upset a learner. It should always be honest and you might have to foster your learners' resilience to manage any negative points.

Making decisions

Decisions should be in accordance with the requirements of what has been assessed, i.e. the qualification specification. You must always remain *objective*, i.e. by making a decision based on your learner's competence towards the required criteria. You should not be *subjective*, i.e. by making a decision based on your own opinions or other factors such as your learner's personality. However, some qualifications or job roles might require the learner to demonstrate the correct attitude, behaviours and manners. This could be where it's part of their job role or an apprenticeships programme. Be careful not to compare your learner's performance to your own expectations. If they have met the criteria then they have achieved what they were meant to. If they have achieved more, you can comment on this in a positive way and encourage them to continue to excel.

When making a decision, you will need to base it on everything you have assessed. If you are observing a learner's skills, you could follow this up by asking questions to check their knowledge and understanding. If your learner did not perform according to the requirements or answered questions incorrectly, they might be able to have another attempt (if it's acceptable). It could be that your learner does know the correct response but your question was vague or ambiguous. You might need to rephrase your instructions or questions, or enable your learner to partake in further training before being reassessed.

When making a decision, you will need to ensure that all assessed work is VARCS:

- **V**alid – the work is relevant to what has been assessed and is at the right level.
- **A**uthentic – the work has been produced solely by the learner.
- **R**eliable – the work is consistent over time.
- **C**urrent – the work is still relevant at the time of assessment.
- **S**ufficient – the work covers all of the requirements at the time.

If the above are not ensured, you might make an incorrect judgement and a learner might appeal against your decision.

Example

Meena wanted to follow the VARCS principle when observing her learner, Jo, towards an aspect of the Level 2 Hairdressing qualification. During the observation, Meena was able to see that Jo was performing what was required at the right level (V). As it was only Jo involved with her client, Meena knew what was being done was authentic (A). This particular hairstyle was one Jo had demonstrated before, therefore her work was reliable and consistent over time (R). What Jo demonstrated was current as the activity was performed live (C). When Jo had finished with her client, Meena asked her a few questions to confirm her knowledge and understanding was sufficient to meet the requirements (S).

In this example, Meena ensured all the VARCS aspects had been met by her learner.

When observing your learners, you might notice skills which have been demonstrated that they can use in other situations. It is useful to point out any such transferable skills to help them realise other contexts in which they could use them. You might also see other aspects demonstrated in addition to those planned. If this is the case, make sure you include them in your decision, inform your learner what else they have achieved and update your records accordingly.

If you are assessing work from learners who hand it to you for you to assess later, it would be a good idea to have a system of signing it in and out. Your learner will have put a lot of effort into their work and would like to know that you will take reasonable care with it. When you return their work, you could ask your learner to sign that they have received it. If your learner was to lose their work, you will have your original assessment records to prove that assessment has taken place. If you are assessing work which has been emailed to you or uploaded online for you to access, there will be the facility for you to add electronic comments to it. This will therefore create a record of what was submitted and when, and what comments and feedback were given and when.

Activity

If you are currently assessing, ask a colleague if you can observe an assessment activity they are due to carry out. Look at their assessment plan and the assessment materials they use. Observe how they communicate with their learner and others, how they reach their decisions, provide feedback and complete their records. Shadowing other assessors to see how they carry out their role may help you develop your own assessment practices, decision-making and feedback skills.

Ensuring you choose the right method of assessment to carry out with your learners, and making a decision which is ethical, safe and fair will help support your learners towards their achievement.

Providing feedback

Providing feedback to your learners will help them understand how they are progressing and what they have achieved so far. Using a feedback strategy can help ensure you give it for a reason and with a purpose. This should be in a constructive and developmental way to have an impact. Figure 10.2 shows an example feedback strategy.

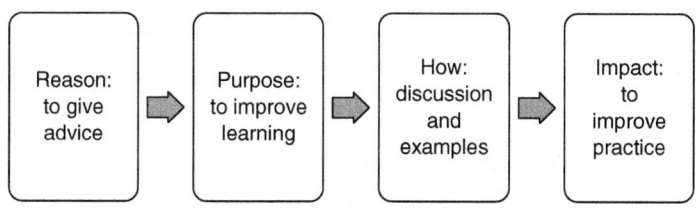

Figure 10.2 Feedback strategy (*Adapted from Hyland, 1998, page 262*)

Example

Aisha noticed that her learner, Vince, kept spelling the word February *as* Febuary. *Her reason for providing feedback was to advise him on how to spell it correctly, with the purpose of improving his learning. She chose to discuss this with him and to show him examples of the correct spelling when included in a sentence (how). The impact would be that Vince could spell the word correctly in future.*

Feedback can help encourage, reassure, boost confidence and motivate learners as well as helping them to learn and develop further. It should aim to improve, and to have an impact upon learning, by identifying any additional requirements and areas for progression.

If you are with your learners, for example, observing an activity, you can give oral feedback immediately. If you are assessing work which has been handed in for marking, you can give written feedback later. You could add ticks to your learner's work to denote something is correct. However, adding notes can help your learner develop further, for example, to point out any errors in spelling, grammar, and/or punctuation. A way of helping your learner to find their own errors, would be to highlight which sentence has an error and ask the learner to see if they can find it themselves. If you don't want to write on their work, you could use sticky notes. If the work is electronic, you could use the comment function to add notes. If you are providing feedback regarding the very first piece of work a learner has submitted, try not to be too harsh. You should want to keep your learner's motivation, but yet remain honest in a supportive way.

When providing feedback, certain key words can help or hinder a learner's progress, as in Table 10.3. Try not to use the words on their own, make sure they are part of a sentence. For example, *'That piece of work was really good and met the standards. However, do check your use of the colon and semi-colon as you sometimes get them the wrong way round'.* Do be careful of giving too much positive feedback, without adding anything developmental, for example, *'your assignment was excellent'.* It doesn't say what was excellent about it or what had been achieved. The learner might become complacent by thinking everything they have done is perfect.

If you are not able to provide feedback in person, you will need to consider that your learner might read or misread your comments and not fully understand them. Try and encourage your learners to get in touch with you if they need to clarify any points regarding your feedback.

Activity

Look at Table 10.3 and see what other words you could add to columns one and two. What words could you use instead of those in column three?

Table 10.3 Examples of key feedback words to use and avoid

When a learner has exceeded the requirements	When a learner has met the requirements	Words to avoid
Brilliant	Achieved	Appalling
Comprehensive	Adequate	Awful
Conscientious	Appropriate	Disgraceful
Creative	Competent	Disappointed
Effective	Consistent	Dreadful
Efficient	Done well	Failed
Engaging	Good attempt	Inadequate
Enthusiastic	Knowledgeable	Inappropriate
Exceeded	Organised	Incompetent
Excellent	Passed	Inconsistent
Exceptional	Prepared	Ineffective
Fantastic	Relevant	Insufficient
Impressive	Satisfactory	Irrelevant
Innovative	Sufficient	Lack of
Insightful	Suitable	Limited
Inspirational	Useful	Not good
Outstanding	Varied	Shocking
Particularly good	Well done	Terrible
Really good		Unclear
Resourceful		Uninspiring
Substantial		Unorganised
Superb		Unsatisfactory
Thorough		Unsuccessful
		Unsuitable
		Vague
		Weak

When providing feedback, whether verbally or in person, try and make sure it is:

- based on facts and not opinions

- clear, genuine and unambiguous

- constructive, developmental and supportive

- detailed regarding what was or wasn't achieved, and what needs improving or developing further

- documented: records must be maintained for audit purposes and proof of progress and achievement

- focused on the activity not the person
- helpful and honest.

The focus of feedback is often likely to be on mistakes rather than strengths. If something constructive or positive is stated first, any developmental or negative comments are more likely to be listened to and acted upon. Starting with a negative point might discourage your learner from listening to anything else that is said. If possible, start with something positive, then state what could be improved upon and finish on a developmental note. This sandwiches the negative aspect between two positive or helpful aspects. However, negative feedback if given skilfully can help your learner if used in the right way. If learning has taken place due to a mistake which has been made by the learner, this can be seen as a positive move.

The advantages of providing feedback are that it:

- can boost your learner's confidence and motivation
- creates opportunities for clarification, discussion and progression
- emphasises progress rather than failure
- enables your learner to appreciate what they need to do to improve or change their practice
- identifies further learning opportunities or actions required
- informs your learner of what they have achieved.

Ongoing constructive feedback which is developmental and has been carefully thought through is an indication of your interest in your learner and of your intention to help them develop and do well in the future. However, don't assume your learner understands everything you have said. You could ask them to repeat some key aspects in their own words to confirm what they have understood.

When providing feedback, try to:

- own your statements by beginning with the word '*I*' rather than '*you*'
- start with something positive, for example, '*I really liked the confident manner in which you delivered your presentation*'
- be specific about what you have seen, for example, '*The way you explained that topic was really interesting due to your knowledge and humour*' or '*I found that the way you explained that topic was rather confusing to me*'
- offer constructive and specific developmental points, for example, '*I would have understood it better if you had broken the subject down into smaller stages*'
- end with something positive or developmental, for example, '*I enjoyed your presentation – you had prepared well and came across as very organised and professional*' or, '*I enjoyed your session; however, issuing a handout summarising the key points would be really helpful to refer to after the session*'.

If you don't have any follow-on points then don't create them just for the sake of it. Conversely, if you do have any negative points or criticism, don't say 'My only negative point is ...' or 'My only criticisms are ...' It's much better to replace these words and say 'Some areas for development could be ...' or 'I'm sure that you will improve once you take into account what we have discussed'.

The role of questioning in feedback

Asking questions when providing feedback can allow your learner to consider their progress and achievements before you tell them. A good way to do this is to ask your learner a question immediately after you have assessed them. For example, 'Carla, how do you feel you have done?' This gives your learner the opportunity to recognise their own mistakes and to learn from them and to reflect on what they could have done differently. You could then build on this throughout the feedback, and discuss what needs to be improved and/or achieved next.

Questioning and feedback should always be adapted to the level of your learners, and be a two-way conversation. You won't help your learners if you are using higher level words or jargon when their level of understanding is lower. You should also be aware of where you give the feedback in case you are interrupted or are in a noisy environment. This might distract you both and some important points might get missed.

Example records for on-the-job and off-the-job feedback are given in Tables 10.4 and 10.5 (on pages 414 and 415) respectively. Your organisation should be able to give you advice as to how much you will need to write and whether this should be in the first or third person.

Record keeping

It is important to keep records of assessment planning, decisions and feedback. This will provide an audit trail of what has taken place, and prove what progress and achievement your learners have made. You will also need to satisfy any company, quality assurance, awarding organisation, funding bodies' or regulatory authorities' audit requirements.

Records will usually need to be kept for a set period, for example, three years. They should be the original records (if hard copies are used), not photocopies or carbon copies. It is fine to give copies to your learners, as it is harder to forge a copy than an original. Unfortunately, there are some learners who might do this; therefore, keeping the originals will ensure your records are authentic.

Keeping full and accurate factual assessment records is also necessary in case one of your learners appeals against an assessment decision you have made. If this happens, don't take it personally – they will be appealing against your decision not you as a person. You will also need to make records available to your internal quality assurer if necessary and any other authorised persons who have an interest in your learner's progress and achievement.

If assessment decisions count towards the achievement of a qualification, it is crucial to keep your feedback records, along with any action identified for each learner.

Table 10.4 Example feedback record (on-the-job)

Feedback record

Learner: Irene Jones

Qualification/unit: Level 1 Certificate in Hospitality & Catering (Unit 101)

Assessor: Jenny Smith

Date: 6 February

Aspects assessed	Feedback	Action required	Target date
Unit 101.3 Be able to help maintain a hygienic, safe and secure workplace	I observed Irene on 6 February at the County Leisure Centre to assess her competence in the workplace. I used the awarding organisation's documents to ensure all the requirements were met. I added additional comments to these regarding what I saw on the day. Irene successfully performed all the requirements of unit 101.3 and I am pleased to inform her she has passed. Irene obtained a witness testimony from her supervisor, which confirmed she had successfully covered the same criteria over a period of time.	Irene and I will meet on 6 April to complete an assessment plan for unit 102 and review her progress to date. In the meantime, Irene will read the supporting handouts for unit 102 and put theory into practice at the Leisure Centre.	6 April
Unit 101.4. Know how to maintain a hygienic, safe and secure workplace	I asked oral questions to check Irene's knowledge and I have digitally recorded her responses as evidence of achievement. I held a discussion with Irene based on the knowledge requirements, which was also recorded. This has been saved on the hard drive under Irene's name and today's date. All the questions were answered correctly and met the requirements of 101.4.		
Achievements	**Learning outcomes**	**Assessment criteria**	
Unit 101	101.3 Be able to help maintain a hygienic, safe and secure workplace. 101.4 Know how to maintain a hygienic, safe and secure workplace. (101.1 and 101.2 have previously been achieved)	3.1 – 3.5 4.1 – 4.19	

Table 10.5 Example feedback record (off-the-job)

Feedback and action record

Learner: Marcia Indira
Qualification/unit: Level 2 Business, Administration and Finance

Assessor: Abbi Cross
Date: 30 October

Aspects assessed	Feedback	Action required	Target date
2.1 – Generate a range of ideas for a business enterprise	I like the ideas you have generated for your business; you have come up with some very original concepts. I feel your idea could become a real business opportunity. Do be careful when you are word processing your work as you have a few spelling errors. For example, where for were and been for being. If you were putting a proposal together to talk to investors you must ensure it is correct and professional. You could consider looking at various enterprise websites to help with your idea.	No action required	
2.2 – Compare the viability of the business enterprise ideas	You have looked at the viability of your business by researching what is available elsewhere, and compared your ideas to them. I like the way you have presented your response using graphs and tables. You do seem to have a really good idea that would benefit a lot of people. I would recommend in future you use some colours rather than just black and white to make your points stand out.	No action required	
2.3 – Select and develop a business idea	You selected your idea as proposed in 2.1 and have now followed your ideas through to the development of a business plan. Your plan is very professional looking and has taken into consideration everything we have discussed during the sessions. I enjoyed watching your presentation to your peers regarding your idea and how it will progress to the investment stage. Peer feedback was positive and your own self-evaluation was fair. You have now successfully achieved learning outcome 2 – well done! We will create a separate action plan for the next learning outcome.	No action required	
Achievements	**Learning outcomes**	**Assessment criteria**	
Unit 1: Business Enterprise	2: Be able to develop a business enterprise idea	2.1 Generate a range of ideas for a business enterprise 2.2 Compare the viability of the business enterprise ideas 2.3 Select and develop a business idea	

Records must always be kept safe and secure; your car boot or a shelf at home is not a good idea, nor is a corner of the staffroom or in an open-plan office. Awarding organisations expect records to be securely managed, be they electronic or paper based. All records should comply with your organisation's requirements, such as confidentially, and any relevant legislation.

A useful record to track overall learner achievement is known as an assessment tracking sheet. Table 10.6 is an example of a tracking sheet for four learners, each working towards five units of a qualification. It can be used as an *at a glance* method of seeing the achievement of all learners and be manual or electronic.

Table 10.6 Example assessment tracking sheet

Assessment tracking sheet					
Assessor: Jenny Smith					
Qualification: Level 1 Certificate in Hospitality & Catering					
Learner name and registration number	Aspects assessed				
	101	**102**	**103**	**104**	**105**
Chang, Hanadi 4524UDBQ	11 June Pass		8 March Pass	10 May Refer 15 May Pass	
Hamed, Aamir 1674UEME		7 May Pass			
Jones, Irene 1234ABCD	6 Feb Pass				
Wilson, Pete 7985IENF	15 Jan Pass	4 Feb Pass			

What are the requirements at your organisation for record keeping? Are there any other requirements, for example, from an awarding organisation or an external body? What records will you use, how will you store them and who will need access to them and why?

Self-assessment checklist

Do I know about the following?

If not, re-read this chapter, or research the texts and websites listed at the end.

☐ The difference between assessment for learning and assessment of learning

☐ The assessment cycle

☐ The difference between formative and summative assessment

☐ The difference between formal and informal assessment

☐ What to consider when planning for assessment

☐ Assessment planning on the job and off-the-job

☐ What the acronyms SMART and VARCS mean

☐ Different assessment types and methods

☐ The difference between peer and self-assessment

☐ Different questioning techniques

☐ How to minimise risks

☐ How to make decisions, provide feedback and maintain records

Summary

This chapter has explored what assessment is and how you can use different types and methods with learners.

You should now be able to assess learners, make decisions and provide feedback. You should also know about how to use various questioning skills, along with the risks that might be involved within the assessment process.

You might like to carry out further research by accessing the books and websites listed at the end of this chapter, particularly if you are working towards a higher level teaching qualification.

This chapter has covered the following topics:

- The purpose of assessment

- Assessment both on- and off-the-job

- Assessment types and methods

- Questioning techniques

- Minimising risks

- Making decisions and providing feedback

References and further information

Gravells, A. (2016) *Principles and Practices of Assessment*. London: Learning Matters SAGE.

Hyland, F. (1998) The Impact of Teacher Written Feedback on Individual Writers. *Journal of Second Language Writing*, 7(3): 255–86

Koc, S. and Xiongyi, Liu (2015) *Assessment in Online and Blended Learning Environments*, Charlotte, USA: Information Age Publishing.

Ofqual (2009) *Authenticity – A Guide for Teachers*. Coventry: Ofqual.

Ollin, R. and Tucker, J. (2016) *The Vocational Assessor Handbook* (6th edition). London: Kogan Page.

Read, H. (2016) *The Best Assessor's Guide*. Bideford: Read On Publications Ltd .

To, J. (2016) 'This is not what I need': Conflicting assessment feedback beliefs in a post-secondary institution in Hong Kong. *Research in Post-Compulsory Education,* 21 (4).

Tummons, J. (2011) *Assessing Learning in the Lifelong Learning Sector*. Exeter: Learning Matters.

Wilson, L. (2012) *Practical Teaching: A Guide to Assessment and Quality Assurance*. Andover: Cengage Learning.

Websites

Apprenticeship assessment plans – https://tinyurl.com/kem7f5s

Apprenticeship standards – https://tinyurl.com/ojtkqs4

Assessment in education – www.tandfonline.com/toc/caie20/24/1

Assessor resources – www.anngravells.com/resources/assessment123

Institute for Apprenticeships – www.gov.uk/government/organisations/institute-for-apprenticeships

Peer and self-assessment – www.nclrc.org/essentials/assessing/peereval.htm

Plagiarism – www.plagiarism.org and www.plagiarismadvice.org

Reading list for assessors – www.anngravells.com/reading-lists/assessment

11

Quality assurance

Introduction

Quality assurance is about having systems in place to ensure the products and services your learners access are the best they can be. The *product* is the programme, qualification or set of standards that the learner is working towards. The *service* is everything which underpins the product and supports the learner. If quality assurance does not take place, there could be risks to the accuracy, consistency and fairness of training and assessment practice. Quality assurance should be a continual process with the aim of maintaining and improving the products and services offered.

This chapter will explore the various aspects of internal and external quality assurance along with the risks involved. What to do in the event of an appeal is covered, as is how to standardise practice with others to ensure a consistent and fair service.

This chapter will cover the following topics:

- Quality assurance in further education and skills contexts
- Internal quality assurance
- External quality assurance
- Minimising risks
- Appeals, complaints and disputes
- Standardisation of practice

Quality assurance in further education and skills contexts

Quality *assurance* can be defined as a system which guarantees the quality of the products or services offered. Within further education and skills contexts, the product is that which a learner is hoping to achieve (i.e. a qualification or to maintain standards of working practices). The service is the support the learner or employee receives from their supervisor, teacher, trainer, assessor and others. The quality assurance process should seek to avoid problems, and stabilise and improve the products and services offered to learners. It can be thought of as a *proactive* system to resolve any issues as they occur. This is in contrast to quality *control* which seeks to find problems and is usually *reactive* after the event. A good quality system will have structures in place to enable situations to be dealt with as they happen, rather than afterwards when it might be too late. Quality *improvement* can be achieved by monitoring and evaluating the quality systems in place. *Internal* quality assurance (IQA) will form part of the overall quality assurance system and mainly relates to teaching, learning and assessment processes and practice.

Activity

Discuss with a colleague or a friend the differences between quality assurance, quality control and quality improvement. You might like to research the terms further to see how they might impact upon your role.

An education or training organisation might follow a *quality cycle*, as in Figure 11.1, to ensure all aspects of their provision are planned, delivered, assessed and evaluated. Following the aspects in the quality cycle could ensure the best provision of all the products and services offered. An organisation's quality cycle might involve the aspects as in Figure 11.1, which could be overseen by a quality manager. Not all of these aspects might occur in the organisation you are working in, but it would be worth finding out which do. If you are involved with quality in your organisation, you will need to know what your role will include, for example:

- arranging standardisation activities
- dealing with appeals, complaints and disputes
- liaising with external inspectors
- holding team meetings and producing an agenda and minutes
- managing and implementing surveys and analysing the responses
- observing colleagues
- preparing for external quality assurance (EQA) visits and following up action points
- producing management reports
- supporting and developing colleagues.

Your role might also include ascertaining and providing information for the organisation's self-assessment report (SAR) and quality improvement plan (QIP) if they have them. These documents might be called something different depending upon where you work.

If carried out correctly, the quality process should safeguard the credibility of the qualification, programmes or standards offered. It's much more difficult to audit poor quality out of a system, than to build good quality in.

Quality assurance is not just a means to an end or something that has to be done because someone says so. There should be a purpose for each aspect which will ensure everything runs smoothly. Aspects should be evaluated regularly to enable changes and/or improvements to take place as necessary.

Example

A training organisation monitors the practice of their teachers and assessors by observing them during sessions with their learners. As the observations take place regularly, any issues can be identified and resolved straight away. If the observations did not take place, problems might not be identified. Learners might therefore be dissatisfied and the organisation's high standards would not be maintained.

A quality cycle will often cover activities which are in addition to, or which complement those which might occur as a part of the *internal quality assurance* process (covered later in this chapter). However, all aspects of the quality cycle are relevant to the way an organisation which offers education and training should operate. For example, if a budget was not agreed prior to a programme commencing, money could run out part way through and the training would be postponed or cancelled.

Extension activity

Look at the quality cycle in Figure 11.1 (on page 422). Which aspects are carried out in your organisation and why? What other aspects might take place and why? What will your role be regarding quality assurance and who will you need to liaise with?

Internal quality assurance

If there is no external formal examination taken by learners, there has to be a system of monitoring the performance of trainers and assessors and the experiences of the learners. If not, assessors might make incorrect judgements or pass a learner who hasn't met the requirements, perhaps because they were biased towards them or they had made a mistake.

Internal quality assurance (IQA) relates to the monitoring of all the teaching, learning and assessment activities which learners, trainees or employees will undertake. It also includes

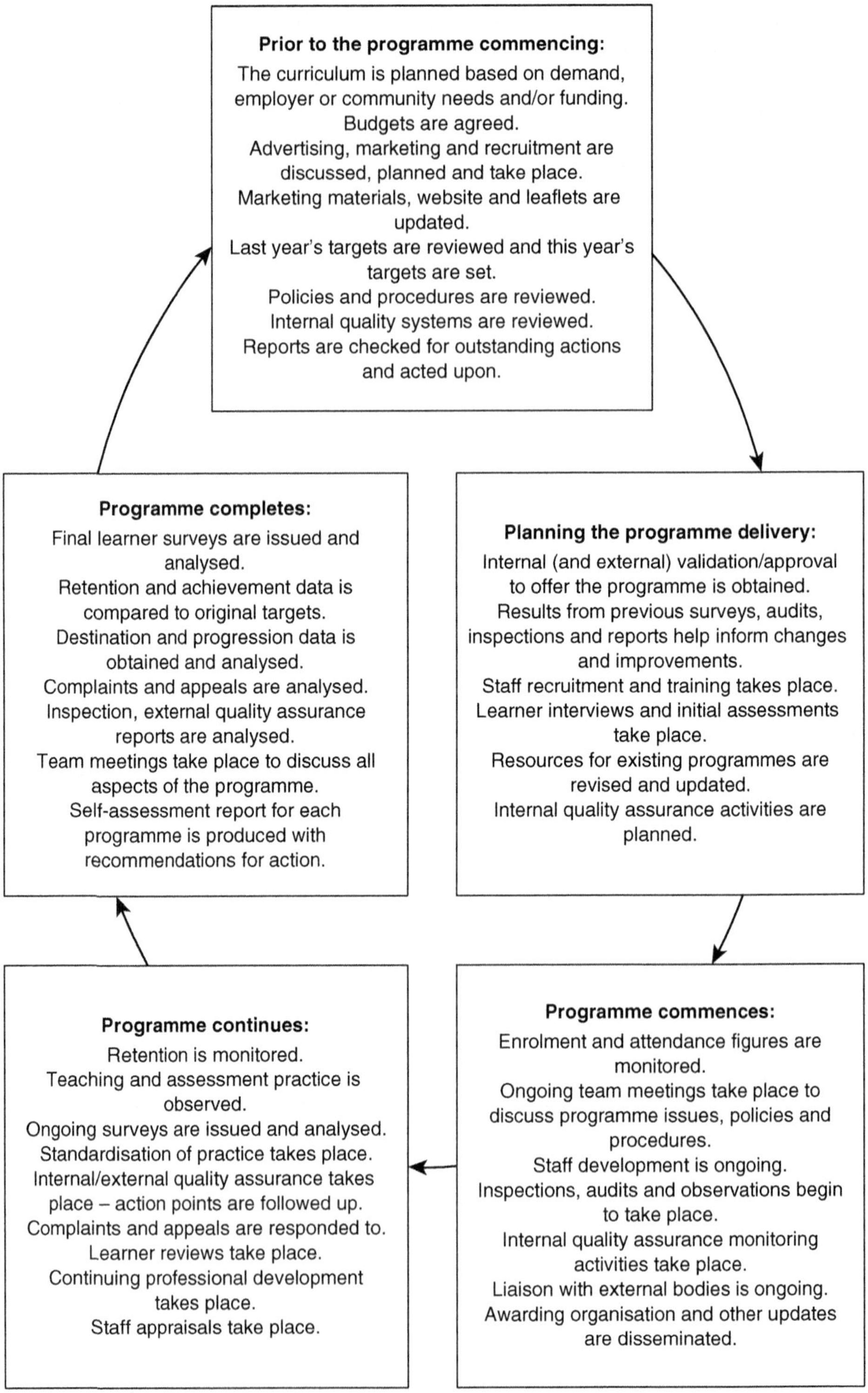

Prior to the programme commencing:
The curriculum is planned based on demand, employer or community needs and/or funding.
Budgets are agreed.
Advertising, marketing and recruitment are discussed, planned and take place.
Marketing materials, website and leaflets are updated.
Last year's targets are reviewed and this year's targets are set.
Policies and procedures are reviewed.
Internal quality systems are reviewed.
Reports are checked for outstanding actions and acted upon.

Programme completes:
Final learner surveys are issued and analysed.
Retention and achievement data is compared to original targets.
Destination and progression data is obtained and analysed.
Complaints and appeals are analysed.
Inspection, external quality assurance reports are analysed.
Team meetings take place to discuss all aspects of the programme.
Self-assessment report for each programme is produced with recommendations for action.

Planning the programme delivery:
Internal (and external) validation/approval to offer the programme is obtained.
Results from previous surveys, audits, inspections and reports help inform changes and improvements.
Staff recruitment and training takes place.
Learner interviews and initial assessments take place.
Resources for existing programmes are revised and updated.
Internal quality assurance activities are planned.

Programme continues:
Retention is monitored.
Teaching and assessment practice is observed.
Ongoing surveys are issued and analysed.
Standardisation of practice takes place.
Internal/external quality assurance takes place – action points are followed up.
Complaints and appeals are responded to.
Learner reviews take place.
Continuing professional development takes place.
Staff appraisals take place.

Programme commences:
Enrolment and attendance figures are monitored.
Ongoing team meetings take place to discuss programme issues, policies and procedures.
Staff development is ongoing.
Inspections, audits and observations begin to take place.
Internal quality assurance monitoring activities take place.
Liaison with external bodies is ongoing.
Awarding organisation and other updates are disseminated.

Figure II.I An example of an organisation's quality cycle

aspects such as having relevant and up-to-date policies and procedures. Monitoring could form part of an organisation's quality cycle, as in Figure 11.1. If the organisation offers several programmes, there might be many staff carrying out the IQA role for the different subjects offered. For example, hairdressing, retail and customer service. If so, they will need to liaise with each other to standardise their practice and ensure a consistent service is given to learners and assessors.

IQA monitoring activities will enable you to find out if your trainers and assessors are performing their roles as they should, and to give them advice and support as necessary. Your role might be to monitor the whole process from when a learner commences to when they finish, i.e. the full learner journey. IQA activities can also take place prior to the learner commencing, i.e. by monitoring the application and interview process, to after they have left, i.e. following up on progression opportunities.

Internal quality assurance is not something that is added on to the end of a qualification or a programme of learning. It should be carried out on an ongoing basis with a view to making improvements, or keeping the status quo if everything is satisfactory. Records must be maintained of all monitoring activities to prove they actually took place and to facilitate improvements as necessary.

There are other terms used for internal quality assurance which you might come across. For example, internal *verification* and internal *moderation*. Internal *verification* can be considered a lesser version of IQA and is usually for monitoring the assessment of vocational subjects. The process will seek to sample the work of assessors over time, but not sample all aspects associated with the full learner journey. If there is a problem with the sample, the assessor will need to revisit it with their learners.

Internal *moderation* seeks to sample a proportion of assessed work for a particular aspect and is usually for checking non-vocational subjects. If there are problems with the sample, then the assessor will need to revisit the problem area with every learner, including those outside of the original sample. Internal moderation is sometimes referred to as double marking or re-assessment as it confirms the original assessment decisions were accurate or not.

Verification and moderation tend to be *reactive* after an event, whereas IQA aims to be *proactive* throughout the learner journey. You will need to find out if any aspect of your role will involve verification and/or moderation or if it is based on the IQA process.

Often, internal quality assurers are also experienced trainers and assessors in the subject area they are quality assuring. For example, if the subject area is motor vehicle maintenance, they should not be internally quality assuring other subjects they are not experienced in such as horticulture. The IQA process might be the same for each subject, but the internal quality assurer must be fully familiar with what is being assessed to make a valid and reliable decision. Valid means you are doing what you should, and reliable means you would get similar results each time you did it.

If you are quality assuring an accredited qualification, you will need to read the *assessment strategy* which should be part of the qualification specification. This will state whether you must also be a qualified trainer and/or assessor in the same subject that you will internally quality assure. It will also state if assessors and IQAs need relevant experience and/or qualifications in the particular subject the learners are working towards. You should also be fully familiar with the content in the qualification specification, i.e. what is to be delivered and assessed, as well as any relevant requirements, regulations and standards.

The internal quality assurance cycle

Depending upon the subject to be quality assured, an IQA cycle will usually be followed as in Figure 11.2. This example relates to the monitoring of the teaching, learning and assessment process. The results and findings from all monitoring activities should be discussed with relevant staff and improvements planned and carried out as necessary.

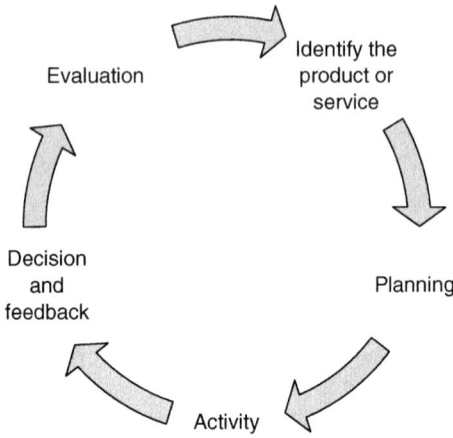

Figure 11.2 Internal quality assurance (IQA) cycle

The IQA cycle can involve the following aspects:

- **Identify the product or service** – ascertain what is to be taught, assessed and internally quality assured and why. For example, are learners working towards a qualification or a programme of learning, or are staff being observed performing their job roles? The criteria will need to be clear, i.e. units from a qualification (product) or the support the learner receives (service). Learners should be allocated to assessors in a fair way, perhaps according to their location or workload.

- **Planning** – devise a sample plan to arrange what will be monitored, from whom and when. Plan the dates to observe trainer and assessor performance, hold team meetings and standardisation activities. Information will need to be obtained from assessors to assist the planning process, and risks taken into account such as assessor knowledge, qualifications and experience.

- **Activity** – carry out the IQA activities such as sampling learners' work, talking to learners, staff, supervisors and witnesses, observing trainer and assessor performance, sampling assessment records and decisions and preparing for EQA visits. Activities also include holding meetings and standardisation events, supporting and training relevant staff and communicating with others involved in the assessment and IQA process.

- **Decision and feedback** – make a judgement as to whether the trainer or assessor has performed satisfactorily and made valid and reliable decisions. Provide developmental feedback as to what was good or what could be improved. Agree action points if necessary and follow them up.

- **Evaluation** – carry out a review of the assessment and IQA process to determine what could be improved or done differently. Agree action plans if necessary; implement and follow up. Follow any action plans from external quality assurers or inspectors. Write self-assessment reports as necessary to link in with the quality cycle.

Throughout the cycle, standardisation of practice between assessors, and internal quality assurers should take place; this will help ensure the consistency and fairness of all decisions. Feedback should also be obtained from learners and others involved in the assessment process. Records must be maintained of all activities for audit requirements.

Activity

Look at the previous bulleted list following Figure 11.2. Describe how each aspect of the cycle will impact upon your role as an IQA. Is there anything you are unsure of? If so, talk to a colleague or a friend to try and find out about it.

As an internal quality assurer only *samples* various activities, there is the possibility that some aspects might be missed. Imagine this taking place in a bakery; the quality assurer would not sample every item by tasting each one made. They would only taste a sample from each baker, otherwise there would be nothing left to sell. This means there are often risks involved with sampling (covered later in this chapter). These should be considered when planning what will be internally quality assured, when and how. For example, if an assessor is new to their role, their work should be sampled more.

Roles and responsibilities of an internal quality assurer

Your main role will be to carry out the IQA process according to what is being assessed. For example, the qualification, programme of learning, work tasks, job specification or standards the learners are working towards. You will also need to maintain full and accurate records and follow relevant regulations and guidelines. Your own roles and responsibilities may or may not include those in the IQA cycle as in Figure 11.2. There might be a quality assurance manager in your organisation who will be responsible for some of the aspects. You will therefore need to know:

- what you are going to internally quality assure

- who you will monitor and why

- when and where the monitoring activities will take place

- how you will go about monitoring them and maintaining relevant records.

If you are currently quality assuring, you will probably know this already, if you are new, you will need to find this out.

Activity

If you are currently carrying out the IQA role, complete numbers 1 and 2 below, if not, just do number 1.

1   *Obtain a copy of what is to be quality assured. For example, the qualification specification, programme of learning, work tasks or job specification. Have a look at the requirements for trainers, assessors and IQAs regarding their qualifications and experience. Read through the content which will be assessed to ensure you are fully familiar with it.*

2   *Find out who the staff are that you will be responsible for as an IQA and obtain their contact details. If you are quality assuring an accredited or an endorsed qualification, you will need to make sure the awarding organisation is kept up to date with any changes to staffing and resource details.*

The type of employment contract you have and where you are based may have an influence on how often you see your assessors and the types of monitoring activities you will perform. This will differ if you are full time, part time, freelance or self-employed, and if you are based in the same location as your assessors or not. Your staff might have different types of contracts too and perhaps be working for more than one organisation. It's therefore important to find this out to ensure that they are following the requirements of your organisation. Sometimes, if staff work for more than one organisation the procedures and documents used will differ, and the wrong ones might be used by accident. It's also possible that you might have to perform some tasks such as administration, in your own time.

The internal quality assurer role might include the following (in alphabetical order):

- advising, observing, supporting and providing developmental feedback to assessors

- creating an IQA policy, rationale and strategy

- ensuring staff interpret, understand and consistently apply the relevant requirements, regulations and standards

- evaluating the programme, taking into consideration feedback from learners, staff and others

- facilitating the standardisation of practice

- identifying issues and trends, for example, if several learners misinterpret the same topic

- interviewing learners, witnesses and other relevant staff

- keeping up to date with changes and developments regarding what is being taught and assessed

- monitoring the full learner journey

- sampling assessment records, learners' work and assessor decisions

- taking part in continuing professional development (CPD)

- working towards a relevant IQA qualification or following certain standards.

Activity

Look at the previous bullet list. Are there any other aspects you feel you should carry out as an IQA? If there are other IQA staff for your subject area, ask them what they do and why. Find out if there is a lead IQA and if so, talk to them to make sure you are all aware of who will do what and when.

Internal quality assurers are often supervisors or managers and are naturally responsible for staff, systems and procedures. However, some are still working as trainers and assessors and performing more than one role. That's absolutely fine as long as they don't IQA their own assessment decisions, as that would be a conflict of interest. Some small teams, i.e. one assessor and one internal quality assurer can swap roles and IQA each other's assessment decisions. Again, it's not a problem unless it's towards an accredited qualification and the awarding organisation deems it is. It could be considered a good way of standardising practice as they will be monitoring each other regularly to ensure consistency.

Example

Angela is the IQA as well as the assessor for a qualification in fabrication and welding. There are 40 learners and one other assessor/IQA: Aleksy. Angela and Aleksy each have a case load of 20 learners and IQA each other's work. They are therefore not quality assuring their own assessment decisions. This has been agreed with the awarding organisation and also helps to standardise their practice as they each see what the other is doing.

The role of technology in internal quality assurance

Information and communication technology (ICT) can be used to support and enhance the IQA process. This is particularly useful when the IQA is located in a different area from their assessors. A virtual learning environment (VLE), electronic portfolio (e-portfolio) or cloud-based system could be used by learners and assessors to upload completed work and records to. This would enable the IQA to sample various aspects remotely at a time to suit. Reports could then be completed electronically, uploaded to the system or emailed as required.

Communication through email or web-based forums can simplify the contact process between the internal quality assurer and their team. There will be times when people are not available at the same time, either for a meeting or a telephone call. Using ICT enables messages to be left which can be responded to when convenient. However, this method of communication does rely on people accessing their messages on a regular basis.

Meetings and standardisation activities could also take place remotely, for example, through video/tele conferencing or webinars. Everyone does not need to be in the same room at the same time for activities to be effective. Materials could be produced and circulated electronically prior to the remote meeting and then discussed when everyone is accessible.

Never assume that staff are familiar with how to use the various aspects of ICT. Training sessions may need to be carried out and resources might need to be updated to support their use.

Activity

Consider what aspects of the IQA role could be carried out using technology. Make a list of the equipment, devices, programs and mobile applications which would be needed. How could you make sure everyone had access to them and knew how to use them? It could be that you would expect your staff to use their own devices if resources are not available.

Some examples of using ICT (with the permission of those involved) include (in alphabetical order):

- making digital recordings or videos of role-play activities or actual case studies. For example, a film of an assessor making a decision and giving developmental feedback to a learner. All assessors could view the recording remotely to comment on strengths and limitations

- making visual recordings of how to complete documents and reports. If an assessor is unsure how to complete a document they could access a video to see an example

- observing live assessment activities via an online visual communication program such as Skype

- recording verbal information, making podcasts or visual recordings of conversations, meetings and/or information regarding updates and changes, to be viewed later by team members

- using a mobile phone/smartphone, tablet or digital camera to record an assessor activity. This is useful if the internal quality assurer cannot be present at the time – the assessor could make a recording and forward it on to them or upload it to an appropriate platform for later access by the IQA

- using blogs, chat rooms, social networking sites, video conferencing, webinars and discussion forums to help staff communicate with each other

- using cloud-based or online systems to store, access and revise various documents and resources

- using emails with integrated video facilities to send visual messages

- using web conferencing to talk to assessors, learners and witnesses if they are quite a distance away

- using webinars to view presentations or review software packages with team members, enabling them to remain in their own locations rather than travel to a central location.

Example

Ling, the IQA, regularly sends emails to communicate with her assessors. As she has a computer with a webcam, she thought she would try something different and use a video email. She accessed a free program at www.mailvu.com. This enabled her to make a quick recording and email it to her assessors. They said her visual message had more impact than just reading text.

ICT can be a useful tool for learning, assessment and quality assurance activities. Your assessors will need to know how technology can assist when differentiating assessment activities to meet a particular learner's requirements. For example, using a screen reader or text enlargement software for a learner who is partially sighted. *Assistive or adaptive technology* is the term used to denote devices and their use for people with disabilities or difficulties. It can lead to greater independence by providing enhancements to or changing the methods of use. This should enable learners to accomplish tasks they might not have been able to do without it. You might therefore need to find out if any of your assessors need relevant training to support their learners. Alternatively, your assessors might wish to use assistive or adaptive technology for their own role (covered in Chapter 8).

There should be a code of practice for the use of ICT for both staff and learners to follow. You will need to locate and read this and ensure your assessors are familiar with it too. For example, if assessors are using online applications for assessment purposes, they should not be accessing their personal social media accounts at the same time. Following the code will help ensure that the use of technology is reasonable and safe.

Examples of completed IQA reports which an IQA might use, along with an IQA rationale and strategy are included in Gravells A (2016) *Principles and Practices of Quality Assurance.*

External quality assurance

External quality assurance (EQA) relates to the monitoring of training, assessment and IQA processes within a centre which has been approved by an awarding organisation (AO) to deliver and assess their qualifications. Any organisation can become an approved centre, for example, colleges, charities, public, private and voluntary organisations, businesses or prisons, providing they meet the qualification and the AOs requirements. An AO will need to follow the Ofqual (2015) General Conditions of Recognition (in England) to ensure centres are operating correctly.

Some training providers might offer in-house programmes of learning to their staff and not be an approved centre with an AO. They might therefore appoint a person to act like an EQA to monitor the assessment and IQA activities taking place, for example, a large organisation offering training programmes which has several sites in different locations. However, the EQA role is not just about monitoring, it's also about supporting the centre staff, and giving advice and guidance to help them get things right. At some point, you might have contact with an EQA, perhaps during their visit, via a remote verification, on the telephone or by email. If you have any questions, don't wait until the next planned visit but keep in touch in the interim period. The EQA will need to be notified of any staffing or resource changes when they occur.

Your learners, when they successfully complete a qualification, will receive a certificate with the awarding organisation's name on, as well as the centre's name. Therefore, the EQA must ensure everything is in order, or their reputation as well as the centre's could be brought into disrepute.

External quality assurance must take place on behalf of an awarding organisation to ensure the learners who have been registered with them have received a quality service. It also seeks to ensure that training, assessment and internal quality assurance have been conducted in a consistent, safe and fair manner.

- **Consistent:** all staff are using similar assessment methods and making similar decisions across all learners. All learners have an equal chance of receiving an accurate assessment decision.

- **Safe:** the methods used to assess and internally quality assure are ethical, there is little chance of plagiarism by learners, the work can be confirmed as authentic, confidentially was taken into account, learning was not compromised, nor was the learner's experience or potential to achieve. (Safe in this context does not relate to health and safety but to the robustness and reliability of the assessment and IQA methods used.)

- **Fair:** the methods used are appropriate to all learners at the required level, taking into account any particular learner needs. Activities are fit for purpose, and planning, decisions and feedback are justifiable and equitable.

There needs to be a system of monitoring the performance and decisions of staff within a centre. If not, they might make incorrect judgements, or pass a learner who hasn't met all the requirements, perhaps because they were biased towards them, or have made a mistake.

Example

Jeff had been assessing the Level 3 Work Based Horse Care and Management qualification for a number of years as part of a team of four. The EQA was due to visit shortly and the lead IQA had asked him to help prepare for the visit. This would be good practice for Jeff as he was working towards his IQA qualification. He first checked the last EQA report to make sure all the action points had been met. He then looked at the EQA visit plan to make sure everything that had been asked for would be available. This included obtaining the requested learners' work, copies of minutes of meetings, standardisation records, and the updated appeals procedure. The EQA had also asked to observe a feedback session between the IQA and Jeff, and to visit a learner in their workplace. Jeff was able to arrange all of this without any problems. The subsequent EQA visit went smoothly and no action points were given.

Roles and responsibilities of an external quality assurer

The main role will be to maintain compliance on behalf of the awarding organisation and regulatory authorities. An EQA will complete a report which will identify aspects of good practice, as well as any relevant action and improvement points. Action points must be carried out by an agreed date and relate to qualification and regulatory requirements. If they are not carried out, a sanction can be imposed upon the centre: for example, not allowing them to claim any certificates until the issues are resolved. Improvement points are matters which have been discussed to help a centre improve, but which would not result in a sanction if not met.

The role might include (in alphabetical order):

- advising and supporting centre staff on an ongoing basis (not just during visits)

- communicating with centre staff and the awarding organisation on an ongoing basis

- completing a report of what was sampled, highlighting any action and improvement points, and judging whether the centre has a low, medium or high risk rating (action points are enforceable whereas improvement points are not, risk ratings will be covered later in this chapter)

- ensuring a centre's policies, procedures, systems and resources meet relevant requirements, regulations and standards

- ensuring centre staff interpret, understand and consistently apply the requirements
- ensuring learners are registered with the awarding organisation within the required timescale (learners who are not registered should not be sampled)
- ensuring quality throughout the learner journey within a centre
- ensuring the accuracy and consistency of trainer, assessor and internal quality assurers' practice
- evaluating and approving centres to offer qualifications, releasing certification rights when they are performing satisfactorily (known as direct claims status (DCS)) or recommending the removal of DCS if necessary
- giving guidance to centre staff regarding the qualification criteria, relevant requirements, regulations and standards
- identifying issues and trends, for example, if all assessors are misinterpreting the same aspect or making the same mistakes
- keeping full and accurate confidential records
- monitoring and auditing the full learner journey from commencement to completion, e.g. information, advice and guidance (IAG), recruitment, initial assessment, induction, training, formative and summative assessment, decision-making, feedback, support for progression opportunities
- monitoring risk within a centre, e.g. when new qualifications are introduced or if there is a high staff turnover
- observing training, assessment and IQA practice
- planning what will be monitored and when and communicating this to all concerned within the awarding organisation's timescales
- sampling assessed and internally quality assured learners' work (and records) according to a planned strategy, and making decisions based on facts
- training staff and giving support and advice, for example, an additional visit to a centre if required
- updating own CPD regarding subject knowledge and EQA practice.

It might be that you are an EQA as well as an IQA and/or assessor. This is good practice as it helps maintain your professional development. However, you cannot be the EQA for a centre you work at as this would be a conflict of interest. You must also not ask a centre to do something the way that you would like it done. If a centre is meeting the awarding organisation's requirements, then that should be acceptable.

Preparing for an EQA visit

If you are internally quality assuring an accredited qualification or endorsed programme from an AO, you will be visited by an EQA at some point. How often these visits take place, the duration, and the activities carried out, will depend upon the requirements of the qualification and how active your organisation is. The EQA or a representative from the AO will make contact to arrange a suitable date and time for the visit. There will be timescales for the EQA to follow when contacting you for information and for sending you their visit and sample plan. They will probably have formal documentation which they will send to you which will outline the information they require prior to the visit. This might include:

- a list of trainers, assessors, witnesses, IQAs along with their locations and CPD records

- copies of minutes of meetings and records of standardisation activities

- details of learners, their locations and registration and/or unit completion and certification dates.

The EQA will use this information to plan what they want to see and from whom. They will be able to compare your learners' names and registration/certification dates with those on the AO's database. If any information is different, this will highlight an anomaly for them to check with you.

Activity

If you are currently working as an IQA, find out when the next EQA visit is due for the qualification you are involved with. Find out what your role will be before and during the visit. Make a list of any questions or points that you would like clarifying by the EQA.

Once the EQA has the relevant information to prepare for their visit, they will send you a visit plan. This will reflect what they will want to achieve during their visit and might include:

- looking at assessment, IQA and other supporting documents and records

- meeting the team

- observing assessor and IQA practice

- sampling learners' work and assessment decisions

- talking to learners and witnesses.

The EQA will not always want to see completed learner work. They might request to see learners' work which has been formatively as opposed to summatively assessed, to check ongoing learner progress. They might also ask for assessed work which has been sampled by you as the IQA on an interim rather than a summative basis. They should sample the same unit from different assessors to ensure consistency, and sample across all units, assessors and locations. A variety of assessment methods, evidence and records might also be sampled.

If this is the first visit by the EQA, they may require a lot more information than for a routine visit. However, they should still convey what they need to see in advance. There will be certain things you will need to prepare and you could involve your team members to help you fulfil these. You should refer to any previous EQA reports to ensure all action points have been met (if applicable). If any have not been met you might be given a sanction. This means certification rights could be removed; therefore, you can no longer claim certificates for learners who have successfully completed.

The following checklist, which is in alphabetical order, lists the documents you should have available (if relevant) prior to the EQA visit. Records can be electronic or paper based but they must follow data protection and confidentiality requirements. While your EQA might not wish to look at all of the following, it's useful to be prepared.

Checklist – documents which are useful for an EQA visit

- [ ] *Action plans, assessment plans or individual learning plans (ILPs) for each learner*
- [ ] *Assessment tracking sheet showing all assessors, all learners and dates of achievement*
- [ ] *Assessor and IQA induction records*
- [ ] *Copies of registration and certification details for all learners*
- [ ] *Equal Opportunities/Equality and Diversity policy and monitoring data*
- [ ] *Evidence of completed action points from the previous EQA sample*
- [ ] *Evidence of learner support/particular assessment requirements being met*
- [ ] *Feedback from learners, for example, evaluations and survey results, along with actions taken*
- [ ] *Identification checks and learner authenticity statements confirming the work is their own*
- [ ] *Initial and diagnostic assessment records for each learner*
- [ ] *IQA planning and tracking sheet*
- [ ] *IQA records: interim and summative feedback, observations of assessors, discussions with learners and others such as witnesses*
- [ ] *IQA policy, rationale and strategy*

- ☐ *Learner induction materials*

- ☐ *Learner portfolios (or electronic portfolios) with assessment plans, decisions and feedback records. The EQA will want to know how you store your records securely. Extra portfolios should be available in case the EQA decides to carry out an additional random sample*

- ☐ *Learning support details*

- ☐ *List of assessment sites/locations and work placements*

- ☐ *List of IQAs/assessor names and contact details*

- ☐ *Minutes of assessor/IQA meetings*

- ☐ *Organisation chart*

- ☐ *Overall learners' start dates, registration dates, unit completion dates, end dates, certification dates*

- ☐ *Records of any appeals and complaints*

- ☐ *Records of standardisation activities*

- ☐ *Relevant policies and procedures*

- ☐ *Reviews of learners' progress and/or tutorial records*

- ☐ *Staff CVs, certificates and CPD records*

- ☐ *Training materials, i.e. scheme of work, session plans, resources and a list of equipment used by the learners.*

To help you prepare for the visit, you could refer to the report form that the EQA will use on the day. If you've been visited before, you will be able to look back at the last report. If not, you could ask the EQA if you can see an example report form. You might like to meet with your assessors in advance of the visit, look at a sample of their work and use the report form as a trial activity to see if you meet all the points. You should ensure you have evidence of meeting any action points which were stated on the previous report. If you are asked something by an EQA and you answer 'yes', make sure you have the documentation or electronic records to prove it.

Other aspects to prepare in advance include informing reception staff of the name, date and time of arrival of the EQA and arranging a suitable room for use during the visit. You might also need to communicate with the EQA regarding public transport and/or parking arrangements. All the required documents should be placed in the room (or be accessible) and all requested staff should be available as needed. You should remain professional throughout the visit and be helpful regarding the EQA's requests. If you think you have been asked to do something which you feel is not relevant, you will need to be confident enough to challenge the EQA.

Roisin, the EQA, asked that a particular unit of the qualification be observed three times. Harry, the IQA, knew that only one was needed. He therefore asked Roisin to show him where it said that three observations were needed. When she looked at the qualification specification, she noticed Harry was right in that only one was needed. Had he not challenged her, she might have created an action point in her report when it was not necessary. An EQA can make recommendations for improvement but cannot force you to do something that is not a requirement.

An EQA can only ask you to do what is required by the awarding organisation, the regulators and any relevant guidelines and legislation for your subject. Never be afraid of challenging them and asking them to show you in writing where it says they must do something.

You might find the visit will be quite tiring as you will be asked lots of questions. You might also need to escort the EQA to different locations to meet staff and learners. Conversely, the EQA might want to be left alone when sampling work and records. At the end of the visit, the EQA should talk you through their findings and the content of their report. They should discuss and agree any action and improvement points with you. Action points will be sanctionable if not met, whereas improvement points are just for development. The EQA might leave you with a copy of their report, or it might be sent to you via the AO afterwards. Alternatively, it might be accessible online but you should be informed when and how you can access it.

Examples of completed EQA documents are included in Gravells A (2016) *Principles and Practices of Quality Assurance*.

Extension activity

If you assess or IQA an accredited qualification, ask if you can see the most recent EQA report which your organisation has received. Have a look at the comments which were made and any supporting action or improvement points. Do you need to change anything you are doing as a result? You might like to discuss the content of the report with other assessors or your IQA.

Minimising risks

It's important to monitor and manage possible risks to ensure adequate support can be given to assessors, and that learners are not disadvantaged in any way. Just ask yourself what could possibly go wrong and, if you can think of something, then there is a risk. Whenever possible, it's best to be proactive by managing any risks that might occur throughout the assessment process, rather than being reactive to a situation after the event. You really need to be in regular contact with your assessors to build up a trusting relationship where they feel able to inform you of any concerns they might have. If you are not aware of any situations which might pose a risk to assessment, a situation could become quite serious.

Risks relate to anything which might disadvantage a learner in some way rather than health and safety risks. Being aware of these might enable you to prevent situations occurring.

Activity

What should you look for as an IQA that could develop into a risk if not checked? Discuss your responses with a colleague or a friend and then compare them to the following list.

Possible risks for an IQA to look out for (in alphabetical order):

- a lack of confidence by the assessor to make correct decisions

- a lack of standardisation activities leading to one assessor giving more of an advantage to a learner than another assessor of the same subject

- a learner's lack of confidence, or resistance to be assessed

- action points from external reports not being carried out by the target date

- an assessor not taking into account a learner's particular needs

- an unsuitable environment for assessment to take place

- answers to questions being obtained inappropriately by learners

- assessing written work too quickly and not noticing errors, cheating or plagiarism

- assessor expertise, knowledge and competence not being kept up to date or failure to note that new staff are working towards an assessor qualification. Unqualified staff might need their decisions countersigning. Staff should have appropriate job specifications and development plans, otherwise they won't know what is expected of them to perform their role correctly

- assessors using leading questions to obtain the correct answers they require

- assessors who might be under or over assessing compared to other assessors

- assistive technology for learners with particular needs being used wrongly or used to give too much support

- awarding organisations prescribing assessment methods which might not complement the qualification, a learner's needs or the learning environment

- changes to qualifications, standards, documents, records, policies and procedures: staff need to be kept up to date

- feedback to the learner which is unhelpful or ineffective

- high turnover of staff resulting in inconsistent support to learners

- how quickly (or how slowly) learners complete a particular assessor compared to others

- instructions too complex or too easy for a learner's ability

- insufficient or incorrect action/assessment planning with learners

- lack of resources or time to perform the assessment role correctly

- learners creating a portfolio of evidence which is based on quantity rather than quality, i.e. submitting too much evidence which does not fully meet the requirements (or exceeds the requirements)

- learners plagiarising or copying the work of others or taking it from the internet or textbooks without correctly referencing it

- locations of learners and assessors which might make them inaccessible at times

- marking and grading carried out incorrectly by assessors

- misinterpreting the assessment requirements and/or criteria (by learners and assessors)

- numbers of learners allocated to assessors is too high, leading to rushed assessments

- resources and equipment: lack of accessibility, availability and safe use

- time pressures and targets put upon assessors and learners

- type of qualification or programme being assessed; problem areas or units

- types of evidence provided by learners, e.g. a reliance on too many personal statements or witness testimonies which are not backed up by assessment decisions

- unreliable witness testimonies from the workplace or a lack of support to witnesses

- unsuitable assessment methods, i.e. an observation when questions would suffice

- unsuitable assessment types, i.e. formative being used instead of summative

- unwelcome disruptions and interruptions when assessing, such as noise or telephone calls

- use of (or lack of) appropriate holistic assessments and recognition of prior learning (RPL)

- use of (or lack of) technology and how reliable it is for assessment purposes

- whether bilingual assessments could lead to any issues, or language barriers which might impede communication

- whether evidence and records are stored electronically or are paper based, and are safe and secure, in case they can be accessed by unsuitable people

- whether the learners have been registered with an awarding organisation (if applicable) as assessment decisions might not be valid otherwise.

All these points can impact upon the amount of IQA activities which need to be carried out, with whom and when. You should also consider any risks regarding your own role. If you are also working as an assessor, please see Chapter 10 for relevant assessment risks.

Example

Brayden, the IQA, was monitoring the assessed work of learners for the same aspect of a qualification but from three different assessors. He noticed one assessor, Margie, had accepted something which she shouldn't have. The other two assessors had made the correct decision. When he spoke to Margie, he found out she was not up to date with the recent changes to the qualification. Margie had therefore made an invalid decision. If Brayden had not sampled this aspect, there would have been a risk that the learner could have achieved the qualification when they had not completed everything correctly.

As an IQA, you will need to make sure the practice of all your team members, plus yourself, is current. All judgements by everyone involved must be valid and reliable.

Extension activity

Find out what the procedures are at your organisation regarding assessment and IQA risks. What risks might occur to learners, yourself and others? What can you do to prevent these occurring? What should you do if you experience something which could cause a risk to a learner's progress and achievement?

Appeals, complaints and disputes

An appeal is usually about an assessment decision which a learner would like to be reconsidered. A complaint is likely to be about a situation or a person, and a dispute about a difference of opinion. Learners who appeal or complain should be able to do so without fear of recrimination. Confidentiality should be maintained where possible to ensure an impartial outcome and the learner should feel protected throughout the full process. If anyone does make an appeal or a complaint, this should not affect the way they are treated, and the outcome should not jeopardise their current or future achievements. Any other relevant persons should be informed of all situations which might lead to an appeal, complaint or dispute.

Examples of appeals, complaints and disputes and ways of avoiding them could become part of the staff development process. The findings from all issues can be used as a basis to prevent similar situations occurring in the future. If you are assessing or quality assuring an accredited qualification, the awarding organisation will have advice about what to do. This should be in their qualification specification or available on their website.

What do you think you can do to avoid any appeals, complaints and disputes regarding the subject you are involved with? Is this something you can communicate to your colleagues to ensure a consistent approach? If so, do this and then discuss it at your next team meeting.

Appeals

At some point during the assessment process, a learner may wish to appeal against a decision. Information regarding the appeals policy and procedure could be displayed on your organisation's noticeboards, in a learner handbook or be available via the intranet or VLE. Learners will need to know who they can go to, and that their issue will be followed up within a given timescale. The process will involve various stages and have deadlines, such as seven days to lodge an appeal, seven days for a response, and all stages should be documented. Usually, an appeals process is made up of four stages: assessor; internal quality assurer; manager; external quality assurer (if applicable). The nature of the appeal can be used to inform future practice to hopefully prevent further appeals.

| Example |

Cheng had lodged a formal appeal straight to the IQA, Louise, regarding his assessor's decision for a unit from the Level 2 Customer Service qualification. He felt he should have passed as he had supplied all the required evidence. Louise spoke to the assessor and reviewed Cheng's evidence. It transpired that the assessor was correct in asking for a further piece of evidence. Louise spoke to Cheng and explained that four pieces of evidence were required and he had only submitted three. He accepted Louise's decision and agreed to supply a further piece of evidence. Cheng then retracted his appeal and wished he had followed the correct procedure by speaking to his assessor first.

Some organisations will provide an appeals pro-forma for learners to complete, which ensures all the required details are obtained, or encourages an informal discussion with the assessor first. Statistics should be maintained regarding all appeals and complaints; these will help your organisation when reviewing its policies and procedures, and should be provided to relevant external inspectors if requested.

Having a climate of respect and honesty can lead to issues being dealt with informally rather than procedures having to be followed, which can be upsetting for all parties concerned.

Complaints

A complaint might occur from a learner, for example, if an assessor has lost their work or it has not been returned to them on time. The learner might complain orally to the assessor or IQA first but then put in a formal complaint if they are not satisfied with the response. As with appeals, there should be a policy and procedure for complaints with which you and your learners are familiar.

If you are concerned that a learner might make a complaint against you, talk to your supervisor and keep records of the situation. Take care not to become too informal with your learners or have friendly chats when no one else is around, which could be misinterpreted.

Disputes

A dispute might occur, for example, if you assess a piece of work from a learner and think that they have plagiarised an aspect from another source. You would need to check this very carefully first. It might be that they have used a quote in a piece of academic writing but omitted to reference it. In this case, it would not have been intentional and you can provide feedback to your learner about the importance of referencing. It might be that they need further training in how to do this. There are specialist programs and software which can be used to submit learners' electronic work to. They will scan the work to determine how much of it has occurred elsewhere. However, if your learner has plagiarised something deliberately, you will need to deal with them carefully, otherwise they may start a dispute which could get out of control. You might find it best to discuss your concerns with someone else first, before you confront your learner. Always remain factual and calm, getting angry will not help the situation.

As with appeals and complaints, there should be a policy and procedure for disputes with which you and your learners are familiar.

Extension activity

Locate your organisation's policies and procedures for appeals, complaints and disputes. Read them to make sure you are familiar with the content and what to do if a situation occurs. If you are not working with an accredited qualification, find out what your organisation expects you to do. If your qualification is accredited, find out what relevant information the awarding organisation provides to support you, and how they would get involved if necessary.

Standardisation of practice

Standardisation of practice is a way of ensuring reliability and fairness between all staff who are in contact with learners. This should enable a consistent experience for all learners from the time they commence to the time they achieve or leave. You should standardise your decisions and the way you complete your records with other staff, particularly where more than one is involved in the same subject area. It is also an opportunity to ensure all staff are interpreting the qualification and assessment requirements accurately. Standardisation enables people to work as a team rather than on their own, and to give an equitable service to all learners.

However, assessors need to take into account the individual needs of their learners, and the settings in which assessment takes place. For example, if a learner is being assessed in a health and social care setting with a client, it might be more appropriate to obtain a reflective account or a witness testimony. An observation carried out by an assessor could upset the client in this situation. Therefore, the number of observations or pieces of evidence from different learners for the same aspect of a qualification could differ. Unless there are written requirements as to the type of evidence and number of observations required, assessors can make their own decisions depending upon the situation.

Activity

If you are currently quality assuring, find out when the next standardisation event will take place, along with the activities which will be carried out. Prior to the event, ensure that you are fully familiar with what is going to be standardised. Think of some questions to ask your colleagues, for example, the best way to assess a particular aspect, or how much IQA should take place for each unit or aspect assessed.

Benefits of standardisation

The main benefit is that it gives a consistent experience to all learners no matter who their trainer or assessor is. It's also a good way of maintaining professional development and ensuring compliance and accountability with awarding organisations' and regulatory authorities' requirements.

Other benefits include (in alphabetical order):

- an opportunity to discuss changes and developments
- assessment decisions are fair for all learners
- clearly defined roles and responsibilities of all involved
- compliance with relevant codes of practice and regulations
- confirmation of own practice
- consistency and fairness of judgements and decisions
- empowerment of teachers, trainers, assessors and IQAs
- giving staff the time to meet formally
- maintaining an audit trail of what has been standardised
- meeting quality assurance requirements
- re-assessment to spot errors or incorrect decisions by assessors, or even plagiarism or cheating by learners

- setting action plans for the development of training and assessment activities

- sharing of good practice

- spotting trends or inconsistencies

- succession planning if staff are likely to leave

- upholding the credibility of the delivery and assessment process and practice.

Attending a standardisation event will give you the opportunity to share good practice and to compare your decisions with those of your colleagues. This will ensure you have interpreted the requirements accurately, that the learner evidence is appropriate and that the assessment and IQA records are completed correctly. Even if you don't learn anything new, it will hopefully confirm you are doing things correctly. Please see Table 11.1 (on page 444) for an example standardisation record, which has been completed for work that has been assessed. For the purpose of future-proofing the book, a year has not been added to the date. When completing any documents yourself, you should always add the year, as well as the day and month, to create a full audit trail.

Standardisation events are not team meetings; the latter are to discuss issues relating to the management of the programme such as awarding organisation updates, targets, success rates and learner issues.

Standardisation activities can include (in alphabetical order):

- agreeing the interpretation of qualification requirements (or what is to be taught/assessed)

- collaborating on schemes of work, session plans, course materials and resources

- comparing how documents and records have been completed

- creating assessment activities, materials, assignments, questions and recommended answers

- designing or revising assessment and quality assurance documents

- discussing decisions made by other assessors/IQAs

- discussing the qualification/programme job requirements

- interpreting policies and procedures

- new staff shadowing experienced staff

- peer observations and feedback to ensure consistency of practice

- preparing materials for induction and initial assessments

- role-play activities such as assessment planning; making a decision; giving feedback; dealing with a complaint (and visually recording for later viewing).

It's important to standardise practice to be fair to all learners. For example, if you assess a vocational qualification you might decide to carry out two observations with each of your learners and give them a written test; whereas another assessor might only carry out

Table 11.1 Example standardisation record for assessed work

	Standardisation record for assessed work		
Learner: A Brown	Original assessor: J Smith		
Qualification/unit: Level 2 Customer Service	Standardising assessor: M Singh		
Aspect/s standardised: Unit 101 evidence and assessment records	Date: 16 February		
Checklist	**Yes**	**No**	**Comments/Action required**
Is there an agreed assessment plan with SMART targets?	Y		Your plan had very clear SMART targets with realistic dates for achievement.
Are the assessment methods appropriate and sufficient? Which methods were used?	Y		You could reduce the number of observations in the workplace if you can rely on the witness testimonies. Observation, questioning, products and witness testimonies have been used.
Does the evidence meet ALL the required criteria?	Y		All assessment criteria have been met though the various assessment methods.
Does the evidence meet VARCS?	Y		You have ensured all these points; you also took into consideration an aspect that you hadn't planned to assess, but that naturally occurred during an observation.
Is there a feedback record clearly showing what has been achieved? (Is it adequate and developmental?)	Y		Your feedback is very thorough and confirms your learner's achievements. However, you could be more developmental to guide your learner towards ways of improving her current practice.
Has subsequent action been identified? (if applicable)		N	The feedback record showed what had been achieved and what feedback had been given. However, no further action had been identified. You need to plan which units will be assessed next and set target dates for their achievement.

Checklist	Yes	No	Comments/Action required
Do you agree with the assessment decision?	Y		I agree with the decision you made; however, I do feel you could have reduced the number of workplace observations.
Are all relevant documents signed and dated? (Including countersignatures if applicable)		N	As you are still working towards your assessor award, you need to ensure your decisions have been checked and countersigned by a qualified assessor.
Are original assessment records stored separately from the learner's work?		N	You have given your original to your learner; you need to ensure that you keep the original and give your learner a copy. The original can be kept electronically or be paper based, but must be secure for three years in the assessor office.

General comments:

Although there are a few Ns in the checklist, this does not affect my judgement as I agree with your decision for this learner. You agreed a SMART assessment plan with your learner which was followed through with assessment and feedback. All your records are in place; however, don't forget to keep originals in the office and give your learner a copy. This is part of our organisation policy due to some learners having amended the original in their favour. It's harder to amend a copy as the pen colour is more prominent.

Make sure you set clear targets for future development and assessment opportunities when you provide feedback. It's better to do it at this point while you are with your learner to enable a two-way conversation to take place and to agree suitable target dates.

As you are still working towards your assessor award, you need to ensure your decisions have been checked and countersigned by a qualified assessor. Please do this by the end of the month.

Comments from original assessor in response to the above:

I agree with your feedback, I had forgotten about keeping original records and only giving a photocopy to my learner; I will ensure I do this in future. I wasn't able to get hold of my countersignatory as he was on holiday; I will make sure he reads my records and signs them upon his return. I will then take a copy ready to use as evidence for my assessor award. I realise that I must give more developmental feedback and agree future targets when I am with my learner.

Key: SMART: specific, measurable, achievable, relevant, timebound
           VARCS: valid, authentic, reliable, current, sufficient

one observation and ask a few oral questions. There are times when an individual learner's needs should be taken into account which will lead to a difference in assessment activities. However, all learners should be entitled to the same assessment experience, no matter which assessor they have been allocated.

Example

Avraam was a newly qualified assessor who had just been appointed in his first role. The team of assessors met once a month to discuss the units of the qualification. This ensured they were all interpreting the requirements in the same way and making correct decisions. Avraam attended the next meeting and was given the opportunity to reassess a unit which had already been assessed by someone else. This activity helped him to understand the requirements and to see how the documentation was completed.

Records should always be maintained of standardisation activities and any identified actions, which should be acted upon in the required timescale. An external quality assurer may want to view the records if it's applicable to the qualification.

It's important to keep up to date with any changes regarding qualifications as the content will be revised every few years. Awarding organisations issue regular updates, either electronic or paper based. Once you receive these, you will need to discuss them with your colleagues, perhaps during a team meeting to ensure that you all interpret them the same way.

Using technology for standardisation purposes

Technology can be used for standardisation purposes and is ideal if not all the team members can attend a meeting or an activity at the same time or are located in different buildings. When standardising the decisions assessors have made based on electronic evidence, it's important to be sure the work does belong to the learner, and that the assessor has confirmed the authenticity of it.

Some examples of using technology for standardisation purposes include:

- holding meetings via Skype or videoconferencing facilities to discuss the interpretation of aspects of a programme or qualification
- using online webinars to help standardise delivery and assessment approaches
- creating, updating and sharing documents online, e.g. schemes of work, session plans and course materials
- making visual recordings of how to complete forms and reports. If a staff member is unsure how to fill in a form they could access a video to see an example
- recording standardisation activities and uploading them to an intranet or virtual learning environment (VLE) for viewing/listening to later.

Find out what activities are used for standardisation purposes and the types of records used to document them. Have a look at Table 11.1 to see if it compares to anything you currently use. Consider how you could carry out some standardisation activities using technology, then try them.

Self-assessment checklist

Do I know about the following?

If not, re-read this chapter, or research the texts and websites listed at the end.

☐ The difference between quality assurance, quality control and quality improvement

☐ How aspects of quality assurance will impact on my role

☐ What the internal quality assurance process involves and why

☐ The difference between verification, moderation and quality assurance monitoring

☐ The roles and responsibilities of an IQA

☐ The role of technology in IQA

☐ What the external quality assurance process involves and why

☐ How to prepare for an EQA visit

☐ How to minimise risks

☐ How to deal with appeals, complaints and disputes

☐ How to standardise practice

☐ How to use technology for standardisation purposes

Summary

This chapter has explored how quality assurance could be a continual process to maintain and improve the products and services offered. This should be carried out as proactively as possible, rather than being reactive when it might be too late to rectify something.

You should now be able to carry out quality assurance activities and standardise your practice with others. You should also know how to deal with any appeals, complaints and disputes which may arise, and minimise risks.

You might like to carry out further research by accessing the books and websites listed at the end of this chapter, particularly if you are working towards a higher level teaching qualification.

This chapter has covered the following topics:

- Quality assurance in further education and skills contexts
- Internal quality assurance
- External quality assurance
- Minimising risks
- Appeals, complaints and disputes
- Standardisation of practice

References and further information

Gravells, A. (2016) *Principles and Practices of Quality Assurance*. London: Learning Matters SAGE.

Ofqual (2009) *Authenticity – a Guide for Teachers*. Coventry: Ofqual.

Pontin, K. (2012) *Practical Guide to Quality Assurance*. London: City & Guilds.

Read, H. (2012) *The Best Quality Assurer's Guide*. Bideford: Read On Publications Ltd.

Wilson, L. (2012) *Practical Teaching: A Guide to Assessment and Quality Assurance*. Andover: Cengage Learning.

Wood, J. and Dickinson, J. (2011) *Quality Assurance and Evaluation in the Lifelong Learning Sector*. Exeter: Learning Matters.

Websites

IQA resources – www.anngravells.com/resources/iqa12

Ofqual General Conditions of Recognition (2015) – http://tinyurl.com/qfg3pum

Ofsted inspection reports – https://tinyurl.com/3o7xgho

Plagiarism – www.plagiarism.org

Reading list for quality assurers – www.anngravells.com/reading-lists/quality

Skype – www.skype.com

12

Evaluating and improving practice

Introduction

Evaluation is about measuring the effectiveness of something, for example, the way you teach and assess. To help you evaluate your practice you can obtain data and statistics as well as feedback from learners and others. When analysed, this information can be used to help you improve your own practice and the experiences of your learners.

This chapter will explore how to obtain information and feedback, and how to reflect on your practice. How to keep up to date with your skills and knowledge is also covered.

This chapter will cover the following topics:

- Evaluation in further education and skills contexts
- Obtaining data and gaining feedback
- Self-evaluation
- Reflective practice
- Theories of reflective practice
- Continuing professional development

Evaluation in further education and skills contexts

Further education and skills contexts include a wide variety of learner age ranges, contexts and environments. For example, 14–16 year olds in a school, 16–19 year olds in a college or training environment, right up to adults of any age in the workplace, a prison or other type of environment. Whichever type of programme or qualification you deliver and/or assess, short or long term, no matter when or where, it is important to evaluate everything you have been involved with. This is to help you make improvements for yourself, and your current and your future learners.

Evaluation is not another term for assessment; evaluation is *of the programme* whereas assessment is *of the learners*. Evaluation includes feedback from your learners and others to help you improve your own practice and the overall learner experience. Assessment is specific towards learners' achievements and how they can improve, develop and progress.

Evaluation is a quality assurance tool for a *product* or a *service*. If you are delivering and/or assessing a qualification or a programme of learning, then that is the *product*. The facilities of the organisation and the support your learners receive relate to the *service*. Your learners should have the opportunity to evaluate the product and service at some point, perhaps by completing a survey.

Other people will also be able to give you feedback, such as your mentor, line manager or supervisor. You might also have an inspector or quality assurer who will observe you at some point. As a result, you will receive feedback to help you develop in your role, as well as feedback which will help improve the product and the service your learners receive.

Activity

What do you understand by the term evaluation? *If you are currently teaching, what aspects are evaluated at your organisation and why? What would you recommend could take place and why?*

Evaluation should be an ongoing process throughout all aspects of teaching, learning and assessment. It can be informal by talking to others or formal by using a survey. Either way, the process should help you realise how effective things were, and what you could change or improve. It will also help you to identify any problem areas, enabling you to do things differently next time. Using feedback from others, and gaining information and data are the key to a good evaluation process. Never assume everything is going well just because you think it is.

Example

Brendan has just been promoted to the role of training manager in his place of work. He has been asked by his boss to devise a way of evaluating the in-house training which takes place with apprentices. He has decided to create an online survey, which each apprentice can complete anonymously, at three key points in their programme. He will devise the questions then email the survey weblink to them at the appropriate times. The survey he uses will automatically analyse the data for him. This will give him valuable feedback on which to act both during and after the training has taken place. He will carry out a staff appraisal and an observation with each trainer twice a year, which will lead to a development plan if necessary. Brendan will also carry out a standardisation activity at the monthly trainer meetings to help ensure all trainers are being consistent with the way they train and assess their apprentices.

In this example, Brendan is being proactive and seeking information while learning is taking place, rather than being reactive to a situation after the event.

Evaluation can take many forms, for example, self-, peer, learner and employer evaluation. Self-evaluation can involve completing a learning journal or diary, which demonstrates how you dealt with critical incidents and what you would do differently next time. Please see Table 12.2 (on page 466) later in this chapter for an example of a learning journal. For the purpose of future-proofing the book, a year has not been added to any dates within the documents. When completing any documents yourself, you should always add the year, as well as the day and month, to create a full audit trail.

Peer evaluation can include observations such as your mentor watching one of your sessions and giving you feedback.

Learner evaluation can include obtaining feedback at the end of a session or the end of a course. You could even ask your learners to design their own questions to put to their peers. Depending upon their age range and maturity, this might be a fun activity for them to participate in. They could even analyse the responses and compile a report of recommendations.

Employer evaluation includes appraisals and reviews of progress. You will probably participate in an appraisal or a performance review system at some point. This is a valuable opportunity to discuss your learning, development, any training or support you may need, and to set performance targets. It is also a chance to reflect upon your achievements and successes. Having the support of your organisation will help you decide what is relevant to your development as a teacher or a trainer, your job role and your specialist subject. You could share your ideas with colleagues if it's something everyone could benefit from.

You can evaluate your practice to ensure:

- a professional service is given to learners and others
- the teaching, learning and assessment process is fair to all
- you are meeting organisational and regulatory requirements
- you are meeting any performance targets
- you can learn from any incidents.

You can evaluate aspects such as:

- how effective was my planning and preparation?

- how well did I communicate with the learners and others?

- how effective were the delivery and assessment approaches I used?

- how did I stretch and challenge my learners?

- how effective were the resources, equipment and materials I used?

- how efficient was my record keeping, i.e. did I keep adequate records showing a full audit trail of my learners' progress and achievement?

- how well did the learners perform, i.e. did they achieve what they should have?

- how many learners left the course prior to achievement and why?

- how were the learners able to progress after completing the course?

You can do this by:

- carrying out questionnaires and surveys with all involved

- analysing data and statistics such as enrolment, retention, achievement, destinations and progression

- analysing appeals and complaints

- talking to learners and others

- looking for trends or patterns to find out why things are occurring.

Extension activity

What aspects could you evaluate for: a) your own performance; and b) the qualification or programme you are involved with? What evaluation methods would you use and why? What would you do with the information you receive?

Obtaining data and gaining feedback

Obtaining data and gaining feedback regarding learners' progress towards the product, and their satisfaction regarding the services received, is a crucial part of the evaluation process. This information will help you to deal with any problems or issues as necessary, if it forms part of your job role. You can use the information to share with colleagues and to improve the product and service, as well as your own professional development. Even if this is not part of your role, it's useful to know what should be taking place. Positive feedback can be used in publicity and promotional materials. Negative feedback should be responded to and acted upon as soon as possible. There isn't room in this chapter to explain all the different ways of obtaining data, gaining feedback and analysing it; therefore, just the basics will be covered. Please see the textbooks and websites listed at the end for further information.

Obtaining data

To help you evaluate your programme, you could obtain data and statistics regarding your learners, for example, enrollment, retention, achievement, destination and progression figures. You might have to ask someone to give you this data if you don't have access to it yourself. Data and feedback from others can help ensure the products and services have been successful (or not) and help to inform future planning. If your programme hasn't been successful, i.e. several learners either left or didn't achieve, your organisation might decide not to offer the programme again. Retention and achievement rates could affect the amount of funding received to offer a programme in future.

Data can also be obtained from assessment results. If you assess a programme which requires grades to be given to learners, you could analyse the data regarding their achievements. This could simply be by adding up the numbers of grades given. For example, out of a group of 24 learners, 12 received an A, 8 received a B and 4 achieved a C.

Grades are not always expressed as letters, they could be one or more of the following:

- 1, 2, 3, 4, 5

- A, B, C, D, E

- competent/not yet competent

- distinction, credit, pass, fail

- pass, refer, fail

- percentages

- satisfactory, good, outstanding.

You will need to check with your organisation or look in the qualification specification (if applicable) to see what grading should be used.

Once you have analysed your data, you will need to consider what has contributed towards it. For example, if you had a group of 30 learners who all achieved an A grade, was this due to your excellent teaching and assessing, the skills and knowledge of your learners or by being too lenient with your grades when marking? If you had a group of 15 learners who all failed an assignment, you could ask yourself the same questions. However, it could be that the assignment questions were worded in a confusing way, or you had given the assignment too early in the programme. If most of a group averaged a grade of 50 per cent for an assignment, whereas a colleague's group's averaged 80 per cent, this could be because misleading or ambiguous information was given. Asking yourself these questions will help you ascertain if you are producing assessments that are fit for purpose, and if not, you will need to do something about it. This might include amending your teaching or assessment methods or rewording assignment questions.

Example

Audrey's group of 20 level 5 learners were progressing well during their first year working towards a teaching qualification. However, at the beginning of the second year, six did not return. When she contacted them to ask why, they all stated they felt the course was too hard. This was not Audrey's fault, as the initial assessment process had not indicated that these particular learners should have been on the level 4 programme. Audrey was able to persuade them to take the lower level, and they were all subsequently successful. She informed the relevant department to update their initial assessment procedures.

This example shows that the interview and initial assessment process was not as detailed as it should have been, and will need reviewing for future applicants.

Gaining feedback

There are many different ways of gaining feedback from learners and others involved in the learning process. Some could be carried out face to face, online, via the telephone, the internet, or by post and could include:

- discussions
- interviews
- observations
- questionnaires
- surveys.

Talking to your learners informally will help you realise how successful the learning process has been. It will also help you find out what they think about the services, such as a library, refreshment facilities, parking and other aspects. This can be carried out individually during tutorial reviews, at break times, or with groups before or after your sessions. Your learners are the best judges of whether they are getting what they feel they need. If given the opportunity, they may give you more feedback in an informal situation. If your organisation is inspected by Ofsted in England, they are keen on the *learner voice*. This is the involvement of learners and potential learners in shaping the learning opportunities that are available to them. Learner voice initiatives seek to include the learner by enabling them to express their concerns, needs and views in a safe way. This could be by the use of anonymous questionnaires or online surveys. Organisations should respond appropriately to the issues that are raised, and provide feedback as to any developments and changes as a result. This places the learner at the centre of policy and practice.

Surveys and questionnaires

A *survey* is a way of gathering information and data that could involve a wide variety of collection methods. For example, analysing previous data, observing staff, and/or obtaining statistical information.

A *questionnaire* is way of gathering information and data which usually involves oral or written questions given to an individual.

Both are useful ways of formally obtaining feedback from learners and others. If you use surveys and questionnaires, you will need to consider what you want to find out, who you will ask, when you will do it and why. Don't just ask questions for the sake of it, and don't just give them to those you know will give you a positive response. This will make the results biased. You should also take ethics into consideration when planning to use any type of survey. This is to ensure no harm comes to anyone as a result of what you will do or will ask. Your organisation will be able to give you advice regarding this. Everyone should be given the opportunity to be involved and then left to decide if they wish to respond or not. You will also need to consider the timing. For example, you might want to gain some feedback regarding the interview and initial assessment process. It would be no good carrying this out at the end of a course as it relates to what happens at the beginning.

You could give your learners a questionnaire at the end of their programme or an event if it's a short session. Always build in time to your session for this to take place, otherwise your learners might take away the questionnaire and forget to return it. Alternatively, you could create a confidential online survey with an agreed completion date, which could be completed in the learners' own time. If you are delivering a longer-term programme, it's best to gain feedback early on so that you can act upon anything, if necessary, while the learners are still with you.

Feedback can be obtained from other people, besides your learners, which can help improve the learners' experiences. For example, from:

- employers
- colleagues
- inspectors
- learning assistants
- librarians
- managers
- mentors
- other teachers and assessors
- quality assurers
- support staff
- workplace supervisors.

Anonymity for those completing a survey or a questionnaire (known as *respondents*) could lead to your gaining more truthful responses if the person knows they will not be identified. However, if the respondent works closely with you, this might not be the case. The same goes for telephone, text message or face-to-face questioning. Electronic surveys that are emailed back will denote who the respondent is; however, postal ones will not (unless a reference code has been added to them). There are lots of online programs that can be used that will guarantee anonymity and will also analyse the results of quantitative data. Some of these offer a free basic service such as www.surveymonkey.com. You could carry out a small-scale survey with just a few learners to see how it works first. This is called a *pilot* and allows you to make any changes before a full survey is carried out.

When creating a survey, you will need to consider what method you will use to gain feedback, how you will use it, and who you will choose and why. Make sure you thank your learners for their contributions. Always inform your learners how their feedback has led to changes and improvements. If the latter have not yet taken place, let your learners know what will happen and when.

Question techniques

When devising questions for a survey or a questionnaire, you will need to gauge the language and level to suit your respondents. You might be able to use jargon or complex terms with colleagues, but not always with your learners. The type of question is also crucial as to the amount of information you need. Using a *closed* question, i.e. a question only requiring a yes or no response, will not give you as much information as an *open* question, which enables the respondent to give a detailed answer.

Example

Did you receive a detailed assessment plan? YES/NO

Was the assessment activity as you expected? YES/NO

Did you receive feedback? YES/NO

Was your assessor supportive? YES/NO

Although these questions will enable you to add up the number of YES and NO answers, they would not help you to understand what it was that led to the responses. Learners might just choose YES to be polite. Adding up the number of YES and NO responses will give you *quantitative data*. Think of this as the *quantity* of something, i.e. in terms of the total number of YES and NO responses.

The questions would be better rephrased as open questions to encourage learners to answer in detail. This would give you *qualitative data*, therefore giving you more information to act on. Think of this as the *quality* of something, which gives you information to work with rather than just statistics. A better way of wording the questions in the previous example would be:

Example

How detailed was your assessment plan?

What assessment activity was used and why?

How did you receive feedback?

How supportive was your assessor?

These questions enable the learner to expand on their responses and gives you more information to act on. When designing surveys or questionnaires use the KISS method: *Keep It Short and Simple.* Don't overcomplicate your questions, for example, by asking two unrelated questions in one sentence, or by making the questionnaire so long that someone will not want to complete it.

Activity

Research different ways of devising questions and gaining responses using surveys or questionnaires (online or paper based). What would be the best method to use with your learners and why?

Using open questions beginning with *who, what, when, where, why* and *how* (WWWWWH) will ensure you gain good quality answers. If you would rather use closed questions with yes/no responses, you could ask a further question to enable the learner to elaborate on why they answered yes or no.

Example

Was the assessment activity as you expected? YES/NO

Why was this?

Adding an extra question as in the example might gain the information you need, providing the learner chooses to respond.

A closed question could also be followed by a response scale of 1–5. Learners could choose 1 being *no* or *low* up to 5 being *yes* or *high*. Alternatively, you could give respondents other options such as:

1.   Strongly disagree

2.   Disagree

3.   Neither agree nor disagree

4.   Agree

5.   Strongly agree

Example

Did the programme fulfil your expectations?   1   2   3   4   5

The tendency might be to choose number 3 as it is in the middle. Removing one number makes the response more definitive one way or the other.

Example

Did the programme fulfil your expectations?   1   2   3   4

Alternatively you could use smiley faces, but this would only give three options.

Example

Did the programme fulfil your expectations?   ☹   ☺   ☺

When using surveys and questionnaires, make sure you set a date for their completion (and for their return if they are not completed online). Try not to be disappointed if you don't get as many responses as you had hoped for. However, if you give people time to complete them, perhaps immediately after a meeting with them, they can hand it in straight away rather than take it away and forget about it. This will not ensure anonymity though. Online surveys and questionnaires enable people to complete them while with you, or in their own time, and could give anonymity. Always inform your respondents why you are asking them to complete the survey or questionnaire and what the information will be used for. If it doesn't have any meaning or benefit for them, they might not complete it.

Activity

Design a short survey which you could use with your own learners either now or in the future, and use an appropriate questioning technique. Consider what information you would like to know and why and then devise your questions carefully. You could use a free online program such as Survey Monkey® at www. surveymonkey.com. If you have the opportunity, use it with a small group of learners as a pilot and remember to set a target date for the return of responses.

Analysing and responding to feedback

When the target date for submission has passed, you will be able to analyse and interpret the results. The whole process is meaningless if you don't do something with the feedback. If you have used an electronic program, it will have analysed the *quantitative* data for you, for example, by giving you percentages, bar charts or graphs. You will just need to read and summarise any *qualitative* responses to open questions which were asked.

If you haven't used an electronic program, you will need to count up all the responses to closed questions, and then summarise the responses to any open questions. You could use a blank survey form which was the same as the one issued. You can mark how many responses you received as in the following example where ten responses were analysed for four closed questions.

Example

Did you receive a detailed assessment plan? YES/NO	YES ЦНТ III	NO II
Was the assessment activity as you expected? YES/NO	YES ЦНТ II	NO III
Did you receive feedback? YES/NO	YES ЦНТ IIII	NO I
Was your assessor supportive? YES/NO	YES ЦНТ IIII	NO I

In this example, the assessor received quantitative data, but nothing qualitative to substantiate why the learners had chosen the YES/NO response. It could be that the learners who said NO didn't understand the questions. Alternatively, there might have been a personality clash between them and the assessor and they were saying NO just to be antagonistic. If possible, always ask an open question to follow up any closed questions. Although it might be time consuming to read and summarise the responses, you will have something more to work with.

Once you have analysed your responses, you may need to write a report with a supporting action plan and target dates. This might go to managers and/or others involved in the learning process. Make sure you follow up any action points with the people identified (if it's not you) who will carry them out. Informing the respondents of the results and subsequent action keeps them up to date with developments and shows that you take their feedback seriously.

Analyse the pilot survey you carried out as part of the last activity. Are there any surprises or are the results as you expected? Do you need to re-word or change any of the questions? If so, revise the survey, then issue it to the rest of your group of learners. Set a target date for return, analyse the results and create a report and action plan based on your findings.

Self-evaluation

Self-evaluation is a way of continually thinking about your own practice to ensure you are carrying out your role effectively. When evaluating your practice, you will need to consider how your own behaviour has impacted upon others, what you could do to improve, and then put this into practice. The word *self* would make you think that you need to do it on your own. However, what you think and what others think might be quite different. If you self-evaluate that you have delivered a fantastic session as none of your learners fell asleep, this might be very different to what they actually experienced. When you carry out the self-evaluation process, you could consider the perspectives of other people besides your learners. This will help you become more objective with your judgements of yourself, rather than being subjective, i.e. only taking your point of view into consideration.

Activity

How can you self-evaluate towards meeting the requirements of your job role? For example, by keeping a diary, a reflective journal or by making notes after each session you deliver. What would be the best option for you and why?

To help you improve in your job role, self-evaluation could take place after each session you deliver. This will enable you to consider your strengths, areas for development and any action required. An example is given in Table 12.1 of a teacher who has used an observation form to evaluate their session. This might be something that you do as part of a micro-teach session or teaching practice (if you are working towards a teaching qualification). If not, it's good practice to do something similar when you have the opportunity.

If you can evaluate each session after you have delivered it, you might be able to realise things you were not aware of. For example, you could ask yourself if you used eye contact with each learner and addressed everyone by name at some point during the session. If your answer is *no* then next time, ensure that you do. Another question to ask yourself is *'How do I know that learning has taken place?'* If you can't answer this, you will need to make some changes to your delivery and assessment approaches.

You might have heard of the term *360 degree feedback*, which is a way of evaluating performance. It can help contribute to the self-evaluation process and staff appraisals. It includes obtaining feedback from your immediate work circle.

Table 12.1 Example self-evaluation form

Did I?	Yes/No	Comments
introduce myself and create a rapport with the learners	yes	I already had my name on the board and was wearing a name badge. I used the introduction as the basis to explain the topic. I put learners at ease by asking what experience they had of non-verbal communication skills, therefore getting them all to talk at the beginning.
state the aim and objectives (or tasks) of the session	yes	This was stated on the first PowerPoint slide, I felt I explained it clearly. It was also on the first flip chart sheet which remained on display throughout the session. I had a session plan which helped keep me focused upon the activities and the timings.
use equipment/resources/handouts appropriately	yes	I set out the room before the learners arrived and arranged it for group work. Sufficient handouts were prepared in advance. I had also pre-prepared the flip chart and checked the PowerPoint was working.
communicate clearly (verbally and non-verbally)	yes	I felt I delivered the session using a suitable tone and pitch. I demonstrated aspects of verbal and non-verbal body language, sometimes in a humorous way. I checked that everyone could see and hear me.
act confidently and professionally	yes	I was a little nervous at first; however, as soon as I started talking about the topic I was familiar with, I was able to relax. This helped me act confidently. I felt I delivered the session in a professional way due to being confident. I included everyone and used a variety of approaches. I had planned what I could remove from the session had I been running out of time, and what I could add in if I was short of time. As it happened, my timing was slightly short so I was able to use all the planned activities and allow for more questions.
ask open questions to check knowledge	yes	I used open questions to check that learners were engaged, and the PPP method to ensure that learning was taking place by each individual. (Pose, Pause, Pick)
involve and include everyone during the session	yes	I ensured I asked a question to each learner and I used eye contact with everyone throughout the session.

(Continued)

461

Table 12.1 (Continued)

Did I?	Yes/No	Comments
demonstrate subject knowledge	yes	Non-verbal communication skills is something I train people about at work, therefore I felt I was able to demonstrate this subject knowledge with ease.
use a variety of teaching, learning and assessment approaches	yes	I used a teacher-led discussion; I asked verbal questions throughout (in different ways). I explained the topics and involved the learners in a practical task. I observed the learners during the activities and checked they had answered the written questions.
take into account: health and safety; equality and diversity; learning preferences, and any individual learner needs	yes	I considered health and safety when setting up the room. My choice of approaches demonstrated consideration of all learning preferences. I explained equality and diversity as part of the topic and ensured my handouts represented all aspects of society. The learner who is diabetic did not need to leave the room; I catered for the learner who has dyslexia by giving everyone a pastel coloured handout.
assess that learning took place	yes	I asked oral questions and observed the role-play activities. Each learner was able to correctly answer written and oral questions and state what they had learnt from the session.
summarise my session and refer to the aim and objectives (or tasks)	yes	I re-visited the aim and objectives (which were on the flip chart and the summary PowerPoint slide) to confirm they had been achieved.
tidy the area afterwards	yes	I removed the flip chart paper, closed down the PowerPoint and tidied the area. I asked the learners to put the desks back to how they were prior to the session.

Strengths	Planning the session to cater for all learners. I knew I had 9 learners: 6 male and 3 female aged 24-48. One learner has dyslexia, therefore the handout was printed on pastel paper for all learners. The learners also appreciated that I offered to email the handouts to them after the session.
	Using my session plan to remain focused and run to time. Using good quality handouts which were issued at the right time. Engaging learners in the topic and making the subject fun and interesting. Remaining calm and acting confidently and professionally.
Areas for development	Building up my self-confidence so I don't appear too nervous. Using more of the Pose Pause Pick method of questioning.
	I had used open questions but I found myself using some closed questions too. These only gave a YES or NO response which didn't really tell me what learning had taken place.
Action required	Improve my skills of using PowerPoint to incorporate links to websites and short videos. Learn how to add animations and pictures to the PowerPoint slides.

Haedish, a trainee economics teacher, was due to take part in a staff appraisal with the human resources manager in a couple of months. She had been told the 360 degree approach would be used. She wasn't sure what this would involve. Upon asking, she was advised to obtain feedback from her immediate colleagues such as her peers, team members, supervisor and line manager. She would also need to obtain feedback from her learners and her mentor. The human resource department supplied her with templates for this purpose, and told her she would need to analyse the data and feedback prior to the meeting.

The rationale for 360 degree feedback is that managers might not always fully understand the workload and contributions of their staff. Feedback from others can be as valuable as traditional hierarchical feedback from managers. However, you may need to be open to accepting the feedback and not become defensive when offered advice.

Extension activity

Take a look at Appendix 2 – Checklist for teachers and trainers. Although not all of the aspects might apply to your job role, check which ones you do and don't do. For the latter, what can you do to make sure that you can meet them (if they are applicable)? You don't know what you don't know, until it's pointed out to you.

Reflective practice

Reflective practice is about becoming more self-aware, which should give you increased confidence and improve the links between the theory and practice of teaching, learning and assessment. It should become a part of your everyday activities enabling you to analyse and focus on things in greater detail. All reflection should lead to an improvement in practice. However, there may be events you would not want to change or improve as you felt they went well. If this is the case, reflect as to *why* they went well and use your thoughts to improve future sessions.

When you look in a mirror, you will see your own reflection; you might look at yourself and think you want to change something, for example, what you are wearing, or you may choose not to change anything. Reflections in a mirror enable you to *visually* see something you might want to change. Reflecting upon your teaching enables you to *think* about what you have done, how you did it and why you decided to do it a certain way, with a view to changing or improving it in the future.

Often, taking time to reflect on your sessions or incidents within them, enables you to plan different ways of doing things. Don't blame yourself if things don't go quite to plan; it's alright to take risks sometimes and make impromptu changes to your session (as long as it's safe to do so). You can then consider afterwards why you did this and whether it worked or not. You always need to take into account your learners, as what might work with one group may not work with another. Try not to blame others for incidents that happen within your sessions, you are the person in control and you must take responsibility. If you blame others, you may not feel the need to make any changes yourself. However, don't blame yourself either, but accept responsibility, learn from mistakes and incidents and try something different next time. However, your session might go really well, so reward yourself with praise and keep up your good practice.

Aspects you might like to reflect upon include (in alphabetical order):

- a conversation with a colleague which left you thinking about something they said

- a discussion with your mentor or observer and the advice they gave you

- a meeting you attended where you felt significant aspects were addressed

- a recent session you have taught

- an aspect of a session which went well, or did not go well

- an assessment activity which went well, or did not go well

- an incident with a learner which didn't go how you had planned

- changes within the organisation, to your job role, or to the subject you teach and assess

- something you have read or seen which will impact upon your role.

Activity

What do you understand by the term reflection? *Carry out a search via the internet, if you have access, or read relevant textbooks. Are there any requirements for your job role that need you to reflect, either in an informal or a formal way? What do you think you should reflect on and why?*

A straightforward method of reflection is to have the *experience*, then *describe* it, *analyse* it and *revise* it (**EDAR**) as in Figure 12.1. This method incorporates the: *who, what, when, where, why* and *how* approach (WWWWWH) and should help you consider ways of changing and/or improving.

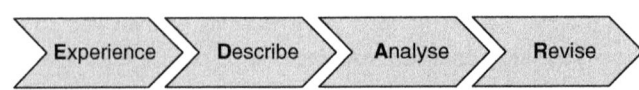

Figure 12.1 The EDAR process

- *Experience: a significant event or incident you would like to change or improve.*

- *Describe: aspects such as who was involved, what happened, when it happened and where it happened.*

- *Analyse: consider the experience more deeply and ask yourself how it happened and why it happened.*

- *Revise: think about how you would do it differently if it happened again, and then try this out if you have the opportunity.*

It should become a habit to reflect, for example, by mentally running through the EDAR points after a significant event. Please see Table 12.2 (on page 466) for an example of a completed learning journal based on EDAR.

As you become more experienced and analytical with reflective practice, you will progress from thoughts of *I didn't do that very well,* to aspects of more significance such as *why* you didn't do it very well and *how* you could change something as a result. You may realise you need further training or support in some areas, therefore partaking in relevant continuing professional development (CPD) could help. As a result, you might find your own skills improving; for example, giving more effective, constructive and developmental feedback to your learners. Whenever you undertake any CPD, always think as to how you can apply what you have learnt to your practice.

Extension activity

Read the completed learning journal in Table 12.2. Do you think it has been completed in an analytic way or is it mainly descriptive? Do the revisions proposed adequately reflect what needs to be done? If not, what else might this teacher need to do?

Theories of reflective practice

There are many reflective practice theories, which have been based on ideas, thoughts, experiences and research. Some are quite old, but are trusted; others are fairly recent. This section will briefly explain some of these in (hopefully) an easy to understand way. They are in no particular order and are often contradictory depending upon the perspective of the theorist. You will need to make your own mind up whether you think they will influence what you do, or you may even come up with your own theory or idea to challenge existing ones. There are many more besides those listed here and there are some weblinks at the end of this chapter if you wish to research further.

Table 12.2 Example completed learning journal

Learning Journal	
Name: Devra Cohen	**Date:** 20th October
Experience significant event or incident	Last night was the first session with a new group and I felt it didn't go well. I focused too much on what I wanted to do and too little on how and what the group wanted to learn. Some of the learners stayed behind to ask a lot of questions that I thought I had addressed in the session. A few said they were confused and thought the programme would not meet their expectations.
Describe who, what, when, where	There were 16 learners aged 29 to 65 attending an evening class (Accountancy for Beginners) from 6-9 p.m. The session took place in a classroom with a broken data projector, windows that wouldn't open and not enough chairs.
Analyse why, how (i.e. the impact on learning)	I should have arrived earlier to check that the data projector was working properly as this delayed the session by 10 minutes. I had to move some chairs from the room across the corridor and leave the door wedged open to let fresh air in. Had I sorted this out prior to the learners arriving, they would not have known of the problems. The class would then have started promptly and I would not have been flustered.
	I had too much administrative work to get through, the learners had to fill in an enrolment form, I needed to carry out an initial assessment of their prior learning and ascertain if anyone had any individual needs. I also wanted them to complete a learning preference questionnaire but there wasn't enough time. I had a list of things I wanted to get through, including agreeing the ground rules but I forgot to do these as I was rushing things. As a result I felt I looked very unprofessional.
	The icebreaker went well but was a bit hurried due to the late start. I had an induction checklist which kept me focused, but it was 7.30 p.m. before I realised the learners needed a break. By this time, some of them were not paying attention to me but talking to others. I felt not a lot of learning took place as I was focusing too much on the administration and the programme requirements.
Revise changes and/or improvements required	I have realised the first session is not about me and the paperwork I need to complete, but about what the learners want to know and learn about the subject.
	I will arrive earlier to ensure there are enough chairs and that the data projector is working. I will apologise at the beginning of next week's session and I will ask what the learners' expectations are and explain how I can meet them. We will discuss and agree the ground rules next week.
	In future, I will interview all learners in advance and ask them to complete the enrolment form, learning preference questionnaire and initial assessment prior to the first session. This will help me ascertain all the information I need to help plan my first session, and make it go more smoothly. It will also ensure the learners are on the right programme. I have reported the windows to the caretaker. I will allow extra time in my session plan to account for questions and answers, and ensure the focus is upon their learning rather than my teaching.

Schön (1983)

Schön suggests two methods of reflection:

- reflection *in* action

- reflection *on* action.

Reflection *in* action happens at the time of the incident, is often instinctive and allows for immediate changes to take place. It is about being *reactive* to a situation and dealing with it straight away.

Reflection *on* action takes place after the incident and is a more conscious process. This allows you time to think about the incident, consider a different approach or to talk to others about it before making any changes. It is about being *proactive* and considering measures to prevent the situation happening again in the future.

Example

Siobhan was teaching a group of adults attending college as part of a day-release business studies programme. During one session, she had underestimated how fast they would learn. The learners were getting through the activities much more quickly than she had originally planned. At break time, she accessed and printed some challenging activities, which she then used with the group. This enabled her to reflect immediately, ensuring the session was effective and meeting the learners' needs. Siobhan therefore carried out reflection in action.

Brookfield (1995)

Brookfield identified the importance of being *critical* when reflecting. He advocated four points of view when looking at your practice, which he called *critical lenses*. These lenses are from the point of view of:

- the teacher

- the learner

- colleagues

- theories and literature.

Using these points makes the reflection critical, by first looking at it from your own point of view; second, how your learners perceived your actions and what they liked and disliked; third, the view from colleagues, e.g. your mentor is taken into consideration. This enables you to have a critical conversation about your actions, which might highlight things you hadn't considered. Fourth, you should link your reflections to theories and literature, comparing your own ideas with others' ideas.

Julia, a trainee teacher, came away from a one-to-one training session feeling it hadn't gone well. From her point of view (the teacher's lens) her learner George hadn't been paying attention. Julia tried to think why this was and came to the conclusion he was acting this way because she was being observed by her mentor today (the learner's lens). Afterwards, Julia asked him why he hadn't been paying attention. To her surprise, he responded by saying the work wasn't challenging him enough. Julia's mentor felt the same as the learner; he could see George had appeared bored (the colleague's lens). This helped Julia realise she needed to broaden George's learning experiences further. She decided to look at Schön's (1983) theory of reflection in action/reflection on action (the theories and literature lens). As a result, Julia will be able to reflect immediately she realises there is a problem (Schön's in action theory) rather than waiting until afterwards (Schön's on action theory).

Reflection can be helped by a *critical friend* who is willing to question, challenge and offer sympathetic support and advice to overcome any problems or issues. You could pair up with a colleague to question, challenge and support each other. This support can be useful in establishing actions to overcome barriers; however, you do need to be open to receiving criticism. Critical friends can be used to engage in conversation or to review each other's reflective writing, for example, their journals. In the latter case, the critical friend would read your journal entries and make comments, which should challenge your thinking or ways of doing things. This should then promote a positive change in your reflective practice and your professional practice.

Johns (2006)

Johns uses guided questions in his model for structured reflection. The questions are posed and answers are written in a reflective diary. *Cue questions* focus on the experience, for example, the *here and now* of the experience, the causes of the experience, the context/background to the experience and the key processes related to this experience. The subsequent questions focus on *what* was the purpose of the actions, feelings and consequences for all involved. The *influencing factors* are then explored, for example, what influenced the decision-making. The final question is *could I have dealt better with the situation?* This explores the choices available that led to the situation. Using this questioning method will help you understand the influencing factors behind your actions.

Kolb (1984)

Kolb proposed a four-stage theory, known as the *experiential learning cycle* as in Figure 12.2. Part of reflection is about knowing what you need to change. If you are not aware of something that needs changing, you will continue as you are until something serious occurs. The cycle is a way by which people can understand their experiences, and as a result, modify their behaviour. It is based on the idea that the more often a person reflects on a task, the more often they have the opportunity to modify and refine their efforts. The process of learning can begin at any stage and is continuous, i.e. there is no limit to the number of cycles that can be made in a learning situation. This theory suggests that without reflection, people would continue to repeat their mistakes.

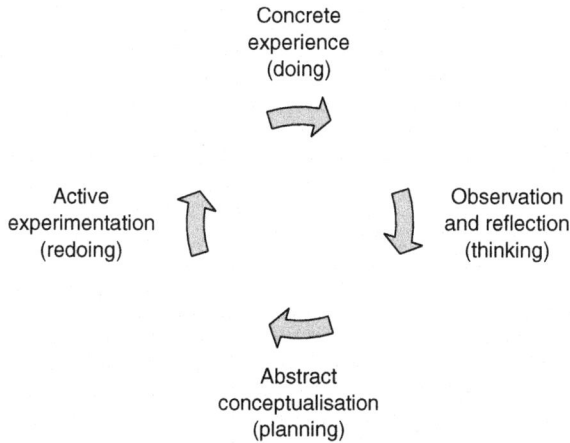

Figure 12.2 Kolb's (1984) experiential learning cycle

- Concrete experience is about experiencing or immersing yourself in the task and is the first stage in which a person simply carries out the task assigned. This is the *doing* stage.

- Observation and reflection involve stepping back from the task and reviewing what has been done and experienced. Your values, attitudes and beliefs can influence your thinking at this stage. This is the stage of *thinking* about what you have done.

- Abstract conceptualisation involves interpreting the events that have taken place and making sense of them. This is the stage of *planning* how you will do it differently.

- Active experimentation enables you to take the new learning and predict what is likely to happen next, or what actions should be taken to refine the way the task is done again. This is the *redoing* stage based upon experience and reflection.

Example

Wang is working towards an accounting course that has an examination at the end. If he fails he will not know why he has failed. He will need to wait another three months before he can retake the examination. During the course, he could experience the learning process, but not reflect upon what he might be doing wrong that may lead to his failing the examination. He is therefore not able to modify his behaviour and try again. If he took a course with ongoing assessment instead of an examination at the end, he would have the opportunity to go through the full cycle. He would have the experience, reflect upon it due to ongoing feedback, think how he could improve, and then experiment to try again.

You are probably familiar with the saying *you learn by experience*. You might find that doing a task, then thinking about it, leads you to plan how you would do it differently next time. Redoing and reflecting on tasks should help improve your practice.

Activity

Consider something that you could do with your learners which is different to what you would normally do, such as a role play-activity. Work through Kolb's cycle by trying it out, reflecting on it, planning what you could differently and then trying it again. What have you learnt from this?

Gibbs (1988)

Gibbs also advocates the use of a reflective cycle as in Figure 12.3. His cycle uses *headings* to generate thought processes. The headings prompt you to consider aspects such as:

- What happened?
- What was I feeling at the time?
- What could I have done differently?

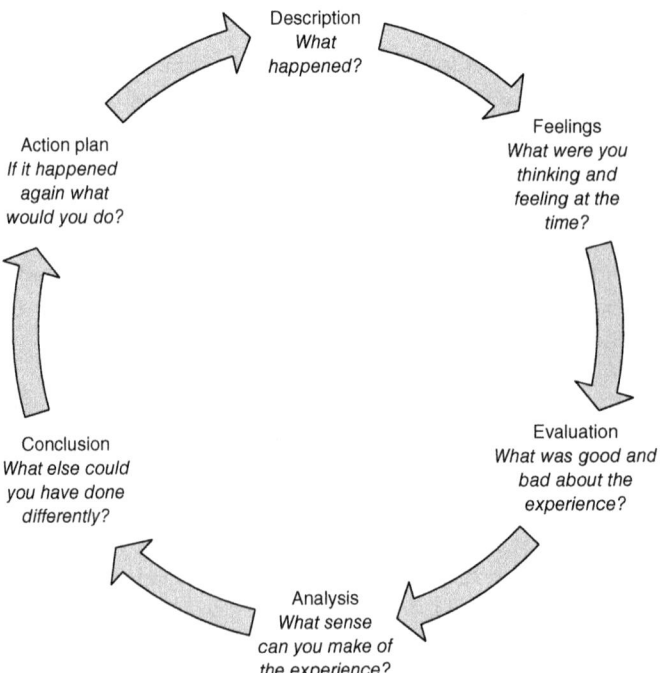

Figure 12.3 Gibbs' (1988) reflective cycle

Using these headings and questions will help you to evaluate your practice.

Griffiths and Tann (1992)

Griffiths and Tann introduced a cycle of reflection with different time frames, as in Figure 12.4. They state that without a conscious effort, the most immediate reactions to experiences can overwhelm the opportunity for deeper consideration and learning. They describe their reflective cycle as:

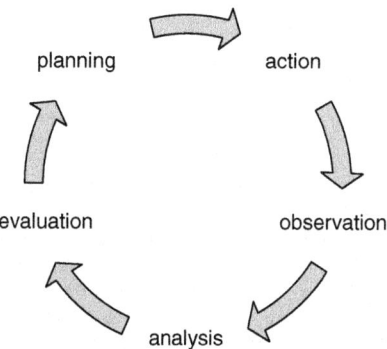

Figure 12.4 Griffiths and Tann's (1992) model of reflection

These aspects go through five levels or time frames:

1. rapid reaction (immediate)

2. repair (short pause for thought)

3. review (time out to reassess, hours or days)

4. research (systematic, focused, weeks/months)

5. re-theorise/re-formulate (abstract, rigorous, over months/years).

Example

Val had adapted a colleague's handout to give to her learners. When she used it, she realised the content was set at too high a level as her learners were asking a lot of questions. She therefore told them she had issued the handout far too early in the programme and facilitated a discussion based on the topic instead. This was a rapid reaction to the situation and was therefore immediate reflection.

Lewin (1951)

Lewin developed a force field analysis technique to help understand change processes. It is useful for planning and implementing change and attempting to overcome resistance to change. Lewin assumed that in any situation there are both *driving* and *restraining* forces that influence any changes that may occur. Driving forces are those which affect a situation and push it in a particular direction, they can be negative or positive, for example, incentives when targets are met. Restraining forces are those which act to hold back or decrease the driving forces, and are often negative, for example, apathy or fear of failure. Equilibrium is reached when the sum of the driving forces equals the sum of the restraining forces. However, this equilibrium can be affected by subsequent changes in the relationship between the driving and the restraining forces.

Using a diagrammatic approach can help generate a force field analysis if you need to analyse change. The driving forces and restraining forces are identified with arrows to denote different strengths, indicating how weak or strong they are, as in the following example.

Example

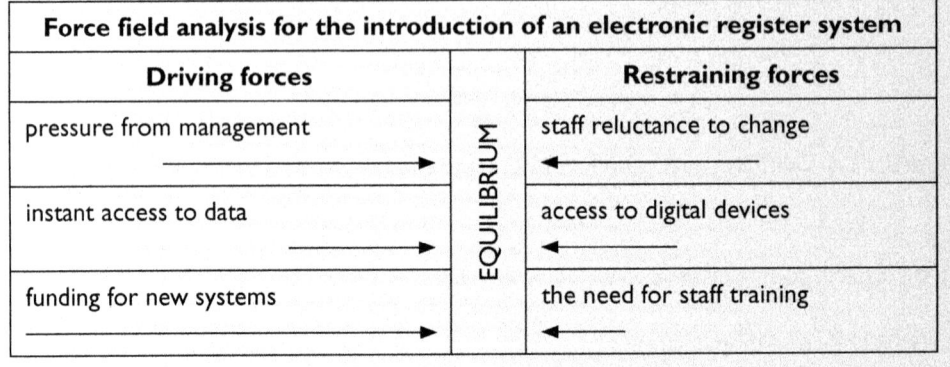

Force field analysis for the introduction of an electronic register system		
Driving forces	EQUILIBRIUM	**Restraining forces**
pressure from management ⟶		staff reluctance to change ⟵
instant access to data ⟶		access to digital devices ⟵
funding for new systems ⟶		the need for staff training ⟵

To achieve change, three steps should be followed:

1. The organisation must amend the driving and restraining forces that hold it in its current state.

2. An imbalance should be introduced to the forces to enable the change to take place. This can be achieved by increasing the driving forces and reducing the restraining forces, or both.

3. When the change is complete, the forces are brought back into an equilibrium and a new current state is achieved.

The ability to manage change comes with experience and knowledge. Change is a regular occurrence within education and training. The pressure for change could come from the government, from regulatory bodies or from within your own organisation. Whatever the change, it will be inevitable it will take place; therefore, you need to embrace it, communicate any concerns and ensure you find out the facts to move forward with it. Fear of the unknown may make you apprehensive and worried. However, try not to be anxious or become stressed; if you are unsure of anything, just talk to a colleague. The best way to embrace change is to look towards the future and the benefits the change will bring. While you might not agree with the changes, they are being brought in to improve or amend a situation for a particular reason, and all staff should be committed towards them. If your job role will change substantially, make sure you are fully aware of what these changes are and how you are expected to implement them. Being unsure of how changes will affect you personally and professionally can cause resentment towards others. Never be afraid to ask questions to clarify any concerns you have. Being positive about change and moving forward with your organisation can lead to new experiences, rewards and increased job satisfaction.

Ecclestone (1995)

Ecclestone states

> there is a danger of reflective practice becoming nothing more than a *mantra*, a comforting and familiar wrap as opposed to a professional tool for exploration. ... People might also want – or need – reflection because they seek interest, inspiration, cultural breadth, critical analysis and reasoning, social insight and awareness, challenge and critique, or to create new knowledge.
>
> (Ecclestone, 1995, page 150)

If you can take reflective practice seriously, embrace change and maintain your personal and professional development, you should see an improvement in your practice. This will hopefully result in a positive impact upon your learners' progress and achievement, as well as your own.

Tripp (1993)

Tripp stated: *When something goes wrong, we need to ask what happened and what caused it to happen* (1993, page 54). The guiding principle is to change the incident into a question.

You may be familiar with the term *critical incident analysis*. A critical incident is something you interpret as a problem or a challenge in a particular context, rather than a routine occurrence.

Example

Pablo has a group of 25 learners, eight of whom always arrive five minutes late to his session. When Pablo asked them why, he ascertained that they finished another class at the same time as this one was due to start. They therefore did not have enough time to move from one room to another without being late. Pablo agreed with everyone in the group to start and finish the session slightly later. This enabled the group to be together at the beginning, minimising the disruption.

Changing the incident in this example to a question becomes *learners repeatedly arrive late to my session* to *why do learners repeatedly arrive late to my session?* In this way, critical incidents can become major turning points. Asking *why* enables you to work on finding a solution.

Critical incident analysis is a way of dealing with these challenges and exploring incidents that occur. This will help to understand them better and find alternative ways of reacting and responding to them.

Often, a critical incident is personal to an individual. Incidents only become critical, that is, problematic, if the individual sees them in this way. It is after the event that it is defined as critical. Carrying out a critical incident analysis can help you question your own practice and enable it to develop and improve.

Reviewing your progress regularly will help you learn about yourself and what you could do differently or improve. For example, how you react to different situations or learners, how patient you are and what skills you may need to develop. You might also decide you need further training or support to improve your subject knowledge or teaching skills.

Extension activity

Reflect upon the next session you either attend (if you are not yet teaching) or that you facilitate with your learners. Evaluate how the session went, what was good about it and how you reacted to certain situations. Use one or more of the theories mentioned in this chapter section to help you identify areas for improvement and/or development. If you have time, research other theories such as Kirkpatrick's (1994) Four Levels, Stufflebeam's (2007) Evaluation Theory, or Martin's (1996) Critical Incidents.

Continuing professional development

Continuing professional development (CPD) can be anything that you do that helps you improve your practice and keep up to date. It shows you are a committed professional and it should help improve your skills, knowledge and understanding regarding your specialist subject. CPD should relate to your job role as well as the subjects you deliver, and can be based on the results of evaluation and feedback. It's useful to add relevant CPD activities to your curriculum vitae, particularly if you are applying for a job or a promotion.

There are constant changes in training and education; therefore, it is crucial to keep up to date and embrace them. Examples include changes to the qualifications or standards you deliver, changes to policies and practices within your organisation, regulatory requirements, and government initiatives.

Activity

Is the programme, qualification or set of standards you use likely to be updated at some time? If so, when will this be and how can you keep up to date with what will change?

Having some knowledge of possible influences upon your role could help you anticipate and embrace the changes when they happen. This could become part of your ongoing CPD, which can be formal or informal, planned well in advance or be opportunistic. However, it should have a real impact upon your role and lead to an improvement in your practice. CPD is more than just attending events or carrying out research. It is also about using evaluation and reflection, which results in positive improvements.

Your organisation might have a strategy for CPD, which will prioritise activities they consider are important to improving standards. They may or may not provide any funding for them. However, you can partake in lots of activities which are free or cost very little. For example, online courses, observing colleagues, researching websites, reading journals and textbooks.

Improving own skills and knowledge

Carrying out the self-evaluation and reflection processes should help you to identify what you might need to improve upon. This could relate to skills, i.e. by taking part in work experience in the industrial area for the subject you teach. Alternatively, it could relate to knowledge, i.e. reading and researching your subject to find out what the latest developments are. Whatever your new experiences are, it's best to share them with your colleagues so that everyone can benefit. However, financial or budget cuts might mean that you can't take any time off from your current role to participate. You might therefore have to do it in your own time, and/or fund it yourself.

You could carry out a SWOT analysis to help you understand where you are at the moment. SWOT stands for **s**trengths, **w**eaknesses, **o**pportunities and **t**hreats.

Strengths and weaknesses can be considered as internal (i.e. within the organisation), whereas opportunities and threats can be considered as external (outside of the organisation). Strengths and opportunities can be helpful, whereas weaknesses and threats can be harmful. A SWOT analysis is useful for identifying your own strengths and weaknesses, as well as the opportunities available and the threats faced.

Activity

Complete the SWOT boxes below regarding your current job role. Once completed, what do you think you need to do to help your development and/or improve your practice? How might you achieve this?

	Helpful	**Harmful**
Internal	*Strengths*	*Weaknesses*
External	*Opportunities*	*Threats*

Carrying out a SWOT analysis is fine for finding things out, but you need to do something with the results. Listing strengths and weakness, while identifying opportunities and threats is of no use if you don't use them for a reason. You will need to decide what that reason is, and whether it's for yourself and/or others you work with. Once identified, you can apply the strengths and take advantage of the opportunities. You will also need to minimise the weaknesses and threats or get rid of them altogether. This might be a long-term project and you may need to work with others to achieve it.

Creating a personal development plan for yourself is a way of formalising what you will do and when as part of your CPD. You can review how you are progressing and update and amend it as you wish. When you have achieved something, it's useful to update your CPD record. Table 12.3 is an example of a personal development plan for short-, medium-, and long-term targets.

Table 12.3 Example personal development plan

Personal development plan				
Name: Abbi Cross		Organisation: Excellence Training College		
Targets	**Aim or activity**	**Start date**	**Review date**	**Completion date** *(update CPD record)*
Short term	Attend standardisation event for units 101, 102 and 103	06 Jan	27 April	06 Jan
	Carry out an internet search for my subject to see what resources and videos are available.	09 Jan		
Medium term	Attend First Aid training day	10 Feb	2 April	10 Feb
	Attend staff training event for trainers and assessors	20 Mar		20 Mar
Long term	Achieve a teaching qualification at level 5	12 Jan	23 Dec	

There are many CPD activities you could carry out, for example:

- attending events and training programmes
- attending meetings and standardisation activities
- collaborative working
- e-learning and online activities
- evaluating feedback from learners, peers, assessors and others
- formally reflecting on experiences and documenting how it has improved practice
- improving own skills such as English, maths and ICT
- keeping up to date with relevant legislation
- membership of professional associations or committees
- mentoring and coaching new staff
- observing colleagues
- networking (online and in person)
- reading textbooks and journals

- reflecting on own progress
- researching developments or changes to your subject
- secondments
- self-reflection
- shadowing colleagues
- sharing ideas with colleagues
- standardisation activities
- studying for relevant qualifications
- subscribing to and reading relevant journals and websites

- team teaching
- updating specialist subject skills and knowledge
- using social media to follow/inform others of relevant and current information
- using new and emerging technology
- voluntary work
- work experience placements
- writing or reviewing books and articles.

Activity

Look at the previous bullet list and decide which of the activities would be relevant to you, then create a personal development plan as in Table 12.3. What other activities could you carry out which would contribute towards your CPD?

It's a good idea to maintain a record of all CPD undertaken to prove you are remaining current within your role and your subject area. This is something you might have to formalise for your organisation or to remain active with a professional association to which you belong. You could keep a paper copy such as the one shown in Table 12.4 (on page 478) or an electronic record. Using a reference number for each activity enables you to cross-reference the activities to your documentation. For example, number 1 could be minutes of meetings, number 2 could be a certificate, number 3 a record of achievement and so on. Adding the reference number to the relevant documents or file names also enables you to locate them when necessary. Besides keeping your CPD record up to date, you could write a more detailed reflection of what you learnt and how it impacted upon your job role.

The amount of detail you need to write will differ depending upon your organisation's requirements. Maintaining your CPD will ensure you are not only competent at your job role, but are also up to date with the latest developments regarding your specialist subject and teaching, learning and assessment approaches.

Always keep a copy of any documentation relating to your training and CPD. You may need to provide this to funding bodies, awarding organisations, professional associations or regulatory bodies if requested.

If you work in education, CPD should relate not only to teaching, learning and assessment practices, but also to changes in education policies as well as your specialist subject. This is known as being a 'dual professional'. You are a professional teacher and assessor as well as a professional in the subject you teach and assess.

Table 12.4 Example CPD record

Continuing professional development record

Name: Abbi Cross

Organisation: Excellence Training College

Date	Activity and venue	Duration	Justification towards job role and subject area	Action required	Ref. no.
06 Jan	Attendance at a standardisation event for units 101, 102 and 103	2.5 hrs	Helped me understand the changes to the qualification	Discuss the changes with other staff at the next team meeting	1
09 Jan	Searched online for useful resources and videos for my subject area	1 hr	Gained new ideas and resources to use with learners	Try using them during sessions	2
12 Jan	Commenced level 5 teaching qualification	4 hrs	Found out about the course, what is expected, and how much teaching practice I need to evidence	Set up a teaching practice log	3
10 Feb	Attendance at a First Aid training day.	6 hrs	To ensure I am current with First Aid in case someone has an accident	Inform all staff and learners that I am a first aider	4
20 Mar	Attendance at in-house event for trainers and assessors. We discussed the types of records we use and how they could be improved, along with updates to policies and procedures	3 hrs	Ensured I am up to date	Find out how to access the latest electronic documents. Re-read the updated policies and procedures	5

Example

Ackram teaches painting and decorating. He keeps up to date with the subject by reading trade magazines, subscribing to relevant online networking sites, belonging to a professional trade association and communicating with colleagues. He keeps up to date with teaching and assessment skills by attending relevant CPD training workshops, belonging to a professional teaching association and subscribing to relevant online updates.

Prior to planning or undertaking any CPD, you might like to ask yourself the following questions:

- Why am I doing it and what will I gain as a result?

- How will others benefit, such as my learners?

- Is it really relevant and/or necessary that I do it?

- Is there any funding available for me to undertake CPD?

- How much of my own time and/or money will I need to invest?

- How can I apply the CPD I have done to my practice?

- Can I share it with others; if so, who?

- Who can support me and give me advice while I undertake it?

- What will the role of my manager/mentor be?

- Are there any organisational implications as a result of my undertaking CPD?

- When is the best time to review my progress, and update my action plan and CPD record?

You might think of a few more questions besides those listed. The important point is that all CPD should have an impact, not just be something that you do because you think you should or someone tells you to.

Keeping up to date

Keeping up to date with what's happening in your subject specialist area will help you to pass on the latest information to your learners and colleagues. You will also need to keep up to date with developments that will impact upon your job role, such as how emerging technology can be utilised to benefit the learning and assessment process. Making contacts and networking with others is a great way to get to know people who you could collaborate with. This could be to share resources, discuss developments in the sector and provide mutual help and support.

Activity

How can you keep up to date with your specialist subject, emerging technology and developments with teaching, training and assessment? If you are currently teaching, make a list of colleagues and other people who you could network with. How can you keep in touch and how can you share information and resources to everyone's benefit? Find out what professional associations and networks are available for you to join. Details of some of these can be found in the Introduction chapter.

Useful websites for CPD

The following websites are useful to gain up-to-date information regarding developments in the further education and skills sector. However, websites change frequently so they might not all be available when you check them. Most of them enable you to register for free electronic updates or contain links to useful free courses, research and resources.

- Ann Gravells' Padlet – lots of useful educational reports and documents – https://pad let.com/AnnGravells/j8ie1yhzsn5u

- Association of Colleges (AOC) – www.aoc.co.uk

- Association of Employment and Learning Providers (AELP) – www.aelp.org.uk

- Association for Research in Post Compulsory Education (ARPCE) – http://arpce.org.uk/

- British Educational Research Association (BERA) – www.bera.ac.uk

- Centre for Vocational Education Research (CVER) – http://cver.lse.ac.uk/events/default.asp

- Chartered Institution for Further Education (CIFE) – www.fecharter.org.uk

- Department for Education (DfE) – www.gov.uk/government/organisations/depart ...

- Edge Foundation – www.edge.co.uk

- Education and Training Foundation (ETF) – www.et-foundation.co.uk

- Equality and Diversity Forum (EDF) – www.edf.org.uk

- Education and Skills Funding Agency (ESFA) – https://www.gov.uk/government/organisations/education-and-skills-funding-agency

- ESOL resources – http://esol.excellencegateway.org.uk/?platform=hoo ...

- Excellence Gateway (teaching and learning resources) – www.excellencegateway.org.uk

- FE Advice – www.feadvice.org.uk

- FE Careers – www.fecareers.co.uk

- FE News – www.fenews.co.uk

- FE Week – http://feweek.co.uk

- Further Education Tutorial Network (FETN) – http://fetn.org.uk/

- Government updates: Education and Learning – www.gov.uk/browse/education

- Learning and Skills Research Network (LSRN) – https://lsrn.wordpress.com/

- Learning and Work Institute (LWI formerly NIACE) – www.learningandwork.org.uk

- Learning Futures – http://lfuturesnews.co.uk

- Lifelong Learning Platform (Europe) – http://lllplatform.eu

- National Careers Service – https://nationalcareersservice.direct.gov.uk

- Ofqual – www.ofqual.gov.uk

- Ofsted – www.ofsted.gov.uk

- Pearson Policy Watch – https://uk.pearson.com/about-us/news-and-policy/po ...

- Research and Practice in Adult Literacies (RaPAL) – https://rapal.org.uk

- Society for Education and Training (SET) – https://set.et-foundation.co.uk/home

- Teacher Educator UK – https://teachereducatoruk.wikispaces.com

- Times Educational Supplement Online (TES) – www.tes.com/uk

- Tutor Voices (TV) – www.facebook.com/groups/tutorvoices

- University of the Third Age (U3A) – www.u3a.org.uk

- UKFEChat – www.ukfechat.com

- Workers' Educational Association (WEA) – www.wea.org.uk

Social networking

You could join free social network sites such as LinkedIn, which is a professional networking site (www.linkedin.com). Here you will find groups you can join specifically aimed at your specialist subject. If you can't find one when searching the site, you can create your own. You can post questions, respond to queries and join in regular discussions. Other social media sites might also be useful for professional purposes.

Following relevant people or organisations via social media will enable you to keep up to date with what's currently taking place (covered in Chapter 8).

Activity

Access some of the websites and blogs listed in the previous bullet lists and subscribe to any relevant electronic updates.

A good point to remember is that failure is not when you get something wrong, but when you stop trying to get it right. Aim to be the best you can be. The demands of your job might affect what you do and how you feel. When you are with your learners you should remain professional and give them a learning experience which they will remember and benefit from.

Extension activity

Decide on a system for documenting your CPD if you don't already have one. You could use a form as in Table 12.4 or you could design your own. Add some recent activities to it and reflect upon each activity you have carried out. Write how each activity has impacted upon your role.

Self-assessment checklist

Do I know about the following?

If not, re-read this chapter, or research the texts and websites listed at the end.

☐   How to obtain data to help analyse aspects such as retention and achievement

☐   Different ways of obtaining feedback from learners and others

☐   The difference between a survey and a questionnaire

☐   How to analyse and respond to feedback

☐   How to use self-evaluation

☐   What reflective practice involves

☐   Different theories of reflective practice

☐   How to reflect upon my practice

☐   What CPD is and how it can positively impact on my role

☐   How to network with others

☐   How to keep up to date with developments regarding my specialist subject

☐   How to maintain records of CPD

Summary

This chapter has explored how to evaluate and improve your practice.

You should now be able to obtain data and feedback and analyse it with a view to improving your practice and the experience of your learners. You should also know about various reflective practice theories and how to keep up to date with changes to your specialist subject.

You might like to carry out further research by accessing the books and websites listed at the end of this chapter, particularly if you are working towards a higher level teaching qualification.

This chapter has covered the following topics:

- Evaluation in further education and skills contexts

- Obtaining data and gaining feedback

- Self-evaluation

- Reflective practice

- Theories of reflective practice

- Continuing professional development

References and further information

Bell, J. and Waters, S. (2014) *Doing your Research Project* (6th edition). New York: McGraw Hill.

Brookfield, S.D. (1995/2017) *Becoming a Critically Reflective Teacher.* San Francisco, CA: Jossey Bass.

Denscombe, M. (2014) *The Good Research Guide* (5th edition). New York: McGraw Hill.

Ecclestone, K. (1995) The Reflective Practitioner: Mantra or Model for Emancipation. *Studies in the Education of Adults,* 28(2).

Gibbs, G. (1988) *Learning by Doing: A Guide to Teaching and Learning Methods.* Oxford Further Education Unit.

Gregson, M. and Hillier, Y. (2015) *Reflective Teaching in Further, Adult and Vocational Education.* London: Bloomsbury.

Griffiths, M. and Tann, S. (1992) Using Reflective Practice to Link Personal and Public Theories. *Journal of Education for Teaching,* 18(1): 69–84.

Johns, C. (2006) *Engaging Reflection in Practice: A Narrative Approach.* Oxford: Blackwell Publishing.

Kirkpatrick, D.L. and Kirkpatrick, J.D. (1994/2006) *Evaluating Training Programs.* Oakland, CA: Berrett-Koehler Publishers.

Kolb, D.A. (1984) *Experiential Learning: Experience as the Source of Learning and Development.* New Jersey: Prentice-Hall.

Lewin, K. (1951) *Field Theory in Social Science.* New York: Harper and Row.

Martin, K. (1996) Critical Incidents in Teaching and Learning. *Issues of Teaching and Learning,* 2 (8).

Roffey-Barentsen, J. and Malthouse, R. (2013) *Reflective Practice in Education and Training* (2nd edition). London: Learning Matters SAGE.

Rushton, I. and Suter, M. (2012) *Reflective Practice for Teaching in Lifelong Learning.* Maidenhead: Open University Press.

Scales, P. et al. (2011) *Continuing Professional Development in the Lifelong Learning Sector.* Maidenhead: Open University Press.

Schön, D. (1983) *The Reflective Practitioner.* London: Temple Smith.

Sellars, M. (2017) *Reflective Practice for Teachers*. London: SAGE.

Stufflebeam (2007) *Evaluation Theory, Models and Applications*. San Francisco: Jossey Bass.

Tripp, D. (1993/2012) *Critical Incidents in Teaching: Developing Professional Judgement*. London: Routledge.

Wood, J. and Dickinson, J. (2011) *Quality Assurance and Evaluation in the Lifelong Learning Sector*. Exeter: Learning Matters.

Websites

360 degree feedback – https://tinyurl.com/l8ztkgf

Brilliant Teaching and Training in FE and Skills: A Guide to Effective CPD for Teachers, Trainers and Leaders – http://tinyurl.com/ocsef6o

Ethical Guidelines for Educational Research – https://tinyurl.com/muahyn8

Excellence Gateway Improving Teaching – http://improving-teaching.excellencegateway.org.uk

Guidelines for CPD – https://tinyurl.com/os92nqe

Review of CPD – https://tinyurl.com/os92nqe

Online surveys – www.surveymonkey.com and www.smartsurvey.co.uk

Questionnaire design – https://tinyurl.com/mfqvc23

Reading list for reflection and CPD – www.anngravells.com/reading-lists/reflection-and-cpd

Self-evaluation – https://tinyurl.com/k6stxhb

Ofsted, *Teaching, Learning and Assessment in Further Education and Skills – What Works and Why* (2014) – http://tinyurl.com/pf52qlx

13

Delivering a micro-teach session

Introduction

A micro-teach session is a short taught session. It is usually with your peer group, learners or colleagues, as part of working towards a formal teaching or training qualification.

This chapter will explore how you can prepare, plan and facilitate a micro-teach session, as well as assess that learning has taken place. Obtaining feedback from your observer to help evaluate your practice is also covered.

At the end of the chapter you will find a checklist to help you with your micro-teach session.

This chapter will cover the following topics:

- Preparing for the session
- Planning the session
- Facilitating the session
- Assessing learning, making decisions and giving feedback
- Receiving feedback
- Evaluating the session

Preparing for the session

If you are working towards a teaching or training qualification, you will be required to demonstrate your skills, knowledge and understanding at some point. This could be to your peer group (or your learners or colleagues at work). The micro-teach session might be called something else, such as a short session, a presentation or a mini training session. It could be part of a teaching qualification, a train the trainer course, or as part of a job interview. Whatever it's called, it's all about demonstrating what you know and can do.

Think of the micro-teach session as a learning experience for you, and a chance to put all your new-found knowledge and skills into practice. It's very rare that someone will fail their micro-teach session, as it's a chance to learn from mistakes. It's also rare that everyone's session will be perfect first time. Yours might be the same, you might make mistakes; however, it's how you deal with them that matters. If something goes wrong, just be honest about it and carry on with the session. Never give up, and don't be tough on yourself. There might be the opportunity to deliver another session on another day, should the need arise. Your assessor will be able to explain the process to you.

If the session is to your peer group, it might be because you are classed as *pre-service,* i.e. not yet working with learners of your own. Your peer group will therefore become your learners for the micro-teach session, and might also give you feedback at the end. However, you might be able to deliver a session to your current learners or colleagues if you are *in-service.* This means you will be in your own working environment.

The length of the session, date, time and place should be agreed in advance with your assessor, also called an observer. They will make notes and/or use an observation checklist. There's an example of one later in this chapter. You might like to ask if you can see theirs in advance, to help ensure you can meet all the points. The observer might also be your teacher from the course, or another appropriate person. They might sit at the back of the room, or they might want to be part of the group. Your observer (or yourself) could make a visual recording of your session. This will enable you to view it in your own time to help you evaluate how you performed. You might see things you were not aware of: for example, saying *erm,* using a lot of hand gestures or not using enough eye contact with your learners. Try not to be put off by having a camera in the room, you could embrace it as a way of developing yourself further. You might have to provide storage media for the recording, i.e. a memory stick, card or a disk. Alternatively, it might be saved to a hard drive or to the cloud. If this is the case, make sure you find out how you can access the recording afterwards.

It might be that you will deliver your session where your observer is not present in the same room. For example, they might be observing you live via the internet. If this is the case, make sure you find out in advance what the procedure will be and how you can obtain feedback afterwards.

You may feel nervous, which is quite normal. However, try to imagine you are acting a role and this might help boost your confidence and calm your nerves. You are the teacher in this situation; you need to be in control and not let any personal issues affect you. If you are organised and have checked the room and equipment in advance, hopefully you won't encounter any problems. Try to relax, but stay focused on what you are doing and, above all, try and enjoy yourself. If you are passionate about your subject and excited to pass on your skills and knowledge, your enthusiasm will hopefully help the session go well.

You will need to plan and prepare carefully in advance; don't underestimate how much time this may take. This will prove good practice for when you are teaching several sessions with different learners. However, over time, you can reuse and adapt your materials if you are delivering the same session but with different learners.

Make sure your session can flow logically through the introduction, development and summary stages (covered in Chapter 4). You should be able to demonstrate the use of a range of teaching and learning approaches, communication methods, resources and assessment methods.

Micro-teach rationale

You might find it useful to create a rationale to help you prepare for your session. This could take the form of *who, what, when, where, why* and *how* (WWWWWH).

Example

Who: *9 learners: 6 male and 3 female aged 24–48.*

What: *Aim: to introduce learners to non-verbal communication skills.*

When: *9th October, 6 p.m. for 30 minutes.*

Where: *Classroom 5, main building.*

Why: *Objectives:*

1.   *State two methods of non-verbal communication*

2.   *Identify aspects of good and bad body language*

3.   *Discuss experiences regarding assumptions made from body language*

How:

Introduction

*   *Introduce myself and my background, explain the aim and objectives.*

*   *Ask if anyone has any prior knowledge or experience of non-verbal communication skills.*

Development

*   *Explain different methods of non-verbal communication and facilitate a group activity to achieve objective 1.*

*   *Explain and demonstrate appropriate (good) and inappropriate (bad) body language signals.*

(Continued)

(Continued)

- *Use a handout of example body language pictures to achieve objective 2, then discuss with learners.*

- *Discuss assumptions regarding body language and the learners' own experiences to achieve objective 3.*

Conclusion

- *Summarise the session and relate to the aim and objectives.*

- *If time, ask if anyone has any further questions.*

- *Thank the learners for their contributions.*

Using a rationale like the one in this example will help you create your session plan with appropriate objectives or tasks for your learners to achieve (covered in Chapter 4). It should also help you consider other aspects such as which resources you will use and how you will assess that learning has taken place.

Deciding a topic to deliver

You might be required to deliver an aspect of the specialist subject you ultimately wish to teach; or you might be told of a subject to use which you might need to research in advance. Alternatively, you might be able to deliver anything you wish, such as a hobby or something that interests you. An example for an academic topic is: *identifying key dates in history*, or for a vocational topic: *creating a hairstyle*. Whatever topic you choose, you will need to carefully plan what you will be doing, what your learners will be doing, and how long each aspect of your session will take. You will also need to assess that learning has taken place and you will need to allocate time to this. As your session might be quite short, don't try to fit in too much.

If you are unsure about what to deliver, have a chat in advance with your observer. They might be able to help you with some ideas to get you thinking about something that will be appropriate. Table 13.1 lists some topics that people have used for their micro-teach session in the past. Looking at the list might give you some ideas; however, do remember that you need to check that learning is taking place – it's not just about you talking.

Activity

Think of a topic you would like to use for your micro-teach session. Write a rational using the WWWWWH approach. If your topic is academic, think how you can make it interesting and interactive. If your topic is vocational, think how you could demonstrate a skill, i.e. to one person in front of the group, or to everyone.

Table 13.1 Examples of topics used by learners for their micro-teach session

• Aromatherapy	• Folding napkins	• Poetry
• Astrology	• Food hygiene	• Reflexology
• Astronomy	• Hand massage	• Road signs
• Backgammon	• Highway code	• Tai Chi moves
• Bandaging a wound	• Historical key dates	• Taking a photo
• Basic dance moves	• How to eat healthily	• Tying laces
• Basket weaving	• Icing cup cakes	• Salsa dancing
• Bird watching	• Interpreting road signs	• Sign language
• Calligraphy	• Kite making	• Using a digital camera
• Creating a hairstyle	• Life of bees	• Using internet search
• Creating a hanging basket	• Lip reading	engines
• Creative writing	• Making a sandwich	• Vitamins and minerals
• Dog grooming	• Manual handling	• Weights and measures
• Drawing a portrait	• Map reading	• Yoga moves
• Fire prevention	• Origami	• Zumba dancing
• First aid		

To help you prepare for your session, you might find it useful to ask your observer the following questions:

- How long will my session be?

- When and where will it take place, and at what time?

- Who will observe me and will they (or can I) make a visual recording?

- Will you need to see my session plan in advance?

- What if I change my mind about what I'm going to deliver?

- How should I dress?

- What equipment and resources are available for me to use?

- How many people will I be delivering to?

- Do I need to know their learning preferences or any individual needs?

- Can I find out in advance what prior knowledge and/or experience my learners have of my topic?

- Can I show a video clip? If so, how long can it last?

- What will I need to bring with me, e.g. board markers, clock, pens and paper?

- Will I have time beforehand to set up the area, e.g. move tables, check my resources and equipment?

- Will I have internet access if I need it?

- If I use an electronic presentation, should I email it to you or bring it on a memory stick or card?

- Is there somewhere I can get handouts photocopied in advance?

- Should I start with an icebreaker and ground rules?

- Do I have to explain the housekeeping information, e.g. fire exits and toilets?

- What kind of assessment activities should I use?

- How will I receive feedback afterwards?

Pre-service micro-teach session

As a pre-service teacher you will usually be delivering to a group of your peers who will become your learners for the micro-teach session. This might be the first time you have taught a group of people and your peers will probably be very encouraging towards you. You might not experience any behaviour issues, as your peers will want to be supportive. You might also become a learner for your peers when they deliver their sessions.

If you have chosen to deliver a topic you know well, your knowledge should help your confidence. You will probably be in the same environment you have been learning in, such as a classroom. Alternatively, you could be at a central meeting point if you have been studying through a distance learning programme. Hopefully you will have met your peers previously and feel comfortable with them. If not, it would be useful to introduce yourself to them beforehand, to help everyone relax. If you are due to deliver your session after someone else, you will probably be thinking about your own micro-teach session rather than focusing upon theirs. Try not to do this as it may make you more nervous. Being well prepared and having self-confidence and knowledge of your topic should help alleviate any worries.

In-service teaching session

If you are currently employed as a teacher, you will be classed as in-service and you might be able to deliver a session to your own learners in your usual teaching environment. If you are in a different role, such as a workplace trainer, you might be able to deliver a session to your colleagues in your place of work. You will need to check if these options are possible with the person who will observe you. It might be that they are unable to observe you in a different location or that they want everyone to deliver a micro-teach session to their peer group. This might be to give everyone the same opportunity by not giving others an unfair advantage in any way.

If you can deliver a session to your own learners or colleagues, you will already know them and have some experience of what to do. Delivering a session to your own learners or colleagues might therefore be fairly straightforward. However, you might need to embed aspects of English, maths and digital skills (covered in Chapter 5), and/or any other requirements of your organisation such as British Values (covered in Chapter 9).

You may want to introduce the observer to your learners, and state they are observing you, not them. Having a stranger in the room might lead to some learner behaviour issues. If so, you must deal with these as soon as they arise. Your session could last longer than the time your observer will be present; they might therefore miss the beginning or ending and arrive part way through. If possible, try to plan the session to allow time to talk to your observer either before and/or afterwards. This will enable you to justify any aspects they may have missed and to receive their feedback.

Extension activity

Look at the bulleted list (on pages 489 and 490) and find out the answers to the questions which are relevant to you. Think of any other questions you would like to ask, and discuss these, and any concerns you have with your observer.

Planning the session

Once you know your topic for the session, you will need to create a plan, usually known as a session plan or a lesson plan (covered in Chapter 4). You may need two copies, one for yourself and one for your observer. However, you might prefer to have your plan stored on an electronic device instead of a printed copy. As long as you can see and refer to it easily you should be fine. You might want to highlight some key words or timings so that you can glance at them quickly, to help you keep on track.

Activity

What do you think makes a good micro-teach session? Make a list and discuss your responses with a colleague or a friend. Think of the session from the learners' perspective as well as from your own. Compare your responses to the following list – you might have thought of more, which is good.

Some examples of what makes a good micro-session include:

- teacher's knowledge, confidence, professionalism, passion and enthusiasm

- setting of a realistic aim and achievable objectives (or tasks)

- inclusion of all learners, e.g. discussing their experiences, involving them in relevant and varied activities, asking questions, giving appropriate support as necessary

- treating all learners as individuals

- keeping to timings, i.e. starting and finishing on time

- preparation and use of quality materials

- if it was enjoyable and interesting

- assessment of learning

- helpful feedback to individuals.

Your plan should have a clear *aim* (what you want your learners to achieve), which is then broken down into *objectives* (how your learners will achieve your aim, or the tasks they will carry out). It should show what you expect your learners to achieve expressed in a way that will enable you to determine that learning has taken place. For example, your learners might *explain*, and/or *demonstrate* something. Knowing whether you are delivering a practical session, i.e. skills, or a theory session, i.e. knowledge, will help you choose appropriate objectives at the right level for your learners.

Session plan

You can refer to your written rationale to help you create your session plan. The plan will usually consist of a template, which you will complete. You might have to use one that is provided for you or you might like to design your own. An example is given in Table 13.2. For the purpose of future-proofing this book, a year has not been added to any dates within the documents. When completing any documents yourself, you should always add the year, as well as the day and month to create a full audit trail.

Your observer will probably want to see your plan in advance to give you relevant advice and support. They will want to check that your objectives will be achievable by your learners. For example, *State two methods of non-verbal communication*. Using the word *understand* instead of *state* would not help you check that learning has taken place. You will need to use objectives or tasks that demonstrate learning has taken place. It's very difficult to assess understanding, unless you ask your learners to do something.

Structure

Your session should be structured to have a beginning (the introduction), a middle section (the development), and an ending (the conclusion). These should show a logical progression of teaching, learning and assessment. Timings should be allocated to each of the activities you plan to use in each section. You need to think about what you will do, and what your learners will do. Your learners should be active, not passive, whenever possible. You should not be speaking for the majority of the session. If you are delivering a 30-minute session and talking for most of it, how will you know what has been learnt? You may find it useful to note what you can remove or reduce if you are overrunning on time, or what you can include if you have spare time, as in Table 13.2.

Once you have your plan, you will need to prepare all of the activities, handouts, resources, electronic presentations and assessment activities you intend to use (covered in Chapters 5 and 7). You may need to learn how to use something in advance such as an interactive whiteboard. You should check all electronic presentations and handouts for spelling, grammar and punctuation errors, and ensure text and any pictures positively represent equality and diversity. If you are delivering a 30-minute session and you plan to show a video for 10 minutes, this will not demonstrate how teaching and learning is taking place. Videos are good for visual learners but, if used, keep them short, or you may lose the attention of other learners.

You could carry out a trial run of your session with friends or family. This will help you to check your timings and to see what works or not.

Table 13.2 Example session plan

Teacher/trainer	A N Other	Date	09 October	Venue		Room 5 Main building
Topic	Non-verbal communication skills			Number of learners		9
Aim of session	To introduce learners to non-verbal communication skills					
Group composition	6 male and 3 female aged 24–48 June has dyslexia, therefore the handout will be printed on pastel paper for all learners and will also be available electronically Magda is diabetic and may need to leave the room to take insulin					
Timing	Objectives *Learners will:*	Teacher activities		Learner activities	Resources	Assessment activities
5 mins	Listen to the introduction of the aim and objectives	Introduce self, explain aim and objectives Ask if anyone has any prior knowledge or experience of non-verbal communication skills		Listen, respond and ask questions	Flip chart	Oral questions
8 mins	State two methods of non-verbal communication	Explain different methods of non-verbal communication and facilitate group activity		Listen and make notes Take part in an activity in groups of three	Paper and pens PowerPoint slides 1 and 2	Observation of learners Discussion regarding each groups' responses

(Continued)

Table 13.2 (Continued)

Timing	Objectives Learners will:	Teacher activities	Learner activities	Resources	Assessment activities
9 mins	Identify aspects of good and bad body language	Explain and demonstrate appropriate (good) and inappropriate (bad) body language signals Issue a handout with example body language pictures, then discuss responses	Listen and make notes Complete the handout activity individually Mark each other's responses	PowerPoint slide 3 Handout	Learners mark each other's responses Discussion regarding responses
5 mins	Discuss experiences regarding assumptions made from body language	Discuss assumptions regarding body language and the learners' own experiences	Discuss and offer opinions and experiences (reduce discussion time if overrunning)	PowerPoint slide 4	Discussion
3 mins	Listen to the recap Ask questions	Summarise the session, relate to the aim and objectives on the flip chart If time, ask if anyone has any further questions Thank the learners for their contributions	Listen to the summary, ask questions (If spare time – each learner to state one significant point they have learnt from the session)	PowerPoint slide 5 Flip chart	Oral questions if time

You might find that what you planned to cover in 30 minutes takes less, or more time. A clock or a watch in a visible place will help you keep track. You might find that time will go quickly during your session, particularly if you are asked lots of questions by your learners. Questions are good, as it shows your learners are interested. However, they do not show what they have learnt.

Try to have a contingency plan in case anything goes wrong or if you overrun or are short of time.

Example

Sangita had prepared a short electronic presentation to use during her session. In case of the equipment not working on the day, she had printed a paper copy to refer to. If her learners also asked for a copy, she could offer to email it to them. She was conscious that she might get asked lots of questions throughout the session, so she planned how she could cut down the timing of an activity if this happened. She also prepared an extra activity in case some learners finished earlier than others.

In this example, Sangita hoped she had prepared for all eventualities.

If possible, check in advance and/or arrive early to see that everything is available and working in the room you will be in. You may want to rearrange the area beforehand to enable everyone to see and hear you. You might find your peers are willing to help with this. Time for setting up and clearing away afterwards should be outside of your allocated delivery time.

Extension activity

Obtain the session planning document you are required to use for your micro-teach session. Complete it using the rationale you created earlier, or with something else. Allocate timings to each of the activities. Think of an additional activity you could use if you have spare time, or consider what you can reduce or remove if you run short of time. Create any handouts you will use and check that any resources you will use are appropriate.

Facilitating the session

Hopefully, you will be given a little time before commencing your session to set up the area, check your resources and focus yourself ready to start. If you are being visually recorded, check who will do this and whether they need time to set up the equipment beforehand. Keep your session plan handy to check your timings, and ask your learners if they can see and hear you before you commence. When you are ready, you can commence your session and go logically through the introduction, development and conclusion stages.

Introduction

Before you speak, take a few deep breaths, smile at your learners and use eye contact with everyone. Hopefully, your learners will smile back at you and this will help you to relax a little. You can then introduce yourself by saying *Hello, my name is ...* , followed by your aim and objectives (or tasks). You might like to keep these on display throughout your session, perhaps on a piece of flipchart paper on the wall. Alternatively, you could display them on a screen and refer to them at the beginning and ending of the session.

There's no need to tell your learners if you are nervous, as it probably won't show. Be aware of your posture, and speak a little more loudly and slowly than normal. Being anxious or nervous may make you speak softly or quickly. If you feel you are shaking, it is highly likely no one will notice. If your mind suddenly goes blank, take a couple of deep breaths for a few seconds and look at your session plan to help you refocus; it might seem a long time to you but it won't to your learners.

It's good if you can establish a rapport with your learners and engage and interact with them from the start. Asking the question *'What experience, if any, do you have?'* is a good way of including your learners from the start. This helps you check any prior knowledge or skills they may have. You can then draw on this during the session, perhaps by asking them some questions about it. Make sure you communicate effectively with everyone at some point during the session, and use eye contact, but do keep an eye on the time. If your topic includes acronyms or jargon words, make sure you explain them clearly.

You will also need to ensure you can meet any individual needs of those in your group. If possible, you could ascertain details in advance if you have the opportunity.

Example

Jonathan knows one member of his group, Jen, has dyslexia. He plans to give a handout to everyone and he knows Jen prefers to read text on a pastel coloured background. He will therefore make sure all the handouts he issues are on pastel coloured paper for everyone in the group.

In this example, Jen was not singled out for any reason and no one else need know she has dyslexia. You could note any individual needs on your plan as your observer might need to see how you are differentiating for them.

If you feel you might forget something during your session, make sure you use a highlight pen beforehand to mark key words on your plan. Alternatively, you could use cue cards with key words on which you can quickly glance at. Standing rather than sitting might help your confidence and your voice projection. Do keep things simple, there's no point in complicating things, or doing too much too quickly. Conversely, don't expect too much from your learners as your topic may be very new to them. If this is the first time you have met your learners, you might want to carry out a short icebreaker with them or ask them to introduce themselves to you if you have the time. However, if your peer group know each other already, they will be familiar with each other, the ground rules and any other requirements such as fire drills. Your observer should have informed you if you need to use an icebreaker or agree any ground rules. These can be time consuming and might not be necessary during a micro-teach session. You might like to encourage your learners to ask questions if they need to clarify any points; however, you will constantly need to keep a check on the time.

Activity

If you have access to the internet, watch the short video regarding facilitating a micro-teach session: http://tinyurl.com/AnnMicro. You could also search for 'micro-teach sessions', which previous trainee teachers have uploaded to YouTube. When watching them, note what is good and what could be improved and why.

Development

You can develop your session by using a variety of teaching and learning approaches and activities to keep your learners engaged and motivated. Do make sure all your learners are included and not left out of anything for any reason. If you are short of time, using eye contact with each individual, and using their name is a quick way of including them. You will need to summarise and recap regularly to reinforce your points; never be afraid of repeating yourself.

If you wish to use technology during your session, it's best to check in advance that everything is working, and that your learners have access if they need to. If you expect your learners to use their own devices for an activity, you will need to find out who has, or does not have one. You will also need to check for internet access if necessary.

Think of your micro–teach session as a learning experience. If you make a mistake, move on and don't draw attention to it, your learners might not notice. However, don't bluff your way out of anything; always be honest. Do keep an eye on the body language of your learners in case they appear bored. If so, you will need to catch their attention, perhaps by asking a question directed at someone by name.

The timing of activities needs to be followed carefully; if you are only delivering a 15-minute session, you may not have time to carry out a group activity. If you do set activities, think what you will be doing while your learners are busy, for example, moving around the room and observing or asking questions shows you are in control. Standing at the front doing nothing doesn't look good. Make sure you set a time limit for your learners to complete any activities, and keep to it. Longer sessions benefit from a mixture of teaching and learning approaches and different activities. If you have delivered a practical task, you will need to observe that your learners have gained the skills to demonstrate what you have taught. However, you will also need to check they have the understanding to explain why they are doing it that way.

Conclusion

The conclusion is the summary to your session once teaching and learning have taken place. This should be given in a succinct way and related back to your aim and objectives. If you have time, you can summarise learning with a short quiz or a multiple-choice test. This is a good way to check knowledge and understanding. You might like to ask your learners if they have any questions. However, you may be met with silence, or they might have lots of questions, which will then impact upon your time. If you find you have covered everything and have spare time, you could ask each member of the group to state *one significant thing* they feel they have learnt from the session. This is a good way of filling in spare time if necessary and shows you what each individual has learnt. You could issue a handout which summarises your session which you can give out at the end. If you issue it during the session your learners may look at it and not focus on what is happening at the time.

If you are unsure of how to end your session, simply say *'Thank you, I've enjoyed my session with you today and I hope you have learnt something new'*. This will indicate to your group you have finished. There's no need to say *'That's it, I've finished'* or *'I'm glad that's over'*. Remember to stay professional right to the end and tidy the area afterwards. If you have been visually recorded, make sure you obtain the storage media, or know how to access the recording so that you can view it later.

Extension activity

Rehearse your micro-teach session by delivering it to a few trusted people such as friends or family members. Make sure you have your session plan and all relevant resources to hand. Although this is a role-play activity, treat it seriously and work through all your planned teaching, learning and assessment activities. Afterwards, ask for some feedback as to how they felt the session went.

Assessing learning, making decisions and giving feedback

At some point during your micro-teach session you will need to assess that learning has taken place by each individual. You will probably not be using formal assessment activities, as your learners might not be working towards a qualification (unless you are an in-service teacher delivering a session with your own learners). You will, therefore, need to use informal activities to ensure learning has taken place. However, as the session will be quite short, you might find it difficult to assess how much learning has actually taken place. It could be that your learners (your peers from the group) already know a bit about your topic beforehand. The micro-teach session is more of a simulated experience than an actual experience, but it will give you valuable practice at planning, facilitating and assessing learning.

Assessment should take place at key points during the session, for example, by asking open questions to check knowledge (ones that begin with *who, what, when, where, why* and *how*). Try to use names when talking to your learners and, if possible, address everyone in the group. Don't just focus on a particular learner who you know can give you the correct answer. Having your learners' names written down in advance will help. Try to use the PPP (Pose, Pause, Pick) method when asking questions. This is where you pose a question, pause for a few seconds (allowing everyone in the group to think of an answer) and then pick a learner. If you do it the other way around by mentioning someone's name first, everyone else might not think of an answer as they know they won't be asked. If you have a small group, you could plan to ask one open question to each learner at some point during the session. You may need to prepare these questions in advance, even if you don't use them all. Alternatively, if mini whiteboards are available (or pieces of A4 paper if not) you could ask a question, and each learner can write their response on it. They can then hold them up for you to see.

Activity

Find out how many people will be your learners for the micro-teach session. If your group is small, write enough open questions to cover everyone, based on the topic you will use. If the group is large, think of a few questions whereby your learners could respond by writing on A4 sheets of paper and holding them up for you to see.

If you have demonstrated a practical skill, you will need to ensure your learners can then carry it out. This will be by observing them to check their skills and asking questions to check their knowledge. If you have a large group, you could choose to focus on demonstrating the task to one learner, while everyone else watches. You can then assess that same learner and give them feedback. Depending upon time and the amount of resources you have, the others in the group could then have a go. You would need to observe them too and also give them feedback. You might wish to discuss with your observer in advance what approach you should take depending upon the time you have.

Example

Serena demonstrated how to create a hanging basket with a variety of plants. She only had enough resources for herself and one learner. She chose Pat to come to the front of the group to carry out the task at the same time as she demonstrated it. The rest of the group were able to see what was happening, but were not able to carry out the task. Serena could observe and ask questions to Pat to check her skills and knowledge. However, she could only ask questions to the rest of the group to check their knowledge, as she could not assess their skills. She gave everyone a handout at the end of the session with pictures and text showing the process of how to create a hanging basket.

In this example, one learner was able to demonstrate skills and knowledge, but the rest of the group were only able to demonstrate knowledge. You may need to check with your observer in advance if you plan to use this approach during your session.

The following are some assessment activities you could use to assess skills and knowledge with your learners (in alphabetical order):

- completing gapped handouts or word searches
- discussions in pairs
- drawing a picture or designing a poster
- group tasks to achieve an objective
- multiple-choice tests
- observation of a practical task
- puzzles
- questions – written or oral
- quizzes
- role plays.

The type of activity you use might depend upon the time you have available and the level of learning taking place. For the purpose of your micro-teach session, you might be able to inform your group that they are all total beginners. They could play along and this would make things easier for you, but would not be realistic. For example, you could use a gapped handout: a page of text with missing words which the learners need to complete. It might be that your learners would have known the missing words before attending your session. Other lower level assessment activities such as quizzes, puzzles and word searches could be fun and can be completed individually, in pairs or in groups. However, you will need to assess what each individual has achieved when they are working as part of a group. You will also need to ensure your assessment activities are at the right level. If you have a group of high-level learners, they might not appreciate having to complete a gapped handout.

Making decisions

Once you have carried out an assessment activity, you will need to make a decision as to whether learning has taken place (or not). This will perhaps be from the learners' answers to oral questions, or by observing them demonstrating a task. If learners have carried out a task individually, you will need to check and confirm they have done it correctly. If it's been carried out as part of a group activity, you will need to check who did what, and again, confirm success or otherwise.

Don't forget that assessment should not be in isolation from teaching and learning and can occur at any time. Don't just leave it until the end of your session.

Giving feedback

You will need to give your learners feedback in a constructive and developmental way. If you don't, they won't know if they have been successful or not. During the micro-teach session the assessment activities will have been quite short. This will have helped you see straight away if your learners have been successful or not. It's probable that most learners will have been successful. However, if you have a learner that hasn't, you still need to let them know. *For example, 'Well done Olga for attempting the task; however, you didn't quite achieve it today. You could practise it in your own time if you get the chance'.*

When giving feedback, clearly state what each person has learnt and give advice for further development if necessary. You won't have a lot of time for this, particularly if you have a large group. You might want to ask your observer what they recommend regarding how you can provide feedback. It might be that you are able to assess and provide feedback to a few of the learners in the group, rather than to everyone individually. The others might therefore be classed as observers rather than learners.

Further information regarding assessment, making decisions and giving feedback can be found in Chapter 10.

You should remain professional when you finish your session, pack away your resources and equipment and re-join your peer group.

Extension activity

Design an activity that you could use to assess your learners during your micro-teach session. For example, a quiz, a multiple-choice test or a task learners can complete (covered in Chapters 5 and 8).

Receiving feedback

After your session you should receive feedback from your observer. This might be immediately, or after all your peers have delivered their sessions. You may find that your observer will ask you how you felt the session went before giving you their feedback. This will enable you to consider what went well and what you could have done differently. Don't be afraid of being honest with yourself, the micro-teach session is a learning opportunity.

If your observer begins to give you feedback while you are still packing away after your session, you might be so relieved it's over, that you don't fully take on board what is being said. Try to focus and listen carefully to anything that is said to you, as it may prove useful.

Some people are good at receiving feedback, others are not and they might become defensive or unwilling to accept what has been said.

Activity

Think back to the last time someone gave you feedback regarding something you had done. Did you listen carefully and act on what they said? Or did you become defensive and not really listen to them? How can you ensure you listen carefully to all the feedback you receive at the end of your micro-teach session?

It's useful to ask your observer a few questions to clarify any points you are unsure of. Try not to interrupt them or become too defensive and don't take anything personally as the feedback will be given with the aim of helping you improve. It should be about the session, not you as a person. You should also receive written feedback, which will be useful to refer to later. This might take the form of a summary of your strengths, areas for development and any action required. Alternatively, the feedback might be written on an observation report as in Table 13.3 or be completed electronically and emailed to you later.

Example

Strengths

- *Your session plan had realistic timings and was very detailed with the use of a clear aim and objectives.*
- *You were well prepared and organised. The electronic presentation was very clear with just the right amount of text on each slide and supported with diagrams and pictures.*
- *You engaged your learners from the start and maintained their attention throughout.*
- *Your passion and enthusiasm for your subject helped you to convey your confidence and professionalism.*
- *All learners achieved the objectives.*

Areas for development

- *Ask more open questions when possible.*
- *Issue a copy of your PowerPoint as a handout (or electronic version) so that your learners can follow the slides and make notes as necessary.*
- *You could have referred to the textbooks you had brought in, perhaps it was nerves that made you forget this.*

Action required

- *Prepare some open questions in advance which you could use with your learners.*
- *Be careful of your timings, particularly at the end when learners were asking questions. If you think you might run out of time, you need something you can remove or reduce the time of. If your learners start asking lots of questions, you could tell them you will talk to them at break time.*

Table 13.3 Example observer's feedback

Did the teacher?	Yes/No	Comments
Introduce themselves and create a rapport with their learners	Y	You already knew the learners as you have been attending the course with them; however, you gave some background information regarding your experience and qualifications regarding your subject. You created a good rapport with the learners by relating the topic to their own experiences. You let them know they could ask questions at any time. You ensured everyone was seated comfortably, could see what you were doing and hear you from the back of the room.
State the aim and objectives (or tasks) of the session	Y	You began the session by stating your aims and objectives using a PowerPoint slide as a visual aid. You checked if anyone had any prior knowledge at this point. You could keep the objectives on display throughout the session by using a flipchart or issuing a copy of your presentation as a handout. You should refer back to the objectives, particularly when an activity has been completed which meets them. You can also use objectives as a good assessment tool by asking learners which ones they feel they have just met.
Use equipment/ resources/handouts appropriately	Y	You prepared well beforehand by creating your PowerPoint and two different handouts. You arrived early to ensure all the equipment was working correctly. You set out the handouts, session plan and notes where you could see and access them throughout the session. You also brought in relevant textbooks in case anyone was interested in any further reading (however, you forgot to mention this). You had saved your presentation to the hard drive and had a backup copy on a memory stick just in case anything went wrong. You also used a remote pointing device which ensured you could move around the room while still operating the presentation slides.
Communicate clearly (verbally and non-verbally)	Y	You spoke clearly during the session and explained the topic in a way that all learners, no matter what their prior knowledge, were able to understand. Your body language was positive, although your voice did at times go a little soft.
Act confidently and professionally	Y	You acted very confidently and professionally which was helped by your vast knowledge of your subject. You were a little nervous at first; however, as you progressed, your confidence grew. You had dressed appropriately in order to appear professional.

(Continued)

Table 13.3 (Continued)

Did the teacher?	Yes/No	Comments
Ask open questions to check knowledge	Y	You prompted your learners to ask you questions throughout; however, you didn't ask many open questions to check the understanding of individual learners.
Involve and include everyone during the session	Y	You made eye contact with everyone, used their names when you could and made sure they were all able to take part in the activity. You also used a group activity and checked everyone knew what they were doing.
Demonstrate subject knowledge	Y	You demonstrated a thorough knowledge of your subject and your passion for it came across as the session developed.
Use a variety of teaching, learning and assessment approaches	Y	You used a mixture of talking, practical activities, an electronic presentation, handouts and questioning.
Take into account: health and safety; equality and diversity; learning preferences and individual learner needs	Y	The room was a comfortable temperature and bright, the area was clear of any possible hazards and you asked your learners to put their bags under the table out of the way. Your learners consisted of a range of learning preferences. These were accommodated by the approaches you used during your session. Your pictures represented people from all aspects of society. You catered well for your learner who has dyslexia by providing the handout on pastel coloured paper for everyone.
Assess that learning took place	Y	Although you didn't ask many open questions, you did ask questions which elicited responses, and the practical activity ensured you could observe that learning was taking place. You could have used a quiz at the end to enable a few more questions to be asked in an informal and fun way.
Summarise the session and refer to the aim and objectives (or tasks)	Y	You gave a summary at the end of the session using a PowerPoint slide, you confirmed the objectives had been achieved and you asked for some learner feedback. Your learners agreed they had achieved the objectives. You gave the opportunity for further questions and your learners responded well. However, you over ran the time by five minutes.
Tidy the area afterwards	Y	You packed everything away at the end of the session and left the area tidy for the next micro-teach session.

Your peers might also have the opportunity to give you feedback. They might complete the same form as your observer, use a different one, or just give oral feedback. They might not be as skilful at giving feedback as your observer. They will be commenting on how they felt as a learner as well as what they felt about the session. Don't take anything personally, but listen for aspects you could improve upon.

You could use the feedback forms to refer to, to help inform your self-evaluation after the session. If you are given these forms prior to another of your peer's micro-teach sessions, put them away to read later. You won't want to distract from what is going on in the room. You might also have the opportunity to provide feedback to your peers after their micro-teach session.

Extension activity

Look at Table 13.3 and read the comments from the observer. Do you feel they are written in a constructive way? If this feedback had been given to you, how would you feel, and what would be your action points as a result?

Evaluating the session

Evaluating how your session went is an important aspect of your own learning and development. You will need to take into account the feedback from your observer and your peers. You might think you have done really well, but you might have received some helpful advice during the feedback process, which could help you to improve further. Do read all the feedback forms you receive and don't be upset by anything you feel is negative. The feedback is not meant to be personal about you; it's meant to be helpful about the session. You might like to make some notes to summarise the feedback you have received, this will help when evaluating your practice. There might be a specific form or template for you to complete to evaluate your session.

Activity

Find out if there is a form or a template you will need to complete to evaluate the feedback you have received. Have a look at it and ask your observer to clarify any points you are unsure of. Can you group any aspects into themes, which will help you when evaluating? For example, communication, teaching and learning approaches, behaviour, and assessment.

Hopefully, you enjoyed your micro-teach session and it has confirmed you do want to have a career as a teacher. However, the experience might have made you think that it just isn't for you at this point in time. Conversely, it might make you more determined to improve and develop further. If you have any concerns, make sure you talk to your observer. If you don't do very well during your session, think of it as a learning experience and consider how you could do things differently next time.

Example

Ojas was quite nervous prior to delivering his 30-minute micro-teach session. He had chosen to talk about the history of calligraphy. He used an electronic presentation, which contained 24 slides, and he talked through all of them. He overran the time and did not ask any questions or make the session interactive in any way. As a result, no assessment took place to check what had been learnt. His observer gave him constructive feedback to this effect. He was offered the chance to deliver the same session, but in a different way on another date. Ojas at first thought he didn't want to carry on with the course. However, he wanted to persevere and his observer and peers gave him lots of encouragement. He changed the session so that he was only talking at the beginning and the end. The middle section enabled all the group to practise using calligraphy. Ojas was able to observe that learning was taking place and he gained positive feedback afterwards.

In this example, Ojas was pleased he had the opportunity to deliver his session again. He realised that it's not about what he does as much as what the learners do.

When evaluating your session, you could consider your strengths, areas for development and any action which might be required. You could consider this from a teaching perspective as well as from your subject specialism perspective.

You could also ask yourself some specific questions such as:

- what went well and why?
- what didn't go well and why?
- what happened that I didn't expect to happen?
- how did I manage my timings and any interruptions?
- what would I do differently if I delivered this same session again?

Answering these questions may help you to evaluate your delivery and focus on how you can improve.

If your session has been visually recorded, watch the playback in your own time. You may see things you didn't realise you had done, which can help the evaluation process.

Extension activity

Consider the feedback you received from your friends or family after your practice micro-teach session. Did you achieve your aim effectively? Were the objectives achieved? Did you keep to your timings or did anything unforeseen happen? Consider what you would change or modify prior to delivering your actual micro-teach session.

Micro-teach checklist

Beforehand

☐   *Decide on a topic that you feel knowledgeable about and confident to deliver, one that is suitable for your group of learners. Try not to change your mind too often about what you plan to do.*

☐   *Find out how many learners there will be and any particular needs they may have.*

☐   *Find out when and where you will be delivering, at what time and for how long.*

☐   *Prepare your plan in advance, ensuring you have a clear aim (what you want to achieve) and SMART objectives (or tasks). Don't use the words* know *or* understand *when creating objectives as they are difficult to assess. It would be useful to ask your observer to comment on your plan beforehand.*

☐   *Plan what will be covered during the beginning, middle and ending sections of your session, and allocate timings to each activity. You will need to keep your learners engaged, active and motivated so that the session is focused upon their learning.*

☐   *Keep things simple – don't try to achieve too much too soon as time will go quickly. Equally, don't expect too much from your learners as they might be new to your topic and will not want to be rushed.*

☐   *Prepare an extra activity in case you have spare time, along with extension activities to stretch and challenge the more capable learners, if applicable.*

☐   *Know what you can reduce or remove if you run short of time.*

☐   *Prepare all your resources, check for spelling, grammar, punctuation and sentence construction errors in handouts and electronic presentations. If you use pictures, make sure they positively represent all aspects of equality and diversity. Check you are not infringing copyright in any way, and reference any text and/or pictures you have used from books, journals or the internet.*

☐   *Rehearse your session with friends or family to check your timings.*

☐   *Plan ahead – practise using the relevant technology, equipment and/or resources beforehand.*

☐   *Photocopy handouts and materials as required; reserve equipment if necessary.*

☐   *Have a contingency plan in case something goes wrong or isn't available, for example, a printed copy of an electronic presentation.*

☐   *Have spare pens and paper.*

☐   *Check if you can arrive early to prepare the room, equipment and resources.*

During

☐   *Set up the area to suit your topic so that all learners can see and hear you.*

☐   *Have a watch or clock handy to keep track of the time.*

(Continued)

(Continued)

☐ *Keep your session plan in view so that you can look at it when necessary to make sure you are on track with your timings or to look at key words.*

☐ *Relax, take a few deep breaths and focus on what you are going to do. Leave all personal issues behind.*

☐ *When you start, smile and use eye contact with everyone; introduce yourself, your topic and your aim. Check that everyone can hear and see you.*

☐ *State the objectives (or tasks) clearly and/or have them written down somewhere for referring back to when they are achieved and at the end of the session.*

☐ *Check for prior knowledge and/or experience and draw on this throughout your session (go from the known to the unknown).*

☐ *Speak a little slower and louder than normal.*

☐ *Deliver your topic confidently, remaining focused, staying in control, acting professionally and trying to relax while enjoying the experience.*

☐ *Engage your learners by asking questions and involving them when you can.*

☐ *Watch the body language of your learners – do they appear interested or bored?*

☐ *Project your energy, enthusiasm and passion for your subject.*

☐ *Pace the session according to your learners, involve them so the session is centred on them and not you. Differentiate activities as necessary and take into account any particular needs.*

☐ *Make sure you involve every learner at some point during your session, i.e. by using their names, asking an individual question, and using eye contact.*

☐ *Limit the use of jargon and acronyms and explain each one when used.*

☐ *Ask open questions to test knowledge and understanding (ones that begin with who, what, when, where, why and how).*

☐ *Use the PPP question technique: Pose, Pause, Pick.*

☐ *Check learning has taken place by carrying out some form of assessment activity, for example, observation, written or oral questions.*

☐ *If you set a group activity, think about what you will be doing while your learners are active and give a target time for completion.*

☐ *Always confirm achievement (or otherwise) to each individual, and give constructive feedback.*

☐ *At the end of your session, allow time for questions from your learners, but keep an eye on the time as you could easily overrun.*

☐ *When summarising, recap your aim and objectives (or the tasks the learners have achieved).*

☐ *It is useful to provide a handout to summarise your topic with further information, for example, relevant textbooks and a website list.*

☐ *If you are unsure how to end your session, simply say 'Thank you, I've enjoyed my session with you today'.*

Afterwards

☐ *Tidy the area.*

☐ *Listen to the feedback from your observer (and peers if applicable).*

☐ *Don't be annoyed with yourself if you made any mistakes, the micro-teach session is a developmental learning opportunity.*

☐ *Evaluate what went well and why, and what didn't go well and why, and take into consideration the feedback you have received.*

☐ *Make sure you complete any required documentation and submit it by the target date.*

Self-assessment checklist

Do I know about the following?

If not, re-read this chapter, or research the texts and websites listed at the end.

☐ What a micro-teach session is

☐ How to prepare a rationale for my session

☐ What topic I could use for my session

☐ The difference between a pre-service and in-service session

☐ What makes a good micro-teach session

☐ How to create a session plan

☐ What resources and equipment I will use

☐ What I will do and what my learners will do during the three stages of the session

☐ How I will assess that learning has taken place

☐ How I will provide feedback to my learners regarding achievement

☐ How I will receive feedback from my assessor and my peers after my session

☐ How I will evaluate my session

Summary

This chapter has explored how you can plan and prepare for your micro-teach session.

You should now be able to facilitate a short session and assess that learning has taken place. You should also know how to evaluate your practice with a view to making improvements.

You might like to carry out further research by accessing the books and websites listed at the end of this chapter, particularly if you are working towards a higher level teaching qualification.

This chapter has covered the following topics:

- Preparing for the session

- Planning the session

- Facilitating the session

- Assessing learning, making decisions and giving feedback

- Receiving feedback

- Evaluating the session

References and further information

Duckworth, V. (2014) *How to be a Brilliant FE Teacher.* Abingdon: Routledge.

Powell, S. and Tummons, J. (2011) *Inclusive Practice in the Lifelong Learning Sector.* Exeter: Learning Matters.

Race, P. (2014) *Making Learning Happen.* London: SAGE.

Rogers, A. and Horrocks, N. (2010) *Teaching Adults* (4th edition). Maidenhead: Open University Press.

Wallace, S. (2011) *Teaching, Tutoring and Training in the Lifelong Learning Sector* (4th edition). Exeter: Learning Matters.

Wilson, L. (2014) *Practical Teaching: A Guide to Teaching in the Educational and Training Sector.* Andover: Cengage Learning.

Websites

Ann Gravells micro-teach video – http://tinyurl.com/AnnMicro

Oxford Learning Institute – Giving and receiving feedback – http://tinyurl.com/688tfev

Reading list for teaching and learning – www.anngravells.com/reading-lists/teaching

14

Teaching practice

Introduction

Teaching practice is about having the opportunity to experience what the role of a teacher involves. This might be if you are new to the role and/or working towards a teaching qualification. This will usually be for a certain amount of time and will help you to gain in confidence. An assessor will observe you for some of this time with the aim of helping you to improve.

This chapter will explore what teaching practice is all about, and how you can prepare for it. What to do prior to being observed and how you can benefit from the experience are covered, as are the minimum core skills of literacy, language, numeracy, and information communication technology (ICT). These are skills that all teachers should be able to demonstrate as part of their role.

This chapter will cover the following topics:

- What is teaching practice?
- The minimum core
- Preparing to be observed
- During the observation
- After the observation
- Evidencing teaching practice

What is teaching practice?

Teaching practice is about demonstrating your skills and knowledge as a teacher or a trainer. This can be with individuals and/or groups of learners, and can be in any further education and skills environment, for example, a classroom, a workshop or the workplace. It's called *practice* as anyone undertaking it is not yet qualified. It will give actual experience of what it's like to be a teacher, in a real teaching and learning environment.

If you haven't taught before, it can be a bit daunting the first time, but it can be an exciting prospect. Teaching practice is a great way for you to try out everything you have been learning during your time taking a teaching qualification.

Effective teaching practice should include:

- using different teaching practice locations, settings or contexts

- teaching across more than one level of learning

- teaching a variety of learners and age ranges

- teaching individuals and groups

- gaining subject-specialist knowledge from mentors and observers.

All teaching qualifications will require you to take part in some form of teaching practice for a set amount of time. If you are already in a teaching role, you should be able to work with your current learners to build up your time. If you train people on-the-job at your place of work, you might be able to include it. It's best to talk to your teacher first, to see what they recommend. If you are not yet teaching, they might be able to advise you how to gain your teaching practice hours. Usually, the hours you deliver should be with real learners in real situations and not with another teacher helping you. However, if your teaching practice includes an element of *micro-teaching*, you might be able to deliver a session to your peer group (covered in Chapter 13).

Activity

Find out how many teaching practice hours you will need to carry out as part of the teaching qualification you will take. Can they be with individual learners, do they need to include groups, or both? Where will the teaching practice take place and who will be your contact person to arrange them? Once you know all this information, you can begin to plan what you will do and when.

You will be observed for some of the teaching practice hours at different points throughout your training programme. This will enable you to demonstrate how you are improving over time and to learn from any mistakes.

You might need to keep a log of your hours and link these to your supporting evidence as in Table 14.3 at the end of this chapter on page 533. The evidence you provide should include all the documentation and resources you have used to facilitate your sessions (one piece of evidence can be referred to several times) as well as your observer's feedback reports. It's useful to carry out a self-evaluation after each session you have delivered, taking into account your strengths, areas for development, and any actions or improvements required. This might form part of a reflective learning journal or a diary that you maintain throughout the time you are working towards the qualification (covered in Chapter 12). Try to be analytical and reflective, rather than just being descriptive when you are writing, and make reference to relevant theories of teaching, learning and assessment (covered in Chapter 2).

People involved throughout the teaching practice experience

There may be several people involved throughout your teaching practice experience. These might include:

- a mentor

- administrators and support staff

- an assessor and/or observer

- other observers such as internal quality assurers

- your supervisor at the teaching practice location

- your teacher.

A mentor

Ideally, you should have a mentor, someone who is a specialist in the subject you wish to teach. They will be able to give you appropriate advice and support throughout your time taking the teaching qualification. They should also be able to observe some of your sessions and give you valuable feedback. This should cover not only your teaching, learning and assessment approaches, but also subject-specific information. They could also help you link your role to any professional standards you might need to meet.

You could also observe your mentor to gain useful ideas for delivering your subject. If a mentor isn't allocated to you, you could ask a colleague if they would be willing to take on the role. If you are not happy with the person who has been allocated to you, you might be able to change to someone else.

Example

Lisa is a fairly new geography teacher in a college, having worked there part time for three months. Her mentor, Zac, has been teaching for six years and has welcomed Lisa into his sessions to observe his practice. He is very helpful and supportive and meets Lisa once a month to discuss her progress and any concerns. As a result, Lisa has learnt a lot more about teaching and learning, as well as gaining further knowledge of geography.

Administrators and support staff

You may need to liaise with various administrators and support staff at some point during your teaching practice. This might be to notify reception when your observer will be visiting, arrange for photocopying to be carried out and to liaise with support staff when necessary.

An assessor and/or an observer

Your teacher might not observe all of your teaching practice sessions. There might be an assessor or another observer either from the organisation you are taking the qualification with, or elsewhere. You will need to find out who they are to arrange when they will visit. They will also need to communicate with the teacher of your qualification to inform them of your progress and achievement.

Other observers

If you are in-service, there might be occasions when quality assurers and/or inspectors will observe you. An internal quality assurer might observe you to satisfy themselves that you are making valid and reliable assessment decisions. An external quality assurer from an awarding organisation might observe you to see that you are following their requirements. Inspectors will want to see how you are meeting certain requirements, for example those from Ofsted (in England). They might not provide feedback directly to you; however, at some point, you should be able to find out what their findings are. An inspector may appear unannounced; therefore, it's always best to be prepared.

A colleague might observe you as part of an appraisal or a review process. This might or might not be arranged in advance. Don't be concerned, just do what you normally would do. You should get the opportunity to discuss their observation at some point, and to agree an action plan for your development if necessary.

You might like to observe your colleagues or peers who teach different subjects to help you appreciate other ways of how teaching, learning and assessment can take place. Even though it's not the same subject to yours, you might gain some good ideas of activities to carry out with your own learners. You could also ask them to observe you and give you some feedback. If you have a learning support assistant who helps particular learners during your session, you could ask them for feedback. They might see things that you don't.

Being observed by others before you are formally observed should help you relax a little when the time comes for a formal observation. However, any observations by mentors or others might not count towards the formally observed practice of a teaching qualification. You don't need to put on a show for any of your observers, you should just be the best you can be, all of the time.

Your supervisor at the teaching practice location

If you are currently working as a teacher, i.e. you are classed as in-service, you might have a supervisor at your place of work. This person might also be your mentor. You should feel able to talk to them about any concerns you have and to ask advice when necessary. You should also liaise with them to inform them when you will be formally observed as part of your teaching qualification. They might want to meet your observer to discuss your progress with them.

If you are not currently working as a teacher, i.e. you are classed as pre-service, you might have been allocated to an organisation for the purposes of your teaching practice. You will need to find out where this is, who the contact person is and what is expected of you. You might feel strange going into unfamiliar surroundings; however, if you have a supportive supervisor, they should help put you at your ease. You might not be able to teach on your own until you have been shadowed by your supervisor for a period of time. You might then be asked to cover classes for absent colleagues if you feel confident. If this is the case, you will need to obtain their scheme of work and course documents to continue effectively with the programme.

Your teacher

Your teacher might observe you at some point during your time taking the teaching qualification. They will discuss with you the dates and times they will visit, and what they will expect when there. It could be that you need to learn something at a particular time to be able to demonstrate it during your teaching practice. If it hasn't been planned yet by your teacher, you could talk to them to find out how you can cover the topic sooner.

Extension activity

If you are currently teaching or training others, ask a colleague (or your mentor if you have one) to observe one of your sessions. Inform your learners that they are there to watch you, not them. Listen to the feedback they give you afterwards and make a note of what you could improve or change.

The minimum core

When carrying out your teaching practice, you might need to demonstrate the *minimum core* personal skills of:

- language and literacy
- numeracy
- information and communication technology (ICT).

These are aspects which every teacher should know, understand and be able to use. They apply if you are working towards a teaching qualification in England. However, it's good practice as part of your teaching role whether it's a requirement or not. If you don't possess good knowledge and skills in these areas, you may have difficulty supporting the developmental needs of your learners.

The minimum core aims to:

- *clarify the expected minimum level of literacy, language, numeracy and ICT skills of further education teachers*

- *emphasise that learners' literacy, language, numeracy and ICT skills may need to be developed for them to achieve their chosen qualification*

- *encourage the development of inclusive practices to meet the needs of all learners*

- *highlight the benefits of using embedded approaches in developing learners' literacy, language, numeracy and ICT skills*

- *promote collaborative practice between vocational specialists and literacy, language, numeracy and ICT specialists*

- *provide links to useful reading, resources and CPD activities to support teachers' own skills and those of their learners (ETF, 2016, page 4).*

Developing and improving your personal skills in these areas will enable you to consider how to best teach your subject in ways which also support the development of your learners' skills. You may need to meet the needs of your learners whose levels of literacy, language, numeracy and ICT skills might otherwise jeopardise or hinder their learning. You, therefore, need to ensure your own skills and knowledge are adequate, to help improve those of your learners.

Example

Lewis was due to deliver a media studies session to 20 learners. He was going to be observed as part of his teaching practice hours and wanted his observer to see him using technology. He felt he needed to improve his skills at using the interactive whiteboard as he wanted his learners to use it during a project. He asked a colleague to give him a training session beforehand, which helped his confidence. His observed session went well, he came across as competent, and he was able to encourage his learners to use the technology too.

It's not a problem if you don't know how to use something. Just ask someone for help or guidance, for example, your mentor, a colleague or your supervisor.

The knowledge and understanding required for you to demonstrate your competence in the minimum core personal skills should be taught as part of the teaching qualification you are undertaking. The taught aspects are often referred to as *Section A*, with your personal skills referred to as *Section B*. This is due to the referencing of the sections of the document they are listed in.

Activity

Take a look at Sections 1B, 2B and 3B for Language and Literacy, Numeracy, and ICT in the following document to see how you can address the minimum core personal skills.

The Education and Training Foundation Minimum Core Guidance (2016) can be accessed at the shortcut https://goo.gl/Th9vp4

If you are not competent or confident with the minimum core personal skills, you might be making errors and not know any different. When planning your sessions, consider how you will demonstrate the skills. Also consider which skills you want your learners to demonstrate, for example, the use of language and literacy when they are writing. When reviewing their work, you can comment on any errors of spelling, grammar and punctuation to help your learners improve.

You might like to take additional learning programmes yourself, perhaps if you need to develop your digital skills or you feel your spelling and grammar need to be improved. When you are teaching, your learners will trust and believe you. If you spell words incorrectly, your learners might think the spelling is correct just because you are their teacher and they expect you to be right.

Evidencing the minimum core skills

To evidence the minimum core skills, you will need to demonstrate your personal skills in the areas of language, literacy, numeracy and ICT. Your observer will be looking for aspects of these when they visit you.

For example:

Language and literacy

You should have knowledge about language and of the four skills of speaking, listening, reading and writing, and be able to show you understand these by putting them into practice. For example, by (in alphabetical order):

- communicating with learners (verbally and non-verbally)

- creating and using interactive learning resources such as quizzes, crosswords or word searches

- giving explanations and descriptions

- listening and responding to learners

- summarising and clarifying information

- using appropriate language

- using spelling, punctuation and grammar correctly

- writing, e.g. on the board, on flipcharts, on OHP transparencies, visual presentations and in handouts and documents.

Evidence you could provide includes your scheme of work, session plans, activities you have designed for learners to use, resource materials, handouts and electronic presentations.

Numeracy

You should have knowledge about numerical communication and processes and be able to show you understand these by putting them into practice. For example, by (in alphabetical order):

- analysing statistical information correctly

- calculating marks and grades correctly

- calculating the correct numbers of resources for the group

- creating mathematical problem-solving tasks

- dividing learners into small groups efficiently

- ensuring that learners meet any time constraints

- timing how long presentations and activities will take.

Evidence you could provide includes statistical analyses, reports, retention, achievement and success data, and financial and other calculations.

ICT

You should have knowledge about information and communication technology and processes, and be able to show you understand these by putting them into practice. For example, by (in alphabetical order):

- creating videos, podcasts, blogs and vlogs for your specialist subject

- keeping up to date with your specialist subject area by using the internet and digital resources

- producing learning materials by using technology

- receiving, assessing and giving feedback regarding learners' work which has been submitted electronically

- recording discussions with a smartphone or audio device

- using digital devices, computers and smartphones to support teaching, learning and assessment

- using email to communicate with learners and others

- using ICT for electronic presentations and/or using an interactive whiteboard

- using online programs to check for plagiarism in learners' work

- using social media in an appropriate way

- using the internet for research

- using various devices, programs and apps with learners

- using virtual learning environments (VLEs) such as Moodle to support learning.

Evidence you could provide includes visual recordings of practical uses of programs and online applications, either printed or saved documents such as handouts and activities for learners to carry out.

If you are already qualified in English and maths, you may be able to use your certificates as evidence, for example:

- Key Skills in Communication at level 2 or above

- Ordinary (O) level or GCSE English (A*–C or 9–4)

- National literacy and numeracy tests at level 2 or above

- Functional skills in English or maths at level 2 or above

- Ordinary (O) level or GCSE mathematics (A*–C or 9–4, or CSE Grade 1 mathematics).

You will need to discuss any qualifications you have with your assessor, to enable them to check whether they are acceptable, or whether you need to demonstrate any personal skills further. If you wish to apply for Qualified Teacher Learning and Skills Status (QTLS) in England (covered in the Introduction chapter), you will need to evidence your literacy and numeracy skills to at least level 2.

Extension activity

Take a look at the minimum core personal skills checklist in Table 14.1 (on pages 520 and 521), which is adapted from **The Education and Training Foundation Minimum Core Guidance (2016)**. *Note how you demonstrate the skills when delivering your teaching practice sessions. You don't have to complete all of them during one session. If you haven't yet taught any sessions, make a note of how you think you will be able to evidence them.*

Table 14.1 Minimum core personal skills checklist

Language and literacy personal skills:	Demonstrated by:
Speaking	
☐ Using communication techniques to help convey meaning and to enhance the delivery and accessibility of the message ☐ Showing the ability to use language, style and tone in ways that suit the audience and recognise use by others ☐ Using appropriate communication techniques to reinforce, check and support learning ☐ Using non-verbal communication to convey meaning and receive information, and recognise use by others	
Listening	
☐ Listening attentively and responding sensitively	
Reading	
☐ Finding, and selecting from, a range of information sources ☐ Using a range of reading strategies ☐ Identifying the key information, themes and concepts in a text, and the use of note-taking to record the information	
Writing	
☐ Writing fluently, accurately and legibly ☐ Selecting an appropriate format and style of writing ☐ Using spelling and punctuation accurately to make the meaning clear ☐ Understanding and using the conventions of grammar consistently when producing written text	
Numeracy personal skills:	*Demonstrated by:*
Communication	
☐ Communicating with others about numeracy in an open and supportive manner ☐ Assessing own, and other people's, understanding of numeracy ☐ Expressing yourself clearly and accurately ☐ Communicating about numeracy in a variety of ways that suit and support the intended audience, and recognising such use by others ☐ Reinforcing oral communication of numeracy, checking how the information is received and supporting the understanding of those listening	

Numeracy personal skills: (Continued)	Demonstrated by:
Processes	
☐ Using strategies to make sense of a situation requiring the application of numeracy ☐ Processing and analysing data ☐ Using numerical skills and content knowledge required to support learners ☐ Making decisions about own skills and the numeracy content required for the professional role ☐ Understanding the validity of different methods ☐ Considering accuracy, efficiency and effectiveness when solving problems and reflecting on what has been learnt ☐ Making sense of data ☐ Selecting an appropriate format and style for communicating findings	
Information and communication technology (ICT) personal skills:	**Demonstrated by:**
Communication	
☐ Communicating with others about ICT in an open and supportive manner ☐ Assessing own, and other people's, understanding ☐ Expressing yourself clearly and accurately ☐ Communicating with/about ICT to suit and support the intended audience, and recognising such use by others ☐ Using appropriate techniques to reinforce oral communication, checking how well the information is received, and supporting the understanding of those listening	
Processes	
☐ Selecting, interacting with, and using ICT systems relevant to role ☐ Finding, selecting and exchanging information ☐ Developing and presenting information relevant to role	

Preparing to be observed

You will be formally observed on several occasions throughout the time you are working towards a teaching qualification. This is to see how you are progressing, how you are meeting the requirements of the qualification and how you are enabling learning to take place. You might also be regularly observed throughout your teaching career as part of your organisation's quality assurance processes. There will be a formal policy and procedure for this, which you might like to find out about.

The time length of each observation might vary, for example, half an hour, one hour, or more. If you are taking any optional units as part of a teaching qualification, you may be subject to extra observations. In addition to this, you might be observed by your mentor, a colleague, an internal and/or external quality assurer or an inspector. However, the results of these might not always count towards your teaching qualification. When preparing to be observed, you might like to carry out the actions in the following checklist (if applicable):

Checklist for preparing to be observed

☐ *Confirm the date, time and location with your observer.*

☐ *Ask to see the assessment checklist or observation report that will be used. It's useful to see what your observer is looking for. If you have a copy of a previous report, read it to refresh your memory and to ensure you have addressed any action or development points.*

☐ *Inform any other staff such as your supervisor and/or mentor.*

☐ *Inform reception of your observer's name; you might need to reserve a parking space for them, inform them of public transport, and/or confirm directions to the venue. Your observer might also need to sign in and out of the building, wear a name badge, and be informed about relevant health and safety procedures.*

☐ *If your observer is due to arrive prior to your session, arrange to meet them beforehand.*

☐ *If you will have started your session before your observer's arrival, make sure they know where to go, and prepare yourself to be interrupted when they do arrive.*

☐ *Check you have the necessary documents and resources. These might include your scheme of work, session plan, group profile, handouts and other resources. Your observer might ask for electronic or hard copies in advance.*

☐ *Check all the equipment you plan to use is in working order.*

☐ *Wear appropriate clothing for the subject you will deliver.*

☐ *Prepare your room so that there is somewhere for your observer to sit. They will need a position away from you and your learners, but where they can see what is going on. They might also need to wear some specialist clothing if applicable, for example, a laboratory coat or safety goggles.*

☐ *Arrange for a quiet place to talk to your observer after your session. If they are not staying until the end, ask when you will have the opportunity to receive their feedback.*

Activity

Ask your teacher or observer if you can have a copy of the document that they will refer to when they observe you. Have a look at it and make sure you understand all the aspects. If you are in any doubt regarding anything, ask for clarification.

Table 14.2 (on pages 524 and 525) is an example of an observation report; however, this might be very different to the one used with you. Some observers might not use a checklist but just make notes. Primarily, your observer will be looking to see that you achieve the criteria for the teaching qualification you are working towards, and that learning is taking place. They will also be looking at areas in which they can give you guidance and support to help you improve and develop.

Prior to the observation, you could make a visual recording of yourself to look for aspects you do well, and areas you could develop. You will need to let your learners know that you are making a recording and that it's to help you. You will need their permission if they are included and it's best to check with your organisation to make sure you are allowed to do it.

Some observers might also use the Ofsted grading characteristics when observing and giving feedback (in England). This might result in their giving your session a grade of 1, 2, 3 or 4. Grade 1 is the highest, and grade 4 is the lowest. Alternatively, they might state that your session was outstanding, good, requires improvement or was inadequate (respectively to the 1–4 grades). The overall results of teaching observations as part of an official Ofsted inspection report will not grade the quality of teaching, learning and assessment of individuals, only organisations. You should be informed before your observation whether or not it will be graded. However, the feedback you receive should be more important than any grade, as this should help you to improve and develop further. Don't be demoralised if you receive a grade lower than you expected; it's all part of your learning experience. The feedback should be used to help you reflect upon, and develop the teaching, learning and assessment process.

All observers will want to satisfy themselves that you are using teaching, learning and assessment approaches and activities effectively. They will want to see that learning is taking place, that you are including all your learners during the session and differentiating for any particular needs.

Example

Roberta was due to be observed next week for one hour, the full length of her session with her group of learners taking history. This was the first time she was to be observed and she wanted to make a good impression. She had prepared her session plan to cover a mixture of teaching and learning activities. She had prepared lots of handouts, would use the interactive whiteboard, and carry out an activity to enable her learners to use their own devices. She showed her plan to her mentor, who reminded her to include some checks that learning was taking place. She hadn't allocated any time to assessing learning; she was just so focused on demonstrating her teaching skills that she had forgotten to check if learning was taking place.

Table 14.2 Example observation report

	Date:
Name of teacher/trainer:	**Venue:**
Name of observer:	**Number of learners:**
Length of session:	**Aim of session:**
Length of observation:	

	Comments/action required
Did the trainee teacher?	
Planning and preparation *Use an appropriate scheme of work, session plan, group profile, risk assessments and other documentation as necessary*	
Introduction to the session *Explain the aim, objectives or tasks* *Link to the previous session (if applicable)* *Check prior skills, knowledge and understanding* *Use a starter activity*	
Teaching and learning *Demonstrate subject knowledge* *Create an inclusive learning environment where all learners could participate at an appropriate level* *Use a variety of teaching and learning approaches and activities* *Differentiate learning and support individual needs* *Communicate appropriately and effectively* *Act professionally and deal with any issues as they arose* *Engage and motivate learners* *Stretch and challenge learners* *Demonstrate aspects of the minimum core* *Embed English, maths and ICT* *Take into account aspects such as safeguarding, equality and diversity, employability and the Prevent Duty (as applicable)*	

Resources

Use resources to enhance the subject, promote equality, value diversity and meet the individual needs of learners

Use relevant equipment and materials in a safe way

Use visual aids, handouts and other resources effectively

Assessment

Use suitable assessment types, e.g. initial, formative, summative

Use appropriate assessment methods, e.g. questions, observation, peer- and self-assessment to check learning was taking place

Make decisions to ensure the validity, authenticity, reliability, currency, and sufficiency of assessment evidence produced by each learner

Give constructive and developmental feedback to individual learners

Maintain records

Conclusion of the session

Summarise the objectives or tasks achieved

Link to the next session (if applicable)

Use a closing activity

Allow time for learner questions

Provide opportunities for learners to provide feedback

Leave the area tidy

Overall feedback

Strengths	
Areas for development	
Action required	Target dates

You might feel that you need to demonstrate all of the teaching qualification criteria during one observed session. This won't be the case, as your observer will be able to see how you perform your role throughout all the observed sessions over time. If you try to do too much, you might end up focusing on the teaching rather than the learning taking place.

Final checks prior to the observation

Make sure all the materials you have prepared are of good quality, are varied, address inclusivity and differentiation, and are free from spelling, grammar and punctuation errors. Don't try and prepare too much at the risk of showing off, or use any equipment you are not totally comfortable with. Make sure you have a spare activity in case you have extra time available, and extension activities to stretch and challenge learners when necessary. Always have a contingency plan, i.e. hard copies of an electronic presentation in case of an equipment malfunction. You could also consider which activities you could reduce or remove if you are running out of time. Check the environment and equipment beforehand, and complete any health and safety checks or risk assessments. Make sure you have enough of everything for the number of learners you expect, plus a spare if possible.

Your session plan should show a clear aim (what you want to achieve) and SMART objectives or tasks (covered in Chapter 4) which your learners will carry out. You should also state how you will check that learning will take place, i.e. the different assessment methods you will use. If possible, it would be useful to ask your observer to comment on your session plan beforehand.

Above all, don't panic, keep calm and don't try to do too much. You are still learning, and you will need to work at things over time. If you make a mistake, it's fine and it shows you are human. Just be honest with yourself and learn from it.

Extension activity

Find out who is going to observe you, when this will be, and for how long. Make a list of a few questions that you would like answered beforehand. For example, what if they arrive after you have started the session? Ask these questions to your observer prior to the visit and find out how you will receive feedback afterwards.

During the observation

Being observed, even if you are an experienced teacher, can be a bit worrying or stressful, as you will want to deliver a perfect session. However, you are being observed every time you deliver a session by your own learners, it's just that they don't give you formal feedback afterwards. If you are nervous, don't let your learners know, as they probably won't notice; there's also no need to tell your observer, as they will be expecting you to be confident at what you do. You are human though, and if you make a mistake, your observer will be watching to see that you put it right.

Your observer will probably arrive early to talk to you beforehand about the observation process, the documentation they will be completing and to inform you when they will give you feedback. If so, you can take this time to ask any questions you might have and to tell them about the session you are about to teach. Your session might last longer than the time your observer will be present. They might, therefore, miss the beginning or ending. If possible, you should try and plan the session to allow time to talk to your observer either before, afterwards or preferably both.

You might want to give your observer details of your individual learners, perhaps in the form of a group profile. This will show how you will be differentiating to meet their individual needs, along with strategies to support them. Your observer may also want to see your record of attendance/register, and other relevant administrative documents. These might be electronic rather than hard copies, but they should still be accessible.

You might want to inform your learners in advance that the session is to be observed, and that you expect them to behave in their usual way. Otherwise, they might feel they should be quiet, not ask any questions, or ask too many questions to appear helpful, which will give a false impression of what normally occurs. Your observer may want to talk to your learners at some point, and might ask you to leave the room while they do this. Don't be concerned, this is quite normal; they like to find out what your learners are experiencing and how your teaching is having an impact upon their learning.

Activity

What will you tell your learners prior to your observer arriving? How will you set up the environment so that your observer can see everything that you and your learners do?

You could introduce your observer to your learners at the beginning and state they are observing the session, not them as individuals. Having a stranger in the room might lead to some behaviour issues if you haven't forewarned your learners. If so, you must deal with these as soon as they arise and do it in a professional manner. Just be yourself. If you are asked a question by a learner you don't know the answer to, say you will find out afterwards, and then make sure you do.

Try not to look at your observer while they are with you, they are not part of your group and will not participate in any activities. Don't embarrass them by trying to involve them. They will be making lots of notes throughout the session; therefore, try not to be concerned if they don't appear to be watching you all the time, they will still be listening to what's going on. If you can, forget that they are there and ignore them, your learners should be the focus of your session not your observer.

Your observer might be seeing the very first session of a programme, in which case you will have several administrative duties to perform, including an induction to the programme, an icebreaker, and the setting of ground rules. If you are being observed during one of several sessions, you will need to complete the register and include a link to the previous session. You will need to allow time for learner questions and/or a starter activity at the beginning. Make sure you start promptly, remain in control and act professionally at all times.

Keep your session plan handy either as a hard copy or on an electronic device. You could highlight key points which you can glance at quickly to make sure you are on track. Don't worry if you don't follow your session plan exactly. As your session progresses you will naturally adapt the timings and activities to meet the needs of your learners. Your observer will not mind if you don't keep to your timings as it will show you are being flexible to meet the needs of your learners.

You may find that you rush things if you are nervous and finish much more quickly than you had planned. If so, you could have a spare activity to use. Depending upon the level of your learners, you could give them a crossword, a multiple-choice quiz, or they could hold a small group or paired discussion regarding the pros and cons of a relevant topic. Whatever you do, don't forget to check how much learning is taking place.

Ensure your learners are engaged throughout and that learning is taking place. Ask lots of open questions to different learners (by name) to check their knowledge. You could have a list of your learners' names and tick them off once you have asked a question. This is fine if your group is not too large, and keeps a check on how you have included each learner. Try and use a variety of teaching and learning approaches and activities to stretch and challenge learners. If possible, use technology to support the teaching and learning process. Above all, make sure learning has taken place. If you are not using formal assessment activities, make sure you use informal activities which will enable your learners to demonstrate the progress they have made during the session.

Example

Martha had planned to use a peer group assessment activity with her group of welding learners who are aged 16–19. She placed her group of 20 learners into pairs, and asked each to provide feedback to the other after they had completed a welding activity. As she walked around the room, she soon realised she had not given them any advice regarding how to give constructive feedback. She had just expected them to be able to do this. Unfortunately, she could not listen to the feedback each learner was giving, as it was all happening at the same time in the room. However, she could hear that everyone was being very polite and giggling. Martha wasn't able to see the amount of individual learning that had taken place and soon learnt that she needed to make changes for the next time she used peer feedback. Her observer gave her some helpful tips after the observation.

It's crucial to use assessment activities which will work to check that learning has taken place. In this example, the learners had fun, but the teacher did not know what they had learnt, or what progress had been made.

At the end of your session you will need to confirm what has been learnt by linking to the objectives or tasks. You can then explain what will be covered during the next session (if applicable) and set any homework or other activities to be carried out during self-study time. Always plan to finish on time, otherwise your learners might decide to leave before you have completed. If the room needs to be left tidy, involve your learners in this before the session finishes. You can then talk to your observer after your learners have left, providing time has been arranged for this.

What teaching, learning and assessment activities will you plan to use during your next observed teaching practice session and why? What tips would you give a new teacher? Compare your tips to those listed in Appendix 3.

After the observation

If your observer stays until the end of your session, they should be able to give you oral feedback when your learners have left. If this is not possible, make sure you ask your observer when you will receive their feedback, which might be oral, electronic or paper based. Ideally, the feedback should be given in a quiet area which will enable you to listen and focus upon what is said. You might also like to make some notes. Don't be afraid of asking your observer to pause while you make them. There will be a lot of information to take in, and they might be happy for you to digitally record the feedback so that you can listen to it again later.

Hopefully, the feedback you receive will reassure you that you are teaching correctly, and that learning is taking place. However, if you receive some negative feedback don't take it personally, your observer has only seen a snapshot of what you are capable of. You might be given a grade, for example, 1, 2, 3 or 4, or told the session is a pass or refer. If you receive a low grade or refer, you should be given developmental advice and support to enable you to work towards a higher grade and a pass next time.

Activity

If your observer has told you that they will use the Ofsted grading system of 1–4, take a look at the grade descriptors in the document: **Further Education and Skills Inspection Handbook** *(2016) at the shortcut link:* **http://tinyurl.com/zsh57e2.** *Make a note of anything you are unsure of and talk to your observer about it.*

You might be given a copy of your observer's completed report, which you should read carefully. It would be useful to refer to this when writing your self-evaluation of how you felt the session went. Your observer might have identified some points for your further training and development which you hadn't considered. As part of your teaching qualification, you might be required to keep a diary or a learning journal (covered in Chapter 12). This will help you reflect upon what you did, or did not do, over time. You might like to show it to your mentor or your supervisor to gain their feedback and advice.

Some questions to ask yourself as part of the self-evaluation process could include:

- How well did I plan and prepare my session?
- How well did I perform and how did I feel about what I did?
- What went well, what didn't go well and why?
- Did I use a variety of teaching and learning approaches?
- Did I check that learning was taking place?
- Were my learners motivated and actively engaged with the topics?
- Did I meet the observation criteria? If not, how can I meet them, or exceed them next time?
- What have I found out about myself?
- What happened that wasn't meant to happen, and how did I deal with it?
- How were my timings compared to my session plan?
- If I was to deliver this same session again, what would I change and why?
- What can I improve upon and why?

You might find it useful to ask yourself the questions in the previous bullet list after every session, and not just after an observed session. Make sure you are honest, there's no point being otherwise as you will only be misleading yourself. Don't be hard on yourself either, teaching practice is a chance to learn from your mistakes, and to improve what you are doing. Your observer should be experienced at what they do and their advice will prove valuable to your career.

Your observer might ask you how you felt the session went, to see if you noticed the things they noticed, before they tell you. They might also give you feedback from their discussion with your learners (if they spoke to them). You should take the opportunity to ask questions about how you can improve the way learning takes place, or what you could do differently next time. An honest dialogue will prove very useful to your long-term development. You might hear some feedback you don't agree with, but don't get defensive. Your observer will have seen your delivery from a different perspective to yourself.

Example

Pauline felt she had delivered a successful session. However, towards the end, she gave out an activity for her learners to complete which many of them could not do in the time left. She became a little flustered as she was being observed and was not sure what to do. Some of her learners began packing up their things. She knew she needed to take control; therefore, she asked everyone to remain in the room, and told those that had not completed yet to finish the activity as homework, which she would check at the next session. Those that had completed could hand it in on their way out. This still meant she had to rush her summary of the session. Her observer gave her some feedback afterwards about how she could manage her timings.

It could be that you thought everything was going well but feedback from your learners to your observer stated otherwise. Try not to argue with your observer, but ask them to clarify how they made their judgement. If you really don't agree with your observer's decision you could appeal. However, observations are a tool to help you improve your teaching and the learner experience, and you should respect the judgement of your observer. Arguing with them will not help the situation. If you do appeal, you will need to have good reasons as to why you disagreed with their decision.

A further observation date might be arranged to enable your observer (or an alternative observer) to visit. This might be an additional observation, or part of your allocated observation hours. Always refer to your last observation's feedback when preparing for a future observation. Remember that you are on a learning journey, and you won't get everything right first time. Don't be disheartened; teaching is a very rewarding career and everyone has to start somewhere.

Afterwards, you could discuss the observation process and the feedback you received with your mentor and/or supervisor. They might be able to reassure you if you are feeling sensitive, or give you some valuable advice and guidance.

Extension activity

If you have been observed already, summarise the feedback you have received so far. What are the trends, i.e. is there something that occurs each time that you need to work on? Set yourself an action plan of what your strengths and areas for development are. What will you do as a result?

Evidencing teaching practice

While you are carrying out your teaching practice you will accumulate a lot of documents. These can be used as evidence, or proof, of what you have achieved. Your observer will not see all of your sessions; therefore, you need to prove that you have delivered a certain number of teaching practice hours with learners. Your sessions might not have been perfect, which is not a problem. Teaching practice is a chance to try out new things, and to learn from your mistakes. If something didn't work, you just need to reflect why, and consider what you could do differently.

The evidence you could provide to support your teaching practice can include (in alphabetical order):

- action plans/individual learning plans

- assessment plans, activities, feedback and decision records

- evidence of demonstrating the minimum core

- group profile

- initial and diagnostic assessment results

- learning journals or diaries

- learning support records

- notes/emails showing liaison and communication with others

- observer's reports, checklists and feedback

- resources such as copies of electronic presentations, handouts, learner activities

- schemes of work

- screenshots of virtual learning environments, website pages or other sites and electronic resources you have created or contributed to

- self-evaluation reports

- session plans

- witness testimony, i.e. from your mentor.

All the evidence you provide should be accessible to your observer if they ask for it. You might keep some or all of it electronically, or place copies in a ring binder or file. If you save it electronically, make sure it is safe and secure, and make backup copies.

Activity

Make a list of the evidence you think you could provide to support your teaching practice. Where and how will you file it, so that it is accessible when needed?

Teaching practice log

You may need to keep a log of the amount of time spent undertaking your teaching practice. The log could link your evidence to each session as in Table 14.3. You might be given a form to complete for this or you could design your own. You could give each piece of evidence a number, which will refer to where it's filed (whether this is electronically or as a hard copy). Each piece of evidence could be used many times, for example, a scheme of work (i.e. number 1 in the example is used twice).

Table 14.3 Example teaching practice log

Date & time	No of learners & subject	Location	Length of session	Evidence reference
5th October 3 p.m.	15 Level 2 Certificate in Customer Service	Room 7	2 hours	1 – scheme of work 2 – session plan one 3 – group profile 4 – handout 5 – self-evaluation form
9th November 3 p.m.	15 Level 2 Certificate in Customer Service	Room 7	2 hours	1 – scheme of work (same one) 6 – session plan two 7 – handout 8 – copy of electronic presentation 9 – self-evaluation form
10th November 7 p.m.	12 Level 1 Award in IT User Skills	Room 1 ICT building	1.5 hours	10 – scheme of work 11 – session plan 12 – group profile 13 – handout 14– group activity 15 – assessment activity 16 – self-evaluation form 17 – completed minimum core personal skills checklist 18 – observer's report (covers one hour)

Extension activity

Design a teaching practice log like that in Table 14.3. If you are currently teaching, start keeping a record of what you are doing and link it to your evidence. You might also wish to reflect upon each session you have delivered to consider your strengths, areas for development, and any actions or improvements required.

Self-assessment checklist

Do I know about the following?

If not, re-read this chapter, or research the texts and websites listed at the end.

☐ What teaching practice involves

☐ The people who will support me through my teaching practice, and how I can benefit from them, for example, a mentor

☐ The other staff who I will need to liaise with throughout my teaching practice time

☐ Who will observe me and the criteria they will use to assess me

☐ What the minimum core is and how I can evidence it

☐ What I need to prepare prior to being observed

☐ What I should tell my learners prior to being observed

☐ What will happen during the observation

☐ What will happen after the observation

☐ How and when I will receive feedback from my observer

☐ How I can reflect upon my teaching practice

☐ How I can evidence my teaching practice

Summary

This chapter has explored what teaching practice is and how you can benefit from it.

You should now be able to plan and prepare for teaching practice and take into account the feedback from your observer. You should also know about the minimum core skills of literacy, language, numeracy and ICT.

You might like to carry out further research by accessing the books and websites listed at the end of this chapter, particularly if you are working towards a higher level teaching qualification.

This chapter has covered the following topics:

*   What is teaching practice?

*   The minimum core

*   Preparing to be observed

*   During the observation

*   After the observation

*   Evidencing teaching practice

References and further information

Duckworth, V., Wood, J., Dickinson, J. and Bostock, J. (2010) *Successful Teaching Practice in the Lifelong Learning Sector*. Exeter: Learning Matters.

ETF (2016) *Minimum Core Guidance*. London: Education and Training Foundation.

LSIS (2013) *Qualification Guidance for Awarding Organisations – Assessed Observations of Practice Within Education and Training Suite of Qualifications*. Coventry: Learning and Skills Improvement Service.

Ofsted (2015) *The Common Inspection Framework: Education, Skills and Early Years.* Manchester: Ofsted.

Ofsted (2016) *Further Education and Skills Inspection Handbook.* Manchester: Ofsted.

O'leary, M. (2013) *Classroom Observation: A Guide to the Effective Observation of Teaching and Learning.* Abingdon: Routledge.

O'leary, M. (2016) *Reclaiming Lesson Observation: Supporting Excellence in Teacher Learning.* Abingdon: Routledge.

Race, P. and Pickford, R. (2007) *Making Teaching Work.* London: SAGE.

Websites

Ann Gravells – videos to support teaching, learning and assessment – http://tinyurl.com/jrdqolb

Computer free support – www.learnmyway.com/subjects

Digital Unite computer support – http://digitalunite.com/guides

Free online English audit – http://sagepub.net/LM/audit/audeng.asp

Free online maths audit – http://sagepub.net/LM/audit/audmat.asp

Initial assessment for using technology – http://wip.exeter.ac.uk/collaborate/itest/

The Education and Training Foundation Minimum Core Guidance (2016) – https://goo.gl/Th9vp4

Reading list for the minimum core – www.anngravells.com/reading-lists/minimum-core

APPENDIX I

Abbreviations and acronyms
(some of these are only applicable in England)

AAIA	Association for Achievement and Improvement through Assessment
AAO	Apprentice Assessment Organisation
ACL	Adult and Community Learning
ADD	Attention Deficit Disorder
ADHD	Attention Deficit and Hyperactivity Disorder
ADS	Adult Dyslexia Support
AELP	Association of Employment and Learning Providers
AET	Award in Education and Training
AfL	Assessment for Learning
AI	Awarding Institution
AO	Awarding Organisation
AoC	Association of Colleges
AoL	Assessment of Learning
AP	Action Plan/Assessment Plan
APL	Accreditation of Prior Learning
ASD	Autism Spectrum Disorder
BEd	Bachelor of Education
BKSB	Basic Key Skills Builder
BYOD	Bring Your Own Device
CA	Classroom Assistant
CAT	Credit Accumulation and Transfer
CAVTL	Commission on Adult Vocational Teaching and Learning
CCEA	Council for the Curriculum, Examinations and Assessment (Northern Ireland)
CET	Certificate in Education and Training
CETT	Centre for Excellence in Teacher Training
Cert Ed	Certificate in Education
CIEA	Chartered Institute for Educational Assessors
CIF	Common Inspection Framework

CIPD	Chartered Institute of Personnel and Development
CL	Community Learning
CLA	Copyright Licensing Authority
COSHH	Control of Substances Hazardous to Health
CPD	Continuing Professional Development
CQFW	Credit and Qualification Framework for Wales
CRB	Criminal Records Bureau (now part of DBS)
CRC	Certificate of Unit Credit
DBS	Disclosure and Barring Service
DCELLS	Department for Children, Education, Lifelong Learning and Skills (Wales)
DET	Diploma in Education and Training
DfE	Department for Education
DSO	Designated Safeguarding Officer
E&D	Equality and Diversity
EBD	Emotional and Behavioural Difficulties
ECDL	European Computer Driving Licence
EDAR	Experience, Describe, Analyse, Revise
EDIP	Explain, Demonstrate, Imitate, Practice
EFA	Education Funding Agency
EHCP	Education, Health and Care Plan
EHRC	Equality and Human Rights Commission
EI	Emotional Intelligence
EPA	End Point Assessment
EQA	External Quality Assurance/Assurer
ESFA	Education and Skills Funding Agency
ESOL	English for Speakers of Other Languages
ETF	Education and Training Foundation
ETS	Education and Training Sector
FAQ	Frequently Asked Questions
FE	Further Education
FELTAG	Further Education Learning Technology Action Group
FHE	Further and Higher Education
FHEQ	Framework for Higher Education Qualifications
GCSE	General Certificate of Secondary Education
GDPR	General Data Protection Regulation
GLH	Guided Learning Hours
GTC	General Teaching Council
H&S	Health and Safety
HE	Higher Education
HEA	Higher Education Academy
HEI	Higher Education Institution
HSE	Health and Safety Executive

IAG	Information, Advice and Guidance
IAC	Independent Assessment Centre
IAO	Independent Assessment Organisation
IAP	Individual Action Plan
ICT	Information and Communication Technology
IDP	Individual Development Plan
IfA	Institute for Apprenticeships
IIP	Investors In People
ILA	Individual Learning Account
ILM	Institute for Leadership and Management
ILP	Individual Learning Plan
ILT	Information and Learning Technology
IQ	Intelligence Quotient
IQA	Internal Quality Assurance/Assurer
ISA	Independent Safeguarding Authority (now part of DBS)
IT	Information Technology
ITE	Initial Teacher Education
ITOL	Institute of Training and Occupational Learning
ITP	Independent Training Provider
ITT	Initial Teacher/Trainer Training
IWB	Interactive Whiteboard
LA	Local Authority
LAR	Learner Achievement Record
LDD	Learning Difficulties and/or Disabilities
LGBT	Lesbian, Gay, Bisexual and Transgender
LLN	Literacy, Language and Numeracy
LRC	Learning Resource Centre
LSA	Learning (or Learner) Support Assistant
LSCB	Local Safeguarding Children Board
LSIS	Learning and Skills Improvement Service (no longer operational)
LST	Learning and Skills Teacher
LWI	Learning and Work Institute
MLD	Moderate Learning Difficulties
MOOCs	Massive Open Online Courses
MOODLE	Modular Object-Oriented Dynamic Learning Environment
NAS	National Apprenticeship Service
NEET	Not in Education, Employment or Training
NEU	National Education Union
NLH	Notional Learning Hours
NLP	Neuro Linguistic Programming
NOS	National Occupational Standards
NQF	National Qualification Framework

NQT	Newly Qualified Teacher
NRDC	National Research and Development Centre for adult literacy and numeracy
NTA	Non-teaching Assistant
NVQ	National Vocational Qualification
NYA	Not yet achieved
OHP	Overhead projector
OER	Open Education Resources
Ofqual	Office of Qualifications and Examinations Regulation
Ofsted	Office for Standards in Education, Children's Services and Skills
OU	Open University
PAT	Portable Appliance Testing
PCET	Post Compulsory Education and Training
PDBW	Personal development, behaviour and welfare
PDP	Personal Development Plan/Portfolio
PGCE	Post Graduate Certificate in Education
PLP	Personal Learning Plan
PLTS	Personal Learning and Thinking Skills
POCA	Protection of Children Act (1999)
PPE	Personal Protective Equipment
PPP	Pose, Pause, Pick
PSHE	Personal, Social and Health Education
QCF	Qualifications and Credit Framework (replaced with RQF)
QIP	Quality Improvement Report
QSR	Qualification Success Rates
QTLS	Qualified Teacher Learning and Skills (further education and skills sector)
QTS	Qualified Teacher Status (schools sector)
RARPA	Recognising and Recording Progress and Achievement in non-accredited learning
RIDDOR	Reporting of Injuries, Diseases and Dangerous Occurrences Regulations
RLJ	Reflective Learning Journal
RoC	Rules of Combination
RPL	Recognition of Prior Learning
RQF	Regulated Qualifications Framework
RWE	Realistic Working Environment
SAR	Self-Assessment Report
SEND	Special Educational Needs and Disabilities
SET	Society for Education and Training
SCN	Scottish Candidate Number
SCQF	Scottish Credit and Qualifications Framework

SL	Student Loan
SLC	Subject Learning Coach
SMART	Specific, Measurable, Achievable, Relevant and Timebound
SoW	Scheme of Work
SP	Session Plan
SSB	Standard Setting Body
SSC	Sector Skills Council
STEM	Science, Technology, Engineering and Maths
SWE	Simulated Working Environment
SWOT	Strengths, Weaknesses, Opportunities and Threats
T&L	Teaching and Learning
TA	Transactional Analysis or Teaching Assistant
TAQA	Training, Assessment and Quality Assurance
TEL	Technology Enhanced Learning
TLA	Teaching, Learning and Assessment
TQT	Total Qualification Time
TNA	Training Needs Analysis
TQFE	Teaching Qualification Further Education (Scotland)
UCU	University and College Union
ULN	Unique Learner Number
VARCS	Valid, Authentic, Reliable, Current, Sufficient
VARK	Visual, Aural, Read/write, Kinaesthetic
VET	Vocational Education and Training
VB	Vetting and Barring
VLE	Virtual Learning Environment
WBL	Work Based Learning
WEA	Workers' Educational Association
WWWWWH	Who, What, When, Where, Why and How

Checklist for teachers and trainers

Depending upon your job role, not all of the following will apply.

Identifying Needs

Do I...?

- ☐ Know who I will be teaching, i.e. details of all learners and any specific requirements or needs they may have

- ☐ Know anything about the learners which might affect my teaching or their learning

- ☐ Need to carry out an initial and/or diagnostic assessment with learners

- ☐ Need to use a learning preference questionnaire with learners

- ☐ Need to agree an action plan or individual learning plan with learners

- ☐ Need to create a group profile

- ☐ Need to liaise with anyone else such as a learner's work placement supervisor

- ☐ Need to learn anything myself before I can teach the subject

Planning learning

Do I...?

- ☐ Feel confident and able to plan to teach my subject

- ☐ Know who can I get support from when I need it

- ☐ Need to obtain a copy of the programme of learning, qualification specification, work tasks, job specification or set of standards which will be taught and assessed

- ☐ Have an induction checklist of points to discuss with learners during the first session

- ☐ Need to consider the domain of learning, for example, psycho-motor, cognitive and/or affective (skills, knowledge, attitudes respectively) when deciding what to teach and how

(Continued)

(Continued)

☐ Plan to differentiate, e.g. what *all, most* and *some* learners will achieve each session

☐ Need to create a scheme of work which shows a logical progression of learning

☐ Need to create a session plan with a logical beginning, middle and ending

☐ Need to create individual learning plans

☐ Need to create SMART objectives or tasks for learners to work towards

☐ Plan to embed English, maths and digital skills rather than teach them separately

☐ Know when and where I will be teaching, to how many learners and for how long

☐ Need to prepare the learning environment in a particular way

☐ Need to carry out any risk assessments or necessary equipment checks

☐ Need a clock or a watch to keep track of time

☐ Need to reserve or obtain any specialist equipment or resources

☐ Have the opportunity to use technology within the session for teaching, learning and assessment, or encourage learners to bring their own devices to use

☐ Need to know any organisational procedures such as accidents, appeals, health and safety, equality and diversity, safeguarding and Prevent Duty requirements

☐ Need to find out where facilities are such as refreshment areas, toilets, smoking areas, fire assembly points

☐ Need to send out any pre-programme information and/or inform reception staff where to direct learners

☐ Need to arrange refreshments, transport or parking in advance and/or inform anyone else about it

☐ Need to devise suitable learning, assessment activities and resources, and get these photocopied or uploaded to an online site for electronic access

☐ Need to check spelling, grammar and punctuation of visual presentations, worksheets and handouts

☐ Have a contingency plan in case anything goes wrong

☐ Have extra activities if learners and/or the session finishes earlier than planned

Facilitating learning

Can I...?

☐ Ensure the environment is suitable, e.g. heating, lighting, ventilation, seating arrangements and access

☐ Arrive early to set up and check equipment and/or obtain resources

- ☐ Lead by example to give a professional impression
- ☐ Complete any necessary administrative duties, e.g. the register/record of attendance
- ☐ Introduce the session aim and objectives (or tasks)
- ☐ Recap the previous session (if applicable)
- ☐ Use an icebreaker, energiser or starter activity
- ☐ Negotiate and reinforce ground rules
- ☐ State the times of breaks and how long they will be
- ☐ Check the prior skills, knowledge and understanding of learners regarding the current topic
- ☐ Use a variety of teaching and learning approaches, activities and resources to include, involve and differentiate for all learners, taking into account equality and diversity
- ☐ Link topics to the session aim as well as to practical situations (i.e. theory to practice)
- ☐ Keep the topics logical and progressive
- ☐ Link and recap key points regularly
- ☐ Keep learners interested and suitably stretched, challenged and motivated
- ☐ Be passionate and enthusiastic about my subject
- ☐ Manage behaviour and disruption as it occurs
- ☐ Manage situations which might impact upon learning such as external noise
- ☐ Take any additional learners' needs into consideration and support learners as necessary
- ☐ Remember to use learners' names
- ☐ Integrate appropriate use of information technologies
- ☐ Make formative assessment interesting and fun
- ☐ Provide ongoing constructive and developmental feedback
- ☐ Ask open questions (ones beginning with *who, what, when, where, why* and *how*)
- ☐ Use an extension activity for learners who finish tasks earlier than others, or need stretching and challenging further
- ☐ Allow time for learners' questions
- ☐ Summarise the session and recap the aim and objectives (or tasks)
- ☐ Link to the next session (if applicable)
- ☐ Use a closing activity
- ☐ Leave the venue tidy
- ☐ Maintain all relevant records
- ☐ Liaise with others involved with the learner, e.g. in the workplace

Assessing learning

Can I...?

☐ Devise formative assessment activities relevant to the topics

☐ Obtain summative assessment activities from the awarding organisation (if applicable) or devise my own

☐ Ensure the validity and reliability of all assessment activities and decisions

☐ Assess learners on an individual basis, or attribute individual learning from group activities

☐ Differentiate assessment activities to meet any particular learner needs (when allowed)

☐ Provide feedback to learners on an individual basis in a constructive manner

☐ Liaise with others involved in the assessment process (if required)

☐ Review learner progress, e.g. by using tutorial reviews and discussions

☐ Keep records of individual progress, achievement and feedback given

☐ Track progress of all assessment grades and dates of achievement for each learner

Evaluating learning

Did I...?

☐ Deliver a beginning, middle and end to the session

☐ Follow the timings on the session plan, if not, what would I change and why

☐ Use a structured and logical approach

☐ Establish and maintain a rapport, putting learners at ease

☐ Engage and motivate learners

☐ Project energy, enthusiasm and passion for the subject

☐ Remain in control and deal with any difficult or unexpected situations appropriately

☐ Appear confident and professional with a positive and helpful attitude

☐ Speak clearly and confidently

☐ Dress and act appropriately

☐ Use eye contact with all learners at some point

☐ Fidget or fiddle with anything, if so, how can I prevent this

☐ Listen actively

☐ Answer questions or agree to find answers if I couldn't

☐ Recap key points regularly

☐ Use appropriate body language and non-verbal communication

☐ Limit the use of jargon or acronyms

☐ Use a variety of teaching, learning and assessment approaches and activities

☐ Differentiate for different learners' abilities, needs and levels

☐ Achieve the planned aim, enabling the learners to achieve their objectives (or tasks)

☐ Follow all regulations and codes of practice

☐ Enable learners to provide feedback regarding the session

☐ Enjoy the session, if not, why not

☐ Reflect on the session content, along with the teaching, learning and assessment process to make improvements for the future

☐ Ensure my subject knowledge is up to date, along with that of relevant legislation, policies and procedures

Tips for new teachers and trainers

- Keep things simple: don't try to achieve too much too soon, or expect your learners to either. They don't know what you know. They need time to assimilate new skills and knowledge and to understand the *how* and *why* of this new learning. You will find you may need to keep repeating and recapping things, which might be frustrating at first, but will help learning to take place.

- Be organised: always have a contingency plan in case anything goes wrong; for example, if a piece of equipment stops working you could hold a discussion instead.

- Get to know the people who can help you when necessary, e.g. the support staff and technicians.

- Give a professional impression to your learners whenever you are in contact with them. They will learn important aspects of how to behave and act from watching and listening to you. This is often referred to as the *hidden curriculum*, so lead by example, for instance, by arriving early, dressing appropriately and leaving the area tidy.

- Check the spelling, grammar and punctuation of any visual presentations, worksheets or handouts you issue. If your learners spot an error, they might think it's correct just because you are their teacher.

- If you feel nervous, your learners probably won't even notice. Try and act confidently, use eye contact and speak a litter louder than normal to command attention.

- Use an appropriate icebreaker to help your learners get to know each other at the start of a course.

- Agree ground rules or learning contracts from the first meeting with your learners, for example, arriving on time and respecting others' opinions. Try not to impose them, but discuss them in a way that lets your learners agree them. This should help them to take ownership, help with any potential behaviour problems and lead to a respectful working environment. If a ground rule is broken, remind everyone of their existence and why they are important.

- Start your session by recapping the previous session (if applicable) and asking if any questions have arisen in the meantime. You can then state your aim and link to the objectives (or tasks) of the current session.

- You could use a starter activity at the beginning of each session. This could be a quiz which your learners can carry out in small groups. It could be based on the topics covered in the last session or any homework or research you asked your learners to carry out. If a learner is late to the session for any reason, they only miss the starter activity, not any important aspects.

- Treat your learners as individuals and use their names whenever possible.

- Involve all your learners during discussions and activities; find out what they know already by discussing their experiences and how they relate to the subject. Learners can learn from each other as well as from you, particularly if you have learners of different age ranges and levels of experience within the same group.

- Ask your learners to take a learning preference questionnaire, the results can help you plan your sessions to ensure you are being inclusive, yet differentiating for their needs. A short free online questionnaire is available at www.vark-learn.com. You might like to try it yourself beforehand.

- Use a variety of different teaching, learning and assessment approaches and activities. These should engage, inspire, motivate and enthuse your learners. Don't just stick to one style because you find it easy. Vary the pace of your session and watch the body language of your learners to notice if boredom is setting in.

- Try and make your sessions fun and interactive when you can. Add value to your subject by drawing on your own experiences and using anecdotes to bring the subject to life.

- Have an extra activity ready in case you have spare time during a session, or if a learner finishes a task before others. Equally, have something you can remove from your session if you over run time. You can always give it as self-study material or carry it over to the next session.

- Try and incorporate technology into your sessions and in-between your sessions. You could consider letting your learners use their own devices. Ground rules might need to be agreed for their proper use, i.e. not accessing personal social networking sites.

- Your learners are not your friends so you should not become involved with their personal lives. It's best to avoid joining their social networking sites.

- You should assess continually throughout your session not just at the end. Always make a judgement based only upon what needs to be assessed.

- Ask open questions such as ...'How do you ....?' This will achieve a knowledgeable response rather than asking a question beginning with 'Do you ....?' which will usually only elicit a *yes* or a *no* answer. A learner may say 'yes' just because this is what they think you want to hear, but it won't tell you what has actually been learnt.

- If ever a learner asks you a question and you don't know the answer, say you will find out. Then make sure you tell them the answer next time you see them, or e-mail them in the meantime. It's fine not to know everything and you don't need to bluff your way out of answering difficult questions.

- When providing feedback, try and start with something positive so that you don't demoralise your learner. Even if they haven't achieved something, you can still be constructive. For example, *'Well done for trying; however, you might like to think about doing it a different way next time.'* You can then discuss different ways of achieving the task.

- End your session by asking questions to check your learners' understanding, and allow time for them to ask you questions.

- Link to the objectives (or tasks) which have been achieved, and state what will be covered in the next session.

- Consider using a closing activity, such as asking your learners in turn to state one thing from the session that has had the most impact upon them.

- Keep on top of your administration duties and keep your records up to date. If your learner loses their work you will need your records to prove what they have achieved. Your organisation should inform you what records you need to keep and how, i.e. in hard copy format or electronically. Awarding organisations expect records to be kept safe and secure.

- Never be afraid to ask for advice from experienced colleagues. You could ask to sit in during one of their sessions to see how they manage the learning process.

- Don't be too hard on yourself, even if you make a mistake. Your learners might not notice, but if they do, you will need to be honest to help retain their respect.

- Keep your own subject knowledge up to date as well as that relating to developments in technology.

- Reflect after each session to think about what went well, what didn't and why. This will help you improve for the future.

- Above all, be prepared, patient, positive and passionate about teaching your subject to others.

- Stay happy and healthy, remain focused and enjoy the experience.

INDEX

Page references followed by (t) refer to a table

360 degree feedback 460–3